I'LL COOK WHEN PIGS FLY

and they do in Cincinnati!

**JUNIOR LEAGUE OF
CINCINNATI**

Women building better communities

Bits and Bites of Queen City Cuisine
prepared for you by the Junior League of Cincinnati

JUNIOR LEAGUE OF CINCINNATI
Women building better communities

Belief statement of the Junior League of Cincinnati
*We believe children need opportunities that foster self-confidence and success.
We believe children need the respect and support of a responsible role model.
We believe children need to be encouraged to read and write.*

Strengthening Childhood Environments is the focus area of the *Junior League of Cincinnati,* whose purpose is to improve the quality of life in our community by developing the leadership potential of women as trained volunteers, responsive to community needs. Proceeds will benefit children in the Greater Cincinnati area.

Library of Congress Card Catalog #
98-66413

ISBN 0-9607078-2-4

Copyright' 1998, Junior League of Cincinnati

Cincinnati, Ohio

First printing	May 1998	15,000 copies
Second printing	June 1999	15,000 copies
Third printing	August 2000	20,000 copies
Fourth printing	August 2003	15,000 copies

WIMMER
COOKBOOKS
ConsolidatedGraphics
1-800-548-2537

About the Cover

"The ability to draw is common enough, and political pundits are a dime a dozen. But a mind that loves curiosities, that turns over every rock, that wonders how spaghetti stains got on the ceiling -THAT is the mind of a great cartoonist."

Since drawing his first editorial cartoon for *The Cincinnati Enquirer* in June of 1976, **Jim Borgman** has been studying the spaghetti stains left by politicians and newsmakers six times a week to the delight of readers in 200 newspapers all across America.

Over the course of his career, Borgman has won every major award in his field including, in 1991, the prestigious Pulitzer Prize. Among his other honors: the Sigma Delta Chi Award (1995 and 1978), the Golden Plate (1992), the National Headliner Award (1991), the Ohio Governor's Award (1989), and perhaps most colorfully, the Thomas Nast Prize (1980), for which he took home his weight in wine from the vineyards of Landau, Germany, birthplace of the father of political cartooning.

Maybe the most professionally flattering are those awards given to him by his fellow cartoonists in the National Cartoonists Society who four times (1987, 1988, 1989 and 1994) voted him Best Editorial Cartoonist in America. In 1993, Borgman received the profession's highest honor, the Reuben Award, as Outstanding Cartoonist of the Year. Awards aside, Borgman is proudest of having mused 350 miles across the frozen tundra of northern Alaska and of having one of his cartoons in the Oval Office.

Born February 24, 1954 in Cincinnati and a product of its blue-collar schools and neighborhoods, Jim Borgman is a 1976 summa cum laude with Phi Beta Kappa honors graduate of Kenyon College. One week after graduation, Borgman was hired to begin as the *Enquirer's* daily cartoonist on the strength of the weekly cartoon he had drawn for the *Kenyon Collegian,* making him, he says, "the first Kenyon art major ever to repay his student loan."

Jim Borgman's work is notable for its warmth, compassion and paradoxically, for its biting edge. Borgman squirms at any attempt to label him politically, calling himself a "progressive iconoclast with a dirt-under-my fingernails conservative streak." He attributes his cartoons less to ideology than to a contrary nature. "If the crowd starts leaning one way, I instinctively lean the other way. These cartoons are not final pronouncements. They are works in progress, all of them, done in the spirit of firing up the American debate."

King Features Syndicate distributes Jim Borgman's cartoons to about 200 newspapers, including *The Washington Post, Chicago Tribune, Los Angeles Times, New York Daily News, USA Today, Philadelphia Inquirer, Newsday,* and the *Atlanta Constitution.* His work frequently appears in the *New York Times "Week in Review"* and *Newsweek.* At the request of *The Washington Post,* Borgman drew a weekly political comic strip, *"Wonk City,"* from 1994-1996, which was syndicated to an additional 60 papers. He is co-author of the comic strip, *"Zits."*

Collections of his work in book form are: *Smorgasborgman* (1982); *The Great Communicator* (1985); *The Mood of America* (with James F. McCarty) (1986); *Jim Borgman's Cincinnati* (1992); and *Disturbing the Peace* (1995). All are available through Colloquial Books, PO Box 20045, Cincinnati, Ohio 45220. Original artwork is represented by The Framery on Hyde Park Square.

About the Photographers

Helen Adams

Helen Adams specializes in portraits of children and families. Her pictures tell a story, with each portrait revealing not only beauty, but personality, humor, and heart. Some of her subjects include President and Mrs. Clinton, Vice President and Mrs. Gore, President and Mrs. Bush, Elizabeth Dole, Boomer Esiason, and Barry Larkin. A member of the Professional Photographers of America, Helen's photographs have been featured in magazines such as *All About Kids, 50 Plus, Arthritis Today, Ohio Magazine,* and *Presbyterians Today.* Her work for various organizations includes Children's Hospital Medical Center, Deaconess Hospital, Lighthouse Youth Services, Maple Knoll Village, Manhattan National Life, The YWCA, The Andrew Jergens Foundation, Beech Acres, and The Arthritis Foundation. Helen graduated from the College of Mount St. Joseph in 1983 with a degree in graphic design.

Robert A. Flischel

Robert A. Flischel is a graduate of Xavier University and the Pazovski School of Photography. His photographs have appeared in national publications such as *Smithsonian* (Cover), *National Geographic Traveler, Time, Travel and Leisure, USA Today Magazine, Audubon, Forbes, Life* (Pictures of the Year 1994), *Preservation Magazine,* and two books, *Perspectives* (Cincinnati) and *Cincinnati, Northern Kentucky, Then and Now.* In addition to his work with corporate, commercial and portrait commissions, he is founding trustee and president of the Board of the Art League of Cincinnati, founding trustee of Radio Reading Service and past board member of the Regional Chapter of the American Society of Media Photographers.

Paula Norton

Award-winning photographer Paula Norton, owner of Norton Photography, specializes in the Polaroid-related processes of image and emulsion transfers. A graduate of the Gebhardt School of Commercial Art and Photography, her work has appeared in national publications such as *Peterson's Photographic, Viewcamera,* and *Graphis Photo.* In addition to teaching photography on a part-time basis at the Art Academy, she is on the board of Images Center for Photography, a Cincinnati-based nonprofit organization devoted to fine art photography, and is involved with the YWCA Art Gallery. Books in which she has been published are *Cincinnati Crowning Glory,* and the *Towery Report-Northern Kentucky.* Corporate clients include the Cincinnati Chamber of Commerce, Nike, Fidelity Investments, and Jacor Communications.

J. Miles Wolf

J. Miles Wolf has been photographing Cincinnati and places across the U.S. and abroad for over 17 years. As a native Cincinnatian, he intuitively captures spectacular scenes of the city and the surrounding region. He has won many prestigious awards for his photographs and publications, including several first place awards for local annual photo contests *Light-Up Cincinnati* and *WEBN Fireworks.* His limited edition photographs are in numerous corporate collections, such as Cincinnati Bell, Cincinnati Gas and Electric Company, Procter and Gamble, West Shell Realtors, and the University of Cincinnati. Primarily focusing on cityscapes, landscapes, architecture and nature, his photographs consist of rich and deep hues emphasized by the dye-bleached (Cibachrome) printing process. He personally oversees the production of his work to guarantee high quality.

J. Miles Wolf operates two galleries located in downtown Cincinnati: Wolf Gallery of Photography, 41 West Fifth Street, and Wolf Photographic Arts, 708 Walnut Street. Wolf Gallery of Photography features J. Miles Wolf limited edition photographs and posters, note cards, and books. Wolf Photographic Arts has an annual schedule of various photography exhibitions highlighting up-and-coming and established local, regional and national photographers. Wolf Photographic Arts offers a full-service custom photography lab. Both Wolf galleries have professional matting and framing services available.

Aimee Dumont-Elmaker

Marianne Scott Emmert

Laurie Ann Frank

Meg Galvin

Nancy Hartman

Margie Hauser

Colleen Hempel

Nicole King

Karen Kremzar

Tina Kroenke

Janet Kirk

Allison Kurtz

Lindsay Lackney

Julia Massarelli

Jenny Moore

Julie Neiheisel

Sandy Rabe

Tish Renz

Joanne Sloneker

Julie Snow-Reese

Elizabeth Staley

Cynthia Stanford

Susan Stearns

Sally Tamborski

Tina Walters

Judy Wells

photograph by J. Miles Wolf

Foreword

When you work at a zoo that feeds 8,500 animals every day, you get to learn a little bit about food and nutrition. And while it's true that animals generally eat food that is better for them than the average person, hardly anybody eats as well as you will if you prepare the recipes in this cookbook. They are a wonderful reflection of Cincinnati.

This is a town known for chili, ribs and bargain hot dogs at ball games, all of which ARE legendary, and tasty. But the really great thing about the Cincinnati area is the breadth and depth of both regional and international cuisine you can find here. There are even a plethora of low-rent bean and rice restaurants, which are my personal favorites. However, when the Junior League of Cincinnati publishes their recipes, there is nothing low-rent about it. Exceptional is the best word to describe their programs and their food.

Here's the deal - after you have a couple of meals from this cookbook, come see me at the Cincinnati Zoo so we can compare the menu with what we feed our orangutans and aardvarks. I dare you.

Thane Maynard
The Cincinnati Zoo & Botanical Garden

Legend has it that once pigs ruled the world. Well, at least Cincinnati, that is. While it's a well known fact that our contributions put this river city on the map, it might appear that now, all that's left of hog heaven are four majestic winged pigs paying homage from their lofty perches on a riverfront sculpture. But I'll let you in on a little secret.

The truth is: in Cincinnati pigs do fly. I should know, that's me on the front cover. My name's Porkopolis, but my friends call me Cincy. In this town, it's not what you know, but who ya know, baby, so stick with me and I'll show you what we do for fun around here while I'm taking you on a culinary journey of what's cookin' and who's cookin' it.

I'm not just talkin' chili and barbecue. I'm talkin' almost 400 scrumptious recipes layered in between photographs by famous local photographers. I'm talkin' spicy quotes from who's who here. I'm talkin' decadent desserts that put the "sin" in Cincinnati.

Most of all, I'm talkin' FOOD and FUN. Join me while I tempt you with tasty morsels and succulent bits and bites of Cincinnati history and trivia. Just consider me your meal ticket to the best of Queen City cuisine. Pigs rule!

Cincy

Table of Contents

Favorite recipes from previous JLC cookbooks are designated by:

 Cincinnati Celebrates    RiverFeast

Eden Park gazebo with the Cincinnati Art Museum in the background

photograph by Robert A. Flischel

APPETIZERS... *Famous Firsts*

The John A. Roebling Suspension Bridge, completed in 1866, served as a prototype for the Brooklyn Bridge.

Photograph by Robert A. Flischel

JOHN A. ROEBLING SUSPENSION BRIDGE

On the first day that the John A. Roebling Suspension Bridge was open for pedestrian traffic, 120,000 people, which was over half the population of Cincinnati, paid a 3 cent toll to cross it.

Parmesan Puffs

1 (16 ounce) loaf white bread
1 cup mayonnaise
1 cup (4 ounces) grated
   Parmesan cheese
2 tablespoons chopped fresh
   parsley

¼ cup minced onion
garlic powder, to taste
1 (10 ounce) jar marinated
   artichoke hearts, drained
   and chopped

- Trim crusts from bread slices.

- Combine mayonnaise, cheese, parsley, onion, garlic powder and artichokes, mixing well.

- Spread portion of mixture on each bread slice. Cut each slice into quarters and place on baking sheet.

- Broil until artichoke mixture is bubbly.

- Makes 48.

Bacon Biscuit Puffs

1 (8 ounce) can refrigerated
   biscuits
2 cups (8 ounces) grated
   cheddar or Swiss cheese
½ cup mayonnaise (additional
   mayonnaise may be needed
   to reach desired consistency)

1 small onion, chopped
1 (3 ounce) jar bacon bits
2 tablespoons sugar
¼ to ½ teaspoon garlic salt
5 drops hot pepper sauce

- Separate each biscuit into 3 pieces. Place on baking sheet.

- Combine cheese, mayonnaise, onion, bacon bits, sugar, garlic salt and hot pepper sauce, mixing well. Place spoonful of mixture, spreading evenly, on each biscuit round.

- Bake at 350 degrees for 10 minutes or until golden.

- Makes 30.

For variety, change ingredients with the season. Replace bacon and onion with 1 cup chopped red bell pepper, 1 bunch of green onions chopped and ½ cup chopped fresh basil or ⅓ cup chopped fresh thyme.

Queen City of the West

Nicholas Longworth, the city's first millionaire, owned vineyards planted with Catawba grapes, which he called the Garden of Eden. Stretching from what is now Mount Adams to Alms Park, these vineyards were famous for their wines. Longworth sent a bottle of his sparkling Golden Wedding Champagne to the poet Henry Wadsworth Longfellow, who wrote:

*"...the richest and best
Is the wine of the
West*

*That grows by the
beautiful river...
And this song of
the wine*

*This greeting of mine
The winds and the
birds shall deliver*

*To the Queen
of the West*

*In her garlands
dressed*

*On the banks of the
beautiful river."*

Artichoke Pepper Puffs

3 large shallots, chopped
2 cloves garlic, minced
3 tablespoons chopped chives
2 tablespoons butter
1 (14 ounce) can artichoke bottoms, drained and diced
6 slices bacon, cooked until crisp, and crumbled
3 tablespoons chopped fresh basil
½ cup (2 ounces) freshly grated Parmesan cheese
½ cup (2 ounces) grated Jarlsberg cheese
½ cup mayonnaise
1 tablespoon lemon juice
¼ teaspoon sugar
¼ teaspoon salt
¼ teaspoon black pepper
6 red or yellow bell peppers
¼ cup olive oil
2 tablespoons red wine vinegar
salt and black pepper, to taste

- Sauté shallots, garlic and chives in butter over medium heat until softened. Place in mixing bowl.

- Add artichokes, bacon, basil, Parmesan cheese and Jarlsberg cheese, tossing to combine.

- Stir in mayonnaise, lemon juice, sugar, salt and black pepper, mixing well. Chill mixture.

- Remove stems and seeds from peppers. Cut into 2-inch squares and place in single layer in baking dish.

- Drizzle oil and vinegar on pepper pieces and season with salt and black pepper.

- Bake at 350 degrees for 15 minutes, stirring after 7 minutes. Remove from oven and let stand until cool.

- Mound spoonful of artichoke mixture on each pepper piece. Arrange on baking sheet. Broil until puffed and bubbly. Let stand until cool.

- Makes 48.

Swiss Cheese Balls

 These cheese balls are worth the fuss.

**3 cups (12 ounces) finely
 grated Swiss cheese
2 tablespoons all-purpose flour
½ teaspoon salt
1 teaspoon Worcestershire
 sauce**

**3 tablespoons minced chives
6 egg whites, stiffly beaten
corn flake crumbs
oil to deep fry**

- Combine cheese, flour, salt, Worcestershire sauce and chives.

- Fold egg whites into cheese mixture. Shape into small balls and roll in corn flake crumbs.

- Deep fry cheese balls in oil at 375 degrees for 1 minute.

- Remove from oil and drain on paper towel.

- Makes 36 to 48.

Festive Chicken and Spinach Cups

**48 slices white bread
1 pound cooked boneless
 chicken, shredded
1 (10 ounce) package frozen
 chopped spinach, thawed
 and pressed dry**

**2 cups (8 ounces) shredded
 Gruyère cheese
6 green onions, chopped
⅔ cup sun dried tomatoes in
 oil, drained and chopped
½ teaspoon salt
¼ teaspoon ground red pepper**

- Using 2½ to 3-inch biscuit cutter, cut bread slices into circles. Roll each to flatten.

- Press bread circles firmly in lightly buttered cups of muffin pans.

- Bake at 400 degrees for about 6 minutes or until lightly browned.

- Remove from pans, cool on wire rack and place on baking sheet.

- Combine chicken, spinach, cheese, onion, tomatoes, salt and red pepper, mixing well.

- Spoon mixture into bread cups.

- Bake at 350 degrees for 10 minutes.

- Makes 48.

City Hall

Samuel Hannaford, Cincinnati's most prominent 19th century architect, designed the Romanesque building, which was dedicated in 1893. He was influenced by the work of Henry Hobson Richardson, who is perhaps best known for his design of the Trinity Church in Boston.

Ginger Chicken Bacon Wraps

¾ pound boned skinless chicken breast
¼ cup orange marmalade
2 tablespoons soy sauce
½ teaspoon ginger

⅛ teaspoon garlic powder
12 slices bacon
1 (8 ounce) can whole water chestnuts

- Cut chicken into 24 bite-sized pieces.

- Combine marmalade, soy sauce, ginger and garlic powder in mixing bowl. Add chicken and marinate for 30 minutes.

- Place bacon slices on unheated broiler pan. Broil 4 to 5 inches from heat for 1 to 2 minutes or until partially cooked but not crisp. Drain grease from pan. Cut bacon slices in halves.

- Cut water chestnuts in halves. Drain marinade from chicken.

- Wrap bacon strip around 1 chicken chunk and ½ water chestnut, securing with wooden pick. Place on broiler pan.

- Broil for 3 to 5 minutes.

- Makes 24.

Festive Deviled Eggs

 Don't forget to serve these at your next picnic!

15 eggs, hard-cooked
⅓ cup chopped pimento-stuffed green olives

1 cup chopped pecans
1 small onion, minced
¾ cup mayonnaise

- Cut 12 eggs in halves. Remove yolks and set whites aside.

- Chop egg yolks and remaining 3 eggs. Add pecans, onion, olives and mayonnaise, mixing well.

- Spoon filling into egg whites. Chill before serving.

- Makes 24.

Crab Swiss Bites

1 (7½ ounce) can crab meat, drained and flaked
2 tablespoons finely chopped green onion
1 cup (4 ounces) grated Swiss cheese
½ cup mayonnaise

1 teaspoon lemon juice
½ teaspoon curry powder
1 (5 ounce) can water chestnuts, drained and finely chopped
1 (8 ounce) can refrigerated biscuits

- Combine crab meat, onion, cheese, mayonnaise, lemon juice, curry powder and water chestnuts, mixing well.

- Separate each biscuit into 3 pieces and place on baking sheet.

- Place spoonful of crab mixture on each biscuit round.

- Bake at 400 degrees for 10 to 12 minutes or until golden brown.

- Makes 30.

Simmered Mushrooms

 These mushrooms really cook down. Your kitchen will smell wonderful.

2 cups water
4 beef bouillon cubes
4 chicken bouillon cubes
2 cups butter
4 cups burgundy
5 pounds whole mushrooms, cleaned

1½ tablespoons Worcestershire sauce
1 teaspoon dill weed
1 teaspoon black pepper
1 teaspoon garlic powder
1 tablespoon monosodium glutamate

- In stockpot or large saucepan, bring water to a boil. Add bouillon cubes and butter, stirring until dissolved.

- Add burgundy, mushrooms, Worcestershire sauce, dill weed, black pepper, garlic powder and monosodium glutamate to butter liquid.

- Bring to a boil, reduce heat and simmer, covered for 5 to 6 hours or uncovered for 3 to 5 hours.

- Drain most of liquid from mushrooms and serve warm.

- Serves 20.

The Palace's Grilled Portobello with Sun-dried Tomato Risotto

Mushrooms
½ cup balsamic vinegar
½ cup red wine
1 clove garlic

4 large portobello mushrooms, stems removed
salt and black pepper, to taste

Risotto
½ cup chopped onion
¼ cup butter
1 cup Arborio rice
½ cup white wine
3 cups chicken broth or water

½ cup sun-dried tomatoes, cut julienne
¾ cup (3 ounces) shredded Parmesan cheese
fresh chives or herb for garnish

Mushrooms
- Combine vinegar, wine, garlic, salt and black pepper in glass bowl.
- Add mushrooms to liquid and marinate for 1 hour.
- Drain mushrooms and place on grill.
- Grill for about 5 minutes or until tender. Remove from heat and set aside.

Risotto
- Sauté onion in butter in heavy saucepan for about 4 minutes or until translucent.
- Add rice to onion and cook, stirring often, for 3 minutes.
- Stir in white wine. Gradually add chicken broth, stirring in a small amount at a time and allowing its absorption by the rice before adding additional broth; additions will take 20 to 30 minutes.
- After all liquid is absorbed, add tomatoes and cheese. Season with salt and black pepper.
- Place scoop of rice in center of each serving plate. Place warm mushroom on rice. Garnish with chives or herb.
- Serves 4.

Sausage Chili Cheese Tarts

¾ pound sweet Italian sausage
½ cup medium hot salsa
½ cup (2 ounces) shredded
  Monterey Jack cheese
½ cup (2 ounces) shredded
  sharp cheddar cheese

½ (4 ounce) can diced green
  chilies
24 wonton wrappers
sour cream for garnish
chopped green onion for
  garnish

- Remove sausage from casing. Cook, stirring to crumble, until browned. Drain excess fat.

- Add salsa, Monterey Jack and cheddar cheeses and chilies to sausage. Simmer for about 5 minutes or until mixture is thickened.

- Press wonton wrappers into cups of miniature muffin pans. Spoon sausage mixture into wrappers.

- Bake at 350 degrees for 10 minutes.

- Remove tartlets from muffin pans and place on baking sheet.

- Bake for additional 10 minutes or until bottoms of tartlets are browned.

- Garnish with small dollop of sour cream and sprinkle of onion.

- Makes 24.

Shrimp Rounds

24 slices white bread
24 cooked shrimp
½ cup mayonnaise

½ cup (2 ounces) grated
  Parmesan cheese
1½ tablespoons chopped fresh
  dill, optional

- Using 2½ to 3-inch biscuit cutter, cut bread slices into circles.

- Place a shrimp on top of each bread round and place on broiler pan.

- Combine mayonnaise, cheese and dill, mixing well. Mound a spoonful of mayonnaise mixture on top of shrimp.

- Broil until golden brown.

- Makes 24.

Strike One

Credited with suggesting that the umpire raise his right hand to signal a strike, William Ellsworth Hoy was also the first baseball player inducted into the American Athletic Association of the Deaf Hall of Fame.

The Sky's the Limit

The 16-story Ingalls Building at Fourth and Vine streets was the world's first reinforced concrete framework skyscraper (1902). While many people expected it to collapse, including a city editor who stood outside all night when it was completed, it is still standing, and is now a National Historic Civil Engineering Landmark.

Sweet Mustard Kielbasa

 Men can't get enough of these tangy sausages.

2 (16 ounce) rings smoked kielbasa sausage
2 cups dry white wine
¼ cup firmly-packed brown sugar
¼ cup Dijon mustard
¼ cup brandy
¼ teaspoon black pepper
¼ cup plus 6 tablespoons chopped fresh parsley

- Cut kielbasa in ½-inch slices. Place in single layer in skillet and cook until browned, turning once.

- Add wine to kielbasa. Bring to a boil and cook, uncovered, for 10 to 12 minutes or until wine is nearly evaporated and liquid appears glazed.

- Stir in brown sugar, mustard, brandy and black pepper. Cook for 1 minute.

- Add parsley to kielbasa and toss to mix.

- Serve hot or at room temperature with French baguette bread slices.

- Serves 12.

Cherry Tomato Poppers

1½ (16 ounce) packages bacon
2 pints cherry tomatoes
½ cup mayonnaise
½ cup chopped green onion

- Cook bacon until crisp. Drain on paper towel, crumble and place in mixing bowl.

- Using tip of small knife, core tomatoes. Remove some of pulp and discard.

- Add mayonnaise and onion to bacon and mix well.

- Using small knife, stuff portion of mixture into each tomato.

- If tomatoes tend to roll, slice a thin layer from bottom.

- Makes 60 to 80.

Sun-dried Tomato Crostini

1 cup sun-dried tomatoes,
  packed without oil
1 teaspoon dried whole
  rosemary, crushed
water
1 tablespoon olive oil

24 (½ inch thick) slices French
  baguette bread
½ teaspoon onion powder
½ cup (2 ounces) crumbled
  feta cheese
1 tablespoon chopped fresh
  parsley

- Place tomatoes and rosemary in 1-quart microwave-safe dish. Add water to cover tomatoes.

- Microwave, covered, at high setting (100%) for 5 to 7 minutes or until water boils. Remove from oven and let stand, covered, for 10 minutes. Drain well.

- Using food processor, process tomatoes for 10 seconds or until chunky consistency.

- Brush oil evenly on bread slices. Sprinkle with onion powder.

- Spread tomato mixture evenly on bread slices. Top each with 1 teaspoon cheese and place on baking sheet.

- Bake at 350 degrees for 5 minutes. Sprinkle with parsley.

- Makes 24.

Basil Clams

20 cherry stone clams,
  scrubbed and on half shell

10 basil leaves, cut in halves
5 slices bacon, cut in quarters

- Place clams on broiler pan.

- Place ½ basil leaf on each clam and top with bacon piece. Bacon should be slightly larger than clam shell.

- Broil until bacon is cooked.

- Makes 20.

Smoked Turkey Tortilla Rollups

1 (8 ounce) package cream cheese, softened
½ cup chopped fresh chives
¼ teaspoon garlic salt
1 (10 count) package large flour tortillas

1 pound thinly-sliced smoked turkey
1 bunch spinach, stems removed
2 cups (8 ounces) grated smoked mozzarella cheese
1 cup salsa
1 cup mayonnaise

- Blend cream cheese, chives and garlic salt. Thinly spread mixture on one side of each tortilla, covering entire surface.

- On each tortilla, arrange 2 slices smoked turkey, then add 3 spinach leaves and sprinkle with mozzarella cheese.

- Roll each tortilla snugly into tube shape. Cut in 1-inch slices, securing each with wooden pick.

- Combine salsa and mayonnaise. Serve tortilla rollups with sauce for dipping.

- Makes 60 to 70.

Cincinnati Sin

1 (8 ounce) package cream cheese, softened
1½ cups sour cream
2 cups (8 ounces) grated cheddar cheese
1 (5 ounce) can minced ham, drained

1 (4 ounce) can green chilies
½ cup chopped green onion
1 (10 ounce) package frozen chopped spinach, thawed and drained
1 round loaf Hawaiian or sourdough bread

- Combine cream cheese, sour cream, cheddar cheese, ham, chilies, onion and spinach, mixing well.

- Cut slice from top of bread loaf. Carefully remove center of loaf, leaving 1-inch shell to form bowl. Reserve center pieces.

- Spoon cheese mixture into bread bowl. Wrap in aluminum foil and place on baking sheet.

- Bake at 350 degrees for 1 hour.

- Cut reserved bread pieces and top slice into chunks and use for dipping.

- Serves 16.

Three Cheese Round

2 (8 ounce) packages cream cheese or Neufchâtel cheese, softened	½ cup (2 ounces) shredded Gruyère cheese
1¼ teaspoons Italian seasoning	¼ cup finely chopped pecans
⅛ teaspoon black pepper	¾ cup chopped fresh parsley, divided
2 tablespoons dried tomato bits	¾ cup (3 ounces) crumbled Roquefort cheese

- Combine cream cheese, Italian seasoning, black pepper and tomato bits. Using electric mixer at medium speed, mix until smooth.

- Line lightly oiled 6x4x2-inch loaf pan with plastic wrap, leaving 2-inch overhang on each side.

- Spread about ⅓ of cheese mixture in loaf pan, smoothing to fill corners. In order listed, add layers of Gruyère cheese, pecans, ⅓ cream cheese mixture, ½ cup parsley, Roquefort cheese and remaining ⅓ cream cheese mixture.

- Pull plastic wrap edges over loaf to cover and chill for at least 8 hours.

- To unmold, lift loaf from pan and invert on serving plate. Remove plastic wrap and sprinkle with remaining ¼ cup parsley. Let stand until room temperature to serve.

- Serves 25.

Gorgonzola-Almond Spread

8 slices bacon, chopped	1 (4 ounce) package Gorgonzola cheese
2 cloves garlic, minced	2 tablespoons chopped chives
1 (8 ounce) package cream cheese, softened	3 tablespoons smoked almonds
¼ cup half and half	

- In skillet, cook bacon until nearly crisp. Add garlic and cook until bacon is crisp. Drain excess fat.

- Combine cream cheese and half and half, mixing until smooth. Add bacon, garlic, Gorgonzola cheese and chives, stirring until blended. Spoon mixture into 2-cup casserole.

- Bake, covered with aluminum foil, at 350 degrees for 20 minutes.

- Sprinkle almonds on cheese mixture. Serve with crackers and vegetables.

- Serves 8.

Recipe can be assembled a day in advance and stored in refrigerator.

College of Mt. St. Joseph

One of the first Catholic colleges in the state to offer the baccalaureate degree for women, The College of Mt. St. Joseph graduated the first nine women in 1924. Today it is a coeducational college.

Exhilarating

In 1891, the Christian Moerlein brewery introduced the first light beer in Cincinnati, a lager which they promised to be "exhilarating, stimulating, rejuvenating, wholesome, delicious and pure." The lager was welcome in a city whose citizens reportedly consumed 2½ times the national average of beer.

Baked Bread Bowl Dip

 *This is one of the most requested recipes. After the* *dip is consumed, we cut the bowl into wedges and broil the pieces to serve with soup.*

1 round loaf sheepherder's bread	2 cups sour cream
1 bunch green onions, chopped	2 cups (8 ounces) grated cheddar cheese
12 cloves garlic, minced and divided	1 (14 ounce) can artichoke hearts, drained and quartered
2 tablespoons butter	1 loaf French bread
1 (8 ounce) package cream cheese	½ cup butter, softened

- Cut 5-inch slice from top of bread. Carefully remove center of loaf, leaving 1-inch shell to form bowl. Reserve slice to use as lid on bowl.

- Sauté green onions and ½ of garlic in 2 tablespoons butter until onions are softened.

- Cut cream cheese into cubes and place in bowl. Add onion and garlic mixture, sour cream and cheddar cheese, mixing well.

- Fold artichokes into cheese mixture. Spoon filling into bread bowl. Cover with bread slice and wrap in double layer of heavy-duty aluminum foil. Place on baking sheet.

- Bake at 350 degrees for 2 hours.

- While stuffed bread bowl is baking, cut French bread into ¼-inch slices.

- Blend ½ cup butter with remaining garlic. Spread mixture thinly on each bread slice.

- Reassemble bread slices to form loaf on sheet of foil. Wrap to enclose.

- Bake French bread loaf with bread bowl for final 30 minutes.

- Remove both loaves from oven. Discard bread lid and place bowl on serving platter. Surround with French bread slices. Serve hot.

- Serves 10 to 12.

Back to Back No Hitters

"It's only been done once, and it was a Red's pitcher who did it. Cincinnati's Johnny Vander Meer took the mound in June, 1938, and threw that rare, once in a lifetime masterpiece, a no hit, no run victory. The amazing thing is, the very next time he took the mound (just four days later), somehow, Vander Meer did it again. Two no-hitters in a row. Hasn't been done before or since."

Charles Henderson
The Downtowner

Ohio's First President

The first President of the United States to claim Ohio as his birthplace, William Henry Harrison married the daughter of John Cleves Symmes, one of the proprietors of the Symmes Purchase.

Blue Cheese Cake

1 cup crushed cheese crackers
2 (8 ounce) packages cream
   cheese softened
½ cup (2 ounces) crumbled
   blue cheese
3 eggs
¼ cup all-purpose flour
¼ teaspoon salt

¼ cup picante sauce
1 cup sour cream
½ cup chopped green onion
   with tops
½ cup chopped walnuts
parsley sprigs, tomato roses or
   sliced green onion for
   garnish

- Prepare the cake the day before serving.

- Sprinkle cracker crumbs on bottom and sides of buttered 8-inch springform pan.

- Combine cream cheese, blue cheese, eggs, flour, salt, picante sauce and sour cream, mixing well. Fold onions into mixture.

- Spread cheese mixture in prepared pan. Sprinkle with walnuts.

- Bake at 375 degrees for 1 hour.

- Chill cake overnight. Remove from pan, place on serving platter and garnish with parsley, tomato roses or green onions. Let stand until room temperature to serve.

- Serves 20.

Walnut-Glazed Brie

⅔ cup finely chopped walnuts
¼ cup Kahlúa liqueur
3 tablespoons brown sugar

½ teaspoon vanilla
1 (14 ounce) Brie round

- Spread walnuts in pie plate or baking pan. Bake at 350 degrees, stirring occasionally, for 10 to 12 minutes or until toasted.

- Add liqueur, brown sugar and vanilla to walnuts. Set aside.

- Reduce oven temperature to 325 degrees.

- Remove and discard top rind from cheese. Place cheese round in shallow baking dish and top with walnut mixture.

- Bake for 8 to 10 minutes or until cheese is softened and thoroughly heated. Serve immediately with assorted crackers and pear slices.

- Serves 12 to 15.

To Market, To Market, To Buy a Fat Pig

Opened on November 28, 1933, Albers Super Market on Hamilton was the first supermarket in the United States.

Bearcats Shine

Floodlights mounted on wooden telephone poles illuminated the first night college football game in 1923 as the University of Cincinnati Bearcats hosted Kentucky Wesleyan at U.C.

 *Stuffed Edam Cheese*

  Very attractive and unusual.

Cincinnati

Cincinnati's first settlers arrived at what is now Yeatman's Cove at the end of 1788. They called the town they planned to build Losantiville, a combination of phrases from Greek, Latin, and French to mean town opposite the Mouth of the (Licking) River. Within two years, their town had been chosen as the site for a federal fort, Ft. Washington. In 1790, Governor of the Northwest Territory Arthur St. Clair, a revolutionary war veteran, changed the name to Cincinnati, after the Revolutionary military organization, Order of Cincinnatus. That's how the city got its name. You can see the statue of Cincinnatus, the Roman citizen-soldier, at Sawyer Point Park.

1 (4 pound) whole Edam cheese
1 cup minced onion
2 tablespoons butter
1 pound ground round
1 teaspoon salt
¼ teaspoon cayenne pepper
1½ cups peeled, seeded and chopped tomatoes
2 eggs, beaten
½ cup chopped pimento-stuffed green olives
½ cup soft bread crumbs
2 tablespoons chopped parsley

- Begin preparation of cheese the day before serving.

- Peel wax coating from cheese and cut 1½-inch slice from top. Using spoon, scoop center from cheese, leaving ½-inch thick shell. Enclose shell and top slice in plastic wrap and chill.

- Grate reserved cheese (amount should measure about 2 cups) and set aside.

- Sauté onion in butter in skillet until soft and translucent. Add beef and cook until browned, stirring to crumble.

- Add salt, pepper and tomatoes to beef mixture. Cook for 3 minutes.

- Remove from heat and stir in grated cheese, eggs, olives, bread crumbs and parsley. Check seasonings.

- Chill mixture, covered, overnight.

- Two to three hours before serving, unwrap cheese shell and slice. Place in bowl and cover with cold water. Let stand for 1 hour, then drain.

- Spoon filling into cheese shell, top with slice and wrap tightly in aluminum foil. Place in deep casserole, filling space around cheese shell with crumpled foil.

- Bake at 375 degrees for 1 hour. Let stand for 30 minutes before unwrapping and serving. If cheese does not hold shape, wrap tightly in foil and freeze for a few minutes until firm.

- Serves 12 to 16.

Mexican Cheesecake

 So good that it could be used as a main dish.

²/₃ cup finely crushed tortilla
  chips
2 tablespoons margarine,
  melted
1 cup cottage cheese
3 (8 ounces) packages cream
  cheese, softened
4 eggs

1½ cups (6 ounces) grated
  cheddar cheese
1 (4 ounce) can chopped
  green chilies, drained
1½ cups sour cream, divided
1 cup jalapeño-cheddar dip
1 cup diced tomato
½ cup sliced green onion
½ cup sliced black olives

- Combine tortilla crumbs and margarine. Press mixture in bottom of 9-inch springform pan.

- Bake at 325 degrees for 15 minutes. Set crust aside.

- Using hand mixer at high speed, whip cottage cheese until smooth.

- Add cream cheese to cottage cheese and mix at medium speed until smooth.

- Add eggs, 1 at a time, mixing well after each addition.

- Fold in cheddar cheese and chilies. Pour mixture into prepared pan.

- Bake at 325 degrees for 1 hour.

- Combine 1 cup sour cream and jalapeño-cheddar dip, mixing well. Spread mixture on cheesecake and continue baking for 10 minutes.

- Allow cheesecake to cool for at least 1 hour before removing sides of springform pan.

- Garnish with tomatoes, green onion, olives and dollops of remaining ½ cup sour cream. Cut into wedges and serve with crackers.

- Serves 16 to 20.

"Art Palace of the West"

This was how the Cincinnati Art Museum was heralded in 1886 when it earned the distinction of being the first general art museum west of the Alleghenies to be established in its own Richardson-Romanesque style building. Constructed by architect James McLaughlin in Eden Park atop Mt. Adams, the museum houses over 5,000 years of world art distinguished by its extremely high quality. One of the premier collections of African objects as art in the United States was showcased here in 1890 in the Carl Stegelman Collection.

Pesto Walnut Cheesecake

Pesto

2 large cloves garlic, minced
1½ cups tightly-packed chopped spinach leaves
¼ cup chopped fresh parsley
½ cup chopped fresh basil

⅔ cup (2¾ ounces) freshly grated Parmesan cheese
⅔ cup chopped walnuts
¼ cup olive oil

Cheesecake

1 (8 ounce) plus 1 (3 ounce) package cream cheese, softened
¾ cup ricotta cheese

2 cups (8 ounces) crumbled goat cheese
3 eggs, at room temperature
½ cup sour cream

Chips

½ cup butter, softened
¼ cup (1 ounce) freshly grated Parmesan cheese

2 cloves garlic, minced
1 (12 ounce) package pita bread

Pesto

- Using food processor, grind garlic, spinach, parsley, basil, Parmesan cheese and walnuts to form paste.

- Add olive oil and continue processing for 2 minutes. Set aside.

Cheesecake

- Using electric mixer, combine cream cheese, ricotta cheese and goat cheese, mixing well.

- Add eggs, 1 at a time, beating well after each addition. Blend in sour cream.

- Pour batter into buttered 8½-inch springform pan.

- Bake at 350 degrees for 45 to 55 minutes. Top should be puffed, golden and firm.

- Cool cheesecake completely before removing sides of pan.

- Spread pesto over surface. Cover with plastic wrap and chill until ready to serve.

Chips

- Combine butter, Parmesan cheese and garlic.

- Split pita rounds, then cut each round into quarters. Thinly spread butter mixture on each wedge and place on broiler pan.

- Broil until golden brown.

(Pesto Walnut Cheesecake continued)

- Place cheesecake in center of serving plate and surround with pita wedges.

- Serves 16 to 20.

Pesto can be stored in airtight container in refrigerator for up to 1 month.

Roquefort Mousse

1 packet unflavored gelatin	2 tablespoons minced pimento
¼ cup lemon juice	1 tablespoon minced capers
1 cup boiling water	1 teaspoon grated onion
1 (4 ounce) package Roquefort cheese	salt and black pepper, to taste
1 cup grated cucumber	1 cup whipping cream, whipped
¼ cup minced fresh parsley	parsley sprigs for garnish

- Soften gelatin in lemon juice. Add boiling water, stir until dissolved and set aside.

- Mash Roquefort cheese. Blend in cucumber, parsley, pimento, capers and onion. Season with salt and black pepper.

- Add gelatin to cheese mixture. Chill until partially firm.

- Fold whipped cream into mixture. Spoon into 6 cup mold. Chill for 4 hours or until very firm.

- Invert on chilled serving platter and remove mold. Garnish with parsley and serve with crackers or melba toast.

- Serves 16 to 18.

For luncheon, use ring mold and fill center with seafood salad. Garnish with paprika-dusted parsley sprigs.

Not a Bird, Not a Plane...

A hot air balloon launched the first air mail out of Cincinnati on the Fourth of July, 1835. Eighty-seven years later, Grisard Field employees in Blue Ash received the first air mail brought by plane.

Mr. President, Your Honor

William Howard Taft was the only person to become both President of the United States, 1909-1912, and Chief Justice of the Supreme Court, 1921-1930.

Curry Pâté

2 (8 ounce) packages cream
  cheese, softened
1 cup (4 ounces) grated
  cheddar cheese
2 tablespoons sherry
½ teaspoon salt
4 teaspoons curry powder
1 cup finely chopped chutney
¼ cup chopped chives

• Combine cream cheese, cheddar cheese, sherry, salt and curry powder, mixing well. Spoon mixture onto serving plate and shape to form a circle.

• Chill for 30 minutes.

• Just before serving, spread chutney on top of cheese circle and sprinkle with chives. Serve with crackers.

• Makes 4 cups.

Hot Jalapeño Crab Dip

 An expensive dip but worth every penny.

½ medium-sized red bell
  pepper, chopped
1½ teaspoons olive oil
1 (14 ounce) can artichoke
  hearts, drained and chopped
1 cup mayonnaise
½ cup (2 ounces) freshly
  grated Parmesan cheese
¼ cup thinly sliced green
  onion
1 tablespoon Worcestershire
  sauce
1 tablespoon minced pickled
  jalapeño peppers
1 teaspoon lemon juice
¼ teaspoon celery salt
1 (8 ounce) can lump crab
  meat, drained
salt
black pepper

• Sauté bell pepper in oil in skillet over medium-high heat for about 3 minutes or until lightly browned. Place bell pepper in mixing bowl.

• Add artichokes, mayonnaise, Parmesan cheese, green onion, Worcestershire sauce, jalapeño peppers, lemon juice and celery salt, stirring to combine.

• Fold in crab meat. Season with salt and black pepper.

• Spread mixture in 8-inch pie plate.

• Bake at 350 degrees for 20 to 25 minutes. Serve with toasted thin slices of French bread.

• Serves 8 to 10.

Hot Bacon and Swiss Dip

1 (8 ounce) package cream
  cheese, softened
½ cup mayonnaise
1 cup (4 ounces) grated Swiss
  cheese

2 tablespoons chopped green
  onion
8 slices bacon, cooked until
  crisp and crumbled

- Combine cream cheese, mayonnaise, Swiss cheese and onion, mixing well. Spread mixture in 9-inch microwave-safe pie plate.

- Microwave on high setting (100%) for 4 minutes or until thoroughly heated.

- Sprinkle with bacon bits and serve with pita chips.

- Makes 2½ cups.

Creamy Crab Dip

1 (6 ounce) can lump crab
  meat
1 (8 ounce) package cream
  cheese, softened
1 tablespoon onion juice

¼ teaspoon curry powder
1 teaspoon paprika
¼ cup chopped fresh parsley
⅔ cup chopped pecans

- Drain crab meat, reserving 3 tablespoons liquid. Using fork, flake crab meat to separate.

- Combine crab meat, reserved liquid, cream cheese, onion juice and curry powder, mixing until smooth. Spread mixture in oven-safe chafing dish.

- Sprinkle paprika, parsley and pecans on crab meat mixture.

- Bake at 350 degrees for 20 minutes.

- Serve hot with melba toast.

- Makes 2½ cups.

Dip can be assembled a day in advance and stored in refrigerator. Bring to room temperature before baking.

Fire Alarm

In 1852, Cincinnati had the very first paid, professional fire department, with the first successful horsedrawn steam fire engine. The Cincinnati Fire Museum is located downtown in a 1907 fire house listed on the National Register.

Kemper Log House

Rev. James Kemper was the first Presbyterian minister ordained north of the Ohio River. In Walnut Hills, he built what is one of the oldest buildings in Ohio. Now known as the Kemper Log House, it was moved to Sharon Woods.

Caviar Pie

3 cups egg salad
1 cup sour cream, at room temperature

1 (2 to 4 ounce) jar domestic caviar
1 cup minced onion

- Spoon egg salad on center of serving plate, shaping into circle 1 inch deep.
- Spread sour cream evenly and completely over egg salad.
- Sprinkle caviar on sour cream. Place onion around rim and in center.
- Serve with potato chips.
- Serves 12.

Hot Tamale Dip

1 (15 ounce) can beef tamales
1 (6 ounce) jar picante dip
1 (16 ounce) package processed cheese food, cubed

1 (16 ounce) can chili without beans

- Remove and discard tamale wrappers and mash with fork.
- In saucepan, combine tamales, picante dip, cheese and chili. Cook over low heat, stirring occasionally, until cheese is melted and blended.
- Serve hot with tortilla chips.
- Serves 12 to 16.

photograph by Robert A. Flischel

The Melanarch Bridge, built in 1884 in Eden Park, is the first concrete bridge in the world.

Ranch Hand Round-Up

 This actually gets better the longer it ages.

2 (15 ounce) cans black beans, drained
1 (15 ounce) can white and yellow corn, drained
1 (4 ounce) can sliced black olives, drained

1 (4 ounce) can diced green chilies, drained
¼ cup chopped green olives
½ cup chopped red onion
½ cup chopped fresh cilantro
½ cup vinaigrette salad dressing

- Prepare the day before serving.

- Combine beans, corn, black olives, chilies, green olives, onion and cilantro. Add dressing and mix well.

- Chill overnight.

- Serve at room temperature with tortilla chips.

- Makes 6 cups.

Barbecue Popcorn Mix

2 teaspoons onion powder
1½ teaspoons chili powder
1½ teaspoons lemon pepper
1 teaspoon garlic powder
½ teaspoon dry mustard
¼ teaspoon paprika

¼ teaspoon salt
18 cups popped corn
6 cups fish-shaped crackers
3 cups pretzel sticks
3 cups peanuts
¼ cup butter, melted

- Combine onion powder, chili powder, lemon pepper, garlic powder, mustard, paprika and salt. Set aside.

- In large roasting pan, combine popcorn, crackers, pretzels and peanuts, mixing well.

- Drizzle butter over popcorn mixture, tossing to coat. Sprinkle spice mixture on popcorn and mix thoroughly.

- Bake at 250 degrees for 45 minutes, stirring at 15 minute intervals.

- Makes 30 cups.

"I'll Have a Big Boy, Please"

David Frisch opened his Big Boy franchise here in 1947. Inspired by the propeller-driven commercial airliners that flew in and out of Lunken Airport, he named the restaurant Frisch's Mainliner.

May I Have This Dance?

Cincinnati's Chicken Dance at Oktoberfest holds the 1994 Guinness World Book of Records title as the largest "Birdie Dance." As lively German music wafted through the air, 48,000 revelers strutted their feathers to earn the title.

Nuts and Bolts

  Your party guests won't be able to get enough of this! It's addictive.

2 (8 ounce) packages cheese crackers
3 to 4 cups mixed nuts
1 cup pecans
4 cups freshly popped corn
2 (8.5 ounce) packages sesame chips
2 (15 ounce) cans coconut chips

1 (6 ounce) package pretzel sticks
1 cup margarine, melted
1 teaspoon salt
½ teaspoon garlic salt or 1 clove garlic, crushed
1 teaspoon curry powder
dash of hot pepper sauce
1 tablespoon Worcestershire sauce

- In large roasting pan, combine crackers, nuts, pecans, popped corn, sesame chips, coconut chips and pretzels.

- Mix butter, salt, garlic, curry powder, hot pepper sauce and Worcestershire sauce together. Drizzle over snack mixture, tossing to coat.

- Bake at 250 degrees for 1 hour, stirring at 15 minute intervals.

- Spread mixture on paper towel to cool. Store in tightly-covered cans or jars.

- Makes 20 cups.

Eighth Street Spires

photograph by Robert A. Flischel

BEVERAGES... *Drinks With a Twist*

The Tyler Davidson Fountain is located in the heart of downtown on Fountain Square.

Photograph by Robert A. Flischel

TYLER DAVIDSON DRINKING FOUNTAIN?

Given to the city as a gift from Henry Probasco as a memorial to his brother-in-law, Henry Tyler Davidson, the bronze fountain was cast by August Von Kreling in Germany. It was originally designed to dispense ice-cold drinking water cooled by a 2,000 foot coil pipe underneath the structure. At one time, four cups, attached by chains, hung from the four fountains.

Apricot Punch

4 teaspoons instant iced tea granules
¼ cup sugar
1¼ cups apricot nectar
½ teaspoon bitters

2 cups cold water
1 cup frozen lemonade concentrate, thawed
½ cup apricot preserves
1 (2 liter) bottle ginger ale

- Combine iced tea granules, sugar, apricot nectar, bitters, and water, mixing thoroughly.

- Stir in lemonade and preserves.

- Just before serving, add ginger ale and ice.

- Serves 12 to 16.

Raspberry Scrub

4 (8 ounce) packages frozen raspberries

1 (6 ounce) can frozen lemonade concentrate, thawed
2 (32 ounce) bottles ginger ale

- Warm raspberries in saucepan over medium heat for 10 minutes or until thawed. Drain through sieve, pressing with wooden spoon to extract juice. Discard seeds. Let stand until cool.

- Combine raspberry juice with lemonade.

- Just before serving, add ginger ale.

- Serves 12 to 18.

"Beer was not sold in bottles until 1850. Before then, if a person wished to buy beer, he went to the neighborhood tavern with a bucket or pot made especially for holding beer, had it filled, and brought the brew home."

Don Deming
Historian

Cherry Berry Slush

1 (12 ounce) package frozen red raspberries, thawed
½ (16 ounce) package frozen pitted unsweetened dark cherries, thawed

1 (6 ounce) can frozen apple juice concentrate, thawed
1 (24 ounce) bottle lemon-lime carbonated drink, chilled
lime slices for garnish

- Using blender, process raspberries with juice until smooth. Strain and discard seeds.

- Process cherries with juice until smooth.

- Combine raspberry puree, cherry puree and apple juice concentrate. Place in freezer-proof bowl and freeze until firm.

- For each serving, scrape fruit juice mixture to measure ¾ cup slush and add ½ cup lemon-lime drink. Garnish with lime slice.

- Serves 6.

 # Bola

4 cups strawberries, stemmed
4 cups sliced, peeled peaches
1 cup peach juice
½ cup lemon juice
¾ cup sugar
½ to 1 cup brandy or kirsch

grated peel of 1 lemon
grated peel of 1 orange
½ cup vodka
2 (32 ounce) bottles chilled Chablis blanc

- Prepare the day before serving.

- Combine strawberries and peaches. Add peach juice, lemon juice, sugar and brandy or kirsch. Marinate at room temperature overnight.

- Just before serving, pour mixture into chilled punch bowl. Add lemon peel, orange peel, vodka and wine.

- Serve over ice.

- Serves 16 to 24.

Cardinal Bowl

1 medium grapefruit
2 small or 1 large orange
1 lemon
1 lime, optional
½ cup water
½ cup sugar

2 (32 ounce) bottles white Rhine or Sauterne wine, chilled
1 (32 ounce) bottle brut or extra-dry champagne, chilled

- Thinly peel grapefruit, orange, lemon and lime. Place peel in bowl, cover with water and chill for 4 to 12 hours.

- Press juice from fruit, strain and add sugar, stirring to dissolve sugar.

- Drain liquid from peel and add to fruit juice. Pour into chilled punch bowl.

- Just before serving, add wine and champagne.

- Serves 16 to 20.

Cranberry Margaritas

 This is a festive holiday drink.

1 cup cranberry juice
½ (scant) cup sugar
1½ cups fresh or frozen cranberries

¾ cup lime juice
¾ cup tequila
½ cup triple sec
3 cups cracked ice

- Using ½ of ingredients at a time, combine cranberry juice, sugar, cranberries, lime juice, tequila, triple sec and ice in blender container. Blend until slushy. Repeat with remaining ingredients.

- To serve, dip rims of cups or glasses in water or cranberry juice, then dip in 3 tablespoons sugar in shallow dish to coat rims. Pour juice mixture into prepared cups or glasses.

- Serves 4 to 6.

On the Vine

Whether you're a wine connoisseur, or simply like a glass of wine now and then, there are several local wineries that are earning award-winning respect across the country: Meier's Wine Cellars in Silverton, Moyer Winery, Valley Vineyards in Morrow, Vinkolet Winery and Vineyard on Colerain Avenue, and Chateau Pomije in Indiana.

"My fondest memories ever are: growing up in Hyde Park, visiting neighbors, running errands for Mrs. Adam's in return for cherry lifesavers, taking care of Mr. Kispert's lawn ($3.00 a day and I thought I was king), my collection of pop bottles, at age 7 having a bologna and mustard sandwich and a 7-ounce coke at Mrs. Stein's grocery and sitting between the iceman and the postman."

Jim Tarbell
Arnold's Bar and Grill

White Wine Sangría

 Perfect for an annual girls' night out.

½ cup water
1 cup sugar
1 stick cinnamon
2 lemons: 1 juiced and 1 sliced

2 oranges: 1 juiced and
1 sliced
1 (32 ounce) bottle white or
red wine

- Combine water, sugar and cinnamon stick in saucepan. Bring to a boil, reduce heat to medium and cook for 5 minutes. Remove from heat and let stand until cool. Discard cinnamon stick.

- Gradually add lemon and orange juice to syrup, stirring to blend.

- Add fruit slices and wine.

- Chill before serving.

- Serves 6 to 8.

 ## Coffee Liqueur

 A delightful Christmas gift. Make the week before Thanksgiving for Christmas stocking stuffers.

3¾ cups sugar
1 (1½-inch) vanilla bean,
broken in pieces
2 cups water

3¾ tablespoons instant coffee
granules
¼ cup boiling water
1 (32 ounce) bottle vodka

- Combine sugar, vanilla pieces and water in saucepan. Simmer for 30 minutes without stirring.

- Dissolve coffee granules in boiling water. Add to vanilla liquid. Strain to remove vanilla bean pieces.

- Add vodka to coffee mixture. Pour into small collector bottles, let stand until cool, then cork.

- Store in dark cool place for 4 weeks.

- Makes 8 cups.

 ## Coffee Punch

 A summer party punch.

½ **gallon coffee ice cream**
1 **(28 ounce) bottle carbonated cream soda drink**

1 **(28 ounce) bottle ginger ale**

- Place ice cream in punch bowl and allow to soften slightly.

- Slowly pour equal amounts of cream soda and ginger ale over ice cream. Mix gently to prevent excess foaming.

- Serves 10.

Champura

 Mexican Chocolate

½ **cup semi-sweet chocolate chips**
1 **tablespoon instant coffee granules**
½ **teaspoon vanilla**
¼ **teaspoon cinnamon**

2 **cups hot milk**
½ **cup rum**
whipped cream for garnish
cinnamon or marshmallows for garnish

- Combine chocolate chips, coffee granules, vanilla, cinnamon and hot milk in blender container. Blend until chocolate is melted.

- Add rum to chocolate liquid. Serve hot, garnished with whipped cream and dash of cinnamon or marshmallow.

- Serves 3 or 4.

 *Christmas Cheer*

Up Close

Located in the heart of downtown, Fountain Square is a favorite gathering place, and the Tyler Davidson Fountain is the centerpiece. The Genius of Water is the central figure, from whose outstretched hands water flows. Four of the figures depict a farmer leaning upon his plow, a mother bathing her child, a citizen extinguishing fire, and a daughter offering water to her father. Four bas-reliefs by Frederick von Muller are at the base, representing navigation, milling, fishing and power. There are children in the niches at each corner of the pedestal, suggesting the pleasures of water: a girl with a string of pearls, a boy putting on ice skates, one playing with a shell and another finding corals.

1 cup gin
½ cup orange juice
¼ cup grenadine

1 tablespoon whipping cream
sugar, optional

- Combine gin, orange juice, grenadine, cream and sugar, mixing well.
- Chill until very cold. Serve over ice in glasses.
- Serves 4.

Close-up of figure in the Tyler Davidson Fountain

photograph by Robert A. Flischel

SOUPS AND SAUCES... *Stirrin' It Up*

Paddle wheelers at the Tall Stacks celebration.

Photograph by J. Miles Wolf

"Although famous for our chili, our soups and sauces really create a stir, too. Spoon it, slurp it, stir it, but for pig's sake, savor it."

Cincy

"Although many may accuse Cincinnatians of having conservative palates, some of our favorite dishes are actually quite adventurous. Muddy-colored mock turtle soup, for instance, is flavored sweet and sour with floating garnishes of chopped hard-boiled eggs and lemon slices. Crispy fried sauerkraut balls are both intensely tart and rich. And Cincinnati chili offers an array of subtle Middle Eastern flavors in a familiar Midwestern form. Even lowly goetta is more exciting than its cousin, scrapple, because of its oaty crunch."

Chuck Martin
Food Editor
The Cincinnati Enquirer

Asparagus Soup

6 cups chicken broth
2 pounds fresh asparagus, chopped
2 leeks, chopped

salt and black pepper
sour cream for garnish
bacon bits for garnish

- In large saucepan, combine broth, asparagus and leeks. Cook until vegetables are tender.

- Pour into food processor container and puree until smooth.

- Season with salt and black pepper. Serve warm with dollop of sour cream and sprinkle of bacon bits.

- Serves 8 to 10.

Three Bean Chili

 A nice meatless entrée. Very tasty.

½ cup chopped onion
½ cup chopped celery
⅓ cup chopped green bell pepper
1 tablespoon olive oil
1 (28 ounce) can tomatoes, chopped and with liquid
1 (15 ounce) can tomato sauce
1 teaspoon sugar
½ teaspoon salt
⅛ teaspoon black pepper
2 teaspoons chili powder

1 teaspoon cumin
1 teaspoon ground cumin
¼ teaspoon garlic powder
⅛ teaspoon cayenne pepper
1 (16 ounce) can Great Northern beans, rinsed and drained
1 (15½ ounce) can kidney beans, rinsed and drained
1 (15½ ounce) can garbanzo beans, rinsed and drained

- In large skillet, sauté onion, celery and bell pepper in oil until vegetables are tender.

- Add tomatoes, tomato sauce, sugar, salt, black pepper, chili powder, cumin, ground cumin, garlic powder and cayenne pepper. Stir in Northern beans, kidney beans and garbanzo beans.

- Simmer for 30 to 45 minutes.

- Serves 8 to 10.

Sunday Supper Soup

"The beauty of Greater Cincinnati and the surrounding Ohio River Valley perhaps is best experienced by taking a cruise on the mighty Ohio River."

Beth Charlton
Greater Cincinnati
Convention and
Visitors Bureau

Meatballs
1½ pounds ground beef
1 egg, lightly beaten
3 tablespoons water
½ cup dry bread crumbs

¼ teaspoon salt
1 tablespoon chopped parsley
2 tablespoons butter

Soup
1 (10½ ounce) can condensed
  beef broth, undiluted
1 (28 ounce) can tomatoes,
  chopped and with liquid
1 (1⅜ ounce) packet onion
  soup mix

1 cup sliced carrots
¼ cup chopped celery tops
¼ cup chopped parsley
¼ teaspoon black pepper
¼ teaspoon dried oregano
¼ teaspoon dried basil
1 bay leaf

- Prepare meatballs by combining beef, egg, water, bread crumbs, salt and parsley, mixing lightly. Shape into 24 balls.

- In 5-quart Dutch oven, brown meatballs in butter, a single layer at a time and turning to brown all sides. Remove meatballs and drain excess fat from pan.

- Pour broth and tomatoes into Dutch oven. Add soup mix, carrots, celery, parsley, black pepper, oregano, basil and bay leaf.

- Bring to a boil, reduce heat and simmer, covered, for 20 minutes. Add meatballs and simmer for additional 20 minutes. Remove bay leaf and discard.

- Serve with crisp green salad and warm French bread chunks to absorb broth.

- Serves 6 to 8.

Traditional Cincinnati Chili

2 pounds ground beef
4 medium sized minced onions
1 clove garlic, minced, or
   1 teaspoon garlic powder
1 (8 ounce) can tomato sauce
4 cups water
2 dashes Worcestershire sauce
1½ tablespoons vinegar

salt and black pepper, to taste
¼ cup chili powder
1 teaspoon ground red pepper
1 teaspoon cinnamon
5 bay leaves
35 whole allspice
1 (16 ounce) can kidney beans

- In Dutch oven, brown beef with onion and garlic, stirring to crumble. Drain excess fat.

- Stir in tomato sauce, water, Worcestershire sauce, vinegar, salt, black pepper, chili powder, red pepper and cinnamon.

- Enclose bay leaves and allspice in cheesecloth bag, secure tightly and add to soup.

- Bring to a boil, stirring frequently. Add beans, reduce heat and simmer, covered, for 3 hours.

- Serves 6 to 8.

White Chili

2 pounds boned skinless
   chicken breasts, diced
1 teaspoon olive oil
1 (48 ounce) jar Great
   Northern beans, undrained

1 (16 ounce) jar salsa
2 cups (8 ounces) shredded
   Monterey Jack cheese
1 cup (4 ounces) shredded
   jalapeño pepper cheese

- In skillet, sauté chicken in oil until cooked.

- Combine chicken, beans and salsa in stock pot. Stir in cheeses.

- Simmer, stirring frequently, for 20 to 30 minutes or until flavors are blended and chili is thoroughly heated.

- Serves 6.

Chili recipe can be doubled and can be frozen.

On Chili

"Is there anything else, besides Skyline?"

WCPO News Anchor
Carol Williams

Chili Parlors

Cincinnatians are known to be quite pig-headed about their choice of chili parlors, and their secret family recipes. From the first chili parlor that opened in the twenties to at least one in every neighborhood, they're everywhere. Whether it's Gold Star, Skyline, Chili Time, the Chili Company, or a mom and pop operation like Empress, Camp Washington, or Delhi Chili, if you've lived here long enough, it becomes an addiction. A five-way is a plate of piping hot spaghetti layered with beans, chili, onions and a mound of grated cheese. Delete an ingredient or two, and you're into a four-way, or a three-way. Then, of course, there's the cheese coneys, miniature hot dogs on steamed buns loaded with chili and cheese, and maybe onions and mustard.

Garland's Chili

5 pounds diced stewing beef	1 tablespoon ground cumin
2 pounds bulk pork sausage	2 cups water
1 (12 ounce) can beer	3 green bell peppers, sliced
3 tablespoons salt	2 large onions, chopped
2 tablespoons black pepper	4 (28 ounce) cans tomatoes,
2 tablespoons oregano	chopped, with liquid
¼ cup chili powder	2 (4 ounce) cans green chilies,
1 tablespoon garlic salt	drained and chopped

- In large skillet, brown beef in 3 batches, stirring to crumble. After each batch, place beef in stock pot and drain excess fat from skillet. Brown sausage, drain excess fat and add sausage to beef.

- Blend beer with salt, black pepper, oregano, chili powder, garlic salt and cumin to form a paste. Stir into meat mixture.

- Simmer, covered, for 30 minutes, stirring frequently.

- Add water, bell pepper, onion, tomatoes and chilies to meat mixture.

- Simmer, covered, for 4½ hours; do not boil and add more water if necessary. For last 15 minutes, remove cover and increase heat to evaporate excess liquid.

- Serves 12 to 16.

Cucumber Soup

2½ cucumbers, peeled, seeds removed and chopped	½ cup sour cream
	salt and black pepper, to taste
½ cup chopped onion	curry powder, to taste
2 cups chicken broth	cucumber slices for garnish
¾ to 1 cup cottage cheese	parsley sprigs for garnish

- In saucepan, combine cucumbers, onion and broth. Cook until vegetables are tender.

- Pour soup into blender container. Add cottage cheese, sour cream, salt, black pepper and curry powder. Blend until smooth.

- Chill soup until very cold. Garnish individual servings with cucumber slices and parsley.

- Serves 4.

"Many years ago, when I was a little boy, we lived next door to a slaughter-house in Camp Washington, Lohrey Packing House. They specialized in pigs — only pigs. Farmers used to bring their pigs down to Spring Grove Avenue. The packing house would send men down there to the stockyards— they would pick out 100 or so pigs, and they would literally drive them over a mile, down Spring Grove Avenue, through the streets in Camp Washington, and some more streets until they got to Sydney, where the packing house was. I mean, these men didn't have any special equipment or anything, just some sticks to keep the pigs in control until they got to the slaughter-house.

Such a noise, from all the squealing pigs. There were over 100 of these things. It was unbelievable—it would be like a sea of pigs comin' at you.

Zucchini Turkey Chili Stew

1 pound ground turkey
  sausage
2 cups chopped celery
2 pounds zucchini, unpeeled
  and sliced
1 large onion, chopped
1 clove garlic, minced
tomato juice or beef broth

1 (28 ounce) can tomatoes,
  crushed and with juice
1 (16 ounce) can pork and
  beans
1 green bell pepper, chopped
1 packet chili seasoning mix
1 (16 ounce) can whole kernel
  corn, undrained
grated Parmesan cheese

- In Dutch oven over medium-low heat, brown turkey, stirring to crumble.

- Add celery, zucchini, onion and garlic. Cook for 10 minutes, adding juice or broth if liquid is needed.

- Stir in tomatoes, pork and beans, bell pepper and chili seasoning. Add juice or broth to just cover vegetables. Simmer, covered, for 20 minutes.

- Add corn, remove cover and simmer for 10 minutes.

- Sprinkle individual portions with Parmesan cheese.

- Serves 6.

Of course, all the kids, I mean, all the kids, in the neighborhood– we'd get out on the street to see this. It was like a parade. That was my one ambition in life. Someday I wanted to grow up to be a pig driver. I never made it."

Jim Key
Executive Vice
President of Sales
and Marketing
Enerfab Corporation

"Homemade chili with all the fixings is best in front of a roaring fire in the dead of winter."

Rob Goering
Hamilton County
Treasurer

photograph by Paula Norton

Taste of Cincinnati

Tuscan Bean Soup

2 cups dried white beans	1 teaspoon salt
water	1 teaspoon black pepper
¾ cup chopped onion	2 teaspoons basil
1 teaspoon minced garlic	2 teaspoons oregano
1 tablespoon vegetable oil	2 teaspoons rosemary
2 cups finely chopped carrots	1 teaspoon thyme
2 cups finely chopped celery	8 cups water
4 cups chopped tomatoes	8 cups thinly sliced cabbage

- Place beans in stock pot and add water to cover. Bring to a boil and cook for 2 minutes. Remove from heat and let stand, covered, for 1 hour. Drain, remove from pot and set aside.

- Sauté onion and garlic in oil in pot for 4 minutes. Add celery and carrots and cook for 2 minutes.

- Stir in tomatoes, salt, black pepper, basil, oregano, rosemary and thyme. Add 8 cups water and beans.

- Bring to a boil, reduce heat and simmer for 1 hour. Add cabbage and simmer for 1 additional hour.

- Serves 24.

Avgolemono

Greek Egg and Lemon Soup

 Delicious served hot or cold.

10 cups chicken broth	2 eggs, separated
1 (16 ounce) package orzo pasta (less ⅓ cup)	juice of 3 large lemons

- In large saucepan, bring broth to a boil. Add orzo, reduce heat and simmer until tender.

- Remove pan from heat, cover and let stand a few minutes; broth should not be boiling hot when adding remaining ingredients.

- Using whisk, whip egg whites until frothy. Add egg yolks and whip until frothy. Add lemon juice to yolks and whip again until frothy.

- Gradually add a ladle of hot broth to egg mixture and whip until frothy. Stir egg mixture into remaining broth with orzo. Let stand for 10 minutes before serving.

- Serves 8.

Fabulous Lentil Soup

3 medium sized onions,
  chopped
3 carrots, coarsely grated
¾ teaspoon dried marjoram,
  crumbled
¾ teaspoon dried thyme,
  crumbled
2 tablespoons vegetable oil
1 (28 ounce) can tomatoes,
  coarsely chopped and with
  juice

3½ cups canned beef broth
3½ cups water
1½ cups dried lentils, rinsed
½ teaspoon salt
½ teaspoon black pepper
¾ cup dry white wine
2 tablespoons dried parsley
  flakes
1 cup (4 ounces) grated
  cheddar cheese, optional

- In large saucepan, sauté onion, carrots, marjoram and thyme in oil for 5 minutes, stirring frequently.

- Add tomatoes, broth, water and lentils. Bring to a boil, reduce heat and simmer, covered, for 1 hour or until the lentils are tender.

- Stir in salt, black pepper, wine and parsley. Simmer for a few additional minutes. Sprinkle with cheese.

- Serves 8.

photograph by J. Miles Wolf

Porkopolis

The humble pig once nudged the lively Midwestern city of Cincinnati into prominence as the pork-packing capital of the world. The bustling Ohio city was called Porkopolis in the early-to-mid 1800's because of her position as a leader in a vital national industry which provided food, employment and exports. Pork from Cincinnati fed everyone - from slaves in plantations in the south to princes in their palaces in Europe. And housewives from San Francisco to New York boasted of having Cincinnati ham for Sunday dinner because it was well known for its reliable quality.

Broccoli Chicken Soup

1 bunch broccoli
¾ cup chopped onion
2 stalks celery with leaves, thinly sliced
1 tablespoon butter
½ cup chopped parsley
⅓ cup uncooked long-grain rice
4 cups chicken broth, divided

¾ pound chicken, cooked and shredded
1 cup evaporated milk
1 teaspoon salt
¼ teaspoon black pepper
⅛ teaspoon cayenne pepper
1 cup (4 ounces) shredded Gruyère cheese
¼ cup (1 ounce) freshly grated Parmesan cheese

- Cut flowerets from broccoli stalks, measure 2 cups and set aside. Peel and chop stalks. Add enough to remaining flowerets to measure 3 cups.

- In large saucepan over medium heat, sauté 3 cups broccoli flowerets and stalks, onion and celery in butter for 3 minutes.

- Stir in parsley, rice and 2 cups broth. Simmer over medium heat for 20 minutes or until most of liquid is absorbed and rice is tender.

- Pour vegetable mixture into blender, puree and set aside.

- In large saucepan, bring remaining 2 cups broth to a boil. Reduce heat to medium, add chicken and 2 cups broccoli flowerets. Simmer for 8 minutes.

- Add milk, pureed vegetables, salt, black pepper and cayenne pepper. Cook for 2 to 3 minutes. Gradually add Gruyère cheese, stirring well after each addition and heating until cheese is blended. Sprinkle Parmesan cheese on individual servings.

- Serves 6.

Burrito Joe's Chicken Tortilla Soup

⅔ cup diced green bell pepper
⅔ cup diced yellow onion
1 tablespoon olive oil
2 teaspoons minced garlic
2 teaspoons kosher salt
1 teaspoon black pepper
1 teaspoon dried oregano
1 teaspoon ground cumin
2 teaspoons dried thyme
1 teaspoon cayenne pepper

2 cups chicken broth
4 cups crushed canned
  tomatoes
2⅔ cups reduced-fat sour
  cream
¾ pound chicken, cooked and
  shredded
½ cup chopped cilantro
6 (6 inch) corn tortillas
1 cup vegetable oil for frying

- In Dutch oven, lightly sauté bell pepper and onion in oil. Add garlic, kosher salt, black pepper, oregano, cumin, thyme and cayenne pepper. Sauté for additional 3 minutes.

- Stir broth into vegetables. Bring to a boil, reduce heat and simmer for 15 minutes.

- Add tomatoes and simmer for additional 15 minutes.

- Pour 2 cups warm soup liquid into bowl. Whisk sour cream into soup, then add mixture to remaining soup in Dutch oven. Stir in chicken and cilantro.

- Cut tortillas into 2-inch strips. Heat oil to 350 degrees in saucepan or skillet. In small batches, fry tortilla strips until crisp and golden brown. Drain on paper towel.

- Garnish individual servings of soup with tortilla strips.

- Serves 8 to 10.

"My favorite memory as a kid was going to Over-the-Rhine to visit my mother's relatives who lived in a 4 or 5-story walkup, it just seemed like a huge house then. I know that the kitchen was huge, it fit in the whole back of the house. It was so big, it had an attic fan on the side of the wall to vent out when they were cooking for the holidays.

One of their favorite things to cook was big soups, and everything seemed like it was a 50-gallon pot to me, so cooking chicken soup as a kid must have been responsible for my interest in cooking now. It is the most vivid thing about cooking in my mind now. I can't remember yesterday's recipe like I can remember sitting in this kitchen, completely overwhelmed. The table fit 18 people, you know, it was so much bigger than life."

*Doug Hart
Owner and Vice
President
Hart Productions*

Ogle's Chicken Soup

A Cubeful of Sugar

Remember that sugar cube with the pink medicine on it at the doctor's office? That was the live polio virus vaccine breakthrough of Dr. Albert Sabin, after whom the Convention Center is named. The earlier Salk vaccine had been delivered by injection.

1 (2½ to 3 pound) broiler-fryer, cut up, or 1½ pounds boned skinless chicken breasts
⅕ head cabbage, chopped
1 head endive, chopped
2 leeks (white portion only), chopped
1 small onion, chopped
2 cups chopped celery
2 cups chopped carrots
chopped fresh parsley, to taste
1 tablespoon dried basil
1 teaspoon minced garlic

2 tablespoons olive oil
1 (15 ounce) can chick peas, drained
2 medium zucchini, cubed
½ (12 ounce) package refrigerated cheese and basil tortellini
¼ cup parsley
½ (12 ounce) package refrigerated cheese tortellini
salt and black pepper, to taste
freshly grated Parmesan cheese for garnish
sourdough or Caesar croutons

- Cook chicken in water ample to provide broth for soup consistency; season water with herbs to taste. Remove bones from cooked chicken and discard; cut meat into cubes and set aside with cooking broth.

- In Dutch oven, sauté cabbage, endive, leeks, onion, celery, carrots, basil and garlic in oil for about 10 minutes, stirring occasionally.

- Add chicken, broth, chick peas and zucchini. Bring to a boil, reduce heat and simmer for 10 minutes.

- Stir in tortellini and parsley, season with salt and black pepper and simmer for 10 to 20 minutes or until tortellini is tender.

- Serve with Parmesan cheese and croutons.

- Serves 6.

Soup can be assembled the day before serving, except for addition of tortellini. Store in refrigerator and reheat, add tortellini and cook as directed.

Peach Soup

3 cups frozen or canned peaches with juice

1 cup sour cream
½ teaspoon almond extract

- Combine peaches, sour cream and almond extract in blender container. Blend until smooth.

- Chill thoroughly and serve cold.

- Serves 3.

Garlic Cream Soup Gratin

 This is an original Italian family recipe.

1 medium sized onion, diced
12 large cloves garlic,
  quartered
2 tablespoons butter
2 tablespoons all-purpose flour
3 cups beef broth
1 cup plus 2 tablespoons
  whipping cream

salt and freshly ground black
  pepper, to taste
nutmeg, to taste
1 teaspoon lemon juice
1 teaspoon oregano
4 slices French baguette bread
2 tablespoons freshly grated
  provolone cheese

- In Dutch oven, sauté onion and garlic in butter until tender. Stir in flour and cook until golden brown.

- Add broth and cream to sauce. Simmer, covered, for 20 minutes.

- Check soup for onion and garlic pieces; puree by pressing through a sieve or mashing with fork and return to soup. Season with salt, black pepper, nutmeg and lemon juice.

- Toast bread slices, sprinkle with provolone cheese, place on baking sheet and bake at 350 degrees for a few minutes until cheese is melted.

- Ladle soup into individual bowls, top each with slice of cheese bread and sprinkle with oregano.

- Serves 4.

Creamy Pumpkin Soup

3 cups fresh pureed pumpkin
  or canned pumpkin
3 cups fresh pureed tomatoes
  or canned tomatoes
3 cups soy milk

1 tablespoon margarine
1 teaspoon cider vinegar
hot pepper sauce, to taste
salt and black pepper, to taste

- In Dutch oven, combine pumpkin, tomatoes, soy milk, margarine, vinegar, hot pepper sauce, salt and black pepper. Simmer for at least 1 hour, stirring frequently.

- Serves 6 to 8.

Soup can be prepared in a slow cooker.

Greater Cincinnati

The southernmost portion of Ohio, the northernmost portion of Kentucky, and the southeastern portion of Indiana all comprise the Greater Cincinnati area. This helps to explain why the airport, which is located in Kentucky, is called the Cincinnati/Northern Kentucky International Airport. It encompasses 3,866 square miles and 1.7 million people, earning the title of the second largest city in Ohio and the 23rd largest in the country. The population of the city itself is 364,000.

 *Crab Chowder*

"The Ohio River Valley where Cincinnati and Northern Kentucky are situated has long been known as a land of special promise. For centuries, various American Indian tribes revered the lush valley where several smaller rivers join the Ohio River to be sacred hunting grounds. Indians from throughout the Midwest would travel to what is now Cincinnati to hunt the huge herds of bison and other game that frequented the area.

Word soon spread about this 'promised land' as European immigrants began to travel west the last half of the 18th century. Part of the Northwest Territory ceded to the United States in 1783 by England, the area where Cincinnati now exists was considered among the most fertile land on the continent.

As the only spot along the Ohio River where the steep hills did not come to the river's banks, the area was the natural setting for a great city. On December 28, 1788, a group of hearty pioneers beached their riverboats directly across the Ohio River from the mouth of Kentucky's Licking River, and Cincinnati was born.

1 small green bell pepper, chopped	1 teaspoon hot pepper sauce
1 medium sized onion, chopped	1 bay leaf
1 leek, chopped	2 teaspoons chicken bouillon granules
½ cup chopped white celery	6 cups milk
¼ cup butter	1 cup sherry or dry white wine
1 teaspoon garlic salt	1 pound crab meat
1 teaspoon seasoned salt	1 tablespoon arrowroot
1 teaspoon thyme	1 tablespoon water
⅛ teaspoon nutmeg	3 tablespoons chopped parsley

- In Dutch oven, sauté bell pepper, onion, leek and celery in butter until tender but not browned.

- Stir garlic salt, seasoned salt, thyme, nutmeg, hot pepper sauce, bay leaf, bouillon and milk into vegetables. Bring to a boil, add wine, reduce heat and simmer for 15 to 20 minutes.

- Add crab meat to soup.

- Blend arrowroot with water and add to soup. Cook, stirring constantly, until slightly thickened.

- Sprinkle individual servings with parsley.

- Serves 6.

The Palace's Roasted Pear Soup with Gorgonzola and Walnuts

12 pears, peeled and cut in
  halves
1 onion, diced
2 tablespoons butter
1 sprig rosemary
1 cup white wine

¼ cup port wine
4 cups chicken broth
salt and black pepper, to taste
1 cup (4 ounces) crumbled
  gorgonzola cheese
¼ cup toasted walnuts

- Place pear halves on baking sheet and spray with vegetable cooking spray. Bake at 350 degrees for about 25 minutes.

- While pears are baking, sauté onion in butter in Dutch oven, cooking until transparent. Stir in rosemary and cook for about 2 minutes

- Add wine to onions and cook until liquid is reduced by ⅓. Stir in broth and bring to a boil.

- Add pears and simmer for about 30 minutes. Pour into blender container (in two or more batches), blend briefly and strain. Season with salt and black pepper.

- Garnish individual servings with sprinkle of gorgonzola cheese and walnuts.

- Serves 8.

Wild Spinach Soup

The botanical name for wild spinach is Chenopodium. Also called Lamb's Quarter and Pig's Weed, wild spinach grows everywhere in midsummer-in the garden, along the roadside, in fields and on the farm. Avoid picking a sprayed crop.

½ pound wild spinach or 10
  ounces cultivated spinach,
  washed and chopped
2 large potatoes, cubed
2 large carrots, chopped
1 large onion, chopped

2 large stalks celery, chopped
6 cups chicken broth or water
1 tablespoon margarine
1 clove garlic, minced
salt and black pepper, to taste

- In stock pot, combine spinach, potatoes, carrots, onion, celery and broth or water. Bring to a boil, reduce heat and simmer for at least 1 hour.

- Stir in margarine, garlic, salt and black pepper.

- Serves 6.

Sheeba's Potato Soup

 The Queen of Sheeba would be proud of this creation.

5 pounds potatoes, peeled and quartered	1 teaspoon black pepper, or to taste
3 or 4 large onions, chopped	2 teaspoons garlic salt or to taste
6 stalks celery, chopped	3 tablespoons Cavender's Greek Seasoning
4 carrots, chopped	instant mashed potato flakes
6 chicken bouillon cubes	grated cheddar cheese for garnish
½ cup butter	chopped green onion for garnish
water	crumbled bacon pieces for garnish
3 cups milk	
1 cup half and half	
¼ cup Worcestershire sauce	
3 tablespoons chopped parsley	

- In stock pot, combine potatoes, onion, celery, carrots, bouillon and butter. Add water to just cover vegetables. Bring to a boil, reduce heat and simmer until vegetables are tender, adding small amounts of water as needed.

- Using potato masher, mash potatoes to desired consistency.

- Stir in milk, half and half, Worcestershire sauce, parsley, black pepper, garlic salt and Cavender's Greek Seasoning, mixing well. Add potato flakes, a small amount at a time, until soup is desired consistency.

- Garnish individual servings with cheddar cheese, green onion and bacon.

- Serves 8 to 10.

Versatile Vegetable Sauce

½ cup butter	2 cups sour cream
½ cup (2 ounces) grated Parmesan cheese	¼ cup chopped chives
1 teaspoon salt	⅓ cup chopped cucumber

- Combine butter, Parmesan cheese and salt, mixing until smooth.

- Blend in sour cream, chives and cucumber.

- Makes 3 cups.

Use as topping for asparagus, broccoli, cauliflower, green beans or sliced parsnips or to cream succotash or peas, corn and onions.

Spinach and Watercress Soup

1 large white onion, chopped
3 tablespoons butter
2 baking potatoes, peeled and
   cubed, or 6 medium new
   potatoes, peeled and cut in
   halves
2 (14½ ounce) cans chicken
   broth

1 teaspoon salt
½ teaspoon black pepper
½ teaspoon nutmeg
2 (10 ounce) packages frozen
   chopped spinach, thawed
1 bunch watercress, chopped
2 cups half and half

- In Dutch oven, sauté onion in butter until tender.

- Add potatoes, broth, salt, black pepper and nutmeg. Simmer for 30 minutes.

- Remove from heat and stir in spinach and watercress. Dividing into 3 or 4 batches, pour mixture into blender container and puree.

- Combine puree and half and half. Serve hot or cold.

- Serves 10.

 ## Cold Squash Soup

 A refreshing summer soup.

1½ pounds yellow squash, sliced
4 onions, chopped
2½ cups chicken broth,
   divided

1 cup sour cream
salt and black pepper, to taste
fresh dill, to taste

- In saucepan, combine squash, onion and 2 cups broth. Bring to a boil, reduce heat and simmer for about 30 minutes or until vegetables are soft.

- Pour soup into blender and puree. Pour into bowl and stir in remaining ½ cup broth, sour cream, salt and black pepper.

- Chill, covered, for several hours. Garnish individual servings with dill.

- Serves 6.

The past twenty-eight years have been wonderful. The Heimlich Institute is now a permanent Cincinnati institution thanks to the support of the people of our city. We're proud to be Cincinnatians."

Dr. Henry Heimlich President of the Heimlich Institute, Dr. Henry Heimlich is perhaps most famous for the Heimlich maneuver. He is also one of the few living persons listed in dictionaries. Norman Vincent Peale has said that Dr. Heimlich has saved more lives than any other person.

Butternut Squash Soup

2 heads garlic with skin
2 pounds butternut squash
1 large red onion, quartered
1 tablespoon plus 2 teaspoons chopped fresh thyme
3 tablespoons chopped fresh basil
3 tablespoons chopped fresh parsley

3 tablespoons olive oil
1 (14½ ounce) can chicken broth
½ cup whipping cream
1 teaspoon salt
⅛ teaspoon black pepper
½ teaspoon nutmeg

- Cut ⅓ inch from top of garlic heads and place, cut side down, in large baking dish. Cut squash into chunks, discard seeds, and place, cut side down, in baking dish. Add onion and sprinkle with thyme, basil, parsley and oil.

- Bake at 350 degrees for 1½ hours.

- Cool squash slightly. Remove pulp and discard skin. Discard skin from onion. Squeeze pulp from garlic. Combine vegetable pulp in food processor and add herbs.

- Add broth, whipping cream, salt, black pepper and nutmeg. Process until smooth. Serve warm.

- Serves 4 to 6.

Beer Marinade for Summer Grilling

1 (12 ounce) can beer
1 cup fresh lime juice
2 tablespoons Worcestershire sauce
1 teaspoon hot pepper sauce

2 tablespoons lime zest
¼ cup firmly packed brown sugar
1 bay leaf
2 tomatoes, diced

- Combine beer, lime juice, Worcestershire sauce, hot pepper sauce and lime zest in glass bowl. Stir in brown sugar, bay leaf and tomatoes.

- Use to marinate about 2 pounds beef, pork or chicken 3 to 12 hours before grilling. Reserve marinade for basting while cooking, then boil remainder for about 5 minutes to reduce and use as sauce.

- Makes 2⅔ cups.

Cheesy Cream of Zucchini

8 slices bacon, diced
1 cup chopped green onion
½ cup chopped green bell
  pepper
2 tablespoons chopped
  pimento
5 cups sliced and quartered
  zucchini
2 cups chicken broth

½ cup butter or margarine
½ cup all-purpose flour
5 cups milk or half and half
½ teaspoon salt
1 teaspoon black pepper
1 teaspoon Worcestershire
  sauce
2 cups (8 ounces) grated
  cheddar cheese

- In Dutch oven, cook bacon until crisp. Remove with slotted spoon and set aside.

- Sauté onion, bell pepper and pimento in bacon drippings until onion is tender.

- Add zucchini and chicken broth. Bring to a boil, reduce heat and simmer for 20 minutes.

- In stock pot, melt butter. Stir in flour and cook for 2 minutes. Blend in milk or half and half, salt, black pepper and Worcestershire sauce.

- Gradually add cheddar cheese to milk, stirring until melted. Add zucchini with broth and bacon.

- Serves 10.

Check Your Thermometer

The average temperature ranges from 30 degrees in January to 76 degrees in July. The annual average temperature is 54 degrees in Cincinnati.

"Cheese coneys are my favorite Cincy food, because they're just plain good! No mustard or onion though-I'm a purist."

*John Morris Russell
Associate Conductor
Cincinnati Symphony
Orchestra*

Dill Sauce for Grilled Salmon

¼ cup reduced-fat mayonnaise
2 tablespoons reduced-fat sour
  cream
1½ teaspoons lemon juice

1½ teaspoons milk
1 teaspoon dill weed
⅛ teaspoon black pepper

- Combine mayonnaise, sour cream, lemon juice, milk, dill weed and black pepper, blending until smooth.

- Chill until ready to serve.

- Makes ½ cup.

Raisin Sauce

2 cups apples, peeled and chopped
1 cup raisins
½ cup vinegar
½ cup water

1 cup firmly packed brown sugar
ground cinnamon, to taste
whole cloves, to taste

- Combine apples, raisins, vinegar, water, brown sugar, cinnamon and cloves in saucepan. Bring to a boil and cook until mixture is caramelized.

- Serve warm on baked ham slices.

- Makes 4 cups.

Sun-dried Cranberry and Red Wine Sauce

Sauce sometimes seems mysterious and difficult to make-but not this one. It's foolproof and will really add to holiday beef, lamb and even ham.

½ cup chopped onion
2 or 3 cloves garlic, chopped
½ cup chopped mushrooms
1 tablespoon olive oil
4 cups beef broth
1 teaspoon orange zest (no white)
2 cups red wine

1 tablespoon chopped fresh thyme or 1 teaspoon dried thyme
½ cup sun-dried cranberries
1 cup orange juice
½ cup port wine
2 tablespoons cold butter
salt and black pepper, to taste

- In stock pot, sauté onion, garlic and mushrooms in oil until onions are transparent.

- Add broth, zest, red wine and thyme. Bring to a simmer and cook until consistency of light sauce. Strain sauce and return to stock pot.

- Stir in cranberries, orange juice and port wine. Bring to a simmer and cook for 8 to 10 minutes.

- Remove from heat and whisk in butter; sauce should thicken slightly. Season with salt and black pepper. Keep warm until ready to serve.

- Makes 4 cups

"Cincinnati is a beautiful city; cheerful, thriving, and animated. I have not often seen a place that commends itself so favorably and pleasantly to a stranger at the first glance; with its clean houses of red and white, its well-paved roads, and footways of bright tile. The streets are broad and airy, the shops extremely good, the private residences remarkable for their elegance and neatness. There is something of invention and fancy in the varying styles of these latter erections, which is perfectly delightful, as conveying an assurance that there are such qualities still in existence. The disposition to ornament these pretty villas and render them attractive, leads to the culture of trees and flowers, and the laying out of well-kept gardens, the sight of which, to those who walk along its streets, is inexpressibly refreshing and agreeable.

Cranberry Fruit Sauce

 Make this with blackberries or blueberries and you will have a sauce that money cannot buy!

1½ cups sugar
¾ cup cold water
1 (12 ounce) package fresh
 cranberries
¼ cup plus 1 teaspoon orange
 or citrus marmalade or
 blackberry or blueberry jam
 or combination of 2

juice of 1½ lemons
3 tablespoons almonds,
 blanched and chopped,
 optional

- Combine sugar and water in saucepan. Bring to a boil, skim and remove foam, and simmer for 5 minutes.

- Stir in cranberries and cook for 3 to 5 minutes or until all have popped and are transparent. Remove from heat.

- Add marmalade, mixing to melt. Stir in lemon juice.

- Add almonds to cooled sauce.

- Makes 3 cups.

Hollandaise Sauce

2 tablespoons half and half
2 tablespoons strained fresh
 lemon juice

2 egg yolks
½ cup butter

- Combine half and half, lemon juice and egg yolks in microwave-safe bowl, whisking to blend.

- Microwave cook on high power (100%) for 2 minutes.

- Whisk in butter, 1 pat a time.

- Serves 4.

Serve on asparagus, broccoli, cauliflower, egg's Benedict and turkey mornay. Sauce can be adapted for custards, gravies, puddings and white sauces.

I was quite charmed with the appearance of the town, and its adjoining suburb of Mount Auburn, from which the city, lying in an amphitheater of hills, forms a picture of remarkable beauty."

Charles Dickens

Barbecue Sauce

 Homemade...there is none better.
Always a hit at the barbecues.

1 cup ketchup	**1 tablespoons liquid smoke**
1 cup water	**1 small onion, minced**
¼ cup cider vinegar	**1 small clove garlic, minced**
1 tablespoon Worcestershire sauce	**2 tablespoons brown sugar**
2 tablespoons molasses	**2 tablespoons dry mustard**
	1 tablespoon chili powder

- Combine ketchup, water, vinegar, Worcestershire sauce, molasses and liquid smoke in saucepan.

- Add brown sugar, mustard and chili powder, whisking until smooth. Stir in onion and garlic.

- Simmer for 20 minutes.

- Makes 2½ cups.

Japanese Fish Barbecue Sauce

 Grilling fresh fish filets is rapidly gaining in popularity. This sauce works well with almost any fish and especially well with swordfish, tuna and salmon. It has no oil.

1 cup teriyaki sauce	**4 to 6 cloves garlic, minced**
½ cup honey	**2 tablespoons cornstarch**
½ cup soy sauce	**3 tablespoons cold water**
1 teaspoon minced ginger	

- Combine teriyaki sauce, honey, soy sauce, ginger and garlic in saucepan. Blend cornstarch with water and add to liquid mixture.

- Bring to a boil over medium heat, stirring constantly. Remove from heat and let stand to cool to room temperature.

- To use, brush both sides of 8 to 10 filets with sauce. Grill 1 side over medium high heat for 2 minutes, turn, brush with sauce, and cook to desired doneness, brushing with additional sauce.

- Makes 2⅓ cups.

Homemade Herbed Mayonnaise

10 spinach leaves
2 tablespoons chopped green
   onion
¼ cup chopped watercress
¼ cup chopped fresh parsley
1 tablespoon dried tarragon

1 cup water
1 egg
½ teaspoon dry mustard
½ teaspoon salt
1 teaspoon lemon juice
1 cup vegetable oil

- Prepare mayonnaise at least 1 day before using.

- Combine spinach, onion, watercress, parsley, tarragon and water in saucepan. Bring to a boil and cook for 2 minutes. Strain well to remove all excess moisture.

- Place vegetable mixture in food processor. Add egg, mustard and salt. Blend thoroughly. Add lemon juice.

- With processor running at high speed, gradually add oil in steady stream. Chill overnight.

- Makes 2½ cups.

Peppermint Marshmallow Sauce

 Best served over Graeter's double chocolate chip ice cream. Just sit back and wait for the sugar buzz to take you away.

1 (7 ounce) jar marshmallow
   creme
¼ cup finely crushed
   peppermint candies

¼ cup milk
⅛ teaspoon peppermint
   extract
red food coloring

- Combine marshmallow creme, peppermint candy and milk in saucepan. Cook over very low heat, stirring constantly, until blended. Remove from heat.

- Stir in peppermint extract and a few drops of food coloring.

- Chill, covered. Stir well just before serving.

- Makes 1⅓ cups.

$$

Pork could be used as currency in many businesses which exchanged the meat for such items as newspaper subscriptions, groceries, and in Kentucky, real estate.

Jezebel Sauce

1 (6 ounce) jar pineapple
  preserves
1 (6 ounce) jar apple jelly
1 (½ ounce) can dry mustard

1 (6 ounce) jar white
  horseradish sauce
1 teaspoon black pepper

- Combine preserves, jelly, mustard, horseradish sauce and black pepper, mixing well.
- Spread cream cheese on cracker and top with sauce.
- Makes 2 cups.

 # Pesto Sauce

2 cups tightly packed fresh
  basil leaves
¼ cup (1 ounce) freshly grated
  Parmesan cheese

4 garlic cloves, cut in halves
1 tablespoon pine nuts
salt and black pepper, to taste
⅔ cup olive oil

- In food processor or blender container, combine basil, Parmesan cheese, garlic, pine nuts, salt and black pepper.
- Blend, gradually adding oil in steady stream, until sauce is thickened and smooth.
- Makes 2 cups.

Mocha Brandy Sauce

6 (1 ounce) squares semi-
  sweet chocolate
½ (1 ounce) square bitter
  chocolate

½ cup strong black coffee
1 tablespoon brandy

- Combine chocolates and coffee in top of double boiler. Over hot water, stir to melt chocolate.
- Blend in brandy and mix until smooth. Serve sauce hot over ice cream.
- Makes 1 cup.

As the Pig Flies...

The Cincinnati/ Northern Kentucky International Airport is ranked as the world's fastest growing airport. Offering over 500 daily nonstop departures to 110 cities worldwide, including nonstop service to London, Frankfurt, Montreal, Paris, Brussels, Toronto and Zurich, you can get just about anywhere from here.

SALADS... *Lettuce Entertain You*

The Baum-Longworth-Taft House, known today as the Taft Museum, is an excellent example of American Palladian architecture. A National Historic Landmark, it was built about 1820 by builders and artisans.

Photograph by Robert A. Flischel

"Salads have elevated vegetarian foods to new heights and sophistication. They are for everyone who enjoys exciting food inventively prepared and presented with style."

Shawn Bleh
Owner
Indigo Casual Gourmet Fare

Cantonese Chicken Salad

 This exotic salad is perfect on a warm summer night.

Dressing

3 tablespoons dry white wine
2 tablespoons unsweetened pineapple juice
2 tablespoons fresh lemon juice

2 tablespoons light brown sugar
1½ tablespoons curry powder
2 teaspoons soy sauce
1 teaspoon onion powder
2 cups mayonnaise

Salad

2 heads lettuce, shredded
1 cup chopped celery
¼ cup chopped fresh cilantro
1¾ cups chow mein noodles
¼ cup vegetable oil
1¾ pounds boned skinless chicken breasts

¾ pound water chestnuts, sliced and drained
1¾ cups snow peas
2 cups curry dressing (see above)
½ cup slivered almonds
10 radishes, thinly sliced
2 green onions, finely chopped

- Prepare dressing by combining wine, pineapple juice, lemon juice, brown sugar, curry powder, soy sauce, onion powder and mayonnaise, mixing well. Set aside.

- Combine lettuce, celery and cilantro in serving bowl. Sprinkle noodles on salad greens.

- Slice chicken into 2-inch strips. Stir fry in oil in skillet over medium heat for about 2 minutes or until lightly browned.

- Add water chestnuts and snow peas to chicken. Stir fry for 1 minute.

- Using slotted spoon, remove chicken mixture from skillet and arrange on salad greens and noodles. Add 2 cups dressing and toss well. Garnish with almonds, radishes and onions.

- Serves 6 to 8.

Note: Extra dressing may be passed at the table.

Bird's Eye View

Internationally known Wildlife Artist John A. Ruthven attended the Cincinnati Art Academy. He painted three bald eagles for the White House during the Ford, Reagan and Bush presidencies. Perhaps best known for his cardinals, Ruthven has cited the influence of John James Audubon in his work.

Fine Feathered Friends

James John Audubon worked as a taxidermist for Cincinnati's "Western Museum" in 1819 and 1820, now the Museum of Natural History and Science at Union Terminal. Years later his love of birds and habit of sketching culminated in "Birds of America," which made him a household name.

Thai Chicken Salad

 Serve with fresh rolls and wine.

Dressing
1/3 cup vegetable oil
2 tablespoons peanut butter
4 teaspoons soy sauce
4 teaspoons cider vinegar
1 1/2 teaspoons sugar

1/4 teaspoon crushed red
   pepper flakes
1 tablespoon water
3 green onions, chopped

Salad
2 cups cooked chicken, cut in
   bite-sized pieces
Boston red leaf lettuce, torn in
   bite-sized pieces
1/2 cucumber, peeled and sliced

4 radishes, thinly sliced
1 (11 ounce) can mandarin
   oranges, drained
1/2 cup peanuts

- Prepare dressing by combining oil, peanut butter, soy sauce, vinegar, sugar, red pepper, water and onions, mixing until peanut butter is well blended and sugar is dissolved. Set aside.

- Place chicken in bowl. Add dressing and mix to coat thoroughly.

- Place lettuce in serving bowl. Sprinkle cucumber and radishes on lettuce. Place chicken with dressing on vegetables. Garnish with oranges and peanuts.

- Serves 4.

Celestial Chicken Salad

 Bacon, mushrooms and pecans are a welcome addition to traditional chicken salad.

Dressing

1 cup mayonnaise
1 cup sour cream

2 tablespoons lemon juice
½ teaspoon salt

Salad

4 cups diced cooked chicken
4 slices bacon, cooked and
    diced
2 cups diced celery

1 (4½ ounce) jar whole
    mushrooms, drained
½ cup toasted pecans

- Prepare dressing by combing mayonnaise, sour cream, lemon juice and salt, mixing until smooth. Set aside.

- Combine chicken, bacon, celery, mushrooms and pecans.

- Add dressing and toss well. Chill before serving.

- Serves 6 to 8.

Shrimp and Crab Meat Salad

 People won't stop raving!

1 (24 ounce) loaf white
    sandwich bread
butter, softened
1 onion, grated
4 hard-cooked eggs, chopped

2 (6 ounce) cans salad shrimp,
    drained
2 (8 ounce) cans crab meat,
    drained and flaked
1 cup diced celery
2 cups mayonnaise

- Begin preparation of salad the day before serving.

- Trim crusts from bread. Butter each slice. Stack 4 slices, then cut 7 slices in each direction to form cubes. Continue with entire loaf.

- Combine bread with onion and eggs, mixing lightly. Cover and chill overnight.

- Three to four hours before serving, add shrimp, crab meat, celery and mayonnaise to bread mixture, tossing to mix but do not overmix. Chill until ready to serve.

- Serves 10 to 12.

Union Terminal

Union Terminal, an art-deco train terminal built during the Depression, is home to the Cincinnati Museum Center. Magnificent mosaic murals depicting American life, by German-born artist Winold Reiss, surround the concourse and largest half-dome rotunda in the Western Hemisphere (spanning 180 feet and measuring 106 feet high). Murals by French artist Pierre Bourdelle are showcased on lacquered linoleum panels. Union Terminal houses the Cincinnati History Museum, Museum of Natural History and Science, Robert D. Lindner Family OMNIMAX Theater, the Cincinnati Historical Society Library, Children's Museum Exhibits and The Cincinnati Railroad Club.

Crab and Shrimp Salad

Dressing

2 teaspoons lemon juice	2 tablespoons Dijon mustard
¾ cup mayonnaise	3 tablespoons dill weed
½ cup sour cream	¼ teaspoon seasoned salt

Salad

2 (8 ounce) packages thin egg noodles	2 (6 ounce) cans cocktail shrimp, rinsed and drained
2 (8 ounce) cans crab meat, drained and flaked	2 teaspoons lemon juice
	½ cup chopped green onion
	½ cup chopped celery

- Prepare dressing by combining lemon juice, mayonnaise, sour cream, mustard, dill and seasoned salt, mixing until smooth. Set aside.

- Prepare noodles according to package directions. Drain, rinse well with cold water and drain thoroughly.

- Sprinkle lemon juice on crab and shrimp. Add noodles, green onion and celery.

- Fold dressing into seafood mixture, stirring just until coated.

- Serves 6 to 8.

Smoked Turkey Salad

Dressing

¾ cup mayonnaise	½ teaspoon black pepper
¾ cup sour cream	¼ cup toasted sliced almonds
½ teaspoon salt	

Salad

4 cups cubed, smoked turkey	1 cup red seedless grapes, cut in halves
1 cup (4 ounces) diced, smoked Gouda cheese	½ cup diced celery
	Bibb lettuce leaves

- Prepare dressing by combining mayonnaise, sour cream, salt, black pepper and almonds, mixing well. Set aside.

- Combine turkey, cheese, grapes and celery. Add dressing to turkey mixture and toss gently. Chill thoroughly.

- Serve portions of salad on lettuce leaves.

- Serves 6.

The Palace's Grilled Shrimp Salad

Dressing

½ cup cider vinegar
½ cup white vinegar
3 cloves garlic
2 tablespoons sugar
1 slice red bell pepper, chopped
½ small carrot, chopped

1 teaspoon black pepper
1 teaspoon Dijon mustard
1 tablespoon dried basil
1 tablespoon dried oregano
2 cups olive oil
2 cups vegetable oil

Salad

24 shrimp
4 ears corn
1 red bell pepper
1 yellow bell pepper
1 green bell pepper
1 small red onion, thinly sliced

1 medium beefsteak tomato,
  diced
¼ pound mesclun mix
1 wheel Boursin cheese
fresh chives for garnish

- Prepare dressing by combining cider vinegar, white vinegar, garlic, sugar, bell pepper, carrot, black pepper, mustard, basil and oregano in blender container. Blend until puree consistency.

- Gradually add olive oil and vegetable oil. Set aside.

- Peel and devein shrimp. Grill until cooked and set aside.

- Steam corn until tender. Cut kernels from cobs and set aside.

- Roast bell peppers. Peel, remove seeds and cut into julienne strips.

- Combine corn, bell peppers, onion, tomato and mesclun mix. Add 1 cup dressing and toss lightly.

- Place salad mixture in center of plate. Crumble cheese on salad, arrange shrimp around edge and garnish with chives.

- Serves 4.

Steamboat Era Phrases

"Steamboats developed high, flute-shaped stacks to throw the hot cinders and smoke away from passengers. People who were wealthy enough to travel on a steamboat became known as 'high falutin' folks.' They are traveling with their 'high faluting friends' or a steamboat is 'well-stacked' are a few phrases which evolved.

Stacks on many steamboats would bend in order to pass under a railroad bridge. 'You've got to bend a little to get where you're going' was a phrase which became popular.

The huge paddle wheels were steam-driven, and since the pressure inside the steam boiler tended to get high from time to time, it had to be relieved through a check valve. Relieving that pressure was naturally called 'letting off steam,' and it came to describe the human emotion of getting rid of tension."

Don Deming
Steamboat Historian

"Cincinnati was built on transportation, and the railroads were, and are a large part of that. They took us from here to war and back again, separated and united families, and moved the goods that built our nation. We occupy and maintain the former control tower at Union Terminal that overlooks the railroad yards. Surrounded by glass on three sides, we have a dramatic view of the lower Mill Creek Valley and all the rail yards it contains. We were founded in 1938, and we're the last original tenant of Union Terminal. Check the Museum Center for our hours, we're the largest reference library of rail-oriented books and materials in the Midwest."

Patrick Rose
President
The Cincinnati
Railroad Club

A New Twist on Tuna Salad

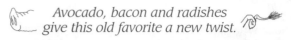 Avocado, bacon and radishes give this old favorite a new twist.

Dressing
1⅓ cups mayonnaise
1 cup plus 1 tablespoon buttermilk
⅓ teaspoon salt
1 teaspoon black pepper

1 teaspoon garlic salt
1 teaspoon monosodium glutamate
2 tablespoons chopped fresh parsley

Salad
6 cups torn salad greens
1 ripe tomato, cut in chunks
2 hard-cooked eggs, sliced
½ ripe avocado, peeled and sliced
1 cup (4 ounces) shredded Monterey Jack cheese

5 radishes, sliced
1 (6½ ounce) can tuna, drained
½ (16 ounce) package bacon, cooked crisp, drained and crumbled

- Prepare dressing by combining mayonnaise, buttermilk, salt, black pepper, garlic salt, monosodium glutamate and parsley, mixing well. Set aside.

- Combine salad greens, tomato, eggs, avocado, Monterey Jack cheese, radishes, tuna and bacon, tossing to mix. Do not season.

- Add dressing to individual portions of salad.

- Serves 6 to 8.

Havarti Tortellini Salad

Dressing

3 tablespoons red wine vinegar
½ cup olive oil
1 teaspoon minced fresh basil
1 clove garlic, minced

1 teaspoon Dijon mustard
¼ teaspoon salt
¼ teaspoon black pepper

Salad

1 (10 ounce) package tortellini
¼ cup packed, chopped, fresh parsley
1 cup (4 ounces) cubed Havarti cheese

¼ pound salami, shredded
1 large red bell pepper, chopped
½ cup black olives, sliced
3 green onions with tops, sliced

- Prepare dressing by blending vinegar, oil, basil, garlic, mustard, salt and black pepper in blender or food processor. Set aside.

- Prepare tortellini according to package directions. Drain, rinse well with cold water and drain thoroughly.

- Combine tortellini, parsley, cheese, salami, bell pepper, olives and green onion. Add dressing and toss gently.

- Chill for 2 hours.

- Serves 6.

"Early pioneers traveled to the 'Outlands' and were called 'Outlanders.' Easterners thought their behavior and clothing (topped with a coonskin cap) were outlandish.

Early river travelers traveled on rafts, using oars known as rifs. These poor immigrants were known as 'rif raf.'

Many of those who settled in the hills were named Wilbur, William, Wilhelm, etc. and were all called 'Billys.' The word 'hillbilly' was born."

Don Deming
Steamboat Historian

photograph courtesy of Cincinnati Museum Center

Union Terminal

Spicy Pasta Salad

 This hearty salad is an excellent main dish.

Dressing

1 (10 ounce) can diced tomatoes

1 (4 ounce) can green chilies, drained

½ cup fat-free Italian salad dressing

2 teaspoons salt-free herb seasoning

Salad

1 (8 ounce) package tricolor rotini pasta

½ pound turkey sausage, cooked and diced

1 (15 ounce) can kidney beans, drained

1 (8 ounce) can whole kernel corn, drained

2 medium tomatoes, chopped

1 small red bell pepper, chopped

½ cup sliced green onion

1 (2¼ ounce) can black olives, drained and sliced

1 cup (4 ounces) shredded low-fat cheddar cheese

- Prepare dressing by combining tomatoes, chilies, salad dressing and herb seasoning, mixing well. Set aside.

- Prepare pasta according to package directions. Drain, rinse well with cold water and drain thoroughly.

- Combine pasta, sausage, beans, corn, tomatoes, bell pepper, green onion, olives and cheese. Drizzle dressing over salad and toss gently.

- Chill until ready to serve.

- Serves 8.

Sherried Wild Rice Salad

Dressing
1 egg, beaten
1 teaspoon sugar
¼ teaspoon salt
2 cups olive oil

2 cups vegetable oil
½ cup vinegar
½ cup sherry
2 large cloves garlic, crushed

Salad
3 cups uncooked wild rice
1 clove garlic
2 green onions with tops, sliced
1 cup frozen peas, thawed

8 cherry tomatoes, quartered
1 (8½ ounce) can artichokes, drained and chopped
salt and black pepper, to taste
1 cup pecan pieces

- Prepare dressing by combining egg, sugar and salt. Using electric mixer, beat until smooth. Alternately add olive oil, vegetable oil and vinegar, blending well after each addition. Continue beating while gradually adding sherry. Stir in garlic. Chill.

- Prepare rice according to package directions. Let stand until cool.

- Rub garlic clove on inside of large wooden salad bowl.

- Combine rice, green onion, peas, tomatoes, artichokes, salt and black pepper in bowl, tossing gently.

- Drizzle enough dressing over salad to coat just before serving and toss gently. Garnish with pecans and pass remaining dressing.

- Serves 8.

Robert D. Lindner OMNIMAX Theater

World-class film entertainment is found at the spectacular Robert D. Lindner OMNIMAX Theater at the Cincinnati Museum Center, which boasts a five-story, 72-foot diameter domed screen, and the most sophisticated digital sound system in the world.

Children's Museum Exhibits

Exhibits from the Children's Museum captivate young imaginations at the Cincinnati Museum Center.

J's Fresh Seafood Hawaiian Asparagus Salad with Papaya Relish

If you mention Hawaiian food around most people, they think of cubes of pineapple in the recipe and little umbrellas on top. The reality is that Hawaii has many fantastic native ingredients readily available. Hawaii also boasts a broad range, multi-ethnic society, possibly the most diverse in the world-an excellent source for recipes.

**32 asparagus spears, trimmed
ice water
½ cup rice vinegar
1 cup vegetable oil
salt and white pepper, to taste
2 tablespoons chopped,
    pickled ginger
2 teaspoons chopped garlic**

**1 yellow bell pepper, cut in
    julienne strips
1½ medium sized tomatoes,
    peeled, seeded and diced
1 papaya, peeled and diced
Romaine or radicchio leaves
2 tablespoons toasted or black
    sesame seeds**

- Blanch asparagus in 1½ quarts boiling water, then submerge in ice water to halt cooking. Drain well.

- Whisk vinegar, oil, salt, white pepper, ginger and garlic together. Pour dressing over asparagus, bell pepper, tomatoes and papaya. Marinate for 3 to 4 hours.

- Mix salad and arrange portions on Romaine or radicchio leaves. Garnish with sesame seeds.

- Serves 4.

Black Bean Salad

 A great salad to serve with a Mexican meal.

Dressing
¼ cup plus 2 tablespoons olive oil
3 tablespoons lemon juice

¼ cup plus 1 tablespoon chopped cilantro
¼ teaspoon salt
1 teaspoon black pepper

Salad
2 (15 ounce) cans black beans, drained
1 red bell pepper, cut in ¼-inch pieces

2 plum tomatoes, cut in ¼-inch cubes
3 scallions, sliced
2 large yellow bell peppers

- Prepare dressing by combining oil, lemon juice, cilantro, salt and black pepper, mixing well. Set aside.

- Combine beans, red bell pepper, tomatoes, scallions and dressing, tossing gently to coat vegetables.

- Let stand, loosely covered, at room temperature for 1 hour before serving.

- Cut yellow bell peppers in halves and remove seeds and core. Spoon salad into pepper halves for individual servings.

- Serves 4.

Shh!

The Cincinnati Historical Society Library is one of the best kept secrets in Cincinnati. Whether you're a serious scholar or simply inquisitive, you're virtually guaranteed to find something of interest. From genealogy and business records to maps and architectural drawings, the library holds an exciting cache of treasures. News films, radio broadcasts, and television programming from the past four decades await you, as do works by many noted photographers such as Paul Briol, Daniel J. Ransohoff, Felix Koch and George Rosenthal. Best of all, its free, and open to the public.

Broccoli Slaw

Dressing
½ cup sugar
½ cup vegetable oil
⅓ cup white vinegar
¼ cup water
2 flavor packets from ramen
   noodle soup

Salad
1 cup almond slivers
2 (3 ounce) packages oriental
   flavor ramen noodle soup
1 cup shelled sunflower seeds
1 bunch green onions,
   chopped
1 (16 ounce) package broccoli
   slaw

- Prepare dressing by combining sugar, oil, vinegar, water and flavor packets, mixing well. Set aside.

- Toast almonds until lightly browned. Crush ramen noodles into tiny pieces and mix with almonds and sunflower seeds.

- Mix green onion and broccoli together.

- To serve, combine almond mixture with vegetables, drizzle with dressing, and toss thoroughly.

- Serves 8 to 10.

Use slivered instead of sliced almonds, do not cook the ramen noodles, and use shelled sunflower seeds...these are mistakes people have actually made with this recipe.

Cucumber and Peanut Salad

 *This unique combination is excellent.
Everyone is always surprised by its consistency.*

2 large cucumbers, peeled,
   seeds removed and chopped
2 teaspoons garlic salt
3 cups plain yogurt
2 teaspoons garlic salt
½ teaspoon ground cumin

¼ teaspoon black pepper
¼ teaspoon cayenne pepper
2 teaspoons chopped fresh dill
1½ cups peanuts, chopped
¼ teaspoon paprika

- Combine cucumbers and garlic salt, tossing to mix. Chill for 1½ hours. Drain excess liquid and blot with paper towel to absorb liquid.

- Mix yogurt, garlic salt, cumin, black pepper, cayenne pepper and dill together. Pour mixture over cucumbers and toss to mix.

- Chill salad for several hours. Before serving, add peanuts and paprika, tossing to mix well.

- Serves 12.

Italian Mushroom and Bean Salad

Dressing
¼ cup vinegar
¼ cup vegetable oil
½ teaspoon salt

½ teaspoon basil
½ teaspoon oregano

Salad
1 (8 ounce) package frozen
   baby lima beans
1 (8 ounce) package frozen
   green beans

8 mushrooms, sliced
4 green onions, chopped
2 tablespoons parsley,
   chopped

- Prepare dressing by combining vinegar, oil, salt, basil and oregano, mixing well. Set aside.

- Separately prepare lima beans and green beans according to package directions. Drain well.

- Combine beans, mushrooms and green onion.

- Drizzle dressing over vegetables and mix thoroughly.

- Cover and chill for 4 hours before serving.

- Serves 6.

Two-Cheese Potato Salad

 This is a potato salad with a kick.

Dressing
1 cup large curd cottage cheese
1 cup sour cream

2 teaspoons prepared mustard
2 teaspoons seasoned salt

Salad
2 (16 ounce) packages frozen diced potatoes
1 cup water
½ cup Italian salad dressing
16 green onions, sliced

1 cup chopped celery
1 red bell pepper, chopped
3 hard-cooked eggs, chopped
1 cup (4 ounces) blue cheese, crumbled

- Place potatoes in large skillet. Add water and salad dressing. Simmer, covered, until liquid is absorbed and potatoes are tender.

- Spoon potatoes into large bowl and chill for 35 minutes.

- Combine potatoes, green onion, celery, bell pepper and eggs, gently tossing to mix.

- Prepare dressing by combining cottage cheese, sour cream, mustard and seasoned salt. Add mixture to vegetables and toss gently.

- Sprinkle blue cheese on salad for garnish.

- Chill before serving.

- Serves 8.

Rio Egg Salad

 This simple salad is colorful and tasty.
It is typical fare of Rio.

Dressing

1 cup mayonnaise

2 tablespoons chopped fresh
dill

1 teaspoon salt

1 teaspoon black pepper

Salad

1 (16 ounce) package frozen
mixed vegetables: corn,
carrots, lima beans, peas
and/or green beans

12 hard-cooked eggs, chopped

- Prepare dressing by combining mayonnaise, dill, salt and black pepper. Set aside.

- Steam vegetables according to package directions. Drain, rinse with cold water and drain thoroughly.

- Add eggs to vegetables.

- Spoon dressing over vegetables and eggs, mixing well.

- Chill before serving.

- Serves 6.

Bermuda Salad Bowl

½ (16 ounce) package bacon,
cooked crisp and crumbled

1 small head cauliflower, cut
in bite-sized pieces

1 large Bermuda onion, sliced

½ cup pimento-stuffed green
olives, sliced

½ cup Italian salad dressing

1 head iceberg lettuce, torn in
bite-sized pieces

1 cup (4 ounces) blue cheese,
crumbled

- Combine bacon, cauliflower, onion, olives and salad dressing, mixing well.

- Chill for 2 hours.

- Just before serving, add lettuce and blue cheese, tossing to mix.

- Serves 6 to 8.

Marinated Vegetable Salad

 A good substitute for potato salad at barbecues.

Dressing
½ cup mayonnaise
2 tablespoons chili sauce

1 tablespoon lemon juice
1 teaspoon dill

Salad
2 cups coarsely chopped broccoli
2 cups coarsely chopped cauliflower
2 cups sliced carrots
1 (8 ounce) bottle Italian salad dressing

2 cups cherry tomatoes, cut in halves
2 (6 ounce) jars marinated artichoke hearts, drained and quartered

- Begin preparation of salad the day before serving.

- Separately blanch broccoli, cauliflower and carrots in boiling water, plunge in ice water and drain well.

- Marinate vegetables in Italian dressing overnight.

- Drain vegetables and add tomatoes and artichokes.

- Prepare dressing by combining mayonnaise, chili sauce, lemon juice and dill, mixing well.

- Add dressing to vegetables and toss to mix.

- Serves 16.

Jo's Salad Dressing

 This flavorful dressing is marvelous with an assortment of vegetables.

1 cup mayonnaise
½ cup chili sauce
1 teaspoon lemon juice
1½ teaspoons grated onion

1 teaspoon horseradish
¼ teaspoon salt
⅛ teaspoon black pepper
¼ teaspoon dried tarragon

- Combine mayonnaise, chili sauce, lemon juice, onion and horseradish. Stir in salt, black pepper and tarragon.

- Store in refrigerator.

- Makes 1½ cups.

Greek Salad

 Healthy, elegant and delicious too!

Dressing
¼ cup plus 1 tablespoon
  olive oil
¼ cup red wine vinegar

½ teaspoon salt
¼ teaspoon black pepper
½ teaspoon oregano

Salad
3 large tomatoes
1 cucumber, sliced
1 medium-sized green bell
  pepper, diced
1 small onion, sliced

8 pitted black olives
2 heads Romaine lettuce, torn
  in bite-sized pieces
⅔ cup (2 to 3 ounces)
  crumbled feta cheese

- Prepare dressing by combining oil, vinegar, salt, black pepper and oregano, mixing well. Set aside.

- Combine tomatoes, cucumber, bell pepper, onion, olives and lettuce.

- Drizzle dressing over vegetables, add cheese and toss to mix.

- Serves 6.

Green Salad with Curried Fruit

Dressing
⅓ cup red wine or red wine
  vinegar
½ cup olive oil
1 clove garlic, minced

2 tablespoons brown sugar
2 tablespoons minced chives
1 tablespoon curry powder
1 teaspoon soy sauce

Salad
1 bunch red leaf lettuce, torn
  in bite-sized pieces
1 cup packed spinach leaves,
  stems removed and torn in
  bite-sized pieces

1 cup red seedless grapes, cut
  in halves
1 (11 ounce) can mandarin
  oranges, drained
1 avocado, sliced
¼ cup sliced almonds, toasted

- Prepare dressing by combining wine or vinegar, oil, garlic, brown sugar, chives, curry powder and soy sauce, mixing well. Set aside.

- Combine lettuce, spinach, grapes, oranges, avocado and almonds.

- Drizzle dressing over salad and toss to mix.

- Serves 6 to 8.

Reminiscences of Levi Coffin

"Our house was large and well adapted for secreting fugitives. Very often, slaves would lie concealed in upper chambers for weeks without boarders or frequent visitors at the house knowing anything about it. My wife had a quiet, unconcerned way of going about her work as if nothing unusual was on hand, which was calculated to lull every suspicion of those who might be watching and who would have been at once aroused by any sign of secrecy or mystery.

When my wife took food to the fugitives, she generally concealed it in a basket and put some freshly ironed garments on top to make it look like a basketful of clean clothes."

Levi Coffin, circa 1847 submitted by Martha Eustis Totten, fourth generation niece of Levi Coffin, the Ohio Quaker who was known for a time as the "President of the Underground Railroad."

Indigo's Hyde Parker Salad

Dressing

¾ cup red wine vinegar
2 cups olive oil
3 tablespoons minced garlic
1 tablespoon salt
1 tablespoon black pepper

1 tablespoon coarsely ground
  mustard
1 tablespoon crushed red
  pepper flakes

Salad

4 medium portobello
  mushrooms, sliced
¾ pound Romaine lettuce, torn
  in bite-sized pieces

¼ pound sun-dried cranberries
1 cup (4 ounces) crumbled
  feta cheese

- Prepare dressing by combining vinegar, oil, garlic, salt, black pepper, mustard and red pepper, whisking until emulsified. Set aside.

- Arrange mushrooms in single layer on baking sheet.

- Bake at 400 degrees for 5 to 6 minutes.

- Place lettuce in individual salad bowls. Arrange warm mushrooms on lettuce, sprinkle with cranberries and cheese and drizzle with dressing. (Use 1 cup dressing and store remaining 2 cups in refrigerator.)

- Serves 4.

Scarlett Dressing

 Forget the salad! This makes a great dip!

1 cup sour cream
1 small onion, minced
1 clove garlic, crushed, optional
½ cup finely diced, cooked
  beets

¼ cup plus 1 tablespoon
  undrained horseradish
1½ tablespoons sugar
1½ teaspoons salt

- Combine sour cream, onion, garlic, beets and horseradish. Blend in sugar and salt, mixing thoroughly.

- Chill before serving. Serve with assorted salad greens and cucumber slices.

- Makes 1¾ cups.

Henry Farny

Henry Farny was a sketch artist for Harpers Weekly. He detailed the life of America's Indians and did illustrations for McGuffy's Eclectic Readers, and was known as one of the "Cincinnati 10", an internationally known group of local artists.

Pecan Spinach Salad

Dressing
½ cup sour cream
3 tablespoons vinegar
½ cup sugar

2 teaspoons horseradish
½ teaspoon salt
½ teaspoon dry mustard

Salad
1 pound spinach, stems
   removed and torn in bite-
   sized pieces
1 (16 ounce) carton cream-style
   small curd cottage cheese
1 cup (4 ounces) grated Swiss
   cheese

1 medium-sized red onion,
   thinly sliced
¾ cup sliced fresh mushrooms
½ (16 ounce) package bacon,
   cooked crisp and crumbled
½ cup chopped pecans

- Prepare dressing by combining sour cream, vinegar, sugar, horseradish, salt and dry mustard, whisking to blend. Set aside.

- Combine spinach, cottage cheese, Swiss cheese, onion, mushrooms, bacon and pecans in serving bowl.

- Add dressing to vegetable and cheese mixture, tossing gently to mix.

- Serves 8.

Sandy's Favorite Salad Dressing

½ cup peanut oil
1 teaspoon Worcestershire
   sauce
3 drops hot pepper sauce
2 cloves garlic, minced

1 tablespoon sugar
1 teaspoon seasoned salt
¼ teaspoon lemon pepper
½ teaspoon dry mustard
⅛ teaspoon paprika

- Combine oil, Worcestershire sauce, hot pepper sauce and garlic in jar with tight-fitting lid. Add sugar, seasoned salt, lemon pepper, mustard and paprika, shaking to mix well.

- Serve on green salad.

- Makes ¾ cup.

The Cincinnati Art Museum

Extensive collections of Near and Far Eastern art, Native American and African art, furniture, glass, silver, costume and folk art grace the galleries of the Cincinnati Art Museum (CAM), located in Eden Park atop Mt. Adams. Outside of Jordan, the CAM holds the only major collection of ancient Nabatean Art.

Sketch Artist

Sketch artist Caroline Williams produced a series of black and white sketches that were published in the Cincinnati Enquirer. Several of these Cincinnati scenes and landmarks have been reproduced on plates, which are now collector's items.

Teller's House Salad

Dressing

½ cup raspberry vinegar	2 tablespoons minced onion
¼ cup sugar	1¾ cup peanut oil
¾ teaspoon salt	2 tablespoons poppy seed

Salad

20 leaves Bibb lettuce	2 tablespoons pine nuts, toasted
½ pound watercress sprigs	
2 tablespoons dried cranberries	2 cups (8 ounces) crumbled Gorgonzola cheese

- Prepare dressing by combining vinegar, sugar, salt and onion in food processor container. Very gradually add peanut oil while processor is running. Pulse in poppy seed. Set aside.

- Arrange 5 lettuce leaves on each dinner plate in fan shape. Place water cress in center. Sprinkle cranberries, pine nuts and cheese on watercress.

- Drizzle dressing over salad. (Use 1 cup dressing and store remaining 1 cup in refrigerator.)

- Serves 4.

Best-Ever Roquefort Dressing

 This is a favorite dip with corn chips.

2 cups (8 ounces) crumbled blue cheese	1 teaspoon hot pepper sauce
4 cups mayonnaise	1 teaspoon steak sauce
1 cup buttermilk	1 clove garlic, minced
2 tablespoons onion juice	½ teaspoon salt
2 teaspoons Worcestershire sauce	1 teaspoon garlic salt

- Prepare dressing the day before serving.

- Combine blue cheese, mayonnaise, buttermilk, onion juice, Worcestershire sauce, hot pepper sauce, steak sauce and garlic. Stir in salt and garlic salt, blending well.

- Chill for at least 24 hours before serving.

- Makes 7 cups.

Bacon Dressing

 Dressing can be served on any vegetables. Because it has a "chicken soup" base, it offers flavor without excess fat.

6 or 7 slices bacon, chopped	¼ teaspoon salt
3 cups water	½ teaspoon white pepper
¾ cup vinegar	½ cup chopped onion
2 tablespoons chicken bouillon	½ cup all-purpose flour
1½ cups sugar	

- In skillet, cook bacon until browned. Using slotted spoon, remove bacon and set aside; reserve drippings in skillet.

- In large saucepan, combine water, vinegar, bouillon, sugar, salt and white pepper. Bring to a boil over medium heat. Add bacon.

- Sauté onion in bacon drippings until soft but do not brown. Stir in flour and cook for 2 to 3 minutes to form roux.

- Add roux to sauce, blending until smooth. Cook for 5 minutes.

- Store in refrigerator.

- Serve on chopped cabbage, green beans or potatoes.

- Makes 4 to 5 cups.

 # Creamy Raspberry Dressing

⅔ cup mayonnaise	4 teaspoons sugar
2 tablespoons raspberry vinegar	1 teaspoon salt

- Combine mayonnaise and vinegar. Add sugar and salt, mixing until dissolved.

- Makes ¾ cup.

Hauck House Museum

The Hauck House Museum is located on what was once known as Millionaire's Row on Dayton Street. Famous local brewer John Hauck lived there, and the museum is a fine example of a wealthy lifestyle in the late 1800's.

Gilbert Young

Painter, muralist, and graphic artist Gilbert Young's paintings have appeared on the sets of "The Cosby Show," "A Different World," and Whoopi Goldberg's movie, "Made in America." He attended the University of Cincinnati.

Avocado Salad

1 (3 ounce) package lime
  gelatin
1 cup boiling water
1 (3 ounce) package cream
  cheese, softened and cubed
1 large avocado, chopped
1 cup (scant) mayonnaise

1 cup finely chopped celery
2 teaspoons lemon juice
1 teaspoon onion juice or
  1 tablespoon grated onion
½ teaspoon salt
black pepper, to taste
garlic salt, to taste

- Dissolve gelatin in boiling water. Stir cream cheese, avocado and mayonnaise into hot gelatin. Let stand until cool and slightly thickened.

- Whip gelatin mixture until smooth and frothy. Add celery, lemon juice, onion, salt, black pepper and garlic salt, mixing well. Pour into serving dish.

- Chill until firm.

- Serves 6.

Pickled Beet Mold

2 (3 ounce) packages lime
  gelatin
2 cups boiling water
4 (16 ounce) cans shoestring
  beets, drained and juice
  reserved

¼ cup plus 2 tablespoons
  vinegar
1 teaspoon salt
1½ cups diced celery
4 teaspoons grated onion
2 tablespoons prepared
  horseradish or mayonnaise

- Dissolve gelatin in boiling water. Stir in 1½ cups beet juice, vinegar and salt, mixing well.

- Chill until partially firm.

- Add beets, celery and onion to gelatin. Pour into serving dish and chill until firm.

- Serve with horseradish or mayonnaise or a mixture of 1 tablespoon of each.

- Serves 12 to 14.

Apricot Salad

Salad
2 (3 ounce) packages apricot
  gelatin
2 cups boiling water
2 cups cold water
½ cup chopped pecans
2 bananas, sliced

1 (16 ounce) can crushed
  pineapple, drained and juice
  reserved
1 cup chopped apricots
1 cup miniature marshmallows

Topping
½ cup pineapple juice
½ cup sugar
2 tablespoons all-purpose flour
2 tablespoons butter
1 egg

1 (3 ounce) package cream
  cheese, softened
1 cup whipping cream,
  whipped

- Dissolve gelatin in boiling water. Stir in cold water. Chill until slightly thickened.

- Add pecans, bananas, pineapple, apricots and marshmallows to gelatin, mixing well. Pour into shallow serving dish and chill until firm.

- Prepare topping. In small saucepan, combine pineapple juice, sugar, flour, butter and egg. Cook until thickened.

- Remove from heat, add cream cheese and whip until smooth.

- Add whipped cream to sauce and mix well. Spread topping evenly on salad and chill until ready to serve.

- Serves 12.

Roll Out the Barrels

The Oldenberg-American Museum of Brewing History and Arts, inside the Oldenberg Brewery at the Drawbridge Estate in Kentucky, houses a large collection of brewing memorabilia. Tours of the Oldenberg microbrewery are available daily. Other microbreweries in town include Main Street Brewery and the Barrelhouse in the Over-the-Rhine district.

Tom Wesselmann

Among America's most celebrated and respected artists, University of Cincinnati Alumnus Tom Wesselmann, along with Andy Warhol and Roy Lichtenstein, was in the forefront of America's Pop Art movement.

Blueberry Layer Mold

 Great for a Fourth of July picnic.

1 (3 ounce) package lemon gelatin
4¼ cups boiling water, divided
1 cup half and half
1 teaspoon vanilla
3 tablespoons powdered sugar

1 (8 ounce) package cream cheese, softened
2 (3 ounce) packages black raspberry gelatin
2 (16 ounce) cans blueberries, drained

- Dissolve lemon gelatin in 1¼ cups boiling water.

- Combine gelatin, half and half, vanilla, powdered sugar and cream cheese in blender container. Process until well blended.

- Pour into oiled 2-quart ring mold and chill until firm.

- Dissolve black raspberry gelatin in 3 cups boiling water.

- Stir blueberries into gelatin. Pour into mold on congealed cream mixture.

- Chill until firm. Invert on serving dish and remove mold.

- Serves 12.

Pineapple Salad

2 eggs, well beaten
3 tablespoons all-purpose flour
¼ cup sugar

2 (15 ounce) cans pineapple chunks, drained and juice reserved
2 cups miniature marshmallows

- In saucepan, combine eggs, flour and sugar, mixing well. Stir in juice from 1 can pineapple.

- Cook, stirring constantly, over medium heat until thickened. Let stand until cool.

- Drain second can pineapple, reserving juice for other use. Combine pineapple and marshmallows in bowl. Pour sauce over mixture.

- Serves 6.

Cranberry Salad

 The dressing can be used on
pumpkin pie or other fruits.

Dressing
1 cup miniature marshmallows
1 (3 ounce) package cream
   cheese, softened

1 cup whipping cream

Salad
2 cups fresh cranberries
1 cup water
1¼ cups sugar
1 (3 ounce) package cherry
   gelatin

1 cup red seedless grapes, cut
   in halves
1 (8 ounce) can crushed
   pineapple, drained
½ cup chopped walnuts
1½ cups frozen strawberries,
   thawed and drained

- Prepare dressing and salad the day before serving. Combine marshmallows, cream cheese and unwhipped cream, blending well.

- Chill overnight.

- In saucepan, combine cranberries, water and sugar. Bring to a boil, reduce heat and cook until cranberries pop. Let stand to cool slightly.

- Stir in gelatin granules, mixing to dissolve. Let stand until cool.

- Add grapes, pineapple, walnuts and strawberries to cranberry mixture. Spoon into serving dish and chill overnight.

- Just before serving, whip dressing. Serve dollops on salad portions.

- Serves 10 to 12.

As the Story Goes...

Counselor-at-Law Abe Lincoln was in Cincinnati trying a case when he came across Nicholas Longworth in the garden. Mistaking him for the gardener, Abe gave him a quarter for the tour. Nick, also an attorney, after identifying himself, said that it was the most honest money he ever made. That's supposedly why there's a statue of Abe in Lytle Park, facing the house.

Grapefruit Salad

Taft Tidbits

Now known as the Taft Museum, the Taft House was built and owned by merchant Martin Baum until he lost his fortune in the bank panic of 1820. The house was briefly known as Belmont, a girl's school, until it was purchased by art patron Nicholas Longworth.

Did You Know. . .

That published family histories, Cincinnati and Hamilton County directories and 19th century census information is on hand at the Cincinnati Historical Society Library at the Cincinnati Museum Center? That company records of businesses that built this city are available? That you can peruse maps, blueprints and renderings of over 50 of the city's 19th and 20's century architectural firms, or browse through manuscripts, books and periodicals? Just sign in, and ask the caretakers of Cincinnati's celebrated past.

Dressing

½ cup sugar
¼ cup plus 2 tablespoons
  all-purpose flour
3 egg yolks, beaten

1 cup pineapple juice
juice of 1 lemon
12 marshmallows
1 cup whipping cream

Salad

2 (3 ounce) packages lemon
  gelatin
1 cup boiling water
3 large pink grapefruit

1 or 2 (15 ounce) can
  pineapple chunks with juice
juice of 1 lemon
½ cup chopped pecans
pinch of salt

- Dissolve gelatin in boiling water and set aside.

- Cut grapefruit in halves. Remove all pulp and juice, adding to enough pineapple, pineapple juice and lemon juice to measure 4 cups.

- Add pecans and salt to fruit mixture. Stir in gelatin.

- Scrape grapefruit shells to remove all membrane. Pour gelatin mixture into shells, place in pan to keep upright and chill until firm.

- Prepare dressing by combining sugar and flour in top of double boiler. Add egg yolks, pineapple juice and lemon juice, blending well.

- Cook over hot water until thickened. Add marshmallows and stir until melted.

- Chill until ready to serve. Whip cream and fold into dressing, blending thoroughly.

- Cut grapefruit halves in half again to make 12 servings. Serve dollop of dressing on each portion.

- Serves 12.

Raspberry Ring

1 (10 to 12 ounce) package
  frozen raspberries, thawed
2 (3 ounce) packages
  raspberry gelatin
2 cups boiling water

1 pint vanilla ice cream
1 (6 ounce) can frozen
  lemonade concentrate
¼ cup chopped pecans
2 cups fresh blueberries

- Drain raspberries, reserving juice, and set aside.

- Dissolve gelatin in boiling water. Add ice cream, a spoonful at a time, stirring after each addition until melted.

- Add lemonade and reserved raspberry juice to ice cream mixture. Chill until partially firm.

- Stir raspberries and pecans into gelatin. Pour into 6-cup ring mold and chill until firm.

- Dip ring into warm water, invert on serving plate and remove mold. Fill center with blueberries.

- Serves 10 to 12.

Sunshine Fruit

 This salad looks wonderful in a fresh watermelon basket or in cantaloupe halves.

1 cantaloupe
½ honeydew melon
¼ cup sugar
¼ cup fresh lime juice
2 tablespoons fresh lemon
  juice

1 teaspoon orange-flavored
  liqueur
1½ teaspoons grated lime peel
1 cup black or red seedless
  grapes
1 kiwi, peeled and sliced
1 cup sliced strawberries

- Using melon baller, remove pulp from cantaloupe and honeydew and set aside.

- Combine sugar, lime juice, lemon juice, liqueur and lime peel, mixing well. Stir in melon, grapes, kiwi and strawberries, tossing gently.

- Chill for at least 2 hours, stirring once.

- Serve fruit in melon halves or basket.

Rookwood

Internationally known for its jewel porcelain pottery, Rookwood Pottery was founded by Maria Longworth Storer in 1880, who named it after her father's country estate on Edwards and Grandin roads. Henry Farny, who later achieved fame as a painter of American Indian subjects, was once one of the Rookwood artists. Although the Rockwood Pottery is no longer in business, its site is now a restaurant of the same name, where patrons can dine in the original beehive kilns. Now, anything "Rookwood" is a sought-after collectible, including vases, ornaments and garden pottery. Examples of Rookwood's architectural line can still be seen today in the Carew Tower arcade and in the Union Terminal lunchroom.

Stewed Tomato Salad

 An old favorite at the church picnics.

Dressing
½ **cup mayonnaise**
½ **cup sour cream**
½ **teaspoon horseradish**

¼ **teaspoon salt**
½ **teaspoon black pepper**

Salad
1 (14½ ounce) can stewed
   tomatoes
1 (3 ounce) package
   strawberry gelatin
1 teaspoon vinegar

½ **teaspoon salt**
1 **tablespoon lemon juice**
2 **dashes Worcestershire sauce**
1 **cup chopped pimento-
   stuffed green olives**
1 **cup chopped pecans**

- Prepare dressing by combining mayonnaise, sour cream, horseradish, salt and black pepper, mixing well. Chill.

- In saucepan, bring tomatoes to a boil, reduce heat and simmer for 2 minutes.

- Add gelatin, vinegar and salt into tomatoes, stirring to dissolve gelatin. Remove from heat.

- Blend in lemon juice, Worcestershire sauce, olives and pecans. Pour into oiled 4-cup ring mold. Chill until firm.

- Dip ring into warm water, invert on serving plate and remove mold. Serve slices of salad with dollop of dressing.

- Serves 6 to 8.

BREAD... *Loafin' Around*

"Find something to care about and live a life that shows it."

**Thane Maynard
Director of Education
Cincinnati Zoo and
Botanical Garden**

Herb Biscuits

2 cups all-purpose flour
1 tablespoon baking powder
1 teaspoon onion salt
¼ cup chopped fresh parsley

¼ cup minced chives
⅓ cup vegetable shortening
¾ cup milk

- Sift flour, baking powder and salt together. Add parsley and chives.

- Using pastry blender, cut shortening into dry ingredients until texture is the consistency of coarse corn meal.

- Make a well in center of mixture. Pour in milk and stir to form soft dough that leaves the sides of bowl.

- Place on lightly floured surface, sprinkle with flour and knead 8 to 10 times. Roll to ½-inch thickness. With floured 2½-inch round cutter, cut biscuits from dough and place 1 inch apart on ungreased baking sheet. Re-roll trimmings and cut biscuits.

- Bake at 375 degrees for 12 to 15 minutes or until lightly browned.

- Makes 12.

Italian Rolls

1 (16 ounce) package hot roll
  mix
1 cup hot (120 degrees) water
2 tablespoons butter
1 egg
½ cup pine nuts

⅓ cup (1⅓ ounces) freshly
  grated Parmesan cheese
¼ cup chopped fresh parsley
2 tablespoons chopped fresh
  basil
2 cloves garlic, minced
2 tablespoons butter, melted

- Prepare hot roll mix according to package directions, using water, butter and egg. Knead dough, then let rest according to directions.

- Combine pine nuts, Parmesan cheese, parsley, basil and garlic.

- On lightly-floured surface, roll dough to 18x18-inch square. Brush with melted butter and sprinkle with pine nut mixture.

- Roll up dough, moistening edge and pressing to seal. Cut crosswise into 12 slices and place, cut side down, in lightly greased baking pan.

- Bake according to package directions. Serve warm.

- Makes 12.

Parmesan Corn Bread

1 cup boiling water
¼ cup bulgur
1 cup all-purpose flour
1 cup yellow corn meal
⅓ cup (1½ ounces) grated
    Parmesan cheese
2 tablespoons sugar
1 tablespoon baking powder
½ teaspoon fennel

½ teaspoon dried basil,
    crushed
2 eggs
1 cup milk
¼ cup olive oil
⅓ cup chopped sun-dried
    tomatoes
⅓ cup chopped red onion
corn meal

- Pour boiling water over bulgur. Let stand for 5 minutes and drain.

- In large mixing bowl, combine flour, 1 cup corn meal, Parmesan cheese, sugar, baking powder, fennel and basil.

- Beat eggs slightly. Blend in milk and oil and add bulgur.

- Make a well in center of dry ingredients. Add egg mixture and stir just until moistened. Fold in tomatoes and onion.

- Spread batter in loaf pan which has been sprinkled with corn meal.

- Bake at 375 degrees for 40 minutes, cover loosely with aluminum foil and bake for additional 10 to 15 minutes. Remove from pan and cool on wire rack.

- Serves 8.

Oatmeal Bread

 This loaf is a dark, fairly dense crusty bread.

2¼ cups bread flour
½ cup uncooked rolled oats
1½ teaspoons salt
¼ cup molasses

1 cup water
1 tablespoon butter
1 teaspoon active dry yeast

- Place flour, oats and salt in bread machine. Add molasses, water and butter.

- Select the 4-hour basic baking mode. Place yeast in yeast dispenser.

- Makes 1 loaf.

Tarragon Bread Sticks

3 cups all-purpose flour,
divided
1 tablespoon brown sugar
2 tablespoons finely chopped
fresh parsley
2 teaspoons salt
1 teaspoon celery seed,
crushed

1 teaspoon dried tarragon,
crushed
1 packet active dry yeast
1 cup water
2 tablespoons butter
¼ cup sesame seeds
1 egg white
1 tablespoon water

- In large mixing bowl, combine 2 cups flour, brown sugar, parsley, salt, celery seed, tarragon and yeast.

- Heat water with butter until lukewarm (110 to 115 degrees). Stir into dry ingredients and add enough of remaining 1 cup flour to form soft dough that begins to leave sides of bowl.

- On lightly-floured surface, knead dough for 5 to 8 minutes or until smooth and elastic.

- Place in lightly-oiled bowl, turn once and cover loosely with plastic wrap. Let rise until doubled in bulk.

- Divide dough into 4 portions, then separate each into 6 pieces. Roll each piece into 8-inch length and place 1 inch apart on greased baking sheet. Let rise, covered, for 15 minutes.

- Toast sesame seeds at 325 degrees for 10 minutes. Combine egg white and 1 tablespoon water. Brush on bread sticks and sprinkle with sesame seeds.

- Bake at 400 degrees for 20 minutes or until golden brown. Remove from baking sheets and cool on wire racks.

- Makes 24.

"Sexiest Zoo in America"

*Because of the success of its breeding programs, **Newsweek** dubbed the Cincinnati Zoo "the sexiest zoo in the country." It holds the national record for the most lowland gorillas born in captivity with 45, captive births of black rhinos with 17, and is home to the Komodo dragon and the only three Sumatran rhinoceros in the United States. The white tiger, a genetic variation of the typical orange color, is another one of the Zoo's internationally recognized breeding successes.*

Explore a world of wonder in Jungle Trails, the Zoo's outstanding rain forest exhibit, where bonobos and orangutans lurk in the misty fog-enshrouded jungles of Africa and Asia. Journey a few steps farther into a steamy island cove inhabited by the world's largest lizards, the Komodo dragons. Or peer into the luminous eyes of a jaguar and see baby walruses up-close.

Swiss Cheese Bread

 Freezes well and is excellent for sandwiches or toast.

1 cup milk
2 tablespoons sugar
1 tablespoon salt
1 tablespoon butter or margarine

1 packet active dry yeast
1 cup warm (110 to 115 degrees) water
5 cups all-purpose flour
2 cups (8 ounces) grated Swiss cheese

- Scald milk with sugar, salt and butter or margarine in saucepan.

- In large mixing bowl, dissolve yeast in warm water. Combine with warm milk liquid.

- Beat in 2 cups flour and cheese, then stir in remaining 3 cups flour or amount necessary to form stiff dough.

- On lightly-floured surface, knead for 8 to 10 minutes or until smooth and elastic, adding only enough additional flour to prevent dough from sticking.

- Place dough in greased bowl, rotating to coat. Cover and let rise for 1½ to 2 hours or until doubled in bulk.

- Punch dough down, divide in 2 portions and knead each a few times. Shape into 2 loaves and placed in greased 9x5x3-inch loaf pans. Cover and let rise in a warm place for 30 minutes to 1 hour or until doubled in bulk.

- Bake at 350 degrees for about 50 minutes. Remove from pans and cool on racks.

- Makes 2 loaves.

Smoked Mozzarella
Red Pepper Muffins

1¾ cups all-purpose flour
3 tablespoons sugar
2 teaspoons baking powder
2 teaspoons salt
1 egg, beaten
¾ cup milk
¼ cup vegetable oil

½ cup (2 ounces) grated
   smoked mozzarella cheese
⅓ cup chopped roasted red
   pepper
⅓ cup minced onion
¼ teaspoon coarsely ground
   black pepper
corn meal

- In large mixing bowl, combine flour, sugar, baking powder and salt.

- Combine egg, milk and oil, blending thoroughly. Make a well in dry ingredients and pour egg mixture into well. Mix just until dry ingredients are moistened.

- Fold in mozzarella cheese, red pepper, onion and black pepper.

- Spoon batter into muffin cups which have been lightly greased and generously sprinkled with corn meal, filling cups ⅔ full. Sprinkle batter with additional black pepper and corn meal.

- Bake at 400 degrees for 20 minutes or until golden brown. Serve warm.

- Makes 10 to 12.

Lawn bowling on Victory Parkway

photograph by Robert A. Flischel

Spring Grove Cemetery

On the National Registry of Historic Sites, 37 Civil War generals, 26 mayors, and eight Ohio governors are buried in Spring Grove Cemetery, which is also one of Cincinnati's most beautiful landmarks, nature preserves and world-class arboretums. Lakes, trees and flowers greet visitors at every turn.

"Musical manna, like Wonder Bread, builds your spiritual body in twelve ways - joy, strength, passion, compassion, love, faith, grace, desire, pain, gratification, confidence, and hope."

John Morris Russell
Associate Conductor
Cincinnati Symphony
Orchestra

Spinach Bread

 This bread requires a knife and fork.

1 (8 ounce) package French rolls
½ cup butter, softened, divided
1 medium sized onion, chopped
1 (6 ounce) package sharp cheddar cheese

1 (10 ounce) package frozen chopped spinach, thawed and drained
1 teaspoon Worcestershire sauce
black pepper, to taste
2 cups (8 ounces) shredded mozzarella cheese

- Split rolls lengthwise in halves. Spread with ¼ cup butter and set aside.

- Sauté onion in remaining ¼ cup butter until softened. Stir in cheese and heat until cheese is melted. Remove from heat.

- Add spinach, Worcestershire sauce and black pepper to cheese mixture. Spread on cut surfaces of French rolls, sprinkle with mozzarella cheese and place on baking sheet.

- Bake at 350 degrees for 8 minutes.

- Makes 12.

Apple Bread

3 cups all-purpose flour
1 teaspoon baking soda
½ teaspoon salt
1 cup vegetable oil
2 cups sugar

3 eggs
2 cups chopped tart apples
2 teaspoons vanilla
1 cup chopped nuts

- Combine flour, baking soda and salt. Set aside.

- In large mixing bowl, blend oil, sugar and eggs, beating until thoroughly combined. Stir in dry ingredients, apples and vanilla. Fold in nuts.

- Spread batter in 2 ungreased 8x4x3-inch loaf pans.

- Bake at 350 degrees for 50 to 60 minutes or until wooden pick inserted near center comes out clean. Cool in pans for 10 minutes, remove and cool on wire rack. Serve warm or cold.

- Makes 2 loaves.

☀ *Polenta*

1 small onion, minced
½ cup butter
2 cups chicken broth
1 drop hot pepper sauce
½ cup white wine
1 cup yellow or white corn
  meal
½ teaspoon Worcestershire
  sauce

1 cup (4 ounces) grated Swiss
  or Parmesan cheese
5 tablespoons dried parsley,
  divided
2 or 3 pimentos, diced
½ teaspoon garlic salt
1 teaspoon seasoned salt
4 eggs
¼ cup (1 ounce) grated cheese

- In large skillet, sauté onion in butter until translucent.

- Add broth and hot pepper sauce. Bring to a boil.

- Stir in wine and bring to a boil. Stir in corn meal and simmer for about 5 minutes or until mushy.

- Add Worcestershire sauce, Swiss or Parmesan cheese, 3 tablespoons parsley, pimento, garlic salt and seasoned salt.

- Beat in eggs, 1 at a time. Pour batter into buttered shallow casserole. Sprinkle with ¼ cup cheese and remaining 2 tablespoons parsley.

- Bake at 350 degrees for 35 to 40 minutes or until firm.

- Serves 8.

"We did not inherit the earth from our ancestors. We are borrowing it from our children."

Native American
Saying

Park City

Cincinnati was once rated second only to Paris in the number of parks. Today, there are over 150 city parks, encompassing 5,580 acres and ranging in size from the floral triangles beautifying roadways at intersections to the 1,460 acre Mt. Airy Forest.

The Cincinnati Park System includes many acres of undeveloped land held as preserves. These include Buttercup Valley, with a trail system, Bradford-Felters, Tanglewood and Hillside. There are also five nature centers: California Woods, Avon Woods, LaBoiteaux Woods, Trailside Nature Center and Caldwell. All five have education centers staffed by naturalists available for educational programs.

Dancin' the Night Away

Italian Renaissance Ault Park Pavilion hosted dances in the 1930's and 40's. So did Mt. Echo Park in western Cincinnati. Perhaps the most famous dance spot of all, however, was Moonlite Gardens at Old Coney Amusement Park, where many a romance had its beginning. And while on the subject of wine and roses, many Cincinnati parks are built on old vineyard land. Alms Park is one of these. If you search, you just might find evidence of an old wine cellar.

President's Grove

The oak trees at Eden Park came as seedlings from Mt. Vernon, home of George Washington, right around the turn of the century.

 Soft Pretzels and Dip

 This is a perfect treat to eat while watching your favorite sporting event.

2 packets active dry yeast	1 egg
2 cups warm (110 to 115 degrees) water	6 to 7 cups all-purpose flour
½ cup sugar	1 egg yolk
2 teaspoons salt	2 tablespoons water
¼ cup butter or margarine, softened	coarse salt
	1½ cups mayonnaise
	3 tablespoons Dijon mustard

- In large warm bowl, dissolve yeast in warm water. Add sugar, 2 teaspoons salt, butter or margarine, egg and 3 cups flour. Beat until smooth. Add enough additional flour to form stiff dough.

- Store, tightly covered with aluminum foil, for 2 hours in refrigerator.

- Divide dough in 2 portions, then cut each half into 16 pieces. On lightly-floured surface, roll each to 20-inch pencil-shaped length. Arrange in pretzel shape on lightly greased baking sheet.

- Brush with mixture of egg yolk and 2 tablespoons water. Sprinkle lightly with coarse salt.

- Let rise, covered, in a warm place, for about 25 minutes or until doubled in bulk.

- Bake at 400 degrees for 15 minutes or until lightly browned. Cool on wire racks.

- Prepare dip by combining mayonnaise and mustard.

- Makes 30 to 36.

☀ *Apricot Nut Bread*

1 cup dried apricots	1 cup sugar
water	2 tablespoons vegetable oil
2 cups all-purpose flour	1 egg
2 teaspoons baking powder	¼ cup water
½ teaspoon baking soda	¼ cup orange juice
1 teaspoon salt	½ cup chopped pecans

- Soak apricots in water to cover for about 30 minutes. Drain well and cut into ¼-inch pieces.

- Sift flour, baking powder, baking soda and salt together.

- In large mixing bowl, cream sugar and oil together until smooth. Beat in egg and stir in water and orange juice.

- Stir dry ingredients into egg mixture and add nuts and apricots. Let stand for 20 minutes.

- Spread batter in greased 9x5x3-inch loaf pan (or two small loaf pans).

- Bake at 350 degrees for 45 to 60 minutes. Cool in pans for 10 minutes, remove and cool on wire rack.

- Makes 1 loaf.

Buttermilk Pecan Bread

2 cups all-purpose flour	1 egg, well beaten
¾ teaspoon baking powder	2 tablespoons butter, melted
½ teaspoon baking soda	1 cup buttermilk
½ teaspoon salt	1 cup broken pecans
1 cup firmly packed brown sugar	

- Sift flour, baking powder, baking soda and salt together.

- In large mixing bowl, gradually add brown sugar to egg, beating until light. Blend in butter.

- Alternately add dry ingredients and buttermilk to egg mixture. Stir in nuts.

- Spread batter in greased 9x5x3-inch loaf pan.

- Bake at 350 degrees for 1 hour. Cool in pan for 10 minutes, remove and cool on wire rack.

- Makes 1 loaf.

'The city's prime river overlooks -Eden Park and Mt. Echo-are great places to bring your lunch and watch the river. My favorite view is the overlook at Mt. Echo, with the Ohio River in front of me and that beautiful Italian Renaissance pavilion and this incredible perennial garden. I like it best when the white Japanese anemones are blooming behind me."

*Vivian Wagner
Supervisor of Nature
Education
Cincinnati Parks*

First Park Over an Expressway

Cincinnatians were so devoted to Lytle Park that when expressway plans threatened to destroy it, citizens rallied to have it rebuilt over the I-71 expressway (Lytle Tunnel), making it the first park to be built over an expressway.

Cinnamon-Carrot Bread

 A good snack for after school.

2 cups all-purpose flour
2 teaspoons baking powder
1 teaspoon baking soda
1 teaspoon cinnamon
¾ cup sugar
¼ cup firmly packed brown sugar

¾ cup vegetable oil
2 eggs, beaten
1 cup grated carrots
¾ cup chopped pecans
½ teaspoon vanilla

- Sift flour, baking powder, baking soda and cinnamon together.

- In large mixing bowl, cream sugar, brown sugar and oil together until smooth.

- Add dry ingredients to creamed mixture, mixing well. Gradually beat in eggs. Stir in carrots, pecans and vanilla, mixing well.

- Spread batter in greased 9x5x3-inch loaf pan.

- Bake at 350 degrees for 1 hour. Cool in pan for 10 minutes, remove and cool on wire rack.

- Makes 1 loaf.

Olive Walnut Bread

5 cups all-purpose flour
2½ tablespoons baking powder
⅔ cup sugar
1 teaspoon salt
½ teaspoon ground savory
2 eggs, beaten

2 cups milk
2 cups sliced pimento-stuffed green olives
2 cups broken walnuts
¼ cup chopped pimento

- In large mixing bowl, sift flour, baking powder, sugar, salt and savory together.

- Beat eggs with milk until well blended. Add to dry ingredients, stirring just until moistened.

- Fold in olives, walnuts and pimento.

- Spread batter in 2 greased 9x5x3-inch loaf pans.

- Bake at 350 degrees for 55 to 60 minutes. Cool in pans for 5 minutes, remove and cool on wire rack.

- Makes 2 loaves.

Pumpkin Bread

3⅓ cups all-purpose flour
3 cups sugar
2 teaspoons baking soda
1 teaspoon salt
2 teaspoons pumpkin pie spice
nutmeg, to taste
cinnamon, to taste

2 cups canned pumpkin
4 eggs, beaten
1 cup vegetable oil
⅔ cup cold water
1 cup chopped pecans
2 cups semisweet chocolate
  chips

- Sift flour, sugar, baking soda, salt, pumpkin pie spice, nutmeg and cinnamon together.

- In large mixing bowl, combine pumpkin, eggs, oil and water, blending well.

- Add dry ingredients to pumpkin mixture, mixing thoroughly. Fold in pecans and chocolate chips.

- Spread batter in 3 well-greased 8x5x3-inch loaf pans.

- Bake at 350 degrees for 1 hour. Cool in pans for 10 minutes, remove and cool on wire rack.

- Makes 3 loaves.

photograph by Robert A. Flischel

Reading in Burnet Woods

Army Campground

In World War I, Eden Park was used as a campground for the Third Regulars of the United States Army.

Hauck Botanic Garden

"That is a marvelous place. You have to visit there in the spring when it's blooming. Mr. Hauck lived there. He bought several adjoining homes and tore down the houses. He was a collector, but what he collected were trees and bushes. He would even go to some of the older estates, like in Clifton, in particular, that were being destroyed or torn down, and he would salvage some of the venerable shrubs."

*Vivian Wagner
Supervisor of Nature
Education
Cincinnati Parks*

Slip Sliding Away

Three Cincinnati parks have concrete slides, including Ault Park, which has a great view of Lunken Airport. The other two are Fernbank Park and Burnet Woods. Like many other walls and structures, these were built during the Works Projects Administration (WPA) during the Depression.

Strawberry Nut Bread with Strawberry Butter

3 cups all-purpose flour
2 cups sugar
1 teaspoon baking soda
1 teaspoon salt
1 teaspoon cinnamon
4 eggs, beaten

¼ cup vegetable oil
2 (10 ounce) packages frozen strawberries, thawed and juice reserved
1 cup chopped nuts of choice
½ cup butter, softened
¾ cup powdered sugar

- In large mixing bowl, combine flour, sugar, baking soda, salt and cinnamon. Make a well in center of dry ingredients.

- Pour eggs, oil and strawberries into well. Mix thoroughly. Stir in nuts.

- Spread batter in 2 greased 9x5x3-inch loaf pans or 5 miniature pans.

- Bake at 350 degrees for 50 to 60 minutes for large loaves or 20 to 25 minutes for small loaves. Cool in pans for 10 minutes, remove and cool on wire rack.

- Combine ½ cup strawberry juice, butter and powdered sugar. Mix by hand or in food processor until smooth.

- Makes 2 loaves.

Krohn Conservatory

The butterfly exhibit is a favorite at the Krohn Conservatory, as is the lily display at Easter and the poinsettia display during the winter holidays. Also of note are the 5,000 exotic plants housed in the Palm House, Desert House, Tropical House and Orchid House.

ENTREES... *The Main Event*

The Cincinnati Red Stockings, America's first professional
baseball team, began play in 1869.

Photograph by J. Miles Wolf

"Cincinnati has all the amenities of a big city, including great theater, sports and entertainment, along with a charming small town feel."

Robert Goering
Hamilton County Treasurer

The Maisonette
Beef Bourguignonne

½ pound salt pork, cut in
 1-inch cubes
24 very small onions
4 pounds chuck beef, cut in
 2-inch cubes
2 tablespoons all-purpose flour
2 cups burgundy wine (or less)
3 cloves garlic, chopped
10 peppercorns
1 bay leaf
½ teaspoon thyme

2 tablespoons tomato paste,
 optional
water
1 carrot
1 stalk celery
4 sprigs parsley
1 leek
½ pound mushrooms
3 tablespoons butter, optional
2 tablespoons cognac, optional
3 tablespoons chopped parsley
1 cup croutons, optional

- In Dutch oven, cook salt pork until browned. Remove pork and drain fat except for ¼ cup. Sauté onion in fat until browned. Remove onion.

- Sauté beef in remaining fat, turning to brown on all sides. Sprinkle beef with flour. Add salt pork, wine, garlic, peppercorns, bay leaf, thyme, tomato paste and enough water to completely cover the beef.

- With string, tie together carrot, celery, parsley and leek to form bouquet garni. Place in center of beef mixture.

- Bake at 325 degrees for 1 hour and 40 minutes or until beef is tender, stirring occasionally and added more wine or water if necessary.

- While beef is cooking, sauté mushrooms in butter. Remove bouquet garni and bay leaf. Add mushrooms and onion. Bake for additional 20 minutes. Check seasoning.

- Just before serving, add cognac, parsley and croutons. Serve with noodles or vegetables.

- Serves 8 to 10.

But of Course, Mon Cher

The Maisonette on Sixth Street downtown may be Cincinnati's only Mobil five-star restaurant, but in 1998, it became the only restaurant ever to earn five stars for 34 consecutive years.

"Life is too short. I'm here to work hard and have fun."

*Jean-Robert de Cavel
Executive Chef
The Maisonette*

Opening Pitch

"Long time Reds broadcaster Joe Nuxhall holds a baseball record which may never be broken. In 1944, while still enrolled at Hamilton High School, Joe took the mound for the Reds at the tender age of 15 years, 10 months. He continued to pitch for sixteen more years."

Charles Henderson
The Downtowner

Beef Paprika

2 pound beef chuck or round, cut in 1-inch cubes
1 cup chopped onion
1 small clove garlic, minced
¼ cup vegetable shortening
¾ cup ketchup
2 tablespoons Worcestershire sauce
1 tablespoon brown sugar
2 teaspoons salt
2 teaspoons paprika
½ teaspoon dry mustard
dash of cayenne pepper
1¾ cups water, divided
2 tablespoons flour

- In large skillet, sauté beef, onion and garlic in shortening, turning to brown beef on all sides and until onion is tender.

- Add ketchup, Worcestershire sauce, brown sugar, salt, paprika, mustard, cayenne pepper and 1½ cups water. Simmer, covered, for 1½ hours.

- Blend flour and remaining ¼ cup water until smooth. Gradually add to cooked beef and sauce, stirring to blend. Bring to a boil, stirring constantly, and cook for 1 minute.

- Serve with noodles.

- Serves 6 to 8.

Blue Cheese Flank Steak

½ cup olive oil
¼ cup lemon juice
1 tablespoon grated onion
1 clove garlic, minced
½ teaspoon hot pepper sauce
2 tablespoons chopped parsley
1 teaspoon salt
1 teaspoon marjoram
1 teaspoon thyme
1 pound flank steak, scored
¼ cup butter
2 tablespoons chopped chives
2 tablespoons crumbled blue cheese

- Combine oil, lemon juice, onion, garlic, hot pepper sauce, parsley, salt, marjoram and thyme.

- Place steak in glass dish, add marinade and let stand for at least 4 hours, turning steak occasionally.

- Drain marinade from steak. Broil or grill for 5 minutes on each side.

- Combine butter, chives and blue cheese, blending well.

- Just before serving, spread blue cheese topping on steak.

- Serves 3.

Beef in Herb Wine Sauce

3 or 4 medium sized onions, sliced
2 tablespoons bacon drippings
2 pounds sirloin tip or other lean beef, cut in 1½-inch cubes
1½ tablespoons all-purpose flour
1 cup beef bouillon, divided

1½ cups dry red wine, divided
1 teaspoon salt
½ teaspoon black pepper
¼ teaspoon marjoram
½ teaspoon oregano
¼ teaspoon thyme
½ pound fresh mushrooms
¼ cup butter

- In Dutch oven, sauté onion in bacon drippings until yellow. Remove with slotted spoon and set aside.

- Add beef to pan, sprinkle lightly with flour and cook, turning to brown cubes on all sides.

- Stir in ¾ cup bouillon, 1 cup red wine, salt, black pepper, marjoram, oregano and thyme. Simmer, tightly covered, or bake at 300 degrees for about 2 hours, gradually adding remaining ¼ cup bouillon and ½ cup wine.

- Sauté mushrooms in butter. Add with onion to beef and cook additional 20 to 30 minutes or until beef is tender.

- Serves 8.

"My favorite Cincinnati tradition is Reds Opening Day. My favorite meal is prime rib, creamed spinach and mashed potatoes."

U.S. Congressman John Boehner

※ Carbonnade À La Flamande

4 pounds lean beef, cut in
  2x1x½-inch slices
½ cup all-purpose flour
½ cup vegetable oil
2 pounds large onions, thickly
  sliced
6 cloves garlic, crushed
3 tablespoons dark brown
  sugar

¼ cup red wine vinegar,
  divided
½ cup chopped parsley
2 small bay leaves
1 tablespoon salt
black pepper, to taste
2 teaspoons thyme
2 (10½ ounce) cans beef broth
2 (12 ounce) cans beer

• Coat beef with flour. In skillet, brown beef slices, a few at a time, in oil; place in large casserole.

• Sauté onion and garlic in oil, adding more oil if needed, until tender. Add onion and garlic to beef. Stir in sugar, 2 tablespoons vinegar, parsley, bay leaves, salt, black pepper and thyme.

• Drain excess oil from skillet. Add broth and heat over low heat, stirring to loosen browned bits. Pour over beef and add beer.

• Bake, covered, at 325 degrees for about 2 hours. Remove bay leaves and stir in remaining vinegar before serving.

• Serves 6.

Beef Waimea

4 pounds stewing beef, cubed
1 lemon, sliced
1 large onion, sliced
salt and black pepper, to taste
1 (12 ounce) bottle beer
¾ cup ketchup

2 tablespoons vinegar
3 drops hot pepper sauce
2 tablespoons Worcestershire
  sauce
¼ cup firmly packed brown
  sugar

• Place beef in shallow roasting pan. Arrange lemon and onion slices on beef and season with salt and black pepper.

• Bake at 450 degrees for 30 minutes. While beef is browning, prepare sauce.

• In small saucepan, combine beer, ketchup, vinegar, hot pepper sauce, Worcestershire sauce and brown sugar, blending well. Simmer for 5 minutes. Pour sauce on beef.

• Bake at 350 degrees for 1 to 1½ hours or until beef is tender, basting at 20 minute intervals (if sauce covers beef, basting is unnecessary).

• Serves 8.

Paprika Beef Roll

3 pounds round steak, cut in
  2 pieces
salt and black pepper, to taste
paprika
¼ pound fresh mushrooms,
  thinly sliced
1 large onion, sliced
1 (4 ounce) jar pimento,
  drained and chopped

1 (12 ounce) package stuffing
  mix
½ cup butter, melted
1 tablespoon boiling water
1 egg, beaten
1 (6 ounce) jar pimento-
  stuffed green olives
¼ cup butter
6 whole mushrooms
1 cup red wine

- Using mallet, pound steak until thin. Rub salt, pepper and liberal amount of paprika into steaks.

- On each steak, layer sliced mushrooms, onion and pimento. Crush stuffing mix and sprinkle evenly on vegetables.

- In small bowl, whisk melted butter, boiling water and egg. Quickly drizzle mixture on stuffing crumbs.

- Arrange olives in row on long side of each steak; roll up from that edge. Secure firmly with string at each end and in center. Season with salt and black pepper.

- Sauté steak in ¼ cup butter in roasting pan, turning to brown on all sides. Place whole mushrooms around steak rolls and sprinkle lightly with salt, black pepper and paprika. Add wine.

- Bake, covered, at 350 degrees for 2 hours, basting with pan juices at 20 minute intervals. Serve hot or cold.

- Serves 6.

"If it was a @#S5&! Sandwich you'd have held on to it!"

Enraged Tom Seaver, after a chubby Reds' teammate dropped an important fly ball.

Beef Carbonnade

½ (16 ounce) package bacon, diced
1 medium sized onion, chopped
3 to 4 pounds stewing beef, cut in cubes
1 teaspoon Worcestershire sauce
1 teaspoon seasoned salt
1 teaspoon garlic salt
dash of hot pepper sauce
black pepper, to taste

1 bay leaf
½ cup all-purpose flour
½ cup tomato puree
½ cup currant or cranberry jelly
2 (12 ounce) bottles beer
1 tablespoon beef bouillon granules
½ pound fresh mushrooms, sliced
1 cup canned pearl onions

- In Dutch oven, cook bacon until done. Add onion and cook until transparent; do not brown.

- Sauté beef in bacon drippings until no longer red; do not brown. Stir in Worcestershire sauce, seasoned salt, garlic salt, hot pepper sauce, black pepper and bay leaf.

- Sprinkle flour on beef and stir to blend. Add tomato puree, jelly, beer and bouillon, mixing well.

- Bring to a boil, reduce heat and simmer for 1½ to 2 hours, adding mushrooms and onions after 45 minutes.

- Serves 6 to 8.

Beef with Pea Pods

¼ cup soy sauce
1 tablespoon dry sherry
1 tablespoon cornstarch
1 teaspoon sugar
1 pound flank steak, cut
   in thin strips
¼ teaspoon seasoned salt

¼ cup vegetable oil
¼ cup sliced onion
pinch of grated ginger root
½ teaspoon salt
¼ pound fresh pea pods or
   1 (6 ounce) package frozen
   pea pods, thawed

- Combine soy sauce and sherry. Blend in cornstarch, sugar and seasoned salt, stirring until dissolved.

- Place steak in glass dish and add marinade, turning to coat well. Drain marinade.

- Sauté steak with onion in oil in skillet, browning quickly.

- Add ginger root, salt and pea pods. Cook just until tender. Serve on rice.

- Serves 4.

Barbecued Beef Brisket

 This meat is delicious served hot or cold.

1 (3 to 5 pound) beef brisket
1 teaspoon onion salt
1 teaspoon celery salt
1 teaspoon garlic salt
1 teaspoon black pepper

1 tablespoon Worcestershire
   sauce
¾ cup prepared barbecue sauce
2 large onions, thinly sliced
onion rolls

- The day before serving, season brisket. Combine onion salt, celery salt, garlic salt and black pepper. Rub seasonings on all surfaces of brisket and place in roasting pan. Sprinkle Worcestershire sauce on brisket. Chill, covered with aluminum foil, overnight.

- Preheat oven to 275 degrees. Bake brisket, covered, for 5 hours.

- Pour barbecue sauce over brisket and place onions around it. Bake, uncovered, for 1 additional hour.

- Let stand for 1 hour before serving. Slice across grain. Serve on onion rolls, using pan sauce as an accompaniment.

- Serves 8.

"My favorite food tradition is Christmas Eve dinner with just my immediate family, which is wife DeDe, son Michael and daughter Michelle. DeDe makes prime rib, twice-baked potatoes, and her famous apple pie. Not a la mode, just 'a la lone.'"

Anthony Munoz, first Cincinnati Bengal to be inducted on the first ballot to the 1998 Football Hall of Fame.

Vegetable-Filled Flank Steak

1¾ pounds flank steak, trimmed
2 cups beef broth
½ cup uncooked regular rice
2 (10 ounce) packages frozen chopped spinach, thawed and drained
½ teaspoon salt, divided
black pepper, to taste
½ teaspoon chopped fresh basil, divided

1 egg
4 carrots, finely shredded
1 carrot, sliced
1 stalk celery, sliced
1 onion, sliced
1½ cups tomato juice
2 tablespoons all-purpose flour
¼ cup cold water
1 tablespoon chopped parsley

- Using mallet, pound steak to form rectangle about 12x14 inches.

- In saucepan, bring broth to a boil. Add rice, reduce heat, and simmer, tightly covered, for about 15 minutes. Drain well, reserving liquid, and set aside.

- Combine spinach, ⅛ teaspoon salt and a dash of black pepper. Spread mixture in a flat layer 4 inches wide across width of steak.

- Add ¼ teaspoon basil and egg to cooked rice, mixing well. Spoon on spinach, spreading evenly.

- Combine ⅛ teaspoon salt, dash of black pepper, ¼ teaspoon basil and shredded carrots. Spoon on rice, pressing slightly to compact.

- Bring both sides of steak over filling, overlapping slightly. Secure with wooden picks.

- Scatter sliced carrot, celery and onion in 8-quart Dutch oven. Place rolled steak on vegetables, seam side down. Pour tomato juice and reserved broth into pan.

- Bring to a boil, reduce heat and simmer, covered, for 1½ hours or until meat is tender, basting occasionally with pan liquids.

- Place steak on serving platter and slice to serve.

- Blend flour and ¼ cup cold water until smooth. Gradually add to remaining pan liquids, stirring to blend. Heat on low, stirring frequently until it thickens. Serve warm and pass as accompaniment with steak.

- Serves 4 to 6.

Sauerbraten

2 cups cider vinegar
2 cups water
½ lemon, sliced
2 tablespoons sugar
1 tablespoon salt
2 medium sized onions, sliced
6 bay leaves

12 whole cloves
16 whole peppercorns
3½ pound cross rib roast, rump roast or pot roast
vegetable shortening
20 gingersnaps, crushed
all-purpose flour

- Combine vinegar, water, lemon, sugar, salt, onion, bay leaves, cloves and peppercorns.

- Marinate beef in liquid for 2 to 3 days, turning roast every 12 to 24 hours.

- Remove beef from marinade, strain liquid and reserve.

- Sear beef in small amount of shortening in Dutch oven, turning to brown on all sides. Add reserved liquid and gingersnaps. Simmer for 2 hours.

- Slice beef to serve with gravy formed by pan juices, adding flour if necessary to thicken. Remove bay leaves from gravy.

- Serves 8.

Reuben Casserole

1 (27 ounce) can sauerkraut, drained and rinsed
1 cup sour cream
1 medium sized onion, minced
2 (12 ounce) cans corned beef

4 cups (16 ounces) Swiss cheese, shredded
10 slices dark rye bread, crumbled or cubed
1 cup margarine, melted

- Combine sauerkraut, sour cream and onion. Place in buttered 13x9x2-inch baking pan.

- Crumbling corned beef to separate, layer over sauerkraut mixture. Sprinkle cheese on beef and top with bread crumbs or cubes. Drizzle margarine on bread.

- Bake at 350 degrees for about 45 minutes.

- Serves 6.

The Big Red Machine

One of the dominant teams of the 1970's, The Cincinnati Reds were nicknamed "The Big Red Machine." The team, which won 5 division titles, 4 National League Championships and two World Series (1975 and 1976) included Pete Rose, Johnny Bench, Joe Morgan, Tony Perez, Dave Concepcion, Cesar Geronimo, Ken Griffey Sr. and George Foster.

4,192

Pete Rose hit a line drive into left field to secure hit number 4,192 in 1985 to break Ty Cobb's record, which made him baseball's all time career hit leader.

Beef Rolls Bourbonnaise

 Adapted from a recipe used by the Imperial House in Lexington, Kentucky, 30 years ago.

4 (5 ounce) thin slices beef round or rump roast	all-purpose flour
salt and black pepper, to taste	vegetable shortening
¾ pound ground lean pork or beef	1 bay leaf
2 tablespoons bourbon or Scotch	¼ cup chopped parsley
2 cloves garlic	½ teaspoon thyme
1 teaspoon crushed oregano	¼ cup chopped celery or ½ teaspoon dried celery, optional
1 small onion, minced	1 cup Burgundy wine
	2 cups beef broth

- If necessary, flatten beef slices until thin. Season with salt and black pepper.

- Combine ground meat, bourbon or Scotch, garlic, oregano and onion, mixing well. Spread ¼ of mixture on each beef slice, roll up and secure with string.

- Dust each beef roll with flour. Sear in shortening, turning to brown on all sides. Place in small roasting pan.

- For a clear sauce, combine bay leaf, parsley, thyme and celery in cheesecloth square, tie with string to form bouquet garni and add to pan. Or ingredients can be added separately. Pour wine and broth into pan.

- Bake at 350 degrees, basting frequently, for 2 hours or until tender. Add more broth if necessary to thin sauce.

- Serves 4.

Serve with egg noodles, sprinkled with Parmesan cheese and garnished with parsley.

"As a little boy, I loved to go the Reds games and eat a bratwurst."

Page Busken
Busken Bakery

Fillets of Beef Chasseur

 Great for a crowd, this dish benefits from being prepared a day in advance.

1 large clove garlic, crushed	2 teaspoons tomato paste
1½ teaspoons seasoned salt	½ teaspoon crushed garlic
¼ teaspoon black pepper	¾ cup dry red wine
8 (6 to 8 ounces) filet mignon steaks	1 cup chicken broth
	½ cup beef broth
¼ cup plus 2 tablespoons butter, divided	¼ teaspoon Worcestershire sauce
2 tablespoons brandy	2 tablespoons currant jelly
3 tablespoons all-purpose flour	½ pound fresh mushrooms, sliced

- Combine garlic, salt and black pepper, mixing to form a paste. Place steaks on work surface. Rub paste on both sides of each steak.

- Sauté steaks, 4 at a time, in 2 tablespoons butter in large heavy skillet over moderately high heat, turning to brown on each side. Steak should be raw in center. Add additional butter if necessary. Place steaks in 13x9x2-inch baking dish, leaving 1-inch spaces between pieces.

- Pour brandy into skillet. Cook over medium heat, stirring constantly to loosen browned bits.

- Add remaining ¼ cup butter. When melted and foamy, stir in flour. Reduce heat to low and cook, stirring constantly, until mixture is golden. Stir in tomato paste and garlic; sauce should be thick and grainy.

- Remove from heat and whisk in wine, chicken broth and beef broth. Return to moderate heat and bring to a boil, stirring constantly. Reduce heat and simmer, stirring occasionally, for 10 minutes or until reduced by one third.

- Stir in Worcestershire sauce and jelly. When jelly is melted, stir in mushrooms and adjust seasonings. If too thick, dilute with water, broth or wine. Remove from heat and let stand until completely cool.

- Pour sauce over steaks in casserole (sauce should be about ½ depth of steaks). Refrigerate, covered with aluminum foil, overnight. Let stand at room temperature for 2 hours before baking.

- Bake at 400 degrees for 15 to 20 minutes for medium-rare or 20 to 25 minutes for medium-well doneness.

- Serves 8

Crosley Field

Crosley Field, which stretched from Western Avenue to Findlay and York streets, the former home of the Reds, was actually Redland Field until Powell Crosley Jr., radio magnate, bought controlling interest in the Reds and renamed it. In 1970, the Reds moved to Riverfront Stadium, now Cinergy Field.

Beef Brisket in Beer

1 (3 to 4 pound) beef brisket, trimmed
salt and black pepper, to taste
1 onion, sliced
¼ cup chili sauce
2 tablespoons brown sugar
1 clove garlic, minced
1 (12 ounce) can beer
2 tablespoons all-purpose flour
water

- Season brisket with salt and black pepper. Place in 13x9x2-inch baking dish. Place onion on brisket.

- Combine chili sauce, brown sugar, garlic and beer. Pour over brisket.

- Bake, covered with aluminum foil, at 350 degrees for 3½ hours. Remove foil and bake for additional 30 minutes, basting with juices.

- Place brisket on platter. Skim excess fat from droppings. Measure liquid, add water to equal 1 cup and pour into saucepan.

- Blend flour with ½ cup water. Add to cooking liquid and cook, stirring constantly, over medium heat until thickened and bubbly.

- Slice brisket across grain and serve slices with gravy.

- Serves 8 to 10.

Delicious with buttered noodles or a noodle Kugel.

photograph by Helen Adams

Chuck Roast Barbecue

3 pounds beef chuck
salt and black pepper, to taste
paprika, to taste
1½ teaspoons chili powder
1 large onion, chopped
3 stalks celery, chopped
2 tablespoons vinegar

1 (12 ounce) bottle ketchup
3 tablespoons Worcestershire
  sauce
1½ cups water
2 tablespoons brown sugar
¼ cup lemon juice

- Place beef in roasting pan. Season with salt, black pepper, paprika and chili powder. Place onion and celery on beef.

- Combine vinegar, ketchup, Worcestershire sauce, water, brown sugar and lemon juice, blending well. Pour sauce over beef and vegetables.

- Bake at 325 degrees for 2 to 3 hours or until beef is very tender. Using forks, shred hot beef and return to sauce, stirring to mix.

- Serves 12 to 15.

Babootie

2 pounds ground beef or lamb
2 onions, chopped or grated
2 cloves garlic, chopped
1 (14½ ounce) can tomatoes,
  chopped and with liquid
1½ tablespoons sugar
2 tablespoons curry powder
2 tablespoons vinegar

salt, to taste
2 firm bananas, diced
1 apple, peeled and diced
1 tablespoon apricot jam
¼ cup slivered almonds
tomato juice
4 to 5 cups cooked rice
chutney

- In large skillet, brown beef, stirring to crumble. Drain excess fat.

- Add onion, garlic, tomatoes, sugar, curry powder, vinegar, salt, banana, apple, apricot jam and almonds, mixing well.

- Simmer, stirring occasionally, for 30 minutes. Add tomato juice to thin sauce, if necessary.

- Spoon mixture on individual servings of rice and serve with chutney.

- Serves 8.

Fruit and almonds can be omitted.

I Like Mine With Lettuce and Tomato

The broiled or fried hamburger sandwich in a bun made its first appearance in 1903 at the Louisiana Purchase Exposition (St. Louis Fair), along with the hot dog and the ice-cream cone. German sailors docking in New York City at the turn of the century insisted the local eating stands chop and sandwich their beef in between buns so they could take it aboard the ship in bags. German butchers are also credited with inventing the hot dog in 1852.

Beef and Tomato Pie

1 (8 ounce) package refrigerated biscuits
¾ pound ground beef
1 medium sized onion, chopped
1 green bell pepper, chopped
1 stalk celery, chopped

1 (8 ounce) can tomatoes, undrained
¼ teaspoon salt
¼ teaspoon oregano
¼ cup buttermilk
2 eggs
½ cup (2 ounces) grated sharp cheddar cheese

- Separate biscuits. On lightly floured surface, roll each to ⅛-inch thickness. Place biscuits in bottom and on sides of greased 9-inch pie plate, pressing to form a solid crust.

- In skillet over high heat, cook ground beef with onion, bell pepper and celery, stirring occasionally, until beef is well browned. Drain excess fat.

- Add tomatoes, salt and oregano. Remove from heat.

- Combine buttermilk and eggs, beating to blend. Stir into beef and vegetables. Spoon mixture evenly in biscuit-lined pie plate and sprinkle with cheese.

- Bake at 350 degrees for 20 to 25 minutes or until biscuits are golden and filling is hot and bubbly.

- Serves 6.

Scotti's Scaloppine Ala Marsala con Fungi

 A traditional version of a classic dish, delicious in its simplicity.

½ cup butter
1¼ pounds veal, thinly sliced
all-purpose flour
1 cup Marsala wine

5 fresh mushrooms, thinly sliced
salt and white pepper, to taste
chopped fresh parsley

- Melt butter in large skillet over low flame. Lightly dredge veal in flour. Sauté in butter for 2 minutes on each side; do not overcook.

- Pour wine over veal. Add mushrooms, salt and white pepper. Simmer, covered, for about 5 minutes.

- Arrange veal on serving platter. Top with mushrooms and sprinkle with parsley.

- Serves 4.

Pedro's Special

1 pound ground beef or turkey
1 medium sized onion,
  chopped
1 clove garlic, minced
1 teaspoon olive oil
1 (8 ounce) can tomato sauce
⅓ (46 ounce) can tomato juice

¼ teaspoon oregano
2 tablespoons chili powder
1 (16 ounce) can chili or pinto
  beans, undrained
1 (6 to 8 ounce) package corn
  chips

- In skillet, cook beef or turkey with onion and garlic in olive oil, stirring to crumble meat, until browned. Drain excess fat.

- Stir in tomato sauce, tomato juice, oregano and chili powder.

- In greased 1½-quart casserole, layer ½ of beef mixture, ½ of beans and ½ of corn chips; repeat layers.

- Bake, covered, at 350 degrees for 20 minutes, remove cover and bake for additional 10 minutes.

- Serves 4 to 6.

Baked casserole can be topped with shredded Colby or Jack cheese, shredded lettuce and minced onion.

Zucchini Meat Loaf

2 pounds ground beef or turkey
2 cups coarsely grated
  unpeeled zucchini
1 cup Italian-seasoned bread
  crumbs
½ cup (2 ounces) freshly
  grated Parmesan cheese
1 tablespoon chopped fresh
  parsley

1 small onion, chopped
2 teaspoons beef bouillon
  granules
¼ teaspoon salt
1 cup milk
1 egg, beaten
10 to 20 thin slices zucchini
paprika

- Combine beef or turkey, grated zucchini, bread crumbs, Parmesan cheese, parsley, onion, bouillon, salt, milk and egg, mixing well.

- Divided mixture in 2 portions and press each into a 9x5x3-inch loaf pan.

- Bake at 350 degrees for 1 hour and 5 minutes. Garnish loaves with zucchini slices and sprinkle with paprika. Bake for additional 10 minutes.

- Serves 8.

Left over meat loaf, thinly sliced, makes delicious sandwiches.

Light Lemon Meat Loaf

Meat Loaf

1½ cups chopped onion
3 tablespoons olive oil
2 pounds lean ground beef
1 egg
2 egg whites
2 tablespoons milk

1 cup bread crumbs
1 or 2 cloves garlic, minced
1 teaspoon seasoned salt
¼ cup chopped fresh parsley
¼ teaspoon lemon zest
1 teaspoon black pepper

Glaze

½ cup ketchup
2 tablespoons brown sugar
1 tablespoon Dijon mustard

1 tablespoon fresh lemon juice
½ teaspoon hot pepper sauce

- Sauté onion in oil until tender.

- In large bowl, combine onion with beef and mix lightly.

- Whisk egg, egg whites and milk together. Stir in bread crumbs. Add mixture, garlic, seasoned salt, parsley, lemon zest and black pepper to beef, mixing thoroughly.

- Gently press beef mixture into lightly oiled 9x5x3-inch loaf pan.

- Combine ketchup, brown sugar, mustard, lemon juice and hot pepper sauce, whisking to blend. Pour glaze evenly on beef.

- Bake at 350 degrees for 1¼ hours. Let stand a few minutes before slicing.

- Serves 8.

Extra glaze can be prepared and served with meat loaf.

Barbecued Beef Loaves

Meat Loaves
1½ **pounds ground chuck**
¼ **cup lemon juice**
½ **cup water**
1 **egg, lightly beaten**

4 **slices stale bread, finely diced**
¼ **cup chopped onion**
2 **teaspoons salt**

Sauce
½ **cup ketchup**
⅓ **cup firmly packed brown sugar**
1 **teaspoon dry mustard**

½ **teaspoon ground cloves**
¼ **teaspoon allspice**
lemon slices

- Combine beef, lemon juice, water, egg, bread, onion and salt, mixing well. Shape into 6 individual oval loaves and place in 13x9x2-inch baking pan.

- Bake at 350 degrees for 10 minutes.

- While loaves bake, blend ketchup, brown sugar, mustard, cloves and allspice. Spoon sauce over partially baked loaves. Bake for additional 10 minutes, basting occasionally with sauce.

- Arrange lemon slices on loaves and bake for additional 10 minutes.

- Serves 6.

"I can't believe there's a non-conference rivalry anywhere else more intense than this."

Xavier Basketball Coach Skip Prosser about the Cross-town Shootout
Xavier Magazine

Geschnetzeltes
Swiss Julienne of Veal

 The name of this dish is pronounced Guh-shnet-sel-tis.

2 pounds veal cutlets, cut ½-inch thick	3 tablespoons all-purpose flour
salt and black pepper, to taste	1 cup whipping cream
paprika, to taste	½ cup dry white wine
3 tablespoons butter or margarine	1 cup sliced mushrooms, optional
2 tablespoons chopped shallots or green onion	¼ cup brandy

- Place each cutlet between waxed paper sheets and using mallet, pound to ¼-inch thickness. Season with salt, black pepper and paprika. Cut into 1½x¼-inch strips.

- In large skillet, sauté shallots or green onion in butter until softened. Add veal strips and cook over medium-high heat for about 4 minutes or until no longer pink. Remove veal.

- Stir flour into pan drippings and cook, stirring, until bubbly.

- Gradually blend in cream and wine. Cook, stirring often, until thickened and smooth. Add mushrooms.

- Just before serving, add veal to sauce in skillet or chafing dish. Cook, stirring frequently, for about 5 minutes.

- Heat brandy until warm to touch. Ignite and pour over veal in sauce. Stir until flame expires and serve.

- Serves 6.

Dish can be assembled in advance: prepare veal and sauce, keeping separate and storing in refrigerator until ready to complete. Reheat each before combining.

"Wherever you go, people talk about this game. If you go into a barbershop, that's what people are talking about. Even during the summer people will bring it up."

U.C. Basketball Coach
Bob Huggins

Artichoke and Chicken Casserole

5 pounds chicken, cut up
1½ teaspoons salt
¼ teaspoon black pepper
½ teaspoon paprika
¼ cup plus 2 tablespoons butter, divided
½ pound fresh mushrooms, cut in large pieces

2 tablespoons all-purpose flour
⅔ cup chicken broth or consommé
3 tablespoons sherry or more, to taste
1 (14 ounce) can artichoke hearts, drained

- Season chicken with salt and generously with black pepper. In large skillet, sauté chicken in ¼ cup butter, turning to brown on all sides. Place chicken in casserole.

- Sauté mushrooms in remaining 2 tablespoons butter until tender. Sprinkle flour on mushrooms, stirring to mix. Add broth or consommé and sherry. Cook for 5 minutes.

- Arrange artichokes on chicken. Spoon sauce on artichokes and chicken.

- Bake at 375 degrees for 40 minutes.

- Serves 6.

Chicken Parisienne

10 to 12 chicken breast halves, skin and bone removed
6 to 8 slices baby Swiss cheese
1 (10¾ ounce) can cream of mushroom soup, undiluted
1 (10¾ ounce) can cream of chicken soup, undiluted

1 (4 ounce) can mushrooms, undrained
1 cup sour cream
½ cup cooking sherry, optional
paprika

- Place chicken in 13x9x2-inch baking dish. Arrange cheese slices to cover chicken.

- Blend mushroom soup, chicken soup, mushrooms, sour cream and sherry. Spoon mixture on cheese layer and sprinkle generously with paprika.

- Bake at 350 degrees for 1½ hours or until chicken is tender.

- Serves 6 to 8.

"Anything chicken" is Billy Long's favorite food. He pitched for the White Sox, the Cubs and the Expos.

Ready All, Row!

The U.S. Olympic Rowing team practices in the Olympic Rowing Center, underneath the Montgomery Inn Boathouse on the Ohio River, which features indoor rowing, as well as a state-of-the-art workout facility. Each year, the National Collegiate Rowing Championship is held in East Fork Lake.

Chicken in Phyllo with Béchamel Sauce

Chicken

1 (16 ounce) package frozen phyllo dough
½ cup butter, melted
1 celery heart, finely chopped
½ cup butter
3 medium sized onions, minced

3 or 4 whole chicken breasts, cooked and diced
1 cup chicken broth
2 tablespoons chopped fresh parsley
salt and black pepper, to taste
3 eggs, well-beaten

Sauce

¼ cup butter
¼ cup plus 1 tablespoon all-purpose flour
2½ cups hot chicken broth

1¼ teaspoons salt
¼ fresh lemon juice
3 egg yolks, beaten

- Thaw phyllo dough, in package, in refrigerator overnight. Carefully unroll and cover with slightly damp linen towel or plastic wrap until ready to use. Set melted butter aside.

- In large skillet, sauté celery in ½ cup butter for 5 minutes. Add onion and cook until onion is transparent.

- Stir in chicken and broth. Cook until liquid is absorbed. Remove from heat and let stand until cool.

- Add parsley, salt and black pepper to chicken mixture. Fold in beaten egg.

- Place phyllo dough on baking sheet. Brushing each with melted butter, stack 6 sheets.

- Spread enough chicken mixture on top sheet to just cover surface, leaving 2-inch margin around edges. Roll up, place seam side down, seal edges securely, brush with butter and slice ¾ of the way through the roll to make 8 equal portions. Prepare a second roll in the same way.

- Bake at 350 degrees for 40 minutes or until golden brown.

- As chicken rolls complete baking, prepare sauce. In saucepan, melt butter and stir in flour. Cook over low heat for 3 minutes. Add broth quickly and stir briskly. Season with salt.

- In separate bowl, blend lemon juice and eggs. Add small amount of hot sauce to egg mixture and stir, then add eggs to sauce and mix thoroughly.

- Spoon sauce on individual servings of chicken roll.

- Serves 8.

Crab Stuffed Chicken Breasts

6 chicken breast halves, skin
  and bone removed
salt and black pepper, to taste
½ cup chopped onion
½ cup chopped celery
3 tablespoons butter
¼ cup plus 3 tablespoons dry
  white wine, divided
1 (7 ounce) can crab meat,
  drained, or 1 (6 ounce)
  package frozen cooked crab,
  thawed and drained

½ cup herb seasoned stuffing
  mix
2 tablespoons all-purpose flour
½ teaspoon paprika
2 tablespoons butter, melted
2 packets hollandaise sauce
  mix
1½ cups milk
1 cup (4 ounces) shredded
  Swiss cheese

- Using mallet, pound chicken to flatten. Season lightly with salt and black pepper.

- Sauté onion and celery in butter until tender. Remove from heat. Add 3 tablespoons wine, crab and stuffing mix, tossing to blend.

- Spread portion of crab mixture on each chicken piece, roll up and secure with wooden pick.

- Combine flour and paprika. Dust each chicken roll and place in baking dish. Drizzle with melted butter.

- Bake, uncovered, at 375 degrees for 1 hour. Place chicken on serving platter.

- Prepare sauce mix, using milk according to package directions. When thickened, add remaining ¼ cup wine and cheese and stir until cheese is melted. Ladle some of sauce over chicken and serve remainder.

- Serves 6.

City Chicken

"I love to eat. Cincinnati cooking is very fine. I'm just dying for some good old city chicken, which is pork on a skewer."

Ken LaRose
Butler University
Football Coach
Former Moeller guard

Garlic Chicken with Shiitake Mushrooms

 This was originally a flank steak recipe.

3½ tablespoons soy sauce, divided
3½ tablespoons rice wine vinegar, divided
1 tablespoon sugar
6 chicken breast halves, skin and bone removed

3 tablespoons canola or vegetable oil
1 pound fresh shiitake mushrooms
10 cloves garlic, flattened and thinly sliced
½ cup chicken broth
watercress sprigs for garnish

- Combine 2½ tablespoons soy sauce, 1½ tablespoon vinegar and sugar, stirring until sugar is dissolved.

- Pour marinade over chicken in shallow dish. Let stand at room temperature for 30 minutes, turning pieces once.

- Discard stems from mushrooms and thinly slice caps. In large heavy skillet, stir-fry mushrooms and garlic in very hot oil for 1 minute. Add broth and 2 tablespoons vinegar and stir-fry until mushrooms are softened and liquid is evaporated. Stir in soy sauce and keep sauce warm.

- Drain marinade from chicken. Grill pieces on an oiled rack for 12 to 15 minutes or until done, turning once. Place on cutting board and let stand for 10 minutes.

- Cut chicken into thin slices, place on platter and serve topped with mushroom sauce and garnished with watercress.

- Serves 6.

Mustard Herbed Chicken

 The taste of this dish can vary each time you make it with the new flavored mustards.

4 chicken breast halves, skin
  and bone removed
2 tablespoons olive oil
2 tablespoons red wine vinegar
2 tablespoons dried tarragon

2 tablespoons dried thyme
salt and freshly ground black
  pepper, to taste
2 teaspoons grainy mustard
2 teaspoons Worcestershire
  sauce

- Using mallet, pound chicken to flatten to ¼-inch thickness.

- Combine oil, vinegar, tarragon, thyme, salt, black pepper, mustard and Worcestershire sauce, blending well. Pour into large non-stick skillet and heat over medium high heat.

- Add chicken to liquid and cook for about 5 minutes or until chicken is no longer pink, turning pieces once.

- Serves 4.

Chicken with Spinach

6 chicken breast halves, skin
  and bone removed
2 eggs, beaten
dry bread crumbs
4 tablespoons vegetable oil,
  divided

1 bunch fresh spinach, stems
  removed
1 lemon
1 (8 ounce) package fresh
  mushrooms, chopped
2 onions, sliced
2 tablespoons butter

- Dip chicken in egg, then coat with bread crumbs. In large skillet, sauté chicken in 2 tablespoons oil, turning to brown on both sides.

- Place spinach in large bowl. Squeeze lemon juice over spinach and let stand.

- Place chicken on uncooked spinach.

- Sauté mushrooms and onion in remaining 2 tablespoons oil and butter. Place on chicken. Spinach will cook from heat of chicken and vegetables.

- Serves 6.

All for One and One for All

Children's author Father Francis J. Finn suggested the nickname, "Musketeers" for the athletic program in 1925, in keeping with the motto of the legendary characters, D'Artagnan, Athos, Porthos, and Aramis. Xavier University is now a member of the Atlantic 10 Conference for athletics. It's a tradition for basketball fans attending games to remain standing until Xavier scores their first two points.

Chicken Supremes

1 teaspoon cinnamon
½ teaspoon garlic salt
¼ teaspoon allspice
¼ teaspoon nutmeg
¼ teaspoon white pepper
8 chicken breast halves, skin and bone removed, at room temperature

1 tablespoon butter
1 tablespoon oil
2 tablespoons chopped chives
⅔ cup whipping cream
½ cup dry vermouth
chopped parsley for
    watercress sprigs for garnish

- Combine cinnamon, garlic salt, allspice, nutmeg and white pepper on waxed paper, mixing. Pat and press seasonings on chicken pieces.

- In heavy skillet over medium-low heat, sauté chicken in butter and oil for about 1 minute on each side, just until opaque. Place in shallow casserole.

- Bake, uncovered, at 300 degrees for 10 to 20 minutes (depending on thickness of chicken).

- Sauté chives for 30 seconds in skillet. Whisk in cream and vermouth. Simmer for several minutes or until slightly thickened.

- Pour sauce over baked chicken in casserole or on platter. Garnish with parsley or watercress.

- Serves 8.

Quick Chicken

1 cup orange juice
1 tablespoon grated orange peel
1 cup firmly packed brown sugar
¼ cup butter, melted

¼ teaspoon allspice
½ teaspoon ginger
1 teaspoon dry mustard
6 chicken breast halves, skin and bone removed

- Combine orange juice, peel, brown sugar, butter, allspice, ginger and mustard.

- Place chicken in single layer in 13x9x2-inch baking pan. Pour orange sauce over chicken.

- Bake at 375 degrees for 40 to 45 minutes or until done, basting frequently.

- Serves 6.

Skillet Tomato Chicken

 Simple to prepare, especially for entertaining.

8 chicken breast halves, skin
  and bone removed
½ cup butter
1 large onion, sliced
2 cloves garlic, minced
2 tablespoons all-purpose flour
1 teaspoon salt

1 (28 ounce) can plum
  tomatoes, drained
1 cup sour cream
½ cup (2 ounce) freshly grated
  Parmesan cheese
6 cups cooked noodles

- In large skillet, sauté chicken in butter until tender, turning to cook on each side. Remove from skillet and set aside.

- Sauté onion and garlic in skillet until transparent. Blend in flour and salt, mixing until smooth. Stir in tomatoes and add chicken.

- Cook, covered, for 35 minutes.

- Add sour cream and Parmesan cheese. Simmer just until thoroughly heated; do not boil. Serve with noodles.

- Serves 8

Grilled Chicken Shish Kebabs

½ cup honey
⅓ cup vegetable oil
⅓ cup soy sauce
2 tablespoons water
1 tablespoons vinegar
¼ teaspoon sugar
1 tablespoon minced onion
1 clove garlic, minced

2 to 3 pounds chicken, bone
  removed and cubed for
  skewers
1 red onion, quartered
1 green bell pepper, cut in
  8 pieces
8 to 12 cherry tomatoes

- Prepare marinade the day before serving.

- Combine honey, oil, soy sauce, water, vinegar, sugar, onion and garlic.

- Marinate chicken overnight in refrigerator.

- Reserving marinade for basting, arrange chicken, onion, bell pepper and tomatoes on skewers.

- Grill, basting occasionally with marinade, until chicken is cooked.

- Serves 4.

Record Breaker

During his years at the University of Cincinnati, Jack Twyman broke all but one basketball scoring record. After graduation in 1955, he had a Hall of Fame career in the NBA. His care for incapacitated fellow player Maurice Stokes has been documented in a book and a film.

Pigall's Fusion
Red Wine Chicken Breasts

"My favorite meal is on Christmas Day, and that's because we have the whole family together. It's always been that way, even when I was growing up. Now we have our whole family together. My wife prepares for a couple of days, and we have this big dinner about three in the afternoon. We have turkey, and ham, and she has mashed potatoes, sweet potatoes mashed, she has corn, she has creamed broccoli, and then she has a jello she makes with the cream on top of it, you know, it's frozen. Then we have a salad. . .it's just a great, unbelievable meal. She really takes a lot of pains to do it well—the whole family's together and we just sit around the table and eat and talk for about an hour and we have a great time. You know, I think they always say the family that prays together, stays together. I think the family that eats together, and prays together stays together."

Red wine with chicken? Some may call it weird but it's called "Fusion" because this recipe combines the flavors of the East with American red wine, plus the influence of today's Western style of eating. It's healthy too—there's no added fat in the marinade.

2 cups Merlot, Cabernet Sauvignon or Zinfandel red wine
½ cup hoisin sauce
2 tablespoons dark soy sauce
2 teaspoons minced garlic
2 teaspoons minced ginger

½ cup chopped onion
1 teaspoon five spice powder
½ teaspoon red pepper flakes
4 chicken breast halves with skin
peanut or vegetable oil
4 cups cooked white rice

- Combine wine, hoisin sauce, soy sauce, garlic, ginger, onion, five spice powder and red pepper.

- Marinate chicken for 1 to 2 hours (no longer). Reserving marinade, remove chicken and set aside.

- When ready to grill or broil chicken, pour reserved marinade in saucepan. Bring to a boil, reduce heat and simmer while chicken cooks.

- Brush chicken with peanut or vegetable oil. Grill or broil until done.

- Ladle marinade over individual portions of chicken and rice.

- Serves 4.

Teller's Grilled Chicken with Mango Salsa

Chicken
4 (5 ounce) chicken breast halves, bone and skin removed
¼ pound spinach
1 tablespoon butter vegetable oil

salt and black pepper, to taste
1⅓ cups cooked brown rice
¼ cup Ligham's sauce (sweet spicy chili sauce)
watercress branch

Salsa
¾ pound mango, seed removed, sliced and diced
¼ cup minced red bell pepper

1⅓ tablespoons minced red onion
1½ teaspoons minced fresh cilantro

- Grill chicken until done; do not overcook. Set aside and keep warm.

- Combine spinach, oil, salt and black pepper in steamer. Cook for 1½ minutes.

- Prepare salsa by combining mango, bell pepper, onion and cilantro.

- Place two chicken pieces on rice on individual serving plate. Top with ½ of spinach, add spoonful of salsa, drizzle with Ligham's sauce and garnish with watercress.

- Serves 2.

River Downs at dawn

photograph by Robert A. Flischel

It's the truth, if you sit together and discuss things, you discuss problems, and you pray together too. . . that's what keeps your family together."

Gerry Faust

Assistant Vice President of Public Affairs and Development

University of Akron

Former Football Coach of Moeller High School, University of Notre Dame, and University of Akron.

South of the Border Chicken

4 cups cooked white rice
2 cups sour cream
½ cup mayonnaise
1 (4 ounce) can chopped green chilies, drained
4 cups (16 ounces) shredded or finely diced Monterey Jack cheese
1½ tablespoons chopped fresh cilantro
¼ teaspoon garlic salt
8 chicken breast halves, cooked and cut in bite-size pieces
2 cups (8 ounces) shredded cheddar cheese

- Combine rice, sour cream, mayonnaise, chilies, Monterey Jack cheese, cilantro and garlic salt. Add chicken and mix thoroughly. Spread in greased 4-quart casserole.

- Sprinkle cheddar cheese on chicken mixture.

- Bake at 350 degrees for 30 minutes, remove cover and bake for additional 30 minutes or until bubbly and hot.

- Serves 8.

Chicken Challipa

 Your family will adore this flavorful dish.

2 (10¾ ounce) cans cream of chicken mushroom soup, undiluted
1 cup sour cream
⅔ cup milk
1 (7 ounce) can diced green chilies, drained
1 medium sized onion, diced
4 or 5 green onions, chopped
12 corn tortillas, quartered
4 to 6 chicken breast halves, cooked and shredded or cubed
4 cups (16 ounces) grated Longhorn (Colby) cheese

- Combine soup, sour cream, milk, chilies, onion and green onion. Spread small portion of sauce into greased 13x9x2-inch baking pan. Arrange ½ of tortilla wedges, overlapping slightly, on sauce.

- In order listed, layer all of chicken, ½ remaining sauce, ½ Longhorn cheese, remaining tortillas, sauce and cheese.

- Bake, covered, at 350 degrees for 30 minutes, remove cover and bake at 325 degrees for additional 30 minutes.

- Serves 8.

Indian Chicken

 This is a very popular ladies' luncheon entrée and perfect for a summer's evening dinner-on-the-deck.

¼ cup mayonnaise
1 cup whipping cream, whipped
1½ teaspoons curry powder or, to taste
4 to 6 chicken breasts, cooked and cut in ½-inch strips

Condiments such as toasted coconut, chopped peanuts, diced bananas, diced apple, chopped cucumber, diced tomato, pineapple tidbits, chopped egg white, chutney and chopped green onion

- Blend mayonnaise, whipped cream and curry powder until smooth.

- Arrange chicken on serving platter. Surround with condiments in small bowls.

- Serve sauce in large bowl.

- Diners assemble own servings.

- Serves 6.

Chicken Casserole

5 cups shredded cooked chicken
5 cups diced celery
2 (4 ounce) cans green chilies, drained and chopped
1 (7 ounce) can black olives, drained and sliced
2 cups slivered almonds

3 cups (12 ounces) shredded Monterey Jack cheese, divided
1½ cups mayonnaise
1½ cups sour cream
3 cups crushed potato chips
1 teaspoon salt
½ teaspoon cayenne pepper

- Combine chicken, celery, chilies, olives, almonds and 2 cups Monterey Jack cheese, stirring to mix.

- Blend mayonnaise and sour cream together. Add to chicken mixture and toss. Stir in salt and cayenne pepper. Spread mixture in 4-quart casserole. Sprinkle with remaining cheese and top with potato chips.

- Bake at 350 degrees for 20 to 25 minutes.

- Serves 12.

"I'm very fond of pigs, but I don't find it difficult to eat them."

Robert Runcie
Archbishop of
Canterbury

Chicken Pot Pie

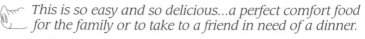 *This is so easy and so delicious...a perfect comfort food for the family or to take to a friend in need of a dinner.*

6 to 8 chicken breast halves, cooked and cut in bite-sized pieces
1 (10 ounce) package frozen peas and carrot mixture, thawed
1 (10¾ ounce) can reduced-fat cream of celery soup, undiluted
1 (10¾ ounce) can reduced-fat cream of chicken soup, undiluted
1 cup chicken broth
1 teaspoon garlic salt
1 teaspoon maggi liquid seasoning
dash of hot pepper sauce
2 unbaked 9-inch pastry shells
1 egg, beaten
2 tablespoons water

• Combine chicken, peas and carrots, celery soup, chicken soup, broth, garlic salt, maggi and hot pepper sauce, mixing well.

• Spread mixture in 1 pastry shell. Using second shell, cover chicken mixture, crimping along edges to seal. Brush with egg mixed with water. Cut slits to vent steam.

• Bake at 400 degrees for 1 hour.

Pork Tenderloin with Bourbon Sauce

 This is an easy recipe that guests love. Make it during the holidays or any busy season as it is easy but tender and delicious.

1 cup soy sauce
1 tablespoon brown sugar
3 tablespoons bourbon
2 (1 to 2 pound) whole pork tenderloins

• Whisk soy sauce, brown sugar and bourbon together.

• Place pork in baking dish. Pour sauce over pork, cover with aluminum foil and marinate for 2 hours.

• Bake at 300 degrees for 1 hour, basting with marinade at 10 minute intervals.

• Serves 4 to 6.

☀ *Holiday Ham*

Sauce
¼ cup dry English mustard
½ cup tarragon vinegar
1½ tablespoons dark rum
3 eggs

¼ cup plus 2 tablespoons
  sugar
¼ cup unsalted butter
½ teaspoon salt
freshly ground black pepper

Ham
1 (10 to 12 pound) boneless
  smoked ham
whole cloves
¼ cup Dijon mustard
1 clove garlic, mashed

¼ cup Chinese duck sauce
  (plum sauce)
splash of orange juice
½ cup firmly packed brown
  sugar

- Prepare sauce the day before serving. Blend mustard, vinegar, dark rum, eggs, sugar, butter, salt and black pepper, mixing well. Chill overnight.

- Score top of ham. Stud with cloves at each "intersection" of scoring lines. Place in roasting pan.

- Blend mustard, garlic and duck sauce with enough orange juice to form syrup consistency. Spread evenly on top and sides of ham. Sprinkle brown sugar on ham.

- Bake at 400 degrees for 1½ hours. Serve warm or at room temperature.

- Serves 20 to 24.

Pork Loin with Cherry Sauce

Pork Loin

1 (4 to 5) pound pork loin roast, boned, rolled and tied
½ teaspoon salt

½ teaspoon black pepper
dash of crushed dried thyme

Sauce

1 cup cherry preserves
¼ cup red wine vinegar
2 tablespoons light corn syrup
¼ teaspoon salt
¼ teaspoon cinnamon

¼ teaspoon nutmeg
¼ teaspoon ground cloves
¼ cup toasted slivered almonds

- Season pork by rubbing with mixture of salt, black pepper and thyme. Place on rack in 13x9x2-inch baking pan.

- Bake, uncovered, at 325 degrees for about 2½ hours.

- While pork is baking, prepare sauce. Combine preserves, vinegar, syrup, salt, cinnamon, nutmeg and cloves in saucepan. Bring to a boil, stirring occasionally, reduce heat and simmer for 2 minutes.

- Stir in almonds. Spoon sauce over pork and bake for additional 30 minutes or until meat thermometer registers 170 degrees. Serve sauce with sliced pork.

- Serves 10 to 12.

"My first job was selling peanuts with Peanut Jim, a Cincinnati icon who sold fresh, roasted peanuts in front of the old Crosley Field before Cincinnati Reds games. It was the only way to enjoy a Cincinnati Reds game. After munching on Peanut Jim's peanuts, while you wanted the Reds to win, you could suffer through a loss with those culinary delights.

He wore a top hat and tails, and was synonymous with Cincinnati Reds baseball. I really enjoyed working with him because I worked on a cash basis, and didn't have to deal with all of those governmental deductibles! At twelve years old, it gave me a real appreciation for cash and carry."

Ken Blackwell
State Treasurer
Former City Mayor

photograph by J. Miles Wolf

The Cincinnati Bengals

Pork Tenderloin
with Cream Currant Sauce

½ cup dry mustard
½ cup salt
1½ tablespoons black pepper
5 (1 to 2 pound) whole pork
   tenderloins
½ cup butter, divided

1 (10 ounce) jar currant jelly
¼ cup plus 1 tablespoon all-
   purpose flour
1 cup half and half
1 cup whipping cream

- Season pork by rubbing with mixture of mustard, salt and black pepper.

- Sauté pork pieces in ¼ cup butter in skillet, turning to brown on each side. Place in baking dish.

- Stir jelly into pan drippings.

- In small saucepan, melt ¼ cup butter. Blend in flour and cook, stirring constantly, until bubbly. Stir in half and half and whipping cream. Bring to a boil and cook for 1 minute, stirring until sauce thickens. Add to jelly mixture and bring to a boil.

- Pour ½ of sauce over pork and reserve remaining sauce.

- Bake pork, tightly covered with aluminum foil, at 325 degrees for 2 hours. Remove from oven and let stand to cool slightly. Cut across grain into slices and place in clean baking dish. Pour reserved sauce over slices.

- Bake, covered, at 275 degrees for 45 minutes.

- Serves 12.

Pig in a Poke, or Pig in a Pocket

"A grilled pork patty smothered in Ribs King barbecue sauce and served in pita bread."

Montgomery Inn
Ribs King

Pig in a Poke

"Something offered in such a way as to obscure its real nature or worth."

Merriam Webster's
Collegiate Dictionary

Pork Tenderloin Lorraine

2 pounds pork tenderloin, cut in strips	1 medium-sized onion, chopped
1/4 cup butter or margarine	1/4 cup butter or margarine, melted
1 cup fine bread crumbs	2 cups beef broth or consommé
1/2 teaspoon salt	2 tablespoons wine vinegar
dash of black pepper	
2 cloves garlic, sliced	

• Sauté pork strips in 1/4 cup butter in ovenproof pan on range top burner, turning to lightly brown on all sides.

• Combine bread crumbs, salt and black pepper. Thoroughly coat pork strips. Add garlic and onion.

• Bake at 400 degrees for 10 minutes, basting 2 or 3 times with melted butter or margarine.

• Reduce oven temperature to 350 degrees. Add broth or consommé to pork. Bake, covered, for 50 minutes; remove cover and bake for 10 minutes or until browned. Place pork on hot platter.

• Stir vinegar into sauce. Simmer for 2 to 3 minutes on range top to reduce liquid slightly. Pour over pork.

• Serves 4 to 6.

Honey Sesame Pork Tenderloin

1/2 cup soy sauce	1/4 cup honey
2 cloves garlic, minced	2 tablespoons brown sugar
1 tablespoon sesame oil	1 pound pork tenderloin
1 teaspoon ground ginger	

• Combine soy sauce, garlic, sesame oil, ginger, honey and brown sugar in large plastic bag.

• Add pork and marinate for 2 hours. Remove from bag and place in baking pan.

• Bake at 350 degrees for 20 to 30 minutes or until well done.

• Serves 2 or 3.

Martini Sauerkraut

½ large onion, chopped
¼ cup butter
1 tart apple, chopped
1 (16 ounce) can or jar
  sauerkraut
1 cup dry white wine
dash of hot pepper sauce
½ teaspoon Worcestershire
  sauce

½ cup gin
½ pound carrots, cut in 2-inch
  pieces
2 or 3 potatoes, quartered
1 pound bulk pork sausage or
  pork chops
1 teaspoon parsley
½ teaspoon seasoned salt

- In Dutch oven, sauté onion in butter until tender. Add apple, sauerkraut, wine, hot pepper sauce, Worcestershire sauce and gin. Simmer for 30 to 45 minutes.

- Separately cook carrots and potatoes in small amount of water until tender. Blanch sausage or brown pork chops.

- In 2-quart casserole, layer sauerkraut mixture, sausage or pork chops and vegetables. Sprinkle with parsley and seasoned salt.

- Bake, covered, at 350 degrees for 30 minutes.

- Serves 4 to 6.

Pork Scaloppine

1 (3 pound) pork tenderloin,
  cut in 1-inch slices
½ cup all-purpose flour
2 tablespoons vegetable oil
2 tablespoons butter
½ cup red wine
¼ cup water
1 (4 ounce) can sliced
  mushrooms, drained

1 medium sized onion,
  chopped
1 clove garlic, minced
salt and black pepper, to taste
¼ teaspoon thyme
¼ teaspoon oregano
¼ teaspoon rosemary

- Dust pork slices with flour. In large skillet, sauté in oil and butter, turning to brown on both sides.

- Add wine, water, mushrooms, onion and garlic to pork. Season with salt, black pepper, thyme, oregano and rosemary.

- Simmer, covered, for 45 minutes, adding more water if necessary.

- Serves 8.

Freezer Burn

"It was like being held in an ice chest. You wanted to get warm, but there was no place to go and no way you could. It wasn't a fun game to play. You were just trying to survive the cold."

*Dan Ross
Bengals Tight End
1982 Freezer Bowl*

The Riverview's
Pork Tenderloin Rio Grande

Pork

1 onion, sliced
⅓ cup chopped garlic
⅓ cup olive oil
2 pounds ground buffalo
2 tablespoons fajita seasoning
½ pound red bell peppers, finely diced or shredded
½ pound yellow bell peppers, finely diced or shredded

5 jalapeño peppers, seeded and diced
¼ cup butter
2 cups (8 ounces) shredded mozzarella cheese
2 cups (8 ounces) shredded Monterey Jack cheese
½ cup chopped cilantro
4 pounds pork tenderloin

Sauce

½ pound jalapeño peppers, seeded and chopped
1 cup butter

2 tablespoons whipping cream
1 teaspoon cornstarch
1 tablespoon cold water

• In large skillet, cook onion and garlic in oil until tender; do not brown. Add buffalo meat and fajita seasoning. Simmer for 10 minutes.

• While cooking meat, cook red bell pepper, yellow bell pepper and 5 jalapeño peppers in butter in saucepan over low heat until tender.

• Combine meat mixture and peppers. Stir in mozzarella cheese, Monterey Jack cheese and cilantro, blending until melted.

• Remove main nerve from tenderloin. Butterfly and pound to flatten. Spread stuffing on tenderloin, roll and place in baking pan.

• Bake at 300 degrees for 15 to 20 minutes.

• Prepare sauce by combining jalapeños and butter in food processor, blending to form green paste.

• In small saucepan, bring cream to a boil. Whip in jalapeño butter. Dilute cornstarch in water and add to sauce. Serve tenderloin with sauce.

• Serves 12.

Sauté of Pork Hongrose

1¼ pounds pork fillets, diagonally cut in ½-inch slices
2 tablespoons clarified butter or 2 tablespoons vegetable oil with 1 tablespoon butter
2 shallots, chopped
1 tablespoon paprika

1 tablespoon all-purpose flour
¼ cup plus 1 tablespoon sherry
½ cup beef broth or consommé
2 ounces fresh whole mushrooms
¼ cup half and half

- In skillet, briefly sauté pork in small batches in butter, turning until no longer pink on both sides. Remove and set aside.

- Cook shallots with paprika in skillet for 2 to 5 minutes. Stir in flour and add sherry and broth or consommé.

- Add pork to sauce. Bring to a boil, reduce heat and simmer for 30 to 40 minutes. Add mushrooms and cook for additional 10 to 15 minutes. Stir in cream, check seasonings and reheat.

- Serves 2 or 3.

Rosemary Pork Chops

 These pork chops are guaranteed to become your summer favorite. The marinade is also good with chicken.

¼ cup Dijon mustard
¼ cup balsamic vinegar
¼ cup lemon juice
6 cloves garlic, minced
3 tablespoons fresh rosemary

¾ teaspoon salt
1 teaspoon freshly ground black pepper
½ cup olive oil
8 pork chops

- Combine mustard, vinegar, lemon juice, garlic, rosemary, salt, black pepper and oil. Pour over pork chops and marinate for 2 hours in refrigerator.

- Drain marinade and grill chops until done.

- Serves 8.

NFL Commissioner Pete Rozelle called it the most exciting of the first 23 games in Super Bowl history. The Bengals lost in Super Bowl XXIII at Miami on January 22, 1989, but it took a 92-yard drive in the final minutes for the favored San Francisco 49ers to escape the upset and claim a 20-16 victory. The game brought a memorable, if unsuccessful, end to a 1988 season highlighted by Boomer Esiason's award as NFL Most Valuable Player and by the unforgettable "Ickey Shuffle."

Burbank's Grilled Southwestern Pork Chops

2 cups canned tomatoes, drained	1 tablespoon honey
2 teaspoons cayenne pepper or to taste	3 tablespoons red wine vinegar
¼ cup chopped onion	¼ cup olive oil
3 to 5 cloves garlic, chopped	1 tablespoon sugar
	8 loin chops, cut 1 to 1¼-inch thick

- Prepare and marinate 1 to 2 days before serving.

- Combine tomatoes, cayenne pepper, onion, garlic, honey, vinegar, oil and sugar in blender or food processor. Puree.

- Place pork chops in single layer in baking dish. Pour marinade over chops. Marinate, covered, in refrigerator overnight or up to 2 days, turning chops twice a day.

- Remove chops from marinade. Grill for about 7 minutes on each side, brushing with marinade, until done.

- Serves 8.

Tomato Pork Chops

4 to 6 pork chops	½ cup water
salt and black pepper, to taste	½ large onion, sliced
1 to 2 tablespoons vegetable oil	1 green bell pepper, sliced
1½ (8 ounce) cans tomato sauce	1 teaspoon lemon juice
	3 cups cooked white rice

- Season pork chops with salt and black pepper. In large skillet, sauté chops, turning to brown on both sides.

- Add tomato sauce, water, onion, bell pepper and lemon juice to chops. Simmer for 45 minutes.

- Serve chops with ladle of sauce on individual servings of rice.

- Serves 4 to 6.

Indonesian Pork

1½ pounds pork, cubed	1 teaspoon ginger
1 tablespoon vegetable oil	¼ cup soy sauce
1 large onion, chopped	1 tablespoon brown sugar
2 green onions, chopped	½ cup water
2 cloves garlic, minced	3 to 4 cups cooked white rice

- In large skillet, sauté pork in oil, turning to brown on all sides.

- Add onion, green onion, garlic and ginger to pork. Simmer for 5 minutes.

- Stir in soy sauce, brown sugar and water. Simmer for 45 minutes.

- Serve pork with sauce on individual servings of rice.

- Serves 6.

Sauce is also good with beef or lamb.

Sauerkraut Bake

1 (16 ounce) package bacon	1 (28 ounce) can tomatoes
1 medium sized onion, chopped	freshly cracked pepper, to taste
¼ cup firmly packed brown sugar	1 (32 ounce) jar sauerkraut, drained and pressed

- In large skillet, cook bacon until crisp. Remove and drain on paper towel.

- Reserve 2 tablespoons bacon drippings in skillet. Add onion and sauté until tender. Stir in brown sugar until melted.

- Drain tomatoes, reserving juice, and chop. Add juice to onion mixture and season with black pepper. Stir in sauerkraut, then spread mixture in 2-quart casserole.

- Bake, covered, at 350 degrees for 40 minutes. Sprinkle with bacon and bake, uncovered, for additional 20 minutes.

- Serves 8.

Paul Brown Stadium

Pro football in Cincinnati enters a new era at the start of the 2000 season, when the Bengals begin play at Paul Brown Stadium. The 67,000-seat riverfront facility features a futuristic design and superior sight-lines and fan amenities. But it also carries a crucial link to the past, as the stadium bears the name of the pro football Hall of Famer who brought the game to town as Bengals founder in 1968.

Sausage Pie with Herbed Cornmeal

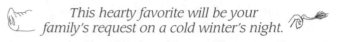

This hearty favorite will be your family's request on a cold winter's night.

1 pound sweet Italian sausage in links, sliced	2 teaspoons chopped cilantro
1½ cups chopped red bell pepper	⅓ cup all-purpose flour
1 large onion, chopped	⅓ cup yellow corn meal
1 (15 ounce) can navy beans, drained	⅓ cup grated Parmesan cheese
1 (14½ ounce) can Mexican stewed tomatoes	¼ teaspoon baking powder
1 (6 ounce) can tomato paste	1 teaspoon garlic salt
¼ cup dry white wine	¼ cup chopped parsley
1 teaspoon sugar	¼ cup chopped chives
	1 egg, beaten
	¼ cup milk
	1 tablespoon vegetable oil

- In large skillet, brown sausage with bell pepper and onion until sausage is no longer pink. Drain excess fat.

- Add beans, tomatoes, tomato paste, wine, sugar and cilantro. Bring to a boil, reduce heat to low and keep warm.

- Combine flour, corn meal, Parmesan cheese, baking powder, garlic salt, parsley and chives, mixing well. Add egg, milk and oil, stirring just until dry ingredients are moistened.

- Place sausage in 12x7½x2-inch baking dish. Drop batter by spoonfuls on sausage.

- Bake, uncovered, at 400 degrees for 12 to 15 minutes or until golden brown.

- Serves 6.

The Maisonette Roasted Chilean Bass

A five-star dish from Cincinnati's very own five-star restaurant.

3 shallots, sliced
1½ cups olive oil, divided
2 tomatoes, chopped
½ cup white wine
⅓ cup tomato juice
salt and black pepper, to taste
22 cloves garlic
2 green bell peppers, divided
2 red bell peppers, divided
⅓ (7 ounce) can black olives, drained
¼ cup grated Parmesan cheese
¼ cup bread crumbs
1 egg
1 yellow squash, diced
1 bulb fennel, diced
1 medium eggplant, diced
1 zucchini
1 thyme branch
6 (5 ounce) Chilean bass filets

- Prepare sauce by sautéing shallots in 1 to 2 tablespoons oil. Add tomatoes and wine. Cook to reduce liquid. Stir in tomato juice and cook to reduce.

- Pour tomato mixture into blender container, add ½ cup oil, season with salt and pepper and blend. Set aside and keep warm.

- Blanche garlic cloves three times and poach them in ½ cup olive oil until tender. Keep warm.

- Prepare crust in food processor, mixing 1 green bell pepper, 1 red bell pepper, black olives, Parmesan cheese, bread crumbs, egg, salt and black pepper.

- Prepare ratatouille by dicing remaining bell peppers and mixing with squash, fennel, eggplant and zucchini. Sauté in oil used for garlic and seasoned with thyme, until vegetables are just tender.

- Place fish in baking pan. Place portion of crust mixture on each and add remaining oil to pan.

- Bake at 350 degrees for 10 minutes.

- To serve, place portion of ratatouille on each dinner plate, add fish and ladle sauce around it, garnish with 3 cloves garlic.

- Serves 6.

Crown Jewel

The Maisonette is the crown jewel of cuisine in Cincinnati. A star among world class restaurants, the Maisonette has won the coveted Mobil Travel Guide's Five Star Award more times than any other restaurant in America. Chef Jean-Robert de Cavel elevates haute cuisine to a new level, directing an international staff in the creation and presentation of continental cuisine, both French and northern Italian, in an elegant, tranquil setting distinguished by a treasury of fine paintings. The owners, the Comisars, personally select the extensive wine list to reflect changing tastes and values from around the world.

 Rolled Fish Filets

1 (16 ounce) fresh or frozen perch filets, thawed	2 tablespoons butter or margarine
1 (10 ounce) package broccoli spears	1 (10¾ ounce) can cream of mushroom soup, undiluted
½ cup cooked shrimp	2 tablespoons Chablis or other dry white wine
⅓ cup chopped onion	⅛ teaspoon dried tarragon, crushed
1 small clove garlic, minced	

- Cook broccoli in small amount of unsalted water just until tender. Drain and set aside.

- Sauté shrimp, onion and garlic in butter until onion is tender. Stir in soup, wine and tarragon.

- On each filet, place portion of broccoli and roll up, securing with a wooden pick. Arrange in spoke fashion in round 1½-quart shallow casserole.

- Pour soup mixture on filets.

- Bake at 350 degrees for 30 minutes.

- Serves 4.

Filets can be assembled several hours in advance and baked just before serving.

Watson's Ale-Battered Cod

 This fish goes great with macaroni and cheese.

1 (8 ounce) package Cantonese mix	pinch of Cajun seasoning
⅓ cup medium to dark amber or red ale	6 to 8 cod filets
	all-purpose flour
	vegetable oil

- Combine Cantonese mix, ale and seasoning, whisking to remove lumps.

- Dip filets into flour, then into batter. Deep fry or pan fry in several inches of oil.

- Serves 4.

Ceviche

2 pounds grouper or snapper
  filets
2 small onions, thinly sliced
¾ teaspoon salt

3 hot peppers, seeds removed
  and sliced in circles
3 cups fresh lemon juice
olive oil
½ cup chopped fresh parsley

- Cut filets in ½-inch wide strips, then cut strips into ½-inch cubes. Place in glass bowl.

- Add onion, salt and hot peppers to fish. Cover with lemon juice, drizzle with oil and sprinkle with parsley, stirring gently to mix.

- Chill, tightly covered, for 24 to 36 hours. Check flavors after 8 to 10 hours, adding more hot peppers or salt to taste.

- Serves 8 to 10.

Marinated Sautéed Scrod Filets

2 tablespoons white wine
2 tablespoons lemon juice
1 tablespoon soy sauce
1 tablespoon olive oil
2 (4 to 6 ounce) scrod filets
¼ cup all-purpose flour

1 tablespoon chopped fresh
  parsley
½ teaspoon garlic salt
black pepper, to taste
1 tablespoon margarine

- Combine wine, lemon juice, soy sauce and oil.

- Place filets in shallow baking dish. Pour marinade over filets and chill for about 2 hours.

- Combine flour, parsley, garlic salt and black pepper.

- Drain filets, dredge in seasoned flour and sauté in margarine until golden brown.

- Serves 2.

Ever Heard of Pig Iron?

"Pig iron is the product resulting from the primary reduction of iron ore in a blast furnace. Pig iron must be modified further with alloys such as carbon, manganese, or others to formulate the final grade of steel desired," says Enerfab Vice President Al Roehr.

The term was used in the 1800's to denote the crude casting of metal. Used to make steel, wrought iron and ingots, it made David Sinton a fortune during the Civil War. His only daughter, Anna Sinton, married Charles Taft, whose father was the Attorney General of the United Sates under President Ulysses S. Grant. They lived in what is now the Taft Museum. Taft's younger half-brother, William Howard Taft, became president in 1909.

☀ Baked Salmon

¾ cup dry white wine	3 minced shallots
½ teaspoon basil	2 slices lemon
¼ teaspoon rosemary	1 stalk celery, leaves only
½ teaspoon tarragon	1 (7 to 10 pound) salmon
½ teaspoon thyme	salt to taste
4 or 5 peppercorns	

- Combine wine, basil, rosemary, tarragon, thyme, peppercorns, shallots, lemon and celery in saucepan. Simmer for 30 minutes; do not boil.

- Season salmon lightly with salt and place on heavy duty aluminum foil in baking pan.

- Pour wine mixture over fish and wrap well with foil.

- Bake at 350 degrees for 8 to 10 minutes per pound. Remove skin before serving.

- Serves 8 to 10.

Spinach Tuna Au Gratin

1 (6 ounce) can tuna, drained and flaked	1 tablespoon lemon juice
⅔ cup dry bread crumbs, divided	3 tablespoons freshly grated Parmesan cheese, divided
1 (10 ounce) package frozen chopped spinach, cooked and drained	¼ teaspoon salt
	⅛ teaspoon black pepper
	½ cup mayonnaise
	paprika

- Combine tuna, ⅓ cup bread crumbs, spinach, lemon juice, 2 tablespoons Parmesan cheese, salt and black pepper, mixing thoroughly.

- Fold mayonnaise into tuna mixture. Spread in 1½-quart casserole.

- Mix remaining ⅓ cup bread crumbs and 1 tablespoon Parmesan cheese. Sprinkle over tuna mixture and garnish with paprika.

- Bake at 350 degrees for 20 minutes.

- Serves 4.

Easy Salmon and Vegetables in Foil

 "I love this dish because you can make it ahead of time, saving any last-minute fuss. Just before dinner, pop the foil envelopes into the oven. Dinner's ready in 15 to 20 minutes." -Joan Lunden

2 red potatoes	salt and black pepper, to taste
1 cup snow peas	2 tablespoons extra-virgin
2 carrots, thinly sliced	olive oil
4 (6 ounce) salmon filets,	¼ small zucchini, sliced
about ½-inch thick	¼ small bulb fennel, thinly
4 teaspoons fresh lemon juice	sliced, optional
2 teaspoons finely chopped	4 teaspoons chopped fresh dill,
fresh ginger, optional	basil, thyme or parsley for
	garnish

- Cook potatoes just until tender, slice and set aside. Blanch snow peas in boiling water for 30 seconds, drain and set aside. Blanch carrots in boiling water for 1 minute, drain and set aside.

- Prepare 4 (16x10 inch) sheets aluminum foil. On each, place 1 filet slightly to the left of the center. Sprinkle with 1 teaspoon lemon juice and ½ teaspoon ginger. Season with salt and black pepper. Drizzle with ½ tablespoon olive oil.

- Place ¼ of each of potatoes, snow peas, carrots, zucchini and fennel on filet.

- Fold foil over filet to form a rectangle and crimp edges tightly. Place on baking sheet.

- Bake at 400 degrees for 15 minutes or just until the salmon is cooked. To serve, place a packet on each dinner plate, slash an X in each to open and sprinkle with 1 teaspoon fresh herbs.

- Serves 4.

Packets can be assembled several hours in advance and stored in refrigerator; increase baking time by 5 minutes. For alternative vegetables, use 1 cup peas, 1 cup corn, 8 stalks blanched small asparagus or 1 cup sliced dehydrated sun-dried tomatoes (not oil-packed).

"We are committed to providing our top players outside of Anaheim to the Cincinnati Mighty Ducks.
The level of competition and style of play in the American Hockey League has proven to be ideal in developing players for the National Hockey League and we look forward to a successful future in Cincinnati."

Jack Ferreira
Anaheim General Manager

The Cincinnati Mighty Ducks play in the 62-year old American Hockey League and are the top affiliate of the Mighty Ducks of Anaheim of the National Hockey League. The American Hockey League features the skill and enthusiasm of some of the best young hockey players in the world. The AHL serves as the premier player development source for the NHL, with 67% of all current NHL players graduates of the AHL.

Grilled Swordfish Steaks with Avocado Butter

Fish

½ cup soy sauce
1 teaspoon lemon zest
¼ cup fresh lemon juice
2 cloves garlic, crushed
2 teaspoons Dijon mustard

½ cup vegetable oil
4 (6 ounce) swordfish steaks
2 lemons, cut in wedges
chopped parsley

Butter

½ cup butter, softened
½ cup mashed avocado
¼ cup plus 1 tablespoon lemon juice

2 tablespoons chopped parsley
2 cloves garlic

• Combine soy sauce, lemon zest, lemon juice, garlic, mustard and oil in food processor. Blend until smooth.

• Place steaks in baking dish, piercing with fork tines. Pour marinade over steaks and let stand for 1 to 4 hours.

• While steaks marinate, prepare butter. Combine butter, avocado, lemon juice, parsley and garlic in food processor. Blend until smooth.

• Place on parchment paper and roll up to form a log. Freeze until ready to serve.

• Remove steaks from marinade. Grill, turning once, until done.

• Place medallion of butter on each serving of fish and garnish with lemon wedges and parsley.

• Serves 4.

Grilled Tuna Steaks

1 cup extra-virgin olive oil
1 cup soy sauce
2 cloves garlic, minced

1 (12 ounce) can beer
8 to 10 tuna steaks

- Combine oil, soy sauce, garlic and beer.

- Place steaks in baking dish. Pour marinade over steaks and let stand for 2 to 3 hours, turning occasionally.

- Remove steaks from marinade. Grill, turning once, until done.

- Serves 8 to 10.

Not Your Average Tuna Casserole

1 (8 ounce) package wide
noodles
1/2 cup butter, divided
1/4 cup plus 1 tablespoon
all-purpose flour
1 teaspoon salt
1/4 teaspoon black pepper
2 1/2 cups milk
1 (8 ounce) package cream
cheese, sliced

1 (6 ounce) can tuna, drained
and flaked
1/2 cup sliced pimento-stuffed
green olives
2 tablespoons chopped fresh
chives
1 (6 ounce) package Muenster
cheese slices
1 1/2 cups herb-seasoned
stuffing mix

- Prepare noodles according to package directions. Drain and set aside.

- Melt 5 tablespoons butter in saucepan. Stir in flour, salt and black pepper. Cook, stirring constantly until bubbly.

- Add milk to sauce. Cook, stirring constantly, until sauce is thickened. Boil for 1 minute.

- Stir cream cheese into sauce and stir until melted. Add tuna, olives and chives. Remove from heat.

- Pour 3/4 cup tuna mixture into 2 1/2-quart casserole. In order listed, layer 1/2 of noodles, 1/2 Muenster cheese, 1/2 tuna mixture, remaining noodles, cheese and tuna mixture.

- Melt remaining 3 tablespoons butter in saucepan. Stir in stuffing mix, tossing lightly. Sprinkle on tuna mixture.

- Bake at 350 degrees for 25 minutes.

- Serves 4.

"The Mighty Ducks offer fans an opportunity to watch some of the best young talent in professional hockey develop their skills as they work their way up to a career in the National Hockey League. AHL games are fast-paced, hard-hitting with an intensity level not found in any of the other minor proleagues."

*Don Helbig
Mighty Ducks Director
of Media Relations*

Creamed Crab Avocado

¼ cup plus 2 tablespoons butter, divided	2 cups crab meat
¼ cup all-purpose flour	2 hard-cooked eggs, chopped
¾ teaspoon salt	½ cup sliced mushrooms, sautéed
⅛ teaspoon black pepper	3 tablespoons sherry
⅛ teaspoon nutmeg	4 ripe avocados, cut in halves, peeled and seeds removed
2 cups milk	⅓ cup cracker crumbs
½ teaspoon grated onion	

- Melt ¼ cup butter in top of double boiler over direct heat. Add flour, salt, black pepper and nutmeg to butter in pan. Cook until bubbly.

- Set pan over boiling water. Gradually add milk, then onion, stirring constantly until thickened and smooth. Stir in sherry. Add crab, eggs and mushrooms. Remove from heat.

- Place avocados in baking pan. Spoon portion of crab mixture into each half.

- Sprinkle with crumbs and drizzle with remaining 2 tablespoons butter.

- Bake at 350 degrees for 20 minutes.

- Serves 6.

Crab Stuffed Potatoes

4 medium baking potatoes	½ teaspoon paprika
½ cup butter	1 (6 ounce) can crab meat
1 cup sour cream	4 cups (16 ounces) grated cheddar cheese
1 teaspoon salt	3 green onions, chopped
⅛ teaspoon black pepper	

- Bake potatoes until tender. Slice lengthwise, remove pulp and place in mixing bowl, leaving potato shell.

- Mash potato pulp, butter, sour cream, salt, pepper and paprika together until smooth.

- Stir in crab meat, cheddar cheese and green onion. Spoon portion of mixture into each potato shell, mounding slightly.

- Bake at 350 degrees for 20 minutes.

- Serves 8.

North Carolina Crab Cakes

 Especially good with fresh blue crab.

Cakes

1 pound fresh or frozen crab meat

2 eggs

½ cup finely chopped green bell pepper

½ cup finely chopped celery

¼ cup minced onion

1 tablespoon chopped fresh parsley

1 tablespoon baking powder

1 tablespoon Worcestershire sauce

1 tablespoon mayonnaise

2 slices fresh bread, cubed

2 to 3 tablespoons vegetable oil

Sauce

¼ cup plus 2 tablespoons chili sauce

1 teaspoon Worcestershire sauce

2 ripe tomatoes, peeled, seeds removed and chopped

1 teaspoon horseradish

1 tablespoon chopped fresh parsley

- Combine crab meat, eggs, bell pepper, celery, onion, parsley, baking powder, Worcestershire sauce, mayonnaise and bread, mixing thoroughly.

- Shape mixture into patties and chill slightly.

- While chilling, prepare cocktail sauce by mixing chili sauce, Worcestershire sauce, tomatoes, horseradish and parsley together. Chill until ready to serve.

- Sauté crab cakes in oil in large skillet, turning to lightly brown on each side.

- Serve with cocktail sauce.

- Serves 4 to 6.

The 48-year-old Cincinnati Gardens seats 10,326 for hockey and is a virtual replica of the historic Maple Leaf Gardens in Toronto, Canada.

Teller's Blue Fin Crab Cakes

4 eggs
1 cup mayonnaise
2 pounds blue fin crab meat
⅓ cup cracker meal or bread
  crumbs
1 or 2 scallions, minced

2 teaspoons dry mustard
1 teaspoon salt and black
  pepper mix
2 teaspoons Old Bay seasoning
  minced fresh parsley, to taste
2 tablespoons garlic oil

- Beat eggs and mayonnaise together in stainless steel bowl. Add crab meat, cracker meal or crumbs, scallions, mustard, salt and black pepper, Old Bay seasoning and parsley, mixing thoroughly.

- Shape mixture into 12 patties and chill.

- Sauté crab cakes in oil in large skillet, turning to lightly brown on each side.

- Serves 6.

The Cincinnati Cobra

Ezzard Charles, also known as the Cincinnati Cobra, was a heavyweight champion in 1949. Union Terminal sits at the end of Ezzard Charles Drive.

Scalloped Oysters

3 cups combination of fresh
  bread crumbs and crushed
  saltine crackers
2 pints fresh oysters
½ cup chopped parsley

1 cup chopped onion
1 cup chopped celery
¼ cup butter, melted
¼ cup half and half

- Spread 1½ cups crumbs in greased 8x8x2-inch baking dish.

- Reserving ¼ cup oyster liquid, drain oysters. Place ½ on crumb layer and sprinkle with parsley, onion and celery. Add remaining crumbs and another layer of oysters.

- Combine butter, half and half and reserved oyster liquid. Drizzle over oysters.

- Bake, covered, at 350 degrees for 20 to 25 minutes.

- Serves 4 to 6.

Broiled Scallops

 Super easy.

2 pounds sea scallops
¼ cup melted butter
3 tablespoons Italian seasoned
   bread crumbs
⅛ teaspoon garlic salt

⅛ teaspoon dry mustard
½ teaspoon paprika
2 tablespoons sherry
lemon slices

- Toss scallops with melted butter. Place on broiler pan.

- Combine bread crumbs, garlic salt, mustard and paprika. Sprinkle on scallops.

- Broil scallops for 5 to 7 minutes or until browned; turn off broiler flame heat but leave scallops in place for 3 to 5 minutes longer.

- Sprinkle scallops with sherry and serve with lemon slices.

- Serves 4.

Scallops can be assembled a couple hours in advance and stored in refrigerator until ready to cook; allow a few minutes extra cooking time.

Shrimp and Artichoke Stir Fry

1 pound medium shrimp,
   peeled and deveined
¼ pound fresh mushrooms
¼ cup olive oil
1 (6 ounce) package frozen
   artichoke hearts, thawed on
   paper towel
3 cloves garlic, minced

½ teaspoon salt
freshly ground black pepper
½ teaspoon dried oregano
2 tablespoons fresh lemon
   juice
2 tablespoons finely chopped
   parsley

- Stir-fry shrimp and mushrooms in oil in wok or large skillet, cooking until shrimp turn pink.

- Add artichoke hearts, garlic, salt, black pepper and oregano, stirring lightly to blend flavors and heating thoroughly. Place in serving bowl.

- Drizzle shrimp mixture with lemon juice, add parsley and toss to mix.

- Serves 4.

Hole in One

If golf or tennis is your game, the Golf Center at Kings Island is the name. The upscale sports center features two public golf courses, a driving range, and professional tennis facilities, where the popular Thriftway ATP Championship, the Kroger Senior Classic and other tournaments are hosted annually.

Shrimp with Mustard and Coriander

2 stalks celery, chopped
1 clove garlic, chopped
1 pound fresh or frozen shrimp, peeled and deveined
2 tablespoons butter
2 teaspoons sesame or olive oil
3 tablespoons fish stock or chicken broth
1 tablespoon Dijon mustard

2 tablespoons dry sherry
1½ tablespoons cornstarch
3 tablespoons cold water
½ cup plus 1 tablespoon whipping cream
freshly ground black pepper
1 to 2 tablespoons chopped fresh coriander
3 to 4 cups cooked long grain and wild rice

- Stir fry celery, garlic and shrimp in mixture of butter and oil in large skillet for 1 minute.

- Add stock or broth, mustard and sherry.

- Blend cornstarch with water and add to shrimp mixture. Bring to a boil, then add cream and black pepper. Sprinkle with coriander. Serve immediately over rice.

- Serves 4.

Baked Seafood Casserole

1 cup cooked or canned crab meat
1 cup cooked or canned shrimp
½ cup chopped green bell pepper
½ cup chopped celery

1 cup mayonnaise
½ teaspoon salt
1 teaspoon Worcestershire sauce
1 cup soft bread crumbs
2 tablespoons butter, melted
garlic powder, to taste

- Combine crab meat, shrimp, bell pepper, celery, mayonnaise, salt and Worcestershire sauce, mixing lightly.

- Spread mixture in 1½-quart casserole.

- Toss bread crumbs with butter and garlic powder. Sprinkle on top of seafood mixture.

- Bake at 350 degrees for 30 minutes.

- Serves 4.

Spicy Shrimp Casserole

3 pounds shrimp, peeled and
 deveined
2 teaspoons salt
1 tablespoon black pepper
1 teaspoon basil
1 teaspoon thyme
½ teaspoon garlic powder
1 tablespoon barbecue sauce
1 tablespoon parsley flakes

1 tablespoon lemon juice
1 tablespoon Worcestershire
 sauce
1½ cups butter
1 (8 ounce) package spaghetti,
 cooked and drained
1 (8 ounce) carton processed
 cheese food, sliced

- Place shrimp in baking dish.

- Combine salt, black pepper, basil, thyme and garlic powder. Sprinkle dry mixture, barbecue sauce, parsley, lemon juice and Worcestershire sauce on shrimp. Cut butter into pats and place on shrimp.

- Bake, uncovered, at 350 degrees for 25 minutes, stirring once or twice.

- Place cooked spaghetti in separate casserole. Pour shrimp and sauce over spaghetti. Top with cheese slices.

- Bake at 350 degrees for about 15 minutes or until cheese is bubbly. Stir to mix ingredients before serving.

- Serves 4 to 6.

"I like our rich heritage here, the Queen City of the Midwest, and the Ohio River and its history. It's a good city to raise children in. I like mock turtle soup, potato pancakes, hot slaw, sour-sweet sauerkraut and Bavarian cabbage like my aunts used to make. We had red cabbage every Thanksgiving along with the turkey."

*Owner Marge Schott
Cincinnati Reds*

photograph by Robert A. Flischel

Seafood and Mushroom Casserole

½ pound fresh mushrooms
⅓ cup butter
2 tablespoons all-purpose flour
1½ cups whole milk
salt and black pepper, to taste
tarragon, to taste

½ pound fresh crab meat, cooked
½ pound fresh shrimp, cooked
¾ cup (3 ounces) grated sharp cheese

- Sauté mushrooms in butter until softened. Drain, reserving liquid, and set mushrooms aside.

- Blend flour with milk in saucepan. Cook over low heat until smooth and creamy. Season with salt, black pepper and tarragon.

- Combine crab meat, shrimp and mushrooms. Fold cream sauce into seafood mixture. Spread in buttered 2-quart casserole and sprinkle with cheese.

- Bake at 325 degrees until cheese is lightly browned and seafood mixture is thoroughly heated.

- Serves 4.

VEGGIES AND RICE... *Savory Sides*

The spectacular Toyota/WEBN fireworks display at the Riverfest celebration lights up the sky every Labor Day weekend.

Photograph by J. Miles Wolf

"Eat your vegetables. That being said, East side, West side, inside, outside, no matter where you are in Cincinnati, something's always cooking. Have fun!"

Cincy

"The most important thing about working in a family business, like fireworks, is to watch out for each other. By sharing meals together, we grow together, for the table is the throne of harmony."

John Rozzi
Rozzi Famous Fireworks

Scalloped Asparagus

3 (16 ounce) cans cut
  asparagus, drained
6 hard-cooked eggs, sliced
1 (6 ounce) can mushrooms,
  drained
1 (2 ounce) jar pimento,
  drained

1 cup (4 ounces) grated
  cheddar cheese
3 (10¾ ounce) cans cream of
  mushroom soup, undiluted
1 cup bread crumbs
paprika

- In buttered 3-quart casserole, layer ½ asparagus, ½ eggs, ½ mushrooms, ½ pimento and ½ cheese; repeat layers.

- Spread soup on top of casserole and sprinkle with bread crumbs and paprika.

- Bake at 350 degrees for 45 minutes.

- Serves 12 to 16.

Asparagus Corn Soufflé

 Fresh corn is truly best.

1 (8 ounce) can asparagus,
  drained
1 (8 ounce) can white corn,
  drained, or 1 cup fresh corn
  kernels

1 (10¾ ounce) can cream of
  mushroom or celery soup,
  undiluted
1 cup mayonnaise
4 eggs, beaten

- Combine asparagus and corn, mashing to blend.

- Mix soup, mayonnaise and eggs together. Stir in vegetables. Pour mixture into 7½-inch soufflé dish. Place soufflé dish in pan of water.

- Bake at 350 degrees for 1 hour.

- Serves 6.

"In 1972, I was contacted by a mutual friend in New York, who introduced me to Calvin Trillin over the phone. This was at a time when Calvin Trillin had a position at **The New Yorker** as a man-at-large. He could travel anywhere on the face of the earth, and write about any subject, and his favorite subject was food. He had been told that chili was an unusual phenomenon in Cincinnati and that it should be covered for **The New Yorker**. I told him the story and invited him here. I was his host for five days, and as a result he put several local restaurants on the map, including Stenger's Café. I also introduced him to Skyline Chili and the Shady Nook Steakhouse near Millville, Oxford, the Barn and Rib Pit downtown, and had a formal dinner party at my home where he was the guest of honor. The whole thing turned into a marvelous piece in **The New Yorker**, which ran five full pages, and became chapter 8 in his first book, **American Fried - Adventures of a Happy Eater**."

Owner Harry Garrison
The Player Piano Shop

Cranberry Baked Beans

½ cup maple syrup
½ cup firmly packed brown sugar
⅓ cup ketchup
1 tablespoon Worcestershire sauce
2 tablespoons prepared mustard

3 or 4 (16 ounce) cans pork and beans, drained
1 (16 ounce) can whole cranberry sauce
2 medium sized onions, chopped
6 to 9 slices bacon, partially cooked, diced and drained

• Combine syrup, brown sugar, ketchup, Worcestershire sauce and mustard, mixing until smooth.

• Stir in beans, cranberry sauce, onions and bacon. Pour mixture into buttered 3-quart casserole.

• Bake at 350 degrees for 2 to 2½ hours.

• Serves 12.

Broccoli and Baby Carrots with Pecan-Crumb Topping

2 bunches broccoli, cut in 3-inch pieces
1 (12 ounce) package baby carrots
boiling water
½ cup butter or margarine, divided

1¼ cups fresh rye bread crumbs
1 cup pecans, toasted and chopped
¾ teaspoon salt, divided
¼ teaspoon black pepper
½ teaspoon dried thyme

• In large saucepan over high heat, add broccoli and carrots to 2-inches boiling water, return to a boil and cook for 5 to 7 minutes or until vegetables are crisp tender.

• While vegetables are cooking, melt ¼ cup butter in large skillet over medium-high heat. Stir in bread crumbs and cook, stirring frequently, for about 5 minutes or until golden and toasted.

• Add pecans, ½ teaspoon salt, black pepper and thyme. Cook, stirring, about 1 minute.

• Drain vegetables, return to saucepan and add remaining ¼ cup butter and ¼ teaspoon salt, tossing to mix. Spoon vegetables into serving dish and sprinkle with crumb mixture.

• Serves 8.

"As a kid, the memories of summers could fill volumes of diaries. For me, every morning was a twenty minute ride to work with my dad. We rarely spoke. It was June. The Fourth of July was coming and he was busy. At ten years old, my work helped relieve some of his anxiety. I learned to make wheels, fountains and American flags. These were what a young boy could do—a lot of hand work, little danger. Besides making fireworks, what I remember most about those summer days was lunch.

While we were making Chrysanthemums, Crossettes and Crackling Star Shells, grandma was home cooking up a midday feast. Every single day, precisely at noon, grandpa's car was waiting for us, my dad, brothers and me. We piled in and drove silently to our ritual. In one short hour, we dined on what she spent all morning preparing. Awaiting us was always soup, salad and crusty Italian bread—hamburgers, chicken, steak, pork chops.

Tortilla Black Bean Casserole

2 cups chopped onion
1½ cups chopped green bell
  pepper
1 (14½ ounce) can tomatoes,
  chopped and with juice
¾ cup picante sauce
2 cloves garlic, minced
2 teaspoons ground cumin
1 (15 ounce) can whole kernel
  corn
2 (15 ounce) cans black beans,
  drained

12 (6 inch) corn tortillas
2 cups (8 ounces) shredded
  reduced-fat Monterey Jack
  cheese
2 cups shredded lettuce,
  optional
2 medium tomatoes, sliced,
  optional
sliced green onion
sour cream or plain yogurt,
  optional

- In large skillet, combine onion, bell pepper, tomatoes, picante sauce, garlic and cumin. Bring to a boil, reduce heat and simmer for 10 minutes.

- Stir in corn and beans. Spread ⅓ vegetable mixture in buttered 13x9x2-inch baking dish.

- In order listed, layer: ½ tortillas, ½ cup cheese, ⅓ vegetable mixture, ½ tortillas, ½ cup cheese, ⅓ vegetable mixture and ½ cup cheese.

- Bake, covered, at 350 degrees for 30 to 35 minutes. Sprinkle with remaining ½ cup cheese.

- Top with lettuce, tomatoes, green onion and sour cream or yogurt. Serve with corn chips or cornbread.

- Serves 6 to 8.

We had olives, salami and sausage. We never had leftovers. Before the hour was up, we were drinking coffee and eating cookies, as if the whole world paused and waited for us to enjoy our feast. We were always back to work before one o'clock.

Growing up in an Italian family that made fireworks meant summer filled with hard work. The Fourth of July deadline loomed over us like an approaching storm at a picnic. It also meant that eating meals together was the source of our togetherness. Our daily lunch time retreat strengthened us, though we rarely spoke during the whole meal. Eventually, grandma got too old and tired to cook. We went to a restaurant every day— the same one, the same table. It wasn't quite the same though."

John Rozzi
The Rozzi Co., Inc.

Fireworks in Cincinnati is synonymous with the Rozzi family, whose famous fireworks are the centerpiece of many celebrations.

Black Bean and Spinach Enchiladas

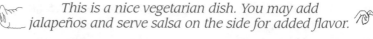

*This is a nice vegetarian dish. You may add
jalapeños and serve salsa on the side for added flavor.*

**2 (15 ounce) cans black beans,
undrained**
1 teaspoon salt
**2 (10 ounce) packages frozen
chopped spinach, thawed
and undrained**
1 cup diced onion
**1 tablespoon butter or
margarine**

**1 (10¾ ounce) can cream of
mushroom soup, undiluted**
¾ cup milk
**3 (4 ounce) cans diced green
chilies, drained**
3 cups sour cream
**3 cups (12 ounces) shredded
Monterey Jack cheese**
16 flour or corn tortillas

- Combine beans, salt and spinach, mixing well. Set aside.

- Sauté onion in butter or margarine until tender. Add to spinach mixture and set aside.

- Blend soup, milk, chilies, sour cream and 1½ cups Monterey Jack cheese, mixing well. Add ½ of mixture to spinach and set remainder aside.

- Spoon portion of spinach mixture in strip across center of each tortilla, roll up and place, seam side down, in 2 lightly greased 13x9x2-inch baking dishes. Spoon remaining sauce over tortilla rolls.

- Bake, uncovered, at 350 degrees for about 25 minutes. Sprinkle with remaining 1½ cups Monterey Jack cheese and bake for an additional 10 minutes.

- Serves 8 to 16.

Enchiladas can be assembled and frozen before baking. Thaw in refrigerator before baking.

Corn and Black Bean Tortilla Cakes

 It will be a hit every time you make it.

1 cup canned black beans, rinsed, drained and blotted dry
1 cup fresh corn
1 cup finely chopped red onion
1½ cups (6 ounces) grated extra sharp white cheddar cheese
1½ cups (6 ounces) grated Monterey Jack cheese
12 (6 or 7 inch) flour tortillas
1 tablespoon olive oil
½ teaspoon cayenne pepper

- Combine beans, corn and onion in large bowl. In separate bowl, combine cheddar cheese and Monterey Jack cheese.

- Place 3 tortillas in a single layer on large baking sheet. Sprinkle about ⅓ cup bean mixture and ⅓ cup cheese mixture on each. Top with second tortilla. Repeat layers twice, pressing tortillas gently to flatten and distribute filling.

- Combine oil and cayenne pepper. Lightly brush seasoned oil on each tortilla stack.

- Bake at 450 degrees for 12 to 15 minutes or until golden brown.

- Cut into wedges and serve with salsa.

- Serves 6.

Tortilla cakes can be assembled, covered well with plastic wrap and stored in refrigerator for up to 6 hours before baking.

Sprouts Supreme

3 pints fresh Brussels sprouts
1 teaspoon sugar
water
1 (10¾ ounce) can cream of chicken soup, undiluted
1 cup mayonnaise
2 tablespoons lemon juice
1 tablespoon grated onion
¼ teaspoon garlic powder
½ teaspoon dill weed
¼ teaspoon dried tarragon
½ teaspoon nutmeg
1 (8 ounce) can sliced water chestnuts, drained
salt and black pepper, to taste
dash of hot pepper sauce
1½ cups crushed crackers
garlic powder, to taste
⅓ cup grated Parmesan cheese
¼ cup butter, melted

- In large saucepan, cook Brussels sprouts with sugar and water to cover for 8 to 10 minutes or until tender.

- While sprouts are cooking, combine soup, mayonnaise, lemon juice, onion, garlic powder, dill weed, tarragon, nutmeg, water chestnuts, salt, black pepper and hot pepper sauce, blending until smooth.

- Drain sprouts and place in buttered 2½-quart casserole. Spoon sauce over sprouts.

- Combine cracker crumbs, garlic powder, Parmesan cheese and melted butter, tossing to blend thoroughly. Sprinkle on sauce.

- Bake at 350 degrees for 20 minutes or until bubbly.

- Serves 8.

Swiss Cheese Spoon Bread

½ cup butter, melted
2 eggs, beaten
1 cup sour cream
1 (15 ounce) can cream-style corn
1 (8 ounce) package corn muffin mix
1 cup (4 ounces) grated Swiss cheese

- Combine butter, eggs, sour cream, corn, muffin mix and Swiss cheese, mixing well. Spread mixture in buttered 2-quart casserole.

- Bake at 375 degrees for 40 minutes or until firm.

- Serves 8.

Carrot Pudding

1 cup butter, softened
½ cup firmly packed brown
  sugar
1 egg
1 tablespoon water
2 cups grated carrots

1½ cups all-purpose flour
½ teaspoon baking powder
½ teaspoon baking soda
½ teaspoon salt
½ teaspoon cinnamon
½ teaspoon nutmeg

- Assemble pudding the day before serving.

- Cream butter and brown sugar until smooth. Blend in egg, water and carrots.

- Sift flour, baking powder, baking soda, salt, cinnamon and nutmeg together. Add dry ingredients to carrot mixture and mix thoroughly.

- Spread batter in ring mold or baking dish. Chill overnight in refrigerator, removing 1 hour before baking.

- Bake at 350 degrees for 1 hour.

- Serves 6.

Carrot Soufflé

1 cup canned carrots, mashed
1 cup sugar
6 eggs, separated
juice of ½ orange
juice of ½ lemon

1 cup grated blanched
  almonds
raspberry preserves
whipped cream
unsweetened fresh or frozen
  raspberries

- Combine carrots, sugar, egg yolks, orange juice, lemon juice and almonds, mixing well.

- Beat egg whites until stiff. Fold into carrot mixture. Spread in greased 1½-quart soufflé dish.

- Bake at 350 degrees for 45 minutes. Let stand in draft-free place until cool.

- Spread with preserves and top with whipped cream. Garnish with raspberries.

- Serves 6.

Shopping in the 21st Century

Acres and acres of produce and meat are showcased at Jungle Jim's, a contemporary urban market located north of the city in Fairfield. From the ordinary to the eclectic, Jungle Jim's fits the bill for both the modern palate and pocketbook. Like George Bernas, owner of the Brandywine Inn says, "If it grows and it's edible, you can bet Jungle Jim's has it, and it's always fresh to boot. I highly recommend shopping there. If you can't find it there, you can't find it anywhere."

Carrots and Zucchini Casserole

1 pound carrots, cut diagonally in ½-inch slices	¾ teaspoon prepared horseradish
4 small zucchini, cut in ¼-inch slices	½ teaspoon salt
6 cups boiling water	½ teaspoon white pepper
½ cup mayonnaise	¾ cup Italian bread crumbs
3 tablespoons grated onion	¾ cup (3 ounces) freshly grated Parmesan cheese
	½ cup butter, melted

- Cook carrots and zucchini in boiling water for 5 minutes or until tender. Drain well, reserving ¼ cup cooking liquid.

- Combine mayonnaise, onion, horseradish, salt, white pepper and reserved cooking liquid. Add carrots and zucchini, tossing to mix well. Spread mixture in 8x8x2-inch baking pan.

- Mix bread crumbs, Parmesan cheese and butter together. Stir ½ cup crumbs into vegetable mixture, then sprinkle remaining crumbs on vegetables.

- Bake at 375 degrees for 15 to 20 minutes.

- Serves 6 to 8.

Cheesy Corn

 Make this using white and yellow corn, fresh from the farm. What a great success it will be at your next family reunion!

1 (8 ounce) regular or reduced-fat cream cheese	3 tablespoons water
¼ cup margarine or butter	3 tablespoons milk
2 (26 ounce) packages frozen corn	2 tablespoons sugar
	6 slices American cheese, optional

- Using microwave, soften cream cheese and margarine or butter together.

- Mix with corn, water, milk, sugar and American cheese in slow cooker.

- Cook on low setting for 3 to 4 hours, checking during final hour. If too liquid, add additional corn, warmed in microwave oven.

- Serves 12.

Corn and Spinach Parmesan

¼ cup minced onion
¼ cup butter, divided
1 (15 ounce) can cream-style corn
1½ cups frozen chopped spinach, thawed and well drained

1 teaspoon vinegar
½ teaspoon salt
¼ teaspoon black pepper
½ cup dry bread crumbs
2 tablespoons grated Parmesan cheese

- Sauté onion in 2 tablespoons butter until tender. Add corn, spinach, vinegar, salt and black pepper. Spread mixture in lightly-buttered 1-quart casserole.

- Melt remaining 2 tablespoons butter in skillet. Add bread crumbs and cheese, mixing lightly. Sprinkle on corn mixture.

- Bake at 400 degrees for 15 to 20 minutes or until lightly browned.

- Serves 6.

Mexican Hominy

 This unique dish is from New Mexico. What a great change of pace!

1 (16 ounce) can yellow hominy, undrained
1 (10¾ ounce) can cream of chicken soup, undiluted

1 (4 ounce) can chopped green chilies, drained
1 cup (4 ounces) cubed processed cheese food

- Combine hominy, soup, chilies and cheese, mixing well. Spread mixture in buttered 1-quart casserole.

- Bake, covered, at 350 degrees for 30 minutes, stir and bake for 20 minutes, remove cover and bake for additional 10 minutes.

- Serves 6.

What's for Dinner's Double Corn Tortilla Casserole

4 cups tomato sauce
1 teaspoon salt
1 tablespoon chili powder
1 teaspoon cumin
1 teaspoon coriander
1 teaspoon crushed red pepper
2 cups buttermilk
4 eggs
30 to 36 corn tortillas
1 (15 ounce) can whole kernel corn, drained
1 (15 ounce) can cream-style corn
2 to 3 cups (8 to 12 ounces) grated cheddar cheese
2 to 3 cups (8 to 12 ounces) grated Monterey Jack cheese
1 (15 ounce) dark red kidney beans, drained
1 bunch green onions, chopped
½ red onion, chopped
½ cup buttered bread crumbs

- Combine tomato sauce, salt, chili powder, cumin, coriander and red pepper, mixing well.

- Blend buttermilk with eggs.

- In order listed in buttered 4-quart casserole, layer: 10 to 12 tortillas, 1½ to 2 cups tomato sauce, whole kernel corn, ½ of cream-style corn, ⅔ cheddar cheese, ½ of green onion, ½ of red onion, 10 to 12 tortillas, 1½ to 2 cups tomato sauce, remaining cheddar cheese, ⅓ of Monterey Jack cheese, beans, remaining cream-style corn, remaining green onion and red onion, remaining tortillas and remaining Monterey Jack cheese.

- Pour buttermilk mixture over layered ingredients. Sprinkle with bread crumbs.

- Bake at 350 degrees for 35 to 50 minutes.

- Serves 16.

Eggplant Casserole

 Gets better when allowed to stand.

1 large eggplant, cut in ½-inch
  slices
¼ cup olive oil
salt and black pepper, to taste
1 large or 2 medium sized
  onions, thinly sliced
1 clove garlic, minced
1½ cups cooked tomatoes
1 green bell pepper, finely
  chopped

1 teaspoon salt
freshly ground black pepper
1 tablespoon chopped fresh
  basil or 1 teaspoon dried
  basil
½ cup toasted bread crumbs
½ cup (2 ounces) grated
  Parmesan cheese

- Sauté eggplant in oil in skillet just until tender. Season with salt and black pepper. Remove from skillet and set aside.

- Sauté onion and garlic in oil just until softened.

- In buttered 2½-quart casserole, layer ½ of eggplant, onion mixture, tomatoes and bell pepper, seasoning with salt, black pepper and basil. Repeat layers.

- Sprinkle bread crumbs on layers.

- Bake, covered, at 300 degrees for 1 hour. Sprinkle with cheese.

- Serves 4 to 6.

Tasty Oktoberfacts

Patrons of Oktoberfest Zinzinnati chow down more than 250 foods, pig out on 87,542 metts, gobble up 16,002 strudels, inhale 20,000 cream puffs, wolf down 23,004 soft pretzels, dig into 2,600 pounds of sauerkraut, scarf down 24,640 potato pancakes, and ingest 64,000 sauerkraut balls.

Eggplant Enchiladas

Gold Star ChiliFest

This two-day festival fires up a weekend of fun downtown for Cincinnati's annual salute to chili madness. The Gold Star ChiliFest features red-hot country artists on the B-105 Free Country Music Stage, dozens of authentic NASCARS on display, tasty chili cuisine by area restaurants, fire fighting demonstrations and sanctioned chili-making competitions. Add plenty of rides, contests and entertainment for the kids, and you have a recipe for a good time.

1 cup chopped onion
2 cloves garlic, minced
vegetable oil
6 cups cubed peeled eggplant
1 cup chopped green bell pepper
1 cup sliced fresh mushrooms
1 teaspoon Worcestershire sauce
2 tablespoons toasted almonds, chopped
1 tablespoon minced fresh parsley
1 teaspoon freshly ground black pepper
1 cup (4 ounces) grated reduced-fat Monterey Jack cheese, divided
¼ cup chicken broth
12 whole wheat flour tortillas

- In large skillet, sauté onion and garlic in small amount of oil until tender.
- Add eggplant, bell pepper, mushrooms and Worcestershire sauce. Cook for 10 to 12 minutes or until eggplant is tender. Remove from heat and stir in almonds, parsley, black pepper and ¾ cup Monterey Jack cheese.
- Heat broth in skillet. Add tortillas, one at a time, and cook, turning once, until softened.
- Spoon portion of eggplant mixture in center of each tortilla, roll and place, seam side down, in baking dish prepared with vegetable cooking spray.
- Sprinkle remaining ¼ cup cheese on rolled tortillas.
- Bake at 350 degrees for 20 minutes.
- Serves 6.

Fennel Gratin

2 pounds fennel bulbs,
  trimmed, quartered and cut
  in julienne strips
1½ cups whipping cream
½ teaspoon salt
¼ teaspoon freshly ground
  black pepper

¼ cup dry bread crumbs
¼ cup (1 ounce) freshly grated
  Parmesan cheese
1½ tablespoons unsalted
  butter

- Place fennel in buttered 10x8x2-inch baking dish or oval gratin dish.

- Whisk cream, salt and black pepper together. Pour over fennel.

- Sprinkle with crumbs, then Parmesan cheese and dot with butter.

- Bake, covered with aluminum foil, at 425 degrees for 20 minutes; remove foil and bake for additional 20 minutes or until liquid is reduced and top is browned.

- Serves 4.

Caesar Green Beans

2 (15 ounce) cans green beans,
  drained
1 tablespoon chopped onion
1 clove garlic, minced
¼ teaspoon salt
⅛ teaspoon black pepper

2 tablespoons vegetable oil or
  bacon grease
3 tablespoons butter, melted
1 tablespoon vinegar
¼ cup dry bread crumbs
¼ cup (1 ounce) freshly grated
  Parmesan cheese

- Combine beans, onion, garlic, salt, black pepper, oil or bacon grease, butter and vinegar, mixing well. Add bread crumbs and Parmesan cheese, tossing to mix.

- Spread mixture in buttered 2-quart casserole.

- Bake at 350 degrees for 40 minutes.

- Serves 6

"At Christmas dinner, we had a tradition of having beets stuffed with hollandaise sauce. You hollow out the little beets and just before you're going to serve them, you put a dab of hollandaise in each little hollow. They're wonderful!"

Marjorie Hiatt
Great Living Cincinnatian
Past Association of
Junior Leagues
President

Tall Stacks

*The romance of the
steamboat era comes
back to life as the
Delta Queen and
other paddle wheelers
from the Ohio,
Missouri and
Mississippi Rivers
converge in Cincinnati
for the Tall Stacks
celebration. The
color, drama and
excitement that this
nationally acclaimed
event brings to the
city is unparalleled.*

Green Beans with Rice

1 (15 ounce) green beans,
  drained
⅓ cup chopped onion
1 tablespoon margarine
1 teaspoon salt
¼ teaspoon black pepper
2 cups hot cooked rice
1 cup sour cream

1 teaspoon dill weed
salt, to taste
1 tablespoon lemon juice
1 tablespoon Worcestershire
  sauce
6 slices bacon, cooked crisp
  and crumbled

- Heat green beans, onion, margarine, salt and black pepper together in
  saucepan until onion is softened. Add rice and toss to mix.

- In separate saucepan, blend sour cream, dill weed, salt to taste, lemon
  juice and Worcestershire sauce. Warm thoroughly.

- Serve sauce over bean mixture, sprinkling with bacon.

- Serves 6.

Teriyaki Bean Special

½ cup chopped onion
¼ cup butter
4 cups cooked green beans,
  well drained
1 (16 ounce) can bean sprouts,
  drained

1 (3 ounce) can chopped
  mushrooms, drained and
  broiled
1 (8 ounce) can sliced water
  chestnuts, drained
1 tablespoon cider vinegar
3 tablespoons soy sauce

- Sauté onion in butter in large skillet until tender.

- Add beans, bean sprouts, mushrooms, water chestnuts, vinegar and soy
  sauce, mixing lightly. Simmer, uncovered, for 15 minutes, stirring
  occasionally.

- Serve with additional soy sauce.

- Serves 6.

The Phoenix's Wild Mushroom and Artichoke Strudel

 This may be used as a side dish or as an appetizer. It's also great as a vegetarian alternative.

1 pound shiitake mushrooms
½ pound crimini mushrooms
½ pound oyster mushrooms
olive oil
salt and black pepper, to taste
½ ounce fresh oregano, chopped
½ ounce fresh rosemary, chopped
½ ounce fresh sage, chopped

2 or 3 shallots, minced
1 to 2 tablespoons crushed garlic
1 teaspoon onion powder
2 (14 ounce) cans artichoke hearts, drained and quartered
1 package frozen phyllo dough sheets, thawed
1 cup butter, melted

- Clean mushrooms and remove stems. In large skillet, separately sauté each type of mushroom until tender, seasoning with salt and black pepper. Remove from skillet and set aside.

- Sauté oregano, rosemary, sage, shallots, garlic and onion powder until wilted. Add to mushrooms.

- Add artichokes to mushrooms.

- Place phyllo dough on flat surface; keep cold moist cloth on dough to prevent it from drying and tearing. Place 1 sheet on surface and brush with melted butter, top with second sheet, brush with butter and repeat with third sheet. Lightly season with salt and black pepper.

- Spread portion of mushroom mixture along bottom ⅓ of dough. Gently roll into log shape, pinching ends to enclose vegetables.

- Repeat with remaining dough and vegetables until all ingredients have been used. Chill logs for about 1 hour.

- Cut logs into ¾-inch pieces and place on baking sheet.

- Bake at 350 degrees until golden brown. Serve immediately.

- Serves 12.

Other mushroom varieties can be used.

Pork, Not Just the Other White Meat

The by-products of pork packing created new industries. Bones were used for buttons; pig bristles were stuffed into mattresses and furniture or made into brushes. The hides were tanned into leather. The lard and tallow from hogs were essential for soap and candle making, and two partners named Procter and Gamble started their business by collecting these by-products from packing houses.

Italian Mushrooms

1 cup unseasoned bread crumbs
1 cup (4 ounces) grated Peccorino Romano cheese
½ cup chopped fresh parsley

2 or 3 cloves garlic, minced or pressed
black pepper, to taste
2 pounds mushrooms, sliced
extra virgin olive oil

- Combine bread crumbs, Romano cheese, parsley, garlic and black pepper, mixing lightly.

- In 2-quart casserole prepared with vegetable cooking spray, alternately layer mushrooms and crumb mixture, ending with crumbs. Drizzle with oil.

- Bake, uncovered, at 350 degrees for 45 minutes, stirring mushrooms occasionally.

- Serves 8 to 10.

Baked Anna Potatoes

 This is a nice change of pace for fixing potatoes. Take them to a dinner party. Everyone will love them. *Very attractive and classy.*

4 Idaho baking potatoes, peeled
2 medium sized yellow onions, thinly sliced
1 (14½ ounce) can chicken broth

¼ cup (1 ounce) grated Parmesan cheese
salt and black pepper, to taste
paprika, to taste

- Partially slice potatoes, cutting ¾ way through and in ⅛-inch slices.

- Place onion in baking dish prepared with vegetable cooking spray. Add broth.

- Place potatoes on onion and sprinkle with Parmesan cheeses, salt, black pepper and paprika.

- Bake, covered, at 375 degrees for 1 hour; remove cover and bake for additional 15 minutes.

- Serves 4.

Stuffed Onions

6 medium sized onions
salted water
vegetable oil
paprika
¼ cup plus 1 tablespoon
 butter, divided
3 tablespoons chopped fresh
 parsley

¼ cup half and half
¼ cup chopped black olives
¾ cup chopped walnuts
½ cup (2 ounces) grated
 Swiss cheese
¼ teaspoon salt
¼ cup dry bread crumbs

- Cut thick slice from top and scoop center from each onion and set aside. Cook onion shells in salted water for 25 minutes. Drain shells and brush each with oil and sprinkle generously with paprika.

- Chop reserved onion. Cook in ¼ cup butter until tender. Stir in parsley, half and half, olives, walnuts, cheese and salt, mixing well.

- Spoon mixture into onion shells and place in shallow baking dish. Sprinkle with mixture of 1 tablespoon butter and bread crumbs.

- Bake at 350 degrees for 15 minutes.

- Serves 6.

Mushrooms Florentine

1 pound fresh mushrooms
2 tablespoons vegetable oil
2 (10 ounce) packages frozen
 chopped spinach, thawed
 and well drained
¼ cup chopped onion

¼ cup butter, melted
1 teaspoon salt
garlic salt, to taste
seasoned salt, to taste
1 cup (4 ounces) grated sharp
 cheddar cheese

- Cut stems from mushrooms. Sauté stem pieces and caps in oil until browned and set aside.

- Place spinach in bottom and sides of shallow 10-inch baking dish. Sprinkle onion, melted butter, salt, garlic salt and seasoned salt on spinach.

- Sprinkle ½ cup cheddar cheese on spinach. Place mushrooms on cheese. Season with garlic salt and sprinkle with remaining ½ cup cheese.

- Bake, uncovered, at 350 degrees for 20 minutes.

- Serves 6 to 8.

The Lilt of Irish Laughter

The Ault Park Celtic Festival, coordinated by Cincinnati Folk Life Director JoAnn Buck, features Irish, Scottish and Welsh music, dancing and workshops.

Gorgonzola Stuffed Potatoes

¼ cup (1 ounce) crumbled Gorgonzola cheese
½ cup sour cream
½ teaspoon black pepper, divided
⅛ teaspoon hot pepper sauce
6 slices bacon, cooked crisp and crumbled
¼ cup coarsely chopped walnuts, toasted
2 tablespoons minced chives
12 small red potatoes
1 tablespoon olive oil
½ teaspoon salt

• Blend Gorgonzola cheese and sour cream. Stir in ¼ teaspoon black pepper, hot pepper sauce, bacon, walnuts and chives. Set aside.

• In small roasting pan, toss potatoes with oil. Season with salt and remaining ¼ teaspoon black pepper.

• Bake at 400 degrees for 30 minutes or until tender.

• Split potatoes lengthwise in halves. Using small melon baller, scoop pulp from center of each potato half, leaving ⅛-inch shell.

• Fill center of each potato shell with generous dollop of cheese and walnut mixture.

• Serves 3 or 4.

Teller's Brown Rice

⅔ pound onion, minced
2½ ounces ginger root
½ cup sesame oil
5 cups water
½ cup soy sauce
1 cup garlic oil
4 cups uncooked brown rice
6 ounces scallions, chopped

• In Dutch oven, sauté onion and ginger root in sesame oil for 2 minutes.

• Add water, soy sauce, garlic oil and rice. Bring to a boil, reduce heat and simmer, covered, until rice is tender and liquid is absorbed.

• Fold scallions into rice.

• Serves 12 to 16.

Swiss Scalloped Potatoes

⅓ cup chopped green onion
1 clove garlic, minced
¼ teaspoon ground red pepper
3 tablespoons butter or
   margarine
1 cup whipping cream
1 cup skim milk
¾ teaspoon salt

¼ teaspoon freshly ground
   black pepper
½ teaspoon nutmeg
2½ pounds red potatoes,
   unpeeled, cut in ⅛-inch slices
1 cup (4 ounces) grated Swiss
   cheese
½ cup (2 ounces) grated
   Parmesan cheese

- In Dutch oven, sauté green onion, garlic and red pepper in butter or margarine, stirring constantly, for 2 minutes.

- Add cream, milk, salt, black pepper and nutmeg, mixing well to blend.

- Add potatoes to sauce. Bring to a boil over medium heat and cook, stirring carefully, for 15 minutes or until potatoes are tender.

- Spoon potatoes and sauce into lightly-buttered 11x7x1½-inch baking dish. Sprinkle with Swiss cheese and Parmesan cheese.

- Bake at 350 degrees for 45 minutes or until bubbly and golden brown. Let stand 15 minutes before serving.

- Serves 8.

Brown Rice and Black Beans

1 medium sized onion,
   chopped
1 tablespoon vegetable oil
1 (14½ ounce) can stewed
   tomatoes
1 (15 ounce) can black beans,
   undrained

1 teaspoon oregano
½ teaspoon garlic powder or
   1 clove garlic, minced
chopped fresh cilantro, to
   taste
1½ cups quick-cooking brown
   rice

- In skillet, sauté onion in oil until tender.

- Add tomatoes, beans, oregano, garlic and cilantro. Bring to a boil.

- Stir in rice. Bring to a boil, reduce heat and simmer, covered, for 5 minutes. Remove from heat and let stand for 5 minutes or until rice is tender.

- Serves 4 to 6.

Rice Balls

3 cups cooked brown rice
1 cup (4 ounces) grated
  Parmesan cheese
4 eggs, beaten
2 tablespoons chopped fresh
  parsley

1 (16 ounce) package
  Monterey Jack cheese, cut in
  1-inch cubes
1 cup seasoned dry bread
  crumbs
vegetable oil
prepared pizza sauce

- Combine rice, Parmesan cheese, eggs and parsley, mixing well.

- Shape ½ cup rice mixture around each cheese cube to form a ball. Roll in bread crumbs.

- Fry rice balls in ½-inch depth oil in heavy skillet, turning often to brown on all sides.

- Serve with pizza sauce.

- Serves 4 to 6.

Spinach and Artichoke Casserole

1 (14 ounce) can artichoke
  hearts, drained and
  quartered
1 tablespoon butter
3 (10 ounce) packages frozen
  chopped spinach, cooked
  and well drained
¾ cup mayonnaise

1 (10¾ ounce) can cream of
  mushroom soup, undiluted
¾ cup sour cream
¼ teaspoon garlic salt
½ teaspoon lemon juice
1 (6 ounce) can sliced
  mushrooms, drained
1½ cups (6 ounces) grated
  Swiss cheese

- Sauté artichokes in butter until wilted. Spread in 13x9x2-inch baking pan.

- Prepare spinach according to package directions. Drain well.

- Combine spinach, mayonnaise, soup, sour cream, garlic salt and lemon juice. Fold in mushrooms. Spread mixture on artichokes and sprinkle with Swiss cheese.

- Bake at 350 degrees for 30 minutes.

- Serves 8.

Spaghetti Squash

1 large spaghetti squash	½ teaspoon black pepper
boiling water	2 tablespoons chopped fresh
2 tablespoons butter	chives
½ teaspoon garlic salt	¾ to 1 cup (3 to 4 ounces)
	grated Parmesan cheese

- Cut squash lengthwise in halves, remove seeds and place squash, cut side down, in 13x9x2-inch baking pan. Add boiling water to 1½-inch depth.

- Bake at 350 degrees for 50 minutes or until tender. Remove from oven and let cool slightly. Using fork tines, remove spaghetti-like strands of squash and place in mixing bowl.

- Add butter, garlic salt, black pepper, chives and Parmesan cheese, tossing to coat squash.

- Serves 8 to 10.

Stuffed Sweet Potatoes

6 medium sized sweet	¼ cup milk
potatoes	1 teaspoon vanilla
vegetable oil	1 cup butter, divided
2 cups firmly packed brown	1 cup walnuts
sugar, divided	⅓ cup all-purpose flour
2 eggs	

- Rub potatoes with oil. Bake at 400 degrees for 1 hour. Let stand until cool enough to handle.

- Cut slice from top of each potatoes and carefully scoop out pulp, leaving shells intact.

- Mash pulp until smooth. Add 1 cup brown sugar, eggs, milk, vanilla and ½ cup butter, mixing well. Spoon mixture into potato shells.

- Combine remaining 1 cup brown sugar, walnuts, flour and remaining ½ cup butter, mixing to form crumbs. Sprinkle on stuffed potatoes and place in baking dish.

- Bake at 350 degrees for 20 minutes.

- Serves 6.

"Our Thanksgiving dinner is a family tradition involving both my family and Rosa's family. Not only is it a time of Thanksgiving, but a fun-filled inter-family cook-off. Those of us who don't do any of the cooking, but are the official tasters, find it to be a blissful experience. My favorite is turkey dressing. There are cooks in both families that do a very special job with the secret spices that they use."

Ken Blackwell
Ohio State Treasurer
Former City Mayor

Tomato Basil Tart

On a Hot Summer's Day

Three waterparks - Coney Island, The Beach, and Surf Cincinnati make a big splash in the summer, in addition to the "Waterworks" at Kings Island.

1 unbaked 9-inch pastry shell
1½ cups (6 ounces) grated Swiss cheese, divided
5 Roma tomatoes or 4 medium tomatoes, cut in wedges and drained
1 cup loosely-packed fresh basil

4 cloves garlic
½ cup regular or reduced-fat mayonnaise
¼ cup (1 ounce) grated Parmesan cheese
⅛ teaspoon white pepper

- Bake pastry shell according to package directions. Sprinkle enough Swiss cheese to just cover bottom of hot shell. Cool on wire rack.

- Arrange tomato wedges in pastry shell.

- Using food processor or knife, finely chop basil and garlic together. Sprinkle on tomatoes.

- Combine mayonnaise, Parmesan cheese and white pepper. Spread on tomatoes and sprinkle with remaining Swiss cheese.

- Bake at 375 degrees for 35 to 40 minutes.

- Serves 6.

photograph by Paula Norton

Oktoberfest dancers

Havarti Tomato Pie

2 unbaked 9-inch pastry shells
¼ cup Dijon mustard
1 (8 ounce) package Havarti
   cheese with dill, sliced
4 to 6 tomatoes, sliced

⅓ cup olive oil
garlic salt, to taste
⅓ cup chopped fresh parsley
¼ cup chopped fresh dill

- Partially bake pastry shells, using package directions but reducing baking time by ½; pastry should be firm but not browned.

- Spread mustard in bottom of pastry shells. Cover with cheese slices and add layers of tomato slices.

- Brush tomatoes with oil. Season with garlic salt and sprinkle with parsley and dill.

- Bake at 375 degrees for 20 to 30 minutes.

- Serves 8 to 10.

Southwest Vegetables

1½ cups fresh white corn
½ cup chopped red onion
½ cup chopped orange or
   yellow bell pepper
½ cup chicken broth
1 cup chopped yellow summer
   squash
1 cup chopped tomatoes

1 cup (4 ounces) grated
   cheddar cheese, divided
⅔ cup corn meal
½ cup milk
2 eggs, beaten
½ teaspoon salt
¼ teaspoon black pepper
¼ teaspoon hot pepper sauce

- In saucepan, combine corn, onion, bell pepper and broth. Bring to a boil, reduce heat and simmer, covered, for 5 minutes.

- Combine squash, tomatoes, ¾ cup cheddar cheese, corn meal, milk, eggs, salt, black pepper and hot pepper sauce. Add vegetables with cooking liquid and mix well.

- Spread mixture in buttered 1½-quart casserole. Top with remaining ¼ cup cheddar cheese.

- Bake at 350 degrees for 45 to 50 minutes.

- Serves 8.

Old Coney

Did you know that Old Coney used to be an apple orchard before its owner turned it into amusement park?

Tomatoes and Spinach

6 scallions, minced
2 or 3 cloves garlic, minced
1 tablespoon butter
2 (10 ounce) packages frozen
   chopped spinach or
   2½ pounds fresh spinach
2 cups dry bread crumbs
6 eggs, beaten
¾ cup butter, melted
½ cup (2 ounces) freshly
   grated Parmesan cheese

1 tablespoon monosodium
   glutamate
salt, to taste
1 teaspoon black pepper
1½ teaspoons thyme
½ teaspoon cayenne pepper
3 or 4 ripe tomatoes, thickly
   sliced
garlic salt, to taste

- In large skillet, sauté scallions and garlic in butter until tender. Set aside.

- Cook spinach according to package directions for 5 minutes. Drain well and chop.

- Combine scallion mixture, spinach, bread crumbs, eggs, melted butter, Parmesan cheese, monosodium glutamate, salt, black pepper, thyme and cayenne pepper, mixing well.

- Arrange tomatoes, seasoned with garlic salt, in single layer in buttered 13x9x2-inch baking dish.

- Place scoop of spinach mixture on each tomato slice.

- Bake at 350 degrees for 15 minutes.

- Serves 8.

 # Sautéed Cherry Tomatoes

½ cup butter
2 tablespoons water

¼ cup firmly packed brown
   sugar
1 pint cherry tomatoes

- In saucepan, melt butter. Blend in water and brown sugar, mixing well.

- Add tomatoes. Cook over medium heat for 3 minutes, stirring once.

- Serves 4 to 6.

For variety, omit water and sugar and add curry powder to butter.

Zucchini Boats

 Inspired by a trip to the Doral Saturnia Spa in Miami, where Good Morning America was broadcast live for a week, this is one of those recipes that taught me how to eat skinny and stay skinny. -Joan Lunden

½ cup minced onion
boiling water
1 cup cooked chopped spinach
2 teaspoons dried oregano
3 cups cooked white or brown rice
2 cups reduced-fat ricotta cheese

salt and black pepper, to taste
4 (8 inch) zucchini
1 cup tomato sauce
¾ cup (3 ounces) coarsely grated reduced-fat mozzarella cheese

- Blanch onion in boiling water for 1 minute. Drain and cool.

- Combine onion, spinach, oregano, rice, ricotta cheese, salt and black pepper, mixing well.

- Cut ends from zucchini, cut lengthwise in halves and remove seeds. Place, cut side down, in baking sheet lightly prepared with vegetable cooking spray.

- Bake at 400 degrees for 8 to 10 minutes or just until squash is tender.

- Mound portion of spinach filling in each zucchini.

- Bake for 10 minutes. Spoon 2 tablespoons tomato sauce on each and sprinkle with mozzarella cheese. Bake for additional 5 minutes.

- Serves 4.

Interstate Alternative

Did you know that there is an alternative to the freeway? Anderson Ferry, located at the bottom of Anderson Ferry Road, transports people and cars across the river to Kentucky.

Jack and Zucchini

1 cup uncooked regular rice
3 cups thinly sliced unpeeled zucchini
boiling water
1 (7½ ounce) can green chilies, drained and chopped
3 cups (12 ounces) grated Monterey Jack cheese
1 large tomato, thinly sliced

salt, to taste
2 cups sour cream
1 teaspoon oregano
1 teaspoon garlic salt
¼ cup chopped green bell pepper
¼ cup chopped green onion
2 tablespoons chopped fresh parsley

- Prepare rice according to package directions. Drain and set aside.

- Cook zucchini in boiling water to cover just until crisp tender. Drain and set aside.

- Spread rice in bottom of 3-quart casserole. In order listed, add layers of chilies, ½ of Monterey jack cheese, zucchini and tomato slices seasoned with salt.

- Combine sour cream, oregano, garlic salt, bell pepper and green onion. Spoon mixture evenly on tomatoes. Sprinkle with remaining Monterey Jack cheese.

- Bake at 350 degrees for 45 to 50 minutes or until hot and bubbly. Garnish with parsley.

- Serves 6 to 8.

Tomato and Corn Casserole

2½ cups shoe peg corn, drained
2½ cups canned tomatoes, drained
½ cup plus 3 tablespoons dry bread crumbs, divided
1½ teaspoon salt

black pepper, to taste
1 teaspoon sugar
2 tablespoons butter, melted
1 tablespoon butter
1 cup (4 ounces) grated cheddar cheese

- Combine corn, tomatoes, ½ cup bread crumbs, salt, black pepper, sugar and melted butter, mixing well.

- Spread mixture in buttered 2-quart casserole. Sprinkle with cheddar cheese and remaining 3 tablespoons bread crumbs. Dot with butter.

- Bake at 350 degrees for 30 minutes.

- Serves 8 to 10.

Italian Zucchini Crescent Pie

 Also works well as a main dish.

4 cups thinly sliced unpeeled
   zucchini
1 cup coarsely chopped onion
½ cup butter
2 tablespoons parsley flakes
½ teaspoon salt
½ teaspoon black pepper
¼ teaspoon garlic powder
¼ teaspoon chopped basil

¼ teaspoon oregano
2 eggs
1 cup (4 ounces) shredded
   mozzarella cheese
1 (8 ounce) package
   refrigerated crescent roll
   dough
2 teaspoons Dijon mustard

- In large skillet, sauté zucchini and onion in butter for about 10 minutes or until tender. Stir in parsley, salt, black pepper, garlic powder, basil and oregano.

- Blend eggs with cheese. Add to vegetable mixture.

- Separate dough into 8 triangles and place in ungreased 10-inch pie plate, 11-inch quiche dish or 12x8x1½-inch baking pan, pressing dough in bottom and along sides to form crust.

- Lightly spread mustard on dough. Spoon vegetable mixture into crust.

- Bake at 375 degrees for 20 minutes or until knife tip inserted near center comes out clean. Cover edges with aluminum foil if necessary to prevent over browning. Let stand for 10 minutes before serving.

- Serves 6.

A Rose By Any Other Name

The Greater Cincinnati Flower Show in Ault Park is the largest open-air flower show in the country.

Zucchini Tart

Just Across the State Line

Nearby Indiana offers several entertainment options. Ski Perfect North is the favorite slogan of avid skiers around town who are looking for a little downhill action. Located just over the state line in Lawrenceburg, Indiana, the slopes are just a short drive from the city. For those less athletically inclined, the Argosy Casino and The Grand Victoria Casino provide a bit of Las Vegas right here in the Midwest.

3 cups (12 ounces) grated
   Swiss cheese, divided
2 cups all-purpose flour
2 cups quick-cooking rolled
   oats
1 cup butter, softened
2¼ pounds zucchini, thinly
   sliced
1 medium sized onion

2 large cloves garlic, crushed
1 large red bell pepper, chopped
2 tablespoons butter
4 eggs, beaten
1 cup sour cream
½ cup (2 ounces) freshly
   grated Parmesan cheese
1 tablespoon chopped fresh
   basil

- Combine 2 cups Swiss cheese, flour, oats and softened butter, blending to form crumbs. Reserving 1 cup of mixture, press remaining crumbs into bottom and on sides of 10-inch spring form pan. Set aside.

- In large skillet over low heat, sauté zucchini, onion, garlic and bell pepper in 2 tablespoons butter until tender.

- Combine eggs, sour cream, remaining 1 cup Swiss cheese, Parmesan cheese and basil, mixing well.

- Spread zucchini mixture in crust-lined pan. Pour egg mixture over zucchini and top with reserved crumbs.

- Bake at 375 degrees for 45 to 60 minutes.

- Serves 8.

PASTA... *Accompaniments*

Designed by Samuel Hannaford, Music Hall was built largely with funds from philanthropist Rueben Springer to house the German Saengerfest for the city's German singing societies. A National Historic Landmark, it is considered to be one of the most acoustically perfect halls in the world.

Photograph by J. Miles Wolf

MUSIC HALL

The patronage of J. Ralph and Patricia Corbett transformed Music Hall into a center for the performing arts in the early 1970's, and today it is home to the Cincinnati Opera, Cincinnati Symphony Orchestra/Pops, May Festival and the Cincinnati Ballet for performances of The Nutcracker.

Lasagna Rollups

1 (16 ounce) package curly
  edge lasagna noodles
1 egg, beaten
1 (15 ounce) carton ricotta
  cheese
2 cups (8 ounces) shredded
  mozzarella cheese
2 medium sized onions,
  chopped
2 large cloves garlic, minced
2 tablespoons olive oil
1 pound ground beef
1 cup packed, chopped fresh
  parsley
2 teaspoons chopped fresh
  basil

2 teaspoons chopped fresh
  oregano
1¼ teaspoons salt, divided
½ teaspoon black pepper,
  divided
2 (15½ ounce) jars spaghetti
  sauce
2 tablespoons butter
2 tablespoons all-purpose flour
1½ cups milk
1 cup (4 ounces) freshly grated
  Parmesan cheese
2 tablespoons chopped fresh
  parsley
2 tablespoons freshly grated
  Parmesan cheese

- Prepare noodles according to package directions, cooking until tender but firm. Drain, plunge noodles in cold water, drain and place strips in single layer on paper towel.

- Combine egg, ricotta cheese and mozzarella cheese.

- In large skillet, sauté onion and garlic in oil until tender. Add ground beef and cook, stirring to crumble, until browned. Drain excess fat.

- Stir in 1 cup parsley, basil, oregano, ¾ teaspoon salt and ¼ teaspoon black pepper.

- Add beef mixture to cheese mixture, stirring to blend.

- Pour 1 jar spaghetti sauce into 3-quart paella pan or lasagna casserole.

- Spread each noodle with a scant ¼ cup of filling and roll up. Cut each in halves and place, cut side down, in sauce.

- Melt butter in saucepan over medium heat. Stir in flour, blending until smooth. Gradually add milk, stirring constantly, and cook until thickened.

- Stir in 1 cup Parmesan cheese, ½ teaspoon salt and ¼ teaspoon black pepper. Spoon sauce over lasagna rolls.

- Pour remaining jar spaghetti sauce over white sauce and sprinkle with 2 tablespoons parsley and 2 tablespoons Parmesan cheese.

- Bake, covered with aluminum foil, at 400 degrees for 20 minutes; remove foil and bake for an additional 10 minutes.

- Serves 8.

Music Hall

Designed by Samuel Hannaford, Music Hall was built largely with funds from philanthropist Rueben Springer to house the German Saengerfest for the city's German singing societies. A National Historic Landmark, it is considered to be one of the most acoustically perfect halls in the world. The patronage of J. Ralph and Patricia Corbett transformed Music Hall into a center for the performing arts in the early 1970's, and today it is home to the Cincinnati Opera, Cincinnati Symphony Orchestra/Pops, May Festival and the Cincinnati Ballet for performances of The Nutcracker.

Nona's Spaghetti Sauce and Meatballs

"When I think of Cincinnati and food, I fondly remember the first time I experienced my wife Ronnie's cooking. It was at a "Party of Note" for the Cincinnati Symphony, prepared for a party of 36 and presented in six delectable courses. I've no doubt that if I hadn't been in love before, I certainly would have been after such a delightful evening of delicious food, not to mention the interesting people I met.

Next, what comes to mind, and it could have even been during the same weekend, was a wonderfully lazy breakfast at Fred and Irma Lazarus' home when Fred, bless him, prepared the best "Matzo Brie" I've had since my own mother's."

Vidal Sassoon

Meatballs

2 pounds ground round	2 eggs, beaten
1 pound ground pork	black pepper, to taste
1 cup (4 ounces) grated cheese	garlic powder, to taste
1 cup bread crumbs	parsley flakes, to taste

Sauce

pork neck bones	garlic powder, to taste
1½ pounds country-style pork ribs	3 (29 ounce) cans tomato sauce
olive oil	2 (15 ounce) cans tomato sauce
parsley flakes	grated Parmesan cheese
black pepper, to taste	

- Prepare sauce by cooking neck bones and ribs in oil in stock pot, browning thoroughly.

- Stir in parsley flakes, black pepper and garlic powder. Cook over low heat for 5 minutes.

- Pour tomato sauce plus 1 large can water and 1 small can water into stock pot. Add additional garlic powder, black pepper and parsley to taste. Simmer for 2 to 3 hours, adding Parmesan cheese about 1 hour before removing from heat. Remove bones.

- Prepare meatballs by combining beef, pork, cheese, bread crumbs and eggs, mixing well. Season with black pepper, garlic powder and parsley flakes.

- Shape mixture into about 24 balls. Sauté in skillet, turning to brown on all sides.

- Add to sauce and simmer until done.

- Serves 6.

South of the Border Manicotti

8 manicotti shells
2 chicken breast halves,
    cooked and diced
1 cup reduced-fat cottage cheese
1 scallion, sliced
3 tablespoons chopped fresh
    parsley or cilantro
1 teaspoon garlic powder
½ teaspoon hot pepper sauce
½ cup (2 ounces) shredded
    reduced-fat Monterey Jack
    cheese
1½ cups salsa

- Prepare manicotti shells according to package directions. Drain and set aside.

- Combine chicken, cottage cheese, scallion, parsley or cilantro, garlic powder and hot pepper sauce, mixing well. Using spoon, stuff mixture into manicotti shells and place in greased 12x8x2-inch baking dish.

- Sprinkle Monterey Jack cheese over shells and top with salsa.

- Bake at 400 degrees for 20 minutes or until shells are hot and cheese is melted.

- Serves 4.

Crab and Pepper Pasta

1 (16 ounce) package penne
    pasta
1 large red bell pepper,
    cut in ½-inch strips
1 large green bell pepper,
    cut in ½-inch strips
1 large yellow bell pepper,
    cut in ½-inch strips
1 large red onion, sliced
½ teaspoon salt
3 tablespoons olive oil
1 tablespoons sugar
3 tablespoons red wine vinegar
1 teaspoon chopped fresh basil
½ teaspoon black pepper
1 pound fresh lump crab meat,
    cooked
½ cup chopped parsley

- Prepare penne pasta according to package directions, cooking to al dente consistency. Drain and set aside, keeping warm.

- In large skillet, cook bell peppers and onion with salt in oil for about 10 minutes or until vegetables are tender.

- Stir in sugar, vinegar, basil and black pepper. Heat thoroughly.

- Toss vegetables with crab meat, pasta and parsley.

- Serves 4.

Singing the Blues

"Blowing into a stovepipe isn't just a novelty, it's a way of life."

Steven Tracy
Going to Cincinnati, A History of the Blues in the Queen City

"Great opera transports the listener. It allows each of us, for a brief moment, to experience human perfection."

Roxanne Qualls
Mayor

Scallops and Pasta

1½ (16 ounce) packages thin
   spaghetti
1½ pounds fresh scallops
1 tablespoon minced garlic
½ cup olive oil

½ cup plus 2 tablespoons
   chopped fresh parsley, divided
¼ teaspoon red pepper flakes
   or to taste
Italian-seasoned bread crumbs
red pepper flakes

- Prepare spaghetti according to package directions. Drain and set aside, keeping warm.

- In skillet over medium heat, sauté garlic in oil until golden. Stir in 2 tablespoons parsley and ¼ teaspoon red pepper flakes.

- Add scallops and sauté quickly, cooking just until scallops turn flat white. Place scallops on cooked spaghetti in serving bowl. Drizzle hot oil over scallops and add remaining ½ cup parsley. Serve with bread crumbs and red pepper flakes.

- Serves 6.

Asparagus Primavera

2 cups (1-inch diagonal slices)
   fresh asparagus
2 cups sliced carrots
1½ cups snow peas
boiling water
½ cup chopped onion
2 cloves garlic, minced
1 tablespoon olive oil

6 cups cooked hot fettuccine
½ cup (2 ounces) grated
   Parmesan cheese, divided
¼ cup chopped fresh parsley
2 tablespoons dry white wine
½ teaspoon salt
½ teaspoon black pepper

- Blanch asparagus, carrots and snow peas in boiling water for 2 minutes, drain and set aside.

- In Dutch oven over medium heat, sauté onion and garlic in oil for 2 minutes or until tender. Remove from heat.

- Stir in blanched vegetables, fettuccine, ¼ cup Parmesan cheese, parsley, wine, salt and black pepper, tossing well. Sprinkle with remaining ¼ cup Parmesan cheese.

- Serves 6.

Pasta with Shrimp Sauce

1 (16 ounce) package pasta
1 small onion, chopped
3 tablespoons extra-virgin
   olive oil
1 pound shrimp, peeled and
   deveined
⅓ cup dry white wine

⅔ pound plum tomatoes,
   peeled and chopped, or
   canned plum tomatoes,
   drained and chopped
salt and freshly ground black
   pepper, to taste
1 tablespoon chopped fresh
   Italian parsley

- Prepare pasta according to package directions, cooking to al dente consistency. While pasta cooks, prepare sauce.

- In large skillet over low heat, sauté onion in oil for about 3 minutes or until translucent, stirring frequently.

- Add shrimp, increase heat to medium and cook, stirring constantly, for 2 minutes. Stir in wine and cook for about 2 minutes or until wine is evaporated.

- Add tomatoes and season with salt and black pepper. Cook for additional 2 minutes.

- Drain pasta and add to tomato sauce. Stir in parsley and cook over medium heat, stirring frequently, for 2 minutes.

- Serves 6.

Shrimp and Pesto

1 (16 ounce) package pasta
1 cup fresh or prepared pesto

1½ pounds shrimp, cooked,
   peeled and deveined
1 or 2 chopped tomatoes

- Prepare pasta according to package directions. While pasta cooks, prepare sauce.

- In skillet, warm pesto. Add shrimp and tomatoes, cooking quickly to heat through.

- Drain pasta well. Add to shrimp mixture and toss to blend.

- Serves 6.

Cooked chicken can be substituted for shrimp.

Seafood Stuffed Shells

1 (12 ounce) package jumbo pasta shells
1 cup chopped onion
2 cloves garlic, minced
1 teaspoon butter
¼ cup all-purpose flour
¾ cup milk
1 (8 ounce) bottle clam juice
½ cup sliced green onion
2 tablespoons minced jalapeño peppers
1 (15 ounce) can cream-style corn
1½ cups (6 ounces) grated Monterey Jack cheese

1 cup ricotta cheese
½ (8 ounce) cream cheese, cubed
¼ cup lemon juice
½ teaspoon cumin
¼ teaspoon black pepper
1 pound medium sized fresh shrimp, peeled and deveined
½ pound fresh lump crab meat, drained and flaked
nutmeg, to taste
2 tablespoons grated Parmesan cheese

- Prepare shells according to package directions, cooking to al dente consistency. Drain, rinse with cold water and set aside.

- In large skillet, sauté onion and garlic in butter for 5 minutes. Stir in flour. Gradually add milk, whisking to blend well.

- Stir in clam juice and cook, stirring constantly, until thickened. Add green onion, jalapeño and corn. Cook for 2 minutes and set aside.

- In food processor, blend Monterey Jack cheese, ricotta cheese and cream cheese together until smooth. Blend in lemon juice, cumin and black pepper.

- Coarsely chop shrimp. Combine with crab meat and stir into cheese mixture, mixing well.

- Spread ¾ cup corn mixture in 3-quart casserole. Spoon 2 teaspoons seafood mixture into each pasta shell. Arrange shells in single layer on corn mixture. Tuck any extra or broken shells in and around stuffed shells.

- Pour remaining sauce over shells and sprinkle lightly with nutmeg and Parmesan cheese.

- Bake at 350 degrees for 30 minutes.

- Serves 6.

Broccoli Linguine and Pine Nuts

1½ pounds broccoli flowerets
  boiling water
1 (8 ounce) package linguine
3 medium sized cloves garlic,
  minced
⅛ teaspoon red pepper flakes

¼ cup plus 1 tablespoon
  olive oil
2 tablespoons lemon juice
⅓ cup (1½ ounces) freshly
  grated Parmesan cheese
salt and black pepper, to taste
¼ cup toasted pine nuts

- Blanch broccoli in boiling water for 3 minutes, drain and set aside.

- Prepare pasta according to package directions. Drain well, set aside and keep warm.

- In large skillet, sauté garlic and red pepper flakes in oil for 1 minute. Add broccoli and sauté, stirring frequently, for 2 minutes.

- Stir in linguine, mixing well. Add lemon juice, Parmesan cheese, salt and black pepper. Just before serving, sprinkle with pine nuts and additional Parmesan cheese.

- Serves 4.

Maya's Sweet Red Pepper Pesto

½ pound red bell pepper, cut
  in chunks
1 (4 ounce) package almonds,
  freshly roasted
1 (3 ounce) package Parmesan
  cheese
1¼ ounces fresh basil
1 teaspoon black pepper

2½ teaspoons chopped fresh
  oregano or 1½ teaspoons
  dried oregano
½ teaspoon minced garlic
1½ teaspoons onion powder
⅔ cup olive oil
salt, to taste

- Using food processor, puree bell pepper and place in mixing bowl.

- Process almonds and Parmesan cheese until fine consistency. Add to bell pepper.

- Process basil, black pepper, oregano, garlic and onion powder with oil, blending well. Season with salt and add to bell pepper mixture, mixing well.

- Serve hot with ravioli, tortellini or other pastas or cold as spread for French baguette bread. If warming, keep direct heat low to avoid clumping cheese.

- Serves 12.

Showboat Majestic

The last of the floating operas, Showboat Majestic reigns supreme as the grande dame of the riverfront. A nostalgic tribute to days gone by, the theater has been showcasing some of the best local talent since 1927. Now permanently anchored at the Public Landing, the Showboat's production season runs April through October.

"The thing I love most about Cincinnati is that it is big enough to be cosmopolitan - with the ballet, symphony, opera and the Aronoff Center, and yet still small enough to be neighborly."

Minette Cooper
Vice Mayor
City of Cincinnati

Watson Bros. Brewhouse Famous Macaroni and Cheese

1 (16 ounce) package penne
  pasta
½ cup cornstarch
4 cups milk
1 cup whipping cream
pinch of white pepper
pinch of black pepper
pinch of cayenne pepper

½ cup finely chopped green
  bell pepper
½ cup finely chopped white
  Spanish onion
4 cups (16 ounces) grated
  cheddar cheese
bread crumbs

- Prepare pasta according to package directions, drain and set aside.

- Dissolve cornstarch in ½ cup milk. In large saucepan over medium heat, combine remaining 3½ cups milk, whipping cream, white pepper, black pepper, cayenne pepper, bell pepper and onion. Bring to a boil, stirring frequently to prevent sticking.

- Add cornstarch paste, blending until smooth, and remove from heat.

- Stir in cheddar cheese, mixing until melted. Add pasta. Spread mixture in shallow baking dish. Sprinkle with bread crumbs.

- Bake at 350 degrees for about 25 minutes or until bubbly and bread crumbs are browned.

- Serves 6 to 8 as main course, 10 as side dish.

Orecchiette Agli Spinaci

2 cups orecchiette pasta
5 ounces spinach
1½ teaspoons chopped garlic
2 teaspoons extra-virgin olive
  oil

4 sun-dried tomato halves, cut
  in julienne strips, or ½ cup
  sun-dried tomato paste
salt and white pepper, to taste
¼ cup (1 ounce) grated
  Parmesan cheese

- Prepare orecchiette according to package directions, cooking to al dente consistency. Drain and set aside. Cook spinach until tender and set aside.

- In saucepan, sauté garlic in oil until sizzling. Stir in spinach, tomatoes, salt and white pepper, tossing well to mix.

- Add orecchiette and toss to blend. Serve with Parmesan cheese.

- Serves 4.

Eggplant Baked Spaghetti

3 cloves garlic, chopped
¼ cup plus 2 tablespoons
   extra-virgin olive oil
1¼ pounds plum tomatoes,
   peeled and chopped, or
   canned plum tomatoes,
   drained and chopped
pinch of ground chili pepper
salt, to taste

5 cups olive oil for deep frying
1¼ pounds slender eggplants,
   trimmed and cut crosswise
   in ¼-inch slices
1 tablespoon unsalted butter
¾ cup fine dry bread crumbs
1 (16 ounce) package
   spaghetti

- In saucepan over low heat, sauté garlic in ¼ cup plus 2 tablespoons oil for 2 minutes, stirring frequently.

- Add tomatoes and chili pepper, stir well and season with salt. Simmer for about 30 minutes or until liquid evaporates.

- In heavy skillet, heat oil for deep frying to 350 degrees. Add eggplant, a few slices at a time, and deep-fry for about 3 minutes or until golden. Remove and drain on paper towels. Season with salt.

- Coat bottom and sides of buttered 9-inch springform pan with bread crumbs. Line bottom and sides with eggplant, overlapping slightly. Reserve any extra slices.

- Prepare spaghetti according to package instructions, cooking to al dente consistency. Drain and place in bowl. Add tomato sauce and leftover eggplant, tossing well to mix.

- Pour spaghetti mixture into eggplant-lined pan, pressing lightly to compact.

- Bake at 350 degrees for about 20 minutes or until lightly browned. Invert on warm platter.

- Serves 6.

Did you know?

The Cincinnati Chamber Music Society plays at the Cincinnati Art Museum and Memorial Hall, and that the Northern Kentucky Symphony performs at the NKU Fine Arts Center.

"Some people carried fiddles with them and would play along the riverbanks and wharfs for pennies. The fiddle was a popular instrument and entertainment for the early settlers. 'Stop your fiddlin' around' was the reprimand which evolved."

Don Deming
Steamboat Historian

A Note From
the Maestro

"My philosophy of
music making is to be
'primus inter pares'
(first among equals)
and bring out the best
of the musicians at
the service of the
composer, here in
Cincinnati and
everywhere."

Jesus Lopez-Cobos
Music Director
Cincinnati Symphony
Orchestra

River and railroad
traffic brought many
street musicians and
songsters to Cincinnati
in the early 1900's.
The abundance of
minstrel and folk
songs, vaudeville and
jug band music,
hokum, and Deep
South piano traditions
inspired Roosevelt
Sykes, Walter Davis,
Baby Bonnie, Pigmeat
Jarrett, and the first
black woman to ever
record vocal blues,
Mamie Smith.

Red Pepper Prosciutto Alfredo

1 (16 ounce) package pasta
2 ounces shallots, chopped
¼ pound prosciutto ham,
  chopped
½ cup garlic oil
2 cups whipping cream

½ cup (2 ounces) freshly grated
  Parmesan cheese, divided
¼ pound red bell pepper,
  chopped
¼ pound snow peas
1 cup pine nuts
½ cup chopped fresh parsley

• Prepare pasta according to package directions, cooking to al dente consistency. Drain well and keep warm.

• In large skillet over medium heat, sauté shallots and prosciutto in oil until tender.

• Stir in cream and simmer until bubbly. Add ¼ cup plus 1 tablespoon Parmesan cheese, bell pepper, snow peas, pine nuts, parsley and pasta, tossing gently to mix.

• Sprinkle with remaining Parmesan cheese.

• Serves 4.

Summer Squash Primavera

1 (16 ounce) package pasta
5 cloves garlic, minced
2 green onions, chopped
¼ cup olive oil
1 red bell pepper, sliced
1 yellow bell pepper, sliced
2 or 3 carrots, sliced
1 small zucchini, sliced

¼ teaspoon salt
¼ teaspoon freshly ground
  black pepper
1 cup chicken broth
1 cup chopped fresh basil
1 cup (4 ounces) freshly grated
  Parmesan cheese
2 tablespoons pine nuts, toasted

• Prepare pasta according to package directions, cooking to al dente consistency. While pasta is cooking, prepare vegetables.

• In large skillet over medium heat, sauté garlic and green onion in oil for 30 seconds. Stir in red bell pepper, yellow bell pepper and carrots, and cook for 2 to 3 minutes. Add squash, salt and black pepper, and cook for 5 minutes.

• Add broth and cook, covered, for 5 minutes or until vegetables are very tender.

• Drain pasta. Add vegetables, basil and Parmesan cheese, tossing to mix. Sprinkle with pine nuts.

• Serves 6.

Pasta with Spinach and Bacon

1 (16 ounce) package rotini
6 slices bacon
3 tablespoons olive oil
2 large cloves garlic, minced
4 cups thinly sliced fresh
   spinach

⅔ cup dry white wine
⅛ teaspoon salt
⅛ teaspoon black pepper
4 Roma tomatoes, thinly sliced
⅓ cup (1⅓ ounces) freshly
   grated Parmesan cheese

- Prepare rotini according to package directions, cooking to al dente consistency. Drain well, reserving ⅓ cup cooking water. Keep rotini warm.

- In large skillet over medium heat, cook bacon until crisp. Remove bacon, crumble, and reserve 2 tablespoons drippings in skillet.

- Add oil to drippings. Sauté garlic for 30 seconds. Add spinach and cook over medium heat, tossing to coat leaves, for 1 minute. Cook, stirring often, for 2 to 3 minutes or until spinach is wilted.

- Stir in wine, salt and black pepper. Simmer for 1 minute.

- Add rotini, tomatoes and reserved cooking water, tossing to blend with sauce. Sprinkle with Parmesan cheese and toss to mix. Sprinkle bacon on pasta.

- Serves 4.

Strolling band at Oktoberfest

photograph by Paula Norton

Whose Alma Mater?

Otto Juettner is the composer of U.C.'s Alma Mater, titled "A Varsity Song." Juettner, a graduate of U.C.'s College of Medicine (1888), also composed the Alma Mater of Xavier University. He earned his undergraduate degree from Xavier in 1885.

Guess what talk show host Jimmy Gherardi's favorite traditional food is? "Pasta, what else? Actually, it's my wife's dish. It's pasta with onions. It's very simple, just pasta with an onion sauce."

*Jimmy Gherardi
J's Fresh Seafood*

Stuffed Spinach Shells

2 (16 ounce) packages jumbo pasta shells
3 (10 ounce) packages frozen chopped spinach
2 medium sized white onions, minced
2 cloves garlic, minced
⅓ cup olive oil
3 (15 ounce) cartons ricotta cheese
2 cups (8 ounces) shredded mozzarella cheese
½ cup (2 ounces) shredded Parmesan cheese
½ cup (2 ounces) shredded Romano cheese
6 eggs, beaten
1 teaspoon lemon juice
1 teaspoon salt or to taste
½ teaspoon black pepper or to taste
3 to 4 cups tomato sauce

- Prepare pasta shells according to package directions, cooking until tender. Drain and set aside. Prepare spinach according to package directions, drain and set aside.

- In skillet, sauté onion and garlic in oil until lightly browned.

- Combine ricotta cheese, mozzarella cheese, Parmesan cheese, Romano cheese, eggs, lemon juice, salt and black pepper, mixing well. Stir in onion and garlic.

- Spread thin layer of tomato sauce in bottom of 2 shallow baking dishes.

- Spoon spinach mixture into pasta shells and place shells upright on tomato sauce.

- Bake, covered with aluminum foil, at 350 degrees for 40 minutes.

- Serves 10 to 12.

For less fat content, use combination of fat-free and reduced-fat ricotta and reduced-fat mozzarella cheeses.

Rotolo

1 (18x11 inch) rectangle
  rotolo egg pasta, homemade
  or pre-packaged
1 egg, beaten
1 cup ricotta cheese
½ teaspoon ground nutmeg
⅛ teaspoon black pepper

1 (10 ounce) package frozen
  chopped spinach, thawed
  and pressed
½ cup (2 ounces) grated
  Parmesan cheese
6 thin slices prosciutto ham
1 (6 ounce) package
  mozzarella cheese slices
½ cup butter or margarine

- Prepare rotolo according to package directions, rolling on lightly floured surface to 18x11-inch rectangle. Set aside.

- Combine egg, ricotta cheese, nutmeg and black pepper. Stir in spinach and Parmesan cheese.

- Spread filling evenly on pasta dough, leaving ½-inch margin around all edges. Layer prosciutto, then mozzarella slices on filling.

- Fold long edges of dough about 1-inch over filling. Moisten short edges with small amount of water. Beginning from short edge, roll up to form 9-inch log. Place on square of cheesecloth, roll to enclose and tie loosely with string.

- Pour water to 1½-inch depth in large Dutch oven and bring to a boil. Carefully add pasta roll, reduce heat and simmer, covered, for 30 to 35 minutes.

- Remove from water and cool for 5 to 10 minutes. Remove cheesecloth, place roll on plate, cover and chill for several hours.

- Cut roll into 12 slices and place, slightly overlapping, in 12x7x2-inch baking dish. Heat butter until lightly browned. Brush slices generously with 2 tablespoons butter.

- Bake at 450 degrees for 5 minutes, brush with additional butter and bake for 5 additional minutes. Serve with remaining butter.

- Serves 6.

Cincinnati Opera

Nicholas Muni took center stage as Cincinnati's Opera's Artistic Director in 1997, replacing James de Blasis, who lead the company with distinction from 1972 to 1996. An acclaimed international stage director of nearly 200 productions, Mr. Muni recently directed the world premiere of **Jackie O,** *based on the life of Jacqueline Kennedy Onassis, with the Houston Grand Opera and Banff Center for the Arts in Alberta, Canada.*

Watson Brothers' Meatless Marinara Sauce

1 medium sized onion, pureed
1 tablespoon chopped garlic
¼ pound finely chopped carrots
1 (2 ounce) can black olives, drained and chopped
½ cup olive oil
1 cup Burgundy or other red wine
2 tablespoons sugar
1 teaspoon salt

1 teaspoon basil
1 teaspoon oregano
1 teaspoon crushed red pepper
1 teaspoon fennel seed
½ teaspoon cayenne pepper
½ teaspoon thyme
1 (29 ounce) can tomato sauce
1 (29 ounce) can tomato puree
1 (28 ounce) can diced tomatoes

- In large stock pot, sauté onion, garlic, carrots and olives in oil until tender.
- Stir in wine, sugar, salt, basil, oregano, red pepper, fennel, cayenne pepper and thyme.
- Add tomato sauce, puree and tomatoes, mixing thoroughly. Simmer for 15 minutes. Serve on cooked pasta of choice.
- Serves 8 to 10.

Greek Pilagi

1 cup vermicelli pasta, broken in short pieces
½ cup margarine or butter, divided

1 (14½ ounce) can chicken broth
2½ cups water
1 cup converted rice
salt and black pepper, to taste

- Brown vermicelli in ¼ cup margarine or butter in saucepan, stirring often.
- Add broth, water and remaining ¼ cup margarine. Bring to a boil and add rice, salt and black pepper.
- Simmer, covered, for 20 to 30 minutes or until liquid is absorbed.
- Serves 6 to 8.

Amount of margarine or butter can be reduced by half.

Penne with Tomato Vodka Cream Sauce

1 (16 ounce) package penne
  pasta
1 small onion, minced
1 large clove garlic, minced
1 tablespoon butter
1 tablespoon olive oil
1 (28 ounce) can plum
  tomatoes, drained, seeds
  removed and chopped

1 cup whipping cream
¼ cup vodka
¼ teaspoon dried crushed red
  pepper
chopped fresh basil, to taste
freshly grated Parmesan
  cheese, to taste

- Prepare pasta according to package directions, cooking to al dente consistency. Drain and keep warm.

- In large skillet, sauté onion and garlic in butter and oil until tender.

- Add tomatoes and cook, stirring frequently, for about 25 minutes or until liquid is evaporated.

- Stir in cream, vodka and red pepper. Bring to a boil and cook for 2 minutes or until thickened.

- Add sauce to pasta, tossing to mix, and sprinkle with basil and Parmesan cheese.

- Serves 4.

Riverbend Music Center

Offering first-class entertainment to music lovers of all ages, Riverbend Music Center is Cincinnati's premier outdoor concert facility. Nestled on the banks of the Ohio River, the picturesque amphitheater was built by world famous architect Michael Graves. This state-of-the-art facility has set a new standard for concert centers throughout the world.

Home Sweet Home

The world renowned Cincinnati Symphony Orchestra calls Riverbend its summer home and delivers many delightful evenings of classical and pop concerts. The biggest names in the entertainment industry, from pop to rock, country to jazz, and middle of the road to alternative are presented by Nederthal.

Pasta with Sun-Dried Tomatoes and Basil

1 (16 ounce) package
   mostaccioli pasta
1 cup chicken broth
1 (2 ounce) package sun-dried
   tomatoes
1 tablespoon olive oil
1 tablespoon all-purpose flour
¼ cup milk
¼ (8 ounce) package cream
   cheese, diced

¼ cup shredded fresh basil or
   2 tablespoons dried basil
½ teaspoon salt
black pepper, to taste
1 teaspoon sugar
¼ cup (1 ounce) freshly grated
   Parmesan cheese
2 large cloves garlic, crushed
freshly grated Parmesan
   cheese, to taste

- Prepare mostaccioli according to package directions, cooking to al dente consistency. Drain and keep warm.

- Heat broth, add tomatoes and let stand to rehydrate.

- Heat oil in large skillet over medium heat. Blend in flour, then add milk and cream cheese.

- Remove tomatoes from broth and set aside. Add broth to white sauce.

- Snip tomatoes into small pieces and add with basil, salt, black pepper, sugar, Parmesan cheese and garlic to sauce. Simmer to blend flavors.

- Combine sauce and pasta, tossing to coat evenly. Serve with additional Parmesan cheese.

- Serves 4.

For variety, add toasted pine nuts, sautéed mushrooms, prosciutto, bacon bits, sautéed onion or frozen peas, cooked.

"Coming home; a strong neighborhood."

Bob Taft
Ohio Secretary of State
On the subject of what
he likes best about Cincinnati

Apple Coffee Cake

2 cups all-purpose flour
1 teaspoon baking soda
dash of salt
¾ cup sugar
2 tablespoons vegetable
   shortening
1 cup sour cream

1 egg
½ teaspoon vanilla
3 or 4 apples, peeled and
   sliced
cinnamon
sugar
butter

- Combine flour, baking soda and salt.

- In large mixing bowl, cream sugar and shortening together until smooth. Beat in sour cream, egg and vanilla.

- Add dry ingredients to egg mixture and mix well. Spread batter in greased 11x9x2-inch baking pan.

- Arrange apple slices on batter. Sprinkle with mixture of cinnamon and sugar and dot with butter.

- Bake at 300 degrees for 45 minutes.

- Serves 8.

Cinnamon Nut Crisps

 This is perfect to serve with breakfast too!

½ cup sugar
½ cup butter, softened
1 egg, separated
1¼ cups all-purpose flour

2 teaspoons cinnamon
¾ cup chopped pecans,
   divided

- In mixing bowl, cream sugar and butter together until smooth. Blend in egg yolk.

- Add flour, cinnamon and ½ cup pecans, mixing well.

- Using floured fingertips, press dough in bottom of 11x7x2-inch baking pan.

- Brush unbeaten egg white on dough and sprinkle with remaining ¼ cup pecans.

- Bake at 350 degrees for 15 minutes, remove from oven, cut into 18 squares and bake for additional 15 minutes or until crisp.

- Makes 18.

Blueberry Coffee Cake with Streusel Topping

1 (18`/ ounce) package yellow cake mix
1 (5`/ ounce) package instant vanilla pudding mix
1 cup reduced-fat sour cream
`/ cup apple sauce
³/ cup lukewarm water
2 cups chopped walnuts
1 cup sugar
2 cups firmly packed brown sugar
2 teaspoons cinnamon
2 cups blueberries
`/ cup powdered sugar
2 to 3 teaspoons skim milk

″ In large mixing bowl, combine cake mix, pudding mix, sour cream, applesauce and warm water, beating until creamy.

″ Combine walnuts, sugar, brown sugar and cinnamon, using fork to mix to streusel consistency.

″ Spread `/  of batter in 13x9x2-inch baking pan prepared with vegetable cooking spray. Sprinkle `/ of blueberries on batter and top with `/ of streusel mixture. Repeat layers.

″ Bake at 350 degrees for 45 minutes or until wooden pick inserted near center comes out clean.

″ Beat powdered sugar and skim milk together until smooth. Drizzle over cooled cake.

″ Serves 12 to 15.

Raspberry Coffee Cake

Cake

1 cup milk
¼ cup butter
¼ cup sugar
½ teaspoon salt
1 egg
1 packet active dry yeast
½ teaspoon brown sugar

¼ cup lukewarm (110 to 115 degrees) water
2 to 3 cups sifted all-purpose flour
1 cup fresh red raspberries
1 cup raspberry preserves
butter, softened

Glaze

1 tablespoon butter
1 tablespoon evaporated milk

½ teaspoon vanilla
1 to 2 cups powdered sugar

- In small saucepan, scald milk. Stir in butter, sugar and salt, mixing until butter is melted. Set aside to cool to lukewarm.

- In large mixing bowl, dissolve yeast with brown sugar in lukewarm water. Add egg to mixture. Let stand for about 5 minutes. Add milk mixture.

- Stir flour into milk liquid, mixing to form stiff dough. Knead thoroughly. Fold in fresh raspberries.

- Place dough in 9x9x2-inch baking pan. Spread with softened butter and top with preserves. Cover with towel and let rise in warm place for 1 hour.

- Bake at 350 degrees for 30 to 45 minutes or until golden brown.

- While cake is baking, prepare glaze by heating butter and milk in small saucepan. Remove from heat and blend in vanilla and powdered sugar, beating well.

- Drizzle glaze over warm coffee cake.

- Serves 6 to 9.

"To teach children anything is wonderful, but to teach children Irish dancing is an honor and the best job in the city of Cincinnati."

*Mary McGing Duckworth
Founder,
The McGing School
of Irish Dancing*

"Foods from Ireland, Scotland and Wales are more 'comfort' foods than sophisticated cuisine. We promise not to serve haggis!"

*JoAnn Buck
Cincinnati Folk Life*

Heavenly Butterscotch Rolls

1 cup milk
2 tablespoons butter
2 tablespoons sugar
pinch of salt
1 cake active yeast
1 egg, separated

3 cups sifted all-purpose flour,
 divided
½ cup butter, melted
1½ to 2 cups firmly packed
 brown sugar

- In small saucepan, scald milk. In large mixing bowl, combine milk, 2 tablespoons butter, sugar and salt. Let stand until lukewarm.

- Add yeast, egg yolk and 1½ cups flour to milk liquid, mixing until smooth.

- Beat egg white until stiff. Alternately add with remaining 1½ cups flour to batter.

- Let dough rise in warm place for 1½ to 2 hours.

- On lightly floured surface, roll dough to ½-inch thickness. Spread with melted butter and ½ of brown sugar. Roll up into long log, cut in 1-inch slices and place, cut side down, in baking pan containing melted butter and remaining brown sugar. Let rise for 30 minutes.

- Bake at 400 degrees for 20 minutes.

- Makes 12 to 18.

"Continental breakfasts are very sparse, usually just a pot of coffee or tea and a teensy roll that looks like a suitcase handle. My advice is to go right to lunch without pausing."

Miss Piggy's Guide to Life (as told to Henry Beard) 1981

White Chocolate
Macadamia Nut Sticky Buns

⅓ **cup milk**
¼ **cup sugar**
½ **teaspoon salt**
¼ **cup butter**
1 teaspoon brown sugar
¼ **cup lukewarm (110 to 115 degrees) water**
1 packet active dry yeast
1 egg
2½ **cups all-purpose flour**

½ **cup butter, softened, divided**
¾ **cup firmly packed brown sugar**
1½ **cups chopped macadamia nuts, divided**
1 cup white chocolate chips
½ **cup firmly packed brown sugar**
½ **teaspoon cinnamon**

- In small saucepan, heat milk just until bubbles form around edge. Remove from heat and add sugar, salt and ¼ cup butter, stirring until butter is melted. Let stand until lukewarm.

- In large mixing bowl, combine 1 teaspoon brown sugar and lukewarm water. Sprinkle yeast on liquid and stir to dissolve. Blend in milk mixture and egg.

- Using electric mixer, beat in 2 cups flour until smooth. Add remaining ½ cup flour by hand, mixing until dough is smooth and leaves sides of bowl.

- On lightly floured surface, knead dough until smooth. Place in lightly greased bowl, turning to coat on all sides. Cover with towel and let rise in warm, draft-free place for 1 to 1½ hours or until dough is doubled in bulk.

- Cream ¼ cup butter with ¾ cup brown sugar. Spread mixture on bottom and sides of 9x9x2-inch baking pan. Sprinkle with ½ cup nuts.

- On lightly floured surface, roll dough to form 16x12-inch rectangle. Spread with remaining ¼ cup butter and sprinkle with remaining ½ cup brown sugar, 1 cup nuts, white chocolate chips and cinnamon.

- Roll up lengthwise. Cut log in 12 slices and place, cut side down, in prepared pan. Cover with towel and let rise in warm place for 1 to 1½ hours or until doubled in bulk.

- Bake at 375 degrees for 25 to 30 minutes or until golden brown. Invert on serving plate, let stand for 1 minute and remove pan.

- Serves 9.

"In England, people actually try to be brilliant at breakfast. That is so dreadful of them. Only dull people are brilliant at breakfast!"

Oscar Wilde,
An Ideal Husband,
1895

**Letter
in the Daily
Telegraph,
1883**

*"Dear Sir: The hymn
'Onward Christian
Soldiers' sung to the
right tune and in a
not-too-brisk tempo,
makes a very good
egg timer. If you put
the egg into boiling
water and sing all five
verses and chorus,
the egg will be just
right when you come
to Amen."*

French Breakfast Puffs

Puffs

⅓ cup butter, softened	1½ teaspoons baking powder
½ cup sugar	½ teaspoon salt
1 egg	¼ teaspoon nutmeg
1½ cups all-purpose flour	½ cup milk

Topping

½ cup butter, melted	1 teaspoon cinnamon
½ cup sugar	

- In large mixing bowl, prepare puffs by creaming butter and sugar together until smooth. Add egg and mix thoroughly.

- Combine flour, baking powder, salt and nutmeg. Add to creamed mixture and stir in milk.

- Spoon batter into greased muffin pans, filling cups ⅔ full.

- Bake at 350 degrees for 20 to 25 minutes.

- Brush hot puffs with melted butter and roll in mixture of sugar and cinnamon. Serve hot.

- Makes 12.

Corn Puff Pancakes

*If you love corn on the cob, you'll love this.
Seems strange for breakfast but it will soon be a
family favorite. You can eat them plain or smothered
in maple syrup, or try them in corn syrup.*

2 eggs, beaten	2 cups pancake mix
1 (15½ ounce) can cream-style corn	½ cup milk
2 tablespoons sugar	3 tablespoons butter

- In large mixing bowl, combine eggs, corn, sugar and pancake mix, beating until smooth. Add milk and blend thoroughly.

- Melt butter in large skillet over medium heat. Add portion of batter and cook, turning when top is bubbly.

- Serves 3 or 4.

Macadamia Nut French Toast

4 eggs, lightly beaten
⅔ cup orange juice
⅓ cup milk
¼ cup sugar
¼ teaspoon nutmeg
½ teaspoon vanilla

1 (16 ounce) loaf Italian bread,
  cut in 1-inch slices
⅔ cup butter, melted
½ cup chopped macadamia
  nuts
powdered sugar

- Assemble the night before serving. In mixing bowl, combine eggs, orange juice, milk, sugar, nutmeg and vanilla, mixing well.

- Fit bread slices into lightly greased 13x9x2-inch baking pan. Pour egg mixture over bread.

- Chill, covered, for 8 hours or overnight, turning bread slices once.

- Pour butter into 15x10x1-inch jelly-roll pan. Place bread in single layer in pan.

- Bake at 400 degrees for 10 minutes, sprinkle with nuts and bake for an additional 10 minutes.

- Sprinkle with powdered sugar and serve with warm maple syrup.

- Serves 6 to 8.

Lemon Ricotta Pancakes

3 eggs, separated
¼ cup butter, melted
¾ cup ricotta cheese
¼ cup all-purpose flour

2 tablespoons sugar
¼ teaspoon salt
1 tablespoon grated lemon
  peel

- In mixing bowl, beat egg whites until stiff and set aside.

- Combine egg yolks, butter, ricotta cheese, flour, sugar, salt and lemon peel, beating well. Fold into egg whites, mixing until batter is free of white streaks.

- Spoon scant ¼ cup batter onto medium hot griddle which has been lightly greased. Cook for about 1½ minutes, turn and cook for about 1 minute. Keep pancakes warm until ready to serve.

- Serves 2.

Golden Gate Bridge

The Golden Gate Bridge was designed by Joseph Strauss, an 1892 graduate of the University of Cincinnati. The south pylon of the bridge holds a brick from the original McMicken Hall at U.C.

Chipped Beef Crêpes

Crêpes
4 eggs
1½ cups milk
½ teaspoon salt

1 cup all-purpose flour
¼ cup butter, melted

Filling
2 tablespoons minced onion
¼ cup butter
1 (4 ounce) package chipped
  dried beef
2 tablespoons all-purpose flour
1 cup milk
1 cup sour cream

1 cup (4 ounces) shredded
  cheddar cheese
1 (4 ounce) can sliced
  mushrooms, drained
2 tablespoons chopped fresh
  parsley

- Prepare crêpes by beating eggs with milk and salt. Add flour and beat until smooth.

- Pour butter into lightly oiled 7 or 8-inch skillet, tilting to distribute.

- Pour thin layer of batter into skillet and cook until lightly browned on 1 side, turn and brown other side. Set aside and keep warm.

- For filling, sauté onion in butter in skillet until onion is transparent. Add beef and frizzle slightly.

- Stir in flour, mixing well. Add milk and stir constantly until thickened and smooth.

- Blend in sour cream, cheddar cheese, mushrooms and parsley. Cook over low heat, stirring, until cheese is melted.

- Spoon filling into crêpes, folding edges over filling.

- Makes 10 to 12.

Crêpes can be prepared in advance and stored in refrigerator or frozen. Place waxed paper between crêpes. Thaw before filling.

"Cincinnati, I thought, was the most beautiful of the inland cities of the Union. From the tower of its unsurpassed hotel the city spreads far and wide its pageant of crimson, purple and gold, laced by silver streams that are great rivers."

Winston Churchill

Crispy Sweet Potato Pancakes with Sour Cream Cilantro Sauce

 These are also wonderful smothered in butter and maple syrup, but skip the sour cream cilantro sauce

Pancakes

3 eggs, beaten	1 pound sweet potatoes,
½ cup plus 1 tablespoon	peeled and shredded
all-purpose flour	1 medium sized onion, minced
½ teaspoon salt	vegetable oil

Sauce

¼ cup pine nuts	¼ cup olive oil
3 cloves garlic	3 tablespoons lime juice
1 bunch cilantro, stems removed	⅛ teaspoon salt
½ jalapeño pepper, seeds	¾ cup sour cream
removed and chopped	

- Prepare pancakes by combining eggs, flour and salt in mixing bowl. Stir in sweet potatoes and onion.

- Drop batter by tablespoons into ¼-inch hot oil in heavy sauce pan. Cook, turning once, for 6 to 8 minutes or until golden on each side. Place on paper towels and keep warm.

- Prepare sauce in food processor, blending pine nuts, garlic, cilantro, jalapeño pepper, oil, lime juice and salt to form smooth paste. Stir in sour cream and serve with pancakes.

- Serves 4.

Gruyère Grits

1 cup quick-cooking grits	¼ teaspoon black pepper
4 cups milk	2 tablespoons butter
1 (8 ounce) package Gruyère	¼ cup (1 ounce) grated
cheese, cubed	Parmesan cheese
¼ teaspoon salt	

- Prepare grits in milk according to package directions. Remove from heat and stir in Gruyère cheese, salt, black pepper and butter.

- Pour grits into 2-quart casserole. Sprinkle with Parmesan cheese.

- Bake at 350 degrees for 30 minutes.

- Serves 6 to 8.

Smoky Egg Casserole

The All New, All Purpose Joy of Cooking

Ethan Becker, who resides in Cincinnati, is co-author of the sixth edition of the Joy of Cooking and the grandson of the original author.

2 tablespoons butter
2 tablespoons all-purpose flour
1¼ cups milk
1 (6 ounce) jar bacon or smoke flavored cheese spread
12 eggs, beaten
1 cup frozen peas, cooked
½ pound fresh mushrooms, sliced

¼ cup chopped pimento
1 tablespoon olive oil
1 cup croutons
6 slices bacon, cooked crisp and crumbled
1 medium tomato, thinly sliced
4 tablespoons chopped fresh chives, divided

- Assemble casserole the night before serving.

- In medium saucepan over low heat, melt butter. Blend in flour and cook for 1 minute. Remove from heat and gradually blend in milk until smooth. Return to low heat and cook, stirring constantly, until thickened.

- Add cheese spread to white sauce and set aside.

- In medium bowl, combine eggs, peas, mushrooms, pimento and 2 tablespoons chives, mixing lightly.

- Heat oil in large skillet. Add egg mixture and cook over medium heat, gently lifting edges to expose uncooked portion to heat.

- Fold cheese sauce into cooked eggs. Spread mixture in buttered casserole. Chill , covered, overnight.

- Bake, uncovered, at 350 degrees for 30 minutes. Sprinkle with croutons and bacon and bake for additional 10 minutes. Garnish with tomato and remaining chives.

- Serves 6.

Chicken Bacon Strata

12 slices white bread, cubed
2 cups shredded cooked
chicken
4 cups crumbled cooked
bacon
¼ cup chopped pimento
½ cup chopped green bell
pepper
½ cup mayonnaise
1 (10¾ ounce) can cream of
chicken soup, undiluted

2 cups (8 ounces) shredded
Swiss cheese
2 cups (8 ounces) shredded
cheddar cheese
4 eggs, beaten
3 cups milk
½ teaspoon salt
½ teaspoon black pepper
¼ teaspoon cayenne pepper
1 teaspoon dry mustard

- Assemble casserole the night before serving.

- Place bread in buttered 13x9x2-inch baking pan.

- Combine chicken, bacon, pimento, bell pepper, mayonnaise and soup, mixing well. Spoon on bread and spread evenly. Sprinkle Swiss cheese and cheddar cheese on soup layer.

- Whisk eggs, milk, salt, black pepper, cayenne pepper and mustard together. Pour over cheese.

- Chill, covered, overnight.

- Bake at 350 degrees for 1 to 1¼ hours.

- Serves 8 to 12.

Eggs Newport

1 (10½ ounce) can cream of
mushroom soup, undiluted
½ cup mayonnaise
½ cup milk
1 teaspoon chopped chives

6 hard-cooked eggs, sliced
8 slices bacon, cooked crisp
and crumbled
4 English muffins, split and
toasted

- In mixing bowl, blend soup and mayonnaise. Gradually add milk and chives, mixing well.

- Layer eggs and soup mixture in 1-quart casserole. Sprinkle with bacon.

- Bake at 350 degrees for 20 minutes. Serve on muffins.

- Serves 4.

Largest Soap Factory

At the turn of the 20th century, Cincinnati had the largest soap factory in the country, as well as the largest playing card factory, trunk factory, tannery, compressed yeast factory, tube and pipe works, printing ink plant, harness and saddlery works, theatrical publishing house, ladies shoe factory, and office furniture factory.

"Although many may accuse Cincinnatians of having conservative palates, some of our favorite dishes are actually quite adventurous. Muddy-colored mock turtle soup, for instance, is flavored sweet and sour with floating garnishes of chopped hard-boiled eggs and lemon slices. Crispy fried sauerkraut balls are both intensely tart and rich. And Cincinnati chili offers an array of subtle Middle Eastern flavors in a familiar Midwestern form. Even lowly goetta is more exciting than its cousin, scrapple, because of its oaty crunch."

Chuck Martin
Food Editor
Cincinnati Enquirer

Slow Cooker Goetta

 This is a true Cincinnati tradition.

5 cups water
2½ cups pin oats
   (not rolled oats)
1 tablespoon salt
½ teaspoon black pepper
1 pound ground beef

1 pound ground pork or
   bulk pork sausage
1½ cups chopped onion
½ teaspoon dried sage
¼ teaspoon thyme
4 bay leaves
½ cup corn meal

- In slow cooker, combine water, oats, salt and black pepper. Cook, covered, on high setting for 1 hour, stirring several times.

- Add beef and pork, crumbling thoroughly. Stir in onion, sage, thyme and bay leaves. Cook for 4 hours on low setting, stirring occasionally.

- Remove cover. Stir in corn meal and cook, uncovered, for 30 minutes.

- Spread mixture in three 9x5x3-inch loaf pans. Cool and store in refrigerator.

- Cut loaves into slices, then fry slices in vegetable oil or butter.

- Serves 18.

Sausage, Zucchini and Bell Pepper Frittata

¼ pound spicy bulk pork
   sausage
6 medium mushrooms, sliced
½ green bell pepper, chopped
1 zucchini, sliced
1 tablespoon olive oil

¼ teaspoon salt
1 teaspoon dried basil,
   crushed
¼ teaspoon red pepper flakes
7 eggs, beaten
1 cup (4 ounces) grated
   mozzarella cheese

- In large skillet, cook sausage, stirring to crumble, until browned.

- Add mushrooms, bell pepper, zucchini, oil, salt, basil and red pepper flakes. Sauté for 3 to 4 minutes.

- Combine sausage mixture, eggs and cheese, mixing well. Pour into greased 10-inch pie plate.

- Bake at 350 degrees for 25 to 30 minutes or until eggs are firm. Serve warm.

- Serves 4.

Ham and Broccoli Bake

1 bunch broccoli, chopped	1 small onion, chopped
10 slices white bread, crusts trimmed	5 eggs, lightly beaten
	3½ cups milk
1 cup (4 ounces) grated cheddar cheese	½ teaspoon salt
	½ teaspoon dry mustard
2 cups diced cooked ham	¼ teaspoon nutmeg

- Steam broccoli until tender, drain and set aside.

- Using doughnut cutter or glass, cut circle from each bread slice. Tear scraps and place in buttered 13x9x2-inch baking dish.

- Layer cheddar cheese, broccoli and ham on bread in dish. Sprinkle with onion and top with single layer of bread rounds.

- In blender container, combine eggs, milk, salt, mustard and nutmeg. Blend for 1 minute. Pour over layered ingredients.

- Chill, covered, for at least 6 hours.

- Bake, uncovered, at 325 degrees for 1 hour.

- Serves 8.

Duke's Egg Casserole

4 cups (16 ounces) grated Colby cheese	3 tablespoons all-purpose flour
	1 (4 ounce) can evaporated milk
4 cups (16 ounces) grated Monterey Jack cheese	½ teaspoon salt
2 (4 ounce) cans chopped mild green chilies, drained	1 egg white
	⅛ teaspoon cream of tartar
4 eggs, separated	

- Combine Colby cheese, Monterey Jack cheese and chilies. Place in 13x9x2-inch baking pan.

- In mixing bowl, combine egg yolks, flour, milk and salt, blending well.

- Whip 5 egg whites with cream of tartar until stiff. Fold into yolk mixture, pour over cheese and mix well with fork.

- Bake at 350 degrees for 1 hour.

- Serves 8 to 12.

Ham Casserole

12 or 13 thin slices white bread
1 pound chipped or shaved ham
3 cups (12 ounces) grated sharp cheddar cheese
3 eggs

3 cups milk
½ teaspoon salt
1 teaspoon dry mustard
1 tablespoon Worcestershire sauce
½ cup margarine, softened
1 cup crushed corn flakes

- Place 6 or 7 slices bread in 13x7x2-inch baking dish. Sprinkle ham on bread, add cheddar cheese and top with remaining bread slices.

- Combine eggs, milk, salt, mustard and Worcestershire sauce. Pour over layered ingredients.

- Mix margarine with corn flakes, adding dash of Worcestershire sauce if desired. Sprinkle on casserole.

- Bake at 300 degrees for 1 hour. Turn off oven heat and leave casserole in oven for additional 30 minutes.

- Serves 6 to 8.

Casserole can be baked the evening before serving and reheated in microwave oven.

Chocolate Waffles

2 cups all-purpose flour
½ cup cocoa
¼ cup sugar
1 tablespoon baking powder

½ teaspoon salt
3 eggs, separated
1¼ cups milk
¼ cup butter, melted

- In large mixing bowl, sift flour, cocoa, sugar, baking powder and salt together.

- Beat egg yolks and add with milk and butter to dry ingredients, stirring until smooth.

- Beat egg whites until stiff. Fold into batter.

- Spoon portion of batter into greased waffle iron and cook until golden brown. Serve with powdered sugar and fresh fruit.

- Serves 6 to 8.

Barbara Bush's Mushroom Quiche

 A favorite of the former President.

1¼ pounds mushrooms, sliced
3 green onions, minced
1 clove garlic, minced
3 shallots, minced
3 tablespoons butter
1¼ teaspoons salt
¼ teaspoon black pepper
1¾ teaspoons basil

1¾ teaspoons oregano
¾ teaspoon marjoram
¼ teaspoon thyme
½ teaspoon dry mustard
4 eggs
¾ cup milk
1 unbaked 9-inch pastry shell

- In large skillet over medium heat, sauté mushrooms, green onion, garlic and shallots in butter until vegetables are softened.

- Stir in seasonings and cook for 2 minutes or until liquid is evaporated. Remove from heat and let stand for 5 minutes.

- Combine eggs with milk, beating well. Stir in mushroom mixture. Pour into pastry shell.

- Bake at 375 degrees for 35 to 45 minutes or until filling is puffed, slightly firm and lightly browned.

- Serves 6.

Sausage Cornbread with Black-eyed Peas

 Down home good!

1 pound mild bulk pork
   sausage
1 red onion, chopped
1 cup yellow corn meal
½ cup all-purpose flour
½ teaspoon baking soda
1 teaspoon salt
2 eggs, beaten

1 cup buttermilk
½ cup vegetable oil
1 cup chopped green bell
   pepper
¾ cup cream-style corn
2 cups (8 ounces) grated
   cheddar cheese
2 cups cooked black-eyed peas

- Cook sausage with onion, stirring to crumble, until browned. Drain excess fat and set aside.

- In mixing bowl, combine corn meal, flour, baking soda and salt.

- Beat eggs, buttermilk and oil together. Add to dry ingredients, mixing just until moistened.

- Stir in sausage and onion, bell pepper, corn, cheddar cheese and peas. Spread mixture in greased 13x9x2-inch baking pan.

- Bake at 350 degrees for 50 minutes or until golden brown.

- Serves 6 to 8.

McGill Masterpiece

 Your guests will never guess the mystery ingredient in this casserole.

1 pound mild bulk pork
   sausage
1 pound hot bulk pork sausage
1 medium sized onion,
   chopped
6 eggs, beaten
2 (10¾ ounce) cans cream of
   celery soup, undiluted

½ cup milk
6 cups crispy rice cereal,
   divided
1½ cups cooked rice
2½ cups (10 ounces) grated
   cheddar cheese
1 tablespoon butter, softened

- Cook sausage, stirring to crumble, until browned. Remove from skillet and set aside. Sauté onion in sausage drippings until tender.

- In mixing bowl, combine eggs, soup and milk, beating until foamy.

- Spread 5 cups cereal in greased 13x9x2-inch baking pan. Spread cooked rice evenly on cereal. Layer sausage with onion on rice and sprinkle with cheese. Spoon egg mixture evenly on cheese layer.

- Toss remaining 1 cup cereal with butter and sprinkle on layered ingredients.

- Bake at 325 degrees for 1 hour. Remove from oven, cover with aluminum foil and let stand for 10 minutes before serving.

- Serves 8 to 10.

Serpentine Wall

The Serpentine Wall on the banks of the Ohio River is the catbird's seat to watch the annual Riverfest fireworks celebration, as well as many of the events on the river. Designed as a floodwall to bank the river, the wall is bordered by the 22-acre Bicentennial Commons. The name comes from the curved concrete wall's appearance.

Sausage and Wild Rice Brunch

½ **pound mild bulk pork sausage**
½ **pound hot bulk pork sausage**
1 **cup chopped celery**
1 **medium sized green bell pepper, chopped**
½ **cup onion, chopped**
2 **cloves garlic, minced**
3 **cups chicken broth**
2 **(10¾ ounce) cans cream of mushroom soup, undiluted**

1 **cup sliced water chestnuts**
1½ **cups sliced fresh mushrooms**
1 **(6 ounce) package long grain and wild rice mix**
¼ **teaspoon chopped fresh thyme**
2 **tablespoons chopped fresh parsley**
½ **cup slivered almonds**

• In large skillet over medium heat, cook sausage, celery, bell pepper, onion and garlic until sausage is browned and vegetables are tender. Drain excess fat.

• Stir in broth, soup, water chestnuts, mushrooms, wild rice mix, thyme and parsley, mixing well.

• Spread mixture in greased 3-quart casserole. Sprinkle with almonds.

• Bake at 350 degrees for 1½ hours.

• Serves 12.

photograph by Robert A. Flischel

Southwestern Brunch Casserole

 This recipe is awesome!

4 (4 ounce) cans chopped mild green chilies, drained

6 corn tortillas, cut in ½-inch strips

1 pound turkey sausage, cooked, crumbled and drained

2 cups (8 ounces) shredded Monterey Jack cheese

½ cup milk

8 eggs

½ teaspoon salt

½ teaspoon black pepper

½ teaspoon garlic salt

½ teaspoon onion salt

½ teaspoon ground cumin

2 large tomatoes, sliced

paprika, to taste

reduced-fat sour cream, optional

salsa, optional

- Assemble casserole the day before serving.

- In greased 13x9x2-inch baking dish, layer ½ of chilies, ½ tortillas, ½ sausage and ½ Monterey Jack cheese; repeat layers with remaining ingredients.

- Combine milk, eggs, salt, black pepper, garlic salt, onion salt and cumin, beating with fork until well mixed. Pour over layered ingredients.

- Arrange tomato slices on casserole and sprinkle with paprika.

- Chill, covered, overnight.

- Bake, uncovered, at 350 degrees for 45 to 55 minutes or until firm in center and lightly browned at edges. Serve with sour cream and salsa.

- Serves 12.

"You will know the truth, and the truth will make you free."

"The saying of Jesus in chapter 8 of St. John's gospel is more than mere pious sentiment; it expresses a deep truth of our human nature. As a liberal arts college, Thomas More exists to help people acquire the skills of being free (In Latin, liberales artes) that they may freely serve God and others."

*Father William F. Cleves
President,
Thomas More College*

Hash Brown Pepper Bake

3 cups frozen shredded
  potatoes
1/3 cup butter, melted
1 cup finely chopped ham
1 cup (4 ounces) shredded
  cheddar cheese
1/4 cup finely chopped red bell
  pepper

1/4 cup finely chopped green
  bell pepper
1/4 cup chopped green onion
2 eggs, beaten
1/2 cup milk
2 teaspoons salt
1/4 teaspoon black pepper

- Thaw potatoes between layers of paper towel to remove excess moisture. Press potatoes in bottom and along sides of ungreased 9-inch pie plate. Drizzle with butter.

- Bake potatoes at 425 degrees for 25 minutes. Cool on wire rack for 10 minutes.

- Combine ham, cheddar cheese, red and green bell pepper and green onion. Spread in potato shell.

- Blend eggs, milk, salt and black pepper. Pour over ham mixture.

- Bake at 350 degrees for 25 to 30 minutes. Let stand for 10 minutes before cutting.

- Serves 6.

Dish can be partially assembled the evening before serving. Prepare potato shell and add ham mixture. Chill overnight. Let stand at room temperature for 30 minutes. Add egg mixture and bake as directed.

"Without question, our favorite family/ food tradition is: every Sunday morning before church, I am a short order cook. And I cook for the kids. We have three young children: Joey, Jon and Elyse. They wake me up early every Sunday. I make everything from pancakes to French Toast to omelettes. For a young family, we already have this tradition, and it's kind of fun. I make them all this fattening stuff, and Missy and I won't eat it."

*Joe Deters
Hamilton County
Prosecutor*

"When I think of Cincinnati and food, I fondly remember the first time I experienced my wife Ronnie's cooking. It was at 'Party of Note' for the Cincinnati Symphony, prepared for a party of 36 and presented in six delectable courses. I've no doubt that if I hadn't been in love before, I certainly would have been after such a delightful evening of delicious food, not to mention the interesting people I met."

Vidal Sassoon

Bridesmaids' Luncheon

Crab Stuffed Chicken Breasts

Marinated Vegetable Salad

Carrot Soufflé

Apricot Nut Bread

French Cream Slices

Cherry Berry Slush

Deck Party

Rosemary Pork Chops

Bermuda Salad Bowl

Gorgonzola Stuffed Potatoes

Tomato Basil Tart

Italian Rolls

Frozen Raspberry Squares

White Wine Sangría

Ladies Luncheon

Celestial Chicken Salad

Raspberry Ring

Stewed Tomato Salad

Parmesan Corn Bread

Lemon Ice Cream Pie

Apricot Punch

"He ordered as one to the menu born."

O'Henry

"My wife, Vicki, is a great cook, but we also like the culinary philosophy of our good friends, Joe Sunderman, the voice of Xavier Basketball, and his wife, Mary Lynn. They believe in the 'three outs' — 'the go out,' 'the grill out,' or 'the carry out.' Lately, we've decided the 'outs' are easier to live by. The 'go out' is usually one of the great Italian restaurants in the city — such as Scalia's, Prima Vista, Barresi's or Nicola's. The 'grill outs' are the great little meat markets and delis in the neighborhoods, such as Bracke's in Mt. Lookout or Hyde Park Meats. The 'carry out' has to be from Bangkok Bistro for Thai food or China Gourmet for Chinese, or Fred and Gary's downtown for lunch carry out. And Nic's Bar and Grill or Zip's have the best hamburgers in town."

Dave Herche

Winter Comfort Foods

Sausage Pie with Herbed Cornmeal

Cranberry Salad

Baked Anna Potatoes

Spaghetti Squash

Buttermilk Pecan Bread

Coffee Liqueur

Tailgate

Barbecue Beef Brisket on Buns

Two-Cheese Potato Salad

Broccoli Slaw

Honey Roasted Chocolate Chippers

Banana Bars

"You Can't East Just One" Oatmeal Cookies

Cocktail Party

Mexican Cheese Cake

Walnut-Glazed Brie

Gorgonzola-Almond Spread

Shrimp Rounds

Simmered Mushrooms

Artichoke Pepper Puffs

Crab Swiss Bites

Festive Chicken and Spinach Cups

Sweet Mustard Kielbasa

Cherry Tomato Poppers

Nuts and Bolts

Sun-dried Tomato Crostini

Cranberry Margaritas

Elegant Picnic

Shrimp and Crab Meat Salad
Pecan Spinach Salad
Cherry Tomato Poppers
Peach Soup
Strawberry Nut Bread with Strawberry Butter
Peach Pecan Pie

Soup Supper

Sheeba's Potato Soup
Broccoli Chicken Soup
White Chili
Parmesan Corn Bread
Three Cheese Round with Crackers
Baked Bread Bowl Dip
Caramel Pecan Cheesecake
Candied Orange Cake
Chocolate Almond Pie
Cardinal Bowl

Brunch

Crispy Sweet Potato Pancakes with Cilantro Sauce
Gruyère Grits
Green Salad with Curried Fruit
White Chocolate Macadamia Nut Sticky Buns
Mimosas

"When I was a little girl, Nan, my grandmother, got me involved in volunteer work. She was always so involved in the community, I remember watching her get all dressed up for evening galas, balls and benefits.
That's what I love about our Cincinnati - our sense of community, commitment and volunteerism."

Judy Dalambakis
Cincinnati Post Columnist - OUR TOWN

Bengal Brunch Buffet

McGill Masterpiece Casserole

Hash Brown Pepper Bake

Slow Cooker Goetta

Gruyère Grits

Macadamia Nut French Toast

Heavenly Butterscotch Rolls

Apple Coffee Cake

Sunshine Fruit

Raspberry Scrub

"Judy, my wife, and I met at the University of Cincinnati when we were students. There was a time when Judy worked in Admissions and I worked for the Alumni Association. We used to organize joint events in distant towns that would introduce prospective students to UC and area alumni. What always brought the alumni out? That local Cincinnati fare - Skyline Chili and Graeter's ice cream. We would ship very large blocks of frozen Cincinnati chili and French Pot ice cream. It was always a ton of work, and messy at times, but our famous and unique local fare was always a sure draw for out-of-town alums of all ages."

Chris Dalambakis
Cincinnati Fire
Museum
Board Member

After the Theatre

Seafood Stuffed Shells

The Palace's Grilled Shrimp Salad

Broccoli and Baby Carrots

Mushrooms Florentine

Tarragon Bread Sticks

Caramel Pecan Cheesecake

Champura "Mexican Chocolate"

Super Bowl Party

Lasagna Rollups

Caesar Green Beans

Green Salad with Sandy's Favorite Dressing

Smoked Mozzarella Red Pepper Muffins

Crunchy Ice Cream Dessert

DESSERTS... *The Final Curtain*

The Aronoff Center for the Arts
Photograph by J. Miles Wolf

"My fondest political memory is the opening of the downtown arts center that now bears my name. It was the culmination of 36 years of public service, and I believe a catalyst for new downtown energy."

Stanley J. Aronoff
Former Ohio State
Senate President

Caramel Apple Walnut Squares

1¾ cups all-purpose flour
1 cup quick-cooked oats
½ cup firmly packed brown
  sugar
½ teaspoon baking soda
½ teaspoon salt
1 cup margarine

1 cup chopped walnuts
20 caramels
1 (14 ounce) can sweetened
  condensed milk
1 (21 ounce) can apple pie
  filling

- In large mixing bowl, combine flour, oats, brown sugar, soda and salt. Cut in margarine until crumb consistency.

- Reserving 1½ cups crumbs, press remainder in 13x9x2-inch baking pan.

- Bake at 375 degrees for 15 minutes.

- Combine caramels and condensed milk in heavy saucepan. Cook over low heat until caramels are melted and mixture is smooth.

- Spoon pie filling on partially baked crust. Spread caramel sauce on apples and sprinkle with reserved crumbs mixed with walnuts.

- Bake for 20 minutes.

- Serves 12.

Delicious served with scoops of ice cream.

"I don't care if its theatre. Or if its music, painting, ballet, opera. Just fall in love with art. Because I think it helps one's life. Art makes us human."

Ed Stern
Director, **Playhouse
in the Park**
The Cincinnati
Enquirer

Berry Cobbler

 Try it accompanied with vanilla ice cream or fresh cream.

¼ cup butter, melted	2 cups whole milk
2 cups all-purpose flour	4 cups fresh blueberries
2¾ cups sugar, divided	4 cups fresh raspberries
1 tablespoon plus 1 teaspoon baking powder	4 cups fresh blackberries
½ teaspoon salt	4 cups strawberries, stemmed and sliced
½ teaspoon nutmeg	

- Melt butter in 4-quart casserole.

- In mixing bowl, combine flour, 2 cups sugar, baking powder, salt and nutmeg. Stir in milk.

- Pour batter on butter in casserole; do not stir. Add berries without stirring. Sprinkle remaining ¾ cup sugar on berries.

- Bake at 400 degrees for 50 to 55 minutes; batter will rise to form crust. If not adequately browned, broil for 1 or 2 minutes.

- Serves 12.

 # Blueberry Buckle

2⅓ cups sifted all-purpose flour, divided	1 egg
2 teaspoons baking powder	½ cup milk
½ teaspoon salt	2 cups blueberries, well drained
1¼ cups sugar, divided	½ teaspoon cinnamon
¼ cup vegetable shortening	¼ cup butter, softened

- Sift 2 cups flour, baking powder and salt together.

- In mixing bowl, cream ¾ cup sugar, shortening and egg together until smooth. Blend in milk, add dry ingredients and fold in blueberries.

- Spread batter in greased and floured 9x9x2-inch baking pan.

- Combine remaining ½ cup sugar with ⅓ cup flour and cinnamon. Cut in butter to form crumb consistency. Sprinkle on batter.

- Bake at 375 degrees for 45 to 50 minutes or until wooden pick inserted near center comes out clean. Serve warm.

- Serves 9.

Blackberry Dream

 Especially good when blackberries are in season.

1 ¾ cups vanilla wafer crumbs,
    divided
2 eggs, separated
1 cup powdered sugar
½ cup butter, softened
¾ cup chopped pecans, divided

2 cups fresh blackberries
    or raspberries
½ cup sugar
1 cup whipping cream,
    whipped

- Prepare dessert the day before serving.

- Sprinkle 1 cup crumbs evenly in 9x9x2-inch baking pan.

- Beat egg whites until stiff and set aside. Beat egg yolks.

- Cream powdered sugar with butter until smooth. Blend in yolks. Fold in egg whites.

- Spread mixture over crumbs in pan and sprinkle with ½ cup pecans.

- Lightly crush berries with sugar and spoon over pecans. Spread whipped cream on berries and sprinkle with remaining ¼ cup nuts mixed with reserved crumbs. Chill for 12 hours.

- Serves 12 to 16.

Big Dave's Bread Pudding with Bourbon Sauce

Pudding

1 loaf French bread
4 cups milk
2½ cups sugar
3 eggs, beaten

2 tablespoons vanilla
1 cup raisins, optional
¼ cup butter, melted

Sauce

½ cup butter
1 cup powdered sugar
1 egg yolk, beaten

1 (5 ounce) can evaporated milk
3 tablespoons bourbon

- Soak bread in milk, crushing to mix thoroughly. Add sugar, eggs, vanilla and raisins, mixing well.

- Pour melted butter into 2-quart casserole. Add bread mixture.

- Bake at 350 degrees until firm.

- While pudding is baking, prepare sauce. Combine butter, powdered sugar, egg yolk and evaporated milk in top of double boiler. Cook over simmering water until thickened. Remove from heat and stir in bourbon.

- Serve sauce over warm pudding.

- Serves 6 to 8.

Miracle Cheesecake Dessert

 The recipe is much lighter in texture than expected.
It is very refreshing and lemon flavored.

Cheesecake

1 (12 ounce) can evaporated milk

1 (3 ounce) package lemon gelatin

1 cup boiling water

3 tablespoons freshly squeezed, strained lemon juice

1 (8 ounce) or 3 (3 ounce) packages cream cheese, softened

1 scant cup sugar

1 teaspoon vanilla

Glaze

1 (10 ounce) package frozen strawberries or raspberries in light syrup, thawed and with juice

2 teaspoons cornstarch

- Pour evaporated milk into mixing bowl and place, with beaters, in freezer until ice crystals form. Beat until peaks form the consistency of whipped cream. Keep cold.

- Dissolve gelatin in boiling water. Let stand until cool. Add lemon juice.

- Beat cream cheese with sugar and vanilla until smooth and creamy. Stir in gelatin and fold in whipped milk.

- Spread mixture in 13x9x2-inch baking dish. Chill until firm.

- Prepare glaze. Drain berries, reserving juice. Combine juice and cornstarch in saucepan and cook, stirring constantly, over low heat until mixture boils. Cook for 1 minute, stirring constantly. Cool sauce, add berries and chill. Spread glaze on cheesecake.

- Serves 12.

If crust is preferred, combine ⅔ cup graham cracker crumbs with ½ cup melted butter. Press in bottom of baking dish. Spread gelatin mixture on crumb layer.

Traditions

Aglamesis Brothers Ice Cream Parlor and Confectionery in Oakley is an old fashioned parlor started by Greek immigrants Thomas and Nicholas Aglamesis, famous for their ice cream and candy.

"Every Friday, after Mrs. Potts' dancing class, we would go to Aglamesis. I was in fifth or sixth grade at the time. And every Friday, Mr. Aglamesis would wait on us. I always got a hot fudge sundae with vanilla ice cream.

Carol Krone Philpott
Owner of The Kiln

Suzie, the only trained gorilla in America lived in her very own apartment at the Cincinnati Zoo. She ate with a spoon and fork, always offering her trainer William Dressman a bite of her sweet dessert.

Cherry Walnut Torte

2¼ cups all-purpose flour, divided
¼ cup plus 1 tablespoon powdered sugar
1 cup butter, softened
2 eggs
1 cup sugar
¼ teaspoon baking powder

pinch of salt
1 teaspoon vanilla
1 (16 ounce) can pitted tart cherries, well-drained
¾ cup coarsely chopped walnuts
powdered sugar

- Prepare crust by blending 2 cups flour, powdered sugar and butter. Press dough in bottom and along sides of 10-inch pie plate.

- Bake at 350 degrees for 20 minutes; crust along sides may slide to bottom of plate. Let stand to cool. Reduce oven temperature to 325 degrees.

- In mixing bowl, beat eggs, vanilla and sugar until thick and frothy. Add remaining ¼ cup flour, baking powder and salt, mixing well. Fold in cherries and walnuts.

- Pour batter into partially baked crust.

- Bake for 40 minutes. Cool, then dust with powdered sugar.

- Serves 6 to 8.

Coffee Soufflé

1½ cups coffee
1 tablespoon unflavored gelatin
⅔ cup sugar, divided
½ cup milk

3 eggs, separated
¼ teaspoon salt
½ teaspoon vanilla
whipped cream

- Combine coffee, gelatin, ⅓ cup sugar and milk in top of double boiler.

- Lightly beat egg yolks. Mix with remaining ⅓ cup sugar and salt and add to liquid in double boiler, mixing well. Cook over simmering water until thickened and smooth.

- Beat egg whites with vanilla. Fold into cooked sauce.

- Pour mixture into mold. Chill until firm. Serve with dollops of whipped cream.

- Serves 6.

Crunchy Ice Cream Dessert

Dessert
½ gallon vanilla ice cream
¼ cup butter
½ cup firmly packed brown
   sugar

2 cups crisp rice cereal
   squares
⅔ cup chopped pecans
⅔ cup flaked coconut

Sauce
1 (6 ounce) package semisweet
   chocolate chips
1 (14 ounce) can sweetened
   condensed milk

1 (7 ounce) jar marshmallow
   creme

- Prepare dessert the day before serving.

- Place ice cream in large bowl and soften at room temperature for 2 hours.

- Melt butter with brown sugar in skillet over medium heat, stirring constantly. Remove from heat.

- Add cereal, pecans and coconut to skillet, mixing well.

- Press ½ of cereal mixture into 13x9x2-inch baking pan. Spread ice cream on cereal layer and top with remaining cereal mixture. Freeze overnight.

- Prepare sauce by melting chocolate chips in top of double boiler over simmering water. Stir in condensed milk and marshmallow creme, heating and stirring until well blended.

- To serve, cut ice cream into squares and top with hot fudge sauce.

- Serves 15.

"Ballet serves as a standard for grace, order and beauty - connecting us to the past, even as the art form stretches to embrace and reflect today's ideas and our vision of the future.

Ballet can tell a story, fascinate and entertain observers; it can also inspire. A human soul and many years of physical training, imbued with powerful music, remind us that we can go beyond perceived physical limitations. Dance, observed at a high level of excellence, sets an example of great hope for our own potential."

Director Victoria Morgan
Cincinnati Ballet

French Cream Slices

 This is such an elegant dessert and worth the effort.

Crust

⅓ cup butter	1 egg, beaten
¼ cup sugar	1½ cups graham cracker
1 (1 ounce) square semi-sweet chocolate	crumbs
	½ cup chopped walnuts
1 teaspoon vanilla	1 cup flaked coconut

Filling

½ cup butter, softened	2 cups powdered sugar
2 tablespoons instant French vanilla pudding mix	3 tablespoons milk

Topping

2 tablespoons butter	8 (1 ounce) squares sweet chocolate

- Prepare crust by combining butter, sugar and chocolate in top of double boiler. Cook over simmering water until chocolate is melted.

- Blend in vanilla and egg. Simmer for 5 minutes. Stir in cracker crumbs, walnuts and coconut. Remove from heat.

- Press mixture in bottom of 13x9x2-inch baking pan. Chill for 15 minutes.

- Prepare filling by combining butter, pudding mix and powdered sugar. Using electric mixer, beat until creamy. Add milk, beating until light and fluffy.

- Spread filling evenly on chilled crust. Chill for additional 15 minutes.

- Prepare topping by melting butter with chocolate in top of double boiler. Cook over simmering water, stirring until well blended.

- Spread chocolate over filling. Chill for additional 30 minutes or until ready to serve.

- Serves 12.

Orange Marmalade Soufflé

3 eggs, separated	¾ cup powdered sugar
3 tablespoons sugar	1 cup whipping cream,
3 tablespoon orange	whipped
marmalade	1 teaspoon vanilla
1 teaspoon orange extract or	1 to 2 tablespoons brandy
frozen orange juice	1 (2 ounce) package slivered
concentrate	almonds, toasted

- Using electric mixer, beat egg whites until stiff. Gradually beat in sugar and add marmalade and extract.

- Pour mixture into top of double boiler. Cook over simmering water for 5 minutes. Cover tightly and do not remove lid.

- Beat egg yolks until light. Beat in powdered sugar. Fold in whipped cream and add vanilla and brandy.

- Invert soufflé on serving platter. Pour sauce around soufflé and sprinkle with almonds. Warm in oven for a few minutes before serving.

- Serves 6.

*Cincinnati's first opera house opened on March 15, 1859. The Pike Opera house, known for it's elegance was destroyed by a fire only seven years after opening with the opera **Martha**.*

Frozen Peach Delight

1 cup mashed peaches, juice	1 cup whipping cream,
drained	whipped
1 cup sugar	1 cup coarse macaroon
1 tablespoon fresh lemon juice	crumbs

- In small mixing bowl, combine peaches, sugar and lemon juice, Fold in whipped cream.

- Place ½ of macaroon crumbs in bottom of 1-quart casserole. Spoon peach mixture on crumbs and top with remaining crumbs.

- Freeze until firm. Cut in wedges or squares to serve.

- Serves 6 to 8.

Peach Blueberry Crisp

10 fresh peaches, peeled and sliced
2 cups fresh blueberries
1 cup sugar
1 teaspoon cinnamon

1½ cups all-purpose flour
½ cup firmly packed brown sugar
½ teaspoon salt
½ cup margarine

- Combine peaches, blueberries, sugar and cinnamon. Spread mixture in greased 13x9x2-inch baking pan.

- Combine flour, brown sugar and salt. Cut in margarine until crumb consistency. Sprinkle mixture on fruit.

- Bake at 350 degrees for 1 hour.

- Serves 8 to 10.

Regal Strawberry Pizza

 A dessert fit for a king.

1 (18½ ounce) package yellow cake mix
¼ cup water
2 eggs
½ cup firmly packed brown sugar
1 teaspoon cinnamon, divided
½ cup crushed pecans

1 (8 ounce) package cream cheese, softened
½ teaspoon vanilla
½ cup sugar
1 quart fresh strawberries, sliced
1 (8 ounce) jar strawberry preserves
Cointreau liqueur

- In large mixing bowl, combine cake mix, water, eggs, brown sugar, ½ teaspoon cinnamon and pecans, mixing well. Divide mixture between 2 foil-lined pizza pans, pressing to form crust.

- Bake at 350 degrees for 20 minutes. Let stand until cool and peel foil from crusts.

- Using electric mixer, combine cream cheese, vanilla, sugar and remaining ½ teaspoon cinnamon, beating until creamy. Spread on cooled crusts.

- Arrange strawberries on cream cheese layer.

- Warm preserves in saucepan. Add enough Cointreau to thin to desired consistency and pour over berries.

- Serves 16 to 20.

Frozen Raspberry Squares

1 cup all-purpose flour
¼ cup firmly packed brown
    sugar
½ cup chopped pecans
½ cup butter, melted

2 egg whites
1 cup sugar
2 cups fresh raspberries
2 tablespoons lemon juice
1 cup whipped cream

- In mixing bowl, combine flour, brown sugar, pecans and butter, mixing until crumb consistency. Spread in 13x9x2-inch baking pan.

- Bake at 350 degrees for 20 minutes, stirring occasionally. Remove from oven. Reserving ⅓ of crumbs, press remainder in bottom of baking pan and set aside.

- In large mixing bowl, combine egg whites, sugar, raspberries and lemon juice. Using electric mixer at high speed, beat for about 10 minutes or until stiff. Fold in whipped cream.

- Spread batter over crumb-lined pan and sprinkle top with reserved crumbs.

- Freeze for 6 hours or overnight.

- Serves 12 to 16.

Strawberries Royale

1½ quarts fresh strawberries,
    sliced or quartered
¼ cup Kirsch
1 (10 ounce) package frozen
    raspberries, thawed

1 cup whipping cream or
    1 cup sour cream
1 tablespoon brown sugar

- Toss strawberries with Kirsch.

- In blender, puree raspberries with juice. Pour over strawberries and toss lightly to mix. Chill for at least 2 hours.

- Combine whipped cream or sour cream with brown sugar.

- Serve fruit in sherbet or parfait glasses, topped with dollop of sweetened cream.

- Serves 8.

"**Enjoy the Arts** has all the ingredients for students of any age to get free and discounted tickets to Cincinnati's arts events. It's the ticket for symphony, opera, ballet, the Broadway Series, the Playhouse in the Park and the visual arts. Call 621-4700."

Director Lisa Mullins
Enjoy the Arts

Fresh Fruit Brûlée

½ pound fresh strawberries, sliced
¼ pound seedless grapes, sliced
1 fresh peach, peeled and sliced

1 cup half and half
¾ cup firmly packed light brown sugar
fresh mint sprigs for garnish

- Arrange strawberries, grapes and peaches in 1-quart casserole.

- Spoon half and half over fruit. Chill for at least 1 hour.

- Sprinkle brown sugar over half and half, smoothing surface.

- Broil for 1 to 2 minutes or until sugar has caramelized.

- Garnish with mint.

- Serves 4.

  # Foolproof Vanilla Taffy

 This old fashioned treat is fun for the whole family.

3 cups sugar
2 cups less 2 tablespoons light corn syrup

1 cup water
2 tablespoons butter
1 teaspoon vanilla

- In heavy 3-quart saucepan with buttered sides, combine sugar, corn syrup and water. Stir with wooden spoon until sugar is dissolved.

- Bring to a boil over medium-high heat, stirring as little as possible: do not scrape pan sides above sugar mixture to prevent sugar crystals but wipe off any crystals. Cook to hard ball stage, 256 degrees on candy thermometer.

- Stir in butter and cook just to 262 degrees. Remove from heat. Pour into buttered chilled shallow pan or platter. With heavy spatula turn edges to center for even cooling.

- As taffy cools, make several cuts on surface. Add vanilla. When cool enough to handle, pull with buttered finger tips and thumbs until taffy changes to shiny ribbon. If too cool, warm in oven for a few minutes.

- Using buttered scissors, cut into bite-sized pieces. Cool and wrap individually in wax paper. Store in airtight containers.

- Makes 2½ pounds.

For cinnamon taffy, add 6 to 8 drops oil of cinnamon while taffy is cooling, kneading taffy with spatula. Red food coloring may also be added to cooking mixture.

Nadelman Legacy Strudel

Ben Nadelman's mother made the best strudel on the face of the earth. She taught Ben how to make it. He didn't want the recipe lost so he taught it to Brenda Benzar Butler. Ben has since died but his mom's recipe lives on!

1 (12 ounce) jar apricot preserves	6 cups all-purpose flour, divided
1 (12 ounce) jar raspberry preserves	1 cup vegetable oil, divided
1 (12 ounce) jar strawberry preserves	2⅔ cup boiling water, divided
2 tablespoons lemon juice	6 cups chopped walnuts, divided
1 cup instant tapioca	6 cups raisins, divided
	cinnamon sugar

- Begin preparation of strudel the day before serving.

- Combine apricot, raspberry and strawberry preserves, lemon juice and tapioca in bowl, blending well. Chill overnight.

- On day of serving, prepare dough in 4 batches. For each, blend 1½ cups flour, ¼ cup oil and ⅔ cup boiling water, mixing with fork until well blended. Roll into ball.

- Divide 1 ball into 3 equal portions, then add 1 of the portions to each of the remaining 3 balls. Divide each of 3 balls into 2 portions, making 6 balls of dough.

- On lightly floured surface, roll out each ball to form 12-inch square, keeping surfaces well-floured.

- Spread portion of preserve mixture on each, leaving 1-inch margin around edges. Sprinkle 1 cup raisins and 1 cup walnuts on each square. Roll up, press ends to seal and place on oiled 15x10x1-inch jelly roll pan. Cut slits at 1-inch intervals across width of each roll.

- Bake at 400 degrees for 20 minutes or until golden brown. Sprinkle generously with cinnamon sugar. Cut warm strudel in slices along steam vents.

- Serves 30 to 36.

"Cooking with jam is a wonderful process, because jam has no cholesterol, it has no fat. All it has is carbohydrates, and relatively small amounts of that. There's twelve grams of sugar per tablespoon. There's an incredible flavor to it, and it makes a great alternative to high fat, high cholesterol products. Is it used at dinner? Unquestionably, you'll see great recipes using it for green beans, using it on swordfish, using it on flank steak. Many people use it on waffles and pancakes. I grew up eating it on French Toast. It's great for making ice cream, or as a topping on ice cream."

Dan Cohen
Clearbrook Farms

 Fresh Apple Cake

 *Great autumn dessert.*

Cake

3 cups all-purpose flour	3 cups chopped unpeeled
1½ teaspoons baking soda	apples
1½ teaspoon salt	1 teaspoon vanilla
2 cups sugar	1 cup chopped walnuts or
1 cup vegetable oil	pecans
2 eggs	

Frosting

1 cup powdered sugar	¼ teaspoon salt
juice of lemon	

- Combine flour, baking soda and salt.

- In large mixing bowl, cream sugar with oil until smooth. Beat in eggs.

- Add dry ingredients to egg mixture, mixing well. Stir in apples, vanilla and walnuts or pecans.

- Spread batter in greased and floured 10-inch tube or fluted tube pan.

- Bake at 350 degrees for 1 hour and 10 minutes.

- While cake is baking, preparing frosting. Beat powdered sugar, lemon juice and salt together until smooth.

- Cool cake in pan for 10 minutes, invert on serving plate and spread with frosting.

- Serves 12.

Taffy Apple Pound Cake

 Make this cake each year after picking apples at Rouster's orchard. This is a wonderful autumn cake.

16 light caramel candies	**1½ cups butter, softened**
3¼ cups all-purpose flour	**1 tablespoon vanilla**
2 teaspoons cinnamon	**6 eggs**
1 teaspoon allspice	**1½ cups coarsely chopped**
4½ cups powdered sugar	** peeled apples**

• Cut each caramel into 8 bits and set aside.

• Sift flour, cinnamon and allspice.

• In large mixing bowl and using electric mixer, beat powdered sugar with butter and vanilla for 3 minutes or until light and fluffy. Add eggs, 1 at a time, beating well after each addition.

• Gradually add dry ingredients to egg mixture, mixing well. Fold in apples and caramels.

• Spread batter in greased and floured 12-cup fluted tube pan.

• Bake at 325 for 1¼ to 1½ hours, checking after 1 hour. Cool in pan for 10 minutes, then invert on serving plate.

• Serves 16.

"The resiliency and power of human muscle comes down to what you eat, how you exercise, and what genes you have inherited. Nutrition is important to dancers because without it we cannot create our art. The quality and quantity of our 'fuel' directly impacts the potential of our movement, water being a top fuel source. I would personally like to recommend a little chocolate everyday."

Director Victoria Morgan
Cincinnati Ballet

Apricot Cake

Cake

1 (18½ ounce) yellow cake mix	1 cup apricot nectar
1 tablespoon sugar	4 eggs, beaten
¾ cup vegetable oil	1 teaspoon fresh lemon juice
	1 cup diced dried apricots

Glaze

1⅓ cups powdered sugar	apricot nectar
¼ cup plus 1 tablespoon	

- In large mixing bowl, combine cake mix, sugar, oil, nectar, eggs and lemon juice, mixing well. Fold in apricots.

- Spread batter in greased and floured 10-inch fluted tube pan.

- Bake at 325 degrees for 1 hour.

- While cake is baking, prepare glaze. Beat powdered sugar and nectar until smooth.

- Using wooden pick, poke holes in top of warm cake in pan. Pour glaze over cake and let stand until cool.

- Serves 12 to 16.

A 16-ounce can of apricots can be pureed and used instead of nectar. Extra nectar can be drizzled over cake. Cake can be garnished with fresh or dried apricot halves.

Jam Cake

Cake

3½ cups all-purpose flour
1 teaspoon ground cloves
1 teaspoon cinnamon
2 teaspoons baking soda
1 cup buttermilk

2 cups sugar
1 cup butter, softened
2 eggs
2 cups blackberries

Frosting

2 cups sugar
4 cups firmly packed brown
  sugar
1 cup milk

1 cup evaporated milk
¼ cup butter
1 teaspoon vanilla

- Combine flour, cloves and cinnamon.

- Blend baking soda and buttermilk.

- In large mixing bowl, cream sugar and butter together until smooth. Add eggs, 1 at a time, beating after each addition.

- Fold blackberries into creamed mixture. Alternately add dry ingredients and buttermilk to blackberry mixture.

- Spread batter in 3 greased and floured 9-inch round baking pans.

- Bake at 350 degrees for 30 minutes.

- While cake is baking, prepare frosting. Combine sugar, brown sugar, milk and evaporated milk in saucepan. Cook over medium heat, stirring constantly, until soft ball forms when dropped in water. Stir in butter and vanilla. Let stand until lukewarm, then beat until smooth.

- Cool cakes in pans for 5 minutes, then cool on wire rack. Spread frosting on cake layers, stack and frost all of cake.

- Serves 12 to 16.

> *"A steamboat is as beautiful as a wedding cake-but without the complications."*
>
> *Mark Twain*

Brownie Nut Cake

 Sinfully delicious.

Cake

1½ cups sifted cake flour	⅓ cup shortening
1¼ cups sugar	¾ cup milk, divided
2 teaspoons baking powder	2 eggs
¾ teaspoon salt	½ cup chopped pecans
¼ cup plus 2 tablespoons sifted cocoa	

Frosting

1 cup sugar	½ cup milk
¼ cup plus 2 tablespoons butter or margarine	½ teaspoon vanilla

- In large mixing bowl, sift cake flour, sugar, baking powder, salt and cocoa together.

- Add shortening and ½ cup milk to dry ingredients. Using electric mixer, beat for 2 minutes. Add eggs and remaining ¼ cup milk, beating for 2 minutes. Fold in pecans.

- Spread batter in greased and floured 9x9x2-inch baking pan.

- Bake at 350 degrees for 30 to 35 minutes.

- While cake is baking, prepare frosting. Cream sugar with butter or margarine in saucepan until smooth. Cook over low heat until sugar is caramelized and very light brown. Add milk and cook until soft ball forms in cold water. Beat until creamy. Stir in vanilla.

- Cool cake in pan. Spread frosting on cake.

- Serves 9.

White Chocolate Cake

Cake

¼ pound white chocolate	4 eggs
2½ cups cake flour	1 cup buttermilk
1 teaspoon baking powder	1 teaspoon vanilla
¼ teaspoon salt	1 cup chopped pecans
2 cups sugar	1 cup flaked coconut
1 cup butter or margarine, softened	

Frosting

1 cup sugar	⅛ teaspoon salt
½ cup margarine	½ teaspoon vanilla
½ (8 ounce) can sweetened condensed milk	

- Melt white chocolate in double boiler over hot water or using microwave method. Set aside to cool slightly.

- Sift flour, baking powder and salt together.

- In large mixing bowl, cream sugar with butter or margarine until light. Stir in melted chocolate. Add eggs, 1 at a time, beating well after each addition.

- Alternately add dry ingredients and buttermilk to egg mixture, beating after each addition. Stir in vanilla, pecans and coconut.

- Spread batter in greased and floured 13x9x2-inch baking pan.

- Bake at 350 degrees for about 50 minutes.

- While cake is baking, prepare frosting. Combine sugar, margarine, milk, salt and vanilla in saucepan. Let stand for 1 hour, stirring occasionally. Cook until soft ball forms in cold water. Cool to lukewarm, then beat until spreading consistency.

- Cool cake in pan. Spread frosting on cake.

- Serves 16 to 20.

Coconut Pound Cake

3 cups sugar
½ cup vegetable shortening
  or sour cream
1 cup butter
6 eggs
3 cups all-purpose flour

1 cup milk
1 cup flaked coconut, divided
½ teaspoon almond flavoring,
  optional
1½ teaspoons coconut
  flavoring

- In large mixing bowl, cream sugar with shortening or sour cream and butter until fluffy.

- Add eggs, 1 at a time, beating well after each addition.

- Alternately add flour and milk to egg mixture, beating after each addition. Stir in ¾ cup coconut, almond and coconut flavoring, beating well.

- Grease 10-inch tube pan and line bottom with wax paper. Spread batter in pan and sprinkle with remaining ¼ cup coconut.

- Bake at 350 degrees for 1 hour and 40 minutes or until wooden pick inserted near center comes out clean.

- Cool in pan for 5 minutes, then invert on wire rack or serving plate.

- Serves 16.

Candied Orange Cake

*"My grandmother made this cake for all of
the holidays. The memories of this cake still bring a
smile to all our faces."*
-Cynthia J. Stanford, Cookbook Chairman

Cake
3½ cups all-purpose flour
½ teaspoon salt
**1 (16 ounce) package orange
  slice candy**
**1 (8 ounce) package pitted
  dates, chopped**
2 cups chopped walnuts

**1 (3½ ounce) can flaked
  coconut**
1 cup butter, softened
2 cups sugar
4 eggs
1 teaspoon baking soda
½ cup buttermilk

Sauce
1¼ cups orange juice

2 cups powdered sugar

- Sift flour and salt together.

- Cut candy slices into ½-inch pieces. Place in large mixing bowl with dates, walnuts, coconut and ½ cup flour mixture, gently tossing to mix and coat.

- In mixing bowl and using electric mixer, cream butter until light. Gradually beat in sugar. Add eggs, 1 at a time, beating well after each addition. Stir in candy mixture.

- Combine baking soda and buttermilk. Alternately add liquid and dry ingredients to egg batter, mixing well after each addition.

- Spread batter in greased and floured 10-inch fluted tube pan.

- Bake at 300 degrees for 1¾ hours.

- While cake is baking, prepare sauce. Using electric mixer, beat orange juice and powdered sugar until smooth.

- Using wooden pick, poke holes in surface of hot cake in pan. Pour sauce over cake, cool to room temperature and chill overnight before removing from pan.

- Serves 16.

The Taft Theatre

Geometrical design and classic ornamentation grace the Taft Theatre, the only Greek design theatre in the Greater Cincinnati area. The two-story foyer is flanked by an open balcony mezzanine on three sides and two grand stairways. Ionic pillars and Pompeiian mural paintings decorate the walls and ceiling panels. Inside the auditorium, the deeply coffered organ grille spanning the proscenium is broken by three allegorical mural panels of heroic size.

The uniquely artistic design of the building combined with the convenient downtown location makes the Taft Theatre ideal for a medium sized show, whether it's alternative, country, comedy, gospel, or oldies. The atmosphere varies as much as the talent. While the crowd may be an intimate Broadway audience one evening, the next night may host an energetic rock show.

Caramel Pound Cake

Cake
3 cups sifted all-purpose flour
¼ teaspoon baking soda
½ teaspoon salt
6 eggs, separated
1 cup butter

3 cups sugar
1 cup sour cream
2 teaspoons vanilla, lemon or
    orange extract

Frosting
2 cups sugar
1 cup butter

1 (5 ounce) can evaporated
    milk

• Sift flour, baking soda and salt together 3 times.

• Using electric mixer, beat egg whites until stiff peaks form. Set aside.

• In large mixing bowl, beat butter until light yellow. Gradually add sugar and beat until fluffy. Add egg yolks, 1 at a time, beating just until incorporated.

• Alternately add dry ingredients and sour cream to egg mixture, beginning and ending with flour mixture.

• Fold in egg whites and flavoring.

• Spread batter in greased and floured 10-inch fluted tube pan or angel food cake pan.

• Bake at 300 degrees for 1½ hours or until done.

• While cake is baking, prepare frosting. In large iron skillet over medium heat, stir sugar until lightly browned and forming crystals. Add butter and continue stirring until butter is melted.

• Add milk and cook, stirring constantly, until soft ball forms in cold water. If crystals remain, pour through strainer and set aside to cool.

• Cool cake in pan for 10 minutes, then invert on wire rack to complete cooling before frosting.

• Cut cold cake into 3 layers. Spread frosting on layers and stack, spreading on top and sides.

• Serves 12 to 16.

Cake is not particularly attractive but has excellent flavor. It is best made a day before serving and kept tightly covered at room temperature.

Autumn Pumpkin Cake

Cake

1 (18½ ounce) package yellow
   cake mix
¾ stick butter, melted
4 eggs, divided
4 cups canned pumpkin
1 cup firmly-packed brown
   sugar

½ teaspoon salt
1 tablespoon cinnamon
2 teaspoons pumpkin pie spice
1 (13 ounce) can sweetened
   condensed milk
2½ teaspoons vanilla

Crumb Topping

½ cup firmly-packed brown
   sugar
¾ stick butter

1 teaspoon cinnamon
1 cup chopped nuts

Topping

1 (8 ounce) carton frozen
   whipped topping, thawed
1 teaspoon vanilla

2 tablespoons brown sugar
1 teaspoon cinnamon

- Reserving 1 cup cake mix for crumb topping, mix remaining cake mix with melted butter and 1 egg until crumbly. Press mixture in bottom of greased 13x9x2-inch baking pan.

- In mixing bowl, combine pumpkin, brown sugar, salt, cinnamon, remaining eggs, pumpkin pie spice, condensed milk and vanilla, beating well. Pour into prepared pan.

- Prepare crumb topping by mixing reserved cake mix, brown sugar, butter, cinnamon and nuts. Sprinkle over batter.

- Bake at 350 degrees for 1 hour or until done.

- Cool in pan until room temperature, then store in refrigerator.

- Prepare topping by mixing whipped topping, vanilla, brown sugar and cinnamon together. Serve dollops of topping on slices of cake.

- Serves 16 to 20.

Poppy Seed Cake with Almond Filling

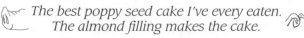 *The best poppy seed cake I've every eaten. The almond filling makes the cake.*

Cake

¾ **cup poppy seeds**	2 **teaspoons baking powder**
¾ **cup water**	1½ **cups sugar**
½ **cup instant nonfat dry milk**	¾ **cup butter, softened**
2 **cups sifted flour**	4 **egg whites, stiffly beaten**

Filling

½ **cup instant nonfat dry milk**	1½ **cups water**
2 **tablespoons cornstarch**	4 **egg yolks, lightly beaten**
¾ **cup sugar**	1 **teaspoon almond extract**

- Soak poppy seeds in water for 2 hours.

- Sift dry milk, flour and baking powder together.

- In large mixing bowl, cream butter and sugar together until light and fluffy.

- Alternately add dry ingredients and poppy seeds with liquid to creamed mixture, beginning and ending with dry ingredients and beating well after each addition.

- Fold in egg whites.

- Spread batter in 2 greased and floured 8-inch round baking pans.

- Bake at 350 degrees for 30 minutes or until surface springs back when lightly touched with fingertip.

- While cake is baking, prepare filling. Combine dry milk, cornstarch and sugar in saucepan. Gradually blend in mixture of water and egg yolks, mixing until smooth. Cook over medium heat, stirring frequently, until thickened and smooth; reduce heat and cook for additional 1 minute. Remove from heat and stir in almond flavoring.

- Cool cake in pans for 5 minutes, then invert on wire rack to complete cooling. Spread cooled frosting between layers and on top and sides of cake.

- Serves 12.

Whiskey Cake

Cake

1 (18½ ounce) package yellow
cake mix
1 (3¼ ounce) package instant
vanilla pudding mix
4 eggs

½ cup water
½ cup vegetable oil
½ cup bourbon or rum
1 cup chopped nuts

Glaze

½ cup bourbon
½ cup butter

½ cup sugar

- In large mixing bowl, combine cake mix and pudding mix. Stir in eggs, water, oil, bourbon or rum and nuts. Using electric mixer, beat for 4 minutes.

- Spread batter in greased 10-inch fluted tube pan.

- Bake at 350 degrees for 50 to 55 minutes.

- While cake is baking, prepare glaze. Combine bourbon, butter and sugar in saucepan. Bring to a boil and cook until sugar is dissolved.

- Cool cake in pan for 10 minutes, then invert on wire rack to complete cooling. Drizzle glaze over cake.

- Serves 12 to 16.

What's the Land Worth?

A Virginian first owned Covington, Kentucky, but swapped it for a keg of whiskey, the second owner exchanged it for a quarter of a buffalo, and finally Thomas Kennedy, a ferry operator, bought it for $750. He sold 150 acres to John and Richard Gano, and Thomas Carneal, who started the town.

Caramel Pecan Cheesecake

On a High Note

The Cincinnati Opera is the oldest summer opera festival in the United States. The first performance was **MARTHA** *on June 27, 1920. They are the second oldest opera company in America. The Metropolitan Opera is the oldest. The Cincinnati Opera performs in Music Hall, which is the fourth largest hall in the U.S. Seating capacity in Music Hall is 3427. The only other larger halls are: Metropolitan Opera House and Fargo-Moorhead Civic Opera, Connecticut Opera, and Lyric Opera/Chicago.*

2 cups finely chopped pecans
1¼ cups sugar, divided
¼ cup butter, melted
26 caramels
2 tablespoons sweetened
   condensed milk

4 (8 ounce) packages cream
   cheese, softened
3 eggs
1 tablespoon vanilla

- Wrap a large sheet of aluminum foil around bottom of 9-inch spring form pan.

- Combine pecans, ¼ cup sugar and melted butter, mixing until moistened. Press pecan mixture evenly in bottom of spring form pan.

- Mix caramels and condensed milk in top of double boiler. Heat over simmering water until caramels are melted. Drizzle caramel sauce over pecan crust.

- In large mixing bowl and using electric mixer, beat cream cheese with 1 cup sugar until creamy. Add eggs, 1 at a time, beating after each addition. Stir in vanilla.

- Pour batter into prepared pan.

- Place cheesecake pan in large baking pan with enough hot water to come up the sides of the pan about one inch.

- Cover the cheesecake pan with foil. Bake at 350 degrees until the top of the cheesecake appears dry and no longer moves in the center when the pan shakes, about 1½ hours.

- Remove cheesecake from the water and let cool 2-3 hours.

- Remove foil from around the edge of the pan. Cover and put in the refrigerator overnight.

- Loosen the edges with a knife first when ready to serve and then release the pan.

- Serves 16.

White Chocolate Cheesecake

1½ cups all-purpose flour
½ cup sugar
½ cup butter
1 (16 ounce) package white
   chocolate, divided
½ cup finely chopped
   macadamia nuts, toasted
1 egg, beaten

⅔ cup whipping cream
1 tablespoon vanilla
3 (8 ounce) packages cream
   cheese, softened
1 (14 ounce) can sweetened
   condensed milk
4 eggs

- In mixing bowl, combine flour and sugar. Cut in butter until consistency of coarse crumbs.

- Grate 4 ounces chocolate and add with nuts and beaten egg to crumbs, mixing well.

- Press mixture in bottom and on sides of 10-inch spring form pan. Chill.

- Chop remaining 12 ounces white chocolate. Mix with whipping cream in top of double boiler and cook over simmering water until chocolate is melted. Stir in vanilla. Keep warm.

- Using electric mixer, beat cream cheese with condensed milk until smooth. Add eggs, 1 at a time, beating well after each addition.

- Stir in melted chocolate. Pour batter into prepared pan.

- Bake at 325 degrees for 1 hour and 20 minutes.

- Using knife tip, separate cake from rim of pan but allow to cool before removing rim. Chill overnight. Garnish with chocolate swirls.

- Serves 12 to 16.

☼ *Chocolate Cookie Cheesecake*

Cake
1¼ cups graham cracker crumbs
⅓ cup unsalted butter, melted
¼ cup firmly packed light brown sugar
1 teaspoon cinnamon
4 (8 ounce) packages cream cheese, softened
1½ cups sugar, divided

2 teaspoons all-purpose flour
6 eggs
3 egg yolks
⅓ cup whipping cream
2 teaspoons vanilla, divided
1½ cups chopped creme-filled chocolate sandwich cookies
2 cups sour cream

Glaze
1 cup whipping cream
1 (8 ounce) package semi-sweet chocolate

1 teaspoon vanilla

- Prepare cake the day before serving.

- Blend cracker crumbs, melted butter, brown sugar and cinnamon together, mixing to form moist crumbs. Press mixture in bottom and on sides of 10-inch spring form pan. Chill for about 30 minutes or until firm.

- In large mixing bowl and using electric mixer, beat cream cheese at low speed until smooth. Beat in 1¼ cups sugar and flour until blended.

- Add eggs and yolks, 1 at a time, beating well after each addition. Stir in cream and 1 teaspoon vanilla.

- Pour ½ of batter in prepared pan. Sprinkle with chopped cookies and top with remaining batter, smoothing with spatula.

- Bake at 425 degrees for 15 minutes, reduce oven temperature to 225 degrees and bake for 50 minutes, covering loosely with aluminum foil if browning too quickly.

- Increase oven temperature to 350 degrees. Blend sour cream, remaining ¼ cup sugar and 1 teaspoon vanilla. Spread over cake and bake for additional 7 minutes.

- Place hot cake in refrigerator. Cover with plastic wrap and chill overnight.

- Prepare glaze by scalding cream in heavy saucepan over medium heat. Add chocolate and vanilla, stirring until chocolate is melted. Chill for 10 minutes.

- Place cake on platter and remove rim. Pour glaze over cake. Chill until ready to serve.

- Serves 12 to 16.

Mint Buttercream Frosting with Dark Chocolate Glaze

Frosting
1 (16 ounce) package
   powdered sugar
½ cup butter, softened

⅛ teaspoon salt
1 teaspoon mint extract
3 to 4 tablespoons milk, divided

Glaze
2 (1 ounce) squares
   unsweetened chocolate

2 tablespoons butter

- Prepare frosting by combining ⅓ of powdered sugar with butter and salt in large bowl. Cream until smooth.

- Add mint extract, 2 tablespoons milk and remaining powdered sugar, blending thoroughly. Gradually add remaining milk until spreading consistency.

- Prepare glaze by melting chocolate with butter in top of double boiler over hot water or using microwave method.

- Spread frosting on cake, then drizzle glaze over frosting. To contain glaze on top of cake, pipe frosting scallop at edge or frost and glaze cake in pan.

Tin Roof Sundae Pie

 Every bit as good as your favorite ice cream parlor delight.

1 cup evaporated milk
1 (6 ounce) package semisweet
   chocolate chips
1 cup miniature marshmallows

vanilla wafers
1 quart chocolate chip ice
   cream, softened
peanuts

- In heavy 1-quart saucepan, combine milk, chocolate chips and marshmallows. Cook over low heat, stirring until chocolate and marshmallows are melted and blended; mixture will be thick. Remove from heat and cool to room temperature.

- Line bottom and sides of 9-inch pie plate with vanilla wafers. Spoon ½ of ice cream over wafers. Spread ½ of chocolate sauce on ice cream. Repeat with remaining ice cream and chocolate sauce. Top with peanuts.

- Freeze until firm.

- Serves 8.

Frozen Blackberry Pie

 Good for young cooks-no cooking required!

1 (8 ounce) package cream cheese, softened	½ teaspoon salt
¾ cup sugar	1 teaspoon vanilla
3 eggs, separated	2 (8 ounce) packages frozen blackberries, thawed
1 cup whipping cream, whipped	2 (9 inch) graham cracker crusts

- Prepare at least 24 hours before serving.

- In mixing bowl, combine cream cheese and sugar, beating until creamy. Blend in egg yolks.

- Add whipped cream to egg mixture. Stir in salt and vanilla. Fold in blackberries with juice.

- Beat egg whites until stiff peaks form. Fold into batter and spread in graham cracker crusts.

- Freeze for at least 24 hours.

- Serves 12.

Toffee Bar Pie

20 round buttery crackers, crushed	1 teaspoon vanilla
½ cup chopped pecans	vanilla ice cream
3 egg whites	3 large chocolate-covered toffee candy bars
1 cup sugar	

- Combine cracker crumbs and pecans.

- Beat egg whites until very stiff. Blend in sugar and vanilla. Fold in crumb mixture.

- Spread batter in bottom and along sides of well-greased 9-inch pie plate.

- Bake at 300 degrees for 25 to 30 minutes. Cool to room temperature.

- Fill shell with ice cream. Crumble candy bars and sprinkle on ice cream.

- Freeze until firm. Remove from freezer 15 to 20 minutes before serving.

- Serves 8.

Chocolate Almond Pie

6 chocolate almond candy bars
22 marshmallows
½ cup milk
¼ teaspoon vanilla
¼ teaspoon almond extract
1 cup whipping cream

1 (5½ ounce) package chocolate wafer cookies, crumbled
½ cup butter, softened
unsweetened chocolate curls for garnish, optional

- Combine candy bars, marshmallows, milk, vanilla and almond extract in top of double boiler. Heat over hot water until chocolate and marshmallows are melted. Chill.

- Mix wafer crumbs and butter to form moist crumbs. Press in bottom and along sides of 9-inch pie plate.

- Whip cream until stiff. Fold into cooled chocolate mixture and spread in prepared pie plate.

- Chill until firm. Garnish with chocolate curls.

- Serves 8.

Pie can be prepared the day before serving.

"Fried chicken, pecan pie, angel food cake and chocolate brownies were first served aboard steamboats."

Don Deming
Steamboat Historian

 *Grasshopper Pie*

 It is an old wive's tale of the Greater Cincinnati Airport to eat this treat to ensure smooth flying.

1 (5½ ounce) package
  chocolate wafer cookies,
  crumbled
½ cup sugar, divided
3 tablespoons butter, melted
1½ teaspoons unflavored
  gelatin
¼ cup plus 1 tablespoon cold
  water

1 egg yolk
¼ cup plus 1 tablespoon
  crème de menthe
¼ cup white crème de cacao
2 cups whipped topping
whipped cream
shaved chocolate

- Combine wafer crumbs, ¼ cup sugar and melted butter to form moist crumbs. Press in bottom and along sides of 9-inch pie plate.

- Bake at 450 degrees for 2 to 3 minutes.

- Soften gelatin in cold water in top of double boiler. Dissolve over hot water and remove from heat.

- Beat sugar and egg yolk into gelatin. Add crème de menthe and crème de cacao. Chill until slightly thickened.

- Fold in whipped topping. Spread in prepared pie plate and chill. Garnish with whipped cream and chocolate shavings.

- Serves 6 to 8.

Lemon Ice Cream Pie

2 cups vanilla wafer crumbs
¼ cup chopped pecans
1 teaspoon apple pie spice
freshly ground nutmeg to taste
¼ cup butter, melted

juice of 3 lemons
1 (14 ounce) can non-fat
   sweetened condensed milk
2 cups vanilla ice cream

- Combine crumbs, pecans, apple pie spice and nutmeg. Add butter, stirring until crumbs are well moistened. Press mixture in bottom and along sides of 10-inch pie plate.

- Bake at 350 degrees for 7 to 10 minutes. Cool to room temperature.

- In mixing bowl, combine lemon juice and condensed milk, stirring until thickened and blended.

- Using electric mixer, add ice cream and beat well. Pour mixture into prepared crust.

- Serves 6 to 8.

 ## Kahlúa Pecan Pie

 A change for an old favorite.

¾ cup sugar
¼ cup butter, softened
1 teaspoon vanilla
2 tablespoon all-purpose flour
3 eggs
½ cup plus 1 teaspoon Kahlúa
½ cup dark corn syrup
¾ cup evaporated milk

1 cup whole or chopped
   pecans
1 unbaked 9-inch pastry shell,
   chilled
½ cup whipping cream,
   whipped
pecan halves

- In mixing bowl, combine sugar, butter, vanilla and flour, mixing well. Add eggs, 1 at a time, beating well after each addition.

- Stir in Kahlúa, syrup, evaporated milk and 1 cup pecans, mixing thoroughly. Spread batter in chilled pastry shell.

- Bake at 400 degrees for 10 minutes, then reduce oven temperature to 325 degrees and bake an additional 40 minutes or until firm.

- Chill pie. Just before serving, garnish with whipped cream and pecan halves.

- Serves 6 to 8.

Lemon Blueberry Sour Cream Pie

 A different and delicious combination.

1 cup plus 2 tablespoons sugar, divided	¼ cup lemon juice
3 tablespoons cornstarch	¼ cup grated lemon peel
dash of salt	1 cup sour cream
1 cup milk	1 cup fresh blueberries
3 eggs, separated	1 baked 9-inch pastry shell
4 tablespoons butter	¼ teaspoon cream of tartar
	½ teaspoon vanilla

- In saucepan, combine ¾ cup sugar, cornstarch and salt. Gradually blend in milk and cook over medium heat, stirring constantly, until boiling and very thickened. Remove from heat.

- Slightly beat egg yolks. Add small amount of custard to egg yolks, then add warmed egg yolk mixture to custard and cook for 2 minutes, stirring constantly.

- Stir in butter, lemon juice and peel. Remove from heat and cool.

- Fold in sour cream. Add blueberries. Spread filling in pastry shell.

- Beat egg whites with remaining ¼ cup plus 2 tablespoons sugar, cream of tartar and vanilla until stiff peaks form. Spread over pie filling.

- Bake at 350 degrees for 12 to 15 minutes.

- Serves 6 to 8.

Cincinnati Skyline

Peach Pecan Pie

 A nice twist that makes grandma's old favorite even more delicious.

3 egg whites	**½ cup chopped pecans**
2 cups sugar, divided	**1 teaspoon vanilla**
12 saltine crackers, rolled to fine crumbs	**4 cups sliced fresh peaches**
½ teaspoon baking powder	**1 cup pecan halves**
	1 cup whipping cream

- In mixing bowl and using electric mixer, beat egg whites until stiff. Gradually add 1 cup sugar, beating constantly.

- Add cracker crumbs, baking powder, chopped pecans and vanilla, mixing well.

- Press mixture in bottom and along sides of buttered 9-inch pie plate.

- Bake at 325 degrees for 30 minutes. Crust will rise while baking and fall while cooling. Let stand until cool.

- Combine peaches and remaining 1 cup sugar, tossing to coat thoroughly. Spoon peaches into baked crust and sprinkle with pecan halves.

- Using electric mixer, whip cream until stiff peaks form. Spread over peach filling. Serve immediately.

- Serves 6.

"Theatre is a mirror which reflects our lives as they are and how we want them to be."

D. Lynn Meyers
Artistic Director
Ensemble Theatre of
Cincinnati

photograph by J. Miles Wolf

Molasses Pumpkin Pie

1 packet unflavored gelatin
¾ cup firmly packed light brown sugar
½ teaspoon salt
½ teaspoon cinnamon
¼ teaspoon ginger
¼ teaspoon nutmeg
1 cup canned pumpkin
¼ cup molasses

1 (5⅓ ounce) can evaporated milk
3 eggs, separated
1 teaspoon vanilla
¼ cup plus 2 tablespoons sugar
1 baked 10-inch deep crust pastry shell
whipped cream

- In 3-quart heavy saucepan, combine gelatin, brown sugar, salt, cinnamon, ginger and nutmeg. Stir in pumpkin, molasses and evaporated milk.

- Cook over medium heat, stirring constantly, until mixture simmers. Remove from heat.

- Lightly beat egg yolks. Slowly add 2 tablespoons hot pumpkin mixture to yolks, stirring constantly; stir warmed yolks into remaining pumpkin mixture, mixing well.

- Cook over medium-low heat, stirring constantly, for about 3 minutes or until thickened. Stir in vanilla. Chill for about 20 minutes or until mixture mounds softly.

- Beat egg whites until stiff but not dry. Gradually add sugar, beating until very stiff. Fold into pumpkin mixture, mixing just until blended.

- Spread filling in pastry shell. Chill for about 3 hours or until firm. Serve with whipped cream.

- Serves 6.

Praline Pumpkin Pie

 Try this at your next Thanksgiving dinner.

3 tablespoons butter, softened
⅓ cup firmly packed brown
   sugar
⅓ cup chopped pecans
1 unbaked 9-inch pastry shell
3 eggs, lightly beaten
1½ cups canned pumpkin
½ cup sugar

½ cup firmly packed brown
   sugar
1½ teaspoons pumpkin pie
   spice
1 teaspoon salt
1 cup evaporated milk
½ cup water
½ cup whipping cream,
   whipped

- In small mixing bowl, cream butter with ⅓ cup brown sugar until smooth. Stir in pecans. Press mixture in bottom of pastry shell.

- Bake at 450 degrees for 10 minutes. Let stand for 10 minutes to cool. Reduce oven temperature to 350 degrees.

- In mixing bowl, combine eggs, pumpkin, sugar, ½ cup brown sugar, pumpkin pie spice and salt.

- Combine evaporated milk and water and add to pumpkin mixture, beating well. Spread filling in pastry shell.

- Bake at 350 degrees for 50 minutes or until knife tip inserted near center comes out clean. Let cool. Serve cooled pie with whipped cream.

- Serves 6 to 8.

"Not enough people are dancing. Nor should everyone be a dancer. But people - not just children - should be dancing and making dance."

Shawn Womack
Antenna Arts Magazine

Cranberry Pie

 This is a Yankee tradition and a well-kept secret in the North.

¾ **tablespoon cornstarch**	3 **tablespoons unsulfured**
⅓ **cup cold water**	**molasses**
1 **cup boiling water**	1½ **cups sugar**
3 **cups fresh cranberries**	3 **tablespoons butter**
	2 **unbaked 9-inch pastry shells**

- Dissolve cornstarch in cold water. Stir into boiling water in mixing bowl.

- Add cranberries, molasses, sugar and butter to cornstarch liquid, mixing well. Spread batter in 1 pastry shell. Arrange second pastry shell over pie filling, crimp edges and cut slits in top pastry to vent steam.

- Bake at 400 degrees for 40 to 50 minutes or until crust is golden brown. Cool before slicing.

- Serves 6 to 8.

photograph by Helen Adams

COOKIES AND BARS... *Encore*

The Taft Theatre hosts a variety of the performing arts–from Children's Theater and dance recital performances to Broadway Series plays and contemporary rock concerts.

Photograph by Robert A. Flischel

"Ballet serves as a standard for grace, order and beauty connecting us to the past, even as the art form stretches to embrace and reflect today's ideas and our vision of the future."

Director Victoria Morgan
Cincinnati Ballet

Apricot Almond Bars

Crust
½ cup sugar
1 cup butter, softened

½ teaspoon vanilla
2 cups sifted all-purpose flour

Filling
1 (12 ounce) jar apricot jam
2 egg whites
½ teaspoon almond extract

1 cup powdered sugar
¼ cup slivered almonds

- Prepare crust by combining sugar, butter and vanilla in mixing bowl, creaming until light and fluffy. Add flour and mix thoroughly.
- Spread dough in 13x9x2-inch baking pan.
- Bake at 350 degrees for 15 minutes. Let stand until cool.
- Carefully spread jam on baked crust.
- Using electric mixer, beat egg whites with almond extract until soft peaks form. Gradually add powdered sugar; mixture will be a glaze consistency. Spread over jam layer and sprinkle with almonds.
- Bake at 400 degrees for 20 minutes or until delicately browned. Cut into bars while warm.
- Makes 24.

Banana Bars

1½ cups all-purpose flour
1 cup sugar
½ teaspoon baking soda
1 teaspoon salt
¼ teaspoon nutmeg
¾ teaspoon cinnamon

¾ cup vegetable shortening
1 egg, beaten
1 cup mashed ripe banana
1¾ cups quick-cooking rolled oats
1 cup chopped walnuts

- In mixing bowl, sift flour, sugar, baking soda, salt, nutmeg and cinnamon together.
- Cut shortening into dry ingredients. Blend in egg and bananas.
- Gradually add oats and walnuts, beating thoroughly.
- Spread batter in greased 13x9x2-inch baking pan.
- Bake at 350 degrees for 25 minutes. Cool in pan and spread with favorite vanilla frosting.
- Makes 24.

Domestic Manners of Americans

Frances Trollope, an English author and critic in 1828, arrived in Cincinnati to open a fancy bazaar. Her business venture failed, but provided her with ample material for her subsequent book, "The Domestic Manners of the Americans." In it, she detailed life in Cincinnati: "I'm sure I should have liked Cincinnati much better if the people had not dealt so very largely in hogs." Constantly having to hold her skirts aside and "brushing by a snout fresh dripping from the kennel" helped entice her to return to England, where her book made a fortune.

☀ *Elegant Kahlúa Bars*

Crust
1½ cups graham cracker
  crumbs
1 cup chopped almonds,
  toasted
½ cup butter

¼ cup sugar
½ cup cocoa
1 egg, lightly beaten
1½ teaspoons vanilla
3 tablespoons Kahlúa

Frosting
¼ cup plus 2 tablespoons
  unsalted butter, softened
1¾ cups powdered sugar

1 tablespoon cream or milk
3 tablespoons Kahlúa

Topping
1½ tablespoons butter

4 (1 ounce) squares semisweet
  chocolate

- Prepare crust by combining cracker crumbs and almonds in large bowl.

- In small saucepan over low heat, melt butter. Stir in sugar, cocoa, egg and vanilla. Cook for 4 minutes or until thickened.

- Pour sauce over crumb mixture and toss to mix. Sprinkle with Kahlúa and mix. Press crumbs in bottom of 11x7x2-inch baking pan. Freeze.

- Prepare frosting by combining butter and sugar in medium bowl, beating until creamy.

- Stir in cream or milk and Kahlúa, mixing well. Spread over crust. Freeze for 2 hours.

- Prepare topping by melting butter and chocolate in small saucepan over low heat. Spread over frosting.

- Cut into bars and refreeze for 30 minutes before serving.

- Makes 15.

Butterscotch Toffee Bars

Bars

1½ cups all-purpose flour
2 teaspoons baking powder
1 teaspoon salt
2 cups firmly packed brown
   sugar
½ cup butter, melted
2 eggs

1 teaspoon vanilla
½ cup flaked coconut
1 cup chopped pecans or
   walnuts
1 cup crushed English toffee
   candy bars

Frosting

¾ cup butter
¾ cup firmly packed brown
   sugar

⅓ cup half and half
1½ teaspoons vanilla
2 cups sugar

- Prepare bars by sifting flour, baking powder and salt together.

- In mixing bowl, combine brown sugar and butter, mixing well. Add eggs, one at a time, beating well after each addition. Stir in vanilla.

- Gradually add dry ingredients to egg mixture, stirring well after each addition. Add coconut, pecans or walnuts and crushed candy.

- Spread dough in 13x9x2-inch baking pan.

- Bake at 350 degrees for 25 minutes. Cool in pan.

- While bars are baking, prepare frosting by melting butter in saucepan over low heat. Stir in brown sugar and heat until sugar is dissolved.

- Add half and half, mixing well. Remove from heat and let stand until cool.

- Add vanilla and sugar, beating until smooth. Spread frosting over cooled bars.

- Makes 24.

If it's sweets and confections that please your eyes, you'll just adore my cakes and pies.

Where the finest and freshest we always use, there are lots in here for you to choose.

Enjoy yourself whatever you do, Recipes are best when they are simple and true.

I know myself that I love what I do.

Jenny Dennis
Bluebird Bakery Owner

Chess Pie Bars

 This is Hattie Mae's prize recipe at her
family's annual North Carolina reunion.

½ cup butter, melted
3 eggs
1 (18½ ounce) package yellow
   cake mix

1 (8 ounce) package cream
   cheese, softened
1 (16 ounce) package
   powdered sugar

- In mixing bowl, combine butter with 1 egg, beating well. Add cake mix and mix thoroughly.

- Press mixture in 13x9x2-inch baking pan.

- Blend remaining 2 eggs with cream cheese and powdered sugar, beating well. Spread batter over cake mix layer.

- Bake at 350 degrees for 30 to 35 minutes. Cool completely before cutting into small squares.

- Makes 32.

For chocolate chess bars, substitute chocolate cake mix for yellow cake mix.

"The most special cake I have ever tasted is the birthday cake my husband, Bobby, made for me the first year we were married. We had no money, so he concocted everything from the ingredients he found in the kitchens at Purdue University student housing. The problem is that there was no recipe. We would probably not want to duplicate those ingredients again, but it was the most wonderful cake I have ever eaten!"

Janie Fleming
Sous Chef

Ricotta Cheese Cookies

Cookies

2 cups sugar	2 teaspoons vanilla
2 cups butter, softened	1 teaspoon salt
3 eggs	4 cups all-purpose flour
1 (15 ounce) carton ricotta cheese	1 teaspoon baking soda

Frosting

2 tablespoons butter, softened	2 cups sifted powdered sugar
2 tablespoons milk	food coloring, optional

- Prepare cookies by combining sugar and butter in mixing bowl. Cream until light and fluffy.

- In separate bowl, combine eggs, cheese, vanilla and salt, mixing well. Add creamed mixture and beat until well mixed.

- Sift flour and baking soda together. Gradually add to egg mixture, beating after each addition.

- Drop dough by ½ teaspoonfuls on ungreased baking sheet.

- Bake at 350 degrees for 10 minutes; do not brown. Cool cookies on wire rack.

- Prepare frosting by combining butter, milk, powder sugar and food coloring. Beat until creamy and spread on cookies.

- Makes 36.

"Baking was always such fun! 'Hello Dollies' were always my favorite cookies to make. My grandchildren gave me a plaque engraved with the words 'World's Best Cookie Baker' in 1975. It still hangs in my kitchen today."

*Helen Wilson,
92 years of age
Oldest Living Member
of the Kenwood
Country Club*

Cherry Coconut Bars

Crust
1 cup all-purpose flour   ¼ cup powdered sugar
½ cup butter

Filling
¾ cup sugar   ½ cup chopped walnuts
3 tablespoons all-purpose flour   ½ cup flaked coconut
½ teaspoon baking powder   ½ cup maraschino cherries,
2 eggs, beaten   cut in halves
2 tablespoons maraschino
   cherry juice

Topping
½ cup butter, softened   1 tablespoon plus 1 teaspoon
1 cup powdered sugar   cherry juice

- Prepare crust by combining flour, butter and powdered sugar, mixing well. Press in bottom of greased 8x8x2-inch baking pan.

- Bake at 350 degrees for 20 minutes.

- Prepare filling by combining sugar, flour, baking powder and cherry juice. Add to eggs and blend well. Stir in walnuts, coconut and cherries.

- Spread filling on partially baked crust.

- Bake at 350 degrees for 25 minutes. Cool in pan.

- Prepare topping by combining butter and powdered sugar in mixing bowl. Using electric mixer, beat for 8 minutes. Add cherry juice, 1 teaspoon at a time, beating well after each addition.

- Spread frosting on bars.

- Makes 16.

Chocolate Delights

½ cup butter
¼ cup plus 1 tablespoon cocoa
¼ cup sugar
1 egg, beaten
1 teaspoon vanilla
2 cups graham cracker crumbs
½ cup chopped nuts

4½ tablespoons butter, divided
2 tablespoons instant vanilla pudding mix
2 cups powdered sugar
3 tablespoons milk
4 (1 ounce) squares unsweetened chocolate

- In large saucepan, melt butter. Add cocoa, sugar, egg and vanilla. Cook over medium heat until thickened. Remove from heat.

- Stir in cracker crumbs and nuts, mixing until blended. Press mixture in bottom of 8x8x2-inch or 9x9x2-inch baking pan. Chill.

- Cream 3 tablespoons butter with pudding mix. Blend in powdered sugar and milk. Spread on chilled crust.

- Melt remaining 1½ tablespoons butter with chocolate. Spread on pudding layer. Cut into bars and chill.

- Makes 16 to 24.

Chocolate Peanut Butter Sandwiches

1 (16 ounce) package townhouse crackers
1 (12 ounce) jar peanut butter

1 (16 ounce) package white chocolate block
1 (16 ounce) package milk chocolate block

- Spread peanut butter generously on ½ of crackers, topping each with second cracker.

- Melt white chocolate in top of double boiler over simmering water. Dip ½ of cracker "sandwich" in chocolate and place on wax paper-lined tray to dry.

- When white chocolate is firm, melt milk chocolate in top of double boiler. Dip opposite end of each "sandwich" in milk chocolate and place on wax paper to dry.

- Makes 36.

"Cincinnati is truly a city of neighborhoods. When all the other bragging is put aside, it is the neighborhoods that continue to sell this community."

Former U.S. Congressman Charlie Luken
Cincinnati: Crowning Glory

Chocolate Malt Bars

 A cold glass of milk is recommended with these rich chocolate bars.

Bars

¾ cup sugar	1 cup all-purpose flour
½ cup vegetable shortening	½ cup chocolate malted milk
1 teaspoon vanilla	powder
2 eggs	½ teaspoon baking powder
1 (1 ounce) square unsweetened	½ teaspoon salt
chocolate, melted	½ cup walnut pieces

Frosting

2 tablespoons butter, softened	dash of salt
¼ cup chocolate malted milk	1 cup powdered sugar
powder	1½ tablespoons half and half

- Prepare bars by combining sugar, shortening and vanilla in mixing bowl, creaming until fluffy. Beat in eggs. Stir in chocolate.

- Sift flour, malted milk powder, baking powder and salt together. Stir into creamed mixture and fold in nuts.

- Spread batter in greased 8x8x2-inch baking pan.

- Bake at 350 degrees for 20 to 25 minutes. Cool in pan.

- Prepare frosting by creaming butter, malted milk powder and salt together until smooth. Gradually beat in powdered sugar and half and half. Spread on bars.

- Makes 16 to 24.

Pixie Cookies

2 tablespoons butter	½ teaspoon vanilla
2 (1 ounce) squares unsweetened chocolate	1 cup sifted all-purpose flour
	1 teaspoon baking powder
1 cup sugar	¼ teaspoon salt
2 eggs	powdered sugar

- Combine butter and chocolate in top of double boiler over simmering water, stirring until melted. Add sugar and mix well. Remove from heat and let stand until cool.

- Blend eggs into chocolate mixture. Stir in vanilla. Pour into large mixing bowl.

- Combine flour, baking powder and salt. Gradually add to egg mixture, mixing well after each addition. Chill dough for 1 hour.

- Roll dough into small balls, then roll in powdered sugar and place on greased baking sheet.

- Bake at 300 degrees for about 12 minutes.

- Makes 36.

Add 1 cup chopped nuts and 1 cup flaked coconut for variety.

Delicious Dates

3 (8 ounce) packages chopped dates	1 cup broken pecans
	9 cups crispy rice cereal
1½ cups butter	1 (7 ounce) package flaked coconut or 2 cups powdered sugar
6 eggs	
2 cups sugar	

- In large saucepan, combine dates and butter. Cook over very low heat, stirring occasionally, for up to 30 minutes or until dates are very soft.

- Combine eggs and sugar. Add to dates, mixing well. Cook over medium heat, stirring constantly, until mixture is bubbly.

- Remove from heat and stir in pecans. Let stand for 15 minutes. Fold cereal into mixture.

- Using a teaspoon, shape mixture into balls. Roll in coconut or powdered sugar and place on wax paper to dry. Store in refrigerator.

- Makes 36.

"Sweets can take a lot of different forms, and pulling taffy can cause blisters. I learned this at an early age when my mother taught me how to make homemade taffy."

Thomas F. Kinder
Voice of the Bengals
for over 30 years.

Honey Roasted Chocolate Chippers

 The Cookbook Committee took the best of two recipes and made these sinful cookies.

¾ cup butter-flavored
    shortening
1¼ cups firmly packed light
    brown sugar
1 teaspoon milk
1 teaspoon vanilla
1 egg, beaten
1½ teaspoons cinnamon
1¾ cups all-purpose flour

1 teaspoon baking powder
¾ teaspoon baking soda
1 teaspoon salt
½ cup uncooked rolled oats
1 (6 ounce) package semisweet
    chocolate chips
¾ cup honey roasted peanuts
4 (2 ounce) chocolate covered
    caramel candy bars, chopped

• In mixing bowl and using electric mixer, cream shortening at medium speed for 2 minutes. Add sugar and continue beating. Add milk, vanilla, egg and cinnamon, beating until well mixed.

• Sift flour, baking powder, baking soda and salt together. Gradually add dry ingredients to egg mixture, mixing well after each addition.

• Stir in oats, chocolate chips, peanuts and chopped candy.

• Drop dough by spoonfuls on baking sheets.

• Bake at 350 degrees for 12 to 15 minutes or until golden brown.

• Makes 30 to 36.

"My mother, Jane Cone Becker Freitag, was a portrait artist. She was commissioned by Cincinnati's most prominent families. She worked exclusively on each portrait for six to eight months in her studio behind our house. She loved her small Victorian studio so much that she had it moved from our old home in East Walnut Hills to our new home at the edge of Eden Park. To her four small children, the tiny studio looked like a grand play house. We would run around banging on the Dutch doors until she would let us in and give us finger paints. She always smelled like oil paints and turpentine. My mother's two greatest passions were painting and baking. My father used to tease her about the paint fumes giving her a sweet tooth. I once had a classmate who always stole my homemade cookies at lunch. One day my mother baked cookies for my class. I guess she didn't get all the turpentine off of her hands before baking the cookies. The cookies tasted like paint. Needless to say, my classmate never took my cookies again."

*Bianca Becker
Gallagher*

Sandy Shipp's Famous Buffalo Chip Cookies

 "As long as my father is around, don't expect to find any extra cookies around the house." -Sandy Shipp, 13, Caterer

1 cup butter, softened	2 teaspoons baking powder
1 cup vegetable shortening	2 teaspoons baking soda
2 cups sugar	2 cups uncooked rolled oats
2 cups firmly packed brown sugar	1 cup flaked coconut
4 eggs	1 (6 ounce) package semisweet chocolate chips
1 tablespoon vanilla	2 cups corn flakes
4 cups all-purpose flour	

- In large mixing bowl and using electric mixer, blend butter and shortening. Add sugar and brown sugar, beating until creamy. Add eggs and vanilla, mixing well.

- Sift flour, baking powder and baking soda together. Gradually add dry ingredients to egg mixture, mixing well after each addition.

- Stir in oats, coconut, chocolate chips and corn flakes.

- Using ¼ cup measure, drop dough on baking sheet, placing 6 cookies on each sheet.

- Bake at 375 degrees for 20 minutes.

- Makes 12 to 15.

Key Lime Squares

 Super easy and oh so elegant.

Crust
1 cup all-purpose flour	⅛ teaspoon salt
¼ cup powdered sugar	½ cup butter

Filling
2 eggs	3 tablespoons all-purpose flour
1 cup sugar	½ teaspoon baking powder
3 tablespoons fresh lime juice	⅛ teaspoon salt
1 teaspoon grated lime peel	2 drops green food coloring

- Prepare crust by combining flour, sugar and salt. Using pastry blender, cut butter into dry ingredients until mixture is consistency of coarse crumbs.

- Press crumbs in bottom of 9x9x2-inch baking pan.

- Bake at 350 degrees for 20 minutes or until golden brown.

- Prepare filling by combining eggs, sugar, lime juice, peel, flour, baking powder, salt and food coloring in mixing bowl. Whisk for 2 minutes to thoroughly blend ingredients.

- Pour filling over partially-baked crust.

- Bake for additional 20 minutes or until firm. Cool in pan and chill before cutting.

- Makes 16 to 25.

"I have always been known as a great cook, but a poor baker. Once I made a batch of cookies for my son's second grade class party. The students waited patiently as the teacher passed out a cookie to each child. Finally the teacher gave the children permission to begin eating. Each child took a bite of their cookie and promptly spit it out. I have never baked again."

Debi Cass
Vice President of the
Junior League of
Cincinnati

"You Can't Eat Just One" Oatmeal Cookies

 People eat these like potato chips and always ask for more.

1 cup sugar
1 cup margarine, softened
1 teaspoon vanilla

1 cup all-purpose flour
2 cups uncooked quick-
   cooking oats

- In mixing bowl, combine sugar, margarine and vanilla, beating until light and fluffy.

- Stir in flour and oats, mixing well.

- Shape dough into 1-inch balls and place on greased baking sheet.

- Bake at 350 degrees for 10 to 12 minutes or until lightly browned.

- Makes 36.

Mixed Nut Bars

Crust
¾ cup firmly packed brown
   sugar
½ cup butter, softened

1½ cups sifted all-purpose
   flour

Filling
½ cup light corn syrup
2 tablespoons butter

1 (6 ounce) package
   butterscotch chips
1½ cups mixed salted nuts

- Prepare crust by creaming brown sugar and butter together. Stir in flour.

- Press dough in bottom of greased 13x9x2-inch baking pan.

- Bake at 350 degrees for 10 minutes.

- Prepare filling in top of double boiler, combining syrup, butter and butterscotch chips. Heat over hot water until chips are melted, stirring to blend.

- Sprinkle nuts on partially-baked crust, using a spoon to gently press into crust. Pour syrup over nuts and crust.

- Bake for an additional 10 minutes. Cool in pan before cutting into squares.

- Makes 24.

Poppy is the seed of a flower grown in Holland, which has a rich fragrance and crunchy, nut-like flavor. It is an excellent topping for breads, rolls and cookies.

Butterscotch Peanut Squares

Crust

½ cup firmly packed brown sugar

½ cup butter
1⅓ cups all-purpose flour

Filling

⅔ cup sugar
⅔ cup light corn syrup

1 (6 ounce) package butterscotch chips
½ cup chunk-style peanut butter
2 cups corn flakes

- Prepare crust by creaming brown sugar and butter together. Stir in flour.

- Press dough in bottom of ungreased 13x9x2-inch baking pan.

- Bake at 350 degrees for 15 minutes.

- Prepare filling in saucepan, combining sugar and corn syrup. Bring to a boil. Remove from heat and stir in butterscotch chips and peanut butter, mixing until chips are melted.

- Fold in corn flakes. Spread mixture on crust. Cool before cutting into squares.

- Makes 24.

Butter Pecan Turtles

Crust

2 cups all-purpose flour
1 cup firmly packed brown sugar

½ cup butter
1 cup pecan halves

Topping

⅔ cup butter
½ cup firmly packed brown sugar

1½ cups semisweet chocolate chips

- Prepare crust by combining flour and brown sugar. Cut in butter and mix until consistency of crumbs.

- Press crumbs in bottom of 13x9x2-inch baking pan. Sprinkle pecans on crust.

- Prepare topping in medium saucepan, heating butter with brown sugar over low heat until bubbly. Pour over pecans.

- Bake at 350 degrees for 20 minutes. Remove from oven. Sprinkle chocolate chips on hot bars and spread as the chips melt. Cool in pan completely before slicing.

- Makes 24.

Peanut Butter Rice Squares

Crust
½ cup light corn syrup
½ cup firmly packed brown
   sugar

1 cup peanut butter
2 cups crispy rice cereal

Filling
¼ cup butter, softened
2 cups powdered sugar
2 tablespoons milk
2 tablespoons vanilla

1 (3¾ ounce) package instant
   vanilla pudding mix
¼ cup butter
1 (6 ounce) package chocolate
   chips

- Prepare crust by combining syrup, brown sugar and peanut butter in medium saucepan. Heat until sugar is melted, stirring to blend. Fold in cereal; do not crush.

- Spread warm mixture in 13x9x2-inch baking pan. Chill.

- Prepare filling by beating softened butter, powdered sugar, milk, vanilla and pudding mix together until creamy. Spread over cereal layer and chill.

- Melt remaining butter with chocolate chips in small saucepan over low heat, stirring to blend. Spread evenly on filling layer. Chill until ready to serve.

- Makes 24.

Southern Pecan Pie Bars

"My mother, Grace Schwab, was a wonderful dessert maker! One of my fondest memories was referred to by my mother as one of her greatest baking failures. One day she put a sponge cake in the oven and insisted that her three young children tread softly around the kitchen. We, of course, forgot. We jumped all around and the cake fell. We called this chewy creation "Gum Cake". We begged my mother to make it again, but she never would."

Jane Schwab Steinway
Pioneer of Greenhills, a
Theodore Roosevelt
Greenbelt Community

Crust
1 (18½ ounce) package yellow cake mix

½ cup butter, melted
1 egg

Filling
⅔ cup reserved cake mix
½ cup firmly-packed brown sugar
1½ cups dark corn syrup

1 teaspoon vanilla
3 eggs, beaten
1 cup chopped pecans

- Reserve ⅔ cup cake mix for filling. In mixing bowl, combine remaining cake mix, butter and egg, blending to form crumbs.

- Press crumbs in bottom of greased 13x9x2-inch baking pan.

- Bake at 350 degrees for 15 to 20 minutes or until golden brown.

- Prepare filling in medium mixing bowl, combining reserved cake mix, brown sugar, syrup, vanilla and eggs. Using electric mixer at medium speed, beat for 2 minutes.

- Pour filling over partially baked crust. Sprinkle with pecans.

- Bake for an additional 30 to 35 minutes or until filling is firm. Cool in pan before slicing.

- Makes 24.

Decadent Walnut Squares

 A hot beverage is a must with this bar cookie.

Crust
½ cup butter, softened
1 (3 ounce) package cream
   cheese softened
¼ cup sugar

1¼ cups all-purpose flour
½ cup chopped walnuts
1 (6 ounce) package
   semisweet chocolate chips

Filling
1½ cups firmly packed brown
   sugar
¼ cup butter, softened
2 eggs
1 cup all-purpose flour
¼ teaspoon baking powder

¼ teaspoon salt
¾ teaspoon instant coffee
   granules
1 teaspoon water
½ cup chopped walnuts

Topping
2 cups whipping cream
2 tablespoons chocolate syrup

½ teaspoon instant coffee
   granules

- Prepare crust by creaming butter, cream cheese and sugar together until smooth. Gradually blend in flour.

- Press dough in bottom of 13x9x2-inch baking pan. Sprinkle with ½ cup walnuts and chocolate chips.

- Prepare filling by combining brown sugar, butter and eggs in large bowl, beating until smooth.

- Sift flour, baking powder and salt together. Gradually add dry ingredients to egg mixture, mixing well after each addition.

- Dissolve coffee granules in water and add to batter. Spread batter evenly on crust and sprinkle with walnuts.

- Bake at 350 degrees for 30 minutes or until lightly browned. Cool in pan.

- Using electric mixer, whip cream with chocolate syrup and coffee granules until stiff peaks form.

- Cut bars into squares and serve each with dollop of flavored whipped cream.

- Makes 24.

> "Katherine and Karl Koch were chefs at WLWT for 15 years and owned the Koch's Restaurant in Norwood. They were both superb cooks. Katherine was such a conservative German baker that she often made her famous seven layer cake into a ten layer cake because she hated to waste the batter. It was our favorite."
>
> Dolores Koch

Walnut Wonders

Crust
½ cup sugar
1 cup unsalted butter, softened

2 cups all-purpose flour

Filling
1 (16 ounce) package brown
   sugar
3 eggs
¼ cup all-purpose flour

1 teaspoon baking powder
1 teaspoon salt
1 teaspoon vanilla
2 cups chopped walnuts

Frosting
2 cups powdered sugar
3 tablespoons milk

2 tablespoons butter, melted
1 teaspoon almond extract

- Prepare crust by creaming sugar and butter together until smooth. Gradually blend in flour.

- Spread dough in greased 15x10x1-inch jelly-roll pan.

- Bake at 350 degrees for 15 minutes.

- Prepare filling by combining brown sugar, eggs, flour, baking powder, salt and vanilla in mixing bowl, blending thoroughly. Stir in walnuts. Spread filling on partially-baked crust.

- Bake for an additional 20 minutes. Cool in pan.

- Prepare frosting by blending powdered sugar, milk, butter and almond extract, beating until smooth. Spread on cooled bars. Cut into squares.

- Makes 35.

"One day while working at our Norwood store I received what I assumed was a prank phone call. In broken English, a man requested an order of 400 loaves of bread to feed his elephants for four days. I said, 'You're kidding!' You want 400 loaves of fresh baked bread to feed elephants? Surely you want day old bread from a bakery thrift shop." He assured me that he wanted our fresh bread. I told him to give me his phone number and I would call him back if this was for real. The man turned out to be Don Larson calling from the Ringling Bros. and Barnum & Bailey Circus in Venice, Florida. I learned a real lesson that day on the need to maintain the health of valuable show animals."

*Russ Adams
Adams Baking
Company*

Bibliography

Luken, Charlie and Mark Bowen. *Cincinnati Crowning Glory.*

Cincinnati Days in History, A Bicentennial Almanac. The Cincinnati Post.

Clubbe, John. *Cincinnati Observed: Architecture and History.* Columbus: Ohio State University Press, 1992.

Doss, Erika. *Spirit Poles and Flying Pigs, Public Art and Cultural Democracy in American Communities.* The Smithsonian Institution Press, 1995.

Giglierano, Geoffrey J. and Deborah A. Overmyer. *The Bicentennial Guide to Greater Cincinnati: A Portrait of Two Hundred Years.* Cincinnati: The Cincinnati Historical Society, 1988.

Hurley, Daniel. *Cincinnati, the Queen City.* Cincinnati: The Cincinnati Historical Society, 1982.

Metcalf, Fred. *The Penguin Dictionary of Modern Humorous Quotations.* St. Ives Place: Clays Ltd., 1986.

Miller, Zane L. *Boss Cox's Cincinnati: Urban Politics in the Progressive Era.* Chicago: University of Chicago Press, 1980.

Steven, Tracy C. *Going to Cincinnati, a History of the Blues in the Queen City.* Illinois: Board of Trustees University of Illinois, 1993.

The WPA Guide to Cincinnati. Cincinnati: Cincinnati Historical Society, 1987.

Special thanks to:

Joan Hock

Mary Conaty Sherrier

Kushleen Conaty

Jennifer Scott

Leslie Cannon

Dr. Judith Spraul-Schmidt, Adjunct Associate Professor of History, University of Cincinnati

Don Deming, Steamboat Historian

Jimmy Gherardi, "Everybody's Cooking with Jimmy and Doc" and J's Fresh Seafood

Patricia "Queen Sheeba" Stanford

Rachel Baker

Extra Credit

Jim Borgman

Helen Adams   Paula Norton

Robert A. Flischel   J. Miles Wolf

Credits

Russ Adams, Adams Baking Company

Larry Annett, Cincinnati Park Board

Stanley Aronoff, Former Ohio Senate President

Patricia K. Beggs, The Cincinnati Opera

George Bernas, Brandywine Inn

Patty Bernert

Ken Blackwell, State Treasurer

Lynn Blaine, Cincinnati Recreation Commission

Jeff Blake, The Cincinnati Bengals

Shawn Bleh, Indigo's

John Boehner, U.S. Congressman

Jean Booze

Jack Brennan, Cincinnati Bengals

Marty Brennaman, The Cincinnati Reds

Brian Brockman, Xavier University

JoAnn Buck, Cincinnati Folk Life

Buz Buse, Greater Cincinnati Chamber of Commerce

Page Busken, Busken Bakery

Elizabeth Cannon, Riverbend, The Crown

Leslie Cannon

Robin Carey Wilson, The Cincinnati Symphony Orchestra

Debbi Cass

Laura Chace, Director, The Cincinnati Historical Library

Beth Charlton , Greater Cincinnati Convention and Visitors Bureau

Stan Chesley

Caleb Clarke

Father William F. Cleves, President, Thomas More College

Rosemary Clooney

Dan Cohen, Clearbrook Farms

Minette Cooper, City Council

Brian Conaty

Nellie Cummins, The Cincinnati Symphony Orchestra

Anita Cunningham, Aboreta Restaurant

Ron Decker, The U.S. Playing Card Company

Chris Dalambakis, The Cincinnati Fire Museum

Judy Dalambakis, The Post

Myron Dale

John Davies

Jean-Robert DeCavel, The Maisonette

Don Deming, Steamboat Historian

Jenny Dennis, The Bluebird Bakery

Charles Desmarais, Contemporary Arts Center

Joe Deters, Hamilton County Prosecutor

Ruthie Deutscher

Downtown Council

Mary McGing Duckworth, The McGing School of Irish Dancing

Meghan Eckstein

Mrs. William A. Effler, Wm. Effler Jewelers

Marilyn Eiser, The U.S. Playing Card Company

Roger Elkus, Big Sky Bread Company

Sara Fenske, P.L.I.

Gerry Faust, University of Akron

Jack Ferreira, Anaheim General Manager

Mary Fisher, Thomas More College

Caroline Gainheasen, The Cincinnati Art Museum

Bianca Becker Gallagher

Harry Garrison

Jimmy Gherardi

Pete Giller

Rob Goering, Hamilton County Treasurer

Greg Hand, University of Cincinnati

Nancy Hazlett

Dr. Henry Heimlich

Don Helbig, Mighty Ducks

Charles Henderson, Cincinnati Reds

Marjorie Hiatt

Dave Herche

Katie, Allie, Jeffrey, Kelsey and Robert Hock

Nan Horton, Robin Imaging Services

Bob Huggins, U.C. Basketball Coach

Amy, Robin Imaging Services

Janice Jones

Jungle Jim's

Ken LaRose, Butler University Football Coach

Joe Kelley, Cincinnati Cyclones/Silverbacks

Jim Key

Ruthie Kinder, Federated Garden Clubs

Thomas F. Kinder, The Bengals

Dolores Koch

Nancy Kohnen, The Cincinnati Fire Museum

Ken LaRose

Andrew Leicester, Bicentennial Commons Artist

Linda Liebau, The College of Mount St. Joseph

Jesus Lopez-Cobos, Cincinnati Symphony Orchestra

Billy Long

Charlie Luken, Former Congressman

Chuck Martin, The Cincinnati Enquirer

Edward Maruska, The Cincinnati Zoo and Botanical Garden

Thane Maynard, The Cincinnati Zoo and Botanical Garden

D. Lynn Meyers, Ensemble Theatre

Chris Milligan

Miss Piggy

Victoria Morgan, Artistic Director, The Cincinnati Ballet

Mary Moyer, Moyer Winery & Restaurant

Ray Mueller

Lisa Mullins, Enjoy the Arts

Anthony Munoz, Former Cincinnati Bengal

Steve Neiheisel

Joe Nuxhall

Meg Olberding, The Cincinnati Museum Center

Elizabeth Oppen, The Contemporary Arts Center

Sara Jessica Parker

Tim Perrino, Showboat Majestic

Joyce Pfarr

Sharon Phillups, Hillshire Farms and Kahn's

Rodger Pille, The Cincinnati Museum Center

Carol Krone Philpott, The Kiln

Martin Plummer, General Manager, P.L.I.

Skip Prosser, Xavier University Basketball Coach

Roxanne Qualls, Mayor

Katie Rankin, The Cincinnati Opera

Ed Rigaud, Underground Railroad Freedom Center

Barbara Rish, The Cincinnati Zoo and Botanical Garden

Jerri Roberts, Taft Museum

Robin Imaging Services

Harry Robinson

Al Roehr

Patrick Rose, The Cincinnati Railroad Club

Pete Rose, Former Cincinnati Red

Dan Ross, The Cincinnati Bengals

John Rozzi, The Rozzi Co., Inc.

Carol Ruff, The Cincinnati Arts Association

John Morris Russell, Cincinnati Symphony Orchestra

Vidal Sassoon

Marge Schott, The Cincinnati Reds Owner

Diane Schrag

Phyllis Schueler

Johnny Scott

Linda Scott

Tom Seaver
Ed Sherrier, NFL Films
Terry Shumrick, Chateau Pomije
Jeffery Siebert, Mighty Ducks
Laura Simpson
Joan Steinberg
Jane Schwab Steinway
Bobbie Sterne, City Council
Ed Stern, Cincinnati Playhouse in the Park
Evelyn Stubbs, The Cincinnati Opera
Maureen and Greg Sweeney
Bob Taft, Ohio Secretary of State
Jim Tarbell, Arnold's Bar and Grill
Dwight Tillery, City Council
Steven Tracy, Author
Jodi Tobin

Vanessa Torbeck, The Cincinnati Ballet
Martha Totten
Jack and Joyce Turigliatto
Ken Ukotter, Summit Country Day School
Laura Varley
Kathy Wade, Jazz Singer
Vivian Wagner, Cincinnati Parks
Sarah Warner, Ensemble Theatre of Cincinnati
Helen Wilson
Robin Carey Wilson, The Cincinnati Symphony
  Orchestra
Kevin "Doc" Wolfe
Shawn Womack
Chad Yelton, The Cincinnati Zoo and
  Botanical Garden
Sam Wyche

COOKBOOK CONTRIBUTORS

Lee Adams
Peggy Adams
Linda Admire
Pat Aikin
Madge Alf
Debbi Alsfelder
Terry Anderson
Jane Andragg
Mary Andrus
Jean Applegate
Marge Artzer
Philipee Audax

Gillian Barton
Meegan Baxter
Sandy Becker
Dee Bennett
Nancy Bennett
Judy Beridon
Jan Beyma
Julie Bishop
Lela Bishop
Fran Bitzer
Justina Block
Dana Bolar
Sally Borchers
Gia Borgerson
Phyllis Bouldin
Marianne Bowe
Laura Branca
Thomas E. Brinkman, Sr.
Pam Buck
Susan Buck
Burbank's Real Bar-B-Q
Leslie Burchenal

Melna Burchenal
Burrito Joe's Restaurant
Kathy Burton
Joyce Buschaus
Thelma Buschenal
Barbara Bush
Susan Bushman
Brenda Benzar Butler
Nancy Byal

Leslie Cannon
Cathy Carmichael
Debi Cass
Mary Cawkins
Tracey Chappelow
Emilie Christie
Cincinnati Celebrates
The Cincinnati Post
Jean Clark
Suzanne Clark
Caroline Cox
Mary Beth Craig
Marylou Crane
Lee Crodes
Joan Crowe
Beth Crowl
Dona Culp

Chris Dalambakis
Francis Darling
Anne Davies
Jean-Robert DeCavel
Beth DeGroft
Sharon Denight
Beth Dennison

M. DeSolar
Maria Devita
Stephanie Diamond
Faith Dilworth
Margaret Ditman
Laura Dolle
Meghan Dolle
Lisa Donofe
Mo Dunne

Patricia Early
Barbara Ebrite
Dorothy Effler
Jill Egan
Marianne Scott Emmert
Tricia Ettinger
Anne Evans
Mrs. Joseph Eveland
*Everybody's Cooking
  with Jimmy and Doc*

Elizabeth Farians
Mary Ferguson
Ida Fisher
Elaine Fishman
Chrissy Fixler
Joan Flugeman
Beth Flynn
Cindy Ford
Betty Forker
Laurie Ann Frank
Irmgard Freeman
Carol Friedman

Meg Galvin
Bev Garland

Tal Gast
Delle Christensen Gay
Sandy George
Laura Getz
Jimmy Gherardi
Mary Gibson
Cindy Glass
Global Culinary Center
Deb Goettsche
Sharon M. Gormas
Michelle Gottschlich
Ellie Graham
Cathy Greene
Kay Greine
Cary Griffin
Sarah Grimmer
Elizabeth Gross

Marsha Haber
Jeanette Hagerman
Donna Hartman
Margie Hauser
Pamela Heckel
Tiffany Hedge
Colleen Hempel
Beth Hendricks
Estelle Hoffman
Betsy Burns Homan
Bridget O. Hubbard
Susan Hueskan
Jane Hutzelman

Indigo's Restaurant

*J's Fresh Seafood
  Restaurant*

Kim Jackson
Betsy Jernigan
Tannie Jester
Sarah Raup Johnson
Janet Jones
Mitzi Jones
Marcia Judge

Darlene Kamine
Lil Keevin
Beth Keller
Anne Stuart Kirkhorn
Jean Kitchen
Jane Klier
Dolores Koch
Marnie Kolojeski
Karen Kremzar
Jean Krieg
Tina Kroenke
Heather Krombholz
Allison Kurtz
Dana Kurtz

Lindsay Lackney
Susan Laubenthal
Doris Lechner
Mary LeRoy
Shirley Lippert
Barbara Littlehale
Gillian Littlehale
Lana Long
Joan Lunden
Charlotte Lunzit

Main Street Brewery
The Maisonette

Julia Massarelli
Maya's
Joan McGill
Janet McMillon
Nadine Mesch
Barbara Minchew
Sally Young Moore
Terri Tatman Morgan
Ginny Myer

National Exemplar
  Restaurant
Jodie Needy
Julie Neiheisel

Sue Oaks

The Palace Restaurant
Cara Pestorius
Susan Pfall
The Phoenix Restaurant
Pigall's Cafe
Sally Porter
Ruthie Price
Jardiniere Printaniere
Laura Pruett

Helen Rebensdorf
Jane Reed
Tish Renz
Grace Richards
Ruth Rickey
Amy Rile
Joyce Riley
Jo Ritzi
RiverFeast

Riverview Restaurant
Karen Shapiro Robinson
Nancy Rogers
Sally Rogers
Rita Rozzi
Marianne Rowe
Barbara Runck

Dorrie Sampson
Mrs. Wallace E. Sarrah, Jr.
Libby Schaeffer
Carolyn Schmidt
Kathy Schmitt
Grace Schwaab
Sylvia C. Schwab
Rosemary Scott
Scotti's Restaurant
Jean Shields
Sandy Shipp
Skyline Chili
Linda Smith
Julie Snow-Reese
Mary Spraul-Uhl
Beth Srofe
Elizabeth Staley
Babs Stanford
Cynthia J. Stanford
Delcia Stanford
Ela Stanford
Hattie Mae Stanford
Lela Stanford
Patricia R. Stanford
Zona Stanford

Gwen St. Clair
Jane Steinway
Nancy Stephens
Patty Stewart
Katie Stine
Bill Strybel
Ellen Sullivan

Kathy Tashjian
Teller's of Hyde Park
Judith TenEyck
Claire Terry
Jeanne Tingle
Martha Totten
Stephanie Trautman
Jane Tredway

Jenny Vance

Jane Wall
Beth Ward
Watson Bros. Brewhouse
Judy Wells
Jeff Wests
What's For Dinner
Amy Whitaker
Mary White
Jennine Winkleman
JoAnn Withrow
Nancy Wolf
Beth Wood

Joyce Yonka
Melissa Young
Natalie Youngquist

Pig Tales, or The True Story of the Four Little Pigs

They were created and canonized by Artist Andrew Leicester, who heard the echoes of their celebrated past as he designed Bicentennial Commons at Sawyer Point Park. They were parodied and immortalized by editorial cartoonist Jim Borgman, who hammed up their potential.

They are the four flying pigs atop crowned smokestacks at the gateway entrance to the 22-acre riverfront park, and are part of the design that won the prestigious Waterfront Center's Top Honors Award in 1989 for interpretive public art. The park salutes the city's history and river heritage, including a depiction of the Ohio River system of locks and dams, tennis and volleyball courts, a children's play area, an amphitheater and skating rink.

"The work is a compendium of different stories and vignettes about the history of Cincinnati and its relationship to the Ohio River, and how it prospered vis-a-vis the river, and the Lake Erie canal that connected down to the Ohio River through Eggleston Avenue. Pig packing, or the pork industry, was essentially one of the primary industries in Cincinnati's past, you know it had the nickname Porkopolis. Procter and Gamble made their original businesses based on pig tallow from the slaughterhouses, from which they made their candles and soaps. So it's a kind of homage to the industrial underpinnings of the community," explains Andrew Leicester.

Although the bustling days of steamboat paddle wheelers and "floating palaces" along the riverfront are long gone, the pig tales remain, and the flying pigs Gateway sculpture stands in whimsical tribute to Cincinnati's colorful past.

photograph by Robert A. Flischel

Index

JUNIOR LEAGUE OF CINCINNATI

Women building better communities

Junior League of Cincinnati
Columbia Center
3500 Columbia Parkway
Cincinnati, Ohio 45226

Name _____

Address _____

City _____ State _____ Zip _____

No. of copies at 21.95 ea.	
Ohio residents only add sales tax 1.54 ea.	
Shipping and handling 4.00 ea.	
TOTAL	

❑ Check enclosed (payable to the Junior League of Cincinnati - Cookbook)

Please charge to:

❑ Visa _____ _____
  Card number   Expiration date

❑ Mastercard _____ _____
  Card number   Expiration date

❑ Check here if gift wrapping is desired at $1.00 each.

To set up a wholesale account, please call (513) 871-9339.

- -

JUNIOR LEAGUE OF CINCINNATI

Women building better communities

Junior League of Cincinnati
Columbia Center
3500 Columbia Parkway
Cincinnati, Ohio 45226

Name _____

Address _____

City _____ State _____ Zip _____

No. of copies at 21.95 ea.	
Ohio residents only add sales tax 1.54 ea.	
Shipping and handling 4.00 ea.	
TOTAL	

❑ Check enclosed (payable to the Junior League of Cincinnati - Cookbook)

Please charge to:

❑ Visa _____ _____
  Card number   Expiration date

❑ Mastercard _____ _____
  Card number   Expiration date

❑ Check here if gift wrapping is desired at $1.00 each.

To set up a wholesale account, please call (513) 871-9339.

Lesson Openers
outline the content and features of each lesson.

A primera vista activities jump-start the lessons, allowing you to use the Spanish you know to talk about the photos.

Communicative goals highlight the real-life tasks you will be able to carry out in Spanish by the end of each lesson.

Supersite

Supersite resources are available for every section of the lesson at **vhlcentral.com**. Icons show you which textbook activities are also available online, and where additional practice activities are available. The description next to the Ⓢ icon indicates what additional resources are available for each section: videos, recordings, tutorials, presentations, and more!

Contextos
presents vocabulary in meaningful contexts.

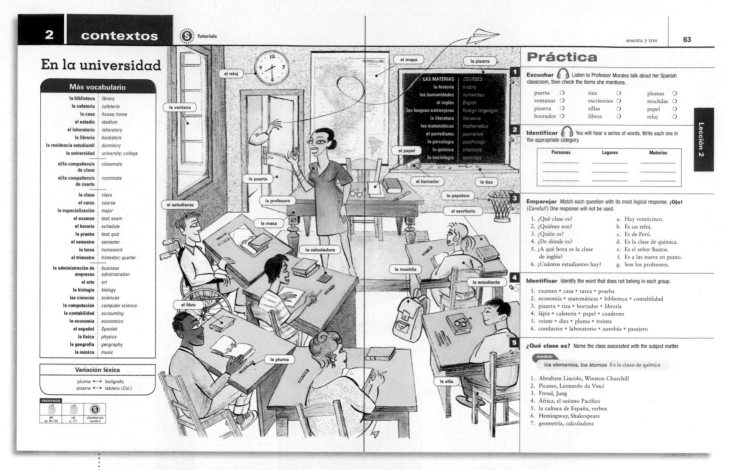

Más vocabulario boxes call out other important theme-related vocabulary in easy-to-reference Spanish-English lists.

Variación léxica presents alternate words and expressions used throughout the Spanish-speaking world.

Illustrations High-frequency vocabulary is introduced through expansive, full-color illustrations.

Recursos The icons in the **Recursos** boxes let you know exactly which print and technology ancillaries you can use to reinforce and expand on every section of every lesson.

Práctica This section always begins with two listening exercises and continues with activities that practice the new vocabulary in meaningful contexts.

Comunicación activities allow you to use the vocabulary creatively in interactions with a partner, a small group, or the entire class.

Supersite

- Vocabulary tutorials
- Audio support for vocabulary presentation
- Worktext activities
- Additional online-only practice activities

- Chat activities for conversational skill-building and oral practice
- Vocabulary activities in Activity Pack

Fotonovela
follows the adventures of a group of students living and traveling in Mexico.

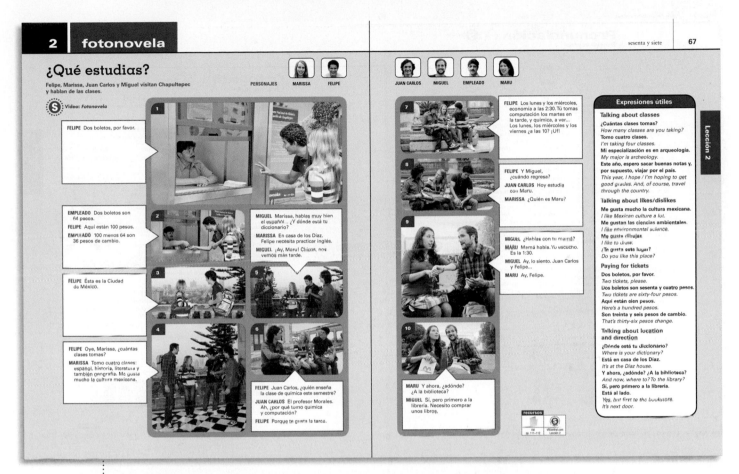

Personajes The photo-based conversations take place among a cast of recurring characters—a Mexican family with two college-age children, and their group of friends.

Icons signal activities by type (pair, group, audio, info gap) and let you know which activities can be completed online.

Fotonovela Video Updated for the Second Edition, the **NEW!** video episodes that correspond to this section are available for viewing online.

Expresiones útiles These expressions organize new, active structures by language function so you can focus on using them for real-life, practical purposes.

Conversations Taken from the **NEW! Fotonovela** Video, the conversations reinforce vocabulary from **Contextos**. They also preview structures from the upcoming **Estructura** section in context and in a comprehensible way.

Supersite

- Streaming video of the **Fotonovela** episode
- Worktext activities
- Additional online-only practice activities

Pronunciación & Ortografía
present the rules of Spanish pronunciation and spelling.

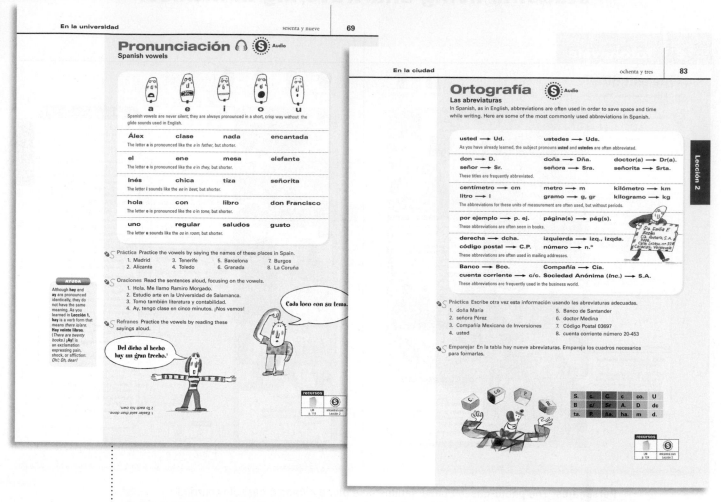

Pronunciación explains the sounds and pronunciation of Spanish in **¡ADELANTE! UNO** and Lessons 1–3 of **¡ADELANTE! DOS**.

Ortografía focuses on topics related to Spanish spelling in Lessons 4–6 of **¡ADELANTE! DOS** and in all of **¡ADELANTE! TRES**.

Supersite

- Audio for pronunciation explanation
- Record-compare worktext activities

Cultura
exposes you to different aspects of Hispanic culture tied to the lesson theme.

En detalle & Perfil(es) Two articles on the lesson theme focus on a specific place, custom, person, group, or tradition in the Spanish-speaking world. In Spanish starting in ¡ADELANTE! DOS Lesson 1, these features also provide reading practice.

Coverage While the **Panorama** section takes a regional approach to cultural coverage, **Cultura** is theme-driven, covering several Spanish-speaking regions in every lesson.

Así se dice & El mundo hispano Lexical and comparative features expand cultural coverage to people, traditions, customs, trends, and vocabulary throughout the Spanish-speaking world.

Supersite

- **Cultura** article
- Worktext activities
- Additional online-only practice activities

- **Conexión Internet** activity with questions and keywords related to lesson theme
- Additional cultural reading

Estructura
presents Spanish grammar in a graphic-intensive format.

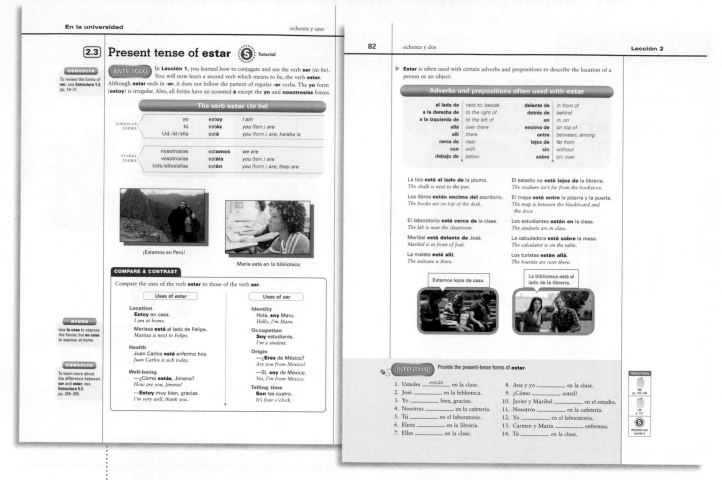

Ante todo Ease into grammar with definitions of grammatical terms, reminders about what you already know of English grammar, and Spanish grammar you have learned in earlier lessons.

Charts To help you learn, colorful, easy-to-use charts call out key grammatical structures and forms, as well as important related vocabulary.

Compare & Contrast This feature focuses on aspects of grammar that native speakers of English may find difficult, clarifying similarities and differences between Spanish and English.

Student sidebars provide you with on-the-spot linguistic, cultural, or language-learning information directly related to the materials in front of you.

Diagrams Clear and easy-to-grasp grammar explanations are reinforced by colorful diagrams that present sample words, phrases, and sentences.

¡Inténtalo! offers an easy first step into each grammar point.

- Animated grammar tutorials
- Worktext activities

Estructura
provides directed and communicative practice.

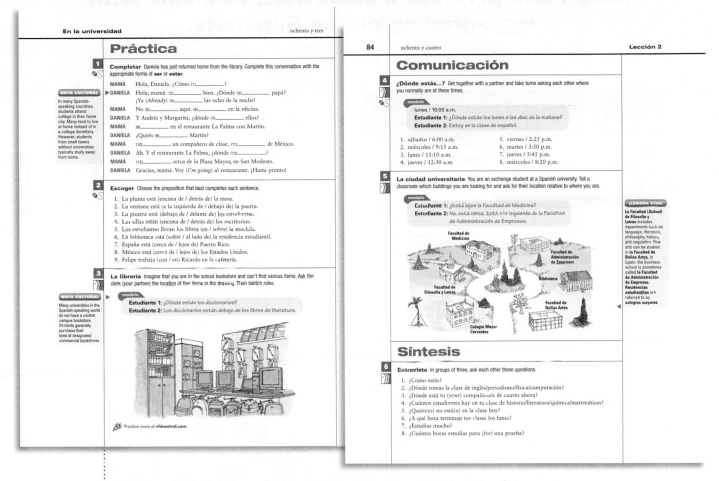

Práctica Guided, yet meaningful exercises weave current and previously learned vocabulary together with the current grammar point.

Information Gap activities You and your partner each have only half of the information you need, so you must work together to accomplish the task at hand.

Comunicación Opportunities for creative expression use the lesson's grammar and vocabulary.

Sidebars The **Notas culturales** expand coverage of the cultures of Spanish-speaking peoples and countries, while **Ayuda** sidebars provide on-the-spot language support.

Síntesis activities integrate the current grammar point with previously learned points, providing built-in, consistent review.

Supersite

- Worktext activities
- Additional online-only practice activities
- Chat activities for conversational skill-building and oral practice
- Grammar and communication activities in Activity Pack

Estructura

Recapitulación reviews the grammar of each lesson and provides a short quiz, available with auto-grading on the Supersite.

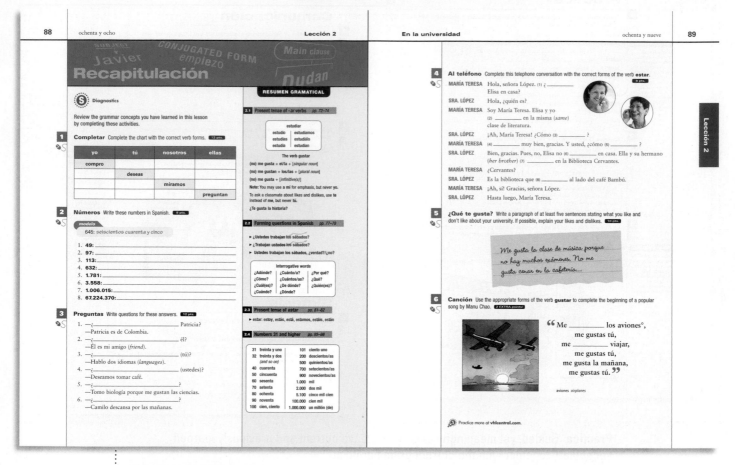

Resumen gramatical This review panel provides you with an easy-to-study summary of the basic concepts of the lesson's grammar, with page references to the full explanations.

Points Each activity is assigned a point value to help you track your progress. All **Recapitulación** sections add up to fifty points, plus two additional points for successfully completing the bonus activity.

Activities A series of activities, moving from directed to open-ended, systematically test your mastery of the lesson's grammar. The section ends with a riddle or puzzle using the grammar from the lesson.

Supersite

- Worktext activities with follow-up support and practice
- Additional online-only review activities
- Review activities in Activity Pack
- Practice quiz

Adelante
Lectura develops reading skills in the context of the lesson theme.

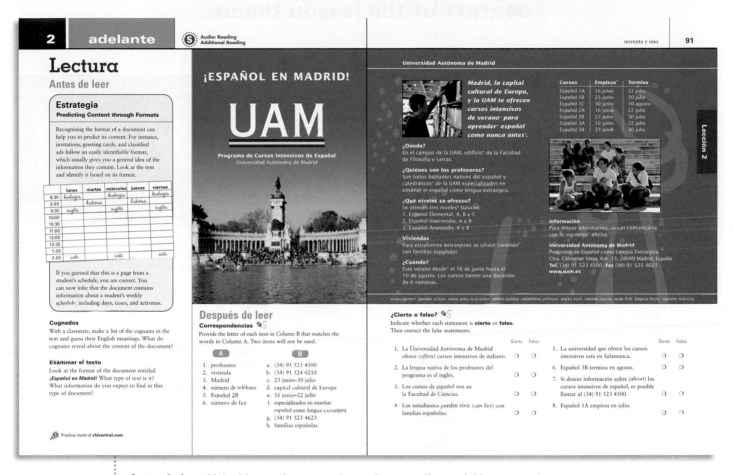

Antes de leer Valuable reading strategies and pre-reading activities strengthen your reading abilities in Spanish.

Readings Selections related to the lesson theme recycle vocabulary and grammar you have learned. The selections in **¡ADELANTE! UNO** and **¡ADELANTE! DOS** are cultural texts, while those in **¡ADELANTE! TRES** are literary pieces.

Después de leer Activities include post-reading exercises that review and check your comprehension of the reading as well as expansion activities.

Supersite

- Audio-sync reading that highlights text as it is being read
- Worktext activities
- Additional reading

Adelante NEW!

Escritura develops writing skills while *Escuchar* practices listening skills in the context of the lesson theme.

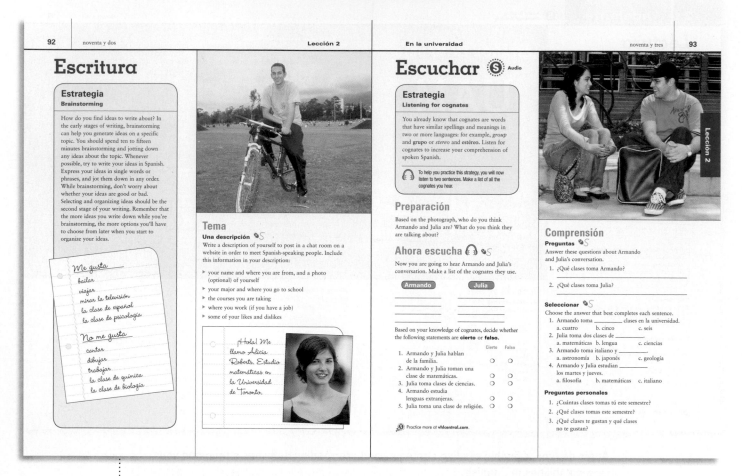

Estrategia Strategies help you prepare for the writing and listening tasks to come.

Escritura The **Tema** describes the writing topic and includes suggestions for approaching it.

Escuchar A recorded conversation or narration develops your listening skills in Spanish. **Preparación** prepares you for listening to the recorded passage.

Ahora escucha walks you through the passage, and **Comprensión** checks your listening comprehension.

Supersite

- Composition engine for writing activity in **Escritura**
- Audio for listening activity in **Escuchar**
- Worktext activities
- Additional online-only practice activities

Adelante **NEW!**

En pantalla and *Flash cultura* present additional video tied to the lesson theme.

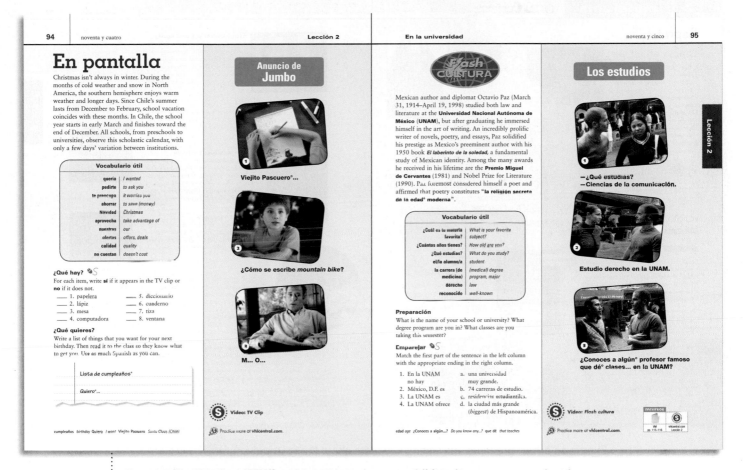

En pantalla

Christmas isn't always in winter. During the months of cold weather and snow in North America, the southern hemisphere enjoys warm weather and longer days. Since Chile's summer lasts from December to February, school vacation coincides with these months. In Chile, the school year starts in early March and finishes toward the end of December. All schools, from preschools to universities, observe this scholastic calendar, with only a few days' variation between institutions.

Vocabulario útil

quería	I wanted
pedirte	to ask you
te preocupa	it worries you
ahorrar	to save (money)
Navidad	Christmas
aprovecha	take advantage of
nuestras	our
ofertas	offers, deals
calidad	quality
no cuestan	doesn't cost

¿Qué hay?

For each item, write **sí** if it appears in the TV clip or **no** if it does not.

___ 1. papelera   ___ 5. diccionario
___ 2. lápiz   ___ 6. cuaderno
___ 3. mesa   ___ 7. tiza
___ 4. computadora   ___ 8. ventana

¿Qué quieres?

Write a list of things that you want for your next birthday. Then read it to the class so they know what to get you. Use as much Spanish as you can.

Lista de cumpleaños°

Quiero°...

cumpleaños *birthday* Quiero *I want* Viejito Pascuero *Santa Claus (Chile)*

Anuncio de Jumbo

Viejito Pascuero°...

¿Cómo se escribe *mountain bike*?

M... O...

Video: TV Clip

Practice more at vhlcentral.com.

Flash CULTURA

Mexican author and diplomat Octavio Paz (March 31, 1914–April 19, 1998) studied both law and literature at the **Universidad Nacional Autónoma de México** (**UNAM**), but after graduating he immersed himself in the art of writing. An incredibly prolific writer of novels, poetry, and essays, Paz solidified his prestige as Mexico's preeminent author with his 1950 book *El laberinto de la soledad*, a fundamental study of Mexican identity. Among the many awards he received in his lifetime are the **Premio Miguel de Cervantes** (1981) and Nobel Prize for Literature (1990). Paz foremost considered himself a poet and affirmed that poetry constitutes "**la religión secreta de la edad° moderna**".

Vocabulario útil

¿Cuál es tu materia favorita?	What is your favorite subject?
¿Cuántos años tienes?	How old are you?
¿Qué estudias?	What do you study?
el/la alumno/a	student
la carrera (de medicina)	(medical) degree program, major
derecho	law
reconocido	well-known

Preparación

What is the name of your school or university? What degree program are you in? What classes are you taking this semester?

Emparejar

Match the first part of the sentence in the left column with the appropriate ending in the right column.

1. En la UNAM no hay   a. una universidad muy grande.
2. México, D.F. es   b. 74 carreras de estudio.
3. La UNAM es   c. residencias estudiantiles.
4. La UNAM ofrece   d. la ciudad más grande (*biggest*) de Hispanoamérica.

edad *age* ¿Conoces a algún...? *Do you know any...?* que dé *that teaches*

Los estudios

—¿Qué estudias?
—Ciencias de la comunicación.

Estudio derecho en la UNAM.

¿Conoces a algún° profesor famoso que dé° clases... en la UNAM?

Video: Flash cultura

Practice more at vhlcentral.com.

En pantalla TV clips, **NEW!** to this edition, give you additional exposure to authentic language. The clips include commercials, newscasts, short films, and TV shows that feature the language, vocabulary, and theme of the lesson.

Presentation Cultural notes, video stills with captions, and vocabulary support all prepare you to view the clips. Activities check your comprehension and expand on the ideas presented.

Flash cultura An icon lets you know that the enormously successful **Flash cultura** Video offers specially shot content tied to the lesson theme.

NEW! Activities Due to the overwhelming popularity of the **Flash cultura** Video, previewing support and comprehension activities are now integrated into the student text.

Super**site**

- Streaming video of **En pantalla** and **Flash cultura**
- Worktext activities
- Additional online-only practice activities

Panorama
presents the nations of the Spanish-speaking world.

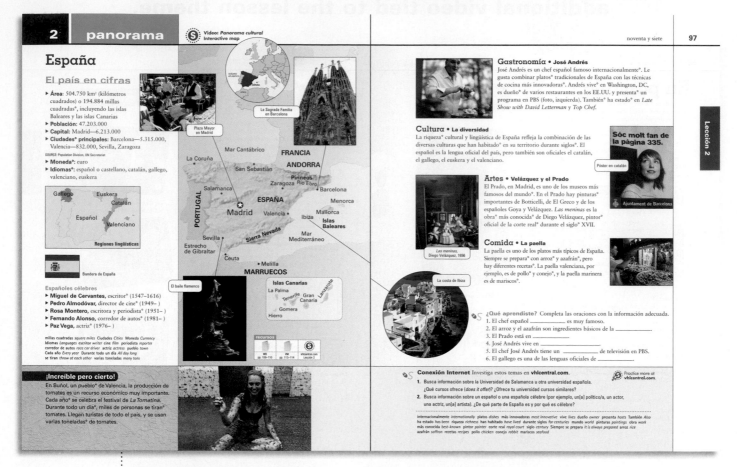

El país en cifras presents interesting key facts about the featured country.

¡Increíble pero cierto! highlights an intriguing fact about the country or its people.

Maps point out major cities, rivers, and geographical features and situate the country in the context of its immediate surroundings and the world.

Readings A series of brief paragraphs explores facets of the country's culture such as history, places, fine arts, literature, and aspects of everyday life.

Panorama cultural **Video** This video's authentic footage takes you to the featured Spanish-speaking country, letting you experience the sights and sounds of an aspect of its culture.

Supersite

• Interactive map

• Streaming video of the **Panorama cultural** program

• Worktext activities

• Additional online-only practice activities

• **Conexión Internet** activity with questions and keywords related to lesson theme

Vocabulario
summarizes all the active vocabulary of the lesson.

Vocabulario The end-of-lesson page lists the active vocabulary from each lesson. This is the vocabulary that may appear on quizzes or tests.

Supersite

- Audio for all vocabulary items
- Vocabulary flashcards with audio

Workbook and Video Manual

2.3 Present tense of estar

1 **Están en...** Answer the questions based on the pictures. Write complete sentences.

1. ¿Dónde están Cristina y Bruno? ___
2. ¿Dónde están la profesora y el estudiante? ___
3. ¿Dónde está la puerta? ___

4. ¿Dónde está la mochila? ___
5. ¿Dónde está el pasajero? ___
6. ¿Dónde está José Miguel? ___

2 **¿Dónde están?** Use these cues and the correct form of **estar** to write complete sentences. Add any missing words.

1. libros / cerca / escritorio
2. ustedes / al lado / puerta
3. calculadora / entre / computadoras
4. lápices / sobre / cuaderno
5. estadio / lejos / residencias
6. mochilas / debajo / mesa
7. tú / en / clase de psicología
8. reloj / a la derecha / ventana
9. Rita / a la izquierda / Julio

Panorama: España

Lección 2
Panorama cultural

Antes de ver el video

1 **Más vocabulario** Look over these useful words before you watch the video.

Vocabulario útil		
antiguo *ancient*	empezar *to start*	niños *children*
blanco *white*	encierro *running of bulls*	pañuelo *neckerchief, bandana*
cabeza *head*	esta *this*	peligroso *dangerous*
calle *street*	feria *fair, festival*	periódico *newspaper*
cohete *rocket (firework)*	fiesta *party, festival*	rojo *red*
comparsa *parade*	gente *people*	ropa *clothing*
correr *to run*	gigante *giant*	toro *bull*
defenderse *to defend oneself*	mitad *half*	ver *to see*

2 **Festivales** In this video, you are going to learn about a Spanish festival. List the things you would probably do and see at a festival.

Mientras ves el video

3 **Ordenar** Number the items in the order in which they appear in the video.

___ a. cohete
___ b. cuatro mujeres en un balcón
___ c. gigante
___ d. toros
___ e. mitad hombre, mitad animal

Después de ver el video

4 **Fotos** Describe the video stills.

Workbook The Workbook section provides additional practice for the **Contextos, Estructura,** and **Panorama** sections.

Video Manual The three Video Manual sections correspond to the **Fotonovela, Panorama cultural,** and **Flash cultura** video programs. These activities provide pre-, while-, and post-viewing practice.

Recursos Within each lesson, **recursos** boxes let you know which Workbook, Lab Manual, and Video Manual materials can be used.

Supersite

• Streaming video of **Fotonovela, Panorama cultural,** and **Flash cultura**

Lab Manual and Notes

contextos — Lección 2

1 Identificar Look at each drawing and listen to the statement. Indicate whether the statement is **cierto** or **falso**.

Cierto Falso   Cierto Falso   Cierto Falso

1. ○ ○   2. ○ ○   3. ○ ○
4. ○ ○   5. ○ ○   6. ○ ○

2 ¿Qué día es? Your friend Diego is never sure what day of the week it is. Respond to his questions saying that it is the day before the one he mentions. Then repeat the correct answer after the speaker. (6 items)

modelo
Hoy es domingo, ¿no?
No, hoy es sábado.

3 Preguntas You will hear a series of questions. Look at Susana's schedule for today and answer each question. Then repeat the correct response after the speaker.

martes 18

- 9:00 economía — Sr. Rivera
- 11:00 química — Sra. Hernández
- 12:15 cafetería — Carmen
- 1:30 prueba de contabilidad — Sr. Ramos
- 3:00 matemáticas — Srta. Torres
- 4:30 laboratorio de computación — Héctor

Notes

Lab Manual The Lab Manual section further practices listening and speaking skills related to the **Contextos**, **Pronunciación**, and **Estructura** materials.

Notes pages The Notes pages at the end of each lesson provide a place to write new vocabulary words and notes.

Supersite
• Audio for Lab Manual activities

Fotonovela Video Program

The cast NEW!

Here are the main characters you will meet in the **Fotonovela** Video:

From Mexico,
Jimena Díaz Velázquez

From Mexico,
Felipe Díaz Velázquez

From Mexico,
María Eugenia (Maru)
Castaño Ricaurte

From Argentina,
Juan Carlos Rossi

From the U.S.,
Marissa Wagner

From Spain,
Miguel Ángel
Lagasca Martínez

Brand-new and fully integrated with your text, the **¡ADELANTE! 2/e Fotonovela** Video is a dynamic and contemporary window into the Spanish language. The new video centers around the Díaz family, whose household includes two college-aged children and a visiting student from the U.S. Over the course of an academic year, Jimena, Felipe, Marissa, and their friends explore **el D.F.** and other parts of Mexico as they make plans for their futures. Their adventures take them through some of the greatest natural and cultural treasures of the Spanish-speaking world, as well as the highs and lows of everyday life.

The **Fotonovela** section in each worktext lesson is actually an abbreviated version of the dramatic episode featured in the video. Therefore, each **Fotonovela** section can be done before you see the corresponding video episode, after it, or as a section that stands alone.

In each dramatic segment, the characters interact using the vocabulary and grammar you are studying. As the storyline unfolds, the episodes combine new vocabulary and grammar with previously taught language, exposing you to a variety of authentic accents along the way. At the end of each episode, the **Resumen** section highlights the grammar and vocabulary you are studying.

We hope you find the new **Fotonovela** Video to be an engaging and useful tool for learning Spanish!

En pantalla Video Program

The **¡ADELANTE!** Supersite features an authentic video clip for each lesson. Clip formats include commercials, news stories, and even short films. These clips, **NEW!** to the Second Edition, have been carefully chosen to be comprehensible for students learning Spanish, and are accompanied by activities and vocabulary lists to facilitate understanding. More importantly, though, these clips are a fun and motivating way to improve your Spanish!

Here are the countries represented in each lesson in **En pantalla**:

¡ADELANTE! UNO	*¡ADELANTE!* DOS	*¡ADELANTE!* TRES
Lesson 1 U.S.	Lesson 1 Argentina	Lesson 1 Argentina
Lesson 2 Chile	Lesson 2 Peru	Lesson 2 Argentina
Lesson 3 U.S.	Lesson 3 Chile	Lesson 3 Mexico
Lesson 4 Peru	Lesson 4 Spain	Lesson 4 Spain
Lesson 5 Mexico	Lesson 5 Colombia	Lesson 5 Mexico
Lesson 6 Mexico	Lesson 6 Spain	Lesson 6 Mexico

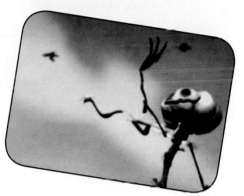

Flash cultura Video Program

In the dynamic **Flash cultura** Video, young people from all over the Spanish-speaking world share aspects of life in their countries with you. The similarities and differences among Spanish-speaking countries that come up through their adventures will challenge you to think about your own cultural practices and values. The segments provide valuable cultural insights as well as linguistic input; the episodes will introduce you to a variety of accents and vocabulary as they gradually move into Spanish.

Panorama cultural Video Program

The **Panorama cultural** Video is integrated with the **Panorama** section in each lesson. Each segment is 2–3 minutes long and consists of documentary footage from each of the countries featured. The images were specially chosen for interest level and visual appeal, while the all-Spanish narrations were carefully written to reflect the vocabulary and grammar covered in the worktexts.

acknowledgments

Acknowledgments

Vista Higher Learning expresses its sincere appreciation to the many instructors and college professors across the U.S. and Canada who contributed their ideas and suggestions.

¡ADELANTE!, Second Edition, is the direct result of extensive reviews and ongoing input from instructors using the First Edition. Accordingly, we gratefully acknowledge those who shared their suggestions, recommendations, and ideas as we prepared this Second Edition.

We express our sincere appreciation to the instructors who completed our online review.

Reviewers

Amy Altamirano South Milwaukee High School South Milwaukee, WI

Barbara Bessette Cayuga Community College

Deborah Bock University of Alaska Anchorage

Teresa Borden Columbia College

Dennis Bricault North Park University

Patrice Burns University of Wisconsin—Milwaukee: School of Continuing Education

Katherine Cash Crown College, MN

Carole A. Champagne, Ph.D. University of Maryland Eastern Shore, Salisbury University

Darren Crasto Houston Community College

Kathie Filby Greenville College

José M. Garcia-Paine, Ph.D. Metropolitan State University of Denver

Nancy Hake Park University

Dominique Hitchcock Norco College

Lola Jerez-Moya Monterey Peninsula College

Aggie Johnson Flagler College

Kevin Kaber University of Wisconsin—Milwaukee: School of Continuing Education

Victoria Kildal Prince William Sound Community College

Isabel Killough Norfolk State University

Teresa Lane Hawai'i Pacific University

Michael Langer Wake Technical Community College

Marilyn Manley Rowan University

Estela Sánchez Márquez East Los Angeles College

Lisa Mathelier Morton College

Lizette S. Moon Houston Community College Northwest

M. Margarita Nodarse, Ph.D. Barry University

Chaiya Mohanty Ortiz Northern Virginia Community College

William Paulino Delaware Technical Community College

Emley Poloche Andrews University

Jeff Ruth East Stroudsburg University

Lisbet Sanchez Mt. San Antonio College

Norma Sánchez California State University Los Angeles

Lowell E. "Buddy" Sandefur Eastern Oklahoma State College

Sarah Shanebrook University of Wisconsin—Milwaukee: School of Continuing Education

Cristina Sparks-Early Northern Virginia Community College

David Thomson Luther College, IA

Jeff Tuttle Northeast Mississippi Community College

Adriana Vecino Bilingual Education Institute

Hugo M. Viera Westfield State University

Sandra Watts University of North Carolina at Charlotte

Charlotte Whittle York School Monterey, CA

Karen L. Woelfle-Potter University of Wisconsin—Milwaukee: School of Continuing Education

Wendy Woodrich Lewis & Clark College

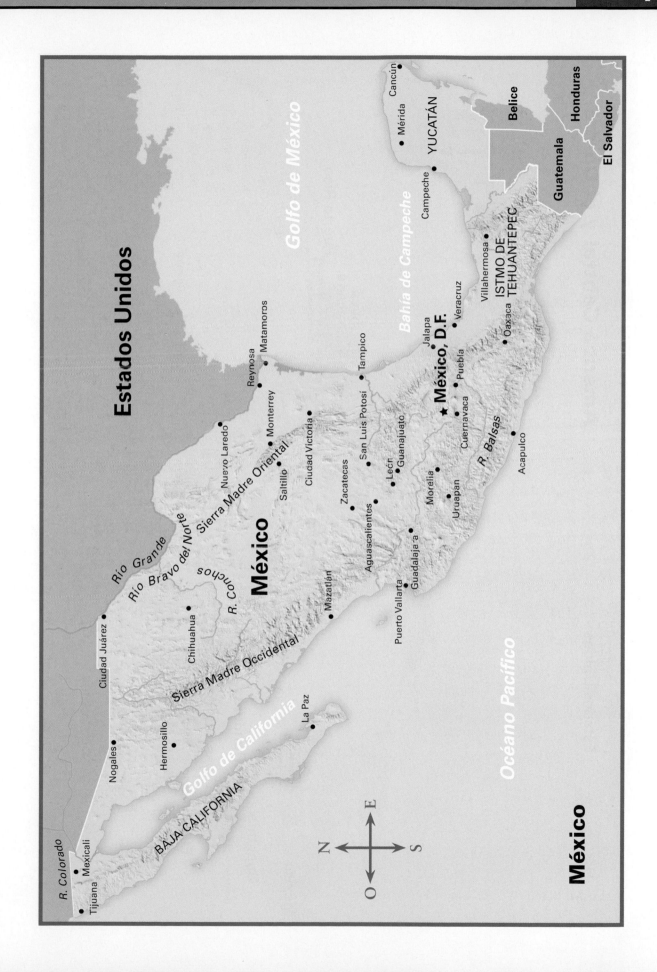

Estados Unidos

Golfo de México

Cancún
Mérida
YUCATÁN
Belice
Honduras
Guatemala
El Salvador

Bahía de Campeche

Campeche

ISTMO DE
TEHUANTEPEC

Villahermosa
Oaxaca
Veracruz
Jalapa
Puebla
México, D.F.
Cuernavaca
Tampico
R. Balsas
Acapulco

Matamoros
Reynosa
Monterrey
Nuevo Laredo

Sierra Madre Oriental

Ciudad Victoria
Saltillo
San Luis Potosí
Zacatecas
León
Guanajuato
Aguascalientes
Morelia
Uruapan
Guadalajara

México

Río Grande
Río Bravo del Norte
R. Conchos

Ciudad Juárez
Chihuahua

Mazatlán
Puerto Vallarta

Sierra Madre Occidental

Golfo de California

La Paz

Nogales
Hermosillo

BAJA CALIFORNIA

R. Colorado
Mexicali
Tijuana

Océano Pacífico

N
E
S
O

México

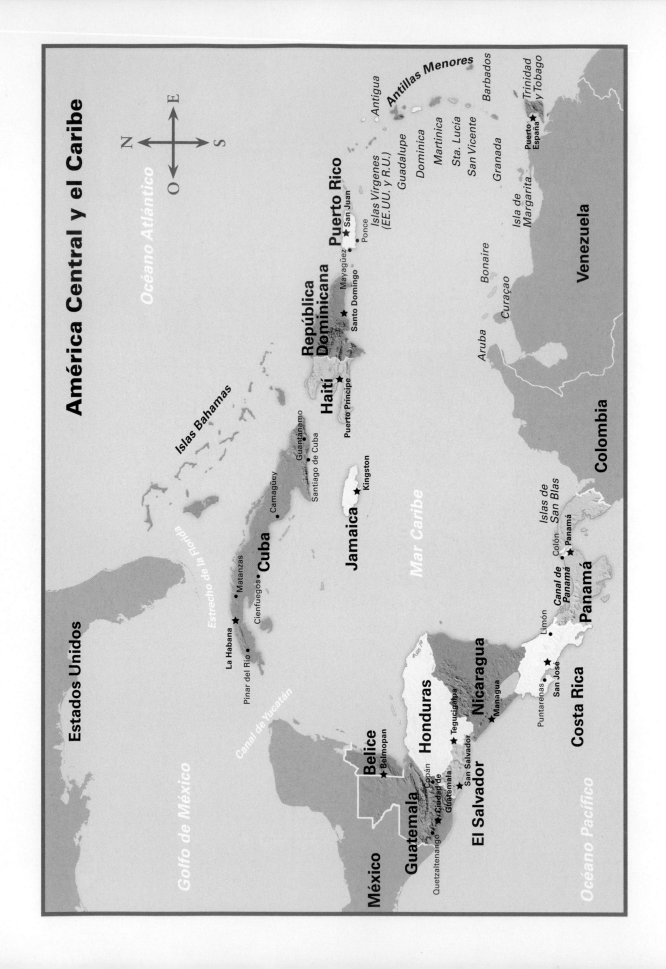

Mar Caribe

Barranquilla
Maracaibo
Caracas ★
Puerto España ★
Trinidad y Tobago

Venezuela

Medellín
Colombia
Bogotá ★
Cáli
Pasto

R. Orinoco

Georgetown ★
Guyana
Paramaribo ★
Cayena •
Surinam
Guayana Francesa

Islas Galápagos

Océano Pacífico

Isla Pinta
Isla Marchena
Isla Genovesa

Isla Isabela

Línea Ecuatorial

ECUADOR

Volcán Darwin
Isla Santiago (San Salvador)

Isla Fernandina

Puerto Ayora
Isla Santa Cruz
Isla San Cristóbal

Santo Tomás
Isla Santa Cruz
Puerto Barquerizo Moreno

Isla Santa María
Isla Española

Quito ★
Ecuador
Guayaquil

Iquitos •

Perú

R. Negro

R. Amazonas
Manaus
Belém •

Cordillera de los Andes

R. Madeira

Recife •

Lima ★
Cuzco •
Lago Titicaca
Arequipa •
Arica •
Iquique •

La Paz ★
Sucre ★
Bolivia

Brasil
Brasilia ★

Océano Pacífico

Antofagasta •
Salta •

R. Paraguay

Paraguay
Asunción ★

R. Paraná

Belo Horizonte •
São Paulo •
Santos •
Río de Janeiro •

Salvador •

Chile

Córdoba •

Valparaíso •
Mendoza •
Santiago ★
Buenos Aires ★

R. Paraná

R. Uruguay

Uruguay
Montevideo •

Porto Alegre •

Concepción •
Argentina

Bahía Blanca •

Océano Atlántico

Cordillera de los Andes

N

O ← → E

S

Puerto Montt •

Estrecho de Magallanes
Punta Arenas •

Islas Malvinas

Tierra del Fuego

América del Sur

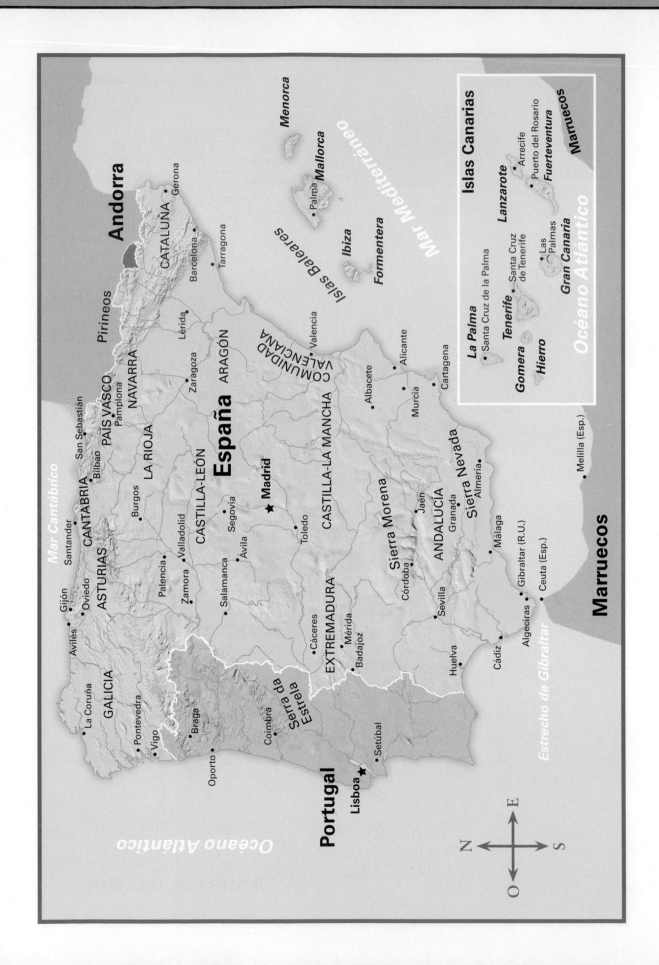

Hola, ¿qué tal?

1

A PRIMERA VISTA

- Guess what the people on the photo are saying:
  a. Adiós.   b. Hola.   c. salsa
- Most likely they would also say:
  a. Gracias.   b. fiesta   c. Buenos días.
- The women are:
  a. amigas   b. chicos   c. señores

Más práctica
Workbook pages 39–48
Video Manual pages 49–54
Lab Manual pages 55–60

Hola, ¿qué tal?

Más vocabulario

Buenos días.	*Good morning.*
Buenas noches.	*Good evening; Good night.*
Hasta la vista.	*See you later.*
Hasta pronto.	*See you soon.*
¿Cómo se llama usted?	*What's your name? (form.)*
Le presento a…	*I would like to introduce you to (name). (form.)*
Te presento a…	*I would like to introduce you to (name). (fam.)*
el nombre	*name*
¿Cómo estás?	*How are you? (fam.)*
No muy bien.	*Not very well.*
¿Qué pasa?	*What's happening?; What's going on?*
por favor	*please*
De nada.	*You're welcome.*
No hay de qué.	*You're welcome.*
Lo siento.	*I'm sorry.*
Gracias.	*Thank you; Thanks.*
Muchas gracias.	*Thank you very much; Thanks a lot.*

Variación léxica

Items are presented for recognition purposes only.

Buenos días.	⟷	Buenas.
De nada.	⟷	A la orden.
Lo siento.	⟷	Perdón.
¿Qué tal?	⟷	¿Qué hubo? (*Col.*)
Chau.	⟷	Ciao; Chao.

recursos

| WB pp. 39–40 | LM p. 55 | vhlcentral.com Lección 1 |

1

ELENA Patricia, éste es el señor Perales.
PATRICIA Encantada.
SEÑOR PERALES Igualmente. ¿De dónde es usted, señorita?
PATRICIA Soy de México. ¿Y usted?
SEÑOR PERALES De Puerto Rico.

2

TOMÁS ¿Qué tal, Alberto?
ALBERTO Regular. ¿Y tú?
TOMÁS Bien. ¿Qué hay de nuevo?
ALBERTO Nada.

3

SEÑOR VARGAS Buenas tardes, señora Wong. ¿Cómo está usted?
SEÑORA WONG Muy bien, gracias. ¿Y usted, señor Vargas?
SEÑOR VARGAS Bien, gracias.
SEÑORA WONG Hasta mañana, señor Vargas. Saludos a la señora Vargas.
SEÑOR VARGAS Adiós.

BERTA Hasta luego, Tere.
TERESA Chau, Berta. Nos vemos mañana.

CARMEN Buenas tardes. Me llamo Carmen.
¿Cómo te llamas tú?
ANTONIO Buenas tardes. Me llamo Antonio.
Mucho gusto.
CARMEN El gusto es mío. ¿De dónde eres?
ANTONIO Soy de los Estados Unidos, de California.

Práctica

1

Escuchar 🎧 Listen to each question or statement, then choose the correct response.

1. a. Muy bien, gracias. b. Me llamo Graciela.
2. a. Lo siento. b. Mucho gusto.
3. a. Soy de Puerto Rico. b. No muy bien.
4. a. No hay de qué. b. Regular.
5. a. Mucho gusto. b. Hasta pronto.
6. a. Nada. b. Igualmente.
7. a. Me llamo Guillermo Montero. b. Muy bien, gracias.
8. a. Buenas tardes. ¿Cómo estás? b. El gusto es mío.
9. a. Saludos a la Sra. Ramírez. b. Encantada.
10. a. Adiós. b. Regular.

2

Identificar 🎧 You will hear a series of expressions. Identify the expression (**a**, **b**, **c**, or **d**) that does not belong in each series.

1. ___ 3. ___
2. ___ 4. ___

3

Escoger For each expression, write another word or phrase that expresses a similar idea.

> **modelo**
> ¿Cómo estás? *¿Qué tal?*

1. De nada. 4. Te presento a Antonio.
2. Encantado. 5. Hasta la vista.
3. Adiós. 6. Mucho gusto.

4

Ordenar Work with a partner to put this scrambled conversation in order. Then act it out.

—Muy bien, gracias. Soy Rosabel.
—Soy de México. ¿Y tú?
—Mucho gusto, Rosabel.
—Hola. Me llamo Carlos. ¿Cómo estás?
—Soy de Argentina.
—Igualmente. ¿De dónde eres, Carlos?

CARLOS _____
ROSABEL _____
CARLOS _____
ROSABEL _____
CARLOS _____
ROSABEL _____

5 **Completar** Work with a partner to complete these dialogues.

> **modelo**
>
> **Estudiante 1:** ¿Cómo estás?
> **Estudiante 2:** *Muy bien, gracias.*

1. **Estudiante 1:** _____
   Estudiante 2: Buenos días. ¿Qué tal?
2. **Estudiante 1:** _____
   Estudiante 2: Me llamo Carmen Sánchez.
3. **Estudiante 1:** _____
   Estudiante 2: De Canadá.
4. **Estudiante 1:** Te presento a Marisol.
   Estudiante 2: _____

5. **Estudiante 1:** Gracias.
   Estudiante 2: _____
6. **Estudiante 1:** _____
   Estudiante 2: Regular.
7. **Estudiante 1:** _____
   Estudiante 2: Nada.
8. **Estudiante 1:** ¡Hasta la vista!
   Estudiante 2: _____

6 **Cambiar** Work with a partner and correct the second part of each conversation to make it logical.

> **modelo**
>
> **Estudiante 1:** ¿Qué tal?
> **Estudiante 2:** ~~No hay de qué.~~ Bien. ¿Y tú?

1. **Estudiante 1:** Hasta mañana, señora Ramírez. Saludos al señor Ramírez.
   Estudiante 2: *Muy bien, gracias.*
2. **Estudiante 1:** ¿Qué hay de nuevo, Alberto?
   Estudiante 2: *Sí, me llamo Alberto. ¿Cómo te llamas tú?*
3. **Estudiante 1:** Gracias, Tomás.
   Estudiante 2: *Regular. ¿Y tú?*
4. **Estudiante 1:** Miguel, ésta es la señorita Perales.
   Estudiante 2: *No hay de qué, señorita.*
5. **Estudiante 1:** ¿De dónde eres, Antonio?
   Estudiante 2: *Muy bien, gracias. ¿Y tú?*
6. **Estudiante 1:** ¿Cómo se llama usted?
   Estudiante 2: *El gusto es mío.*
7. **Estudiante 1:** ¿Qué pasa?
   Estudiante 2: *Hasta luego, Alicia.*
8. **Estudiante 1:** Buenas tardes, señor. ¿Cómo está usted?
   Estudiante 2: *Soy de Puerto Rico.*

> **¡LENGUA VIVA!**
>
> The titles **señor**, **señora**, and **señorita** are abbreviated **Sr.**, **Sra.**, and **Srta.** Note that these abbreviations are capitalized, while the titles themselves are not.
>
> • • •
>
> There is no Spanish equivalent for the English title *Ms.;* women are addressed as **señora** or **señorita**.

 Practice more at **vhlcentral.com**.

Comunicación

7 **Diálogos** With a partner, complete and act out these conversations.

Conversación 1

—Hola. Me llamo Teresa. ¿Cómo te llamas tú?

—_____

—Soy de Puerto Rico. ¿Y tú?

—_____

Conversación 2

—_____

—Muy bien, gracias. ¿Y usted, señora López?

—_____

—Hasta luego, señora. Saludos al señor López.

—_____

Conversación 3

—_____

—Regular. ¿Y tú?

—_____

—Nada.

8 **Conversaciones** This is the first day of class. Write four short conversations based on what the people in this scene would say.

9 **Situaciones** In groups of three, write and act out these situations.

1. On your way out of class on the first day of school, you strike up a conversation with the two students who were sitting next to you. You find out each student's name and where he or she is from before you say goodbye and go to your next class.
2. At the next class you meet up with a friend and find out how he or she is doing. As you are talking, your friend Elena enters. Introduce her to your friend.
3. As you're leaving the bookstore, you meet your parents' friends Mrs. Sánchez and Mr. Rodríguez. You greet them and ask how each person is. As you say goodbye, you send greetings to Mrs. Rodríguez.
4. Make up and act out a real-life situation that you and your classmates can role-play with the language you've learned.

Lección 1

Bienvenida, Marissa

Marissa llega a México para pasar un año con la familia Díaz.

PERSONAJES MARISSA SRA. DÍAZ

 **Video:** *Fotonovela*

MARISSA ¿Usted es de Cuba?

SRA. DÍAZ Sí, de La Habana. Y Roberto es de Mérida. Tú eres de Wisconsin, ¿verdad?

MARISSA Sí, de Appleton, Wisconsin.

MARISSA ¿Quiénes son los dos chicos de las fotos? ¿Jimena y Felipe?

SRA. DÍAZ Sí. Ellos son estudiantes.

DON DIEGO ¿Cómo está usted hoy, señora Carolina?

SRA. DÍAZ Muy bien, gracias. ¿Y usted?

DON DIEGO Bien, gracias.

DON DIEGO Buenas tardes, señora. Señorita, bienvenida a la Ciudad de México.

MARISSA ¡Muchas gracias!

MARISSA ¿Cómo se llama usted?

DON DIEGO Yo soy Diego. Mucho gusto.

MARISSA El gusto es mío, don Diego.

SRA. DÍAZ Ahí hay dos maletas. Son de Marissa.

DON DIEGO Con permiso.

DON DIEGO

SR. DÍAZ

FELIPE

JIMENA

SR. DÍAZ ¿Qué hora es?

FELIPE Son las cuatro y veinticinco.

SRA. DÍAZ Marissa, te presento a Roberto, mi esposo.

SR. DÍAZ Bienvenida, Marissa.

MARISSA Gracias, señor Díaz.

JIMENA ¿Qué hay en esta cosa?

MARISSA Bueno, a ver, hay tres cuadernos, un mapa... ¡Y un diccionario!

JIMENA ¿Cómo se dice mediodía en inglés?

FELIPE "Noon".

FELIPE Estás en México, ¿verdad?

MARISSA ¿Sí?

FELIPE Nosotros somos tu diccionario.

recursos

VM
pp. 49–50

vhlcentral.com
Lección 1

Expresiones útiles

Identifying yourself and others

¿Cómo se llama usted?
What's your name?

Yo soy Diego, el portero. Mucho gusto.
I'm Diego, the doorman. Nice to meet you.

¿Cómo te llamas?
What's your name?

Me llamo Marissa.
My name is Marissa.

¿Quién es...? / ¿Quiénes son...?
Who is...? / Who are...?

Es mi esposo.
He's my husband.

Tú eres..., ¿verdad?/¿cierto?/¿no?
You are..., right?

Identifying objects

¿Qué hay en esta cosa?
What's in this thing?

Bueno, a ver, aquí hay tres cuadernos...
Well, let's see, here are three notebooks...

Oye/Oiga, ¿cómo se dice suitcase en español?
Hey, how do you say suitcase in Spanish?

Se dice *maleta*.
You say maleta.

Saying what time it is

¿Qué hora es?
What time is it?

Es la una. / Son las dos.
It's one o'clock. / It's two o'clock.

Son las cuatro y veinticinco.
It's four twenty-five.

Polite expressions

Con permiso.
Pardon me; Excuse me. (to request permission)

Perdón.
Pardon me; Excuse me. (to get someone's attention or excuse yourself)

¡Bienvenido/a! *Welcome!*

¿Qué pasó?

1 **¿Cierto o falso?** Indicate if each statement is **cierto** or **falso**. Then correct the false statements.

	Cierto	Falso
1. La Sra. Díaz es de Caracas.	○	○
2. El Sr. Díaz es de Mérida.	○	○
3. Marissa es de Los Ángeles, California.	○	○
4. Jimena y Felipe son profesores.	○	○
5. Las dos maletas son de Jimena.	○	○
6. El Sr. Díaz pregunta "¿qué hora es?".	○	○
7. Hay un diccionario en la mochila (*backpack*) de Marissa.	○	○

2 **Identificar** Indicate which person would make each statement. One name will be used twice.

1. Son las cuatro y veinticinco, papá.
2. Roberto es mi esposo.
3. Yo soy de Wisconsin, ¿de dónde es usted?
4. ¿Qué hay de nuevo, doña Carolina?
5. Yo soy de Cuba.
6. ¿Qué hay en la mochila, Marissa?

MARISSA **FELIPE** **SRA. DÍAZ**

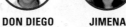
DON DIEGO **JIMENA**

¡LENGUA VIVA!

In Spanish-speaking countries, **don** and **doña** are used with first names to show respect: **don Diego**, **doña Carolina**. Note that these titles, like **señor** and **señora**, are not capitalized.

3 **Completar** Complete the conversation between Don Diego and Marissa.

DON DIEGO Hola, (1)_____.
MARISSA Hola, señor. ¿Cómo se (2)_____ usted?
DON DIEGO Yo me llamo Diego, ¿y (3)_____?
MARISSA Yo me llamo Marissa. (4)_____.
DON DIEGO (5)_____, señorita Marissa.
MARISSA Nos (6)_____, don Diego.
DON DIEGO Hasta (7)_____, señorita Marissa.

4 **Conversar** Imagine that you are chatting with a traveler you just met at the airport. With a partner, prepare a conversation using these cues.

Estudiante 1	Estudiante 2
Say "good afternoon" to your partner and ask for his or her name. →	Say hello and what your name is. Then ask what your partner's name is.
Say what your name is and that you are glad to meet your partner. →	Say that the pleasure is yours.
Ask how your partner is. →	Say that you're doing well, thank you.
Ask where your partner is from. →	Say where you're from.
Say it's one o'clock and say goodbye. →	Say goodbye.

 Practice more at **vhlcentral.com**.

Lección 1

Pronunciación   Audio
The Spanish alphabet

The Spanish and English alphabets are almost identical, with a few exceptions. For example, the Spanish letter **ñ (eñe)** doesn't occur in the English alphabet. Furthermore, the letters **k (ka)** and **w (doble ve)** are used only in words of foreign origin. Examine the chart below to find other differences.

¡LENGUA VIVA!

Note that **ch** and **ll** are digraphs, or two letters that together produce one sound. Conventionally they are considered part of the alphabet, but **ch** and **ll** do not have their own entries when placing words in alphabetical order, as in a glossary.

Letra	Nombre(s)	Ejemplos	Letra	Nombre(s)	Ejemplos
a	a	adiós	m	eme	mapa
b	be	bien, problema	n	ene	nacionalidad
c	ce	cosa, cero	ñ	eñe	mañana
ch	che	chico	o	o	once
d	de	diario, nada	p	pe	profesor
e	e	estudiante	q	cu	qué
f	efe	foto	r	ere	regular, señora
g	ge	gracias, Gerardo, regular	s	ese	señor
			t	te	tú
h	hache	hola	u	u	usted
i	i	igualmente	v	ve	vista, nuevo
j	jota	Javier	w	doble ve	walkman
k	ka, ca	kilómetro	x	equis	existir, México
l	ele	lápiz	y	i griega, ye	yo
ll	elle	llave	z	zeta, ceta	zona

El alfabeto Repeat the Spanish alphabet and example words after your instructor.

Práctica Spell these words aloud in Spanish.

1. nada
2. maleta
3. quince
4. muy
5. hombre
6. por favor
7. San Fernando
8. Estados Unidos
9. Puerto Rico
10. España
11. Javier
12. Ecuador
13. Maite
14. gracias
15. Nueva York

AYUDA

The letter combination **rr** produces a strong trilled sound which does not have an English equivalent. English speakers commonly make this sound when imitating the sound of a motor. This sound occurs with the **rr** between vowels and with the **r** at the beginning of a word: **puertorriqueño, terrible, Roberto,** etc. See **¡ADELANTE! DOS Lección 1**, p. 27 for more information.

Refranes Read these sayings aloud.

Ver es creer.[1]

En boca cerrada no entran moscas.[2]

1 Seeing is believing. 2 Silence is golden.

recursos

LM p. 56   vhlcentral.com Lección 1

1

EN DETALLE

Additional Reading

Saludos y besos en los países hispanos

In Spanish-speaking countries, kissing on the cheek is a customary way to greet friends and family members. Even when people are introduced for the first time, it is common for them to kiss, particularly in non-business settings. Whereas North Americans maintain considerable personal space when greeting, Spaniards and Latin Americans tend to decrease their personal space and give one or two kisses (**besos**) on the cheek, sometimes accompanied by a handshake or a hug. In formal business settings, where associates do not know one another on a personal level, a simple handshake is appropriate.

Greeting someone with a **beso** varies according to gender and region. Men generally greet each other with a hug or warm handshake, with the exception of Argentina, where male friends and relatives lightly kiss on the cheek. Greetings between men and women, and between women, generally include kissing, but can differ depending on the country and context. In Spain, it is customary to give **dos besos**, starting with the right cheek first. In Latin American countries, including Mexico, Costa Rica, Colombia, and Chile, a greeting consists of a single "air kiss" on the right cheek. Peruvians also "air kiss," but

strangers will simply shake hands. In Colombia, female acquaintances tend to simply pat each other on the right forearm or shoulder.

Tendencias

País	Beso	País	Beso
Argentina	💋	España	💋💋
Bolivia	💋	México	💋
Chile	💋	Paraguay	💋💋
Colombia	💋	Puerto Rico	💋
El Salvador	💋	Venezuela	💋/💋💋

ACTIVIDADES

1 **¿Cierto o falso?** Indicate whether these statements are true (**cierto**) or false (**falso**). Correct the false statements.

1. Hispanic people use less personal space when greeting than in the U.S.
2. Men never greet with a kiss in Spanish-speaking countries.
3. Shaking hands is not appropriate for a business setting in Latin America.
4. Spaniards greet with one kiss on the right cheek.
5. In Mexico, people greet with an "air kiss."
6. Gender can play a role in the type of greeting given.
7. If two women acquaintances meet in Colombia, they should exchange two kisses on the cheek.
8. In Peru, a man and a woman meeting for the first time would probably greet each other with an "air kiss."

Leccíon 1

ASÍ SE DICE

Saludos y despedidas

¿Cómo te/le va?	*How are things going (for you)?*
¡Cuánto tiempo!	*It's been a long time!*
Hasta ahora.	*See you soon.*
¿Qué hay?	*What's new?*
¿Qué onda? (Méx., Arg., Chi.); **¿Qué más?** (Ven., Col.)	*What's going on?*

EL MUNDO HISPANO

Parejas y amigos famosos

Here are some famous couples and friends from the Spanish-speaking world.

- **Jennifer López** y **Marc Anthony** (Estados Unidos/Puerto Rico) Both singers, the couple married in 2004 and divorced in 2011. They starred together in the 2007 film *El Cantante.*

- **Gael García Bernal** (México) y **Diego Luna** (México) These lifelong friends became famous when they starred in the 2001 Mexican film *Y tu mamá también.* They continue to work together on projects, such as the 2008 film, *Rudo y Cursi.*

- **Salma Hayek** (México) y **Penélope Cruz** (España) These two close friends developed their acting skills in their countries of origin before meeting in Hollywood.

PERFIL

La plaza principal

In the Spanish-speaking world, public space is treasured. Small city and town life revolves around the **plaza principal**. Often surrounded by cathedrals or municipal buildings like the **ayuntamiento** (*city hall*), the pedestrian **plaza** is designated as a central meeting place for family and friends. During warmer months, when outdoor cafés usually line the **plaza**, it is

La Plaza Mayor de Salamanca

a popular spot to have a leisurely cup of coffee, chat, and people watch. Many town festivals, or **ferias**, also take place in this space. One of the most famous town squares

La Plaza de Armas, Lima, Perú

is the **Plaza Mayor** in the university town of Salamanca, Spain. Students gather underneath its famous clock tower to meet up with friends or simply take a coffee break.

Conexión Internet

What are the plazas principales in large cities such as Mexico City and Caracas?

Go to vhlcentral.com to find more cultural information related to this Cultura section.

ACTIVIDADES

2 **Comprensión** Answer these questions.

1. What are two types of buildings found on the **plaza principal**?
2. What two types of events or activities are common at a **plaza principal**?
3. How would Diego Luna greet his friends?
4. Would Salma Hayek and Jennifer López greet each other with one kiss or two?

3 **Saludos** Role-play these greetings with a partner. Include a verbal greeting as well as a kiss or handshake, as appropriate.

1. friends in Mexico
2. business associates at a conference in Chile
3. friends meeting in Madrid's Plaza Mayor
4. Peruvians meeting for the first time
5. relatives in Argentina

 Practice more at **vhlcentral.com**.

Nouns and articles  Tutorial

Spanish nouns

ANTE TODO A noun is a word used to identify people, animals, places, things, or ideas. Unlike English, all Spanish nouns, even those that refer to non-living things, have gender; that is, they are considered either masculine or feminine. As in English, nouns in Spanish also have number, meaning that they are either singular or plural.

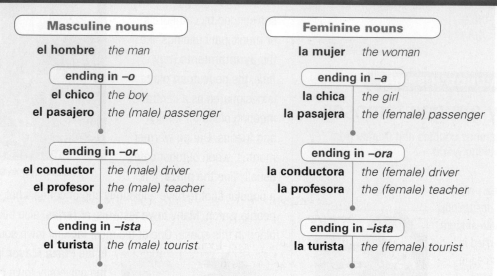

Nouns that refer to living things

Masculine nouns		Feminine nouns	
el hombre	*the man*	**la mujer**	*the woman*
ending in –o		*ending in –a*	
el chico	*the boy*	**la chica**	*the girl*
el pasajero	*the (male) passenger*	**la pasajera**	*the (female) passenger*
ending in –or		*ending in –ora*	
el conductor	*the (male) driver*	**la conductora**	*the (female) driver*
el profesor	*the (male) teacher*	**la profesora**	*the (female) teacher*
ending in –ista		*ending in –ista*	
el turista	*the (male) tourist*	**la turista**	*the (female) tourist*

▶ Generally, nouns that refer to males, like **el hombre**, are masculine, while nouns that refer to females, like **la mujer**, are feminine.

▶ Many nouns that refer to male beings end in **–o** or **–or**. Their corresponding feminine forms end in **–a** and **–ora**, respectively.

el conductor

la profesora

▶ The masculine and feminine forms of nouns that end in **–ista**, like **turista**, are the same, so gender is indicated by the article **el** (masculine) or **la** (feminine). Some other nouns have identical masculine and feminine forms.

el joven
the youth; the young man

la joven
the youth; the young woman

el estudiante
the (male) student

la estudiante
the (female) student

Lección 1

Nouns that refer to non-living things

Masculine nouns		Feminine nouns	
ending in –o		**ending in –a**	
el cuaderno	the notebook	la computadora	the computer
el diario	the diary	la cosa	the thing
el diccionario	the dictionary	la escuela	the school
el número	the number	la maleta	the suitcase
el video	the video	la palabra	the word
ending in –ma		**ending in –ción**	
el problema	the problem	la lección	the lesson
el programa	the program	la conversación	the conversation
ending in –s		**ending in –dad**	
el autobús	the bus	la nacionalidad	the nationality
el país	the country	la comunidad	the community

▶ As shown above, certain noun endings are strongly associated with a specific gender, so you can use them to determine if a noun is masculine or feminine.

▶ Because the gender of nouns that refer to non-living things cannot be determined by foolproof rules, you should memorize the gender of each noun you learn. It is helpful to learn each noun with its corresponding article, **el** for masculine and **la** for feminine.

▶ Another reason to memorize the gender of every noun is that there are common exceptions to the rules of gender. For example, **el mapa** (*map*) and **el día** (*day*) end in **–a**, but are masculine. **La mano** (*hand*) ends in **–o**, but is feminine.

Plural of nouns

▶ To form the plural, add **–s** to nouns that end in a vowel. For nouns that end in a consonant, add **–es**. For nouns that end in **z**, change the **z** to **c**, then add **–es**.

el chic**o** ⟶ los chic**os**   la nacionalida**d** ⟶ las nacionalida**des**

el diari**o** ⟶ los diari**os**   el paí**s** ⟶ los paí**ses**

el problem**a** ⟶ los problem**as**   el lápi**z** (*pencil*) ⟶ los lápi**ces**

CONSULTA

You will learn more about accent marks in **Lección 4, Pronunciación**, p. 193.

▶ In general, when a singular noun has an accent mark on the last syllable, the accent is dropped from the plural form.

la lecci**ón** ⟶ las lecci**ones**   el autob**ús** ⟶ los autob**uses**

▶ Use the masculine plural form to refer to a group that includes both males and females.

1 pasajer**o** + 2 pasajer**as** = 3 pasajer**os**   2 chic**os** + 2 chic**as** = 4 chic**os**

Lección 1

Spanish articles

ANTE TODO As you know, English often uses definite articles (*the*) and indefinite articles (*a, an*) before nouns. Spanish also has definite and indefinite articles. Unlike English, Spanish articles vary in form because they agree in gender and number with the nouns they modify.

Definite articles

▶ Spanish has four forms that are equivalent to the English definite article *the*. Use definite articles to refer to specific nouns.

Masculine		Feminine	
SINGULAR	PLURAL	SINGULAR	PLURAL
el diccionario	**los** diccionarios	**la** computadora	**las** computadoras
the dictionary	*the dictionaries*	*the computer*	*the computers*

Indefinite articles

▶ Spanish has four forms that are equivalent to the English indefinite article, which according to context may mean *a*, *an*, or *some*. Use indefinite articles to refer to unspecified persons or things.

Masculine		Feminine	
SINGULAR	PLURAL	SINGULAR	PLURAL
un pasajero	**unos** pasajeros	**una** fotografía	**unas** fotografías
a (one) passenger	*some passengers*	*a (one) photograph*	*some photographs*

¡LENGUA VIVA!

Feminine singular nouns that begin with a stressed a- or ha- require the masculine articles **el** and **un**. This is done in order to avoid repetition of the *a* sound. The plural forms still use the feminine articles.

el agua *water*
las aguas *waters*
un hacha *ax*
unas hachas *axes*

¡LENGUA VIVA!

Since **la fotografía** is feminine, so is its shortened form, **la foto**, even though it ends in –o.

**¡INTÉNTALO!** Provide a definite article for each noun in the first column and an indefinite article for each noun in the second column.

¿el, la, los o las?	¿un, una, unos o unas?
1. ____la____ chica	1. ____un____ autobús
2. _____ chico	2. _____ escuelas
3. _____ maleta	3. _____ computadora
4. _____ cuadernos	4. _____ hombres
5. _____ lápiz	5. _____ señora
6. _____ mujeres	6. _____ lápices

recursos

WB
p. 41

LM
p. 57

vhlcentral.com
Lección 1

Práctica

1

¿Singular o plural? If the word is singular, make it plural. If it is plural, make it singular.

1. el número
2. un diario
3. la estudiante
4. el conductor
5. el país
6. las cosas
7. unos turistas
8. las nacionalidades

9. unas computadoras
10. los problemas
11. una fotografía
12. los profesores
13. unas señoritas
14. el hombre
15. la maleta
16. la señora

2

Identificar For each drawing, provide the noun with its corresponding definite and indefinite articles.

> **modelo**
> las maletas, unas maletas

1. _____

2. _____

3. _____

4. _____

5. _____

6. _____

7. _____

8. _____

Comunicación

3

Charadas In groups, play a game of charades. Individually, think of two nouns for each charade, for example, a boy using a computer (**un chico**; **una computadora**). The first person to guess correctly acts out the next charade.

 Practice more at **vhlcentral.com**.

1.2 Numbers 0–30   Tutorial

Los números 0 a 30		
0 cero		
1 uno	**11** once	**21** veintiuno
2 dos	**12** doce	**22** veintidós
3 tres	**13** trece	**23** veintitrés
4 cuatro	**14** catorce	**24** veinticuatro
5 cinco	**15** quince	**25** veinticinco
6 seis	**16** dieciséis	**26** veintiséis
7 siete	**17** diecisiete	**27** veintisiete
8 ocho	**18** dieciocho	**28** veintiocho
9 nueve	**19** diecinueve	**29** veintinueve
10 diez	**20** veinte	**30** treinta

AYUDA

Though it is less common, the numbers 16 through 29 (except 20) can also be written as three words: **diez y seis, diez y siete…**

▶ The number **uno** (*one*) and numbers ending in **–uno**, such as **veintiuno**, have more than one form. Before masculine nouns, **uno** shortens to **un**. Before feminine nouns, **uno** changes to **una**.

un hombre ⟶ veinti**ún** hombres   **una** mujer ⟶ veinti**una** mujeres

▶ **¡Atención!** The forms **uno** and **veintiuno** are used when counting (**uno, dos, tres… veinte, veintiuno, veintidós…**). They are also used when the number *follows* a noun, even if the noun is feminine: **la lección uno**.

▶ To ask *how many people* or *things* there are, use **cuántos** before masculine nouns and **cuántas** before feminine nouns.

▶ The Spanish equivalent of both *there is* and *there are* is **hay**. Use **¿Hay…?** to ask *Is there…?* or *Are there…?* Use **no hay** to express *there is not* or *there are not*.

—**¿Cuántos** estudiantes **hay**?
How many students are there?

—**Hay** seis estudiantes en la foto.
There are six students in the photo.

—**¿Hay** chicos en la fotografía?
Are there guys in the picture?

—**Hay** tres chicas y **no hay** chicos.
There are three girls, and there are no guys.

¡INTÉNTALO!   Provide the Spanish words for these numbers.

1. **7** _____
2. **16** _____
3. **29** _____
4. **1** _____

5. **0** _____
6. **15** _____
7. **21** _____
8. **9** _____

9. **23** _____
10. **11** _____
11. **30** _____
12. **4** _____

13. **12** _____
14. **28** _____
15. **14** _____
16. **10** _____

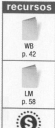

recursos

WB
p. 42

LM
p. 58

S
vhlcentral.com
Lección 1

Práctica

1

Contar Following the pattern, write out the missing numbers in Spanish.

1. 1, 3, 5, ..., 29
2. 2, 4, 6, ..., 30
3. 3, 6, 9, ..., 30
4. 30, 28, 26, ..., 0
5. 30, 25, 20, ..., 0
6. 28, 24, 20, ..., 0

2

Resolver Solve these math problems with a partner.

> **modelo**
>
> 5 + 3 =
> **Estudiante 1:** *cinco más tres son...*
> **Estudiante 2:** *ocho*

AYUDA

+ → más
− → menos
= → son

1. **2 + 15 =**
2. **20 − 1 =**
3. **5 + 7 =**
4. **18 + 12 =**
5. **3 + 22 =**

6. **6 − 3 =**
7. **11 + 12 =**
8. **7 − 2 =**
9. **8 + 5 =**
10. **23 − 14 =**

3

¿Cuántos hay? How many persons or things are there in these drawings?

> **modelo**
>
> Hay tres maletas.

1. _____

2. _____

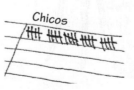

3. _____

4. _____

5. _____

6. _____

7. _____

8. _____

Comunicación

4

En la clase With a classmate, take turns asking and answering these questions about your classroom.

1. ¿Cuántos estudiantes hay?
2. ¿Cuántos profesores hay?
3. ¿Hay una computadora?
4. ¿Hay una maleta?
5. ¿Cuántos mapas hay?

6. ¿Cuántos lápices hay?
7. ¿Hay cuadernos?
8. ¿Cuántos diccionarios hay?
9. ¿Hay hombres?
10. ¿Cuántas mujeres hay?

5

Preguntas With a classmate, take turns asking and answering questions about the drawing. Talk about:

1. how many children there are
2. how many women there are
3. if there are some photographs
4. if there is a boy
5. how many notebooks there are

6. if there is a bus
7. if there are tourists
8. how many pencils there are
9. if there is a man
10. how many computers there are

1.3 Present tense of ser Tutorial

Subject pronouns

ANTE TODO In order to use verbs, you will need to learn about subject pronouns. A subject pronoun replaces the name or title of a person and acts as the subject of a verb. In both Spanish and English, subject pronouns are divided into three groups: first person, second person, and third person.

Subject pronouns			
	SINGULAR		**PLURAL**
FIRST PERSON	**yo** / *I*	**nosotros** *we* (masculine)	
		nosotras *we* (feminine)	
SECOND PERSON	**tú** *you* (familiar)	**vosotros** *you* (masc., fam.)	
	usted (Ud.) *you* (formal)	**vosotras** *you* (fem., fam.)	
		ustedes (Uds.) *you* (form.)	
THIRD PERSON	**él** *he*	**ellos** *they* (masc.)	
	ella *she*	**ellas** *they* (fem.)	

¡LENGUA VIVA!

In Latin America, **ustedes** is used as the plural for both **tú** and **usted**. In Spain, however, **vosotros** and **vosotras** are used as the plural of **tú**, and **ustedes** is used only as the plural of **usted**.

• • •

Usted and ustedes are abbreviated as **Ud**. and **Uds**., or occasionally as **Vd**. and **Vds**.

▶ Spanish has two subject pronouns that mean *you* (singular). Use **tú** when addressing a friend, a family member, or a child you know well. Use **usted** to address a person with whom you have a formal or more distant relationship, such as a superior at work, a professor, or an older person.

Tú eres de Canadá, ¿verdad, David? | **¿Usted** es la profesora de español?
You are from Canada, right, David? | *Are you the Spanish professor?*

▶ The masculine plural forms **nosotros**, **vosotros**, and **ellos** refer to a group of males or to a group of males and females. The feminine plural forms **nosotras**, **vosotras**, and **ellas** can refer only to groups made up exclusively of females.

nosotros, vosotros, ellos

nosotros, vosotros, ellos

nosotras, vosotras, ellas

▶ There is no Spanish equivalent of the English subject pronoun *it*. Generally *it* is not expressed in Spanish.

Es un problema. | Es una computadora.
It's a problem. | *It's a computer.*

The present tense of ser

ANTE TODO   In **Contextos** and **Fotonovela**, you have already used several present-tense forms of **ser** (*to be*) to identify yourself and others, and to talk about where you and others are from. **Ser** is an irregular verb; its forms do not follow the regular patterns that most verbs follow. You need to memorize the forms, which appear in this chart.

The verb **ser** (*to be*)		
SINGULAR FORMS	yo **soy**	*I am*
	tú **eres**	*you are* (fam.)
	Ud./él/ella **es**	*you are* (form.); *he/she is*
PLURAL FORMS	nosotros/as **somos**	*we are*
	vosotros/as **sois**	*you are* (fam.)
	Uds./ellos/ellas **son**	*you are* (form.); *they are*

Uses of *ser*

▶ Use **ser** to identify people and things.

—¿Quién **es** él?
Who is he?

—**Es** Felipe Díaz Velázquez.
He's Felipe Díaz Velázquez.

—¿Qué **es**?
What is it?

—**Es** un mapa de España.
It's a map of Spain.

Es Marissa.

Es una maleta.

▶ **Ser** also expresses possession, with the preposition **de**. There is no Spanish equivalent of the English construction [*noun*] + 's (*Maru's*). In its place, Spanish uses [*noun*] + **de** + [*owner*].

—¿**De** quién **es**?
Whose is it?

—**Es** el diario **de** Maru.
It's Maru's diary.

—¿**De** quién **son**?
Whose are they?

—**Son** los lápices **de** la chica.
They are the girl's pencils.

▶ When **de** is followed by the article **el**, the two combine to form the contraction **del**. **De** does *not* contract with **la**, **las**, or **los**.

—**Es** la computadora **del** conductor.
It's the driver's computer.

—**Son** las maletas **del** chico.
They are the boy's suitcases.

Lección 1

▶ **Ser** also uses the preposition **de** to express origin.

¿De dónde eres?

Yo soy de Wisconsin.

¿De dónde es usted?

Yo soy de Cuba.

—¿**De** dónde **es** Juan Carlos?
Where is Juan Carlos from?

—Es **de** Argentina.
He's from Argentina.

—¿**De** dónde **es** Maru?
Where is Maru from?

—**Es de** Costa Rica.
She's from Costa Rica.

▶ Use **ser** to express profession or occupation.

Don Francisco **es conductor**.
Don Francisco is a driver.

Yo **soy estudiante**.
I am a student.

▶ Unlike English, Spanish does not use the indefinite article (**un, una**) after **ser** when referring to professions, unless accompanied by an adjective or other description.

Marta **es** profesora.
Marta is a teacher.

Marta **es una** profesora excelente.
Marta is an excellent teacher.

Somos Perú

LanPerú

¡INTÉNTALO!　Provide the correct subject pronouns and the present forms of **ser**.

1. Gabriel　　__él__　__es__
2. Juan y yo　　____　____
3. Óscar y Flora　　____　____
4. Adriana　　____　____

5. las turistas　　____　____
6. el chico　　____　____
7. los conductores　　____　____
8. los señores Ruiz　　____　____

Práctica

1

Pronombres What subject pronouns would you use to (a) talk *to* these people directly and (b) talk *about* them to others?

> modelo
>
> un joven tú, él

1. una chica
2. el presidente de México
3. tres chicas y un chico
4. un estudiante
5. la señora Ochoa
6. dos profesoras

2

Identidad y origen With a partner, take turns asking and answering these questions about the people indicated: **¿Quién es?/¿Quiénes son?** and **¿De dónde es?/¿De dónde son?**

> modelo
>
> Selena Gomez (Estados Unidos)
> **Estudiante 1:** ¿Quién es?   **Estudiante 1:** ¿De dónde es?
> **Estudiante 2:** Es Selena Gomez. **Estudiante 2:** Es de los Estados Unidos.

1. Enrique Iglesias (España)

2. Robinson Canó (República Dominicana)

3. Rebecca Lobo y Martin Sheen (Estados Unidos)

4. Carlos Santana y Salma Hayek (México)

5. Shakira (Colombia)

6. Antonio Banderas y Penélope Cruz (España)

7. Taylor Swift y Demi Lovato (Estados Unidos)

8. Daisy Fuentes (Cuba)

3

¿Qué es? Ask your partner what each object is and to whom it belongs.

> modelo
>
> **Estudiante 1:** ¿Qué es?   **Estudiante 1:** ¿De quién es?
> **Estudiante 2:** Es un diccionario. **Estudiante 2:** Es del profesor Núñez.

1.   2.   3.   4.

Comunicación

Lección 1

4

Preguntas Using the items in the word bank, ask your partner questions about the ad. Be imaginative in your responses.

| ¿Cuántas? | ¿De dónde? | ¿Qué? |
| ¿Cuántos? | ¿De quién? | ¿Quién? |

SOMOS ECOTURISTA, S.A.
Los autobuses oficiales de la Ruta Maya

* 25 autobuses en total
* 30 conductores del área
* pasajeros internacionales
* mapas de la región

¡Todos a bordo!

5

¿Quién es? In small groups, take turns pretending to be a famous person from a Spanish-speaking country (such as Spain, Mexico, Puerto Rico, Cuba, or the United States). Use the list of professions to think of people from a variety of backgrounds. Your partners will ask you questions and try to guess who you are.

| actor *actor* | cantante *singer* | escritor(a) *writer* |
| actriz *actress* | deportista *athlete* | músico/a *musician* |

modelo

Estudiante 3: ¿Eres de Puerto Rico?
Estudiante 1: No. Soy de Colombia.
Estudiante 2: ¿Eres hombre?
Estudiante 1: Sí. Soy hombre.
Estudiante 3: ¿Eres escritor?
Estudiante 1: No. Soy actor.
Estudiante 2: ¿Eres John Leguizamo?
Estudiante 1: ¡Sí! ¡Sí!

 Practice more at **vhlcentral.com**.

1.4 Telling time  Tutorial

ANTE TODO   In both English and Spanish, the verb *to be* (**ser**) and numbers are used to tell time.

▶ To ask what time it is, use **¿Qué hora es?** When telling time, use **es + la** with **una** and **son + las** with all other hours.

Es la una.

Son las dos.

Son las seis.

▶ As in English, you express time in Spanish from the hour to the half hour by adding minutes.

Son las cuatro **y cinco**.

Son las once **y veinte**.

▶ You may use either **y cuarto** or **y quince** to express fifteen minutes or quarter past the hour. For thirty minutes or half past the hour, you may use either **y media** or **y treinta**.

Es la una **y cuarto**.

Son las nueve **y quince**.

Son las doce **y media**.

Son las siete **y treinta**.

▶ You express time from the half hour to the hour in Spanish by subtracting minutes or a portion of an hour from the next hour.

Es la una **menos cuarto**.

Son las tres **menos quince**.

Son las ocho **menos veinte**.

Son las tres **menos diez**.

▶ To ask at what time a particular event takes place, use the phrase **¿A qué hora (...)?**
To state at what time something takes place, use the construction **a la(s)** + *time*.

¿A qué hora es la clase de biología?	La clase es **a las dos**.
(At) what time is biology class?	*The class is at two o'clock.*
¿A qué hora es la fiesta?	**A las ocho**.
(At) what time is the party?	*At eight.*

¡LENGUA VIVA!

Other useful expressions for telling time:
Son las doce (del día).
It is twelve o'clock (p.m.).
Son las doce (de la noche).
It is twelve o'clock (a.m.).

▶ Here are some useful words and phrases associated with telling time.

Son las ocho **en punto**.	Son las nueve **de la mañana**.
It's 8 o'clock on the dot/sharp.	*It's 9 a.m./in the morning.*
Es **el mediodía**.	Son las cuatro y cuarto **de la tarde**.
It's noon.	*It's 4:15 p.m./in the afternoon.*
Es **la medianoche**.	Son las diez y media **de la noche**.
It's midnight.	*It's 10:30 p.m./at night.*

¿Qué hora es?

Son las cuatro menos diez.

¿Qué hora es?

Son las cuatro y veinticinco.

¡INTÉNTALO!   Practice telling time by completing these sentences.

1. (1:00 a.m.) Es la _____una_____ de la mañana.
2. (2:50 a.m.) Son las tres _____ diez de la mañana.
3. (4:15 p.m.) Son las cuatro y _____ de la tarde.
4. (8:30 p.m.) Son las ocho y _____ de la noche.
5. (9:15 a.m.) Son las nueve y quince de la _____.
6. (12:00 p.m.) Es el _____.
7. (6:00 a.m.) Son las seis de la _____.
8. (4:05 p.m.) Son las cuatro y cinco de la _____.
9. (12:00 a.m.) Es la _____.
10. (3:45 a.m.) Son las cuatro menos _____ de la mañana.
11. (2:15 a.m.) Son las _____ y cuarto de la mañana.
12. (1:25 p.m.) Es la una y _____ de la tarde.
13. (6:50 a.m.) Son las _____ menos diez de la mañana.
14. (10:40 p.m.) Son las once menos veinte de la _____.

recursos

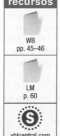
WB
pp. 45–46

LM
p. 60

(S)
vhlcentral.com
Lección 1

Lección 1

Práctica

1   **Ordenar** Put these times in order, from the earliest to the latest.

a. Son las dos de la tarde.

b. Son las once de la mañana.

c. Son las siete y media de la noche.

d. Son las seis menos cuarto de la tarde.

e. Son las dos menos diez de la tarde.

f. Son las ocho y veintidós de la mañana.

2   **¿Qué hora es?** Give the times shown on each clock or watch.

Son las cuatro y cuarto/quince de la tarde.

p.m.   p.m.   p.m.   a.m.

1. _____   2. _____   3. _____   4. _____   5. _____

a.m.   a.m.   p.m.

6. _____   7. _____   8. _____   9. _____ 10. _____

NOTA CULTURAL

Many Spanish-speaking countries use both the 12-hour clock and the 24-hour clock (that is, military time). The 24-hour clock is commonly used in written form on signs and schedules. For example, 1 p.m. is **13h**, 2 p.m. is **14h** and so on. See the photo on p. 33 for a sample schedule.

3   **¿A qué hora?** Ask your partner at what time these events take place. Your partner will answer according to the cues provided.

modelo

la clase de matemáticas (2:30 p.m.)

Estudiante 1: ¿A qué hora es la clase de matemáticas?

Estudiante 2: Es a las dos y media de la tarde.

1. el programa *Las cuatro amigas* (11:30 a.m.)

2. el drama *La casa de Bernarda Alba* (7:00 p.m.)

3. el programa *Las computadoras* (8:30 a.m.)

4. la clase de español (10:30 a.m.)

5. la clase de biología (9:40 a.m.)

6. la clase de historia (10:50 a.m.)

7. el partido (*game*) de béisbol (5:15 p.m.)

8. el partido de tenis (12:45 p.m.)

9. el partido de baloncesto (*basketball*) (7:45 p.m.)

NOTA CULTURAL

La casa de Bernarda Alba is a famous play by Spanish poet and playwright **Federico García Lorca** (1898–1936). Lorca was one of the most famous writers of the 20th century and a close friend of Spain's most talented artists, including the painter Salvador Dalí and the filmmaker Luis Buñuel.

 Practice more at **vhlcentral.com**.

Comunicación

4

En la televisión With a partner, take turns asking questions about these television listings.

> **modelo**
>
> **Estudiante 1:** ¿A qué hora es el documental *Las computadoras*?
> **Estudiante 2:** Es a las nueve en punto de la noche.

TV Hoy – Programación

11:00 am Telenovela: *La casa de la familia Díaz*	**5:00 pm** Telenovela: *Tres mujeres*
12:00 pm Película: *El cóndor* (drama)	**6:00 pm** Noticias
2:00 pm Telenovela: *Dos mujeres y dos hombres*	**7:00 pm** Especial musical: *Música folklórica de México*
3:00 pm Programa juvenil: *Fiesta*	**7:30 pm** La naturaleza: *Jardín secreto*
3:30 pm Telenovela: *¡Sí, sí, sí!*	**8:00 pm** Noticiero: *Veinticuatro horas*
4:00 pm Telenovela: *El diario de la Sra. González*	**9:00 pm** Documental: *Las computadoras*

5

Preguntas With a partner, answer these questions based on your own knowledge.

1. Son las tres de la tarde en Nueva York. ¿Qué hora es en Los Ángeles?

2. Son las ocho y media en Chicago. ¿Qué hora es en Miami?

3. Son las dos menos cinco en San Francisco. ¿Qué hora es en San Antonio?

4. ¿A qué hora es el programa *Saturday Night Live*?; ¿A qué hora es el programa *American Idol*?

6

Más preguntas Using the questions in the previous activity as a model, make up four questions of your own. Then get together with a classmate and take turns asking and answering each other's questions.

Síntesis

7

Situación With a partner, play the roles of a journalism student interviewing a visiting literature professor (**profesor(a) de literatura**) from Venezuela. Be prepared to act out the conversation for your classmates.

Estudiante	**Profesor(a) de literatura**
Ask the professor his/her name.	→ Ask the student his/her name.
Ask the professor what time his/her literature class is.	→ Ask the student where he/she is from.
Ask how many students are in his/her class.	→ Ask to whom the notebook belongs.
Say thank you and goodbye.	→ Say thank you and you are pleased to meet him/her.

Lección 1

Recapitulación

 Diagnostics

Review the grammar concepts you have learned in this lesson by completing these activities.

1 **Completar** Complete the charts according to the models. **14 pts.**

Masculino	Femenino
el chico	la chica
	la profesora
	la amiga
el señor	
	la pasajera
el estudiante	
	la turista
el joven	

Singular	Plural
una cosa	unas cosas
un libro	
	unas clases
una lección	
un conductor	
	unos países
	unos lápices
un problema	

2 **En la clase** Complete each conversation with the correct word. **11 pts.**

 César   Beatriz

CÉSAR   ¿(1) _____ (Cuántos/Cuántas) chicas hay en la (2) _____ (maleta/clase)?

BEATRIZ Hay (3) _____ (catorce/cuatro) [14] chicas.

CÉSAR   Y, ¿(4) _____ (cuántos/cuántas) chicos hay?

BEATRIZ Hay (5) _____ (tres/trece) [13] chicos.

CÉSAR   Entonces (*Then*), en total hay (6) _____ (veintiséis/veintisiete) (7) _____ (estudiantes/chicas) en la clase.

 Ariana   Daniel

ARIANA   ¿Tienes (*Do you have*) (8) _____ (un/una) diccionario?

DANIEL   No, pero (*but*) aquí (9) _____ (es/hay) uno.

ARIANA   ¿De quién (10) _____ (son/es)?

DANIEL   (11) _____ (Son/Es) de Carlos.

RESUMEN GRAMATICAL

1.1 **Nouns and articles** *pp. 12–14*

Gender of nouns

Nouns that refer to living things

	Masculine		Feminine
-o	el chico	-a	la chica
-or	el profesor	-ora	la profesora
-ista	el turista	-ista	la turista

Nouns that refer to non-living things

	Masculine		Feminine
-o	el libro	-a	la cosa
-ma	el programa	-ción	la lección
-s	el autobús	-dad	la nacionalidad

Plural of nouns

► ending in vowel + -s   la chica → las chicas

► ending in consonant + -es   el señor → los señores

   (-z → -ces un lápiz → unos lápices)

► Definite articles: el, la, los, las

► Indefinite articles: un, una, unos, unas

1.2 **Numbers 0–30** *p. 16*

0	cero	8	ocho	16	dieciséis
1	uno	9	nueve	17	diecisiete
2	dos	10	diez	18	dieciocho
3	tres	11	once	19	diecinueve
4	cuatro	12	doce	20	veinte
5	cinco	13	trece	21	veintiuno
6	seis	14	catorce	22	veintidós
7	siete	15	quince	30	treinta

1.3 **Present tense of *ser*** *pp. 19–21*

yo	soy	nosotros/as	somos
tú	eres	vosotros/as	sois
Ud./él/ella	es	Uds./ellos/ellas	son

1.4 **Telling time** *pp. 24–25*

Es la una.	It's 1:00.
Son las dos.	It's 2:00.
Son las tres y diez.	It's 3:10.
Es la una y cuarto/quince.	It's 1:15.
Son las siete y media/treinta.	It's 7:30.
Es la una menos cuarto/quince.	It's 12:45.
Son las once menos veinte.	It's 10:40.
Es el mediodía.	It's noon.
Es la medianoche.	It's midnight.

3 **Presentaciones** Complete this conversation with the correct form of the verb **ser**. **6 pts.**

JUAN ¡Hola! Me llamo Juan. (1) _____ estudiante en la clase de español.

DANIELA ¡Hola! Mucho gusto. Yo (2) _____ Daniela y ella (3) _____ Mónica. ¿De dónde (4) _____ (tú), Juan?

JUAN De California. Y ustedes, ¿de dónde (5) _____ ?

MÓNICA Nosotras (6) _____ de Florida.

4 **¿Qué hora es?** Write out in words the following times, indicating whether it's morning, noon, afternoon, or night. **10 pts.**

1. It's 12:00 p.m.
_____

2. It's 7:05 a.m.
_____

3. It's 9:35 p.m.
_____

4. It's 5:15 p.m.
_____

5. It's 1:30 p.m.
_____

5 **¡Hola!** Write five sentences introducing yourself and talking about your classes. You may want to include your name, where you are from, who your Spanish teacher is, the time of your Spanish class, how many students are in the class, etc. **9 pts.**

_____
_____
_____
_____

6 **Canción** Use the two appropriate words from the list to complete this children's song. **2 EXTRA points!**

cinco	cuántas	cuatro	media	quiénes

"_____ patas° tiene un gato°? Una, dos, tres y _____."

patas *legs* tiene un gato *does a cat have*

Practice more at **vhlcentral.com**.

Lectura

Antes de leer

Estrategia
Recognizing cognates

As you learned earlier in this lesson, cognates are words that share similar meanings and spellings in two or more languages. When reading in Spanish, it's helpful to look for cognates and use them to guess the meaning of what you're reading. But watch out for false cognates. For example, **librería** means *bookstore*, not *library*, and **embarazada** means *pregnant*, not *embarrassed*. Look at this list of Spanish words, paying special attention to prefixes and suffixes. Can you guess the meaning of each word?

importante	oportunidad
farmacia	cultura
inteligente	activo
dentista	sociología
decisión	espectacular
televisión	restaurante
médico	policía

Examinar el texto
Glance quickly at the reading selection and guess what type of document it is. Explain your answer.

Cognados
Read the document and make a list of the cognates you find. Guess their English equivalents, then compare your answers with those of a classmate.

Joaquín Salvador Lavado nació (*was born*) en Argentina en 1932 (mil novecientos treinta y dos). Su nombre profesional es **Quino**. Es muy popular en Latinoamérica, Europa y Canadá por sus tiras cómicas (*comic strips*). Mafalda es su serie más famosa. La protagonista, Mafalda, es una chica muy inteligente de seis años (*years*). La tira cómica ilustra las aventuras de ella y su grupo de amigos. Las anécdotas de Mafalda y los chicos también presentan temas (*themes*) importantes como la paz (*peace*) y los derechos humanos (*human rights*).

Después de leer

Preguntas
Answer these questions.

1. What is Joaquín Salvador Lavado's pen name?
2. What is Mafalda like?
3. Where is Mafalda in panel 1? What is she doing?
4. What happens to the sheep in panel 3? Why?
5. Why does Mafalda wake up?
6. What number corresponds to the sheep in panel 5?
7. In panel 6, what is Mafalda doing? How do you know?

Los animales 🐾

This comic strip uses a device called onomatopoeia: a word that represents the sound that it stands for. Did you know that many common instances of onomatopoeia are different from language to language? The noise a sheep makes is *baaaah* in English, but in Mafalda's language it is **béeeee**.

Do you think you can match these animals with their Spanish sounds? First, practice saying aloud each animal sound in group B. Then, match each animal with its sound in Spanish. If you need help remembering the sounds the alphabet makes in Spanish, see p. 9.

A

1. ___ **gato**   2. ___ **perro**   3. ___ **vacas**   4. ___ **gallo**

5. ___ **rana**   6. ___ **pato**   7. ___ **cerdo**

B

a. kikirikí   b. muuu   c. croac   d. guau

e. cuac cuac   f. miau   g. oinc

Escritura

Estrategia
Writing in Spanish

Why do we write? All writing has a purpose. For example, we may write an e-mail to share important information or compose an essay to persuade others to accept a point of view. Proficient writers are not born, however. Writing requires time, thought, effort, and a lot of practice. Here are some tips to help you write more effectively in Spanish.

DO

- ▶ Try to write your ideas in Spanish
- ▶ Use the grammar and vocabulary that you know
- ▶ Use your textbook for examples of style, format, and expression in Spanish
- ▶ Use your imagination and creativity
- ▶ Put yourself in your reader's place to determine if your writing is interesting

AVOID

- ▶ Translating your ideas from English to Spanish
- ▶ Simply repeating what is in the textbook or on a web page
- ▶ Using a dictionary until you have learned how to use foreign language dictionaries

Tema
Hacer una lista

Create a telephone/address list that includes important names, numbers, and websites that will be helpful to you in your study of Spanish. Make whatever entries you can in Spanish without using a dictionary. You might want to include this information:

- ▶ The names, phone numbers, and e-mail addresses of at least four classmates
- ▶ Your professor's name, e-mail address, and office hours
- ▶ Three phone numbers and e-mail addresses of campus offices or locations related to your study of Spanish
- ▶ Five electronic resources for students of Spanish, such as chat rooms and sites dedicated to the study of Spanish as a second language

Nombre Sally (la chica de Indiana)
Teléfono 655-8888
Dirección electrónica sally@uru.edu

Nombre Profesor José Ramón Casas
Teléfono 655-8090
Dirección electrónica jrcasas@uru.edu
Horas de oficina 12 a 12:30

Nombre Biblioteca 655-7000
Dirección electrónica library@uru.edu

Escuchar S Audio

Estrategia
Listening for words you know

You can get the gist of a conversation by listening for words and phrases you already know.

 To help you practice this strategy, listen to the following sentence and make a list of the words you have already learned.

Preparación

Based on the photograph, what do you think Dr. Cavazos and Srta. Martínez are talking about? How would you get the gist of their conversation, based on what you know about Spanish?

Ahora escucha

Now you are going to hear Dr. Cavazos's conversation with Srta. Martínez. List the familiar words and phrases each person says.

Dr. Cavazos	Srta. Martínez
1. _____	9. _____
2. _____	10. _____
3. _____	11. _____
4. _____	12. _____
5. _____	13. _____
6. _____	14. _____
7. _____	15. _____
8. _____	16. _____

With a classmate, use your lists of familiar words as a guide to come up with a summary of what happened in the conversation.

Comprensión

Identificar

Who would say the following things, Dr. Cavazos or Srta. Martínez?

1. Me llamo…
2. De nada.
4. Gracias. Muchas gracias.
4. Aquí tiene usted los documentos de viaje (*trip*), señor.
5. Usted tiene tres maletas, ¿no?
6. Tengo dos maletas.
7. Hola, señor.
8. ¿Viaja usted a Buenos Aires?

Contestar

1. Does this scene take place in the morning, afternoon, or evening? How do you know?
2. How many suitcases does Dr. Cavazos have?
3. Using the words you already know to determine the context, what might the following words and expressions mean?

   - boleto
   - pasaporte
   - un viaje de ida y vuelta
   - ¡Buen viaje!

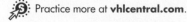

En pantalla

Latinos form the largest-growing minority group in the United States. This trend is expected to continue; the Census Bureau projects that by the year 2050, the Latino population will grow to 30 percent. Viewership of the two major Spanish-language TV stations, **Univisión** and **Telemundo**, has skyrocketed, at times surpassing that of the four major English-language networks. With Latino purchasing power estimated at 1.5 trillion dollars for 2015, many companies have responded by adapting successful marketing campaigns to target a Spanish-speaking audience. Turn on a Spanish-language channel any night of the week, and you'll see ads for the world's biggest consumer brands, from soft drinks to car makers; many of these advertisements are adaptations of their English-language counterparts. Bilingual ads, which use English and Spanish in a way that is accessible to all viewers, have become popular during events such as the Super Bowl, where advertisers want to appeal to a diverse market.

Vocabulario útil	
carne en salsa	*beef with sauce*
copa de helado	*cup of ice cream*
no tiene precio	*priceless*
plato principal	*main course*
un domingo en familia	*Sunday with the family*

Emparejar

Match each item with its price according to the ad. **¡Ojo!** (*Careful!*) One of the responses will not be used.

____ 1. aperitivo   a. quince dólares

____ 2. plato principal   b. ocho dólares

____ 3. postre   c. treinta dólares

                     d. seis dólares

Un comercial

With a partner, brainstorm and write a MasterCard-like TV ad about something you consider priceless. Then read it to the class. Use as much Spanish as you can.

Aperitivo Appetizer Postre Dessert

Anuncio de MasterCard

Aperitivo°...

Postre°...

Un domingo en familia...

S Video: TV Clip

Practice more at **vhlcentral.com**.

The **Plaza de Mayo** in Buenos Aires, Argentina, is perhaps best known as a place of political protest. Aptly nicknamed **Plaza de Protestas** by the locals, it is the site of weekly demonstrations. Despite this reputation, for many it is also a traditional **plaza**, a spot to escape from the hustle of city life. In warmer months, office workers from neighboring buildings flock to the plaza during lunch hour. **Plaza de Mayo** is also a favorite spot for families, couples, and friends to gather, stroll, or simply sit and chat. Tourists come year-round to take in the iconic surroundings: **Plaza de Mayo** is flanked by the rose-colored presidential palace (**Casa Rosada**), city hall (**municipalidad**), a colonial-era museum (**Cabildo**), and a spectacular cathedral (**Catedral Metropolitana**).

Vocabulario útil

abrazo	hug
¡Cuánto tiempo!	It's been a long time!
encuentro	encounter
plaza	city or town square
¡Qué bueno verte!	It's great to see you!
¡Qué suerte verlos!	How lucky to see you!

Preparación

Where do you and your friends usually meet? Are there public places where you get together? What activities do you take part in there?

Identificar

Identify the person or people who make(s) each of these statements.

1. ¿Cómo están ustedes?　　a. Gonzalo
2. ¡Qué bueno verte!　　　　b. Mariana
3. Bien, ¿y vos?　　　　　　c. Mark
4. Hola.　　　　　　　　　　d. Silvina
5. ¡Qué suerte verlos!

Encuentros en la plaza

Today we are at the Plaza de Mayo.

People come to walk and get some fresh air...

And children come to play...

Video: *Flash cultura*

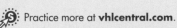
Practice more at **vhlcentral.com.**

recursos

VM pp. 53–54　｜　vhlcentral.com Lección 1

Lección 1

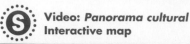

Video: *Panorama cultural*
Interactive map

Estados Unidos

El país en cifras°

▶ **Población° de los EE.UU.:** 310 millones
▶ **Población de origen hispano:** 49 millones
▶ **País de origen de hispanos en los EE.UU.:**

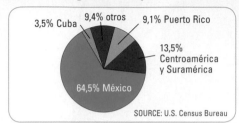

3,5% Cuba
9,4% otros
9,1% Puerto Rico
13,5% Centroamérica y Suramérica
64,5% México

SOURCE: U.S. Census Bureau

▶ **Estados con la mayor° población hispana:**

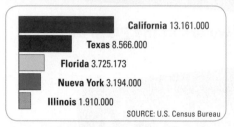

California 13.161.000
Texas 8.566.000
Florida 3.725.173
Nueva York 3.194.000
Illinois 1.910.000

SOURCE: U.S. Census Bureau

Canadá

El país en cifras

▶ **Población de Canadá:** 34 millones
▶ **Población de origen hispano:** 700.000
▶ **País de origen de hispanos en Canadá:**

48% España
9,1% México
34,1% otros
8,8% El Salvador

SOURCE: Statistics Canada

▶ **Ciudades° con la mayor población hispana:**
Montreal, Toronto, Vancouver

en cifras *by the numbers* Población *Population* mayor *largest*
Ciudades *Cities* creció *grew* más *more* cada *every* niños *children*
Se estima *It is estimated* va a ser *it is going to be*

Mission District, en San Francisco

AK
HI

CANADÁ

Vancouver
• Calgary

Ottawa ⭐
• Mont

Toronto •

San Francisco
Las Vegas
Chicago •
Nueva York •

• Los Ángeles

EE.UU.

• San Diego

Washington, D.C. ⭐

San Antonio

Océano Atlántico

Miami

Golfo de México

MÉXICO

Mar Caribe

El Álamo, en San Antonio, Texas

recursos

WB pp. 47–48
VM pp. 51–52
vhlcentral.com Lección 1

¡Increíble pero cierto!

La población hispana en los EE.UU. creció° un
43% entre los años 2000 (dos mil) y 2010
(dos mil diez) (15,2 millones de personas más°).
Hoy, uno de cada° cinco niños° en los EE.UU. es
de origen hispano. Se estima° que en el año 2034
va a ser° uno de cada tres.

SOURCE: U.S. Census Bureau and The Associated Press

Comida • La comida mexicana

La comida° mexicana es muy popular en los Estados Unidos. Los tacos, las enchiladas, las quesadillas y los frijoles frecuentemente forman parte de las comidas de muchos norteamericanos. También° son populares las variaciones de la comida mexicana en los Estados Unidos: el tex-mex y el cali-mex.

Lugares • La Pequeña Habana

La Pequeña Habana° es un barrio° de Miami, Florida, donde viven° muchos cubanoamericanos. Es un lugar° donde se encuentran° las costumbres° de la cultura cubana, los aromas y sabores° de su comida y la música salsa. La Pequeña Habana es una parte de Cuba en los Estados Unidos.

Costumbres • Desfile puertorriqueño

Cada junio, desde° 1951 (mil novecientos cincuenta y uno), los puertorriqueños celebran su cultura con un desfile° en Nueva York. Es un gran espectáculo con carrozas° y música salsa, merengue y hip-hop. Muchos espectadores llevan° la bandera° de Puerto Rico en su ropa° o pintada en la cara°.

Comunidad • Hispanos en Canadá

En Canadá viven° muchos hispanos. Toronto y Montreal son las ciudades° con mayor° población hispana. Muchos de ellos tienen estudios universitarios° y hablan° una de las lenguas° oficiales: inglés o francés°. Los hispanos participan activamente en la vida cotidiana° y profesional de Canadá.

¿Qué aprendiste? Completa las oraciones con la información adecuada (*appropriate*).

1. Hay _____ de personas de origen hispano en los Estados Unidos.
2. Los cuatro estados con las poblaciones hispanas más grandes son (en orden) _____, Texas, Florida y _____.
3. Toronto, Montreal y _____ son las ciudades con más población hispana de Canadá.
4. Las quesadillas y las enchiladas son platos (*dishes*) _____.
5. La Pequeña _____ es un barrio de Miami.
6. En Miami hay muchas personas de origen _____.
7. Cada junio se celebra en Nueva York un gran desfile para personas de origen _____.
8. Muchos hispanos en Canadá hablan _____ o francés.

 Conexión Internet Investiga estos temas en **vhlcentral.com**.

 Practice more at **vhlcentral.com**.

1. Haz (*Make*) una lista de seis hispanos célebres de los EE.UU. o Canadá. Explica (*Explain*) por qué (*why*) son célebres.
2. Escoge (*Choose*) seis lugares en los Estados Unidos con nombres hispanos e investiga sobre el origen y el significado (*meaning*) de cada nombre.

....

comida *food* También *Also* La Pequeña Habana *Little Havana* barrio *neighborhood* viven *live* lugar *place* se encuentran *are found* costumbres *customs* sabores *flavors* Cada junio desde *Each June since* desfile *parade* con carrozas *with floats* llevan *wear* bandera *flag* ropa *clothing* cara *face* viven *live* ciudades *cities* mayor *most* tienen estudios universitarios *have a degree* hablan *speak* lenguas *languages* inglés o francés *English or French* vida cotidiana *daily life*

Saludos

Hola.	*Hello; Hi.*
Buenos días.	*Good morning.*
Buenas tardes.	*Good afternoon.*
Buenas noches.	*Good evening; Good night.*

Despedidas

Adiós.	*Goodbye.*
Nos vemos.	*See you.*
Hasta luego.	*See you later.*
Hasta la vista.	*See you later.*
Hasta pronto.	*See you soon.*
Hasta mañana.	*See you tomorrow.*
Saludos a...	*Greetings to…*
Chau.	*Bye.*

¿Cómo está?

¿Cómo está usted?	*How are you? (form.)*
¿Cómo estás?	*How are you? (fam.)*
¿Qué hay de nuevo?	*What's new?*
¿Qué pasa?	*What's happening?; What's going on?*
¿Qué tal?	*How are you?; How is it going?*
(Muy) bien, gracias.	*(Very) well, thanks.*
Nada.	*Nothing.*
No muy bien.	*Not very well.*
Regular.	*So-so; OK.*

Expresiones de cortesía

Con permiso.	*Pardon me; Excuse me.*
De nada.	*You're welcome.*
Lo siento.	*I'm sorry.*
(Muchas) gracias.	*Thank you (very much); Thanks (a lot).*
No hay de qué.	*You're welcome.*
Perdón.	*Pardon me; Excuse me.*
por favor	*please*

Títulos

señor (Sr.); don	*Mr.; sir*
señora (Sra.); doña	*Mrs.; ma'am*
señorita (Srta.)	*Miss*

Presentaciones

¿Cómo se llama usted?	*What's your name? (form.)*
¿Cómo te llamas?	*What's your name? (fam.)*
Me llamo...	*My name is…*
¿Y usted?	*And you? (form.)*
¿Y tú?	*And you? (fam.)*
Mucho gusto.	*Pleased to meet you.*
El gusto es mío.	*The pleasure is mine.*
Encantado/a.	*Delighted; Pleased to meet you.*
Igualmente.	*Likewise.*
Éste/Ésta es...	*This is…*
Le presento a...	*I would like to introduce you to (name). (form.)*
Te presento a...	*I would like to introduce you to (name). (fam.)*
el nombre	*name*

¿De dónde es?

¿De dónde es usted?	*Where are you from? (form.)*
¿De dónde eres?	*Where are you from? (fam.)*
Soy de...	*I'm from…*

Palabras adicionales

¿cuánto(s)/a(s)?	*how much/many?*
¿de quién...?	*whose…? (sing.)*
¿de quiénes...?	*whose…? (plural)*
(no) hay	*there is (not); there are (not)*

Países

Argentina	*Argentina*
Costa Rica	*Costa Rica*
Cuba	*Cuba*
Ecuador	*Ecuador*
España	*Spain*
Estados Unidos (EE.UU.)	*United States*
México	*Mexico*
Puerto Rico	*Puerto Rico*

Sustantivos

el autobús	*bus*
la capital	*capital city*
el chico	*boy*
la chica	*girl*
la computadora	*computer*
la comunidad	*community*
el/la conductor(a)	*driver*
la conversación	*conversation*
la cosa	*thing*
el cuaderno	*notebook*
el día	*day*
el diario	*diary*
el diccionario	*dictionary*
la escuela	*school*
el/la estudiante	*student*
la foto(grafía)	*photograph*
el hombre	*man*
el/la joven	*youth; young person*
el lápiz	*pencil*
la lección	*lesson*
la maleta	*suitcase*
la mano	*hand*
el mapa	*map*
la mujer	*woman*
la nacionalidad	*nationality*
el número	*number*
el país	*country*
la palabra	*word*
el/la pasajero/a	*passenger*
el problema	*problem*
el/la profesor(a)	*teacher*
el programa	*program*
el/la turista	*tourist*
el video	*video*

Verbo

ser	*to be*

Numbers 0–30	*See page 16.*
Telling time	*See pages 24–25.*
Expresiones útiles	*See page 7.*

  Audio: Vocabulary Flashcards

recursos

LM p. 60

vhlcentral.com Lección 1

contextos

Lección 1

1 Saludos
For each question or expression, write the appropriate answer from the box in each blank.

| De nada. | Encantada. | Muy bien, gracias. | Nos vemos. |
| El gusto es mío. | Me llamo Pepe. | Nada. | Soy de Argentina. |

1. ¿Cómo te llamas? _____
2. ¿Qué hay de nuevo? _____
3. ¿De dónde eres? _____
4. Adiós. _____
5. ¿Cómo está usted? _____
6. Mucho gusto. _____
7. Te presento a la señora Díaz. _____
8. Muchas gracias. _____

2 Conversación
Complete this conversation by writing one word in each blank.

ANA   Buenos días, señor González. ¿Cómo (1)_____ (2)_____?

SR. GONZÁLEZ   (3)_____ bien, gracias. ¿Y tú, (4)_____ estás?

ANA   Regular. (5)_____ presento a Antonio.

SR. GONZÁLEZ   Mucho (6)_____, Antonio.

ANTONIO   El gusto (7)_____ (8)_____.

SR. GONZÁLEZ   ¿De dónde (9)_____, Antonio?

ANTONIO   (10)_____ (11)_____ México.

ANA   (12)_____ luego, señor González.

SR. GONZÁLEZ   Nos (13)_____, Ana.

ANTONIO   (14)_____, señor González.

3 Saludos, despedidas y presentaciones
Complete these phrases with the missing words. Then write each phrase in the correct column of the chart.

1. ¿_____ pasa?
2. _____ luego.
3. _____ gusto.
4. Te _____ a Irene.
5. ¿_____ estás?
6. _____ días.
7. El _____ es mío.
8. Nos _____.

Saludos	Despedidas	Presentaciones

4 **Los países** Fill in the blanks with the name of the Spanish-speaking country that is highlighted in each map.

1. _____

2. _____

3. _____

5 **Diferente** Write the word that does not belong in each group.

1. Hasta mañana.
   Nos vemos.
   Buenos días.
   Hasta pronto.

2. ¿Qué tal?
   Regular.
   ¿Qué pasa?
   ¿Cómo estás?

3. Puerto Rico
   Washington
   México
   Estados Unidos

4. Muchas gracias.
   Muy bien, gracias.
   No muy bien.
   Regular.

5. ¿De dónde eres?
   ¿Cómo está usted?
   ¿De dónde es usted?
   ¿Cómo se llama usted?

6. Chau.
   Buenos días.
   Hola.
   ¿Qué tal?

estructura

1.1 Nouns and articles

1 **¿Masculino o femenino?** Write the correct definite article before each noun. Then write each article and noun in the correct column.

_____ hombre   _____ pasajero   _____ chico

_____ profesora   _____ mujer   _____ pasajera

_____ chica   _____ conductora   _____ profesor

Masculino	**Femenino**
_____	_____
_____	_____
_____	_____
_____	_____

2 **¿El, la, los o las?** Write the correct definite article before each noun.

1. _____ autobús   6. _____ mano

2. _____ maleta   7. _____ país

3. _____ lápices   8. _____ problema

4. _____ diccionario   9. _____ cosas

5. _____ palabras   10. _____ diarios

3 **Singular y plural** Give the plural form of each singular article and noun and the singular form of each plural article and noun.

1. unas fotografías _____   6. unas escuelas _____

2. un día _____   7. unos videos _____

3. un cuaderno _____   8. un programa _____

4. unos pasajeros _____   9. unos autobuses _____

5. una computadora _____   10. una palabra _____

4 **Las cosas** For each picture, provide the noun with its corresponding definite and indefinite articles.

1. _____   2. _____   3. _____   4. _____

1.2 Numbers 0–30

1 **Los números** Solve the math problems to complete the crossword puzzle.

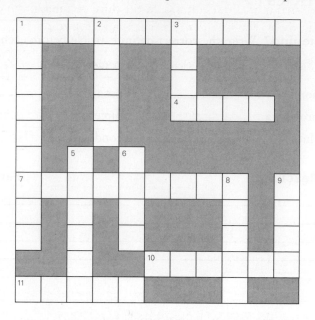

Horizontales

1. veinte más cinco
4. veintiséis menos quince
7. treinta menos catorce
10. veinticinco menos veintiuno
11. once más dos

Verticales

1. once más once
2. seis más tres
3. trece menos trece
5. doce más ocho

6. veintinueve menos diecinueve
8. veintitrés menos dieciséis
9. siete más uno

2 **¿Cuántos hay?** Write questions that ask how many items there are. Then write the answers. Write out the numbers.

> **modelo**
>
> 2 cuadernos
> ¿Cuántos cuadernos hay? Hay dos cuadernos.

1. 3 diccionarios _____

2. 12 estudiantes _____

3. 10 lápices _____

4. 7 maletas _____

5. 25 palabras _____

6. 21 países _____

7. 13 escuelas _____

8. 18 pasajeros _____

9. 15 computadoras _____

10. 27 fotografías _____

1.3 Present tense of **ser**

1 **Los pronombres** In the second column, write the subject pronouns that you would use when addressing the people listed in the first column. In the third column, write the pronouns you would use when talking about them. The first item has been done for you.

Personas	Addressing them	Talking about them
1. el señor Díaz	usted	él
2. Jimena y Marissa	_____	_____
3. Maru y Miguel	_____	_____
4. la profesora	_____	_____
5. un estudiante	_____	_____
6. el director de una escuela	_____	_____
7. tres chicas	_____	_____
8. un pasajero de autobús	_____	_____
9. Juan Carlos y Felipe	_____	_____
10. una turista	_____	_____

2 **Nosotros somos...** Rewrite each sentence with the new subject. Change the verb **ser** as necessary.

> **modelo**
>
> Ustedes son profesores.
> Nosotros *somos profesores.*

1. Nosotros somos estudiantes. Ustedes _____.

2. Usted es de Puerto Rico. Ella _____.

3. Nosotros somos conductores. Ellos _____.

4. Yo soy turista. Tú _____.

5. Ustedes son de México. Nosotras _____.

6. Ella es profesora. Yo _____.

7. Tú eres de España. Él _____.

8. Ellos son pasajeros. Ellas _____.

3 **¡Todos a bordo! (All aboard!)** Complete Jorge's introduction of his travelling companions with the correct forms of **ser**.

Hola, me llamo Jorge y (1)_____ de Cuba. Pilar y Nati (2)_____ de España.
Pedro, Juan y Paco (3)_____ de México. Todos (4)_____ estudiantes.
La señorita Blasco (5)_____ de San Antonio. Ella (6)_____
la profesora. Luis (7)_____ el conductor. Él (8)_____ de Puerto Rico.
Ellos (9)_____ de los Estados Unidos. El autobús (10)_____ de la
agencia Marazul. Todos (11)_____ pasajeros de la agencia de viajes Marazul.
Perdón, ¿de dónde (12)_____ tú, quién (13)_____ ella y de quién
(14)_____ las maletas?

4 **¿De quién es?** Use **ser** + **de** (or **del**) to indicate that the object belongs to the person or people listed.

> modelo
>
> nombre / el pasajero
> **Es el nombre del pasajero.**

1. diccionario / el estudiante _____
2. cuadernos / las chicas _____
3. mano / Sara _____
4. maletas / la turista _____
5. computadoras / los profesores _____
6. autobús / el conductor _____
7. lápices / la joven _____
8. fotografía / los chicos _____
9. computadora / la directora _____
10. país / David _____

5 **¿De dónde son?** Use **ser** + **de** to indicate where the people are from.

> modelo
>
> Ustedes / Costa Rica
> **Ustedes son de Costa Rica.**

1. Lina y María / Colombia _____
2. El profesor / México _____
3. Tú y los jóvenes / Argentina _____
4. Las estudiantes / Estados Unidos _____
5. Ellos / Canadá _____
6. La mujer / Puerto Rico _____
7. Los turistas / España _____
8. Él y yo / Chile _____
9. Nosotras / Cuba _____
10. Usted / Venezuela _____

6 **¿De quién?** Write questions for these answers using the correct interrogative words from the list.

> modelo
>
> **¿De dónde son ellos?**
> Ellos son de España.

cómo	dónde	de quién(es)	por qué
cuándo	de dónde	qué	quién(es)

1. _____
   Los lápices son de Alejandro.
2. _____
   Daniela es de Ecuador.
3. _____
   Es una foto.
4. _____
   Ellas son Claudia y Marta.

1.4 Telling time

1 **La hora** Give the time shown on each clock using complete sentences.

1. _____

2. _____

3. _____

4. _____

5. _____

6. _____

2 **¿Qué hora es?** Use complete sentences to tell the time.

1. 3:40 p.m. _____

2. 6:00 a.m. _____

3. 9:15 p.m. _____

4. 12:00 a.m. _____

5. 1:10 p.m. _____

6. 10:45 a.m. _____

7. 5:05 p.m. _____

8. 11:50 p.m. _____

9. 1:30 a.m. _____

10. 10:00 p.m. _____

Nombre _____

Fecha _____

3 | **El día de Marta** Use the schedule to answer the questions in complete sentences.

8:45 a.m.	Biología
11:00 a.m.	Cálculo
12:00 p.m.	Almuerzo
2:00 p.m.	Literatura
4:15 p.m.	Yoga
10:30 p.m.	Programa especial

1. ¿A qué hora es la clase de biología? _____

2. ¿A qué hora es la clase de cálculo? _____

3. ¿A qué hora es el almuerzo (*lunch*)? _____

4. ¿A qué hora es la clase de literatura? _____

5. ¿A qué hora es la clase de yoga? _____

6. ¿A qué hora es el programa especial? _____

Síntesis

¿Y tú? Answer the questions about yourself and your class using complete sentences.

1. ¿Cómo te llamas? _____

2. ¿De dónde eres? _____

3. ¿Qué hay de nuevo? _____

_____

4. ¿Qué hora es? _____

_____

5. ¿A qué hora es la clase de español? _____

_____

6. ¿Cuántos estudiantes hay en la clase de español? _____

_____

7. ¿Hay estudiantes de México en la clase? _____

_____

8. ¿A qué hora es tu (*your*) programa de televisión favorito? _____

_____

panorama

Estados Unidos y Canadá

1 **¿Cierto o falso?** Indicate if each statement is **cierto** (*true*) or **falso** (*false*). Then correct the false statements.

1. La mayor parte de la población hispana de los Estados Unidos es de origen mexicano.

   _____

2. Hay más (*more*) hispanos en Illinois que (*than*) en Texas.

   _____

3. El estado con la mayor población hispana de los Estados Unidos es California.

   _____

4. Muchos hispanos en Canadá tienen estudios universitarios.

   _____

5. Muchos hispanos en Canadá hablan una de las lenguas oficiales: inglés o portugués.

   _____

6. Hoy, uno de cada cuatro niños en los Estados Unidos es de origen hispano.

   _____

7. Los tacos, las enchiladas y las quesadillas son platos cubanos.

   _____

8. Las ciudades con más población hispana en Canadá son Montreal, Toronto y Vancouver.

   _____

9. Un barrio cubanoamericano importante de Miami se llama la Pequeña Cuba.

   _____

10. Los puertorriqueños de Nueva York celebran su origen con un desfile.

    _____

2 **Completar** Complete the sentences with the correct information from **Panorama** about the Hispanic communities in Canada and the United States.

1. Se estima que en el año 2034 uno de cada tres _____ va a ser de origen hispano.

2. Los hispanos _____ activamente en la vida cotidiana y profesional de Canadá.

3. La Pequeña Habana es una _____ de Cuba en los Estados Unidos.

4. El desfile puertorriqueño es un gran espectáculo con carrozas y música _____, _____ y hip-hop.

5. La comida mexicana es muy _____ en los Estados Unidos.

Nombre _____

Fecha _____

3 **Un mapa** Write the name of each state numbered on the map and provide its Hispanic population (round up population) in millions.

1. _____ (_____ millones de hispanos)

2. _____ (_____ millones de hispanos)

3. _____ (_____ millones de hispanos)

4. _____ (_____ millones de hispanos)

5. _____ (_____ millones de hispanos)

4 **Nosotros somos...** Write the origin of each item listed (**estadounidense, mexicano, cubano,** or **puertorriqueño**).

Origen

1. desfile en Nueva York   _____

2. enchiladas, tacos y quesadillas   _____

3. Pequeña Habana   _____

4. comida tex-mex y cali-mex   _____

5. mayor población hispana de EE.UU.   _____

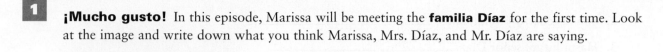

Bienvenida, Marissa

Antes de ver el video

1 **¡Mucho gusto!** In this episode, Marissa will be meeting the **familia Díaz** for the first time. Look at the image and write down what you think Marissa, Mrs. Díaz, and Mr. Díaz are saying.

_____

_____

_____

_____

_____

_____

Mientras ves el video

2 **Completar** Watch **Bienvenida, Marissa** and fill in the blanks in the following sentences.

SRA. DÍAZ ¿(1) _____ hora es?

MARISSA (2) _____ las cuatro menos diez.

DON DIEGO Buenas tardes, (3) _____. Señorita, bienvenida a la Ciudad de México.

MARISSA ¡Muchas gracias! Me (4) _____ Marissa.
¿(5) _____ se llama usted?

DON DIEGO Yo soy Diego, mucho (6) _____.

MARISSA El gusto es (7) _____, don Diego.

DON DIEGO ¿Cómo (8) _____ usted hoy, señora Carolina?

SRA. DÍAZ Muy bien, gracias, ¿y (9) _____?

DON DIEGO Bien, (10) _____.

SRA. DÍAZ Ahí hay (11) _____ maletas. Son de Marissa.

DON DIEGO Con (12) _____.

3 **¿Cierto o falso?** Indicate whether each statement is **cierto** or **falso**.

	Cierto	Falso
1. Marissa es de Wisconsin.	○	○
2. Jimena es profesora.	○	○
3. La señora Díaz es de Cuba.	○	○
4. Felipe es estudiante.	○	○
5. El señor Díaz es de la Ciudad de México.	○	○
6. Marissa no tiene (*doesn't have*) diccionario.	○	○

Después de ver el video

4 **¿Quién?** Write the name of the person who said each of the following sentences.

1. Ellos son estudiantes. _____

2. Son las cuatro y veinticinco. _____

3. Hasta luego, señor Díaz. _____

4. La chica de Wisconsin. _____

5. Bienvenida, Marissa. _____

6. Nosotros somos tu diccionario. _____

7. Hay... tres cuadernos... un mapa... un libro de español... _____

8. Marissa, te presento a Roberto, mi esposo. _____

9. De nada. _____

10. Lo siento, Marissa. _____

11. Hola. _____

12. No hay de qué. _____

13. ¿Qué hay en esta cosa? _____

14. ¿Quiénes son los dos chicos de las fotos? ¿Jimena y Felipe? _____

15. Gracias, don Diego. _____

5 **Ho, ho, hola...** Imagine that you have just met the man or woman of your dreams, and that person speaks only Spanish! Don't be shy! Write what the two of you would say in your first conversation.

_____

_____

_____

_____

_____

_____

_____

6 **En la clase** Imagine that you are in Mexico studying Spanish. Write your conversation with your Spanish professor on the first day you attend the university.

_____

_____

_____

_____

_____

_____

Panorama: Los Estados Unidos

Lección 1
Panorama cultural

Antes de ver el video

1 **Más vocabulario** Look over these useful words and expressions before you watch the video.

Vocabulario útil		
algunos *some, a few*	espectáculos *shows*	millón *million*
beisbolistas *baseball players*	estaciones *stations*	mucha *large*
comparsa *parade*	este *this*	muchos *many*
concursos *contests*	ligas mayores *major leagues*	por ciento *percent*
diseñador *designer*	más *more*	su *their*
disfraces *costumes*	mayoría *majority*	tiene *has*
escritora *writer*		

2 **Deportes** In this video, you are going to learn about some famous Dominican baseball players. In preparation, answer these questions about sports.

1. What sports are popular in the United States? _____

2. What is your favorite sport? _____

3. Do you play any sports? Which ones? _____

Mientras ves el video

3 **Cognados** Check off all the cognates you hear during the video.

___ 1. agosto   ___ 3. celebrar   ___ 5. democracia   ___ 7. festival   ___ 9. intuición

___ 2. carnaval   ___ 4. discotecas   ___ 6. famosos   ___ 8. independencia   ___ 10. populares

Después de ver el video

4 **Responder** Answer the questions in Spanish. Use complete sentences.

1. ¿Cuántos hispanos hay en Estados Unidos?

_____

2. ¿De dónde son la mayoría de los hispanos en Estados Unidos?

_____

3. ¿Quiénes son Pedro Martínez y Manny Ramírez?

_____

4. ¿Dónde hay muchas discotecas y estaciones de radio hispanas?

_____

5. ¿Qué son WADO y Latino Mix?

_____

6. ¿Es Julia Álvarez una escritora dominicana?

_____

Panorama: Canadá   Lección 1

Antes de ver el video

1 **Más vocabulario** Look over these useful words and expressions before you watch the video.

Vocabulario útil		
bancos *banks*	hijas *daughters*	periódico *newspaper*
campo *field*	investigadora científica *research scientist*	que *that*
canal de televisión *TV station*	mantienen *maintain*	revista *magazine*
ciudad *city*	mayoría *majority*	seguridad *safety*
comunidad *community*	ofrecen *offer*	sus *her*
escuelas *schools*	otras *others*	trabajadores *workers*
estudia *studies*	pasa *spends*	vive *live*

2 **Responder** This video talks about the Hispanic community in Montreal. In preparation for watching the video, answer the following questions about your family's background.

1. Where were your parents born? And your grandparents? _____

2. If any of them came to the United States from another country, when and why did they come here?

   _____

3. Are you familiar with the culture of the country of your ancestors? What do you know about their culture? Do you follow any of their traditions? Which ones? _____

   _____

Mientras ves el video

3 **Cognados** Check off all the cognates you hear during the video.

___ 1. apartamento   ___ 3. diario   ___ 5. horas   ___ 7. instituciones   ___ 9. lápiz

___ 2. comunidad   ___ 4. escuela   ___ 6. hoteles   ___ 8. laboratorio   ___ 10. el programa

Después de ver el video

4 **¿Cierto o falso?** Indicate whether these statements are **cierto** or **falso**. Correct the false statements.

1. La mayoría de los hispanos en Montreal son de Argentina. _____

2. En Montreal no hay canales de televisión en español. _____

3. En Montreal hay hispanos importantes. _____

4. Una hispana importante en el campo de la biología es Ana María Seifert. _____

5. Ella vive con sus dos hijas en una mansión en Montreal. _____

6. Ella pasa muchas horas en el museo. _____

7. En su casa mantienen muchas tradiciones argentinas. _____

8. Ella participa en convenciones nacionales e internacionales. _____

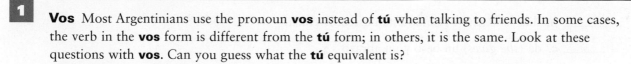

Encuentros en la plaza

Lección 1
Flash cultura

Antes de ver el video

1 **Vos** Most Argentinians use the pronoun **vos** instead of **tú** when talking to friends. In some cases, the verb in the **vos** form is different from the **tú** form; in others, it is the same. Look at these questions with **vos**. Can you guess what the **tú** equivalent is?

> **modelo**
>
> Vos: ¿Cómo te llamás?
> Tú: *¿Cómo te llamas?*

1. Y vos, ¿cómo estás?

   _____

2. ¿De dónde sos?

   _____

2 **¡En español!** Look at the video still. Imagine a conversation between two of these people.

¡Hola! ¿Cómo te va? _____

_____

_____

_____

_____

_____

Mientras ves el video

3 **Completar** What does Silvina say when she meets her friends? Complete these conversations.

A. (3:42–3:51)

CHICO	Hola.
CHICA	¿(1) _____?
CHICA Y CHICO	¡Cuánto tiempo! (*It's been so long!*)
SILVINA	Sí, hace mucho, ¿no?
CHICA	¡Qué (2) _____ verte (*to see you*)!
SILVINA	¿(3) _____ están ustedes? ¿Bien?
CHICA Y CHICO	(4) _____.

B. (4:12–4:19)

SILVINA	Quiero (*I want*) presentarles a mi (5) _____ Gonzalo.
CHICA	Hola, ¿qué (6) _____?
GONZALO	Hola. Gonzalo. ¿Tú cómo te (7) _____?
CHICA	Mariana.
GONZALO	(8) _____, Mariana.

Video Manual

Después de ver el video

4 **Ordenar** Pay attention to Silvina's actions and put them in the correct order.

_____ a. presenta una amiga a Mark

_____ b. dice (*she says*): ¿Como están ustedes? ¿Bien?

_____ c. da (*she gives*) un beso y un abrazo

_____ d. camina (*she walks*) por la Plaza de Mayo

_____ e. dice: ¡Hasta pronto!

5 **¿Quién?** Indicate who would make each of these statements.

Statements	Long-time friends at a plaza	People meeting for the first time
1. ¡Qué bueno verte!		
2. Sí, hace mucho, ¿no?		
3. Les presento a mi amigo.		
4. ¿Cómo estás?		
5. Mucho gusto.		

6 **¡Cuánto tiempo!** Write a conversation you would have with a friend whom you have not seen in a long time. Include the expressions provided.

> ¡Cuánto tiempo!   ¡Qué bueno verte!
> Hace mucho.   ¿Qué tal?

_____

_____

_____

_____

_____

7 **Encuentros en la plaza** Describe two aspects of this episode that caught your attention: people, their physical proximity, activities they do, etc. Then, explain how those are similar or different in your own culture. You may use English.

_____

_____

_____

_____

_____

contextos

Lección 1

1 **Identificar** You will hear six short exchanges. For each one, decide whether it is a greeting, an introduction, or a leave-taking. Mark the appropriate column with an **X**.

> **modelo**
>
> *You hear:* RAQUEL David, te presento a Paulina.
>   DAVID Encantado.
> *You mark:* an **X** under ***Introduction***.

	Greeting	*Introduction*	*Leave-taking*
Modelo		X	
1.			
2.			
3.			
4.			
5.			
6.			

2 **Asociar** You will hear three conversations. Look at the drawing and write the number of the conversation under the appropriate group of people.

3 **Preguntas** Listen to each question or statement and respond with an answer from the list in your lab manual. Repeat the correct response after the speaker.

a. Bien, gracias.   c. Lo siento.   e. Nada.

b. Chau.   d. Mucho gusto.   f. Soy de los Estados Unidos.

pronunciación

The Spanish alphabet

The Spanish and English alphabets are almost identical, with a few exceptions. For example, the Spanish letter **ñ (eñe)** doesn't occur in the English alphabet. Furthermore, the letters **k (ka)** and **w (doble ve)** are used only in words of foreign origin. Examine the chart below to find other differences.

Letra	Nombre(s)	Ejemplo(s)	Letra	Nombre(s)	Ejemplo(s)
a	a	**a**diós	n	ene	**n**acionalidad
b	be	**b**ien, pro**b**lema	ñ	eñe	ma**ñ**ana
c	ce	**c**osa, **c**ero	o	o	**o**nce
ch	che	**ch**ico	p	pe	**p**rofesor
d	de	**d**iario, na**d**a	q	cu	**q**ué
e	e	**e**studiante	r	ere	**r**egular, seño**r**a
f	efe	**f**oto	s	ese	**s**eñor
g	ge	**g**racias, **G**erardo, re**g**ular	t	te	**t**ú
h	hache	**h**ola	u	u	**u**sted
i	i	**i**gualmente	v	ve	**v**ista, nue**v**o
j	jota	**J**avier	w	doble ve	*walkman*
k	ka, ca	**k**ilómetro	x	equis	e**x**istir, Mé**x**ico
l	ele	**l**ápiz	y	i griega, ye	**y**o
ll	elle	**ll**ave	z	zeta, ceta	**z**ona
m	eme	**m**apa			

1   **El alfabeto** Repeat the Spanish alphabet and example words after the speaker.

2   **Práctica** When you hear the number, say the corresponding word aloud and then spell it. Then listen to the speaker and repeat the correct response.

1. nada
2. maleta
3. quince
4. muy
5. hombre
6. por favor
7. San Fernando
8. Estados Unidos
9. Puerto Rico
10. España
11. Javier
12. Ecuador
13. Maite
14. gracias
15. Nueva York

3   **Dictado** You will hear six people introduce themselves. Listen carefully and write the people's names as they spell them.

1. _____

2. _____

3. _____

4. _____

5. _____

6. _____

estructura

1.1 Nouns and articles

1 **Identificar** You will hear a series of words. Decide whether the word is masculine or feminine, and mark an **X** in the appropriate column.

> *modelo*
> You hear: lección
> You mark: an **X** under *feminine*.

	Masculine	Feminine
Modelo		X
1.		
2.		
3.		
4.		
5.		
6.		
7.		
8.		

2 **Transformar** Change each word from the masculine to the feminine. Repeat the correct answer after the speaker. (6 items)

> *modelo*
> el chico
> la chica

3 **Cambiar** Change each word from the singular to the plural. Repeat the correct answer after the speaker. (8 items)

> *modelo*
> una palabra
> unas palabras

4 **Completar** Listen to the following description and write the missing words in your lab manual.

_____ diccionario
un _____
_____ cuadernos
_____ mapa de _____
_____ lápices

1.2 Numbers 0–30

1 **¡Bingo!** You are going to play two games (**juegos**) of bingo. As you hear each number, mark it with an **X** on your bingo card.

Juego 1		
1	3	5
29	25	6
14	18	17
9	12	21

Juego 2		
0	30	27
10	3	2
16	19	4
28	22	20

2 **Números** Use the cue in your lab manual to tell how many there are of each item. Repeat the correct response after the speaker.

> **modelo**
>
> *You see:* 18 chicos
> *You say: dieciocho chicos*

1. 15 lápices
2. 4 computadoras
3. 8 cuadernos
4. 22 días
5 9 lecciones
6. 30 fotos
7. 1 palabra
8. 26 diccionarios
9. 12 países
10. 3 problemas
11. 17 escuelas
12. 25 turistas

3 **Completar** You will hear a series of math problems. Write the missing numbers and solve the problems.

1. _____ + _____11_____ = _____
2. _____ - _____5_____ = _____
3. _____8_____ + _____ = _____
4. _____ - _____12_____ = _____
5. _____3_____ + _____ = _____
6. _____ + _____0_____ = _____

4 **Preguntas** Look at the drawing and answer each question you hear. Repeat the correct response after the speaker. (*6 items*)

1.3 Present tense of **ser**

1 **Identificar** Listen to each statement and mark an **X** in the column for the subject of the verb.

> **modelo**
> *You hear:* Son pasajeros.
> *You mark:* an **X** under **ellos**.

	yo	tú	él	nosotros	ellos
Modelo	_____	_____	_____	_____	**X**
1.	_____	_____	_____	_____	_____
2.	_____	_____	_____	_____	_____
3.	_____	_____	_____	_____	_____
4.	_____	_____	_____	_____	_____
5.	_____	_____	_____	_____	_____
6.	_____	_____	_____	_____	_____

2 **Cambiar** Form a new sentence using the cue you hear as the subject. Repeat the correct answer after the speaker. (*8 items*)

> **modelo**
> Isabel es de los Estados Unidos. (yo)
> *Yo soy de los Estados Unidos.*

3 **Escoger** Listen to each question and choose the most logical response.

1. a. Soy Patricia. b. Es la señora Gómez.
2. a. Es de California. b. Él es conductor.
3. a. Es de Canadá. b. Es un diccionario.
4. a. Es de Patricia. b. Soy estudiante.
5. a. Él es conductor. b. Es de España.
6. a. Es un cuaderno. b. Soy de los Estados Unidos.

4 **Preguntas** Answer each question you hear using the cue in your lab manual. Repeat the correct response after the speaker.

> **modelo**
> *You hear:* ¿De dónde es Pablo?
> *You see:* Estados Unidos
> *You say:* Él es de los Estados Unidos.

1. España 2. California 3. México 4. Ecuador 5. Puerto Rico 6. Colorado

5 **¿Quiénes son?** Listen to this conversation and write the answers to the questions in your lab manual.

1. ¿Cómo se llama el hombre? _____ 4. ¿De dónde es ella? _____
2. ¿Cómo se llama la mujer? _____ 5. ¿Quién es estudiante? _____
3. ¿De dónde es él? _____ 6. ¿Quién es profesor? _____

1.4 Telling time

1 **La hora** Look at the clock and listen to the statement. Indicate whether the statement is **cierto** or **falso**.

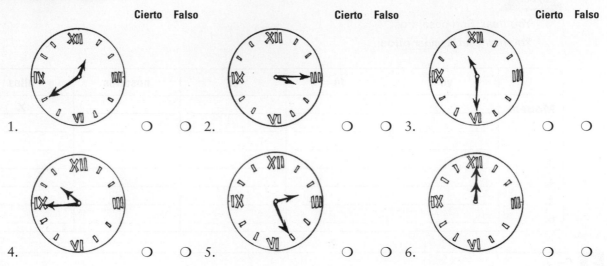

Cierto Falso Cierto Falso Cierto Falso

1. ○ ○ 2. ○ ○ 3. ○ ○

4. ○ ○ 5. ○ ○ 6. ○ ○

2 **Preguntas** Some people want to know what time it is. Answer their questions, using the cues in your lab manual. Repeat the correct response after the speaker.

> **modelo**
>
> *You hear:* ¿Qué hora es, por favor?
> *You see:* 3:10 p.m.
> *You say:* Son las tres y diez de la tarde.

1. 1:30 p.m.   3. 2:05 p.m.   5. 4:54 p.m.
2. 9:06 a.m.   4. 7:15 a.m.   6. 10:23 p.m.

3 **¿A qué hora?** You are trying to plan your class schedule. Ask your counselor what time these classes meet and write the answer.

> **modelo**
>
> *You see:* la clase de economía
> *You say:* ¿A qué hora es la clase de economía?
> *You hear:* Es a las once y veinte de la mañana.
> *You write:* 11:20 a.m.

1. la clase de biología: _____   4. la clase de literatura: _____
2. la clase de arte: _____   5. la clase de historia: _____
3. la clase de matemáticas: _____   6. la clase de sociología: _____

vocabulario

You will now hear the vocabulary found in your textbook on the last page of this lesson. Listen and repeat each Spanish word or phrase after the speaker.

Additional Vocabulary

Additional Vocabulary

Notes

Notes

Notes

En la universidad

2

Communicative Goals

You will learn how to:

- Talk about your classes and school life
- Discuss everyday activities
- Ask questions in Spanish
- Describe the location of people and things

A PRIMERA VISTA
- ¿Hay dos chicos en la foto?
- ¿Hay tres cuadernos o siete?
- ¿Son turistas o estudiantes?
- ¿Qué hora es, la una de la mañana o de la tarde?

En la universidad

Más vocabulario

la biblioteca	library
la cafetería	cafeteria
la casa	house; home
el estadio	stadium
el laboratorio	laboratory
la librería	bookstore
la residencia estudiantil	dormitory
la universidad	university; college
el/la compañero/a de clase	classmate
el/la compañero/a de cuarto	roommate
la clase	class
el curso	course
la especialización	major
el examen	test; exam
el horario	schedule
la prueba	test; quiz
el semestre	semester
la tarea	homework
el trimestre	trimester; quarter
la administración de empresas	business administration
el arte	art
la biología	biology
las ciencias	sciences
la computación	computer science
la contabilidad	accounting
la economía	economics
el español	Spanish
la física	physics
la geografía	geography
la música	music

Variación léxica

pluma ⟷ bolígrafo
pizarra ⟷ tablero (Col.)

recursos

| WB pp. 99–100 | LM p. 117 | vhlcentral.com Lección 2 |

el reloj

la ventana

la puerta

la profesora

el estudiante

la mesa

la calculadora

el libro

la pluma

el mapa
la pizarra

LAS MATERIAS	COURSES
la historia	history
las humanidades	humanities
el inglés	English
las lenguas extranjeras	foreign languages
la literatura	literature
las matemáticas	mathematics
el periodismo	journalism
la psicología	psychology
la química	chemistry
la sociología	sociology

el papel

el borrador
la tiza

la papelera

el escritorio

la mochila

la estudiante

la silla

Práctica

1

Escuchar 🎧 Listen to Professor Morales talk about her Spanish classroom, then check the items she mentions.

puerta	○	tiza	○	plumas	○
ventanas	○	escritorios	○	mochilas	○
pizarra	○	sillas	○	papel	○
borrador	○	libros	○	reloj	○

2

Identificar 🎧 You will hear a series of words. Write each one in the appropriate category.

Personas	Lugares	Materias
_____	_____	_____
_____	_____	_____
_____	_____	_____

3

Emparejar Match each question with its most logical response. **¡Ojo!** (*Careful!*) One response will not be used.

1. ¿Qué clase es?
2. ¿Quiénes son?
3. ¿Quién es?
4. ¿De dónde es?
5. ¿A qué hora es la clase de inglés?
6. ¿Cuántos estudiantes hay?

a. Hay veinticinco.
b. Es un reloj.
c. Es de Perú.
d. Es la clase de química.
e. Es el señor Bastos.
f. Es a las nueve en punto.
g. Son los profesores.

4

Identificar Identify the word that does not belong in each group.

1. examen • casa • tarea • prueba
2. economía • matemáticas • biblioteca • contabilidad
3. pizarra • tiza • borrador • librería
4. lápiz • cafetería • papel • cuaderno
5. veinte • diez • pluma • treinta
6. conductor • laboratorio • autobús • pasajero

5

¿Qué clase es? Name the class associated with the subject matter.

> **modelo**
> los elementos, los átomos *Es la clase de química.*

1. Abraham Lincoln, Winston Churchill
2. Picasso, Leonardo da Vinci
3. Freud, Jung
4. África, el océano Pacífico
5. la cultura de España, verbos
6. Hemingway, Shakespeare
7. geometría, calculadora

Los días de la semana

¿Qué día es hoy (today)?

Hoy es martes.

¿Cuándo (When) es el examen?

Es el viernes.

¡LENGUA VIVA!

The days of the week are never capitalized in Spanish.

• • •

Monday is considered the first day of the week in Spanish-speaking countries.

septiembre

lunes	martes	miércoles	jueves	viernes	sábado	domingo
1	2	3	4	5	6	
7	8	9	10			

CONSULTA

Note that September in Spanish is **septiembre**. For all of the months of the year, go to **Contextos, Lección 5,** p. 248.

6 **¿Qué día es hoy?** Complete each statement with the correct day of the week.

1. Hoy es martes. Mañana es _____. Ayer fue (*Yesterday was*) _____.
2. Ayer fue sábado. Mañana es _____. Hoy es _____.
3. Mañana es viernes. Hoy es _____. Ayer fue _____.
4. Ayer fue domingo. Hoy es _____. Mañana es _____.
5. Hoy es jueves. Ayer fue _____. Mañana es _____.
6. Mañana es lunes. Hoy es _____. Ayer fue _____.

7 **Analogías** Use these words to complete the analogies. Some words will not be used.

arte	día	martes	pizarra
biblioteca	domingo	matemáticas	profesor
catorce	estudiante	mujer	reloj

1. maleta ⟷ pasajero ⊜ mochila ⟷ _____
2. chico ⟷ chica ⊜ hombre ⟷ _____
3. pluma ⟷ papel ⊜ tiza ⟷ _____
4. inglés ⟷ lengua ⊜ miércoles ⟷ _____
5. papel ⟷ cuaderno ⊜ libro ⟷ _____
6. quince ⟷ dieciséis ⊜ lunes ⟷ _____
7. Cervantes ⟷ literatura ⊜ Dalí ⟷ _____
8. autobús ⟷ conductor ⊜ clase ⟷ _____
9. los EE.UU. ⟷ mapa ⊜ hora ⟷ _____
10. veinte ⟷ veintitrés ⊜ jueves ⟷ _____

Practice more at **vhlcentral.com**.

Comunicación

8

Horario Choose three courses from the chart to create your own class schedule, then discuss it with a classmate.

materia	horas	días	profesor(a)
historia	9–10	lunes, miércoles	Prof. Ordóñez
biología	12–1	lunes, jueves	Profa. Dávila
periodismo	2–3	martes, jueves	Profa. Quiñones
matemáticas	2–3	miércoles, jueves	Prof. Jiménez
arte	12–1:30	lunes, miércoles	Prof. Molina

modelo

Estudiante 1: Tomo (*I take*) biología los lunes y jueves, de 12 a 1, con (*with*) la profesora Dávila.

Estudiante 2: ¿Sí? Yo no tomo biología. Yo tomo arte los lunes y miércoles, de 12 a 1:30, con el profesor Molina.

9

Memoria How well do you know your Spanish classroom? Take a good look around and then close your eyes. Your partner will ask you questions about the classroom, using these words and other vocabulary. Each person should answer six questions and switch roles every three questions.

escritorio	mapa	pizarra	reloj
estudiante	mesa	profesor(a)	ventana
libro	mochila	puerta	silla

modelo

Estudiante 1: ¿Cuántas ventanas hay?

Estudiante 2: Hay cuatro ventanas.

10

Nuevos amigos During the first week of class, you meet a new student in the cafeteria. With a partner, prepare a conversation using these cues. Then act it out for the class.

 **Estudiante 1**   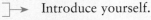 **Estudiante 2**

Greet your new acquaintance.   → Introduce yourself.

Find out about him or her.   → Tell him or her about yourself.

Ask about your partner's class schedule.   → Compare your schedule to your partner's.

Say nice to meet you and goodbye.   → Say nice to meet you and goodbye.

Lección 2

¿Qué estudias?

Felipe, Marissa, Juan Carlos y Miguel visitan Chapultepec y hablan de las clases.

PERSONAJES MARISSA FELIPE

 Video: *Fotonovela*

FELIPE Dos boletos, por favor.

EMPLEADO Dos boletos son 64 pesos.

FELIPE Aquí están 100 pesos.

EMPLEADO 100 menos 64 son 36 pesos de cambio.

MIGUEL Marissa, hablas muy bien el español... ¿Y dónde está tu diccionario?

MARISSA En casa de los Díaz. Felipe necesita practicar inglés.

MIGUEL ¡Ay, Maru! Chicos, nos vemos más tarde.

FELIPE Ésta es la Ciudad de México.

FELIPE Oye, Marissa, ¿cuántas clases tomas?

MARISSA Tomo cuatro clases: español, historia, literatura y también geografía. Me gusta mucho la cultura mexicana.

FELIPE Juan Carlos, ¿quién enseña la clase de química este semestre?

JUAN CARLOS El profesor Morales. Ah, ¿por qué tomo química y computación?

FELIPE Porque te gusta la tarea.

JUAN CARLOS

MIGUEL

EMPLEADO

MARU

FELIPE Los lunes y los miércoles, economía a las 2:30. Tú tomas computación los martes en la tarde, y química, a ver... Los lunes, los miércoles y los viernes ¿a las 10? ¡Uf!

FELIPE Y Miguel, ¿cuándo regresa?

JUAN CARLOS Hoy estudia con Maru.

MARISSA ¿Quién es Maru?

MIGUEL ¿Hablas con tu mamá?

MARU Mamá habla. Yo escucho. Es la 1:30.

MIGUEL Ay, lo siento. Juan Carlos y Felipe...

MARU Ay, Felipe.

MARU Y ahora, ¿adónde? ¿A la biblioteca?

MIGUEL Sí, pero primero a la librería. Necesito comprar unos libros.

recursos

VM
pp. 111–112

vhlcentral.com
Lección 2

Expresiones útiles

Talking about classes

¿Cuántas clases tomas?
How many classes are you taking?
Tomo cuatro clases.
I'm taking four classes.
Mi especialización es en arqueología.
My major is archeology.
Este año, espero sacar buenas notas y, por supuesto, viajar por el país.
This year, I hope / I'm hoping to get good grades. And, of course, travel through the country.

Talking about likes/dislikes

Me gusta mucho la cultura mexicana.
I like Mexican culture a lot.
Me gustan las ciencias ambientales.
I like environmental science.
Me gusta dibujar.
I like to draw.
¿Te gusta este lugar?
Do you like this place?

Paying for tickets

Dos boletos, por favor.
Two tickets, please.
Dos boletos son sesenta y cuatro pesos.
Two tickets are sixty-four pesos.
Aquí están cien pesos.
Here's a hundred pesos.
Son treinta y seis pesos de cambio.
That's thirty-six pesos change.

Talking about location and direction

¿Dónde está tu diccionario?
Where is your dictionary?
Está en casa de los Díaz.
It's at the Díaz house.
Y ahora, ¿adónde? ¿A la biblioteca?
And now, where to? To the library?
Sí, pero primero a la librería.
Está al lado.
Yes, but first to the bookstore.
It's next door.

¿Qué pasó?

1 **Escoger** Choose the answer that best completes each sentence.

1. Marissa toma (*is taking*) _____ en la universidad.
   a. español, psicología, economía y música   b. historia, inglés, sociología y periodismo
   c. español, historia, literatura y geografía
2. El profesor Morales enseña (*teaches*) _____.
   a. química   b. matemáticas   c. historia
3. Juan Carlos toma química _____.
   a. los miércoles, jueves y viernes   b. los lunes, miércoles y viernes
   c. los lunes, martes y jueves
4. Miguel necesita ir a (*needs to go to*) _____.
   a. la biblioteca   b. la residencia estudiantil   c. la librería

2 **Identificar** Indicate which person would make each statement. The names may be used more than once.

1. ¿Maru es compañera de ustedes? _____
2. Mi mamá habla mucho. _____
3. El profesor Morales enseña la clase de química este semestre. _____
4. Mi diccionario está en casa de Felipe y Jimena. _____
5. Necesito estudiar con Maru. _____
6. Yo tomo clase de computación los martes por la tarde. _____

MARU

JUAN CARLOS

MARISSA

MIGUEL

> **NOTA CULTURAL**
>
> **Maru** is a shortened version of the name **María Eugenia**. Other popular "combination names" in Spanish are **Juanjo** (Juan José) and **Maite** (María Teresa).

3 **Completar** These sentences are similar to things said in the **Fotonovela**. Complete each sentence with the correct word(s).

Castillo de Chapultepec	estudiar	miércoles
clase	inglés	tarea

1. Marissa, éste es el _____.
2. Felipe tiene (*has*) el diccionario porque (*because*) necesita practicar _____.
3. A Juan Carlos le gusta mucho la _____.
4. Hay clase de economía los lunes y _____.
5. Miguel está con Maru para _____.

> **NOTA CULTURAL**
>
> The **Castillo de Chapultepec** is one of Mexico City's most historic landmarks. Constructed in 1785, it was the residence of emperors and presidents. It has been open to the public since 1944 and now houses the National Museum of History.

4 **Preguntas personales** Interview a classmate about his/her university life.

1. ¿Qué clases tomas en la universidad?
2. ¿Qué clases tomas los martes?
3. ¿Qué clases tomas los viernes?
4. ¿En qué clase hay más chicos?
5. ¿En qué clase hay más chicas?
6. ¿Te gusta la clase de español?

 Practice more at **vhlcentral.com**.

Pronunciación **Audio**

Spanish vowels

 a **e** **i**  **o**  **u**

Spanish vowels are never silent; they are always pronounced in a short, crisp way without the glide sounds used in English.

Álex	**clase**	**nada**	**encantada**

The letter **a** is pronounced like the *a* in *father*, but shorter.

el	**ene**	**mesa**	**elefante**

The letter **e** is pronounced like the *e* in *they*, but shorter.

Inés	**chica**	**tiza**	**señorita**

The letter **i** sounds like the *ee* in *beet*, but shorter.

hola	**con**	**libro**	**don Francisco**

The letter **o** is pronounced like the *o* in *tone*, but shorter.

uno	**regular**	**saludos**	**gusto**

The letter **u** sounds like the *oo* in *room*, but shorter.

 Práctica Practice the vowels by saying the names of these places in Spain.

1. Madrid
2. Alicante
3. Tenerife
4. Toledo
5. Barcelona
6. Granada
7. Burgos
8. La Coruña

Oraciones Read the sentences aloud, focusing on the vowels.

1. Hola. Me llamo Ramiro Morgado.
2. Estudio arte en la Universidad de Salamanca.
3. Tomo también literatura y contabilidad.
4. Ay, tengo clase en cinco minutos. ¡Nos vemos!

Refranes Practice the vowels by reading these sayings aloud.

Cada loco con su tema.[2]

Del dicho al hecho hay un gran trecho.[1]

AYUDA

Although **hay** and **ay** are pronounced identically, they do not have the same meaning. As you learned in **Lección 1**, **hay** is a verb form that means *there is/are*. **Hay veinte libros**. (*There are twenty books.*) **¡Ay!** is an exclamation expressing pain, shock, or affliction: *Oh!; Oh, dear!*

---

1 Easier said than done.
2 To each his own.

Lección 2

recursos

LM p. 118

vhlcentral.com Lección 2
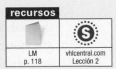

EN DETALLE

Additional Reading

La elección de una
carrera universitaria

Since higher education in the Spanish-speaking world is heavily state-subsidized, tuition is almost free. As a result, public universities see large enrollments. Spanish and Latin American students generally choose their **carrera universitaria** (major) when they're eighteen—which is either the year they enter the university or the year before. In order to enroll, all students must complete a high school degree, known as the **bachillerato**. In countries like Bolivia, Mexico, and Peru, the last year of high school (**colegio***) tends to be specialized in an area of study, such as the arts or natural sciences.

Universidad Central de Venezuela en Caracas

Students then choose their major according to their area of specialization. Similarly, university-bound students in Argentina focus their studies on their studies on specific fields, such as the humanities and social sciences, natural sciences, communication, art and design, and economics and business, during their five years of high school. Based on this coursework, Argentine students choose their **carrera**. Finally, in Spain, students choose their major according to the score they receive on the **prueba de aptitud** (skills test or entrance exam).

University graduates receive a **licenciatura**, or bachelor's degree. In Argentina and Chile, a **licenciatura** takes four to six years to complete, and may be considered equivalent to a master's degree. In Peru and Venezuela, a bachelor's degree is a five-year process. Spanish and Colombian **licenciaturas** take four to five years, although some fields, such as medicine, require six or more.

> ### Estudiantes hispanos en los EE.UU.
>
> In the 2010–11 academic year, over 13,000 Mexican students (2% of all international students) studied at U.S. universities. Colombians were the second-largest Spanish-speaking group, with over 6,000 students.

*¡Ojo! El colegio is a false cognate. In most countries, it means *high school*, but in some regions it refers to an elementary school. All undergraduate study takes place at **la universidad**.

ACTIVIDADES

1 **¿Cierto o falso?** Indicate whether these statements are **cierto** or **falso**. Correct the false statements.

1. Students in Spanish-speaking countries must pay large amounts of money toward their college tuition.

2. **Carrera** refers to any undergraduate or graduate program that students enroll in to obtain a professional degree.

3. After studying at a **colegio**, students receive their **bachillerato**.

4. Undergraduates study at a **colegio** or an **universidad**.

5. In Latin America and Spain, students usually choose their majors in their second year at the university.

6. In Argentina, students focus their studies in their high school years.

7. In Mexico, the **bachillerato** involves specialized study.

8. In Spain, majors depend on entrance exam scores.

9. Venezuelans complete a **licenciatura** in five years.

10. According to statistics, Colombians constitute the third-largest Latin American group studying at U.S. universities.

Lección 2

Clases y exámenes

aprobar	*to pass*
la asignatura (Esp.)	la clase, la materia
la clase anual	*year-long course*
el examen parcial	*midterm exam*
la facultad	*department, school*
la investigación	*research*
el profesorado	*faculty*
reprobar; suspender (Esp.)	*to fail*
sacar buenas/ malas notas	*to get good/ bad grades*
tomar apuntes	*to take notes*

EL MUNDO HISPANO

Las universidades hispanas

It is not uncommon for universities in Spain and Latin America to have extremely large student body populations.

- **Universidad de Buenos Aires** (Argentina) 325.000 estudiantes

- **Universidad Autónoma de Santo Domingo** (República Dominicana) 180.000 estudiantes

- **Universidad Complutense de Madrid** (España) 86.200 estudiantes

- **Universidad Central de Venezuela** (Venezuela) 62.600 estudiantes

PERFIL

La Universidad de Salamanca

The University of Salamanca, established in 1218, is the oldest university in Spain. It is located in Salamanca, one of the most spectacular Renaissance cities in Europe. Salamanca is nicknamed **La Ciudad Dorada** (*The Golden City*) for the golden glow of its famous sandstone buildings, and it was declared a UNESCO World Heritage Site in 1968.

Salamanca is a true college town, as its prosperity and city life depend on and revolve around the university population. Over 38,000 students from all over Spain, as well as abroad, come to study here each year. The school offers over 250 academic programs, as well as renowned Spanish courses for foreign students. To walk through the university's historic grounds is to follow the footsteps of immortal writers like Miguel de Cervantes and Miguel de Unamuno.

Conexión Internet

To which **facultad** does your major belong in Spain or Latin America?

Go to **vhlcentral.com** to find more cultural information related to this **Cultura** section.

ACTIVIDADES

2 **Comprensión** Complete these sentences.

1. The University of Salamanca was established in the year _____.
2. A _____ is a year-long course.
3. Salamanca is called _____.
4. Over 300,000 students attend the _____.
5. An _____ occurs about halfway through a course.

3 **La universidad en cifras** With a partner, research a Spanish or Latin American university online and find five statistics about that institution (for instance, the total enrollment, majors offered, year it was founded, etc.). Using the information you found, create a dialogue between a prospective student and a university representative. Present your dialogue to the class.

 Practice more at **vhlcentral.com**.

2.1 Present tense of -ar verbs

 Tutorial

ANTE TODO In order to talk about activities, you need to use verbs. Verbs express actions or states of being. In English and Spanish, the infinitive is the base form of the verb. In English, the infinitive is preceded by the word *to*: *to study*, *to be*. The infinitive in Spanish is a one-word form and can be recognized by its endings: **-ar**, **-er**, or **-ir**.

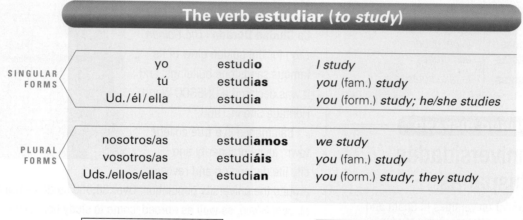

-*ar* verb		-*er* verb		-*ir* verb	
estudiar	*to study*	**comer**	*to eat*	**escribir**	*to write*

▶ In this lesson, you will learn the forms of regular **-ar** verbs.

The verb estudiar (*to study*)

SINGULAR FORMS	yo	estudi**o**	*I study*
	tú	estudi**as**	*you* (fam.) *study*
	Ud./él/ella	estudi**a**	*you* (form.) *study; he/she studies*
PLURAL FORMS	nosotros/as	estudi**amos**	*we study*
	vosotros/as	estudi**áis**	*you* (fam.) *study*
	Uds./ellos/ellas	estudi**an**	*you* (form.) *study; they study*

Juan Carlos estudia ciencias ambientales.

Y tú, ¿qué estudias, Miguel?

▶ To create the forms of most regular verbs in Spanish, drop the infinitive endings (**-ar, -er, -ir**). You then add to the stem the endings that correspond to the different subject pronouns. This diagram will help you visualize verb conjugation.

Conjugation of -*ar* verbs

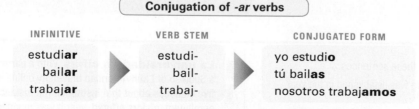

INFINITIVE	VERB STEM	CONJUGATED FORM
estudi**ar**	estudi-	yo estudi**o**
bail**ar**	bail-	tú bail**as**
trabaj**ar**	trabaj-	nosotros trabaj**amos**

Lección 2

Common -ar verbs

bailar	to dance	**estudiar**	to study
buscar	to look for	**explicar**	to explain
caminar	to walk	**hablar**	to talk; to speak
cantar	to sing	**llegar**	to arrive
cenar	to have dinner	**llevar**	to carry
comprar	to buy	**mirar**	to look (at); to watch
contestar	to answer	**necesitar (+ inf.)**	to need
conversar	to converse, to chat	**practicar**	to practice
desayunar	to have breakfast	**preguntar**	to ask (a question)
descansar	to rest	**preparar**	to prepare
desear (+ inf.)	to desire; to wish	**regresar**	to return
dibujar	to draw	**terminar**	to end; to finish
enseñar	to teach	**tomar**	to take; to drink
escuchar	to listen (to)	**trabajar**	to work
esperar (+ inf.)	to wait (for); to hope	**viajar**	to travel

▶ **¡Atención!** Unless referring to a person, the Spanish verbs **buscar**, **escuchar**, **esperar**, and **mirar** do not need to be followed by prepositions as they do in English.

Busco la tarea.
I'm looking for the homework.

Escucho la música.
I'm listening to the music.

Espero el autobús.
I'm waiting for the bus.

Miro la pizarra.
I'm looking at the blackboard.

COMPARE & CONTRAST

English uses three sets of forms to talk about the present: (1) the simple present (*Paco works*), (2) the present progressive (*Paco is working*), and (3) the emphatic present (*Paco does work*). In Spanish, the simple present can be used in all three cases.

Paco **trabaja** en la cafetería.
1. *Paco works in the cafeteria.*
2. *Paco is working in the cafeteria.*
3. *Paco does work in the cafeteria.*

In Spanish and English, the present tense is also sometimes used to express future action.

Marina **viaja** a Madrid mañana.
1. *Marina travels to Madrid tomorrow.*
2. *Marina will travel to Madrid tomorrow.*
3. *Marina is traveling to Madrid tomorrow.*

▶ When two verbs are used together with no change of subject, the second verb is generally in the infinitive. To make a sentence negative in Spanish, the word **no** is placed before the conjugated verb. In this case, **no** means *not*.

Deseo hablar con el señor Díaz.
I want to speak with Mr. Díaz.

Alicia **no** desea bailar ahora.
Alicia doesn't want to dance now.

▶ Spanish speakers often omit subject pronouns because the verb endings indicate who the subject is. In Spanish, subject pronouns are used for emphasis, clarification, or contrast.

—¿Qué enseñan?
What do they teach?

—**Ella** enseña arte y **él** enseña física.
She teaches art, and he teaches physics.

—¿Quién desea trabajar hoy?
Who wants to work today?

—**Yo** no deseo trabajar hoy.
I don't want to work today.

The verb gustar

▶ To express your likes and dislikes, use the expression **(no) me gusta + el/la** + [*singular noun*] or **(no) me gustan + los/las** + [*plural noun*]. Note: You may use the phrase **a mí** for emphasis, but never the subject pronoun **yo**.

Me gusta la música clásica.
I like classical music.

Me gustan las clases de español y biología.
I like Spanish and biology classes.

A mí me gustan las artes.
I like the arts.

A mí no me gusta el programa.
I don't like the program.

▶ To talk about what you like and don't like to do, use **(no) me gusta** + [*infinitive(s)*]. Note that the singular **gusta** is always used, even with more than one infinitive.

No me gusta viajar en autobús.
I don't like to travel by bus.

Me gusta cantar y **bailar**.
I like to sing and dance.

▶ To ask a classmate about likes and dislikes, use the pronoun **te** instead of **me**. Note: You may use **a ti** for emphasis, but never the subject pronoun **tú**.

—¿**Te gusta la geografía?**
Do you like geography?

—Sí, **me gusta**. Y a ti, ¿**te gusta el inglés?**
Yes, I like it. And you, do you like English?

▶ You can use this same structure to talk about other people by using the pronouns **nos**, **le**, and **les**. Unless your instructor tells you otherwise, only the **me** and **te** forms will appear on test materials for this worktext.

Nos gusta dibujar. (nosotros)
We like to draw.

**Nos gustan las clases de español
  e inglés. (nosotros)**
We like Spanish class and English class.

**No le gusta trabajar.
  (usted, él, ella)**
*You don't like to work.
He/She doesn't like to work.*

**Les gusta el arte.
  (ustedes, ellos, ellas)**
*You like art.
They like art.*

Sidebar

¡ATENCIÓN!

Note that **gustar** does not behave like other -ar verbs. You must study its use carefully and pay attention to prepositions, pronouns, and agreement.

AYUDA

Use the construction **a** + [*name/pronoun*] to clarify to whom you are referring. This construction is not always necessary.
A Gabriela le gusta bailar.
A Sara y a él les gustan los animales.
A mí me gusta viajar.
¿**A ti** te gustan las clases?

CONSULTA

For more on **gustar** and other verbs like it, see **¡ADELANTE! DOS** pp. 40–41.

¡INTÉNTALO!   Provide the present tense forms of these verbs. The first items have been done for you.

(**hablar**)

1. Yo ___hablo___ español.
2. Ellos _____ español.
3. Inés _____ español.
4. Nosotras _____ español.
5. Tú _____ español.

(**gustar**)

1. ___Me gusta___ el café. (a mí)
2. ¿_____ las clases? (a ti)
3. No _____ el café. (a ti)
4. No _____ las clases. (a mí)
5. No _____ el café. (a mí)

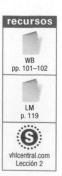

Práctica

1

Completar Complete the conversation with the appropriate forms of the verbs in parentheses.

JUAN ¡Hola, Linda! ¿Qué tal las clases?

LINDA Bien. (1)_____ (Tomar) tres clases... química, biología y computación. Y tú, ¿cuántas clases (2)_____ (tomar)?

JUAN (3)_____ (Tomar) tres también... biología, arte y literatura. El doctor Cárdenas (4)_____ (enseñar) la clase de biología.

LINDA ¿Ah, sí? Lily, Alberto y yo (5)_____ (tomar) biología a las diez con la profesora Garza.

JUAN ¿(6)_____ (Estudiar) mucho ustedes?

LINDA Sí, porque hay muchos exámenes. Alberto y yo (7)_____ (necesitar) estudiar dos horas todos los días (*every day*).

2

Oraciones Form sentences using the words provided. Remember to conjugate the verbs and add any other necessary words.

1. ustedes / practicar / vocabulario
2. ¿preparar (tú) / tarea?
3. clase de español / terminar / once
4. ¿qué / buscar / ustedes?
5. (nosotros) buscar / pluma
6. (yo) comprar / calculadora

3

Gustos Read what these people do. Then use the information in parentheses to tell what they like.

> **modelo**
>
> Yo enseño en la universidad. (las clases)   Me gustan las clases.

1. Tú deseas mirar cuadros (*paintings*) de Picasso. (el arte)
2. Soy estudiante de economía. (estudiar)
3. Tú estudias italiano y español. (las lenguas extranjeras)
4. No descansas los sábados. (cantar y bailar)
5. Busco una computadora. (la computación)

4

Actividades Get together with a classmate and take turns asking each other if you do these activities. Which activities does your partner like? Which do you both like?

> **modelo**
>
> tomar el autobús
> **Estudiante 1:** ¿Tomas el autobús?
> **Estudiante 2:** Sí, tomo el autobús, pero (*but*) no me gusta./ No, no tomo el autobús.

AYUDA

The Spanish **no** translates to both *no* and *not* in English. In negative answers to questions, you will need to use **no** twice:
¿Estudias geografía?
No, no estudio geografía.

bailar merengue	escuchar música rock	practicar el español
cantar bien	estudiar física	trabajar en la universidad
dibujar en clase	mirar la televisión	viajar a Europa

Comunicación

5

Describir With a partner, describe what you see in the pictures using the given verbs. Also ask your partner whether or not he/she likes one of the activities.

> **modelo**
>
> enseñar
> La profesora enseña química. ¿Te gusta la química?

1. caminar, hablar, llevar

2. buscar, descansar, estudiar

3. dibujar, cantar, escuchar

4. llevar, tomar, viajar

6

Charadas In groups of three, play a game of charades using the verbs in the word bank. For example, if someone is studying, you say "**Estudias.**" The first person to guess correctly acts out the next charade.

bailar	cantar	descansar	enseñar	mirar
caminar	conversar	dibujar	escuchar	preguntar

Síntesis

7

Conversación Get together with a classmate and pretend that you are friends who have not seen each other on campus for a few days. Have a conversation in which you catch up on things. Mention how you're feeling, what classes you're taking, what days and times you have classes, and which classes you like and don't like.

 Practice more at **vhlcentral.com**.

2.2 Forming questions in Spanish Tutorial

ANTE TODO There are three basic ways to ask questions in Spanish. Can you guess what they are by looking at the photos and photo captions on this page?

Te gusta mucho la tarea, ¿no?

¿Hablas con tu mamá?

¿Estudia Maru?

Lección 2

▶ One way to form a question is to raise the pitch of your voice at the end of a declarative sentence. When writing any question in Spanish, be sure to use an upside-down question mark (¿) at the beginning and a regular question mark (?) at the end of the sentence.

Statement	Question
Ustedes trabajan los sábados.	¿Ustedes trabajan los sábados?
You work on Saturdays.	*Do you work on Saturdays?*
Carlota busca un mapa.	¿Carlota busca un mapa?
Carlota is looking for a map.	*Is Carlota looking for a map?*

▶ You can also form a question by inverting the order of the subject and the verb of a declarative statement. The subject may even be placed at the end of the sentence.

Statement	Question
SUBJECT VERB	VERB SUBJECT
Ustedes trabajan los sábados.	**¿Trabajan ustedes** los sábados?
You work on Saturdays.	*Do you work on Saturdays?*
SUBJECT VERB	VERB SUBJECT
Carlota regresa a las seis.	**¿Regresa** a las seis **Carlota**?
Carlota returns at six.	*Does Carlota return at six?*

▶ Questions can also be formed by adding the tags **¿no?** or **¿verdad?** at the end of a statement.

Statement	Question
Ustedes trabajan los sábados.	Ustedes trabajan los sábados, **¿no?**
You work on Saturdays.	*You work on Saturdays, don't you?*
Carlota regresa a las seis.	Carlota regresa a las seis, **¿verdad?**
Carlota returns at six.	*Carlota returns at six, right?*

Question words

Interrogative words

¿Adónde?	Where (to)?	**¿De dónde?**	From where?
¿Cómo?	How?	**¿Dónde?**	Where?
¿Cuál?, ¿Cuáles?	Which?; Which one(s)?	**¿Por qué?**	Why?
¿Cuándo?	When?	**¿Qué?**	What?; Which?
¿Cuánto/a?	How much?	**¿Quién?**	Who?
¿Cuántos/as?	How many?	**¿Quiénes?**	Who (plural)?

CONSULTA

You will learn more about the difference between **qué** and **cuál** in *¡ADELANTE! DOS* p. 158.

▶ To ask a question that requires more than a *yes* or *no* answer, use an interrogative word.

¿Cuál de ellos estudia en la biblioteca?
Which of them studies in the library?

¿Adónde caminamos?
Where are we walking?

¿Cuántos estudiantes hablan español?
How many students speak Spanish?

¿Por qué necesitas hablar con ella?
Why do you need to talk to her?

¿Dónde trabaja Ricardo?
Where does Ricardo work?

¿Quién enseña la clase de arte?
Who teaches the art class?

¿Qué clases tomas?
What classes are you taking?

¿Cuánta tarea hay?
How much homework is there?

▶ When pronouncing this type of question, the pitch of your voice falls at the end of the sentence.

¿Cómo llegas a clase?
How do you get to class?

¿Por qué necesitas estudiar?
Why do you need to study?

▶ Notice the difference between **¿por qué?**, which is written as two words and has an accent, and **porque**, which is written as one word without an accent.

¿Por qué estudias español?
Why do you study Spanish?

¡Porque es divertido!
Because it's fun!

▶ In Spanish **no** can mean both *no* and *not*. Therefore, when answering a yes/no question in the negative, you need to use **no** twice.

¿Caminan a la universidad?
Do you walk to the university?

No, **no** caminamos a la universidad.
No, we do not walk to the university.

 **¡INTÉNTALO!** Make questions out of these statements. Use the intonation method in column 1 and the tag **¿no?** method in column 2.

Statement	Intonation	Tag questions
1. Hablas inglés.	¿Hablas inglés?	Hablas inglés, ¿no?
2. Trabajamos mañana.		
3. Ustedes desean bailar.		
4. Raúl estudia mucho.		
5. Enseño a las nueve.		
6. Luz mira la televisión.		

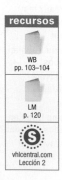
recursos
WB pp. 103–104
LM p. 120
vhlcentral.com Lección 2

Práctica

1 **Preguntas** Change these sentences into questions by inverting the word order.

> **modelo**
>
> Ernesto habla con su compañero de clase.
> ¿Habla Ernesto con su compañero de clase? /
> ¿Habla con su compañero de clase Ernesto?

1. La profesora Cruz prepara la prueba.

2. Sandra y yo necesitamos estudiar.

3. Los chicos practican el vocabulario.

4. Jaime termina la tarea.

5. Tú trabajas en la biblioteca.

2 **Completar** Irene and Manolo are chatting in the library. Complete their conversation with the appropriate questions.

IRENE Hola, Manolo. (1)_____

MANOLO Bien, gracias. (2)_____

IRENE Muy bien. (3)_____

MANOLO Son las nueve.

IRENE (4)_____

MANOLO Estudio historia.

IRENE (5)_____

MANOLO Porque hay un examen mañana.

IRENE (6)_____

MANOLO Sí, me gusta mucho la clase.

IRENE (7)_____

MANOLO El profesor Padilla enseña la clase.

IRENE (8)_____

MANOLO No, no tomo psicología este (this) semestre.

IRENE (9)_____

MANOLO Regreso a la residencia a las once.

IRENE (10)_____

MANOLO No, no deseo tomar una soda. ¡Deseo estudiar!

3 **Dos profesores** In pairs, create a dialogue, similar to the one in **Actividad 2**, between Professor Padilla and his colleague Professor Martínez. Use question words.

> **modelo**
>
> **Prof. Padilla:** ¿Qué enseñas este semestre?
> **Prof. Martínez:** Enseño dos cursos de sociología.

 Practice more at **vhlcentral.com**.

Lección 2

Comunicación

4

Encuesta Your instructor will give you a worksheet. Change the categories in the first column into questions, then use them to survey your classmates. Find at least one person for each category. Be prepared to report the results of your survey to the class.

5

Un juego In groups of four or five, play a game (**un juego**) of Jeopardy®. Each person has to write two clues. Then take turns reading the clues and guessing the questions. The person who guesses correctly reads the next clue.

> **Es algo que...**   **Es un lugar donde...**   **Es una persona que...**
> *It's something that...*   *It's a place where...*   *It's a person that...*

> **modelo**
>
> **Estudiante 1:** Es un lugar donde estudiamos.
> **Estudiante 2:** ¿Qué es la biblioteca?
>
> **Estudiante 1:** Es algo que escuchamos.
> **Estudiante 2:** ¿Qué es la música?
>
> **Estudiante 1:** Es un director de España.
> **Estudiante 2:** ¿Quién es Pedro Almodóvar?

NOTA CULTURAL

Pedro Almodóvar is an award-winning film director from Spain. His films are full of both humor and melodrama, and their controversial subject matter has often sparked great debate. His film **Hable con ella** won the Oscar for Best Original Screenplay in 2002. His 2006 hit **Volver** was nominated for numerous awards, and won the Best Screenplay and Best Actress award for the entire female cast at the Cannes Film Festival.

6

El nuevo estudiante Imagine you are a transfer student and today is your first day of Spanish class. Ask your partner questions to find out all you can about the class, your classmates, and the university. Then switch roles.

> **modelo**
>
> **Estudiante 1:** Hola, me llamo Samuel. ¿Cómo te llamas?
> **Estudiante 2:** Me llamo Laura.
> **Estudiante 1:** ¿Quiénes son ellos?
> **Estudiante 2:** Son Melanie y Lucas.
> **Estudiante 1:** Y él, ¿de dónde es?
> **Estudiante 2:** Es de California.
> **Estudiante 1:** En la universidad hay cursos de ciencias, ¿verdad?
> **Estudiante 2:** Sí, hay clases de biología, química y física.
> **Estudiante 1:** ¿Cuántos exámenes hay en esta clase?
> **Estudiante 2:** Hay dos.

Síntesis

7

Entrevista Imagine that you are a reporter for the school newspaper. Write five questions about student life at your school and use them to interview two classmates. Be prepared to report your findings to the class.

2.3 Present tense of estar  Tutorial

CONSULTA

To review the forms of **ser**, see **Estructura 1.3**, pp. 19–21.

ANTE TODO In **Lección 1**, you learned how to conjugate and use the verb **ser** (*to be*). You will now learn a second verb which means *to be*, the verb **estar**. Although **estar** ends in **-ar**, it does not follow the pattern of regular **-ar** verbs. The **yo** form (**estoy**) is irregular. Also, all forms have an accented **á** except the **yo** and **nosotros/as** forms.

The verb estar (*to be*)		
SINGULAR FORMS		
yo	est**oy**	*I am*
tú	est**ás**	*you* (fam.) *are*
Ud./él/ella	est**á**	*you* (form.) *are; he/she is*
PLURAL FORMS		
nosotros/as	est**amos**	*we are*
vosotros/as	est**áis**	*you* (fam.) *are*
Uds./ellos/ellas	est**án**	*you* (form.) *are; they are*

¡Estamos en Perú!

María está en la biblioteca.

COMPARE & CONTRAST

Compare the uses of the verb **estar** to those of the verb **ser**.

AYUDA

Use **la casa** to express *the house*, but **en casa** to express *at home*.

CONSULTA

To learn more about the difference between **ser** and **estar**, see **Estructura 5.3**, pp. 264–265.

Uses of *estar*

Location
Estoy en casa.
I am at home.

Marissa **está** al lado de Felipe.
Marissa is next to Felipe.

Health
Juan Carlos **está** enfermo hoy.
Juan Carlos is sick today.

Well-being
—¿Cómo **estás**, Jimena?
How are you, Jimena?

—**Estoy** muy bien, gracias.
I'm very well, thank you.

Uses of *ser*

Identity
Hola, **soy** Maru.
Hello, I'm Maru.

Occupation
Soy estudiante.
I'm a student.

Origin
—¿**Eres** de México?
Are you from Mexico?

—Sí, **soy** de México.
Yes, I'm from Mexico.

Telling time
Son las cuatro.
It's four o'clock.

Lección 2

▶ **Estar** is often used with certain adverbs and prepositions to describe the location of a person or an object.

Adverbs and prepositions often used with **estar**

al lado de	next to; beside	**delante de**	in front of
a la derecha de	to the right of	**detrás de**	behind
a la izquierda de	to the left of	**en**	in; on
allá	over there	**encima de**	on top of
allí	there	**entre**	between; among
cerca de	near	**lejos de**	far from
con	with	**sin**	without
debajo de	below	**sobre**	on; over

La tiza **está al lado de** la pluma.
The chalk is next to the pen.

Los libros **están encima del** escritorio.
The books are on top of the desk.

El laboratorio **está cerca de** la clase.
The lab is near the classroom.

Maribel **está delante de** José.
Maribel is in front of José.

La maleta **está allí**.
The suitcase is there.

El estadio no **está lejos de** la librería.
The stadium isn't far from the bookstore.

El mapa **está entre** la pizarra y la puerta.
The map is between the blackboard and the door.

Los estudiantes **están en** la clase.
The students are in class.

La calculadora **está sobre** la mesa.
The calculator is on the table.

Los turistas **están allá**.
The tourists are over there.

Estamos lejos de casa.

La biblioteca está al lado de la librería.

¡INTÉNTALO! Provide the present-tense forms of **estar**.

1. Ustedes ___están___ en la clase.
2. José _____ en la biblioteca.
3. Yo _____ bien, gracias.
4. Nosotras _____ en la cafetería.
5. Tú _____ en el laboratorio.
6. Elena _____ en la librería.
7. Ellas _____ en la clase.
8. Ana y yo _____ en la clase.
9. ¿Cómo _____ usted?
10. Javier y Maribel _____ en el estadio.
11. Nosotros _____ en la cafetería.
12. Yo _____ en el laboratorio.
13. Carmen y María _____ enfermas.
14. Tú _____ en la clase.

Práctica

1

Completar Daniela has just returned home from the library. Complete this conversation with the appropriate forms of **ser** or **estar**.

MAMÁ   Hola, Daniela. ¿Cómo (1)_____?

▶ DANIELA   Hola, mamá. (2)_____ bien. ¿Dónde (3)_____ papá? ¡Ya (*Already*) (4)_____ las ocho de la noche!

MAMÁ   No (5)_____ aquí. (6)_____ en la oficina.

DANIELA   Y Andrés y Margarita, ¿dónde (7)_____ ellos?

MAMÁ   (8)_____ en el restaurante La Palma con Martín.

DANIELA   ¿Quién (9)_____ Martín?

MAMÁ   (10)_____ un compañero de clase. (11)_____ de México.

DANIELA   Ah. Y el restaurante La Palma, ¿dónde (12)_____?

MAMÁ   (13)_____ cerca de la Plaza Mayor, en San Modesto.

DANIELA   Gracias, mamá. Voy (*I'm going*) al restaurante. ¡Hasta pronto!

2

Escoger Choose the preposition that best completes each sentence.

1. La pluma está (encima de / detrás de) la mesa.
2. La ventana está (a la izquierda de / debajo de) la puerta.
3. La pizarra está (debajo de / delante de) los estudiantes.
4. Las sillas están (encima de / detrás de) los escritorios.
5. Los estudiantes llevan los libros (en / sobre) la mochila.
6. La biblioteca está (sobre / al lado de) la residencia estudiantil.
7. España está (cerca de / lejos de) Puerto Rico.
8. México está (cerca de / lejos de) los Estados Unidos.
9. Felipe trabaja (con / en) Ricardo en la cafetería.

3

La librería Imagine that you are in the school bookstore and can't find various items. Ask the clerk (your partner) the location of five items in the drawing. Then switch roles.

modelo

Estudiante 1: ¿Dónde están los diccionarios?
Estudiante 2: Los diccionarios están debajo de los libros de literatura.

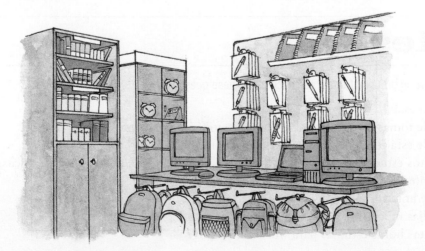

 Practice more at **vhlcentral.com**.

Lección 2

Comunicación

4 **¿Dónde estás...?** Get together with a partner and take turns asking each other where you normally are at these times.

> **modelo**
>
> lunes / 10:00 a.m.
> **Estudiante 1:** ¿Dónde estás los lunes a las diez de la mañana?
> **Estudiante 2:** Estoy en la clase de español.

1. sábados / 6:00 a.m.
2. miércoles / 9:15 a.m.
3. lunes / 11:10 a.m.
4. jueves / 12:30 a.m.

5. viernes / 2:25 p.m.
6. martes / 3:50 p.m.
7. jueves / 5:45 p.m.
8. miércoles / 8:20 p.m.

5 **La ciudad universitaria** You are an exchange student at a Spanish university. Tell a classmate which buildings you are looking for and ask for their location relative to where you are.

> **modelo**
>
> **Estudiante 1:** ¿Está lejos la Facultad de Medicina?
> **Estudiante 2:** No, está cerca. Está a la izquierda de la Facultad de Administración de Empresas.

Facultad de Medicina · Facultad de Administración de Empresas · Facultad de Filosofía y Letras · Biblioteca · Facultad de Bellas Artes · Colegio Mayor Cervantes

Síntesis

6 **Entrevista** In groups of three, ask each other these questions.

1. ¿Cómo estás?
2. ¿Dónde tomas la clase de inglés/periodismo/física/computación?
3. ¿Dónde está tu (*your*) compañero/a de cuarto ahora?
4. ¿Cuántos estudiantes hay en tu clase de historia/literatura/química/matemáticas?
5. ¿Quién(es) no está(n) en la clase hoy?
6. ¿A qué hora terminan tus clases los lunes?
7. ¿Estudias mucho?
8. ¿Cuántas horas estudias para (*for*) una prueba?

(2.4) Numbers 31 and higher  Tutorial

ANTE TODO You have already learned numbers 0–30. Now you will learn the rest of the numbers.

Numbers 31–100

▶ Numbers 31–99 follow the same basic pattern as 21–29.

Numbers 31–100		
31 treinta y uno	40 cuarenta	50 cincuenta
32 treinta y dos	41 cuarenta y uno	51 cincuenta y uno
33 treinta y tres	42 cuarenta y dos	52 cincuenta y dos
34 treinta y cuatro	43 cuarenta y tres	60 sesenta
35 treinta y cinco	44 cuarenta y cuatro	63 sesenta y tres
36 treinta y seis	45 cuarenta y cinco	64 sesenta y cuatro
37 treinta y siete	46 cuarenta y seis	70 setenta
38 treinta y ocho	47 cuarenta y siete	80 ochenta
39 treinta y nueve	48 cuarenta y ocho	90 noventa
	49 cuarenta y nueve	100 cien, ciento

▶ **Y** is used in most numbers from **31** through **99**. Unlike numbers 21–29, these numbers must be written as three separate words.

Hay **noventa y dos** exámenes.
There are ninety-two exams.

Hay **cuarenta y dos** estudiantes.
There are forty-two students.

Hay cuarenta y siete estudiantes en la clase de geografía.

Cien menos sesenta y cuatro son treinta y seis pesos de cambio.

▶ With numbers that end in **uno** (31, 41, etc.), **uno** becomes **un** before a masculine noun and **una** before a feminine noun.

Hay **treinta y un** chicos.
There are thirty-one guys.

Hay **treinta y una** chicas.
There are thirty-one girls.

▶ **Cien** is used before nouns and in counting. The words **un, una,** and **uno** are never used before **cien** in Spanish. Use **cientos** to say *hundreds.*

Hay **cien** libros y **cien** sillas.
There are one hundred books and one hundred chairs.

¿Cuántos libros hay? **Cientos.**
How many books are there? Hundreds.

Numbers 101 and higher

▶ As shown in the chart, Spanish uses a period to indicate thousands and millions, rather than a comma, as is used in English.

Numbers 101 and higher			
101	ciento uno	**1.000**	mil
200	doscientos/as	**1.100**	mil cien
300	trescientos/as	**2.000**	dos mil
400	cuatrocientos/as	**5.000**	cinco mil
500	quinientos/as	**100.000**	cien mil
600	seiscientos/as	**200.000**	doscientos/as mil
700	setecientos/as	**550.000**	quinientos/as cincuenta mil
800	ochocientos/as	**1.000.000**	un millón (de)
900	novecientos/as	**8.000.000**	ocho millones (de)

▶ Notice that you should use **ciento**, not **cien**, to count numbers over 100.

110 = **ciento diez**   118 = **ciento dieciocho**   150 = **ciento cincuenta**

▶ The numbers 200 through 999 agree in gender with the nouns they modify.

324 plum**as**   3.505 libr**os**
trescient**as** veinticuatro plum**as**   tres mil quinient**os** cinco libr**os**

▶ The word **mil**, which can mean *a thousand* and *one thousand*, is not usually used in the plural form to refer to an exact number, but it can be used to express the idea of *a lot*, *many*, or *thousands*. **Cientos** can also be used to express *hundreds* in this manner.

¡Hay **miles** de personas en el estadio!   Hay **cientos** de libros en la biblioteca.
There are thousands of people   *There are hundreds of books*
in the stadium!   *in the library.*

▶ To express a complex number (including years), string together all of its components.

55.422   cincuenta y cinco mil cuatrocientos veintidós

¡LENGUA VIVA!

In Spanish, years are not expressed as pairs of two-digit numbers as they are in English (1979, *nineteen seventy-nine*): 1776, **mil setecientos setenta y seis**; 1945, **mil novecientos cuarenta y cinco**; 2012, **dos mil doce**.

¡ATENCIÓN!

When **millón** or **millones** is used before a noun, the word **de** is placed between the two:
1.000.000 hombres = un millón de hombres
12.000.000 casas = doce millones de casas.

¡INTÉNTALO!   Write out the Spanish equivalent of each number.

1. **102** _____*ciento dos*_____
2. **5.000.000** _____
3. **201** _____
4. **76** _____
5. **92** _____
6. **550.300** _____

7. **235** _____
8. **79** _____
9. **113** _____
10. **88** _____
11. **17.123** _____
12. **497** _____

recursos

WB
pp. 107–108

LM
p. 122

S
vhlcentral.com
Lección 2

Práctica y Comunicación

1

Baloncesto Provide these basketball scores in Spanish.

1. Ohio State 76, Michigan 65
2. Florida 92, Florida State 104
3. Stanford 83, UCLA 89
4. Purdue 81, Indiana 78
5. Princeton 67, Harvard 55
6. Duke 115, Virginia 121

2

Completar Following the pattern, write out the missing numbers in Spanish.

1. 50, 150, 250 ... 1.050
2. 5.000, 20.000, 35.000 ... 95.000
3. 100.000, 200.000, 300.000 ... 1.000.000
4. 100.000.000, 90.000.000, 80.000.000 ... 0

3

Resolver In pairs, take turns reading the math problems aloud for your partner to solve.

> **modelo**
> 200 + 300 =
> **Estudiante 1:** Doscientos más trescientos son...
> **Estudiante 2:** ...quinientos.

AYUDA
+ → más
− → menos
= → son

1. 1.000 + 753 =
2. 1.000.000 − 30.000 =
3. 10.000 + 555 =
4. 15 + 150 =
5. 100.000 + 205.000 =
6. 29.000 − 10.000 =

4

Entrevista Find out the telephone numbers and e-mail addresses of four classmates.

> **modelo**
> **Estudiante 1:** ¿Cuál es tu (your) número de teléfono?
> **Estudiante 2:** Es el 635-19-51.
> **Estudiante 1:** ¿Y tu dirección de correo electrónico?
> **Estudiante 2:** Es a-Smith-arroba-pe-ele-punto-e-de-u. (asmith@pl.edu)

AYUDA
arroba *at* (@)
punto *dot* (.)

Síntesis

5

¿A qué distancia...? Your instructor will give you and a partner incomplete charts that indicate the distances between Madrid and various locations. Fill in the missing information on your chart by asking your partner questions.

> **modelo**
> **Estudiante 1:** ¿A qué distancia está Arganda del Rey?
> **Estudiante 2:** Está a veintisiete kilómetros de Madrid.

 Practice more at **vhlcentral.com**.

Lección 2

Recapitulación

 Diagnostics

Review the grammar concepts you have learned in this lesson by completing these activities.

1 **Completar** Complete the chart with the correct verb forms. `12 pts.`

yo	tú	nosotros	ellas
compro			
	deseas		
		miramos	
			preguntan

2 **Números** Write these numbers in Spanish. `8 pts.`

> **modelo**
> 645: *seiscientos cuarenta y cinco*

1. **49:** _____
2. **97:** _____
3. **113:** _____
4. **632:** _____
5. **1.781:** _____
6. **3.558:** _____
7. **1.006.015:** _____
8. **67.224.370:** _____

3 **Preguntas** Write questions for these answers. `12 pts.`

1. —¿_____ Patricia?
   —Patricia es de Colombia.
2. —¿_____ él?
   —Él es mi amigo (*friend*).
3. —¿_____ (tú)?
   —Hablo dos idiomas (*languages*).
4. —¿_____ (ustedes)?
   —Deseamos tomar café.
5. —¿_____?
   —Tomo biología porque me gustan las ciencias.
6. —¿_____?
   —Camilo descansa por las mañanas.

RESUMEN GRAMATICAL

2.1 Present tense of -ar verbs *pp. 72–74*

estudiar	
estudio	estudiamos
estudias	estudiáis
estudia	estudian

The verb gustar

(no) me gusta + el/la + [*singular noun*]

(no) me gustan + los/las + [*plural noun*]

(no) me gusta + [*infinitive(s)*]

Note: You may use **a mí** for emphasis, but never **yo.**

To ask a classmate about likes and dislikes, use **te** instead of **me**, but never **tú.**

¿Te gusta la historia?

2.2 Forming questions in Spanish *pp. 77–78*

▶ ¿Ustedes trabajan los sábados?
▶ ¿Trabajan ustedes los sábados?
▶ Ustedes trabajan los sábados, ¿verdad?/¿no?

Interrogative words		
¿Adónde?	¿Cuánto/a?	¿Por qué?
¿Cómo?	¿Cuántos/as?	¿Qué?
¿Cuál(es)?	¿De dónde?	¿Quién(es)?
¿Cuándo?	¿Dónde?	

2.3 Present tense of estar *pp. 81–82*

▶ estar: estoy, estás, está, estamos, estáis, están

2.4 Numbers 31 and higher *pp. 85–86*

31	treinta y uno	101	ciento uno
32	treinta y dos	200	doscientos/as
	(and so on)	500	quinientos/as
40	cuarenta	700	setecientos/as
50	cincuenta	900	novecientos/as
60	sesenta	1.000	mil
70	setenta	2.000	dos mil
80	ochenta	5.100	cinco mil cien
90	noventa	100.000	cien mil
100	cien, ciento	1.000.000	un millón (de)

4 **Al teléfono** Complete this telephone conversation with the correct forms of the verb **estar**. `8 pts.`

MARÍA TERESA   Hola, señora López. (1) ¿ _____ Elisa en casa?

SRA. LÓPEZ   Hola, ¿quién es?

MARÍA TERESA   Soy María Teresa. Elisa y yo (2) _____ en la misma (*same*) clase de literatura.

SRA. LÓPEZ   ¡Ah, María Teresa! ¿Cómo (3) _____ ?

MARÍA TERESA   (4) _____ muy bien, gracias. Y usted, ¿cómo (5) _____ ?

SRA. LÓPEZ   Bien, gracias. Pues, no, Elisa no (6) _____ en casa. Ella y su hermano (*her brother*) (7) _____ en la Biblioteca Cervantes.

MARÍA TERESA   ¿Cervantes?

SRA. LÓPEZ   Es la biblioteca que (8) _____ al lado del café Bambú.

MARÍA TERESA   ¡Ah, sí! Gracias, señora López.

SRA. LÓPEZ   Hasta luego, María Teresa.

5 **¿Qué te gusta?** Write a paragraph of at least five sentences stating what you like and don't like about your university. If possible, explain your likes and dislikes. `10 pts.`

Me gusta la clase de música porque no hay muchos exámenes. No me gusta cenar en la cafetería...

6 **Canción** Use the appropriate forms of the verb **gustar** to complete the beginning of a popular song by Manu Chao. `2 EXTRA points!`

❝ Me _____ los aviones°,
me gustas tú,
me _____ viajar,
me gustas tú,
me gusta la mañana,
me gustas tú. ❞

aviones *airplanes*

 Practice more at **vhlcentral.com**.

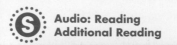
Lectura

Antes de leer

Estrategia

Predicting Content through Formats

Recognizing the format of a document can help you to predict its content. For instance, invitations, greeting cards, and classified ads follow an easily identifiable format, which usually gives you a general idea of the information they contain. Look at the text and identify it based on its format.

	lunes	martes	miércoles	jueves	viernes
8:30	biología		biología		biología
9:00		historia		historia	
9:30	inglés		inglés		inglés
10:00					
10:30					
11:00					
12:00					
12:30					
1:00					
2:00	arte		arte		arte

If you guessed that this is a page from a student's schedule, you are correct. You can now infer that the document contains information about a student's weekly schedule, including days, times, and activities.

Cognados

With a classmate, make a list of the cognates in the text and guess their English meanings. What do cognates reveal about the content of the document?

Examinar el texto

Look at the format of the document entitled *¡Español en Madrid!* What type of text is it? What information do you expect to find in this type of document?

¡ESPAÑOL EN MADRID!

UAM

Programa de Cursos Intensivos de Español
Universidad Autónoma de Madrid

Después de leer

Correspondencias

Provide the letter of each item in Column B that matches the words in Column A. Two items will not be used.

A	B
1. profesores	a. (34) 91 523 4500
2. vivienda	b. (34) 91 524 0210
3. Madrid	c. 23 junio–30 julio
4. número de teléfono	d. capital cultural de Europa
5. Español 2B	e. 16 junio–22 julio
6. número de fax	f. especializados en enseñar español como lengua extranjera
	g. (34) 91 523 4623
	h. familias españolas

 Practice more at **vhlcentral.com**.

Universidad Autónoma de Madrid

Madrid, la capital cultural de Europa, y la UAM te ofrecen cursos intensivos de verano° para aprender° español como nunca antes°.

Cursos	Empieza°	Termina
Español 1A	16 junio	22 julio
Español 1B	23 junio	30 julio
Español 1C	30 junio	10 agosto
Español 2A	16 junio	22 julio
Español 2B	23 junio	30 julio
Español 3A	16 junio	22 julio
Español 3B	23 junio	30 julio

¿Dónde?
En el campus de la UAM, edificio° de la Facultad de Filosofía y Letras.

¿Quiénes son los profesores?
Son todos hablantes nativos del español y catedráticos° de la UAM especializados en enseñar el español como lengua extranjera.

¿Qué niveles se ofrecen?
Se ofrecen tres niveles° básicos:
1. Español Elemental, A, B y C
2. Español Intermedio, A y B
3. Español Avanzado, A y B

Viviendas
Para estudiantes extranjeros se ofrece vivienda° con familias españolas.

¿Cuándo?
Este verano desde° el 16 de junio hasta el 10 de agosto. Los cursos tienen una duración de 6 semanas.

Información
Para mayor información, sirvan comunicarse con la siguiente° oficina:

Universidad Autónoma de Madrid
Programa de Español como Lengua Extranjera
Ctra. Colmenar Viejo, Km. 15, 28049 Madrid, España
Tel. (34) 91 523 4500, **Fax** (34) 91 523 4623
www.uam.es

verano *summer* aprender *to learn* nunca antes *never before* edificio *building* catedráticos *professors* niveles *levels* vivienda *housing* desde *from* Empieza *Begins* siguiente *following*

¿Cierto o falso?

Indicate whether each statement is **cierto** or **falso**.
Then correct the false statements.

	Cierto	Falso
1. La Universidad Autónoma de Madrid ofrece (*offers*) cursos intensivos de italiano.	○	○
2. La lengua nativa de los profesores del programa es el inglés.	○	○
3. Los cursos de español son en la Facultad de Ciencias.	○	○
4. Los estudiantes pueden vivir (*can live*) con familias españolas.	○	○

	Cierto	Falso
5. La universidad que ofrece los cursos intensivos está en Salamanca.	○	○
6. Español 3B termina en agosto.	○	○
7. Si deseas información sobre (*about*) los cursos intensivos de español, es posible llamar al (34) 91 523 4500.	○	○
8. Español 1A empieza en julio.	○	○

Escritura

Estrategia
Brainstorming

How do you find ideas to write about? In the early stages of writing, brainstorming can help you generate ideas on a specific topic. You should spend ten to fifteen minutes brainstorming and jotting down any ideas about the topic. Whenever possible, try to write your ideas in Spanish. Express your ideas in single words or phrases, and jot them down in any order. While brainstorming, don't worry about whether your ideas are good or bad. Selecting and organizing ideas should be the second stage of your writing. Remember that the more ideas you write down while you're brainstorming, the more options you'll have to choose from later when you start to organize your ideas.

Me gusta

bailar
viajar
mirar la televisión
la clase de español
la clase de psicología

No me gusta

cantar
dibujar
trabajar
la clase de química
la clase de biología

Tema

Una descripción

Write a description of yourself to post in a chat room on a website in order to meet Spanish-speaking people. Include this information in your description:

▶ your name and where you are from, and a photo (optional) of yourself

▶ your major and where you go to school

▶ the courses you are taking

▶ where you work (if you have a job)

▶ some of your likes and dislikes

¡Hola! Me llamo Alicia Roberts. Estudio matemáticas en la Universidad de Toronto.

Escuchar Audio

Estrategia
Listening for cognates

You already know that cognates are words that have similar spellings and meanings in two or more languages: for example, *group* and **grupo** or *stereo* and **estéreo.** Listen for cognates to increase your comprehension of spoken Spanish.

 To help you practice this strategy, you will now listen to two sentences. Make a list of all the cognates you hear.

Preparación

Based on the photograph, who do you think Armando and Julia are? What do you think they are talking about?

Ahora escucha

Now you are going to hear Armando and Julia's conversation. Make a list of the cognates they use.

Armando	Julia
_____	_____
_____	_____
_____	_____
_____	_____

Based on your knowledge of cognates, decide whether the following statements are **cierto** or **falso.**

	Cierto	Falso
1. Armando y Julia hablan de la familia.	○	○
2. Armando y Julia toman una clase de matemáticas.	○	○
3. Julia toma clases de ciencias.	○	○
4. Armando estudia lenguas extranjeras.	○	○
5. Julia toma una clase de religión.	○	○

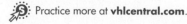

Lección 2

Comprensión

Preguntas
Answer these questions about Armando and Julia's conversation.

1. ¿Qué clases toma Armando?
   _____
2. ¿Qué clases toma Julia?
   _____

Seleccionar
Choose the answer that best completes each sentence.

1. Armando toma _____ clases en la universidad.
   a. cuatro   b. cinco   c. seis
2. Julia toma dos clases de _____.
   a. matemáticas b. lengua   c. ciencias
3. Armando toma italiano y _____.
   a. astronomía   b. japonés c. geología
4. Armando y Julia estudian _____ los martes y jueves.
   a. filosofía   b. antropología c. italiano

Preguntas personales

1. ¿Cuántas clases tomas tú este semestre?
2. ¿Qué clases tomas este semestre?
3. ¿Qué clases te gustan y qué clases no te gustan?

En pantalla

Christmas isn't always in winter. During the months of cold weather and snow in North America, the southern hemisphere enjoys warm weather and longer days. Since Chile's summer lasts from December to February, school vacation coincides with these months. In Chile, the school year starts in early March and finishes toward the end of December. All schools, from preschools to universities, observe this scholastic calendar, with only a few days' variation between institutions.

Vocabulario útil	
quería	I wanted
pedirte	to ask you
te preocupa	it worries you
ahorrar	to save (money)
Navidad	Christmas
aprovecha	take advantage of
nuestras	our
ofertas	offers, deals
calidad	quality
no cuestan	doesn't cost

¿Qué hay?

For each item, write **sí** if it appears in the TV clip or **no** if it does not.

_____ 1. papelera   _____ 5. diccionario
_____ 2. lápiz   _____ 6. cuaderno
_____ 3. mesa   _____ 7. tiza
_____ 4. computadora   _____ 8. ventana

¿Qué quieres?

Write a list of things that you want for your next birthday. Then read it to the class so they know what to get you. Use as much Spanish as you can.

Lista de cumpleaños°

Quiero°...

cumpleaños *birthday* Quiero *I want* Viejito Pascuero *Santa Claus (Chile)*

Anuncio de Jumbo

Viejito Pascuero°...

¿Cómo se escribe *mountain bike*?

M... O...

 Video: TV Clip

Practice more at **vhlcentral.com**.

Mexican author and diplomat Octavio Paz (March 31, 1914–April 19, 1998) studied both law and literature at the **Universidad Nacional Autónoma de México** (**UNAM**), but after graduating he immersed himself in the art of writing. An incredibly prolific writer of novels, poetry, and essays, Paz solidified his prestige as Mexico's preeminent author with his 1950 book *El laberinto de la soledad,* a fundamental study of Mexican identity. Among the many awards he received in his lifetime are the **Premio Miguel de Cervantes** (1981) and Nobel Prize for Literature (1990). Paz foremost considered himself a poet and affirmed that poetry constitutes "**la religión secreta de la edad° moderna**".

Vocabulario útil

¿Cuál es tu materia favorita?	*What is your favorite subject?*
¿Cuántos años tienes?	*How old are you?*
¿Qué estudias?	*What do you study?*
el/la alumno/a	*student*
la carrera (de medicina)	*(medical) degree program, major*
derecho	*law*
reconocido	*well-known*

Preparación

What is the name of your school or university? What degree program are you in? What classes are you taking this semester?

Emparejar

Match the first part of the sentence in the left column with the appropriate ending in the right column.

1. En la UNAM no hay
2. México, D.F. es
3. La UNAM es
4. La UNAM ofrece

a. una universidad muy grande.
b. 74 carreras de estudio.
c. residencias estudiantiles.
d. la ciudad más grande (*biggest*) de Hispanoamérica.

Los estudios

—¿Qué estudias?
—Ciencias de la comunicación.

Estudio derecho en la UNAM.

¿Conoces a algún° profesor famoso que dé° clases... en la UNAM?

Video: *Flash cultura*

recursos

VM
pp. 115–116

vhlcentral.com
Lección 2

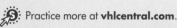
Practice more at **vhlcentral.com**.

edad *age* ¿Conoces a algún...? *Do you know any...?* que dé *that teaches*

Lección 2

España

El país en cifras

▸ **Área**: 504.750 km² (kilómetros cuadrados) o 194.884 millas cuadradas°, incluyendo las islas Baleares y las islas Canarias

▸ **Población**: 47.203.000

▸ **Capital**: Madrid—6.213.000

▸ **Ciudades° principales:** Barcelona—5.315.000, Valencia—832.000, Sevilla, Zaragoza

SOURCE: Population Division, UN Secretariat

▸ **Moneda°:** euro

▸ **Idiomas°:** español o castellano, catalán, gallego, valenciano, euskera

Gallego   Euskera
            Catalán
Español
            Valenciano

Regiones lingüísticas

Bandera de España

Españoles célebres

▸ **Miguel de Cervantes,** escritor° (1547–1616)

▸ **Pedro Almodóvar,** director de cine° (1949–)

▸ **Rosa Montero,** escritora y periodista° (1951–)

▸ **Fernando Alonso,** corredor de autos° (1981–)

▸ **Paz Vega,** actriz° (1976–)

millas cuadradas *square miles* Ciudades *Cities* Moneda *Currency*
Idiomas *Languages* escritor *writer* cine *film* periodista *reporter*
corredor de autos *race car driver* actriz *actress* pueblo *town*
Cada año *Every year* Durante todo un día *All day long*
se tiran *throw at each other* varias toneladas *many tons*

La Sagrada Familia
en Barcelona

Plaza Mayor
en Madrid

Mar Cantábrico
La Coruña
San Sebastián
FRANCIA
ANDORRA
Pirineos
Salamanca   Zaragoza Río Ebro
PORTUGAL   **ESPAÑA**   ● Barcelona
            Madrid   Menorca
            Valencia ●   Mallorca
                        Ibiza **Islas Baleares**
            Sierra Nevada
Sevilla ●   Mar Mediterráneo
Estrecho
de Gibraltar
            ● Ceuta
                ● Melilla
            MARRUECOS

El baile flamenco

Islas Canarias
La Palma   Lanzarote
        Tenerife Gran Canaria
        Gomera
Hierro

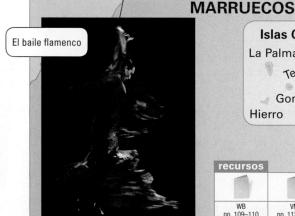

recursos

WB
pp. 109–110

VM
pp. 113–114

Ⓢ vhlcentral.com
Lección 2

¡Increíble pero cierto!

En Buñol, un pueblo° de Valencia, la producción de tomates es un recurso económico muy importante. Cada año° se celebra el festival de *La Tomatina*. Durante todo un día°, miles de personas se tiran° tomates. Llegan turistas de todo el país, y se usan varias toneladas° de tomates.

Gastronomía • José Andrés

José Andrés es un chef español famoso internacionalmente°. Le gusta combinar platos° tradicionales de España con las técnicas de cocina más innovadoras°. Andrés vive° en Washington, DC, es dueño° de varios restaurantes en los EE.UU. y presenta° un programa en PBS (foto, izquierda). También° ha estado° en *Late Show with David Letterman* y *Top Chef*.

Cultura • La diversidad

La riqueza° cultural y lingüística de España refleja la combinación de las diversas culturas que han habitado° en su territorio durante siglos°. El español es la lengua oficial del país, pero también son oficiales el catalán, el gallego, el euskera y el valenciano.

Sóc molt fan de la pàgina 335.

Póster en catalán

Ajuntament de Barcelona

Artes • Velázquez y el Prado

Las meninas,
Diego Velázquez, 1656

El Prado, en Madrid, es uno de los museos más famosos del mundo°. En el Prado hay pinturas° importantes de Botticelli, de El Greco y de los españoles Goya y Velázquez. *Las meninas* es la obra° más conocida° de Diego Velázquez, pintor° oficial de la corte real° durante el siglo° XVII.

Comida • La paella

La paella es uno de los platos más típicos de España. Siempre se prepara° con arroz° y azafrán°, pero hay diferentes recetas°. La paella valenciana, por ejemplo, es de pollo° y conejo°, y la paella marinera es de mariscos°.

La costa de Ibiza

¿Qué aprendiste? Completa las oraciones con la información adecuada.

1. El chef español _____ es muy famoso.
2. El arroz y el azafrán son ingredientes básicos de la _____.
3. El Prado está en _____.
4. José Andrés vive en _____.
5. El chef José Andrés tiene un _____ de televisión en PBS.
6. El gallego es una de las lenguas oficiales de _____.

Conexión Internet Investiga estos temas en **vhlcentral.com**.

Practice more at **vhlcentral.com**.

1. Busca información sobre la Universidad de Salamanca u otra universidad española. ¿Qué cursos ofrece (*does it offer*)? ¿Ofrece tu universidad cursos similares?
2. Busca información sobre un español o una española célebre (por ejemplo, un[a] político/a, un actor, una actriz, un[a] artista). ¿De qué parte de España es y por qué es célebre?

....

internacionalmente *internationally* **platos** *dishes* **más innovadoras** *most innovative* **vive** *lives* **dueño** *owner* **presenta** *hosts* **También** *Also* **ha estado** *has been* **riqueza** *richness* **han habitado** *have lived* **durante siglos** *for centuries* **mundo** *world* **pinturas** *paintings* **obra** *work* **más conocida** *best-known* **pintor** *painter* **corte real** *royal court* **siglo** *century* **Siempre se prepara** *It is always prepared* **arroz** *rice* **azafrán** *saffron* **recetas** *recipes* **pollo** *chicken* **conejo** *rabbit* **mariscos** *seafood*

La clase y la universidad

el/la compañero/a de clase	classmate
el/la compañero/a de cuarto	roommate
el/la estudiante	student
el/la profesor(a)	teacher
el borrador	eraser
la calculadora	calculator
el escritorio	desk
el libro	book
el mapa	map
la mesa	table
la mochila	backpack
el papel	paper
la papelera	wastebasket
la pizarra	blackboard
la pluma	pen
la puerta	door
el reloj	clock; watch
la silla	seat
la tiza	chalk
la ventana	window
la biblioteca	library
la cafetería	cafeteria
la casa	house; home
el estadio	stadium
el laboratorio	laboratory
la librería	bookstore
la residencia estudiantil	dormitory
la universidad	university; college
la clase	class
el curso, la materia	course
la especialización	major
el examen	test; exam
el horario	schedule
la prueba	test; quiz
el semestre	semester
la tarea	homework
el trimestre	trimester; quarter

Las materias

la administración de empresas	business administration
la arqueología	archeology
el arte	art
la biología	biology
las ciencias	sciences
la computación	computer science
la contabilidad	accounting
la economía	economics
el español	Spanish
la física	physics
la geografía	geography
la historia	history
las humanidades	humanities
el inglés	English
las lenguas extranjeras	foreign languages
la literatura	literature
las matemáticas	mathematics
la música	music
el periodismo	journalism
la psicología	psychology
la química	chemistry
la sociología	sociology

Adverbios y preposiciones

al lado de	next to; beside
a la derecha de	to the right of
a la izquierda de	to the left of
allá	over there
allí	there
cerca de	near
con	with
debajo de	below; under
delante de	in front of
detrás de	behind
en	in; on
encima de	on top of
entre	between; among
lejos de	far from
sin	without
sobre	on; over

Palabras adicionales

¿Adónde?	Where (to)?
ahora	now
¿Cuál?, ¿Cuáles?	Which?; Which one(s)?
¿Por qué?	Why?
porque	because

Verbos

bailar	to dance
buscar	to look for
caminar	to walk
cantar	to sing
cenar	to have dinner
comprar	to buy
contestar	to answer
conversar	to converse, to chat
desayunar	to have breakfast
descansar	to rest
desear	to wish; to desire
dibujar	to draw
enseñar	to teach
escuchar la radio/ música	to listen (to) the radio/music
esperar (+ inf.)	to wait (for); to hope
estar	to be
estudiar	to study
explicar	to explain
gustar	to like
hablar	to talk; to speak
llegar	to arrive
llevar	to carry
mirar	to look (at); to watch
necesitar (+ inf.)	to need
practicar	to practice
preguntar	to ask (a question)
preparar	to prepare
regresar	to return
terminar	to end; to finish
tomar	to take; to drink
trabajar	to work
viajar	to travel

Los días de la semana

¿Cuándo?	When?
¿Qué día es hoy?	What day is it?
Hoy es…	Today is…
la semana	week
lunes	Monday
martes	Tuesday
miércoles	Wednesday
jueves	Thursday
viernes	Friday
sábado	Saturday
domingo	Sunday

Numbers 31 and higher	See pages 85–86.
Expresiones útiles	See page 67.

  Audio: Vocabulary Flashcards

recursos

LM
p. 122

vhlcentral.com
Lección 2

contextos

1 **Categorías** Read each group of items. Then write the word from the list that describes a category for the group.

cafetería	clase	laboratorio
ciencias	geografía	materias

1. sándwiches, tacos, sodas, bananas _____

2. mapas, capitales, países, nacionalidades _____

3. literatura, matemáticas, geografía, lenguas extranjeras _____

4. microscopios, experimentos, ciencias, elementos _____

5. física, química, biología, astronomía _____

6. pizarras, tiza, borrador, papelera, escritorios _____

2 **Buscar (To search)** Find school-related words in the grid, looking horizontally and vertically. Circle them in the puzzle, and write the words in the blanks with the correct accents.

S	P	F	I	S	I	C	A	B	Q	G	Ñ	E
O	E	S	P	A	Ñ	O	L	E	U	S	B	R
C	X	B	E	C	O	N	O	M	I	A	I	M
I	A	R	T	E	G	Q	F	A	M	F	O	I
O	M	C	A	C	L	O	U	R	I	V	L	N
L	E	P	R	U	E	B	A	A	C	D	O	G
O	N	U	E	O	N	E	Z	H	A	U	G	L
G	Ñ	D	A	M	C	L	A	S	E	T	I	E
I	E	J	I	L	C	I	E	N	C	I	A	S
A	P	E	R	I	O	D	I	S	M	O	P	I
D	S	T	H	O	R	A	R	I	O	Q	X	A
H	U	M	A	N	I	D	A	D	E	S	M	O

_____   _____

_____   _____

_____   _____

_____   _____

_____   _____

_____   _____

3 **El calendario** Use the calendar to answer these questions with complete sentences.

marzo

L	M	M	J	V	S	D
		1	2	3	4	5
6	7	8	9	10	11	12
13	14	15	16	17	18	19
20	21	22	23	24	25	26
27	28	29	30	31		

abril

L	M	M	J	V	S	D
					1	2
3	4	5	6	7	8	9
10	11	12	13	14	15	16
17	18	19	20	21	22	23
24	25	26	27	28	29	30

> **modelo**
>
> ¿Qué día de la semana es el 8 de abril (*April*)?
> El *8 de abril es sábado.*/Es sábado.

1. ¿Qué día de la semana es el 21 de marzo (*March*)? _____

2. ¿Qué día de la semana es el 7 de abril? _____

3. ¿Qué día de la semana es el 2 de marzo? _____

4. ¿Qué día de la semana es el 28 de marzo? _____

5. ¿Qué día de la semana es el 19 de abril? _____

6. ¿Qué día de la semana es el 12 de marzo? _____

7. ¿Qué día de la semana es el 3 de abril? _____

8. ¿Qué día de la semana es el 22 de abril? _____

9. ¿Qué día de la semana es el 31 de marzo? _____

10. ¿Qué día de la semana es el 9 de abril? _____

4 **Completar** Complete these sentences using words from the word bank.

arte	ciencias	examen	horario	tarea
biblioteca	matemáticas	geografía	laboratorio	universidad

1. La biología, la química y la física son _____.

2. El _____ dice (*says*) a qué hora son las clases.

3. A las once hay un _____ de biología.

4. Martín es artista y toma (*takes*) una clase de _____.

5. Hay veinte calculadoras en la clase de _____.

6. Los experimentos se hacen (*are made*) en el _____.

7. Hay muchos libros en la _____.

8. Los mapas son importantes en el curso de _____.

estructura

2.1 Present tense of **-ar** verbs

1 **Tabla (*Chart*) de verbos** Write the missing forms of each verb.

Present tense					
Infinitivo	**yo**	**tú**	**Ud., él, ella**	**nosotros/as**	**Uds., ellos**
1. cantar	_____	_____	_____	_____	_____
2. _____	pregunto	_____	_____	_____	_____
3. _____	_____	contestas	_____	_____	_____
4. _____	_____	_____	practica	_____	_____
5. _____	_____	_____	_____	deseamos	_____
6. _____	_____	_____	_____	_____	llevan

2 **Completar** Complete these sentences using the correct form of the verb in parentheses.

1. Los turistas _____ (viajar) en un autobús.

2. Elena y yo _____ (hablar) español en clase.

3. Los estudiantes _____ (llegar) a la residencia estudiantil.

4. Yo _____ (dibujar) un reloj en la pizarra.

5. La señora García _____ (comprar) libros en la librería de la universidad.

6. Francisco y tú _____ (regresar) de la biblioteca.

7. El semestre _____ (terminar) en mayo (*May*).

8. Tú _____ (buscar) a tus (*your*) compañeros de clase en la cafetería.

3 **¿Quién es?** Complete these sentences with the correct verb form so that the sentence makes sense.

busco	conversas	esperan	regresamos	trabaja
compran	enseña	necesitas	toman	viajan

1. Nosotras _____ a las seis de la tarde.

2. Muchos estudiantes _____ el curso de periodismo.

3. Rosa y Laura no _____ a Manuel.

4. Tú _____ con los chicos en la residencia estudiantil.

5. El compañero de cuarto de Jaime _____ en el laboratorio.

6. Yo _____ un libro en la biblioteca.

7. Rebeca y tú _____ unas maletas para viajar.

8. La profesora Reyes _____ el curso de español.

4   **Usar los verbos** Form sentences using the words provided. Use the correct present tense or infinitive form of each verb.

1. una estudiante / desear / hablar / con su profesora de biología

   _____

2. Mateo / desayunar / en la cafetería de la universidad

   _____

3. (mí) / gustar / cantar y bailar

   _____

4. los profesores / contestar / las preguntas (*questions*) de los estudiantes

   _____

5. ¿(ti) / gustar / la clase de música?

   _____

6. (nosotros) / esperar / viajar / a Madrid

   _____

7. (yo) / necesitar / practicar / los verbos en español

   _____

8. (mí) / no / gustar / los exámenes

   _____

5   **¿Y tú?** Use complete sentences to answer these yes or no questions.

> **modelo**
>
> ¿Bailas el tango?
> *Sí, bailo el tango./No, no bailo el tango.*

1. ¿Estudias ciencias en la universidad?

   _____

2. ¿Conversas mucho con los compañeros de clase?

   _____

3. ¿Esperas estudiar administración de empresas?

   _____

4. ¿Necesitas descansar después de (*after*) los exámenes?

   _____

5. ¿Compras los libros en la librería?

   _____

6. ¿Te gusta viajar?

   _____

2.2 Forming questions in Spanish

1 **Las preguntas** Make questions out of these statements by inverting the word order.

1. Ustedes son de Puerto Rico.

_____

2. El estudiante dibuja un mapa.

_____

3. Los turistas llegan en autobús.

_____

4. La clase termina a las dos de la tarde.

_____

5. Samuel trabaja en la biblioteca.

_____

6. Los chicos miran un programa.

_____

7. El profesor Miranda enseña la clase de humanidades.

_____

8. Isabel compra cinco libros de historia.

_____

9. Mariana y Javier preparan la tarea.

_____

10. Ellas conversan en la cafetería de la universidad.

_____

2 **Seleccionar** Choose an interrogative word from the list to write a question that corresponds with each response.

adónde	cuándo	de dónde	por qué	quién
cuáles	cuántos	dónde	qué	quiénes

1. _____

Ellos caminan a la biblioteca.

2. _____

El profesor de español es de México.

3. _____

Hay quince estudiantes en la clase.

4. _____

El compañero de cuarto de Jaime es Manuel.

5. _____

La clase de física es en el laboratorio.

6. _____

Julia lleva una computadora portátil.

7. _____

El programa de televisión termina en dos horas.

8. _____

Estudio biología porque hay un examen mañana.

3   **Muchas preguntas** Form four different questions from each statement.

1. Mariana canta en el coro (*choir*) de la universidad.

    _____

    _____

    _____

    _____

2. Carlos busca el libro de arte.

    _____

    _____

    _____

    _____

3. La profesora Gutiérrez enseña contabilidad.

    _____

    _____

    _____

    _____

4. Ustedes necesitan hablar con el profesor de economía.

    _____

    _____

    _____

    _____

4   **¿Qué palabra?** Write the interrogative word or phrase that makes sense in each question.

1. ¿_____ es la clase de administración de empresas?
   Es en la biblioteca.

2. ¿_____ preparas la tarea de matemáticas?
   Preparo la tarea de matemáticas el lunes.

3. ¿_____ es el profesor de inglés?
   Es de los Estados Unidos.

4. ¿_____ libros hay en la clase de biología?
   Hay diez libros.

5. ¿_____ caminas con (*with*) Olga?
   Camino a la clase de biología con Olga.

6. ¿_____ enseña el profesor Hernández en la universidad?
   Enseña literatura.

7. ¿_____ llevas cinco libros en la mochila?
   Porque regreso de la biblioteca.

8. ¿_____ es la profesora de física?
   Es la señora Caballero.

2.3 Present tense of **estar**

1 **Están en...** Answer the questions based on the pictures. Write complete sentences.

1. ¿Dónde están Cristina y Bruno? _____

2. ¿Dónde están la profesora y el estudiante? _____

3. ¿Dónde está la puerta? _____

4. ¿Dónde está la mochila? _____

5. ¿Dónde está el pasajero? _____

6. ¿Dónde está José Miguel? _____

2 **¿Dónde están?** Use these cues and the correct form of **estar** to write complete sentences. Add any missing words.

1. libros / cerca / escritorio

_____

2. ustedes / al lado / puerta

_____

3. calculadora / entre / computadoras

_____

4. lápices / sobre / cuaderno

_____

5. estadio / lejos / residencias

_____

6. mochilas / debajo / mesa

_____

7. tú / en / clase de psicología

_____

8. reloj / a la derecha / ventana

_____

9. Rita / a la izquierda / Julio

_____

3 **¿Ser o estar?** Complete these sentences with the correct present-tense form of the verb **ser** or **estar**.

1. Sonia _____ muy bien hoy.

2. Las sillas _____ delante del escritorio.

3. Ellos _____ estudiantes de sociología.

4. Alma _____ de la capital de España.

5. _____ las diez y media de la mañana.

6. Nosotras _____ en la biblioteca.

4 **El libro** Complete this cell phone conversation with the correct forms of **estar**.

GUSTAVO Hola, Pablo. ¿(1) _____ en la residencia estudiantil?

PABLO Sí, (2) _____ en la residencia.

GUSTAVO Necesito el libro de física.

PABLO ¿Dónde (3) _____ el libro?

GUSTAVO El libro (4) _____ en mi cuarto (*room*), al lado de la computadora.

PABLO ¿Dónde (5) _____ la computadora?

GUSTAVO La computadora (6) _____ encima del escritorio.

PABLO ¡Aquí (*Here*) (7) _____ la computadora y... el libro de física!

5 **Conversación** Complete this conversation with the correct forms of **ser** and **estar**.

PILAR Hola, Irene. ¿Cómo (1) _____?

IRENE Muy bien, ¿y tú? ¿Qué tal?

PILAR Bien, gracias. Te presento a Pablo.

IRENE Encantada, Pablo.

PILAR Pablo (2) _____ de México.

IRENE ¿De qué parte de (*where in*) México (3) _____ ?

PABLO (4) _____ de Monterrey. Y tú, ¿de dónde (5) _____?

IRENE (6) _____ de San Juan, Puerto Rico.

PILAR ¿Dónde (7) _____ Claudia, tu (*your*) compañera de cuarto?

IRENE (8) _____ en la residencia estudiantil.

PABLO Nosotros vamos a (*are going to*) la librería ahora.

PILAR Necesitamos comprar el manual del laboratorio de física.

IRENE ¿A qué hora (9) _____ la clase de física?

PABLO (10) _____ a las doce del día. ¿Qué hora (11) _____ ahora?

PILAR (12) _____ las once y media.

IRENE ¡Menos mal que (*Fortunately*) la librería (13) _____ cerca del laboratorio!

PILAR Sí, no (14) _____ muy lejos de la clase. Nos vemos.

IRENE Hasta luego.

PABLO Chau.

2.4 Numbers 31 and higher

1 **Números de teléfono** Provide the words for these telephone numbers.

> **modelo**
> 968-3659
> nueve, sesenta y ocho, treinta y seis, cincuenta y nueve

1. 776-7799

_____

2. 543-3162

_____

3. 483-4745

_____

4. 352-5073

_____

5. 888-7540

_____

6. 566-3857

_____

2 **¿Cuántos hay?** Use the inventory list to answer these questions about the amount of items in stock at the school bookstore. Use complete sentences and write out the Spanish words for numbers.

Inventario			
libros	320	mochilas	31
cuadernos	276	diccionarios	43
plumas	125	mapas	66

1. ¿Cuántos mapas hay? _____
2. ¿Cuántas mochilas hay? _____
3. ¿Cuántos diccionarios hay? _____
4. ¿Cuántos cuadernos hay? _____
5. ¿Cuántas plumas hay? _____
6. ¿Cuántos libros hay? _____

3 **Mi universidad** Use the information provided to complete the paragraph about your university. Write out the Spanish words for numbers.

> 25.000 estudiantes en total   44 nacionalidades diferentes   1.432 computadoras
> 350 españoles   10.500 libros   126 especialidades

Mi universidad es muy grande, hay (1) _____ estudiantes en el campus. Hay personas de (2) _____ países diferentes y (3) _____ son estudiantes de España. La biblioteca tiene (4) _____ libros de (5) _____ especialidades diferentes. Hay mucha tecnología; hay (6) _____ computadoras en el campus. ¡Me encanta mi universidad!

4 **Por ciento** Use the pie chart to complete these sentences. Write out the Spanish numbers in words.

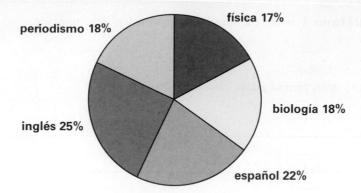

periodismo 18%

física 17%

biología 18%

inglés 25%

español 22%

1. Un _____ por ciento de los estudiantes estudian las ciencias.

2. Un _____ por ciento de los estudiantes estudian inglés o periodismo.

3. Un _____ por ciento de los estudiantes no estudian las ciencias.

4. Un _____ por ciento de los estudiantes no estudian biología.

5. Un _____ por ciento de los estudiantes estudian inglés o español.

6. Un _____ por ciento de los estudiantes no estudian idiomas.

Síntesis

La universidad Imagine that a parent calls a college student during the second week of courses. Write questions that the parent might ask about the son or daughter's schedule, courses, and campus life. Use the cues provided. Then write possible answers.

> **modelo**
>
> ¿A qué hora termina la clase de español?
> *La clase de español termina a las tres.*

- ¿A qué hora...?
- ¿Dónde está...?
- ¿Qué cursos...?
- ¿Trabajas...?

- ¿Estudias...?
- ¿Qué días de la semana...?
- ¿Hay...?
- ¿Cuántos...?

_____

_____

_____

_____

_____

_____

panorama

España

1 **¿De qué ciudad es?** Write the city or town in Spain associated with each item.

1. el Museo del Prado _____
2. el baile flamenco _____
3. la Sagrada Familia _____
4. la Tomatina _____
5. segunda (*second*) ciudad en población _____

2 **¿Cierto o falso?** Indicate whether each statement is **cierto** or **falso**. Then correct the false statements.

1. Las islas Canarias y las islas Baleares son de España.

_____

2. Zaragoza es una de las ciudades principales de España.

_____

3. La moneda de España es el peso.

_____

4. En España hay más de un idioma.

_____

5. La Tomatina es uno de los platos más deliciosos de España.

_____

6. El chef José Andrés vive en Washington, D.C.

_____

3 **El mapa de España** Fill in the blanks with the name of the city or geographical feature.

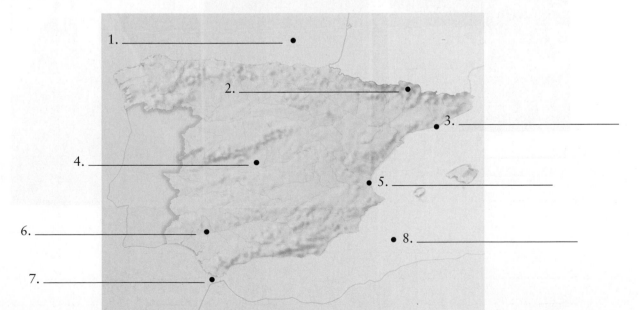

1. _____
2. _____
3. _____
4. _____
5. _____
6. _____
7. _____
8. _____

4 **Profesiones** Complete these sentences with the person's occupation.

1. Fernando Alonso es _____.

2. Rosa Montero es _____.

3. Pedro Almodóvar es _____.

4. Miguel de Cervantes es _____.

5. Paz Vega es _____.

6. Diego Velázquez es _____.

5 **Palabras cruzadas (crossed)** Write one letter on each blank. Then answer the final question, using the new word that is formed.

1. Islas españolas del Mar Mediterráneo

2. Español, catalán, gallego, valenciano y euskera

3. José Andrés es dueño (owner) de varios

4. Museo español famoso

5. Pintor español famoso

6. Obra más conocida de Diego Velázquez

El aeropuerto (airport) de Madrid se llama _____.

6 **Las fotos** Label the object shown in each photo.

1. _____

2. _____

3. _____

¿Qué estudias?

Lección 2
Fotonovela

Antes de ver el video

1 **Impresiones** Based on your impressions of Marissa, Felipe, and Jimena in **Lección 1**, write the names of the classes you think each person is taking or is most interested in. Circle the name of the person you believe is the most studious, and underline the name of the character you believe is the most talkative.

MARISSA	FELIPE	JIMENA
_____	_____	_____
_____	_____	_____
_____	_____	_____

Mientras ves el video

2 **¿Quién y a quién?** Watch **¿Qué estudias?** and say who asks these questions and to whom.

Preguntas	¿Quién?	¿A quién?
1. ¿A quién buscas?	_____	_____
2. ¿Cuántas clases tomas?	_____	_____
3. ¿Qué estudias?	_____	_____
4. ¿Dónde está tu diccionario?	_____	_____
5. ¿Hablas con tu mamá?	_____	_____

3 **¿Qué cosas hay?** Make a check mark beside the actions, items and places shown in **¿Qué estudias?**

____ 1. libros   ____ 5. comprar   ____ 9. pizarra
____ 2. laboratorio ____ 6. tiza   ____ 10. dibujar
____ 3. caminar   ____ 7. hablar   ____ 11. reloj
____ 4. castillo   ____ 8. horario   ____ 12. mochila

4 **Completar** Fill in the blanks.

1. Marissa está en México para _____.
2. Marissa toma cuatro _____.
3. La _____ de Marissa es arqueología.
4. La especialización de Miguel es _____.
5. A Miguel le gusta _____.
6. Marissa _____ muy bien el español.
7. Juan Carlos toma química con el _____ Morales.
8. El profesor Morales enseña en un laboratorio sin _____.
9. A Felipe le gusta estar _____ el reloj y la puerta.
10. Maru _____ con su mamá.

Después de ver el video

5 **Corregir** The underlined words in the following statements are incorrect. Fill in the blanks with the correct ones.

1. <u>Maru</u> es de los Estados Unidos. _____

2. <u>Miguel</u> toma una clase de computación. _____

3. <u>Felipe</u> necesita comprar libros. _____

4. En clase, a Marissa le gusta estar cerca <u>del reloj</u>. _____

5. <u>Felipe</u> es de Argentina. _____

6. Marissa toma español, <u>periodismo</u>, literatura y geografía. _____

7. Felipe busca a Juan Carlos y a <u>Maru</u>. _____

8. Felipe necesita practicar <u>español</u>. _____

6 **Asociar** Write the words or phrases in the box next to the names.

¿A la biblioteca?	cuatro clases	¿Por qué tomo química y computación?
arqueología	Ésta es la Ciudad de México.	Te gusta la tarea.
Buenos Aires	Hola, mamá, ¿cómo estás?	Y sin diccionario.
ciencias ambientales	Me gusta mucho la cultura mexicana.	

1. Marissa _____ _____

2. Felipe _____ _____

3. Juan Carlos _____ _____

4. Maru _____ _____

7 **¿Y tú?** Write a paragraph saying who you are, where you are from, where you study (city and name of university), and what classes you are taking this semester.

_____
_____
_____
_____
_____
_____
_____
_____
_____
_____

Panorama: España

Antes de ver el video

1

Más vocabulario Look over these useful words before you watch the video.

Vocabulario útil		
antiguo *ancient*	empezar *to start*	niños *children*
blanco *white*	encierro *running of bulls*	pañuelo *neckerchief, bandana*
cabeza *head*	esta *this*	peligroso *dangerous*
calle *street*	feria *fair, festival*	periódico *newspaper*
cohete *rocket (firework)*	fiesta *party, festival*	rojo *red*
comparsa *parade*	gente *people*	ropa *clothing*
correr *to run*	gigante *giant*	toro *bull*
defenderse *to defend oneself*	mitad *half*	ver *to see*

2

Festivales In this video, you are going to learn about a Spanish festival. List the things you would probably do and see at a festival.

_____

_____

_____

_____

Mientras ves el video

3

Ordenar Number the items in the order in which they appear in the video.

_____ a. cohete   _____ c. gigante   _____ e. mitad hombre,

_____ b. cuatro mujeres en   _____ d. toros   mitad animal
       un balcón

Después de ver el video

4

Fotos Describe the video stills.

_____

_____

_____

_____

_____

5   **Crucigrama** Complete these sentences and use the words to complete the crossword.

1. El Festival de San Fermín es la combinación de tres fiestas, una de ellas es las _____ comerciales.

2. Las _____ son los eventos favoritos de los niños.

3. La fiesta religiosa en honor a San Fermín, las ferias comerciales y los eventos taurinos son celebraciones _____.

4. Los Sanfermines es una de las _____ tradicionales españolas.

5. Las personas usan ropa blanca y _____ rojos.

6. En los encierros las personas corren delante de diecisiete _____.

7. En las comparsas hay figuras _____ hombre, mitad animal.

8. En los días del festival, hay ocho _____.

9. En las comparsas hay ocho _____.

10. Las comparsas pasan por las _____ de Pamplona.

11. Otras de las figuras tienen (*have*) enormes _____.

Los estudios

Antes de ver el video

Lección 2
Flash cultura

1 **Más vocabulario** Look over these useful words and expressions before you watch the video.

> ### Vocabulario útil
>
> | | |
> |---|---|
> | las ciencias biológicas y de la salud *biological and health sciences* | el cuarto año de la carrera *the fourth year of college* |
> | las ciencias físico-matemáticas *physical and mathematical sciences* | dé clases *teaches* |
> | ¿Conoces a algún ex alumno reconocido? *¿Do you know any renowned alumni?* | los estudios superiores *higher education* |
> | | la psicoterapia *psychotherapy* |

2 **¡En español!** Look at the video still and answer these questions in Spanish. Carlos is in Mexico City; can you guess what place? Who is Carlos talking to? What do you think this person does?

Carlos López, México, D.F.

_____

_____

_____

_____

_____

_____

Mientras ves el video

3 **Conversaciones** Complete these conversations between Carlos López and two students.

CARLOS LÓPEZ   ¿(1) _____ te llamas?

ESTUDIANTE   Héctor.

CARLOS LÓPEZ   Héctor. ¿Y qué estudias?

ESTUDIANTE   (2) _____.

CARLOS LÓPEZ   ¿Y cuál es tu materia favorita?

ESTUDIANTE   Este... ahorita, (3) _____ de Roma.

CARLOS LÓPEZ   ¿De dónde (4) _____?

ESTUDIANTE   De Corea.

CARLOS LÓPEZ   De Corea. ¿Te gusta estudiar en la (5) _____?

ESTUDIANTE   Sí, me gusta mucho (*I like it a lot*).

CARLOS LÓPEZ   ¿Qué estudias?

ESTUDIANTE   Estoy estudiando (6) _____.

4 **Identificar** Indicate which area of study each of these students and alumni is likely to study or have studied.

Ciencias Biológicas y de la Salud   Ciencias Sociales

Ciencias Físico-Matemáticas   Humanidades

Octavio Paz
Escritor

1. _____ 2. _____ 3. _____

Después de ver el video

5 **Oraciones** Complete each statement with the correct option.

autobuses	estudio	profesor
derecho	ex alumno	residencia estudiantil
estudiantes	México, D.F.	universidad

1. _____ es un importante centro económico y cultural.

2. La UNAM es una _____ en la Ciudad de México.

3. La UNAM es como (*like*) una ciudad con _____, policía y gobierno (*government*) propios (*own*).

4. Los _____ de la UNAM son de diferentes países.

5. Hay cuatro áreas principales de _____.

6. Manuel Álvarez Bravo es un _____ famoso de la UNAM.

6 **¡Carlos López de visita (*on a visit*)!** Imagine that Carlos López visits your school and wants to find out about the institution, campus or facilities, classes, and students. Write a brief paragraph about what you would say.

> **modelo**
>
> ¡Hola, Carlos! Me llamo Rosa Estévez y estudio en la Universidad de Toronto.
> Hay muchos estudiantes de diferentes países. Este (*This*) semestre tomo clases...

_____

_____

_____

_____

_____

contextos   Lección 2

1 **Identificar** Look at each drawing and listen to the statement. Indicate whether the statement is **cierto** or **falso**.

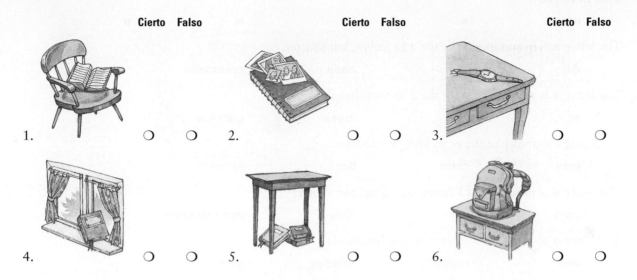

	Cierto	Falso		Cierto	Falso		Cierto	Falso
1.	○	○	2.	○	○	3.	○	○
4.	○	○	5.	○	○	6.	○	○

2 **¿Qué día es?** Your friend Diego is never sure what day of the week it is. Respond to his questions saying that it is the day before the one he mentions. Then repeat the correct answer after the speaker. (*6 items*)

> **modelo**
> Hoy es domingo, ¿no?
> No, hoy es sábado.

3 **Preguntas** You will hear a series of questions. Look at Susana's schedule for today and answer each question. Then repeat the correct response after the speaker.

---

martes 18

○

9:00 economía — Sr. Rivera

11:00 química — Sra. Hernández

12:15 cafetería — Carmen

1:30 prueba de contabilidad — Sr. Ramos

3:00 matemáticas — Srta. Torres

4:30 laboratorio de computación — Héctor

○

pronunciación

Spanish vowels

Spanish vowels are never silent; they are always pronounced in a short, crisp way without the glide sounds used in English.

| a | e | i | o | u |

The letter **a** is pronounced like the a in *father*, but shorter.

| Álex | clase | nada | encantada |

The letter **e** is pronounced like the e in *they*, but shorter.

| el | ene | mesa | elefante |

The letter **i** sounds like the *ee* in *beet*, but shorter.

| Inés | chica | tiza | señorita |

The letter **o** is pronounced like the o in *tone*, but shorter.

| hola | con | libro | don Francisco |

The letter **u** sounds like the *oo* in *room*, but shorter.

| uno | regular | saludos | gusto |

1 **Práctica** Practice the vowels by repeating the names of these places in Spain after the speaker.

1. Madrid
2. Alicante
3. Tenerife
4. Toledo
5. Barcelona
6. Granada
7. Burgos
8. La Coruña

2 **Oraciones** Repeat each sentence after the speaker, focusing on the vowels.

1. Hola. Me llamo Ramiro Morgado.
2. Estudio arte en la Universidad de Salamanca.
3. Tomo también literatura y contabilidad.
4. Ay, tengo clase en cinco minutos. ¡Nos vemos!

3 **Refranes** Repeat each saying after the speaker to practice vowels.

1. Del dicho al hecho hay un gran trecho.
2. Cada loco con su tema.

4 **Dictado** You will hear a conversation. Listen carefully and write what you hear during the pauses. The entire conversation will then be repeated so you can check your work.

JUAN _____

_____

_____

ROSA _____

JUAN _____

ROSA _____

estructura

2.1 Present tense of **-ar** verbs

1   **Identificar** Listen to each sentence and mark an **X** in the column for the subject of the verb.

> **modelo**
> *You hear:* Trabajo en la cafetería.
> *You mark:* an **X** under **yo**.

	yo	tú	él/ella	nosotros/as	ellos/ellas
Modelo	X				
1.					
2.					
3.					
4.					
5.					
6.					
7.					
8.					

2   **Cambiar** Form a new sentence using the cue you hear as the subject. Repeat the correct answer after the speaker. (*6 items*)

> **modelo**
> María practica los verbos ahora. (José y María)
> *José y María practican los verbos ahora.*

3   **Preguntas** Answer each question you hear in the negative. Repeat the correct response after the speaker. (*8 items*)

> **modelo**
> ¿Estudias geografía?
> *No, yo no estudio geografía.*

4   **Completar** Listen to the following description and write the missing words in your lab manual.

Teresa y yo (1) _____ en la Universidad Autónoma de Madrid. Teresa

(2) _____ lenguas extranjeras. Ella (3) _____ trabajar

en las Naciones Unidas (*United Nations*). Yo (4) _____ clases de periodismo.

También me gusta (5) _____ y (6) _____. Los sábados

(7) _____ con una tuna. Una tuna es una orquesta (*orchestra*) estudiantil.

Los jóvenes de la tuna (8) _____ por las calles (*streets*) y

(9) _____ canciones (*songs*) tradicionales de España.

2.2 Forming questions in Spanish

1 **Escoger** Listen to each question and choose the most logical response.

1. a. Porque mañana es la prueba.   b. Porque no hay clase mañana.
2. a. Viaja en autobús.   b. Viaja a Toledo.
3. a. Llegamos el 3 de abril.   b. Llegamos al estadio.
4. a. Isabel y Diego dibujan.   b. Dibujan en la clase de arte.
5. a. No, enseña física.   b. No, enseña en la Universidad Politécnica.
6. a. Escuchan un video.   b. Escuchan música clásica.
7. a. Sí, me gusta mucho.   b. Miro la televisión en la residencia.
8. a. Hay diccionarios en la biblioteca.   b. Hay tres.

2 **Cambiar** Change each sentence into a question using the cue in your lab manual. Repeat the correct response after the speaker.

> **modelo**
>
> *You hear:* Los turistas toman el autobús.
> *You see:* ¿Quiénes?
> *You say:* ¿Quiénes toman el autobús?

1. ¿Dónde?   3. ¿Qué?, (tú)   5. ¿Cuándo?   7. ¿Quiénes?
2. ¿Cuántos?   4. ¿Quién?   6. ¿Dónde?   8. ¿Qué?, (tú)

3 **¿Lógico o ilógico?** You will hear some questions and the responses. Decide if they are **lógico** (*logical*) or **ilógico** (*illogical*).

1. Lógico   Ilógico   3. Lógico   Ilógico   5. Lógico   Ilógico
2. Lógico   Ilógico   4. Lógico   Ilógico   6. Lógico   Ilógico

4 **Un anuncio** Listen to this radio advertisement and answer the questions in your lab manual.

1. ¿Dónde está (*is*) la Escuela Cervantes? _____

_____

2. ¿Qué cursos ofrecen (*do they offer*) en la Escuela Cervantes? _____

_____

3. ¿Cuándo practican los estudiantes el español? _____

_____

4. ¿Adónde viajan los estudiantes de la Escuela Cervantes? _____

2.3 Present tense of **estar**

1 **Describir** Look at the drawing and listen to each statement. Indicate whether the statement is **cierto** or **falso**.

	Cierto	Falso		Cierto	Falso		Cierto	Falso		Cierto	Falso
1.	◯	◯	3.	◯	◯	5.	◯	◯	7.	◯	◯
2.	◯	◯	4.	◯	◯	6.	◯	◯	8.	◯	◯

2 **Cambiar** Form a new sentence using the cue you hear. Repeat the correct answer after the speaker. (*8 items*)

> **modelo**
>
> Irma está en la biblioteca. (Irma y Hugo)
> *Irma y Hugo están en la biblioteca.*

3 **Escoger** You will hear some sentences with a beep in place of the verb. Decide which form of **ser** or **estar** should complete each sentence and circle it.

> **modelo**
>
> *You hear:* Javier (*beep*) estudiante.
> *You circle:* **es** *because the sentence is* **Javier es estudiante**.

1.	es	está	5.	es	está
2.	es	está	6.	eres	estás
3.	es	está	7.	son	están
4.	Somos	Estamos	8.	Son	Están

2.4 Numbers 31 and higher

1 **Números de teléfono** You want to invite some classmates to a party, but you don't have their telephone numbers. Ask the person who sits beside you what their telephone numbers are, and write the answer.

> **modelo**
>
> *You see:* Elián
> *You say:* ¿Cuál es el número de teléfono de Elián?
> *You hear:* Es el ocho, cuarenta y tres, cero, ocho, treinta y cinco.
> *You write:* 843-0835

1. Arturo: _____   5. Simón: _____

2. Alicia: _____   6. Eva: _____

3. Roberto: _____   7. José Antonio: _____

4. Graciela: _____   8. Mariana: _____

2 **Dictado** Listen carefully and write each number as numerals rather than words.

1. _____   4. _____   7. _____

2. _____   5. _____   8. _____

3. _____   6. _____   9. _____

3 **Mensaje telefónico** Listen to this telephone conversation and complete the phone message in your lab manual with the correct information.

> **Mensaje telefónico**
>
> **Para (*For*)** _____
> **De parte de (*From*)** _____
> **Teléfono** _____
> **Mensaje** _____
> _____
> _____
> _____

vocabulario

You will now hear the vocabulary found in your textbook on the last page of this lesson. Listen and repeat each Spanish word or phrase after the speaker.

Additional Vocabulary

Additional Vocabulary

Notes

Notes

La familia

Communicative Goals

You will learn how to:

3

• Talk about your family and friends
• Describe people and things
• Express possession

A PRIMERA VISTA
• ¿Cuántos chicos hay en la foto?
• ¿Hay una mujer a la izquierda? ¿Y a la derecha?
• ¿Hay una cosa en la mano de la mujer?
• ¿Conversan ellos? ¿Trabajan? ¿Viajan?
• ¿Están lejos de su casa?

Más práctica
Workbook pages 161–172
Video Manual pages 173–178
Lab Manual pages 179–184

La familia

Más vocabulario

los abuelos	*grandparents*
el/la bisabuelo/a	*great-grandfather/ great-grandmother*
el/la gemelo/a	*twin*
el/la hermanastro/a	*stepbrother/stepsister*
el/la hijastro/a	*stepson/stepdaughter*
la madrastra	*stepmother*
el medio hermano/ la media hermana	*half-brother/ half-sister*
el padrastro	*stepfather*
los padres	*parents*
los parientes	*relatives*
el/la cuñado/a	*brother-in-law/ sister-in-law*
la nuera	*daughter-in-law*
el/la suegro/a	*father-in-law/ mother-in-law*
el yerno	*son-in-law*
el/la amigo/a	*friend*
el apellido	*last name; surname*
la gente	*people*
el/la muchacho/a	*boy/girl*
el/la niño/a	*child*
el/la novio/a	*boyfriend/girlfriend*
la persona	*person*
el/la artista	*artist*
el/la ingeniero/a	*engineer*
el/la doctor(a), el/la médico/a	*doctor; physician*
el/la periodista	*journalist*
el/la programador(a)	*computer programmer*

Variación léxica

madre ⟷ mamá, mami (*colloquial*)
padre ⟷ papá, papi (*colloquial*)
muchacho/a ⟷ chico/a

La familia de
José Miguel Pérez Santoro

Juan Santoro Sánchez

mi abuelo (*my grandfather*)

Ernesto Santoro González

mi tío (*uncle*)
hijo (*son*) **de Juan y Socorro**

Marina Gutiérrez de Santoro

mi tía (*aunt*)
esposa (*wife*) **de Ernesto**

Silvia Socorro Santoro Gutiérrez

mi prima (*cousin*)
hija (*daughter*) **de Ernesto y Marina**

Héctor Manuel Santoro Gutiérrez

mi primo (*cousin*)
nieto (*grandson*) **de Juan y Socorro**

Carmen Santoro Gutiérrez

mi prima
hija de Ernesto y Marina

¡LENGUA VIVA!

In Spanish-speaking countries, it is common for people to go by both their first name and middle name, such as **José Miguel** or **Juan Carlos.** You will learn more about names and naming conventions on p. 132.

Socorro González de Santoro

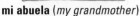

mi abuela (*my grandmother*)

Mirta Santoro de Pérez

mi madre (*mother*)
hija de Juan y Socorro

Rubén Ernesto Pérez Gómez

mi padre (*father*)
esposo de mi madre

José Miguel Pérez Santoro

hijo de Rubén y de Mirta

Beatriz Alicia Pérez de Morales

mi hermana (*sister*)

Felipe Morales Zapata

esposo (*husband*) **de Beatriz Alicia**

Víctor Miguel Morales Pérez

mi sobrino (*nephew*)
hermano (*brother*) **de Anita**

Anita Morales Pérez

mi sobrina (*niece*)
nieta (*granddaughter*) **de mis padres**

los hijos (*children*) **de Beatriz Alicia y de Felipe**

Práctica

1 **Escuchar** 🎧 Listen to each statement made by José Miguel Pérez Santoro, then indicate whether it is **cierto** or **falso**, based on his family tree.

	Cierto	Falso		Cierto	Falso
1.	○	○	6.	○	○
2.	○	○	7.	○	○
3.	○	○	8.	○	○
4.	○	○	9.	○	○
5.	○	○	10.	○	○

2 **Personas** 🎧 Indicate each word that you hear mentioned in the narration.

1. _____ cuñado   4. _____ niño   7. _____ ingeniera
2. _____ tía   5. _____ esposo   8. _____ primo
3. _____ periodista 6. _____ abuelos

3 **Emparejar** Provide the letter of the phrase that matches each description. Two items will not be used.

1. Mi hermano programa las computadoras.
2. Son los padres de mi esposo.
3. Son los hijos de mis (*my*) tíos.
4. Mi tía trabaja en un hospital.
5. Es el hijo de mi madrastra y el hijastro de mi padre.
6. Es el esposo de mi hija.
7. Es el hijo de mi hermana.
8. Mi primo dibuja y pinta mucho.
9. Mi hermanastra enseña en la universidad.
10. Mi padre trabaja con planos (*blueprints*).

a. Es médica.
b. Es mi hermanastro.
c. Es programador.
d. Es ingeniero.
e. Son mis suegros.
f. Es mi novio.
g. Es mi padrastro.
h. Son mis primos.
i. Es artista.
j. Es profesora.
k. Es mi sobrino.
l. Es mi yerno.

4 **Definiciones** Define these family terms in Spanish.

> **modelo**
> hijastro Es el hijo de mi esposo/a, pero no es mi hijo.

1. abuela   5. suegra
2. bisabuelo   6. cuñado
3. tío   7. nietos
4. primas   8. medio hermano

5 **Escoger** Complete the description of each photo using words you have learned in **Contextos.**

1. La _____ de Sara
   es grande.

2. Héctor y Lupita son _____.

3. Maira Díaz es _____.

4. Rubén habla con su _____.

5. Los dos _____ están
   en el parque.

6. Irene es _____.

7. Elena Vargas Soto es _____.

8. Don Manuel es el _____ de
   Martín.

Practice more at **vhlcentral.com**.

Comunicación

6 **Una familia** With a classmate, identify the members in the family tree by asking questions about how each family member is related to Graciela Vargas García

CONSULTA

To see the cities where these family members live, look at the map in **Panorama** on p. 158.

> **modelo**
> **Estudiante 1:** ¿Quién es Beatriz Pardo de Vargas?
> **Estudiante 2:** Es la abuela de Graciela.

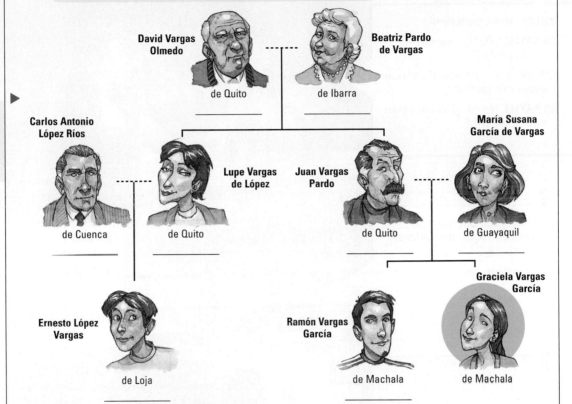

David Vargas Olmedo — de Quito

Beatriz Pardo de Vargas — de Ibarra

Carlos Antonio López Ríos — de Cuenca

Lupe Vargas de López — de Quito

Juan Vargas Pardo — de Quito

María Susana García de Vargas — de Guayaquil

Ernesto López Vargas — de Loja

Ramón Vargas García — de Machala

Graciela Vargas García — de Machala

Now take turns asking each other these questions. Then invent three original questions.

1. ¿Cómo se llama el primo de Graciela?
2. ¿Cómo se llama la hija de David y de Beatriz?
3. ¿De dónde es María Susana?
4. ¿De dónde son Ramón y Graciela?
5. ¿Cómo se llama el yerno de David y de Beatriz?
6. ¿De dónde es Carlos Antonio?
7. ¿De dónde es Ernesto?
8. ¿Cuáles son los apellidos del sobrino de Lupe?

7 **Preguntas personales** With a classmate, take turns asking each other these questions.

1. ¿Cuántas personas hay en tu familia?
2. ¿Cómo se llaman tus padres? ¿De dónde son? ¿Dónde trabajan?
3. ¿Cuántos hermanos tienes? ¿Cómo se llaman? ¿Dónde estudian o trabajan?
4. ¿Cuántos primos tienes? ¿Cuáles son los apellidos de ellos? ¿Cuántos son niños y cuántos son adultos? ¿Hay más chicos o más chicas en tu familia?
5. ¿Eres tío/a? ¿Cómo se llaman tus sobrinos/as? ¿Dónde estudian o trabajan?
6. ¿Quién es tu pariente favorito?
7. ¿Tienes novio/a? ¿Tienes esposo/a? ¿Cómo se llama?

AYUDA

tu *your* (sing.)
tus *your* (plural)
mi *my* (sing.)
mis *my* (plural)
tienes *you have*
tengo *I have*

Lección 3

Un domingo en familia

Marissa pasa el día en Xochimilco con la familia Díaz.

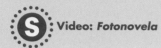
Video: *Fotonovela*

JIMENA Hola, tía Nayeli.

TÍA NAYELI ¡Hola, Jimena! ¿Cómo estás?

JIMENA Bien, gracias. Y, ¿dónde están mis primas?

TÍA NAYELI No sé. ¿Dónde están mis hijas? ¡Ah!

MARISSA ¡Qué bonitas son tus hijas! Y ¡qué simpáticas!

MARISSA La verdad, mi familia es pequeña.

SRA. DÍAZ ¿Pequeña? Yo soy hija única. Bueno, y ¿qué más? ¿Tienes novio?

MARISSA No. Tengo mala suerte con los novios.

FELIPE Soy guapo y delgado.

JIMENA Ay, ¡por favor! Eres gordo, antipático y muy feo.

TÍO RAMÓN ¿Tienes una familia grande, Marissa?

MARISSA Tengo dos hermanos mayores, Zack y Jennifer, y un hermano menor, Adam.

MARISSA Tía Nayeli, ¿cuántos años tienen tus hijas?

TÍA NAYELI Marta tiene ocho años y Valentina doce.

JIMENA

MARTA

VALENTINA

SRA. DÍAZ

TÍO RAMÓN

SR. DÍAZ
MARISSA

SRA. DÍAZ Chicas, ¿compartimos una trajinera?

MARISSA ¡Claro que sí! ¡Qué bonitas son!

SRA. DÍAZ ¿Vienes, Jimena?

JIMENA No, gracias. Tengo que leer.

MARISSA Me gusta mucho este sitio. Tengo ganas de visitar otros lugares en México.

SRA. DÍAZ ¡Debes viajar a Mérida!

TÍA NAYELI ¡Sí, con tus amigos! Debes visitar a Ana María, la hermana de Roberto y de Ramón.

(La Sra. Díaz habla por teléfono con la tía Ana María.)

SRA. DÍAZ ¡Qué bien! Excelente. Sí, la próxima semana. Muchísimas gracias.

MARISSA ¡Gracias, Sra. Díaz!
SRA. DÍAZ Tía Ana María.
MARISSA Tía Ana María.
SRA. DÍAZ ¡Un beso, chau!
MARISSA *Bye!*

recursos
VM pp. 173–174
vhlcentral.com Lección 3

Lección 3

Expresiones útiles

Talking about your family
¿Tienes una familia grande?
Do you have a big family?
Tengo dos hermanos mayores y un hermano menor.
I have two older siblings and a younger brother.
La verdad, mi familia es pequeña.
The truth is, my family is small.
¿Pequeña? Yo soy hija única.
Small? I'm an only child.

Describing people
¡Qué bonitas son tus hijas!
Y ¡qué simpáticas!
Your daughters are so pretty!
And so nice!
Soy guapo y delgado.
I'm handsome and slim.
¡Por favor! Eres gordo, antipático y muy feo.
Please! You're fat, unpleasant, and very ugly.

Talking about plans
¿Compartimos una trajinera?
Shall we share a trajinera?
¡Claro que sí! ¡Qué bonitas son!
Of course! They're so pretty!
¿Vienes, Jimena?
Are you coming, Jimena?
No, gracias. Tengo que leer.
No, thanks. I have to read.

Saying how old people are
¿Cuántos años tienen tus hijas?
How old are your daughters?
Marta tiene ocho años y Valentina doce.
Marta is eight and Valentina twelve.

Additional vocabulary
ensayo *essay*
pobrecito/a *poor thing*
próxima *next*
sitio *place*
todavía *still*
trajinera *type of barge*

¿Qué pasó?

1 **¿Cierto o falso?** Indicate whether each sentence is **cierto** or **falso**. Correct the false statements.

	Cierto	Falso
1. Marissa dice que (*says that*) tiene una familia grande.	○	○
2. La Sra. Díaz tiene dos hermanos.	○	○
3. Marissa no tiene novio.	○	○
4. Valentina tiene veinte años.	○	○
5. Marissa comparte una trajinera con la Sra. Díaz y la tía Nayeli.	○	○
6. A Marissa le gusta mucho Xochimilco.	○	○

2 **Identificar** Indicate which person would make each statement. The names may be used more than once. **¡Ojo!** One name will not be used.

1. Felipe es antipático y feo.
2. Mis hermanos se llaman Jennifer, Adam y Zack.
3. ¡Soy un joven muy guapo!
4. Mis hijas tienen ocho y doce años.
5. ¡Qué bonitas son las trajineras!
6. Ana María es la hermana de Ramón y Roberto.
7. No puedo (*I can't*) compartir una trajinera porque tengo que leer.
8. Tus hijas son bonitas y simpáticas, tía Nayeli.

SRA. DÍAZ **JIMENA**

MARISSA **FELIPE**

TÍA NAYELI

3 **Escribir** In pairs, choose Marissa, Sra. Díaz, or tía Nayeli and write a brief description of her family. Be creative!

MARISSA **SRA. DÍAZ** **TÍA NAYELI**

Marissa es de los EE.UU. La Sra. Díaz es de Cuba. La tía Nayeli es de México.
¿Cómo es su familia? ¿Cómo es su familia? ¿Cómo es su familia?

4 **Conversar** With a partner, use these questions to talk about your families.

1. ¿Cuántos años tienes?
2. ¿Tienes una familia grande?
3. ¿Tienes hermanos o hermanas?
4. ¿Cuántos años tiene tu abuelo (tu hermana, tu primo, etc.)?
5. ¿De dónde son tus padres?

 Practice more at **vhlcentral.com**.

Pronunciación 🎧 Ⓢ Audio

Diphthongs and linking

---

hermano   **niña**   **cuñado**

In Spanish, **a**, **e**, and **o** are considered strong vowels. The weak vowels are **i** and **u**.

---

ruido   **parientes**   **periodista**

A diphthong is a combination of two weak vowels or of a strong vowel and a weak vowel. Diphthongs are pronounced as a single syllable.

mi hijo   **una clase excelente**

Two identical vowel sounds that appear together are pronounced like one long vowel.

la abuela

---

con Natalia   **sus sobrinos**   **las sillas**

Two identical consonants together sound like a single consonant.

---

es ingeniera   **mis abuelos**   **sus hijos**

A consonant at the end of a word is linked with the vowel at the beginning of the next word.

---

mi hermano   **su esposa**   **nuestro amigo**

A vowel at the end of a word is linked with the vowel at the beginning of the next word.

Ⓢ **Práctica** Say these words aloud, focusing on the diphthongs.

1. historia
2. nieto
3. parientes
4. novia
5. residencia
6. prueba
7. puerta
8. ciencias
9. lenguas
10. estudiar
11. izquierda
12. ecuatoriano

Ⓢ **Oraciones** Read these sentences aloud to practice diphthongs and linking words.

1. Hola. Me llamo Anita Amaral. Soy del Ecuador.
2. Somos seis en mi familia.
3. Tengo dos hermanos y una hermana.
4. Mi papá es del Ecuador y mi mamá es de España.

Ⓢ **Refranes** Read these sayings aloud to practice diphthongs and linking sounds.

Cuando una puerta se cierra, otra se abre.[1]

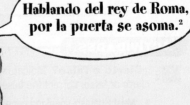

Hablando del rey de Roma, por la puerta se asoma.[2]

2 Speak of the devil and he will appear.
1 When one door closes, another opens.

recursos

LM p. 180   vhlcentral.com Lección 3

Lección 3

Additional Reading

¿Cómo te llamas?

In the Spanish-speaking world, it is common to have two last names: one paternal and one maternal. In some cases, the conjunctions **de** or **y** are used to connect the two. For example, in the name **Juan Martínez de Velasco**, *Martínez* is the paternal surname (**el apellido paterno**), and *Velasco* is the maternal surname (**el apellido materno**); **de** simply links the two. This convention of using two last names (**doble apellido**) is a European tradition that Spaniards brought to the Americas. It continues to be practiced in many countries, including Chile, Colombia, Mexico, Peru, and Venezuela. There are exceptions, however. In Argentina, the prevailing custom is for children to inherit only the father's last name.

When a woman marries in a country where two last names are used, legally she retains her two maiden surnames. However, socially she may take her husband's paternal surname in place of her inherited maternal surname. For example, **Mercedes Barcha**

Gabriel García Márquez   Mercedes Barcha Pardo

Rodrigo García Barcha

Pardo, wife of Colombian writer **Gabriel García Márquez**, might use the names **Mercedes Barcha García** or **Mercedes Barcha de García** in social situations (although officially her name remains **Mercedes Barcha Pardo**). Adopting a husband's last name for social purposes, though widespread, is only legally recognized in Ecuador and Peru.

Most parents do not break tradition upon naming their children; regardless of the surnames the mother uses, they use the father's first surname followed by the mother's first surname, as in the name **Rodrigo García Barcha**. However, one should note that both surnames come from the grandfathers, and therefore all **apellidos** are effectively paternal.

Hijos en la casa

In Spanish-speaking countries, family and society place very little pressure on young adults to live on their own (**independizarse**), and children often live with their parents well into their thirties. For example, about 60% of Spaniards under 34 years of age live at home with their parents. This delay in moving out is both cultural and economic—lack of job security or low wages coupled with a high cost of living may make it impractical for young adults to live independently before they marry.

---

1 **¿Cierto o falso?** Indicate whether these statements are **cierto** or **falso**. Correct the false statements.

1. Most Spanish-speaking people have three last names.

2. Hispanic last names generally consist of the paternal last name followed by the maternal last name.

3. It is common to see **de** or **y** used in a Hispanic last name.

4. Someone from Argentina would most likely have two last names.

5. Generally, married women legally retain two maiden surnames.

6. In social situations, a married woman often uses her husband's last name in place of her inherited paternal surname.

7. Adopting a husband's surname is only legally recognized in Peru and Ecuador.

8. Hispanic last names are effectively a combination of the maternal surnames from the previous generation.

Lección 3

Familia y amigos

el/la bisnieto/a	*great-grandson/daughter*
el/la chamaco/a (Méx.); el/la chamo/a (Ven.); el/la chaval(a) (Esp.); el/la pibe/a (Arg.)	el/la muchacho/a
mi colega (Esp.); mi cuate (Méx.); mi parcero/a (Col.); mi pana (Ven., P. Rico, Rep. Dom.)	*my pal; my buddy*
la madrina	*godmother*
el padrino	*godfather*
el/la tatarabuelo/a	*great-great-grandfather/ great-great-grandmother*

Las familias

Although worldwide population trends show a decrease in average family size, households in many Spanish-speaking countries are still larger than their U.S. counterparts.

- **México** 4,0 personas
- **Colombia** 3,9 personas
- **Argentina** 3,6 personas
- **Uruguay** 3,0 personas
- **España** 2,9 personas
- **Estados Unidos** 2,6 personas

La familia real española

Undoubtedly, Spain's most famous family is **la familia real** (*Royal*). In 1962, then prince **Juan Carlos de Borbón** married Princess **Sofía** of Greece. In the late 1970s, **el Rey** (*King*) **Juan Carlos** and **la Reina** (*Queen*) **Sofía** returned to Spain and helped transition the country to democracy after a forty-year dictatorship. The royal couple has three children: las **infantas** (*Princesses*) **Elena** and **Cristina**, and a son, **el príncipe** (*Prince*) **Felipe**, whose official title was **el Príncipe de Asturias**. In 2004, Felipe married **Letizia Ortiz Rocasolano**, a journalist and TV presenter. They have two daughters, **las infantas Leonor** (born in 2005) and **Sofía** (born in 2007). In 2014, Juan Carlos abdicated the throne in favor of his son.

Conexión Internet

What role do **padrinos** and **madrinas** have in today's Hispanic family?

Go to vhlcentral.com to find more cultural information related to this **Cultura** section.

---

2 **Comprensión** Complete these sentences.

1. Spain's royals were responsible for guiding in _____.
2. In Spanish, your godmother is called _____.
3. Princess Leonor is the _____ of Queen Sofía.
4. Uruguay's average household has _____ people.
5. If a Venezuelan calls you **mi pana**, you are that person's _____.

3 **Una familia famosa** Create a genealogical tree of a famous family, using photos or drawings labeled with names and ages. Present the family tree to a classmate and explain who the people are and their relationships to each other.

 Practice more at **vhlcentral.com**.

3.1 Descriptive adjectives  Tutorial

ANTE TODO Adjectives are words that describe people, places, and things. In Spanish, descriptive adjectives are used with the verb **ser** to point out characteristics such as nationality, size, color, shape, personality, and appearance.

Forms and agreement of adjectives

COMPARE & CONTRAST

In English, the forms of descriptive adjectives do not change to reflect the gender (masculine/feminine) and number (singular/plural) of the noun or pronoun they describe.

*Juan is **nice**.*   *Elena is **nice**.*   *They are **nice**.*

In Spanish, the forms of descriptive adjectives agree in gender and/or number with the nouns or pronouns they describe.

Juan es simpátic**o**.   Elena es simpátic**a**.   Ellos son simpátic**os**.

▶ Adjectives that end in **-o** have four different forms. The feminine singular is formed by changing the **-o** to **-a**. The plural is formed by adding **-s** to the singular forms.

Masculine		Feminine	
SINGULAR	PLURAL	SINGULAR	PLURAL
el muchach**o** alt**o**	los muchach**os** alt**os**	la muchach**a** alt**a**	las muchach**as** alt**as**

¡Qué bonitas son
tus hijas, tía Nayeli!

Felipe es gordo,
antipático y muy feo.

▶ Adjectives that end in **-e** or a consonant have the same masculine and feminine forms.

Masculine		Feminine	
SINGULAR	PLURAL	SINGULAR	PLURAL
el chico inteligent**e**	los chicos inteligent**es**	la chica inteligent**e**	las chicas inteligent**es**
el examen difíci**l**	los exámenes difíci**les**	la clase difíci**l**	las clases difíci**les**

▶ Adjectives that end in **-or** are variable in both gender and number.

Masculine		Feminine	
SINGULAR	PLURAL	SINGULAR	PLURAL
el hombre trabajad**or**	los hombres trabajad**ores**	la mujer trabajad**ora**	las mujeres trabajad**oras**

> Use the masculine plural form to refer to groups that include males and females.

Manuel es alt**o**.   Lola es alt**a**.   Manuel y Lola son alt**os**.

Common adjectives

alto/a	tall	**gordo/a**	fat	**moreno/a**	brunet(te)
antipático/a	unpleasant	**grande**	big; large	**mucho/a**	much; many;
bajo/a	short (in	**guapo/a**	handsome;		a lot of
	height)		good-looking	**pelirrojo/a**	red-haired
bonito/a	pretty	**importante**	important	**pequeño/a**	small
bueno/a	good	**inteligente**	intelligent	**rubio/a**	blond(e)
delgado/a	thin; slender	**interesante**	interesting	**simpático/a**	nice; likeable
difícil	hard; difficult	**joven**	young	**tonto/a**	silly; foolish
fácil	easy	**malo/a**	bad	**trabajador(a)**	hard-working
feo/a	ugly	**mismo/a**	same	**viejo/a**	old

Adjectives of nationality

> Unlike in English, Spanish adjectives of nationality are **not** capitalized. Proper names of countries, however, are capitalized.

Some adjectives of nationality

alemán, alemana	German	**francés, francesa**	French
argentino/a	Argentine	**inglés, inglesa**	English
canadiense	Canadian	**italiano/a**	Italian
chino/a	Chinese	**japonés, japonesa**	Japanese
costarricense	Costa Rican	**mexicano/a**	Mexican
cubano/a	Cuban	**norteamericano/a**	(North) American
ecuatoriano/a	Ecuadorian	**puertorriqueño/a**	Puerto Rican
español(a)	Spanish	**ruso/a**	Russian
estadounidense	from the U.S.		

> Adjectives of nationality are formed like other descriptive adjectives. Those that end in **-o** change to **-a** when forming the feminine.

chin**o** ⟶ chin**a**   mexican**o** ⟶ mexican**a**

The plural is formed by adding an **-s** to the masculine or feminine form.

argentin**o** ⟶ argentin**os**   cuban**a** ⟶ cuban**as**

> Adjectives of nationality that end in **-e** have only two forms, singular and plural.

canadiens**e** ⟶ canadiens**es**   estadounidens**e** ⟶ estadounidens**es**

> To form the feminine of adjectives of nationality that end in a consonant, add **-a**.

alemá**n** ⟶ alema**na**   españo**l** ⟶ españo**la**
japoné**s** ⟶ japone**sa**   inglé**s** ⟶ ingle**sa**

Position of adjectives

▶ Descriptive adjectives and adjectives of nationality generally follow the nouns they modify.

El niño **rubio** es de España.
The blond boy is from Spain.

La mujer **española** habla inglés.
The Spanish woman speaks English.

▶ Unlike descriptive adjectives, adjectives of quantity precede the modified noun.

Hay **muchos** libros en la biblioteca.
There are many books in the library.

Hablo con **dos** turistas puertorriqueños.
I am talking with two Puerto Rican tourists.

▶ **Bueno/a** and **malo/a** can appear before or after a noun. When placed before a masculine singular noun, the forms are shortened: **bueno** → **buen; malo** → **mal.**

Joaquín es un **buen** amigo.
Joaquín es un amigo **bueno.**   ⟶   *Joaquín is a good friend.*

Hoy es un **mal** día.
Hoy es un día **malo.**   ⟶   *Today is a bad day.*

▶ When **grande** appears before a singular noun, it is shortened to **gran,** and the meaning of the word changes: **gran** = *great* and **grande** = *big, large.*

Don Francisco es un **gran** hombre.
Don Francisco is a great man.

La familia de Inés es **grande.**
Inés' family is large.

¡LENGUA VIVA!

Like **bueno** and **grande**, **santo** (*saint*) is also shortened before masculine nouns (unless they begin with **To-** or **Do-**): **San Francisco, San José** (but: **Santo Tomás, Santo Domingo**). **Santa** is used with names of female saints: **Santa Bárbara, Santa Clara.**

¡INTÉNTALO!   Provide the appropriate forms of the adjectives.

simpático

1. Mi hermano es ___simpático___.
2. La profesora Martínez es _____.
3. Rosa y Teresa son _____.
4. Nosotros somos _____.

difícil

1. La química es ___difícil___.
2. El curso es _____.
3. Las pruebas son _____.
4. Los libros son _____.

alemán

1. Hans es ___alemán___.
2. Mis primas son _____.
3. Marcus y yo somos _____.
4. Mi tía es _____.

guapo

1. Su esposo es ___guapo___.
2. Mis sobrinas son _____.
3. Los padres de ella son _____.
4. Marta es _____.

recursos

WB
pp. 163–164

LM
p. 181

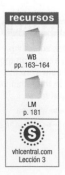

vhlcentral.com
Lección 3

Práctica

1

Emparejar Find the words in column B that are the opposite of the words in column A. One word in B will not be used.

Marcos

Jorge

A	B
1. guapo	a. delgado
2. moreno	b. pequeño
3. alto	c. malo
4. gordo	d. feo
5. joven	e. viejo
6. grande	f. rubio
7. simpático	g. antipático
	h. bajo

2

Completar Indicate the nationalities of these people by selecting the correct adjectives and changing their forms when necessary.

NOTA CULTURAL

Carlos Fuentes (1928–2012) is one of Mexico's best-known writers. His novel *La muerte* (*death*) *de Artemio Cruz* explores the psyche of a Mexican revolutionary.

1. Penélope Cruz es _____.
▶ 2. Carlos Fuentes es un gran escritor (*writer*) de México; es _____.
3. Ellen Page y Avril Lavigne son _____.
4. Giorgio Armani es un diseñador de modas (*fashion designer*) _____.
5. Daisy Fuentes es de La Habana, Cuba; ella es _____.
6. Emma Watson y Daniel Radcliffe son actores _____.
7. Heidi Klum y Boris Becker son _____.
8. Apolo Anton Ohno y Shaun White son _____.

3

Describir Look at the drawing and describe each family member using as many adjectives as possible.

Carlos Romero Sandoval

Josefina Barcos de Romero

Susana Romero Barcos

Tomás Romero Barcos

Alberto Romero Pereda

1. Susana Romero Barcos es _____.
2. Tomás Romero Barcos es _____.
3. Los dos hermanos son _____.
4. Josefina Barcos de Romero es _____.
5. Carlos Romero Sandoval es _____.
6. Alberto Romero Pereda es _____.
7. Tomás y su (*his*) padre son _____.
8. Susana y su (*her*) madre son _____.

 Practice more at **vhlcentral.com**.

Lección 3

Comunicación

4

¿Cómo es? With a partner, take turns describing each item on the list. Tell your partner whether you agree (**Estoy de acuerdo**) or disagree (**No estoy de acuerdo**) with their descriptions. ◄

> *modelo*
>
> San Francisco
> **Estudiante 1:** San Francisco es una ciudad (*city*) muy bonita.
> **Estudiante 2:** No estoy de acuerdo. Es muy fea.

1. Nueva York
2. Steve Carell
3. las canciones (*songs*) de Celine Dion
4. el presidente de los Estados Unidos
5. Steven Spielberg
6. la primera dama (*first lady*) de los Estados Unidos
7. el/la profesor(a) de español
8. las personas de Los Ángeles
9. las residencias de mi universidad
10. mi clase de español

AYUDA

Here are some tips to help you complete the descriptions:
- **Steve Carell es actor de cine y de televisión.**
- **Celine Dion es cantante.**
- **Steven Spielberg es director de cine.**

5

Anuncio personal Write a personal ad that describes yourself and your ideal boyfriend, girlfriend, or mate. Then compare your ad with a classmate's. How are you similar and how are you different? Are you looking for the same things in a romantic partner? ◄

SOY ALTA, morena y bonita. Soy cubana, de Holguín. Estudio arte en la universidad. Busco un chico similar. Mi novio ideal es alto, moreno, inteligente y muy simpático.

AYUDA

casado/a *married*
divorciado/a *divorced*
soltero/a *single; unmarried*

These words and others like them are presented in **¡ADELANTE! DOS**, **Contextos, Lección 3**, p. 144.

Síntesis

6

Diferencias Your instructor will give you and a partner each a drawing of a family. Describe your version of the drawing to your partner in order to find at least five differences between your picture and your partner's.

> *modelo*
>
> **Estudiante 1:** Susana, la madre, es rubia.
> **Estudiante 2:** No, la madre es morena.

3.2 Possessive adjectives  Tutorial

ANTE TODO Possessive adjectives, like descriptive adjectives, are words that are used to qualify people, places, or things. Possessive adjectives express the quality of ownership or possession.

Forms of possessive adjectives

SINGULAR FORMS	PLURAL FORMS	
mi	**mis**	*my*
tu	**tus**	*your* (fam.)
su	**sus**	*his, her, its, your* (form.)
nuestro/a	**nuestros/as**	*our*
vuestro/a	**vuestros/as**	*your* (fam.)
su	**sus**	*their, your* (form.)

COMPARE & CONTRAST

In English, possessive adjectives are invariable; that is, they do not agree in gender and number with the nouns they modify. Spanish possessive adjectives, however, do agree in number with the nouns they modify.

my cousin	*my cousins*	*my aunt*	*my aunts*
mi primo	**mis** primos	**mi** tía	**mis** tías

The forms **nuestro** and **vuestro** agree in both gender and number with the nouns they modify.

nuestr**o** prim**o**	nuestr**os** prim**os**	nuestr**a** tía	nuestr**as** tí**as**

▶ Possessive adjectives are always placed before the nouns they modify.

—¿Está **tu novio** aquí?　　　　　—No, **mi novio** está en la biblioteca.
Is your boyfriend here?　　　　　*No, my boyfriend is in the library.*

▶ Because **su** and **sus** have multiple meanings (*your, his, her, their, its*), you can avoid confusion by using this construction instead: [*article*] + [*noun*] + **de** + [*subject pronoun*].

sus parientes	los parientes **de él/ella**	*his/her relatives*
	los parientes **de Ud./Uds.**	*your relatives*
	los parientes **de ellos/ellas**	*their relatives*

 **¡INTÉNTALO!** Provide the appropriate form of each possessive adjective.

1. Es ____mi____ (*my*) libro.
2. _____ (*My*) familia es ecuatoriana.
3. ____ (*Your*, fam.) esposo es italiano.
4. _____ (*Our*) profesor es español.
5. Es _____ (*her*) reloj.
6. Es _____ (*your*, fam.) mochila.
7. Es _____ (*your*, form.) maleta.
8. _____ (*Their*) sobrina es alemana.

1. ____Sus____ (*Her*) primos son franceses.
2. _____ (*Our*) primos son canadienses.
3. Son _____ (*their*) lápices.
4. _____ (*Their*) nietos son japoneses.
5. Son _____ (*our*) plumas.
6. Son _____ (*my*) papeles.
7. _____ (*My*) amigas son inglesas.
8. Son _____ (*his*) cuadernos.

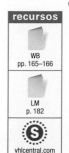
Lección 3

Práctica

AYUDA

Remember that possessive adjectives don't agree in number or gender with the owner of an item; they always agree with the item(s) being possessed.

1

La familia de Manolo Complete each sentence with the correct possessive adjective from the options in parentheses. Use the subject of each sentence as a guide.

1. Me llamo Manolo, y _____ (nuestro, mi, sus) hermano es Federico.
2. _____ (Nuestra, Sus, Mis) madre Silvia es profesora y enseña química.
3. Ella admira a _____ (tu, nuestro, sus) estudiantes porque trabajan mucho.
4. Yo estudio en la misma universidad, pero no tomo clases con _____ (mi, nuestras, tus) madre.
5. Federico trabaja en una oficina con _____ (mis, tu, nuestro) padre.
6. _____ (Mi, Su, Tu) oficina está en el centro de la Ciudad de México.
7. Javier y Óscar son _____ (mis, mi, sus) tíos de Oaxaca.
8. ¿Y tú? ¿Cómo es _____ (mi, su, tu) familia?

2

Clarificar Clarify each sentence with a prepositional phrase. Follow the model.

> **modelo**
>
> Su hermana es muy bonita. (ella)
> La hermana *de ella* es muy bonita.

1. Su casa es muy grande. (ellos) _la casa de ellos es muy grande_
2. ¿Cómo se llama su hermano? (ellas) _____
3. Sus padres trabajan en el centro. (ella) _~~estas~~ los padres de ella trabajan en el centro._
4. Sus abuelos son muy simpáticos. (él) _los abuelos de el es muy simpaticos_
5. Maribel es su prima. (ella) _la prima de ella es Maribel_
6. Su primo lee los libros. (ellos) _el primo de ellos lee los libros_

3

¿Dónde está? With a partner, imagine that you can't remember where you put some of the belongings you see in the pictures. Your partner will help you by reminding you where your things are. Take turns playing each role.

CONSULTA

For a list of useful prepositions, refer to the table *Prepositions often used with* **estar**, in **Estructura 2.3**, p. 82.

> **modelo**
>
> **Estudiante 1:** ¿Dónde está mi mochila?
> **Estudiante 2:** Tu mochila está encima del escritorio.

1. 2. 3.

4. 5. 6.

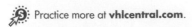

Comunicación

4

Describir With a partner, describe the people and places listed below. Make note of any similarities and be prepared to share them with the class.

> **modelo**
>
> la biblioteca de su universidad
> *La biblioteca de nuestra universidad es muy grande. Hay muchos libros en la biblioteca. Mis amigos y yo estudiamos en la biblioteca.*

1. tu profesor favorito
2. tu profesora favorita
3. su clase de español
4. la librería de su universidad
5. tus padres
6. tus abuelos
7. tu mejor (*best*) amigo
8. tu mejor amiga
9. su universidad
10. tu país de origen

5

Una familia famosa Assume the identity of a member of a famous family, real or fictional (the Kardashians, Clintons, Beckhams, Jolie-Pitts, etc.), and write a description of "your" family. Be sure not to use any names! Then, in small groups, take turns reading the descriptions aloud. The other group members may ask follow-up questions to help them identify the famous person.

> **modelo**
>
> **Estudiante 1:** Hay cuatro personas en mi familia. Mi padre es delgado y muy trabajador. Su trabajo (*job*) es importante; él viaja mucho. Mi madre es guapa e inteligente. Tengo una hermana mayor. Ella y yo estudiamos en una escuela privada. Nuestra casa está en la capital.
> **Estudiante 2:** ¿Son ustedes de la capital?
> **Estudiante 1:** No, somos de Chicago.
> **Estudiante 3:** ¿Eres Sasha Obama?
> **Estudiante 1:** Sí.

Síntesis

6

Describe a tu familia Get together with two classmates and describe your family to them in several sentences (**Mi padre es alto y moreno. Mi madre es delgada y muy bonita. Mis hermanos son...**). They will work together to try to repeat your description (**Su padre es alto y moreno. Su madre...**). If they forget any details, they can ask you questions (**¿Es alto tu hermano?**). Alternate roles until all of you have described your families.

3.3 Present tense of -er and -ir verbs  Tutorial

ANTE TODO In **Lección 2,** you learned how to form the present tense of regular -ar verbs. You also learned about the importance of verb forms, which change to show who is performing the action. The chart below shows the forms from two other important groups, **-er** verbs and **-ir** verbs.

CONSULTA

To review the conjugation of -**ar** verbs, see **Estructura 2.1,** p. 72.

Present tense of -er and -ir verbs

		comer (to eat)	**escribir** (to write)
SINGULAR FORMS	yo	como	escribo
	tú	comes	escribes
	Ud./él/ella	come	escribe
PLURAL FORMS	nosotros/as	comemos	escribimos
	vosotros/as	coméis	escribís
	Uds./ellos/ellas	comen	escriben

▶ **-Er** and **-ir** verbs have very similar endings. Study the preceding chart to detect the patterns that make it easier for you to use them to communicate in Spanish.

Felipe y su tío comen.

Jimena lee.

AYUDA

Here are some tips on learning Spanish verbs:
1) Learn to identify the verb's stem, to which all endings attach.
2) Memorize the endings that go with each verb and verb tense.
3) As often as possible, practice using different forms of each verb in speech and writing.
4) Devote extra time to learning irregular verbs, such as **ser** and **estar**.

▶ Like **-ar** verbs, the **yo** forms of **-er** and **-ir** verbs end in **-o.**

Yo com**o.**   Yo escrib**o.**

▶ Except for the **yo** form, all of the verb endings for **-er** verbs begin with **-e.**

-es	-emos	-en
-e	-éis	

▶ **-Er** and **-ir** verbs have the exact same endings, except in the **nosotros/as** and **vosotros/as** forms.

nosotros ◀ com**emos** / escrib**imos**   vosotros ◀ com**éis** / escrib**ís**

Common -er and -ir verbs

-er verbs		**-ir verbs**	
aprender (a + *inf.*)	*to learn*	**abrir**	*to open*
beber	*to drink*	**asistir (a)**	*to attend*
comer	*to eat*	**compartir**	*to share*
comprender	*to understand*	**decidir (+ *inf.*)**	*to decide*
correr	*to run*	**describir**	*to describe*
creer (en)	*to believe (in)*	**escribir**	*to write*
deber (+ *inf.*)	*should; must; ought to*	**recibir**	*to receive*
leer	*to read*	**vivir**	*to live*

Ellos **corren** en el parque.

Él **escribe** una carta.

¡INTÉNTALO! Provide the appropriate present-tense forms of these verbs.

correr

1. Graciela __corre__.
2. Tú _____.
3. Yo _____.
4. Sara y Ana _____.
5. Usted _____.
6. Ustedes _____.
7. La gente _____.
8. Marcos y yo _____.

abrir

1. Ellos __abren__ la puerta.
2. Carolina _____ la maleta.
3. Yo _____ las ventanas.
4. Nosotras _____ los libros.
5. Usted _____ el cuaderno.
6. Tú _____ la ventana.
7. Ustedes _____ las maletas.
8. Los muchachos _____ los cuadernos.

aprender

1. Él __aprende__ español.
2. Maribel y yo _____ inglés.
3. Tú _____ japonés.
4. Tú y tu hermanastra _____ francés.
5. Mi hijo _____ chino.
6. Yo _____ alemán.
7. Usted _____ inglés.
8. Nosotros _____ italiano.

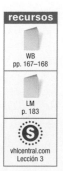

Práctica

 1

Completar Complete Susana's sentences about her family with the correct forms of the verbs in parentheses. One of the verbs will remain in the infinitive.

1. Mi familia y yo _____ (vivir) en Mérida, Yucatán.
2. Tengo muchos libros. Me gusta _____ (leer).
3. Mi hermano Alfredo es muy inteligente. Alfredo _____ (asistir) a clases los lunes, miércoles y viernes.
4. Los martes y jueves Alfredo y yo _____ (correr) en el Parque del Centenario.
5. Mis padres _____ (comer) mucha lasaña los domingos y se quedan dormidos (*they fall asleep*).
6. Yo _____ (creer) que (*that*) mis padres deben comer menos (*less*).

 2

Oraciones Juan is talking about what he and his friends do after school. Form complete sentences by adding any other necessary elements.

> **modelo**
>
> yo / correr / amigos / lunes y miércoles
> *Yo corro con mis amigos los lunes y miércoles.*

1. Manuela / asistir / clase / yoga
2. Eugenio / abrir / correo electrónico (*e-mail*)
3. Isabel y yo / leer / biblioteca
4. Sofía y Roberto / aprender / hablar / inglés
5. tú / comer / cafetería / universidad
6. mi novia y yo / compartir / libro de historia

 3

Consejos Mario and his family are spending a year abroad to learn Japanese. In pairs, use the words below to say what he and/or his family members are doing or should do to adjust to life in Japan. Then, create one more sentence using a verb not on the list.

> **modelo**
>
> recibir libros / deber practicar japonés
> **Estudiante 1:** Mario y su esposa reciben muchos libros en japonés.
> **Estudiante 2:** Los hijos deben practicar japonés.

aprender japonés	decidir explorar el país
asistir a clases	escribir listas de palabras en japonés
beber sake	leer novelas japonesas
deber comer cosas nuevas	vivir con una familia japonesa
¿?	¿?

 Practice more at **vhlcentral.com**.

Comunicación

4

Entrevista In pairs, use these questions to interview each other. Be prepared to report the results of your interviews to the class.

1. ¿Dónde comes al mediodía? ¿Comes mucho?
2. ¿Cuándo asistes a tus clases?
3. ¿Cuál es tu clase favorita? ¿Por qué?
4. ¿Dónde vives?
5. ¿Con quién vives?
6. ¿Qué cursos debes tomar el próximo (*next*) semestre?
7. ¿Lees el periódico (*newspaper*)? ¿Qué periódico lees y cuándo?
8. ¿Recibes muchos mensajes de texto (*text messages*)? ¿De quién(es)?
9. ¿Escribes poemas?
10. ¿Crees en fantasmas (*ghosts*)?

5

¿Acción o descripción? In small groups, take turns choosing a verb from the list. Then choose to act out the verb or give a description. The other members of the group will say what you are doing. Be creative!

abrir (un libro, una puerta, una mochila)
aprender (a bailar, a hablar francés, a dibujar)
asistir (a una clase de yoga, a un concierto de rock, a una clase interesante)
beber (agua, Coca-Cola)
comer (pasta, un sándwich, pizza)
compartir (un libro, un sándwich)

correr (en el parque, en un maratón)
escribir (una composición, un mensaje de texto [*text message*], con lápiz)
leer (una carta [*letter*] de amor, un mensaje electrónico [*e-mail message*], un periódico [*newspaper*])
recibir un regalo (*gift*)
¿?

modelo
Estudiante 1: (*pantomimes typing a keyboard*)
Estudiante 2: ¿Escribes un mensaje electrónico?
Estudiante 1: Sí.

modelo
Estudiante 1: Soy estudiante y tomo muchas clases. Vivo en Roma.
Estudiante 2: ¿Comes pasta?
Estudiante 1: No, no como pasta.
Estudiante 3: ¿Aprendes a hablar italiano?
Estudiante 1: ¡Sí!

Síntesis

6

Horario Your instructor will give you and a partner incomplete versions of Alicia's schedule. Fill in the missing information on the schedule by talking to your partner. Be prepared to reconstruct Alicia's complete schedule with the class.

3.4 Present tense of tener and venir Tutorial

ANTE TODO The verbs **tener** (*to have*) and **venir** (*to come*) are among the most frequently used in Spanish. Because most of their forms are irregular, you will have to learn each one individually.

The verbs tener and venir

		tener	venir
SINGULAR FORMS	yo	ten**go**	ven**go**
	tú	tien**es**	vien**es**
	Ud./él/ella	tien**e**	vien**e**
PLURAL FORMS	nosotros/as	ten**emos**	ven**imos**
	vosotros/as	ten**éis**	ven**ís**
	Uds./ellos/ellas	tien**en**	vien**en**

▶ The endings are the same as those of regular **-er** and **-ir** verbs, except for the **yo** forms, which are irregular: **tengo, vengo.**

▶ In the **tú, Ud.,** and **Uds.** forms, the **e** of the stem changes to **ie,** as shown below.

INFINITIVE	VERB STEM	VERB FORM
tener →	ten- →	tú t**ie**nes
		Ud./él/ella t**ie**ne
		Uds./ellos/ellas t**ie**nen
venir →	ven- →	tú v**ie**nes
		Ud./él/ella v**ie**ne
		Uds./ellos/ellas v**ie**nen

¿Tienes una familia grande, Marissa?

No, tengo una familia pequeña.

▶ Only the **nosotros** and **vosotros** forms are regular. Compare them to the forms of **comer** and **escribir** that you learned on page 142.

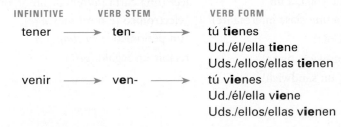

	tener	comer	venir	escribir
nosotros/as	ten**emos**	com**emos**	ven**imos**	escrib**imos**
vosotros/as	ten**éis**	com**éis**	ven**ís**	escrib**ís**

▶ In certain idiomatic or set expressions in Spanish, you use the construction **tener** + [*noun*] to express *to be* + [*adjective*]. This chart contains a list of the most common expressions with **tener**.

Expressions with tener

tener... años	*to be... years old*	**tener (mucha) prisa**	*to be in a (big) hurry*
tener (mucho) calor	*to be (very) hot*		
tener (mucho) cuidado	*to be (very) careful*	**tener razón**	*to be right*
		no tener razón	*to be wrong*
tener (mucho) frío	*to be (very) cold*	**tener (mucha) sed**	*to be (very) thirsty*
tener (mucha) hambre	*to be (very) hungry*	**tener (mucho) sueño**	*to be (very) sleepy*
tener (mucho) miedo (de)	*to be (very) afraid/ scared (of)*	**tener (mucha) suerte**	*to be (very) lucky*

—¿**Tienen** hambre ustedes?
Are you hungry?

—Sí, y **tenemos** sed también.
Yes, and we're thirsty, too.

▶ To express an obligation, use **tener que** (*to have to*) + [*infinitive*].

—¿Qué **tienes que** estudiar hoy?
What do you have to study today?

—**Tengo que** estudiar biología.
I have to study biology.

▶ To ask people if they feel like doing something, use **tener ganas de** (*to feel like*) + [*infinitive*].

—¿**Tienes ganas de** comer?
Do you feel like eating?

—No, **tengo ganas de** dormir.
No, I feel like sleeping.

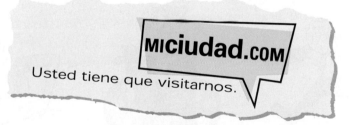

MIciudad.com

Usted tiene que visitarnos.

¡INTÉNTALO!   Provide the appropriate forms of **tener** and **venir**.

tener

1. Ellos ___tienen___ dos hermanos.
2. Yo _____ una hermana.
3. El artista _____ tres primos.
4. Nosotros _____ diez tíos.
5. Eva y Diana _____ un sobrino.
6. Usted _____ cinco nietos.
7. Tú _____ dos hermanastras.
8. Ustedes _____ cuatro hijos.
9. Ella _____ una hija.

venir

1. Mis padres ___vienen___ de México.
2. Tú _____ de España.
3. Nosotras _____ de Cuba.
4. Pepe _____ de Italia.
5. Yo _____ de Francia.
6. Ustedes _____ de Canadá.
7. Alfonso y yo _____ de Portugal.
8. Ellos _____ de Alemania.
9. Usted _____ de Venezuela.

Práctica

 Emparejar Find the expression in column B that best matches an item in column A. Then, come up with a new item that corresponds with the leftover expression in column B.

A	B
1. el Polo Norte	a. tener calor
2. una sauna	b. tener sed
3. la comida salada (*salty food*)	c. tener frío
4. una persona muy inteligente	d. tener razón
5. un abuelo	e. tener ganas de
6. una dieta	f. tener hambre
	g. tener 75 años

 Completar Complete the sentences with the correct forms of **tener** or **venir**.

1. Hoy nosotros _____ una reunión familiar (*family reunion*).
2. Yo _____ en autobús de la Universidad de Quito.
3. Todos mis parientes _____, excepto mi tío Manolo y su esposa.
4. Ellos no _____ ganas de venir porque viven en Portoviejo.
5. Mi prima Susana y su novio no _____ hasta las ocho porque ella _____ que trabajar.
6. En las fiestas, mi hermana siempre (*always*) _____ muy tarde (*late*).
7. Nosotros _____ mucha suerte porque las reuniones son divertidas (*fun*).
8. Mi madre cree que mis sobrinos son muy simpáticos. Creo que ella _____ razón.

 Describir Describe what these people are doing or feeling using an expression with **tener**.

1. _____
2. _____
3. _____

4. _____
5. _____
6. _____

 Practice more at **vhlcentral.com**.

Comunicación

4

¿Sí o no? Indicate whether these statements apply to you by checking either **Sí** or **No**.

	Sí	No
1. Mi padre tiene 50 años.	○	○
2. Mis amigos vienen a mi casa todos los días (*every day*).	○	○
3. Vengo a la universidad los martes.	○	○
4. Tengo hambre.	○	○
5. Tengo dos computadoras.	○	○
6. Tengo sed.	○	○
7. Tengo que estudiar los domingos.	○	○
8. Tengo una familia grande.	○	○

Now interview a classmate by transforming each statement into a question. Be prepared to report the results of your interview to the class.

> **modelo**
>
> **Estudiante 1:** ¿Tiene tu padre 50 años?
> **Estudiante 2:** No, no tiene 50 años. Tiene 65.

5

Preguntas Get together with a classmate and ask each other these questions.

1. ¿Tienes que estudiar hoy?
2. ¿Cuántos años tienes? ¿Y tus hermanos/as?
3. ¿Cuándo vienes a la clase de español?
4. ¿Cuándo vienen tus amigos a tu casa, apartamento o residencia estudiantil?
5. ¿De qué tienes miedo? ¿Por qué?
6. ¿Qué tienes ganas de hacer esta noche (*tonight*)?

6

Conversación Use an expression with **tener** to hint at what's on your mind. Your partner will ask questions to find out why you feel that way. If your partner cannot guess what's on your mind after three attempts, tell him/her. Then switch roles.

> **modelo**
>
> **Estudiante 1:** Tengo miedo.
> **Estudiante 2:** ¿Tienes que hablar en público?
> **Estudiante 1:** No.
> **Estudiante 2:** ¿Tienes un examen hoy?
> **Estudiante 1:** Sí, y no tengo tiempo para estudiar.

Síntesis

7

Minidrama Act out this situation with a partner: you are introducing your boyfriend/girlfriend to your extended family. To avoid any surprises before you go, talk about who is coming and what each family member is like. Switch roles.

Recapitulación

Diagnostics

Review the grammar concepts you have learned in this lesson by completing these activities.

1 **Adjetivos** Complete each phrase with the appropriate adjective from the list. Make all necessary changes. **6 pts.**

antipático	interesante	mexicano
difícil	joven	moreno

1. Mi tía es _____. Vive en Guadalajara.
2. Mi primo no es rubio, es _____.
3. Mi novio cree que la clase no es fácil; es _____.
4. Los libros son _____; me gustan mucho.
5. Mis hermanos son _____; no tienen muchos amigos.
6. Las gemelas tienen quince años. Son _____.

2 **Completar** For each set of sentences, provide the appropriate form of the verb **tener** and the possessive adjective. Follow the model. **12 pts.**

> **modelo**
> Él *tiene* un libro. Es *su* libro.

1. Esteban y Julio _____ una tía. Es _____ tía.
2. Yo _____ muchos amigos. Son _____ amigos.
3. Tú _____ tres primas. Son _____ primas.
4. María y tú _____ un hermano. Es _____ hermano.
5. Nosotras _____ unas mochilas. Son _____ mochilas.
6. Usted _____ dos sobrinos. Son _____ sobrinos.

3 **Oraciones** Arrange the words in the correct order to form complete logical sentences. **¡Ojo!** Don't forget to conjugate the verbs. **10 pts.**

1. libros / unos / tener / interesantes / tú / muy

   _____

2. dos / leer / fáciles / compañera / tu / lecciones

   _____

3. mi / francés / ser / amigo / buen / Hugo

   _____

4. ser / simpáticas / dos / personas / nosotras

   _____

5. a / clases / menores / mismas / sus / asistir / hermanos / las

   _____

RESUMEN GRAMATICAL

3.1 **Descriptive adjectives** *pp. 134–136*

Forms and agreement of adjectives

Masculine		Feminine	
Singular	Plural	Singular	Plural
alto	altos	alta	altas
inteligente	inteligentes	inteligente	inteligentes
trabajador	trabajadores	trabajadora	trabajadoras

▶ Descriptive adjectives follow the noun:
el chico rubio

▶ Adjectives of nationality also follow the noun:
la mujer española

▶ Adjectives of quantity precede the noun:
muchos libros, dos turistas

▶ When placed before a singular masculine noun, these adjectives are shortened.

bueno → buen   malo → mal

▶ When placed before a singular noun, **grande** is shortened to **gran**.

3.2 **Possessive adjectives** *p. 139*

Singular		Plural	
mi	nuestro/a	mis	nuestros/as
tu	vuestro/a	tus	vuestros/as
su	su	sus	sus

3.3 **Present tense of -er and -ir verbs** *pp. 142–143*

comer		escribir	
como	comemos	escribo	escribimos
comes	coméis	escribes	escribís
come	comen	escribe	escriben

3.4 **Present tense of tener and venir** *pp. 146–147*

tener		venir	
tengo	tenemos	vengo	venimos
tienes	tenéis	vienes	venís
tiene	tienen	viene	vienen

Lección 3

4 **Carta** Complete this letter with the appropriate forms of the verbs in the word list. Not all verbs will be used. **10 pts.**

abrir	correr	recibir
asistir	creer	tener
compartir	escribir	venir
comprender	leer	vivir

Hola, Ángel:

¿Qué tal? (Yo) (1) _____ esta carta (this letter) en la biblioteca. Todos los días (2) _____ aquí y (3) _____ un buen libro. Yo (4) _____ que es importante leer por diversión. Mi compañero de apartamento no (5) _____ por qué me gusta leer. Él sólo (6) _____ los libros de texto. Pero nosotros (7) _____ unos intereses. Por ejemplo, los dos somos atléticos; por las mañanas nosotros (8) _____. También nos gustan las ciencias; por las tardes (9) _____ a nuestra clase de biología. Y tú, ¿cómo estás? ¿(Tú) (10) _____ mucho trabajo (work)?

5 **Su familia** Write a brief description of a friend's family. Describe the family members using vocabulary and structures from this lesson. Write at least five sentences. **12 pts.**

> **modelo**
> La familia de mi amiga Gabriela es grande. Ella tiene tres hermanos y una hermana. Su hermana mayor es periodista...

6 **Proverbio** Complete this proverb with the correct forms of the verbs in parentheses. **2 EXTRA points!**

" Dos andares° _____ (tener) el dinero°, _____ (venir) despacio° y se va° ligero°. "

andares *speeds* dinero *money* despacio *slowly*
se va *it leaves* ligero *quickly*

 Practice more at **vhlcentral.com**.

Lectura

Antes de leer

Estrategia

Guessing meaning from context

As you read in Spanish, you'll often come across words you haven't learned. You can guess what they mean by looking at the surrounding words and sentences. Look at the following text and guess what **tía abuela** means, based on the context.

¡Hola, Claudia!
  ¿Qué hay de nuevo?
  ¿Sabes qué? Ayer fui a ver a mi tía abuela, la hermana de mi abuela. Tiene 85 años, pero es muy independiente. Vive en un apartamento en Quito con su prima Lorena, quien también tiene 85 años.

If you guessed *great-aunt*, you are correct, and you can conclude from this word and the format clues that this is a letter about someone's visit with his or her great-aunt.

Examinar el texto

Quickly read through the paragraphs and find two or three words you don't know. Using the context as your guide, guess what these words mean. Then glance at the paragraphs where these words appear and try to predict what the paragraphs are about.

Examinar el formato

Look at the format of the reading. What clues do the captions, photos, and layout give you about its content?

Gente... Las familias

1. Me llamo Armando y tengo setenta años, pero no me considero viejo. Tengo seis nietas y un nieto. Vivo con mi hija y tengo la oportunidad de pasar mucho tiempo con ella y con mi nieto. Por las tardes salgo a pasear° por el parque con él y por la noche le leo cuentos°.

Armando. Tiene seis nietas y un nieto.

2. Mi prima Victoria y yo nos llevamos muy bien. Estudiamos juntas° en la universidad y compartimos un apartamento. Ella es muy inteligente y me ayuda° con los estudios. Además°, es muy simpática y generosa. Si necesito cualquier° cosa, ¡ella me la compra!

Diana. Vive con su prima.

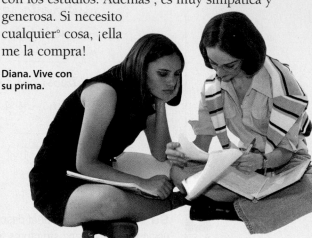

3. Me llamo Ramona y soy paraguaya, aunque° ahora vivo en los Estados Unidos. Tengo tres hijos, uno de nueve años, uno de doce y el mayor de quince. Es difícil a veces, pero mi esposo y yo tratamos° de ayudarlos y comprenderlos siempre°.

Ramona. Sus hijos son muy importantes para ella.

4. Tengo mucha suerte. Aunque mis padres están divorciados, tengo una familia muy unida. Tengo dos hermanos y dos hermanas. Me gusta hablar y salir a fiestas con ellos. Ahora tengo novio en la universidad y él no conoce a mis hermanos. ¡Espero que se lleven bien!

Ana María. Su familia es muy unida.

5. Antes quería° tener hermanos, pero ya no° es tan importante. Ser hijo único tiene muchas ventajas°: no tengo que compartir mis cosas con hermanos, no hay discusiones° y, como soy nieto único también, ¡mis abuelos piensan° que soy perfecto!

Fernando. Es hijo único.

6. Como soy joven todavía°, no tengo ni esposa ni hijos. Pero tengo un sobrino, el hijo de mi hermano, que es muy especial para mí. Se llama Benjamín y tiene diez años. Es un muchacho muy simpático. Siempre tiene hambre y por lo tanto vamos° frecuentemente a comer hamburguesas. Nos gusta también ir al cine° a ver películas de acción. Hablamos de todo. ¡Creo que ser tío es mejor que ser padre!

Santiago. Cree que ser tío es divertido.

salgo a pasear *I go take a walk* cuentos *stories* juntas *together* me ayuda *she helps me* Además *Besides* cualquier *any* aunque *although* tratamos *we try* siempre *always* quería *I wanted* ya no *no longer* ventajas *advantages* discusiones *arguments* piensan *think* todavía *still* vamos *we go* ir al cine *to go to the movies*

Después de leer

Emparejar

Glance at the paragraphs and see how the words and phrases in column A are used in context. Then find their definitions in column B.

A	B
1. me la compra	a. the oldest
2. nos llevamos bien	b. movies
3. no conoce	c. the youngest
4. películas	d. buys it for me
5. mejor que	e. borrows it from me
6. el mayor	f. we see each other
	g. doesn't know
	h. we get along
	i. portraits
	j. better than

Seleccionar

Choose the sentence that best summarizes each paragraph.

1. Párrafo 1
   a. Me gusta mucho ser abuelo.
   b. No hablo mucho con mi nieto.
   c. No tengo nietos.

2. Párrafo 2
   a. Mi prima es antipática.
   b. Mi prima no es muy trabajadora.
   c. Mi prima y yo somos muy buenas amigas.

3. Párrafo 3
   a. Tener hijos es un gran sacrificio, pero es muy bonito también.
   b. No comprendo a mis hijos.
   c. Mi esposo y yo no tenemos hijos.

4. Párrafo 4
   a. No hablo mucho con mis hermanos.
   b. Comparto mis cosas con mis hermanos.
   c. Mis hermanos y yo somos como (*like*) amigos.

5. Párrafo 5
   a. Me gusta ser hijo único.
   b. Tengo hermanos y hermanas.
   c. Vivo con mis abuelos.

6. Párrafo 6
   a. Mi sobrino tiene diez años.
   b. Me gusta mucho ser tío.
   c. Mi esposa y yo no tenemos hijos.

Lección 3

Escritura

Estrategia

Using idea maps

How do you organize ideas for a first draft?
Often, the organization of ideas represents
the most challenging part of the process.
Idea maps are useful for organizing pertinent
information. Here is an example of an idea
map you can use:

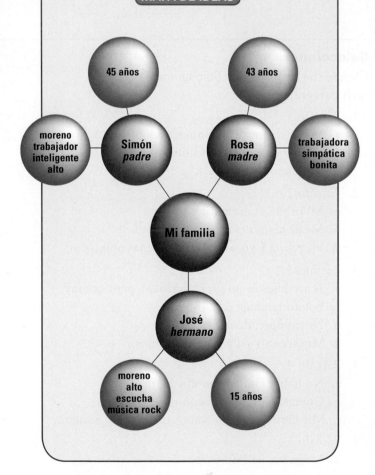

MAPA DE IDEAS

- 45 años
- 43 años
- moreno trabajador inteligente alto
- Simón *padre*
- Rosa *madre*
- trabajadora simpática bonita
- Mi familia
- José *hermano*
- moreno alto escucha música rock
- 15 años

Tema

Escribir un mensaje electrónico

A friend you met in a chat room for Spanish speakers wants
to know about your family. Using some of the verbs and
adjectives you have learned in this lesson, write a brief e-mail
describing your family or an imaginary family, including:

▶ Names and relationships
▶ Physical characteristics
▶ Hobbies and interests

Here are some useful expressions for writing an e-mail or
letter in Spanish:

Salutations

Estimado/a Julio/Julia:	*Dear Julio/Julia,*
Querido/a Miguel/Ana María:	*Dear Miguel/Ana María,*

Closings

Un abrazo,	*A hug,*
Abrazos,	*Hugs,*
Cariños,	*Much love,*
¡Hasta pronto!	*See you soon!*
¡Hasta la próxima semana!	*See you next week!*

Escuchar Audio

Lección 3

Estrategia

**Asking for repetition/
Replaying the recording**

Sometimes it is difficult to understand what people say, especially in a noisy environment. During a conversation, you can ask someone to repeat by saying **¿Cómo?** (*What?*) or **¿Perdón?** (*Pardon me?*). In class, you can ask your teacher to repeat by saying **Repita, por favor** (*Repeat, please*). If you don't understand a recorded activity, you can simply replay it.

 To help you practice this strategy, you will listen to a short paragraph. Ask your professor to repeat it or replay the recording, and then summarize what you heard.

Preparación

Based on the photograph, where do you think Cristina and Laura are? What do you think Laura is saying to Cristina?

Ahora escucha

Now you are going to hear Laura and Cristina's conversation. Use **R** to indicate which adjectives describe Cristina's boyfriend, Rafael. Use **E** for adjectives that describe Laura's boyfriend, Esteban. Some adjectives will not be used.

____ rubio	____ interesante
____ feo	____ antipático
____ alto	____ inteligente
____ trabajador	____ moreno
____ un poco gordo	____ viejo

Comprensión

Identificar

Which person would make each statement: Cristina or Laura?

	Cristina	Laura
1. Mi novio habla sólo de fútbol y de béisbol.	○	○
2. Tengo un novio muy interesante y simpático.	○	○
3. Mi novio es alto y moreno.	○	○
4. Mi novio trabaja mucho.	○	○
5. Mi amiga no tiene buena suerte con los muchachos.	○	○
6. El novio de mi amiga es un poco gordo, pero guapo.	○	○

¿Cierto o falso?

Indicate whether each sentence is **cierto** or **falso**, then correct the false statements.

	Cierto	Falso
1. Esteban es un chico interesante y simpático.	○	○
2. Laura tiene mala suerte con los chicos.	○	○
3. Rafael es muy interesante.	○	○
4. Laura y su novio hablan de muchas cosas.	○	○

 Practice more at **vhlcentral.com**.

En pantalla

In the Spanish-speaking world, grandparents play an important role in the nuclear family structure. Even in the U.S., where retirement communities and nursing homes abound, in Latino families it is often expected that members of the older generation will live with their adult children and grandchildren. This living situation usually brings benefits—financial, emotional, and logistical—that improve the quality of life for everyone involved, and it facilitates the passing on of family history and culture.

Vocabulario útil	
la canción	song
cocinar	to cook
el espíritu	spirit
los frijoles	beans
la lágrima	tear
el milagro	miracle
romántico/a	romantic
se aparece en	appears in
supersticioso/a	superstitious

Preparación

Have you or anyone in your family ever experienced a situation that seemed supernatural? What happened?

Preguntas

Choose the correct answer for each question.

1. ¿Qué hace (*is she doing*) la abuela?
   a. Prepara tortillas.   b. Come tortillas.

2. ¿Quién escucha una canción?
   a. la abuela   b. el nieto

3. ¿Quién se aparece en la tortilla?
   a. el nieto   b. el abuelo

4. ¿Qué tiene el nieto?
   a. sed   b. hambre

Los personajes

Choose one of the characters and write a description of him or her. Use as many adjectives as you can and mention the person's likes and dislikes. Be creative! Then, read your description to a partner.

¿me llamaste? *you called me?*

Tears & Tortillas

Ay, Carlos. Nuestra canción.

¡Beto!... ¡Beto!...

Abuelita... ¿me llamaste?°

Tears & Tortillas forms part of a growing U.S. market for Latino cinema. Director Xóchitl Dorsey's narrative and documentary films have appeared on Showtime and PBS, as well as in various film festivals.

 Video: Short Film

 Practice more at **vhlcentral.com**.

If a Spanish-speaking friend told you he was going to a **reunión familiar,** what type of event would you picture? Most likely, your friend would not be referring to an annual event reuniting family members from far-flung cities. In Hispanic culture, family gatherings are much more frequent and relaxed, and thus do not require intensive planning or juggling of schedules. Some families gather every Sunday afternoon to enjoy a leisurely meal; others may prefer to hold get-togethers on a Saturday evening, with food, music, and dancing. In any case, gatherings tend to be laid-back events in which family members spend hours chatting, sharing stories, and telling jokes.

Vocabulario útil	
el Día de la Madre	*Mother's Day*
estamos celebrando	*we are celebrating*
familia grande y feliz	*a big, happy family*
familia numerosa	*a large family*
hacer (algo) juntos	*to do (something) together*
el patio interior	*courtyard*
pelear	*to fight*
reuniones familiares	*family gatherings, reunions*

Preparación

What is a "typical family" like where you live? Is there such a thing? What members of a family usually live together?

Completar

Complete this paragraph with the correct options.

Los Valdivieso y los Bolaños son dos ejemplos de familias en Ecuador. Los Valdivieso son una familia (1) _____ (difícil/numerosa). Viven en una casa (2) _____ (grande/buena). En el patio, hacen (*they do*) muchas reuniones (3) _____ (familiares/con amigos). Los Bolaños son una familia pequeña. Ellos comen (4) _____ (separados/juntos) y preparan canelazo, una bebida (*drink*) típica ecuatoriana.

tan *so*

—**Érica, ¿y cómo se llaman tus padres?**
—**Mi mamá, Lorena y mi papá, Miguel.**

¡Qué familia tan° grande tiene!

Te presento a la familia Bolaños.

 **Video:** *Flash cultura*

 Practice more at **vhlcentral.com**.

recursos	
VM pp. 177–178	vhlcentral.com Lección 3

Ⓢ Video: *Panorama cultural*
Interactive map

Ecuador

El país en cifras

▶ **Área:** 283.560 km² (109.483 millas²), *incluyendo las islas Galápagos, aproximadamente el área de Colorado*

▶ **Población:** 14.596.000

▶ **Capital:** Quito — 2.035.000

▶ **Ciudades° principales:**
Guayaquil — 2.941.000, Cuenca, Machala, Portoviejo

SOURCE: Population Division, UN Secretariat

▶ **Moneda:** dólar estadounidense

▶ **Idiomas:** español (oficial), quichua
La lengua oficial de Ecuador es el español, pero también se hablan° otras° lenguas en el país. Aproximadamente unos 4.000.000 de ecuatorianos hablan lenguas indígenas; la mayoría° de ellos habla quichua. El quichua es el dialecto ecuatoriano del quechua, la lengua de los incas.

Bandera de Ecuador

Ecuatorianos célebres

▶ **Francisco Eugenio De Santa Cruz y Espejo,** médico, periodista y patriota (1747–1795)

▶ **Juan León Mera,** novelista (1832–1894)

▶ **Eduardo Kingman,** pintor° (1913–1998)

▶ **Rosalía Arteaga,** abogada°, política y ex vicepresidenta (1956–)

Ciudades *cities* se hablan *are spoken* otras *other* mayoría *majority* pintor *painter* abogada *lawyer* sur *south* mundo *world* pies *feet* dos veces más alto que *twice as tall as*

Las islas Galápagos

COLOMBIA

Indígenas del Amazonas

Río Esmeraldas

• Ibarra

Quito ★

Volcán Cotopaxi

Río Napo

Portoviejo •

Volcán Tungurahua

Río Pastaza

Río Daule

Cordillera de los Andes

Guayaquil •

Volcán Chimborazo

Océano Pacífico

Cuenca

Machala

La ciudad de Quito y la Cordillera de los Andes

• Loja

Muchos indígenas de Ecuador hablan quichua.

ESTADOS UNIDOS

OCÉANO PACÍFICO

OCÉANO ATLÁNTICO

ECUADOR

AMÉRICA DEL SUR

PERÚ

Catedral de Guayaquil

recursos

WB pp. 171–172

VM pp. 175–176

Ⓢ vhlcentral.com Lección 3

¡Increíble pero cierto!

El volcán Cotopaxi, situado a unos 60 kilómetros al sur° de Quito, es considerado el volcán activo más alto del mundo°. Tiene una altura de 5.897 metros (19.340 pies°). Es dos veces más alto que° el monte Santa Elena (2.550 metros o 9.215 pies) en el estado de Washington.

Lugares • Las islas Galápagos

Muchas personas vienen de lejos a visitar las islas Galápagos porque son un verdadero tesoro° ecológico. Aquí Charles Darwin estudió° las especies que inspiraron° sus ideas sobre la evolución. Como las Galápagos están lejos del continente, sus plantas y animales son únicos. Las islas son famosas por sus tortugas° gigantes.

Artes • Oswaldo Guayasamín

Oswaldo Guayasamín fue° uno de los artistas latinoamericanos más famosos del mundo. Fue escultor° y muralista. Su expresivo estilo viene del cubismo y sus temas preferidos son la injusticia y la pobreza° sufridas° por los indígenas de su país.

Madre y niño en azul, 1986, Oswaldo Guayasamín

Deportes • El *trekking*

El sistema montañoso de los Andes cruza° y divide Ecuador en varias regiones. La Sierra, que tiene volcanes, grandes valles y una variedad increíble de plantas y animales, es perfecta para el *trekking*. Muchos turistas visitan Ecuador cada° año para hacer° *trekking* y escalar montañas°.

Lugares • Latitud 0

Hay un monumento en Ecuador, a unos 22 kilómetros (14 millas) de Quito, donde los visitantes están en el hemisferio norte y el hemisferio sur a la vez°. Este monumento se llama la Mitad del Mundo° y es un destino turístico muy popular.

Explosión del volcán Tungurahua

¿Qué aprendiste? Completa las oraciones con la información correcta.

1. La ciudad más grande (*biggest*) de Ecuador es _____.
2. La capital de Ecuador es _____.
3. Unos 4.000.000 de ecuatorianos hablan _____.
4. Darwin estudió el proceso de la evolución en _____.
5. Dos temas del arte de _____ son la pobreza y la _____.
6. Un monumento muy popular es _____.
7. La Sierra es un lugar perfecto para el _____.
8. El volcán _____ es el volcán activo más alto del mundo.

Conexión Internet Investiga estos temas en **vhlcentral.com**.

 Practice more at **vhlcentral.com**.

1. Busca información sobre una ciudad de Ecuador. ¿Te gustaría (*Would you like*) visitar la ciudad? ¿Por qué?
2. Haz una lista de tres animales o plantas que viven sólo en las islas Galápagos. ¿Dónde hay animales o plantas similares?

verdadero tesoro *true treasure* **estudió** *studied* **inspiraron** *inspired* **tortugas** *tortoises* **fue** *was* **escultor** *sculptor* **pobreza** *poverty* **sufridas** *suffered* **cruza** *crosses* **cada** *every* **hacer** *to do* **escalar montañas** *to climb mountains* **a la vez** *at the same time* **Mitad del Mundo** *Equatorial Line Monument (lit. Midpoint of the World)*

La familia

el/la abuelo/a	grandfather/grandmother
los abuelos	grandparents
el apellido	last name; surname
el/la bisabuelo/a	great-grandfather/great-grandmother
el/la cuñado/a	brother-in-law/sister-in-law
el/la esposo/a	husband/wife; spouse
la familia	family
el/la gemelo/a	twin
el/la hermanastro/a	stepbrother/stepsister
el/la hermano/a	brother/sister
el/la hijastro/a	stepson/stepdaughter
el/la hijo/a	son/daughter
los hijos	children
la madrastra	stepmother
la madre	mother
el/la medio/a hermano/a	half-brother/half-sister
el/la nieto/a	grandson/granddaughter
la nuera	daughter-in-law
el padrastro	stepfather
el padre	father
los padres	parents
los parientes	relatives
el/la primo/a	cousin
el/la sobrino/a	nephew/niece
el/la suegro/a	father-in-law/mother-in-law
el/la tío/a	uncle/aunt
el yerno	son-in-law

Otras personas

el/la amigo/a	friend
la gente	people
el/la muchacho/a	boy/girl
el/la niño/a	child
el/la novio/a	boyfriend/girlfriend
la persona	person

Profesiones

el/la artista	artist
el/la doctor(a), el/la médico/a	doctor; physician
el/la ingeniero/a	engineer
el/la periodista	journalist
el/la programador(a)	computer programmer

Adjetivos

alto/a	tall
antipático/a	unpleasant
bajo/a	short (in height)
bonito/a	pretty
buen, bueno/a	good
delgado/a	thin; slender
difícil	difficult; hard
fácil	easy
feo/a	ugly
gordo/a	fat
gran, grande	big; large
guapo/a	handsome; good-looking
importante	important
inteligente	intelligent
interesante	interesting
joven (sing.), jóvenes (pl.)	young
mal, malo/a	bad
mismo/a	same
moreno/a	brunet(te)
mucho/a	much; many; a lot of
pelirrojo/a	red-haired
pequeño/a	small
rubio/a	blond(e)
simpático/a	nice; likeable
tonto/a	silly; foolish
trabajador(a)	hard-working
viejo/a	old

Nacionalidades

alemán, alemana	German
argentino/a	Argentine
canadiense	Canadian
chino/a	Chinese
costarricense	Costa Rican
cubano/a	Cuban
ecuatoriano/a	Ecuadorian
español(a)	Spanish
estadounidense	from the U.S.
francés, francesa	French
inglés, inglesa	English
italiano/a	Italian
japonés, japonesa	Japanese
mexicano/a	Mexican
norteamericano/a	(North) American
puertorriqueño/a	Puerto Rican
ruso/a	Russian

Verbos

abrir	to open
aprender (a + *inf.*)	to learn
asistir (a)	to attend
beber	to drink
comer	to eat
compartir	to share
comprender	to understand
correr	to run
creer (en)	to believe (in)
deber (+ *inf.*)	should; must; ought to
decidir (+ *inf.*)	to decide
describir	to describe
escribir	to write
leer	to read
recibir	to receive
tener	to have
venir	to come
vivir	to live

Possessive adjectives	See page 139.
Expressions with *tener*	See page 147.
Expresiones útiles	See page 129.

Audio: Vocabulary Flashcards

recursos
LM p. 184
vhlcentral.com
Lección 3

contextos

1 **La familia** Look at the family tree and describe the relationships between these people.

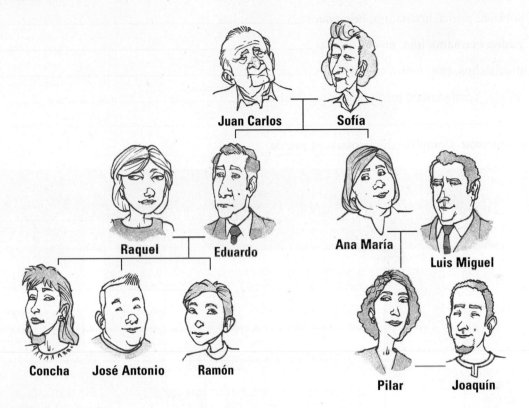

modelo

Eduardo / Concha
Eduardo es el padre de Concha.

1. Juan Carlos y Sofía / Pilar

_____

2. Pilar / Ana María y Luis Miguel

_____

3. Eduardo / Raquel

_____

4. José Antonio y Ramón / Concha

_____

5. Raquel / Pilar

_____

6. Concha, José Antonio y Ramón / Pilar

_____

7. Ana María / Raquel

_____

8. Joaquín / Ana María y Luis Miguel

_____

2 **Diferente** Write the word that does not belong in each group.

1. ingeniera, médica, programadora, periodista, hijastra _____

2. cuñado, nieto, yerno, suegra, nuera _____

3. sobrina, prima, artista, tía, hermana _____

4. padre, hermano, hijo, novio, abuelo _____

5. muchachos, tíos, niños, chicos, hijos _____

6. amiga, hermanastra, media hermana, madrastra _____

3 **Crucigrama** Complete this crossword puzzle.

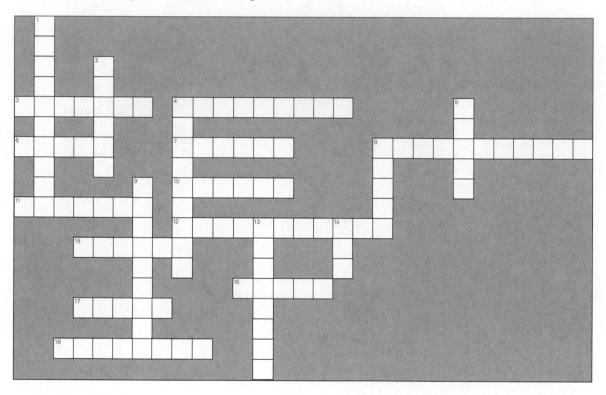

Horizontales

3. el hijo de mi hermano
4. la esposa de mi padre, pero no soy su hijo
6. el hijo de mi hija
7. el esposo de mi hermana
8. hombre que estudió (*studied*) computación
10. la madre de mi padre
11. padre, madre e (*and*) hijos
12. el hijo de mi madrastra, pero no de mi padre
15. doctor
16. Tus nietos son los _____ de tus hijos
17. personas en general
18. la hija de mi esposa, pero no es mi hija

Verticales

1. mujer que escribe (*writes*) para el *New York Times*
2. compañeros inseparables
4. chicos
5. el esposo de mi madre es el _____ de mis abuelos
8. el hijo de mi tía
9. abuelos, primos, tíos, etc.
13. Pablo Picasso y Diego Velázquez
14. el hermano de mi madre

estructura

3.1 Descriptive adjectives

1 **¿Cómo son?** Use the adjective in parentheses that agrees with each subject to write descriptive sentences about them.

> **modelo**
> **(gordo, delgada)**
> Lidia: Lidia *es delgada.*
> el novio de Olga: *El novio de Olga es gordo.*

(simpático, guapos, alta)

1. la profesora de historia: _____

2. David y Simón: _____

3. el artista: _____

(trabajadora, viejo, delgadas)

4. esas (*those*) muchachas: _____

5. el abuelo de Alberto: _____

6. la programadora: _____

2 **Descripciones** Complete each sentence with the correct forms of the adjectives in parentheses.

1. Lupe, Rosa y Tomás son _____ (bueno) amigos.

2. Ignacio es _____ _____ (alto) y _____ (guapo).

3. Lourdes y Virginia son _____ (bajo) y _____ (delgado).

4. Pedro y Vanessa son _____ (moreno), pero Diana es _____ (pelirrojo).

5. Nosotras somos _____ (inteligente) y _____ (trabajador).

6. Esos (*Those*) chicos son _____ (simpático), pero son _____ (tonto).

3 **No** Answer these questions using the adjective with the opposite meaning.

> **modelo**
> ¿Es alta Manuela?
> No, *es baja.*

1. ¿Es antipático don Antonio? _____

2. ¿Son morenas las hermanas de Lupe? _____

3. ¿Es fea la mamá de Carlos? _____

4. ¿Son viejos los primos de Sofía? _____

5. ¿Son malos los padres de Alejandro? _____

6. ¿Es guapo el tío de Andrés? _____

4 **Origen y nacionalidad** Read the names and origins of the people in this tour group. Then write sentences saying what city they are from and what their nationalities are.

> modelo
>
> Álvaro Estrada / Miami, Estados Unidos
> Álvaro Estrada **es de Miami. Es estadounidense.**

1. Lucy y Lee Hung / Pekín, China _____

2. Pierre y Marie Lebrun / Montreal, Canadá _____

3. Luigi Mazzini / Roma, Italia _____

4. Elizabeth Mitchell / Londres, Inglaterra (*England*) _____

5. Roberto Morales / Madrid, España _____

6. Andrés y Patricia Padilla / La Habana, Cuba _____

7. Paula y Cecilia Robles / San José, Costa Rica _____

8. Arnold Schmidt / Berlín, Alemania (*Germany*) _____

9. Antoinette y Marie Valois / París, Francia _____

10. Marta Zedillo / Guadalajara, México _____

5 **Completar** Complete each sentence with the correct form of each adjective in parentheses.

(bueno)

1. La clase de matemáticas es muy _____.

2. Rogelio es un _____ compañero de cuarto.

3. Agustina compra una _____ mochila para (*for*) los libros.

4. Andrés y Guillermo son muy _____ estudiantes.

(malo)

5. Federico es antipático y una _____ persona.

6. Ahora es un _____ momento para descansar.

7. La comida (*food*) de la cafetería es _____.

8. Son unas semanas _____ para viajar.

(grande)

9. Hay un _____ evento en el estadio hoy.

10. Los problemas en esa (*that*) familia son muy _____.

11. La biblioteca de la universidad es _____.

12. La prima de Irma es una _____ amiga.

3.2 Possessive adjectives

1

¿De quién es? Answer each question affirmatively using the correct possessive adjective.

> **modelo**
>
> ¿Es tu maleta?
> *Sí, es mi maleta.*

1. ¿Es la calculadora de Adela? _____

2. ¿Es mi clase de español? _____

3. ¿Son los papeles de la profesora? _____

4. ¿Es el diccionario de tu compañera de cuarto? _____

5. ¿Es tu novia? _____

6. ¿Son los lápices de ustedes? _____

2

Familia Write the appropriate forms of the possessive adjectives indicated in parentheses.

1. _____ (*My*) cuñada, Christine, es francesa.

2. _____ (*Their*) parientes están en Costa Rica.

3. ¿Quién es _____ (*your* fam.) tío?

4. _____ (*Our*) padres regresan a las diez.

5. Es _____ (*his*) tarea de matemáticas.

6. Linda y María son _____ (*my*) hijas.

7. ¿Dónde trabaja _____ (*your* form.) esposa?

8. _____ (*Our*) familia es grande.

3

Clarificar Add a prepositional phrase that clarifies to whom the item(s) belongs.

> **modelo**
>
> ¿Es su libro? (ellos)
> *¿Es el libro de ellos?*

1. ¿Cuál es su problema? (ella)

   _____

2. Trabajamos con su madre. (ellos)

   _____

3. ¿Dónde están sus papeles? (ustedes)

   _____

4. ¿Son sus plumas? (ella)

   _____

5. ¿Quiénes son sus compañeros de cuarto? (él)

   _____

6. ¿Cómo se llaman sus sobrinos? (usted)

   _____

4 Posesiones Write sentences using possessive adjectives to indicate who owns these items.

> **modelo**
>
> Yo compro un escritorio.
> Es mi *escritorio*.

1. Ustedes compran cuatro sillas. _____

2. Tú compras una mochila. _____

3. Nosotros compramos una mesa. _____

4. Yo compro una maleta. _____

5. Él compra unos lápices. _____

6. Ellos compran una calculadora. _____

5 Mi familia Paula is talking about her family. Complete her description with the correct possessive adjectives.

Somos cinco hermanos. Ricardo, José Luis y Alejandro son (1) _____ hermanos. Francisco es (2) _____ cuñado. Es el esposo de (3) _____ hermana mayor, Mercedes. Francisco es argentino. (4) _____ papás viven en Mar del Plata. Vicente es el hijo de (5) _____ hermano mayor, Ricardo. Él es (6) _____ sobrino favorito. (7) _____ mamá se llama Isabel y es española. Ellos viven con (8) _____ familia en Sevilla. José Luis estudia en Monterrey y vive con la tía Remedios y (9) _____ dos hijos, Carlos y Raquel, (10) _____ primos. Alejandro y yo vivimos con (11) _____ papás en Guadalajara. Los papás de (12) _____ mamá viven también con nosotros. Alejandro y yo compartimos (13) _____ problemas con (14) _____ abuelos. Ellos son muy buenos. Y tú, ¿cómo es (15) _____ familia?

6 Preguntas Answer these questions using possessive adjectives and the words in parentheses.

> **modelo**
>
> ¿Dónde está tu amiga? (Barcelona)
> Mi amiga *está en Barcelona*.

1. ¿Cómo es tu padre? (alto y moreno)

   _____

2. José, ¿dónde están mis papeles? (en el escritorio)

   _____

3. ¿Cómo es la escuela de Felipe? (pequeña y vieja)

   _____

4. ¿Son mexicanos los amigos de ustedes? (puertorriqueños)

   _____

5. Mami, ¿dónde está mi tarea? (en la mesa)

   _____

6. ¿Cómo son los hermanos de Pilar? (simpáticos)

   _____

3.3 Present tense of **-er** and **-ir** verbs

1 **Conversaciones** Complete these conversations with the correct forms of the verbs in parentheses.

(leer)

1. —¿Qué _____, Ana?

2. —_____ un libro de historia.

(vivir)

3. —¿Dónde _____ ustedes?

4. — Nosotros _____ en Nueva York. ¿Y tú?

(comer)

5. —¿Qué _____ ustedes?

6. — Yo _____ un sándwich y Eduardo _____ pizza.

(deber)

7. —Profesora, ¿ _____ abrir nuestros libros ahora?

8. —Sí, ustedes _____ abrir los libros en la página (*page*) 87.

(escribir)

9. —¿_____ un libro, Melinda?

10. — Sí, _____ un libro de ciencia ficción.

2 **Frases** Write complete sentences using the correct forms of the verbs in parentheses.

1. (nosotros) (Escribir) muchas composiciones en la clase de literatura.

_____

2. Esteban y Luisa (aprender) a bailar el tango.

_____

3. ¿Quién no (comprender) la lección de hoy?

_____

4. (tú) (Deber) comprar un mapa de Quito.

_____

5. Ellos no (recibir) muchos mensajes electrónicos (*e-mails*) de sus padres.

_____

6. (yo) (Buscar) unas fotos de mis primos.

_____

3 **¿Qué verbo es?** Choose the most logical verb to complete each sentence, and write the correct form.

1. Tú _____ (abrir, correr, decidir) en el parque (*park*), ¿no?

2. Yo _____ (asistir, compartir, leer) a conciertos de Juanes.

3. ¿_____ (aprender, creer, deber) a leer tu sobrino?

4. Yo no _____ (beber, vivir, comprender) la tarea de física.

5. Los estudiantes _____ (escribir, beber, comer) hamburguesas en la cafetería.

6. Mi esposo y yo _____ (decidir, leer, deber) el *Miami Herald*.

4 **Tú y ellos** Rewrite each sentence using the subject in parentheses. Change the verb form and possessive adjectives as needed.

> **modelo**
> Carolina no lee sus libros. (nosotros)
> **Nosotros no leemos nuestros libros.**

1. Rubén cree que la lección 3 es fácil. (ellos)

   _____

2. Mis hermanos aprenden alemán en la universidad. (mi tía)

   _____

3. Aprendemos a hablar, leer y escribir en la clase de español. (yo)

   _____

4. Sandra escribe en su diario todos los días (*everyday*). (tú)

   _____

5. Comparto mis problemas con mis padres. (Víctor)

   _____

6. Vives en una residencia interesante y bonita. (nosotras)

   _____

5 **Descripciones** Look at the drawings and use these verbs to describe what the people are doing.

| abrir | aprender | comer | leer |

1. Nosotros _____ 2. Yo _____

3. Mirta _____ 4. Los estudiantes _____

3.4 Present tense of **tener** and **venir**

1   **Completar** Complete these sentences with the correct forms of **tener** and **venir**.

1. ¿A qué hora _____ ustedes al estadio?

2. ¿_____ tú a la universidad en autobús?

3. Nosotros _____ una prueba de psicología mañana.

4. ¿Por qué no _____ Juan a la clase de literatura?

5. Yo _____ dos hermanos y mi prima _____ tres.

6. ¿_____ ustedes fotos de sus parientes?

7. Mis padres _____ unos amigos japoneses.

8. Inés _____ con su esposo y yo _____ con Ernesto.

9. Marta y yo no _____ al laboratorio los sábados.

10. ¿Cuántos nietos _____ tú?

11. Yo _____ una clase de contabilidad a las once de la mañana.

12. Mis amigos _____ a comer a la cafetería hoy.

2   **¿Qué tienen?** Rewrite each sentence, using the logical expression with **tener**.

1. Los estudiantes (tienen hambre, tienen miedo de) tomar el examen de química.

   _____

2. Las turistas (tienen sueño, tienen prisa) por llegar al autobús.

   _____

3. Mi madre (tiene cincuenta años, tiene razón) siempre (*always*).

   _____

4. Vienes a la cafetería cuando (*when*) (tienes hambre, tienes frío).

   _____

5. (Tengo razón, Tengo frío) en la biblioteca porque abren las ventanas.

   _____

6. Rosaura y María (tienen calor, tienen ganas) de mirar la televisión.

   _____

7. Nosotras (tenemos cuidado, no tenemos razón) con el sol (*sun*).

   _____

8. David toma mucha agua cuando (*when*) (tiene miedo, tiene sed).

   _____

3 **Expresiones con *tener*** Complete each sentence with the correct expression and the appropriate form of **tener**.

tener cuidado	tener miedo	tener mucha suerte	tener que
tener ganas	tener mucha hambre	tener prisa	tener razón

1. Mis sobrinos _____ del perro (*dog*) de mis abuelos.

2. Necesitas _____ con la computadora portátil (*laptop*).

3. Yo _____ practicar el vocabulario de español.

4. Lola y yo _____ de escuchar música latina.

5. Anita cree que (*that*) dos más dos son cinco. Ella no _____.

6. Ganas (*You win*) cien dólares en la lotería. Tú _____.

Síntesis

Tus parientes Choose an interesting relative of yours and write a description of that person. Answer these questions in your description.

- ¿Quién es?
- ¿Cómo es?
- ¿De dónde viene?
- ¿Cuántos hermanos/primos/hijos... tiene?

- ¿Cómo es su familia?
- ¿Dónde vive?
- ¿Cuántos años tiene?
- ¿De qué tiene miedo?

_____

_____

_____

_____

_____

_____

_____

_____

_____

_____

_____

_____

_____

panorama

Ecuador

1 **¿Cierto o falso?** Indicate whether the statements are **cierto** or **falso**. Correct the false statements.

1. Ecuador tiene aproximadamente el área de Rhode Island.

   _____

2. Panamá y Chile limitan con (*border*) Ecuador.

   _____

3. Las islas Galápagos están en el océano Pacífico.

   _____

4. Quito está en la cordillera de los Andes.

   _____

5. Todos (*All*) los ecuatorianos hablan lenguas indígenas.

   _____

6. Rosalía Arteaga es novelista y pintora.

   _____

7. Hay volcanes activos en Ecuador.

   _____

8. Oswaldo Guayasamín fue un novelista ecuatoriano famoso.

   _____

2 **El mapa de Ecuador** Fill in the blanks on this map with the correct geographical names.

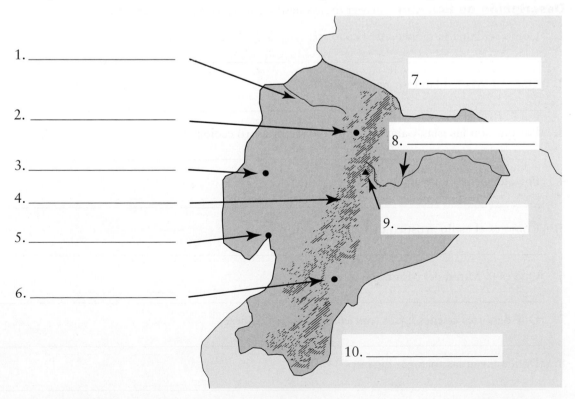

1. _____

2. _____

3. _____

4. _____

5. _____

6. _____

7. _____

8. _____

9. _____

10. _____

3 **Fotos de Ecuador** Label the place shown in each photograph.

1. _____

2. _____   3. _____

4 **Descripción de Ecuador** Answer these questions using complete sentences.

1. ¿Cómo se llama la moneda de Ecuador?

_____

2. ¿Qué idiomas hablan los ecuatorianos?

_____

3. ¿Por qué son las islas Galápagos un verdadero tesoro ecológico?

_____

4. ¿Por qué vienen muchos turistas a Ecuador?

_____

5. ¿Cómo es el estilo artístico de Guayasamín?

_____

6. ¿Qué es la Mitad del Mundo?

_____

7. ¿Qué deportes puedes hacer (*can you do*) en los Andes?

_____

8. ¿Dónde viven las tortugas gigantes?

_____

Un domingo en familia

Lección 3
Fotonovela

Antes de ver el video

1   **Examinar el título** Look at the title of the episode. Based on the title and the image below, imagine what you think you will see.

_____

_____

_____

_____

_____

_____

Mientras ves el video

2   **Completar** Fill in the blanks for each sentence from column A with a word from column B, according to **Un domingo en familia**.

A	B
1. Marta _____ ocho años.	trabajadora
2. Las hijas de Nayeli son simpáticas y _____.	tiene
3. La _____ de Ramón y Roberto se llama Ana María.	vive
4. Jimena dice que Felipe es _____ y feo.	gordo
5. Jimena es muy _____.	bonitas
6. Ana María _____ en Mérida.	hermana

3   **En Xochimilco** Check off each person or thing that appears.

_____ 1. a Biology book   _____ 5. Felipe's uncle   _____ 9. people eating

_____ 2. Marissa's grandparents   _____ 6. a soccer ball   _____ 10. Felipe's girlfriend

_____ 3. Jimena's cousins   _____ 7. trajineras   _____ 11. Jimena's dad

_____ 4. a desk   _____ 8. mariachis   _____ 12. Ana María's son-in-law

4   **¿Cierto o falso?** Indicate whether each statement is **cierto** or **falso**.

	Cierto	Falso
1. Felipe tiene mucha hambre.	O	O
2. El ex novio de Marissa es alemán.	O	O
3. Ana María tiene tres hijos.	O	O
4. Marissa tiene una sobrina que se llama Olivia.	O	O
5. La señora Díaz dice que su cuñada es muy simpática.	O	O

Después de ver el video

5   **Seleccionar** Select the letter of the word or phrase that goes in each sentence.

1. Roberto es el _____ de Felipe y Jimena.
   a. tío   b. primo   c. padre   d. sobrino

2. Los abuelos de Marissa son _____.
   a. ecuatorianos   b. españoles   c. mexicanos   d. alemanes

3. Adam es el _____ de Marissa.
   a. hermano menor   b. tío   c. primo   d. cuñado

4. Carolina tiene una _____ que se llama Ana María.
   a. tía   b. cuñada   c. hermana   d. prima

5. Las _____ de Nayeli son _____.
   a. primas; altas   b. hermanas; trabajadoras   c. hijas; simpáticas   d. sobrinas; guapas

6. La _____ de Nayeli es muy _____.
   a. sobrina; trabajadora   b. abuela; vieja   c. mamá; simpática   d. tía; alta

7. La _____ de Carolina tiene _____.
   a. tía; hambre   b. hija; sed   c. sobrina; frío   d. familia; sueño

8. Marissa decide ir a _____.
   a. la librería   b. la cafetería   c. Mérida   d. el estadio

6   **Preguntas** Answer the questions, using complete sentences.

1. ¿Quién tiene tres hermanos?

2. ¿Cuántos años tiene Valentina, la hija de Nayeli?

3. ¿Quién es hija única?

4. ¿Cómo se llama el hermano de Jimena?

5. ¿Cómo se llama el padre de Felipe?

7   **Preguntas personales** Answer the questions about your family.

1. ¿Cuántas personas hay en tu familia? ¿Cuál es más grande (*bigger*), tu familia o la familia de Jimena?

2. ¿Tienes hermanos/as? ¿Cómo se llaman?

3. ¿Tienes un(a) primo/a favorito/a? ¿Cómo es?

4. ¿Cómo es tu tío/a favorito/a? ¿Dónde vive?

Nombre _____

Fecha _____

Panorama: Ecuador

Lección 3
Panorama cultural

Antes de ver el video

1 **Más vocabulario** Look over these useful words and expressions before you watch the video.

Vocabulario útil		
algunas *some*	otro *other*	todo *every*
científico *scientist*	pingüino *penguin*	tomar fotografías *to take pictures*
guía *guide*	recurso *resource*	tortuga *tortoise*

2 **Foto** Describe the video still. Write at least three sentences in Spanish.

_____

_____

_____

_____

_____

_____

3 **Predecir** Look at the video still from the previous activity and write at least two sentences in Spanish about what you think you will see in this video.

_____

_____

_____

4 **Emparejar** Find the items in the second column that correspond to the ones in the first.

_____ 1. grande   a. near

_____ 2. pequeña   b. about

_____ 3. vieja   c. here

_____ 4. también   d. big

_____ 5. aquí   e. very

_____ 6. sobre   f. old

_____ 7. muy   g. also

_____ 8. cerca de   h. small

_____ 9. para   i. for

Video Manual

Mientras ves el video

5 **Marcar** Check off the verbs you hear while watching the video.

_____ 1. aprender   _____ 5. escribir   _____ 9. tener

_____ 2. bailar   _____ 6. estudiar   _____ 10. tomar

_____ 3. beber   _____ 7. leer   _____ 11. vivir

_____ 4. comprar   _____ 8. recibir

Después de ver el video

6 **Responder** Answer the questions in Spanish. Use complete sentences.

1. ¿En qué océano están las islas Galápagos?

_____

_____

2. ¿Qué hacen los científicos que viven en las islas?

_____

_____

3. ¿Qué hacen los turistas que visitan las islas?

_____

_____

4. ¿Qué proyectos tiene la Fundación Charles Darwin?

_____

_____

5. ¿Cuáles son los animales más grandes que viven en las islas?

_____

_____

6. ¿Por qué son importantes estas islas?

_____

_____

7 **Preferencias** Of all the animals you saw in this video, which was your favorite? Write three sentences in Spanish describing your favorite animal.

_____

_____

_____

_____

La familia

Antes de ver el video

Lección 3
Flash cultura

1 **Más vocabulario** Look over these useful words before you watch the video.

Vocabulario útil	
el canelazo *typical drink from Ecuador*	¡Qué familia tan grande tiene! *Your family is so big!*
la casa *house*	¡Qué grande es tu casa…! *Your house is so big!*
Día de la Madre *Mother's Day*	¿Quién pelea con quién? *Who fights with whom?*
Ésta es la cocina. *This is the kitchen.*	te muestro *I'll show you*
Éste es un patio interior.	Vamos. *Let's go.*
This is an interior patio.	

2 **¡En español!** Look at the video still. Imagine what Mónica will say about families in Ecuador, and write a two- or three-sentence introduction to this episode.

Mónica, Quito

¡Hola, amigos! Bienvenidos a otra aventura de *Flash cultura*. Hoy vamos (*we are going*) a hablar de… _____

_____

_____

_____

_____

_____

_____

Mientras ves el video

3 **Identificar** Identify which family these people belong to: **los Valdivieso**, **los Bolaños**, or both.

Personas	Los Valdivieso	Los Bolaños
1. abuelos	_____	_____
2. novia	_____	_____
3. esposo	_____	_____
4. esposa	_____	_____
5. sobrinos	_____	_____
6. dos hijos y una hija	_____	_____

4   **Emparejar** Watch as Mrs. Valdivieso gives Mónica a tour of the house. Match the captions to the appropriate images.

1. _____   2. _____   3. _____

a. Y éste es el comedor…
   Todos comemos aquí.

b. Vamos, te enseño el
   resto de la casa.

c. Éste es un patio interior.
   Aquí hacemos reuniones
   familiares.

d. Finalmente, ésta es
   la cocina.

e. ¿Qué están haciendo hoy
   en el parque?

Después de ver el video

5   **¿Cierto o falso?** Indicate whether each statement is **cierto** (*true*) or **falso** (*false*).

1. En el parque, una familia celebra el Día de la Madre. _____

2. La familia Valdivieso representa la familia moderna y la familia Bolaños representa la familia tradicional. _____

3. Los Bolaños no viven (*do not live*) en Quito. _____

4. Bernardo tiene animales en su casa. _____

5. Los Valdivieso toman canelazo. _____

6   **¿Qué te gusta?** Imagine that you are one of the Valdivieso children and that Mónica asks you about your likes and dislikes. Select one of the children and write a paragraph using the cues provided.

| bailar | dibujar | hermanos | padres |

_____

_____

_____

_____

7   **Andy, un chico con novia** Andy's parents just found out that he has a girlfriend. Imagine that they are being introduced to her for the first time. Write five questions they would ask her.

_____

_____

_____

_____

contextos

1 **Escoger** You will hear some questions. Look at the family tree and choose the correct answer to each question.

La familia González

Juan Carlos   Sofía

Raquel   Eduardo   Ana María

Luis Miguel

Concha   José Antonio   Ramón

Pilar   Joaquín

1. a. Pilar   b. Concha   5. a. José Antonio y Ramón   b. Eduardo y Ana María
2. a. Luis Miguel b. Eduardo   6. a. Joaquín   b. Eduardo
3. a. Sofía   b. Ana María   7. a. Ana María   b. Sofía
4. a. Raquel   b. Sofía   8. a. Luis Miguel   b. Juan Carlos

2 **La familia González** Héctor wants to verify the relationship between various members of the González family. Look at the drawing and answer his questions with the correct information. Repeat the correct response after the speaker. (*6 items*)

> **modelo**
>
> Juan Carlos es el abuelo de Eduardo, ¿verdad?
> No, Juan Carlos es el padre de Eduardo.

3 **Profesiones** Listen to each statement and write the number of the statement below the drawing it describes.

a. _____   b. _____   c. _____   d. _____

pronunciación

Diphthongs and linking

In Spanish, **a**, **e**, and **o** are considered strong vowels. The weak vowels are **i** and **u**.

    hermano   niña   cuñado

A diphthong is a combination of two weak vowels or of a strong vowel and a weak vowel. Diphthongs are pronounced as a single syllable.

    ruido   parientes   periodista

Two identical vowel sounds that appear together are pronounced like one long vowel.

    la abuela   mi hijo   una clase excelente

Two identical consonants together sound like a single consonant.

    con Natalia   sus sobrinos   las sillas

A consonant at the end of a word is always linked with the vowel sound at the beginning of the next word.

    Es ingeniera.   mis abuelos   sus hijos

A vowel at the end of a word is always linked with the vowel sound at the beginning of the next word.

    mi hermano   su esposa   nuestro amigo

1   **Práctica** Repeat each word after the speaker, focusing on the diphthongs.

1. historia	4. novia	7. puerta	10. estudiar
2. nieto	5. residencia	8. ciencias	11. izquierda
3. parientes	6. prueba	9. lenguas	12. ecuatoriano

2   **Oraciones** When you hear the number, read the corresponding sentence aloud. Then listen to the speaker and repeat the sentence.

1. Hola. Me llamo Anita Amaral. Soy del Ecuador.
2. Somos seis en mi familia.
3. Tengo dos hermanos y una hermana.
4. Mi papá es del Ecuador y mi mamá es de España.

3   **Refranes** Repeat each saying after the speaker to practice diphthongs and linking sounds.

1. Cuando una puerta se cierra, otra se abre.
2. Hablando del rey de Roma, por la puerta se asoma.

4   **Dictado** You will hear eight sentences. Each will be said twice. Listen carefully and write what you hear.

1. _____
2. _____
3. _____
4. _____
5. _____
6. _____
7. _____
8. _____

estructura

3.1 Descriptive adjectives

1 **Transformar** Change each sentence from the masculine to the feminine. Repeat the correct answer after the speaker. (*6 items*)

> **modelo**
> *El chico es mexicano.*
> La chica es mexicana.

2 **Cambiar** Change each sentence from the singular to the plural. Repeat the correct answer after the speaker. (*6 items*)

> **modelo**
> *El profesor es ecuatoriano.*
> *Los profesores son ecuatorianos.*

3 **Mis compañeros de clase** Describe your classmates, using the cues in your lab manual. Repeat the correct response after the speaker.

> **modelo**
> *You hear:* María
> *You see:* alto
> *You say:* María es alta.

1. simpático
2. rubio
3. inteligente
4. pelirrojo y muy bonito
5. alto y moreno
6. delgado y trabajador
7. bajo y gordo
8. tonto

4 **Completar** Listen to the following description and write the missing words in your lab manual.

Mañana mis parientes llegan de Guayaquil. Son cinco personas: mi abuela Isabel, tío Carlos y tía Josefina, y mis primos Susana y Tomás. Mi prima es (1) _____ y (2) _____. Baila muy bien. Tomás es un niño (3) _____, pero es (4) _____. Tío Carlos es (5) _____ y (6) _____. Tía Josefina es (7) _____ y (8) _____. Mi abuela es (9) _____ y muy (10) _____.

5 **La familia Rivas** Look at the photo of the Rivas family and listen to each statement. Indicate whether the statement is **cierto** or **falso**.

	Cierto	Falso
1.	○	○
2.	○	○
3.	○	○
4.	○	○
5.	○	○
6.	○	○
7.	○	○

3.2 Possessive adjectives

1 **Identificar** Listen to each statement and mark an **X** in the column for the possessive adjective you hear.

> **modelo**
>
> *You hear:* Es mi diccionario de español.
> *You mark:* an **X** under **my**.

	my	*your* (familiar)	*your* (formal)	*his/her*	*our*	*their*
Modelo	X					
1.						
2.						
3.						
4.						
5.						
6.						
7.						
8.						

2 **Escoger** Listen to each question and choose the most logical response.

1. a. No, su hijastro no está aquí.
   b. Sí, tu hijastro está aquí.
2. a. No, nuestros abuelos son argentinos.
   b. Sí, sus abuelos son norteamericanos.
3. a. Sí, tu hijo trabaja ahora.
   b. Sí, mi hijo trabaja en la librería Goya.
4. a. Sus padres regresan hoy a las nueve.
   b. Mis padres regresan hoy a las nueve.
5. a. Nuestra hermana se llama Margarita.
   b. Su hermana se llama Margarita.
6. a. Tus plumas están en el escritorio.
   b. Sus plumas están en el escritorio.
7. a. No, mi sobrino es ingeniero.
   b. Sí, nuestro sobrino es programador.
8. a. Su horario es muy bueno.
   b. Nuestro horario es muy bueno.

3 **Preguntas** Answer each question you hear in the affirmative using the appropriate possessive adjective. Repeat the correct response after the speaker. (7 items)

> **modelo**
>
> ¿Es tu lápiz?
> Sí, *es mi lápiz.*

3.3 Present tense of **-er** and **-ir** verbs

1 **Identificar** Listen to each statement and mark an **X** in the column for the subject of the verb.

> **modelo**
>
> *You hear:* Corro con Dora mañana.
> *You mark:* an **X** under **yo**.

	yo	tú	él/ella	nosotros/as	ellos/ellas
Modelo	X				
1.					
2.					
3.					
4.					
5.					
6.					

2 **Cambiar** Listen to the following statements. Using the cues you hear, say that these people do the same activities. Repeat the correct answer after the speaker. (*8 items*)

> **modelo**
>
> Julia aprende francés. (mi amigo)
> **Mi amigo también aprende francés.**

3 **Preguntas** Answer each question you hear in the negative. Repeat the correct response after the speaker. (*8 items*)

> **modelo**
>
> ¿Viven ellos en una residencia estudiantil?
> **No, ellos no viven en una residencia estudiantil.**

4 **Describir** Listen to each statement and write the number of the statement below the drawing it describes.

a. _____ b. _____ c. _____ d. _____

3.4 Present tense of **tener** and **venir**

1 **Cambiar** Form a new sentence using the cue you hear as the subject. Repeat the correct answer after the speaker. (*6 items*)

> **modelo**
> Alicia viene a las seis. (David y Rita)
> *David y Rita vienen a las seis.*

2 **Consejos (*Advice*)** Some people are not doing what they should. Say what they have to do. Repeat the correct response after the speaker. (*6 items*)

> **modelo**
> Elena no trabaja.
> *Elena tiene que trabajar.*

3 **Preguntas** Answer each question you hear using the cue in your lab manual. Repeat the correct answer after the speaker.

> **modelo**
> ¿Tienen sueño los niños? (no)
> *No, los niños no tienen sueño.*

1. sí, (yo)
2. Roberto
3. no, (nosotros)
4. sí, dos, (yo)
5. sí, (mi abuela)
6. mis tíos
7. el domingo

4 **Situaciones** Listen to each situation and choose the appropriate **tener** expression. Each situation will be repeated.

1. a. Tienes sueño.   b. Tienes prisa.
2. a. Tienen mucho cuidado.   b. Tienen hambre.
3. a. Tenemos mucho calor.   b. Tenemos mucho frío.
4. a. Tengo sed.   b. Tengo hambre.
5. a. Ella tiene razón.   b. Ella no tiene razón.
6. a. Tengo miedo.   b. Tengo sueño.

5 **Mi familia** Listen to the following description. Then read the statements in your lab manual and decide whether they are **cierto** or **falso**.

	Cierto	Falso		Cierto	Falso
1. Francisco desea ser periodista.	○	○	4. Él tiene una familia pequeña.	○	○
2. Francisco tiene 20 años.	○	○	5. Su madre es inglesa.	○	○
3. Francisco vive con su familia.	○	○	6. Francisco tiene una hermana mayor.	○	○

vocabulario

You will now hear the vocabulary found in your textbook on the last page of this lesson. Listen and repeat each Spanish word or phrase after the speaker.

Additional Vocabulary

Additional Vocabulary

Notes

Notes

Los pasatiempos

4

contextos

fotonovela

cultura

estructura

adelante

A PRIMERA VISTA
- ¿Es esta persona un atleta o un artista?
- ¿En qué tiene interés, en el ciclismo o en el tenis?
- ¿Es viejo? ¿Es delgado?
- ¿Tiene frío o calor?

Más práctica
Workbook pages 221–232
Video Manual pages 233–238
Lab Manual pages 239–244

Los pasatiempos

Más vocabulario

el béisbol	baseball
el ciclismo	cycling
el esquí (acuático)	(water) skiing
el fútbol americano	football
el golf	golf
el hockey	hockey
la natación	swimming
el tenis	tennis
el vóleibol	volleyball
el equipo	team
el parque	park
el partido	game; match
la plaza	city or town square
andar en patineta	to skateboard
bucear	to scuba dive
escalar montañas (*f., pl.*)	to climb mountains
esquiar	to ski
ganar	to win
ir de excursión	to go on a hike
practicar deportes (*m., pl.*)	to play sports
escribir una carta/ un mensaje electrónico	to write a letter/ an e-mail
leer correo electrónico	to read e-mail
leer una revista	to read a magazine
deportivo/a	sports-related

Variación léxica

piscina ⟷ pileta (*Arg.*); alberca (*Méx.*)
baloncesto ⟷ básquetbol (*Amér. L.*)
béisbol ⟷ pelota (*P. Rico, Rep. Dom.*)

Lee el periódico. (leer)

Pasea en bicicleta. (pasear)

la pelota

el fútbol

la jugadora

Visitan el monumento. (visitar)

Pasean. (pasear)

Toma el sol. (tomar)

Nada. (nadar)

la piscina

Patina en línea.
(patinar)

el jugador

el baloncesto

Práctica

1 Escuchar 🎧 Indicate the letter of the activity in Column B that best corresponds to each statement you hear. Two items in Column B will not be used.

Lección 4

A	B
1. _____	a. leer correo electrónico
2. _____	b. tomar el sol
3. _____	c. pasear en bicicleta
4. _____	d. ir a un partido de fútbol americano
5. _____	e. escribir una carta
6. _____	f. practicar muchos deportes
	g. nadar
	h. ir de excursión

2 Ordenar 🎧 Order these activities according to what you hear in the narration.

_____ a. pasear en bicicleta   _____ d. tomar el sol

_____ b. nadar   _____ e. practicar deportes

_____ c. leer una revista   _____ f. patinar en línea

3 ¿Cierto o falso? Indicate whether each statement is **cierto** or **falso** based on the illustration.

	Cierto	Falso
1. Un hombre nada en la piscina.	○	○
2. Un hombre lee una revista.	○	○
3. Un chico pasea en bicicleta.	○	○
4. Dos muchachos esquían.	○	○
5. Una mujer y dos niños visitan un monumento.	○	○
6. Un hombre bucea.	○	○
7. Hay un equipo de hockey.	○	○
8. Una mujer toma el sol.	○	○

4 Clasificar Fill in the chart below with as many terms from **Contextos** as you can.

Actividades	Deportes	Personas
_____	_____	_____
_____	_____	_____
_____	_____	_____
_____	_____	_____
_____	_____	_____
_____	_____	_____

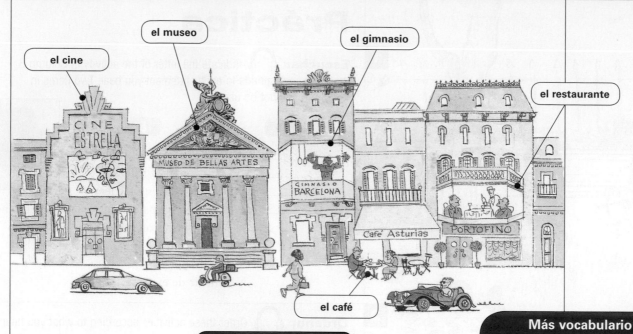

el cine

el museo

el gimnasio

el restaurante

el café

En el centro

Más vocabulario

la diversión	fun activity; entertainment; recreation
el fin de semana	weekend
el pasatiempo	pastime; hobby
los ratos libres	spare (free) time
el videojuego	video game
la iglesia	church
el lugar	place
ver películas (f., pl.)	to watch movies
favorito/a	favorite

5 **Identificar** Identify the place where these activities would take place.

modelo

Esquiamos. Es una montaña.

1. Tomamos una limonada.
2. Vemos una película.
3. Nadamos y tomamos el sol.
4. Hay muchos monumentos.
5. Comemos tacos y fajitas.
6. Miramos pinturas (*paintings*) de Diego Rivera y Frida Kahlo.
7. Hay mucho tráfico.
8. Practicamos deportes.

6 **Preguntar** Ask a classmate what he or she does in the places mentioned below. Your classmate will respond using verbs from the word bank.

modelo

una plaza

Estudiante 1: ¿Qué haces (*do you do*) cuando estás en una plaza?
Estudiante 2: Camino por la plaza y miro a las personas.

beber	escalar	mirar	practicar
caminar	escribir	nadar	tomar
correr	leer	patinar	visitar

1. una biblioteca
2. un estadio
3. una plaza
4. una piscina
5. las montañas
6. un parque
7. un café
8. un museo

 Practice more at **vhlcentral.com**.

Comunicación

Lección 4

7

Crucigrama Your instructor will give you and your partner an incomplete crossword puzzle. Yours has the words your partner needs and vice versa. In order to complete the puzzle, take turns giving each other clues, using definitions, examples, and phrases.

> *modelo*
>
> **2 horizontal:** *Es un deporte que practicamos en la piscina.*
> **6 vertical:** *Es un mensaje que escribimos con lápiz o con pluma.*

8

Entrevista In pairs, take turns asking and answering these questions.

1. ¿Hay un café cerca de la universidad? ¿Dónde está?
2. ¿Cuál es tu restaurante favorito?
3. ¿Te gusta viajar y visitar monumentos? ¿Por qué?
4. ¿Te gusta ir al cine los fines de semana?
5. ¿Cuáles son tus películas favoritas?
6. ¿Te gusta practicar deportes?
7. ¿Cuáles son tus deportes favoritos? ¿Por qué?
8. ¿Cuáles son tus pasatiempos favoritos?

> **CONSULTA**
>
> To review expressions with **gustar,** see **Estructura 2.1,** p. 74.

9

Conversación Using the words and expressions provided, work with a partner to prepare a short conversation about pastimes.

| ¿a qué hora? | ¿con quién(es)? | ¿dónde? |
| ¿cómo? | ¿cuándo? | ¿qué? |

> *modelo*
>
> **Estudiante 1:** *¿Cuándo patinas en línea?*
> **Estudiante 2:** *Patino en línea los domingos. Y tú, ¿patinas en línea?*
> **Estudiante 1:** *No, no me gusta patinar en línea. Me gusta practicar el béisbol.*

10

Pasatiempos In pairs, tell each other what pastimes three of your friends and family members enjoy. Be prepared to share with the class any pastimes you noticed they have in common.

> *modelo*
>
> **Estudiante 1:** *Mi hermana pasea mucho en bicicleta, pero mis padres practican la natación. Mi hermano no nada, pero visita muchos museos.*
> **Estudiante 2:** *Mi primo lee muchas revistas, pero no practica muchos deportes. Mis tíos esquían y practican el golf...*

Fútbol, cenotes y mole

Maru, Miguel, Jimena y Marissa visitan un cenote, mientras Felipe y Juan Carlos van a un partido de fútbol.

PERSONAJES

 MIGUEL

 PABLO

Ⓢ Video: *Fotonovela*

MIGUEL Buenos días a todos.

TÍA ANA MARÍA Hola, Miguel. Maru, ¿qué van a hacer hoy?

MARU Miguel y yo vamos a llevar a Marissa a un cenote.

MARISSA ¿No vamos a nadar? ¿Qué es un cenote?

MIGUEL Sí, sí vamos a nadar. Un cenote... difícil de explicar. Es una piscina natural en un hueco profundo.

MARU ¡Ya vas a ver! Seguro que te va a gustar.

(unos minutos después)

EDUARDO Hay un partido de fútbol en el parque. ¿Quieren ir conmigo?

PABLO Y conmigo. Si no consigo más jugadores, nuestro equipo va a perder.

ANA MARÍA Marissa, ¿qué te gusta hacer? ¿Escalar montañas? ¿Ir de excursión?

MARISSA Sí, me gusta ir de excursión y practicar el esquí acuático. Y usted, ¿qué prefiere hacer en sus ratos libres?

PABLO Mi mamá tiene muchos pasatiempos y actividades.

EDUARDO Sí. Ella nada y juega al tenis y al golf.

PABLO Va al cine y a los museos.

ANA MARÍA Sí, salgo mucho los fines de semana.

FELIPE ¿Recuerdas el restaurante del mole?

EDUARDO ¿Qué restaurante?

JIMENA El mole de mi tía Ana María es mi favorito.

MARU Chicos, ya es hora. ¡Vamos!

ANA MARÍA  **MARU**   **MARISSA**   **EDUARDO**   **FELIPE**   **JUAN CARLOS**   **JIMENA** **DON GUILLERMO**

Lección 4

7

(más tarde, en el parque)

PABLO No puede ser. ¡Cinco a uno!

FELIPE ¡Vamos a jugar! Si perdemos, compramos el almuerzo. Y si ganamos...

EDUARDO ¡Empezamos!

9

(mientras tanto, en el cenote)

MARISSA ¿Hay muchos cenotes en México?

MIGUEL Sólo en la península de Yucatán.

MARISSA ¡Vamos a nadar!

8

(Los chicos visitan a don Guillermo, un vendedor de paletas heladas.)

JUAN CARLOS Don Guillermo, ¿dónde podemos conseguir un buen mole?

FELIPE Eduardo y Pablo van a pagar el almuerzo. Y yo voy a pedir un montón de comida.

10

FELIPE Sí, éste es el restaurante. Recuerdo la comida.

EDUARDO Oye, Pablo... No tengo...

PABLO No te preocupes, hermanito.

FELIPE ¿Qué buscas? *(muestra la cartera de Pablo)* ¿Esto?

recursos

VM
pp. 233–234

vhlcentral.com
Lección 4

Expresiones útiles

Making invitations

Hay un partido de fútbol en el parque. ¿Quieren ir conmigo?
There's a soccer game in the park. Do you want to come with me?

¡Yo puedo jugar!
I can play!

Mmm... no quiero.
Hmm... I don't want to.

Lo siento, pero no puedo.
I'm sorry, but I can't.

¡Vamos a nadar!
Let's go swimming!

Sí, vamos.
Yes, let's go.

Making plans

¿Qué van a hacer hoy?
What are you going to do today?

Vamos a llevar a Marissa a un cenote.
We are taking Marissa to a cenote.

Vamos a comprar unas paletas heladas.
We're going to buy some popsicles.

Vamos a jugar. Si perdemos, compramos el almuerzo.
Let's play. If we lose, we'll buy lunch.

Talking about pastimes

¿Qué te gusta hacer? ¿Escalar montañas? ¿Ir de excursión?
What do you like to do? Mountain climbing? Hiking?

Sí, me gusta ir de excursión y practicar esquí acuático.
Yes, I like hiking and water skiing.

Y usted, ¿qué prefiere hacer en sus ratos libres?
And you, what do you like to do in your free time?

Salgo mucho los fines de semana.
I go out a lot on the weekends.

Voy al cine y a los museos.
I go to the movies and to museums.

Additional vocabulary

la cartera *wallet*   **el hueco** *hole*
un montón de *a lot of*

¿Qué pasó?

1

Escoger Choose the answer that best completes each sentence.

1. Marissa, Maru y Miguel desean _____.
   a. nadar   b. correr por el parque   c. leer el periódico

2. A Marissa le gusta _____.
   a. el tenis   b. el vóleibol   c. ir de excursión y practicar esquí acuático

3. A la tía Ana María le gusta _____.
   a. jugar al hockey   b. nadar y jugar al tenis y al golf   c. hacer ciclismo

4. Pablo y Eduardo pierden el partido de _____.
   a. fútbol   b. béisbol   c. baloncesto

5. Juan Carlos y Felipe desean _____.
   a. patinar   b. esquiar   c. comer mole

NOTA CULTURAL

Mole is a typical sauce in Mexican cuisine. It is made from pumpkin seeds, chile, and chocolate, and it is usually served with chicken, beef, or pork.

2

Identificar Identify the person who would make each statement.

1. A mí me gusta nadar, pero no sé qué es un cenote. _____

2. Mamá va al cine y al museo en sus ratos libres. _____

3. Yo voy a pedir mucha comida. _____

4. ¿Quieren ir a jugar al fútbol con nosotros en el parque? _____

5. Me gusta salir los fines de semana. _____

MARISSA

FELIPE

EDUARDO

PABLO

TÍA ANA MARÍA

NOTA CULTURAL

Cenotes are deep, freshwater sinkholes found in caves throughout the Yucatán peninsula. They were formed in prehistoric times by the erosion and collapse of cave walls. The Mayan civilization considered the **cenotes** sacred, and performed rituals there. Today, they are popular destinations for swimming and diving.

3

Preguntas Answer the questions using the information from the **Fotonovela**.

1. ¿Qué van a hacer Miguel y Maru?

2. ¿Adónde van Felipe y Juan Carlos mientras sus amigos van al cenote?

3. ¿Quién gana el partido de fútbol?

4. ¿Quiénes van al cenote con Maru y Miguel?

4

Conversación With a partner, prepare a conversation in which you talk about pastimes and invite each other to do some activity together. Use these expressions and also look at **Expresiones útiles** on the previous page.

¿A qué hora? *(At) What time?*	**¿Dónde?** *Where?*	**Nos vemos a las siete.** *See you at seven.*
contigo *with you*	**No puedo porque...** *I can't because...*	

▶ ¿Eres aficionado/a a...?   ▶ ¿Por qué no...?   ▶ ¿Qué vas a hacer esta noche?

▶ ¿Te gusta...?   ▶ ¿Quieres... conmigo?

Practice more at **vhlcentral.com**.

Pronunciación  (S) Audio
Word stress and accent marks

pe-lí-cu-la   **e-di-fi-cio**   **ver**   **yo**

Every Spanish syllable contains at least one vowel. When two vowels are joined in the same syllable they form a **diphthong***. A **monosyllable** is a word formed by a single syllable.

bi-blio-te-ca   **vi-si-tar**   **par-que**   **fút-bol**

The syllable of a Spanish word that is pronounced most emphatically is the "stressed" syllable.

pe-lo-ta   **pis-ci-na**   **ra-tos**   **ha-blan**

Words that end in **n, s,** or a **vowel** are usually stressed on the next-to-last syllable.

na-ta-ción   **pa-pá**   **in-glés**   **Jo-sé**

If words that end in **n, s,** or a **vowel** are stressed on the last syllable, they must carry an accent mark on the stressed syllable.

bai-lar   **es-pa-ñol**   **u-ni-ver-si-dad**   **tra-ba-ja-dor**

Words that do not end in **n, s,** or a **vowel** are usually stressed on the last syllable.

béis-bol   **lá-piz**   **ár-bol**   **Gó-mez**

If words that do not end in **n, s,** or a **vowel** are stressed on the next-to-last syllable, they must carry an accent mark on the stressed syllable.

*The two vowels that form a diphthong are either both weak or one is weak and the other is strong.

Práctica Pronounce each word, stressing the correct syllable. Then give the word stress rule for each word.

1. profesor
2. Puebla
3. ¿Cuántos?
4. Mazatlán
5. examen
6. ¿Cómo?
7. niños
8. Guadalajara
9. programador
10. México
11. están
12. geografía

Oraciones Read the conversation aloud to practice word stress.

MARINA   Hola, Carlos. ¿Qué tal?
CARLOS   Bien. Oye, ¿a qué hora es el partido de fútbol?
MARINA   Creo que es a las siete.
CARLOS   ¿Quieres ir?
MARINA   Lo siento, pero no puedo.
        Tengo que estudiar biología.

Refranes Read these sayings aloud to practice word stress.

En la unión está la fuerza.²

Quien ríe de último, ríe mejor.¹

1 He who laughs last, laughs best.   2 United we stand.

recursos

LM p. 240   vhlcentral.com Lección 4

Lección 4

EN DETALLE

S Additional Reading

Real Madrid y Barça:
rivalidad total

Soccer in Spain is a force to be reckoned with, and no two teams draw more attention than **Real Madrid** and the **Fútbol Club Barcelona**. Whether the venue is Madrid's **Santiago Bernabéu** or Barcelona's **Camp Nou**, the two cities shut down for the showdown, paralyzed by **fútbol** fever. A ticket to the actual game is always the hottest ticket in town.

The rivalry between **Real Madrid** and **Barça** is about more than soccer. As the two biggest, most powerful cities in Spain, Barcelona and Madrid are constantly compared to one another and have a natural rivalry. There is also a political component to the dynamic. Barcelona, with its distinct language and culture, has long struggled for increased autonomy from Madrid's centralized government. Under Francisco Franco's rule (1939–1975), when repression of the Catalan identity was at its height, a game between **Real Madrid** and **FC Barcelona** was wrapped up with all the symbolism of the regime versus the resistance, even though both teams suffered casualties in Spain's civil war and the subsequent Franco dictatorship.

Although the dictatorship is long over, the momentum of all those decades of competition still transforms both cities into a frenzied, tense panic leading up to the game. Once the final score is announced, one of those cities is transformed again, this time into the best party in the country.

Rivalidades del fútbol
Argentina: Boca Juniors vs River Plate
México: Águilas del América vs Chivas del Guadalajara
Chile: Colo Colo vs Universidad de Chile
Guatemala: Comunicaciones vs Municipal
Uruguay: Peñarol vs Nacional
Colombia: Millonarios vs Independiente Santa Fe

ACTIVIDADES

1

¿Cierto o falso? Indicate whether each statement is **cierto** or **falso**. Correct the false statements.

1. People from Spain don't like soccer.
2. Madrid and Barcelona are the most important cities in Spain.
3. Santiago Bernabéu is a stadium in Barcelona.
4. The rivalry between Real Madrid and FC Barcelona is not only in soccer.
5. Barcelona has resisted Madrid's centralized government.
6. Only the FC Barcelona team was affected by the civil war.
7. During Franco's regime, the Catalan culture thrived.
8. There are many famous rivalries between soccer teams in the Spanish-speaking world.
9. River Plate is a popular team from Argentina.
10. Comunicaciones and Peñarol are famous rivals in Guatemala.

ASÍ SE DICE

Los deportes

el/la árbitro/a	referee
el/la atleta	athlete
la bola; el balón	la pelota
el campeón/ la campeona	champion
la carrera	race
competir	to compete
empatar	to draw; to tie
la medalla	medal
el/la mejor	the best
mundial	worldwide
el torneo	tournament

EL MUNDO HISPANO

Atletas importantes

World-renowned Hispanic athletes:

- **Rafael Nadal** (España) is a top tennis player. He has won twelve Grand Slam singles titles and the 2008 Olympic gold medal in singles.

- **Dayron Robles** (Cuba), an Olympic champion hurdler, set a world record in the 110-meter hurdles. He is now retired.

- **Carolina Ruiz Castillo** (España), an alpine skier, participated in the 2002, 2006, and 2010 Olympics.

- **Paola Milagros Espinosa Sánchez** (México) has competed in three Olympics (2004, 2008, 2012) in diving. She and her partner, Tatiana Ortiz, won the bronze medal in 2008. In 2012, she won a silver medal with partner Alejandra Orozco.

PERFILES

Lionel Messi y Lorena Ochoa

Lionel Andrés Messi is considered one of the best soccer players of his generation. Born in 1987 in Argentina, Messi suffered a hormone deficiency that conflicted with his athletic dreams. He moved to Spain as a teenager and, at just 17, played his first game for the team **Fútbol Club Barcelona**. He is now the highest-paid player in the Spanish league.

Mexican golfer **Lorena Ochoa**, born in 1981, took up the sport at the age of five and won her first national event two years later. Winner of the LPGA Tour Player of the Year award every year from 2006-2009, Ochoa was ranked number one worldwide among female golfers when she retired in 2010.

Conexión Internet

¿Qué deportes son populares en los países hispanos?	Go to **vhlcentral.com** to find more cultural information related to this **Cultura** section.

ACTIVIDADES

2 **Comprensión** Write the name of the athlete described in each sentence.

1. Es un jugador de fútbol de Argentina. _____

2. Es una chica que practica el golf. _____

3. Es una chica española a la que le gusta esquiar. _____

4. Es una chica mexicana que practica un deporte en la piscina. _____

3 **¿Quién es?** Write a short paragraph describing an athlete that you like, but do not mention his/her name. What does he/she look like? What sport does he/she play? Where does he/she live? Read your description to the class to see if they can guess who it is.

 Practice more at **vhlcentral.com**.

4.1 Present tense of ir  Tutorial

ANTE TODO The verb **ir** (*to go*) is irregular in the present tense. Note that, except for the **yo** form (**voy**) and the lack of a written accent on the **vosotros** form (**vais**), the endings are the same as those for regular present tense **-ar** verbs.

The verb ir (*to go*)

Singular forms		Plural forms	
yo	**voy**	nosotros/as	**vamos**
tú	**vas**	vosotros/as	**vais**
Ud./él/ella	**va**	Uds./ellos/ellas	**van**

▶ **Ir** is often used with the preposition **a** (*to*). If **a** is followed by the definite article **el**, they combine to form the contraction **al**. If **a** is followed by the other definite articles (**la, las, los**), there is no contraction.

> **a + el = al**

Voy **al** parque con Juan.
I'm going to the park with Juan.

Mis amigos van **a las** montañas.
My friends are going to the mountains.

CONSULTA

To review the contraction **de + el**, see **Estructura 1.3**, pp. 20–21.

▶ The construction **ir a** + [*infinitive*] is used to talk about actions that are going to happen in the future. It is equivalent to the English *to be going* + [*infinitive*].

Va a leer el periódico.
He is going to read the newspaper.

Van a pasear por el pueblo.
They are going to walk around town.

AYUDA

When asking a question that contains a form of the verb **ir**, remember to use **adónde**:

¿Adónde vas?
(To) Where are you going?

¡Voy a ir con ellos!

Ella va al cine y a los museos.

▶ **Vamos a** + [*infinitive*] can also express the idea of *let's* (*do something*).

Vamos a pasear.
Let's take a stroll.

¡Vamos a ver!
Let's see!

¡INTÉNTALO! Provide the present tense forms of **ir**.

1. Ellos ___van___.
2. Yo _____.
3. Tu novio _____.
4. Adela _____.
5. Mi prima y yo _____.
6. Tú _____.
7. Ustedes _____.
8. Nosotros _____.
9. Usted _____.
10. Nosotras _____.
11. Miguel _____.
12. Ellas _____.

recursos

WB
pp. 223–224

LM
p. 241

S
vhlcentral.com
Lección 4

Práctica

 Practice more at **vhlcentral.com**.

1 **¿Adónde van?** Everyone in your neighborhood is dashing off to various places.
Say where they are going.

1. la señora Castillo / el centro
2. las hermanas Gómez / la piscina
3. tu tío y tu papá / el partido de fútbol
4. yo / el Museo de Arte Moderno
5. nosotros / el restaurante Miramar

2 **¿Qué van a hacer?** These sentences describe what several students in a college
hiking club are doing today. Use **ir a** + [*infinitive*] to say that they are also going to do the
same activities tomorrow.

> **modelo**
>
> Martín y Rodolfo nadan en la piscina.
> Van a nadar en la piscina mañana también.

1. Sara lee una revista.
2. Yo practico deportes.
3. Ustedes van de excursión.
4. El presidente del club patina.
5. Tú tomas el sol.
6. Paseamos con nuestros amigos.

3 **Preguntas** With a partner, take turns asking and answering questions about where the people are
going and what they are going to do there.

> **modelo**
>
> **Estudiante 1:** ¿Adónde va Estela?
> **Estudiante 2:** Va a la Librería Sol.
> **Estudiante 1:** Va a comprar un libro.

Estela

1. Álex y Miguel

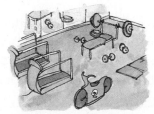

2. mi amigo

3. tú

4. los estudiantes

5. la profesora Torres

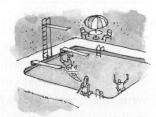

6. ustedes

Comunicación

4

Situaciones Work with a partner and say where you and your friends go in these situations.

1. Cuando deseo descansar…
2. Cuando mi novio/a tiene que estudiar…
3. Si mis compañeros de clase necesitan practicar el español…
4. Si deseo hablar con mis amigos…
5. Cuando tengo dinero (*money*)…
6. Cuando mis amigos y yo tenemos hambre…
7. En mis ratos libres…
8. Cuando mis amigos desean esquiar…
9. Si estoy de vacaciones…
10. Si tengo ganas de leer…

5

Encuesta Your instructor will give you a worksheet. Walk around the class and ask your classmates if they are going to do these activities today. Find one person to answer **Sí** and one to answer **No** for each item and note their names on the worksheet in the appropriate column. Be prepared to report your findings to the class.

modelo
Tú: ¿Vas a leer el periódico hoy?
Ana: Sí, voy a leer el periódico hoy.
Luis: No, no voy a leer el periódico hoy.

Actividades	Sí	No
1. comer en un restaurante chino		
2. leer el periódico	Ana	Luis
3. escribir un mensaje electrónico		
4. correr 20 kilómetros		
5. ver una película de terror		
6. pasear en bicicleta		

6

Entrevista Talk to two classmates in order to find out where they are going and what they are going to do on their next vacation.

modelo
Estudiante 1: ¿Adónde vas de vacaciones (*on vacation*)?
Estudiante 2: Voy a Guadalajara con mis amigos.
Estudiante 3: ¿Y qué van a hacer (*to do*) ustedes en Guadalajara?
Estudiante 2: Vamos a visitar unos monumentos y museos. ¿Y tú?

Síntesis

7

Planes Make a schedule of your activities for the weekend. Then, share with a partner.

▶ For each day, list at least three things you have to do.
▶ For each day, list at least two things you will do for fun.
▶ Tell a classmate what your weekend schedule is like. He or she will write down what you say.
▶ Switch roles to see if you have any plans in common.
▶ Take turns asking each other to participate in some of the activities you listed.

4.2 Stem-changing verbs:  Tutorial
e→ie, o→ue

CONSULTA

To review the present tense of regular **-ar** verbs, see **Estructura 2.1**, p. 72.

•••

To review the present tense of regular **-er** and **-ir** verbs, see **Estructura 3.3**, p. 142.

ANTE TODO Stem-changing verbs deviate from the normal pattern of regular verbs. When stem-changing verbs are conjugated, they have a vowel change in the last syllable of the stem.

INFINITIVE	VERB STEM	STEM CHANGE	CONJUGATED FORM
empezar	empez-	emp**ie**z-	emp**ie**zo
volver	v**o**lv-	v**ue**lv-	v**ue**lvo

▶ In many verbs, such as **empezar** (*to begin*), the stem vowel changes from **e** to **ie**. Note that the **nosotros/as** and **vosotros/as** forms don't have a stem change.

The verb empezar (e:ie) (*to begin*)

Singular forms		Plural forms	
yo	emp**ie**zo	nosotros/as	empezamos
tú	emp**ie**zas	vosotros/as	empezáis
Ud./él/ella	emp**ie**za	Uds./ellos/ellas	emp**ie**zan

Los chicos empiezan a hablar de su visita al cenote.

Ellos vuelven a comer en el restaurante.

▶ In many other verbs, such as **volver** (*to return*), the stem vowel changes from **o** to **ue**. The **nosotros/as** and **vosotros/as** forms have no stem change.

The verb volver (o:ue) (*to return*)

Singular forms		Plural forms	
yo	v**ue**lvo	nosotros/as	volvemos
tú	v**ue**lves	vosotros/as	volvéis
Ud./él/ella	v**ue**lve	Uds./ellos/ellas	v**ue**lven

▶ To help you identify stem-changing verbs, they will appear as follows throughout the text:

empezar (e:ie), volver (o:ue)

Lección 4

Common stem-changing verbs

e:ie		o:ue	
cerrar	to close	**almorzar**	to have lunch
comenzar (a + *inf.*)	to begin	**contar**	to count; to tell
empezar (a + *inf.*)	to begin	**dormir**	to sleep
entender	to understand	**encontrar**	to find
pensar	to think	**mostrar**	to show
perder	to lose; to miss	**poder (+** *inf.*)	to be able to; can
preferir (+ *inf.*)	to prefer	**recordar**	to remember
querer (+ *inf.*)	to want; to love	**volver**	to return

¡LENGUA VIVA!

The verb **perder** can mean *to lose* or *to miss*, in the sense of "to miss a train."

Siempre pierdo mis llaves.

I always lose my keys.

Es importante no perder el autobús.

It's important not to miss the bus.

▶ **Jugar** (*to play a sport or a game*) is the only Spanish verb that has a **u:ue** stem change. **Jugar** is followed by **a** + [*definite article*] when the name of a sport or game is mentioned.

Ella juega al tenis y al golf.

Los chicos juegan al fútbol.

▶ **Comenzar** and **empezar** require the preposition **a** when they are followed by an infinitive.

Comienzan a jugar a las siete.
They begin playing at seven.

Ana **empieza a** escribir una postal.
Ana is starting to write a postcard.

▶ **Pensar** + [*infinitive*] means *to plan* or *to intend to do something*. **Pensar en** means *to think about someone* or *something*.

¿**Piensan** ir al gimnasio?
Are you planning to go to the gym?

¿**En** qué **piensas**?
What are you thinking about?

¡INTÉNTALO! Provide the present-tense forms of these verbs.

cerrar (e:ie)

1. Ustedes ___cierran___.
2. Tú _____.
3. Nosotras _____.
4. Mi hermano _____.
5. Yo _____.
6. Usted _____.
7. Los chicos _____.
8. Ella _____.

dormir (o:ue)

1. Mi abuela no ___duerme___.
2. Yo no _____.
3. Tú no _____.
4. Mis hijos no _____.
5. Usted no _____.
6. Nosotros no _____.
7. Él no _____.
8. Ustedes no _____.

recursos

WB
pp. 225–226

LM
p. 242

Ⓢ
vhlcentral.com
Lección 4

Lección 4

Práctica

1 **Completar** Complete this conversation with the appropriate forms of the verbs. Then act it out with a partner.

PABLO Óscar, voy al centro ahora.

ÓSCAR ¿A qué hora (1)_____ (pensar) volver? El partido de fútbol (2)_____ (empezar) a las dos.

PABLO (3)_____ (Volver) a la una. (4)_____ (Querer) ver el partido.

ÓSCAR (5)¿_____ (Recordar) que (*that*) nuestro equipo es muy bueno? (6)¡ _____ (Poder) ganar!

PABLO No, (7)_____ (pensar) que va a (8)_____ (perder). Los jugadores de Guadalajara son salvajes (*wild*) cuando (9)_____ (jugar).

2 **Preferencias** With a partner, take turns asking and answering questions about what these people want to do, using the cues provided.

modelo
> Guillermo: estudiar / pasear en bicicleta
> **Estudiante 1:** ¿Quiere estudiar Guillermo?
> **Estudiante 2:** No, prefiere pasear en bicicleta.

1. tú: trabajar / dormir

▶ 2. ustedes: mirar la televisión / jugar al dominó

3. tus amigos: ir de excursión / descansar

4. tú: comer en la cafetería / ir a un restaurante

5. Elisa: ver una película / leer una revista

6. María y su hermana: tomar el sol / practicar el esquí acuático

NOTA CULTURAL

Dominó (*Dominoes*) is a popular pastime throughout Colombia, Venezuela, Central America, and the Spanish-speaking countries of the Caribbean. It's played both socially and competitively by people of all ages.

3 **Describir** Use a verb from the list to describe what these people are doing.

| almorzar | cerrar | contar | dormir | encontrar | mostrar |

1. las niñas

2. yo

3. nosotros

4. tú

5. Pedro

6. Teresa

 Practice more at **vhlcentral.com**.

Comunicación

4

Frecuencia In pairs, take turns using the verbs from the list and other stem-changing verbs you know to tell your partner which activities you do daily (**todos los días**), which you do once a month (**una vez al mes**), and which you do once a year (**una vez al año**). Record your partner's responses in the chart so that you can report back to the class.

modelo

> **Estudiante 1:** Yo recuerdo a mi familia todos los días.
> **Estudiante 2:** Yo pierdo uno de mis libros una vez al año.

cerrar	perder
dormir	poder
empezar	preferir
encontrar	querer
jugar	recordar
¿?	¿?

todos los días	una vez al mes	una vez al año

5

En la televisión Read the television listings for Saturday. In pairs, write a conversation between two siblings arguing about what to watch. Be creative and be prepared to act out your conversation for the class.

modelo

> **Hermano:** Podemos ver la Copa Mundial.
> **Hermana:** ¡No, no quiero ver la Copa Mundial! Prefiero ver...

	13:00	14:00	15:00	16:00	17:00	18:00	19:00	20:00	21:00	22:00	23:00
7	Copa Mundial (*World Cup*) de fútbol				República Deportiva	Campeonato (*Championship*) Mundial de Vóleibol: México-Argentina				Torneo de Natación	
8	Abierto (*Open*) Mexicano de Tenis: Santiago González (México) vs. Nicolás Almagro (España). Semifinales			Campeonato de baloncesto: Los Correcaminos de Tampico vs. los Santos de San Luis				Aficionados al buceo		Cozumel: Aventuras	
12	Yo soy Betty, la fea	Héroes		Hermanos y hermanas			Película: **Sin nombre**			Película: **El coronel no tiene quien le escriba**	
13	El padrastro		60 Minutos			El esquí acuático				Patinaje artístico	
17	Biografías: La artista Frida Kahlo			Música de la semana		Entrevista del día: Iker Casillas y su pasión por el fútbol			Cine de la noche: **Elsa y Fred**		

NOTA CULTURAL

Iker Casillas Fernández is a famous goalkeeper for **Real Madrid**. A native of Madrid, he is among the best goalkeepers of his generation.

Síntesis

6

Situación Your instructor will give you and your partner each a partially illustrated itinerary of a city tour. Complete the itineraries by asking each other questions using the verbs in the captions and vocabulary you have learned.

modelo

> **Estudiante 1:** Por la mañana, empiezan en el café.
> **Estudiante 2:** Y luego...

Lección 4

4.3 Stem-changing verbs: e→i   Ⓢ Tutorial

ANTE TODO   You've already seen that many verbs in Spanish change their stem vowel when conjugated. There is a third kind of stem-vowel change in some verbs, such as **pedir** (*to ask for; to request*). In these verbs, the stressed vowel in the stem changes from **e** to **i**, as shown in the diagram.

INFINITIVE	VERB STEM	STEM CHANGE	CONJUGATED FORM
pedir ▶	p**e**d- ▶	p**i**d- ▶	p**i**do

▶ As with other stem-changing verbs you have learned, there is no stem change in the **nosotros/as** or **vosotros/as** forms in the present tense.

The verb pedir (e:i) (*to ask for; to request*)

Singular forms		Plural forms	
yo	pido	nosotros/as	pedimos
tú	pides	vosotros/as	pedís
Ud./él/ella	pide	Uds./ellos/ellas	piden

▶ To help you identify verbs with the **e:i** stem change, they will appear as follows throughout the text:

> **pedir (e:i)**

▶ These are the most common **e:i** stem-changing verbs:

conseguir	**decir**	**repetir**	**seguir**
to get; to obtain	*to say; to tell*	*to repeat*	*to follow; to continue; to keep (doing something)*

Pido favores cuando es necesario.
I ask for favors when it's necessary.

Javier dice la verdad.
Javier is telling the truth.

Sigue con su tarea.
He continues with his homework.

Consiguen ver buenas películas.
They get to see good movies.

▶ **¡Atención!** The verb **decir** is irregular in its **yo** form: **yo digo**.

▶ The **yo** forms of **seguir** and **conseguir** have a spelling change in addition to the stem change **e:i**.

Sigo su plan.
I'm following their plan.

Consigo novelas en la librería.
I get novels at the bookstore.

¡INTÉNTALO!   Provide the correct forms of the verbs.

repetir (e:i)	**decir (e:i)**	**seguir (e:i)**
1. Arturo y Eva __repiten__.	1. Yo __digo__.	1. Yo __sigo__.
2. Yo _____.	2. Él _____.	2. Nosotros _____.
3. Nosotros _____.	3. Tú _____.	3. Tú _____.
4. Julia _____.	4. Usted _____.	4. Los chicos _____.
5. Sofía y yo _____.	5. Ellas _____.	5. Usted _____.

Práctica

1 **Completar** Complete these sentences with the correct form of the verb provided.

1. Cuando mi familia pasea por la ciudad, mi madre siempre (*always*) va a un café y _____ (pedir) una soda.
2. Pero mi padre _____ (decir) que perdemos mucho tiempo. Tiene prisa por llegar al Bosque de Chapultepec.
3. Mi padre tiene suerte, porque él siempre _____ (conseguir) lo que (*that which*) desea.
4. Cuando llegamos al parque, mis hermanos y yo _____ (seguir) conversando (*talking*) con nuestros padres.
5. Mis padres siempre _____ (repetir) la misma cosa: "Nosotros tomamos el sol aquí sin ustedes".
6. Yo siempre _____ (pedir) permiso para volver a casa un poco más tarde porque me gusta mucho el parque.

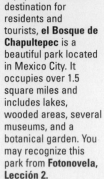

NOTA CULTURAL

A popular weekend destination for residents and tourists, **el Bosque de Chapultepec** is a beautiful park located in Mexico City. It occupies over 1.5 square miles and includes lakes, wooded areas, several museums, and a botanical garden. You may recognize this park from **Fotonovela, Lección 2.**

2 **Combinar** Combine words from the two columns to create sentences about yourself and people you know.

A	B
yo	(no) pedir muchos favores
mi compañero/a de cuarto	nunca (*never*) pedir perdón
mi mejor (*best*) amigo/a	nunca seguir las instrucciones
mi familia	siempre seguir las instrucciones
mis amigos/as	conseguir libros en Internet
mis amigos/as y yo	repetir el vocabulario
mis padres	poder hablar dos lenguas
mi hermano/a	dormir hasta el mediodía
mi profesor(a) de español	siempre perder sus libros

3 **Opiniones** In pairs, take turns guessing how your partner completed the sentences from **Actividad 2**. If you guess incorrectly, your partner must supply the correct answer.

> **modelo**
> **Estudiante 1:** Creo que tus padres consiguen libros en Internet.
> **Estudiante 2:** ¡No! Mi hermana consigue libros en Internet.

CONSULTA

To review possessive adjectives, see **Estructura 3.2**, p. 139.

4   **¿Quién?** Your instructor will give you a worksheet. Talk to your classmates until you find one person who does each of the activities. Use **e:ie**, **o:ue**, and **e:i** stem-changing verbs.

> **modelo**
> **Tú:** ¿Pides consejos con frecuencia?
> **Maira:** No, no pido consejos con frecuencia.
> **Tú:** ¿Pides consejos con frecuencia?
> **Lucas:** Sí, pido consejos con frecuencia.

 Practice more at **vhlcentral.com**.

Comunicación

5

Las películas Use these questions to interview a classmate.

1. ¿Prefieres las películas románticas, las películas de acción o las películas de terror? ¿Por qué?
2. ¿Dónde consigues información sobre (*about*) cine y televisión?
3. ¿Dónde consigues las entradas (*tickets*) para ver una película?
4. Para decidir qué películas vas a ver, ¿sigues las recomendaciones de los críticos de cine? ¿Qué dicen los críticos en general?
5. ¿Qué cines en tu comunidad muestran las mejores (*best*) películas?
6. ¿Vas a ver una película esta semana? ¿A qué hora empieza la película?

Síntesis

6

El cine In pairs, first scan the ad and jot down all the stem-changing verbs. Then answer the questions. Be prepared to share your answers with the class.

1. ¿Qué palabras indican que *Avatar* es una película dramática?
2. ¿Cómo son los dos personajes (*characters*) del póster? ¿Qué relación tienen?
3. ¿Te gustan las películas como ésta (*this one*)? ¿Por qué?
4. Describe tu película favorita con los verbos de la **Lección 4**.

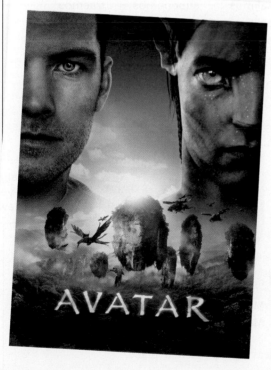

Ganadora de tres premios Óscar

Cuando todas las puertas se cierran, siempre hay una oportunidad para volver a empezar.

Del productor y director de
Titanic y Terminator

Un mundo lejano puede desaparecer, su salvación está en las manos de un hombre que también puede perderlo todo... Incluso el amor.
¿Cuentan con él?

[4.4] Verbs with irregular yo forms Tutorial

ANTE TODO   In Spanish, several verbs have irregular **yo** forms in the present tense. You have already seen three verbs with the **-go** ending in the **yo** form: **decir → digo**, **tener → tengo**, and **venir → vengo**.

▶ Here are some common expressions with **decir**.

decir la verdad	**decir mentiras**
to tell the truth	*to tell lies*
decir que	**decir la respuesta**
to say that	*to say the answer*

▶ The verb **hacer** is often used to ask questions about what someone does. Note that when answering, **hacer** is frequently replaced with another, more specific action verb.

Verbs with irregular yo forms

	hacer *(to do; to make)*	poner *(to put; to place)*	salir *(to leave)*	suponer *(to suppose)*	traer *(to bring)*
SINGULAR FORMS	**hago** haces hace	**pongo** pones pone	**salgo** sales sale	**supongo** supones supone	**traigo** traes trae
PLURAL FORMS	hacemos hacéis hacen	ponemos ponéis ponen	salimos salís salen	suponemos suponéis suponen	traemos traéis traen

Salgo mucho los fines de semana.

Yo no salgo, yo hago la tarea y veo películas en la televisión.

▶ **Poner** can also mean to *turn on* a household appliance.

Carlos **pone** la radio.   María **pone** la televisión.
Carlos turns on the radio.   *María turns on the television.*

▶ **Salir de** is used to indicate that someone is leaving a particular place.

Hoy **salgo del** hospital.   **Sale de** la clase a las cuatro.
Today I leave the hospital.   *He leaves class at four.*

▶ **Salir para** is used to indicate someone's destination.

Mañana **salgo para** México.	Hoy **salen para** España.
Tomorrow I leave for Mexico.	*Today they leave for Spain.*

▶ **Salir con** means *to leave with someone* or *something*, or *to date someone.*

Alberto **sale con** su mochila.	Margarita **sale con** Guillermo.
Alberto is leaving with his backpack.	*Margarita is going out with Guillermo.*

The verbs **ver** and **oír**

▶ The verb **ver** (*to see*) has an irregular **yo** form. The other forms of **ver** are regular.

The verb **ver** (*to see*)

Singular forms		Plural forms	
yo	**veo**	nosotros/as	vemos
tú	ves	vosotros/as	veis
Ud./él/ella	ve	Uds./ellos/ellas	ven

▶ The verb **oír** (*to hear*) has an irregular **yo** form and the spelling change **i:y** in the **tú**, **usted/él/ella**, and **ustedes/ellos/ellas** forms. The **nosotros/as** and **vosotros/as** forms have an accent mark.

The verb **oír** (*to hear*)

Singular forms		Plural forms	
yo	**oigo**	nosotros/as	oímos
tú	oyes	vosotros/as	oís
Ud./él/ella	oye	Uds./ellos/ellas	oyen

▶ While most commonly translated as *to hear*, **oír** is also used in contexts where the verb *to listen* would be used in English.

Oigo a unas personas en la otra sala.	¿**Oyes** la radio por la mañana?
I hear some people in the other room.	*Do you listen to the radio in the morning?*

¡INTÉNTALO!   Provide the appropriate forms of these verbs.

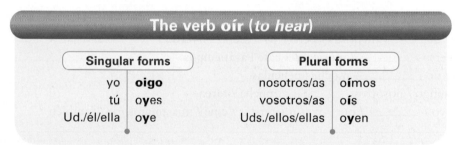

1. salir   Isabel _sale_.   Nosotros _____.   Yo _____.
2. ver   Yo _____.   Uds. _____.   Tú _____.
3. poner   Rita y yo _____.   Yo _____.   Los niños _____.
4. hacer   Yo _____.   Tú _____.   Ud. _____.
5. oír   Él _____.   Nosotros _____.   Yo _____.
6. traer   Ellas _____.   Yo _____.   Tú _____.
7. suponer   Yo _____.   Mi amigo _____.   Nosotras _____.

Lección 4

Práctica

1

Completar Complete this conversation with the appropriate forms of the verbs. Then act it out with a partner.

ERNESTO David, ¿qué (1)_____ (hacer) hoy?

DAVID Ahora estudio biología, pero esta noche (2)_____ (salir) con Luisa. Vamos al cine. Los críticos (3)_____ (decir) que la nueva (*new*) película de Almodóvar es buena.

ERNESTO ¿Y Diana? ¿Qué (4)_____ (hacer) ella?

DAVID (5)_____ (Salir) a comer con sus padres.

ERNESTO ¿Qué (6)_____ (hacer) Andrés y Javier?

DAVID Tienen que (7)_____ (hacer) las maletas. (8)_____ (Salir) para Monterrey mañana.

ERNESTO Pues, ¿qué (9)_____ (hacer) yo?

DAVID Yo (10)_____ (suponer) que puedes estudiar o (11)_____ (ver) la televisión.

ERNESTO No quiero estudiar. Mejor (12)_____ (poner) la televisión. Mi programa favorito empieza en unos minutos.

2

Oraciones Form sentences using the cues provided and verbs from **Estructura 4.4**.

> **modelo**
>
> tú / _____ / cosas / en / su lugar / antes de (*before*) / salir
> Tú *pones las cosas en su lugar antes de salir.*

1. mis amigos / _____ / conmigo / centro
2. tú / _____ / mentiras / pero / yo _____ / verdad
3. Alberto / _____ / música del café Pasatiempos
4. yo / no / _____ / muchas películas
5. domingo / nosotros / _____ / mucha / tarea
6. si / yo / _____ / que / yo / querer / ir / cine / mis amigos / ir / también

3

Describir Use the verbs from **Estructura 4.4** to describe what these people are doing.

1. Fernán

2. los aficionados

3. yo

4. nosotros

5. la señora Vargas

6. el estudiante

 Practice more at **vhlcentral.com**.

Comunicación

4

Tu rutina In pairs, take turns asking each other these questions.

1. ¿Qué traes a clase?
2. ¿Quiénes traen un diccionario a clase? ¿Por qué traen un diccionario?
3. ¿A qué hora sales de tu residencia estudiantil o de tu casa por la mañana? ¿A qué hora sale tu compañero/a de cuarto?
4. ¿Dónde pones tus libros cuando regresas de clase? ¿Siempre (*Always*) pones tus cosas en su lugar?
5. ¿Qué prefieres hacer, oír la radio o ver la televisión?
6. ¿Oyes música cuando estudias?
7. ¿Ves películas en casa o prefieres ir al cine?
8. ¿Haces mucha tarea los fines de semana?
9. ¿Sales con tus amigos los fines de semana? ¿A qué hora? ¿Qué hacen?
10. ¿Te gusta ver deportes en la televisión o prefieres ver otros programas? ¿Cuáles?

5

Charadas In groups, play a game of charades. Each person should think of two phrases containing the verbs **hacer, oír, poner, salir, traer,** or **ver.** The first person to guess correctly acts out the next charade.

6

Entrevista You are doing a market research report on lifestyles. Interview a classmate to find out when he or she goes out with these people and what they do for entertainment.

▶ los/las amigos/as
▶ el/la novio/a
▶ el/la esposo/a
▶ la familia

Síntesis

7

Situación Imagine that you are speaking with your roommate. With a partner, prepare a conversation using these cues.

Estudiante 1	Estudiante 2
Ask your partner what he or she is doing.	Tell your partner that you are watching TV.
Say what you suppose he or she is watching.	Say that you like the show _____. Ask if he or she wants to watch.
Say no, because you are going out with friends, and tell where you are going.	Say you think it's a good idea, and ask what your partner and his or her friends are doing there.
Say what you are going to do, and ask your partner whether he or she wants to come along.	Say no and tell your partner what you prefer to do.

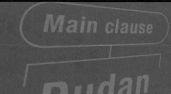

Recapitulación

 **Diagnostics**

Review the grammar concepts you have learned in this lesson by completing these activities.

1 **Completar** Complete the chart with the correct verb forms.   **15 pts.**

Infinitive	yo	nosotros/as	ellos/as
	vuelvo		
comenzar		**comenzamos**	
		hacemos	**hacen**
ir			
	juego		
repetir			**repiten**

2 **Un día típico** Complete the paragraph with the appropriate forms of the verbs in the word list. Not all verbs will be used. Some may be used more than once.   **10 pts.**

almorzar	ir	salir
cerrar	jugar	seguir
empezar	mostrar	ver
hacer	querer	volver

¡Hola! Me llamo Cecilia y vivo en Puerto Vallarta, México. ¿Cómo es un día típico en mi vida (*life*)? Por la mañana bebo café con mis padres y juntos (*together*) (1) _____ las noticias (*news*) en la televisión. A las siete y media, (*yo*) (2) _____ de mi casa y tomo el autobús. Me gusta llegar temprano (*early*) a la universidad porque siempre (*always*) (3) _____ a mis amigos en la cafetería. Tomamos café y planeamos lo que (4) _____ hacer cada (*each*) día. A las ocho y cuarto, mi amiga Sandra y yo (5) _____ al laboratorio de lenguas. La clase de francés (6) _____ a las ocho y media. ¡Es mi clase favorita! A las doce y media (*yo*) (7) _____ en la cafetería con mis amigos. Después (*Afterwards*), yo (8) _____ con mis clases. Por las tardes, mis amigos (9) _____ a sus casas, pero yo (10) _____ al vóleibol con mi amigo Tomás.

4.1 **Present tense of ir**   *p. 196*

yo	voy	nos.	vamos
tú	vas	vos.	vais
él	va	ellas	van

► ir a + [*infinitive*] = *to be going* + [*infinitive*]

► a + el = al

► vamos a + [*infinitive*] = *let's (do something)*

4.2 **Stem-changing verbs e:ie, o:ue, u:ue**   *pp. 199–200*

	empezar	volver	jugar
yo	empiezo	vuelvo	juego
tú	empiezas	vuelves	juegas
él	empieza	vuelve	juega
nos.	empezamos	volvemos	jugamos
vos.	empezáis	volvéis	jugáis
ellas	empiezan	vuelven	juegan

► Other e:ie verbs: cerrar, comenzar, entender, pensar, perder, preferir, querer

► Other o:ue verbs: almorzar, contar, dormir, encontrar, mostrar, poder, recordar

4.3 **Stem-changing verbs e:i**   *p. 203*

	pedir		
yo	pido	nos.	pedimos
tú	pides	vos.	pedís
él	pide	ellas	piden

► Other e:i verbs: conseguir, decir, repetir, seguir

4.4 **Verbs with irregular yo forms**   *pp. 206–207*

hacer	poner	salir	suponer	traer
hago	pongo	salgo	supongo	traigo

► ver: veo, ves, ve, vemos, veis, ven

► oír: oigo, oyes, oye, oímos, oís, oyen

Lección 4

3   **Oraciones** Arrange the cues provided in the correct order to form complete sentences. Make all necessary changes. **14 pts.**

1. tarea / los / hacer / sábados / nosotros / la

_____

2. en / pizza / Andrés / una / restaurante / el / pedir

_____

3. a / ? / museo / ir / ¿ / el / (tú)

_____

4. de / oír / amigos / bien / los / no / Elena

_____

5. libros / traer / yo / clase / mis / a

_____

6. película / ver / en / Jorge y Carlos / pensar / cinc / una / el

_____

7. unos / escribir / Mariana / electrónicos / querer / mensajes

_____

4   **Escribir** Write a short paragraph about what you do on a typical day. Use at least six of the verbs you have learned in this lesson. You can use the paragraph on the opposite page (**Actividad 2**) as a model. **11 pts.**

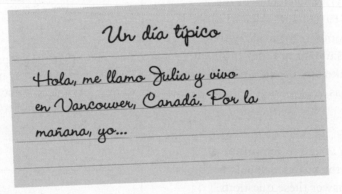

Un día típico

Hola, me llamo Julia y vivo en Vancouver, Canadá. Por la mañana, yo...

5   **Rima** Complete the rhyme with the appropriate forms of the correct verbs from the list. **2 EXTRA points!**

contar	poder
oír	suponer

❝ Si no _____ dormir
y el sueño deseas,
lo vas a conseguir
si _____ ovejas°. ❞

ovejas *sheep*

 Practice more at **vhlcentral.com.**

Lectura

Antes de leer

Estrategia
Predicting content from visuals

When you are reading in Spanish, be sure to look for visual clues that will orient you as to the content and purpose of what you are reading. Photos and illustrations, for example, will often give you a good idea of the main points that the reading covers. You may also encounter very helpful visuals that are used to summarize large amounts of data in a way that is easy to comprehend; these include bar graphs, pie charts, flow charts, lists of percentages, and other sorts of diagrams.

Examinar el texto

Take a quick look at the visual elements of the magazine article in order to generate a list of ideas about its content. Then compare your list with a classmate's. Are they the same or are they different? Discuss your lists and make any changes needed to produce a final list of ideas.

Contestar

Read the list of ideas you wrote in **Examinar el texto**, and look again at the visual elements of the magazine article. Then answer these questions:

1. Who is the woman in the photo, and what is her role?
2. What is the article about?
3. What is the subject of the pie chart?
4. What is the subject of the bar graph?

por María Úrsula Echevarría

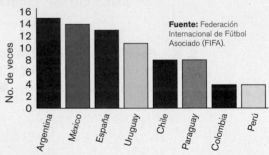

El fútbol es el deporte más popular en el mundo° hispano, según° una encuesta° reciente realizada entre jóvenes universitarios. Mucha gente practica este deporte y tiene un equipo de fútbol favorito. Cada cuatro años se realiza la Copa Mundial°. Argentina y Uruguay han ganado° este campeonato° más de una vez°. Los aficionados siguen los partidos de fútbol en casa por tele y en muchos otros lugares como bares, restaurantes, estadios y clubes deportivos. Los jóvenes juegan al fútbol con sus amigos en parques y gimnasios.

Países hispanos en campeonatos mundiales de fútbol (1930–2010)

Fuente: Federación Internacional de Fútbol Asociado (FIFA).

Pero, por supuesto°, en los países de habla hispana también hay otros deportes populares. ¿Qué deporte sigue al fútbol en estos países? Bueno, ¡depende del país y de otros factores!

Después de leer

Evaluación y predicción

Which of the following sporting events would be most popular among the college students surveyed? Rate them from one (most popular) to five (least popular). Which would be the most popular at your college or university?

_____ 1. la Copa Mundial de Fútbol
_____ 2. los Juegos Olímpicos
_____ 3. el Campeonato de Wimbledon
_____ 4. la Serie Mundial de Béisbol
_____ 5. el Tour de Francia

No sólo el fútbol

En Colombia, el béisbol también es muy popular después del fútbol, aunque° esto varía según la región del país. En la costa del norte de Colombia, el béisbol es una pasión. Y el ciclismo también es un deporte que los colombianos siguen con mucho interés.

Donde el béisbol es más popular

En los países del Caribe, el béisbol es el deporte predominante. Éste es el caso en Puerto Rico, Cuba y la República Dominicana. Los niños empiezan a jugar cuando son muy pequeños. En Puerto Rico y la República Dominicana, la gente también quiere participar en otros deportes, como el baloncesto, o ver los partidos en la tele. Y para los espectadores aficionados del Caribe, el boxeo es número dos.

Donde el fútbol es más popular

En México, el béisbol es el segundo° deporte más popular después° del fútbol. Pero en Argentina, después del fútbol, el rugby tiene mucha importancia. En Perú a la gente le gusta mucho ver partidos de vóleibol. ¿Y en España? Muchas personas prefieren el baloncesto, el tenis y el ciclismo.

Deportes más populares

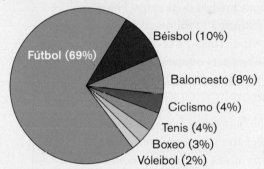

Fútbol (69%)
Béisbol (10%)
Baloncesto (8%)
Ciclismo (4%)
Tenis (4%)
Boxeo (3%)
Vóleibol (2%)

---

mundo *world* según *according to* encuesta *survey* se realiza la Copa Mundial *the World Cup is held* han ganado *have won* campeonato *championship*
más de una vez *more than once* por supuesto *of course* segundo *second* después *after* aunque *although*

¿Cierto o falso?

Indicate whether each sentence is **cierto** or **falso**, then correct the false statements.

	Cierto	Falso
1. El vóleibol es el segundo deporte más popular en México.	○	○
2. En España a la gente le gustan varios deportes como el baloncesto y el ciclismo.	○	○
3. En la costa del norte de Colombia, el tenis es una pasión.	○	○
4. En el Caribe, el deporte más popular es el béisbol.	○	○

Preguntas

Answer these questions in Spanish.

1. ¿Dónde ven el fútbol los aficionados? Y tú, ¿cómo ves tus deportes favoritos?
2. ¿Te gusta el fútbol? ¿Por qué?
3. ¿Miras la Copa Mundial en la televisión?
4. ¿Qué deportes miras en la televisión?
5. En tu opinión, ¿cuáles son los tres deportes más populares en tu universidad? ¿En tu comunidad? ¿En tu país?
6. ¿Practicas deportes en tus ratos libres?

Escritura

Estrategia
Using a dictionary

A common mistake made by beginning language learners is to embrace the dictionary as the ultimate resource for reading, writing, and speaking. While it is true that the dictionary is a useful tool that can provide valuable information about vocabulary, using the dictionary correctly requires that you understand the elements of each entry.

If you glance at a Spanish-English dictionary, you will notice that its format is similar to that of an English dictionary. The word is listed first, usually followed by its pronunciation. Then come the definitions, organized by parts of speech. Sometimes the most frequently used definitions are listed first.

To find the best word for your needs, you should refer to the abbreviations and the explanatory notes that appear next to the entries. For example, imagine that you are writing about your pastimes. You want to write, "I want to buy a new racket for my match tomorrow," but you don't know the Spanish word for "racket." In the dictionary, you may find an entry like this:

> **racket** *s* **1.** alboroto; **2.** raqueta (*dep.*)

The abbreviation key at the front of the dictionary says that *s* corresponds to **sustantivo** (*noun*). Then, the first word you see is **alboroto**. The definition of **alboroto** is *noise* or *racket*, so **alboroto** is probably not the word you're looking for. The second word is **raqueta**, followed by the abbreviation *dep.*, which stands for **deportes**. This indicates that the word **raqueta** is the best choice for your needs.

Tema
Escribir un folleto

Choose one topic to write a brochure.

1. You are the head of the Homecoming Committee at your school this year. Create a pamphlet that lists events for Friday night, Saturday, and Sunday. Include a brief description of each event and its time and location. Include activities for different age groups, since some alumni will bring their families.

2. You are on the Freshman Student Orientation Committee and are in charge of creating a pamphlet for new students that describes the sports offered at your school. Write the flyer and include activities for both men and women.

3. You work for the Chamber of Commerce in your community. It is your job to market your community to potential residents. Write a brief pamphlet that describes the recreational opportunities your community provides, the areas where the activities take place, and the costs, if any. Be sure to include activities that will appeal to singles as well as couples and families; you should include activities for all age groups and for both men and women.

Escuchar Audio

Estrategia
Listening for the gist

Listening for the general idea, or gist, can help you follow what someone is saying even if you can't hear or understand some of the words. When you listen for the gist, you simply try to capture the essence of what you hear without focusing on individual words.

 To help you practice this strategy, you will listen to a paragraph made up of three sentences. Jot down a brief summary of what you hear.

Preparación

Based on the photo, what do you think Anabela is like? Do you and Anabela have similar interests?

Ahora escucha

You will hear first José talking, then Anabela. As you listen, check off each person's favorite activities.

Pasatiempos favoritos de José

1. _____ leer el correo electrónico
2. _____ jugar al béisbol
3. _____ ver películas de acción
4. _____ ir al café
5. _____ ir a partidos de béisbol
6. _____ ver películas románticas
7. _____ dormir la siesta
8. _____ escribir mensajes electrónicos

Pasatiempos favoritos de Anabela

9. _____ esquiar
10. _____ nadar
11. _____ practicar el ciclismo
12. _____ jugar al golf
13. _____ jugar al baloncesto
14. _____ ir a ver partidos de tenis
15. _____ escalar montañas
16. _____ ver televisión

 Practice more at **vhlcentral.com**.

Comprensión
Preguntas

Answer these questions about José's and Anabela's pastimes.

1. ¿Quién practica más deportes?
2. ¿Quién piensa que es importante descansar?
3. ¿A qué deporte es aficionado José?
4. ¿Por qué Anabela no practica el baloncesto?
5. ¿Qué películas le gustan a la novia de José?
6. ¿Cuál es el deporte favorito de Anabela?

Seleccionar

Which person do these statements best describe?

1. Le gusta practicar deportes.
2. Prefiere las películas de acción.
3. Le gustan las computadoras.
4. Le gusta nadar.
5. Siempre (*Always*) duerme una siesta por la tarde.
6. Quiere ir de vacaciones a las montañas.

En pantalla

In many Spanish-speaking countries, soccer isn't just a game; it's a way of life. Many countries have professional and amateur leagues, and soccer is even played in the streets. Every four years, during the World Cup, even those who aren't big fans of the sport find it impossible not to get swept up in "soccer fever." During the month-long Cup, passions only increase with each of the sixty-four matches played. Companies also get caught up in the soccer craze, running ad campaigns and offering promotions with prizes ranging from commemorative glasses to all-expenses-paid trips to the World Cup venue.

Vocabulario útil	
cracks	*stars, aces (sports)*
lo tuvo a Pelé de hijo	*he was a better player than Pelé (coll. expr. Peru)*
Dios me hizo	*God made me*
patito feo	*ugly duckling*
plata	*money (S. America)*
jugando	*playing*

Comprensión

Indicate whether each statement is **cierto** or **falso**.

	Cierto	Falso
1. La familia juega al baloncesto.	○	○
2. No hay mujeres en el anuncio (*ad*).	○	○
3. La pareja tiene cinco hijos.	○	○
4. El hijo más joven es un mariachi.	○	○

Conversación

With a partner, discuss these questions in Spanish.

1. En el anuncio hay varios elementos culturales representativos de la cultura de los países hispanos. ¿Cuáles son?

2. ¿Qué otros elementos culturales de los países hispanos conocen (*do you know*)?

jugaba used to play cuna crib barriga womb Por eso That's why esperaban que yo fuera they expected that I would be el mejor de todos the best of all

Anuncio de Totofútbol

Mi hermano mayor jugaba° desde la cuna°.

Mi segundo hermano, desde la barriga°.

Por eso° esperaban que yo fuera° el mejor de todos°.

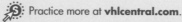 **Video: TV Clip**

 Practice more at **vhlcentral.com**.

¡Fútbol en España!

The rivalry between the teams **Real Madrid** and **F.C. Barcelona** is perhaps the fiercest in all of soccer—just imagine if they occupied the same city! Well, each team also has competing clubs within its respective city: Spain's capital has the **Club Atlético de Madrid**, and Barcelona is home to **Espanyol**. In fact, across the Spanish-speaking world, it is common for a city to have more than one professional team, often with strikingly dissimilar origins, identity, and fan base. For example, in Bogotá, the **Millonarios** were so named for the large sums spent on players, while the **Santa Fe** team is one of the most traditional in Colombian soccer. **River Plate** and **Boca Juniors**, who enjoy a famous rivalry, are just two of twenty-four clubs in Buenos Aires—the city with the most professional soccer teams in the world.

Vocabulario útil

afición	fans
celebran	they celebrate
preferido/a	favorite
rivalidad	rivalry
se junta con	it's tied up with

Preparación

What is the most popular sport at your school? What teams are your rivals? How do students celebrate a win?

Escoger

Select the correct answer.

1. Un partido entre el Barça y el Real Madrid es un _____ (deporte/evento) importante en toda España.

2. Ronaldinho fue (*was*) un futbolista estrella (*soccer star*) del _____ (Barça/Real Madrid).

3. Los aficionados _____ (miran/celebran) las victorias de sus equipos en las calles (*streets*).

4. La rivalidad entre el Real Madrid y el Barça está relacionada con la _____ (religión/política).

(Hay mucha afición al fútbol en España.)

¿Y cuál es vuestro jugador favorito?

—¿Y quién va a ganar?
—El Real Madrid.

Video: Flash cultura

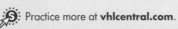
Practice more at **vhlcentral.com**.

recursos
VM pp. 237–238 | vhlcentral.com Lección 4

Lección 4

S Video: *Panorama cultural*
Interactive map

México

El país en cifras

▸ **Área:** 1.972.550 km²
(761.603 millas²), *casi° tres veces°*
el área de Texas

La situación geográfica de México,
al sur° de los Estados Unidos, ha
influido en° la economía y la sociedad de los dos
países. Una de las consecuencias es la emigración
de la población mexicana al país vecino°. Hoy día,
más de 30 millones de personas de ascendencia
mexicana viven en los Estados Unidos.

▸ **Población:** 115.528.000

▸ **Capital:** México, D.F. (y su área
metropolitana)—20.078.000

▸ **Ciudades principales:** Guadalajara
—4.648.000, Monterrey—4.118.000,
Puebla—2.460.000,
Ciudad Juárez—1.470.000

SOURCE: Population Division, UN Secretariat

▸ **Moneda:** peso mexicano

▸ **Idiomas:** español (oficial), náhuatl,
otras lenguas indígenas

Bandera de México

Mexicanos célebres

▸ **Benito Juárez,** héroe nacional (1806–1872)
▸ **Octavio Paz,** poeta (1914–1998)
▸ **Elena Poniatowska,** periodista y escritora
(1933–)
▸ **Julio César Chávez,** boxeador (1962–)

casi *almost* veces *times* sur *south* ha influido en *has influenced*
vecino *neighboring* se llenan de luz *get filled with light* flores *flowers*
Muertos *Dead* se ríen *laugh* muerte *death* lo cual se refleja *which is*
reflected calaveras de azúcar *sugar skulls* pan *bread* huesos *bones*

Cabo San Lucas

ESTADOS UNIDOS

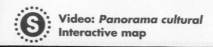

Autorretrato con mono
(*Self-portrait with monkey*),
1938, Frida Kahlo

Ciudad Juárez

Río Grande

Río Bravo del Norte

Golfo de California

Baja California

Sierra Madre Oriental

Sierra Madre Occidental

ESTADOS UNIDOS

MÉXICO

OCÉANO
PACÍFICO

OCÉANO
ATLÁNTICO

AMÉRICA DEL SUR

Monterrey

Océano Pacífico

Puerto
Vallarta

Ciudad de
México

Guadalajara

Puebla

Acapulco

Artesanías
en Taxco, Guerrero

recursos

WB
pp. 231–232

VM
pp. 235–236

S vhlcentral.com
Lección 4

Pirámide de Kukulcán
en Chichén Itzá

¡Increíble pero cierto!

Cada dos de noviembre los cementerios de
México se llenan de luz°, música y flores°. El Día
de Muertos° no es un evento triste; es una fiesta
en honor a las personas muertas. En ese día,
los mexicanos se ríen° de la muerte°, lo cual se
refleja° en detalles como las calaveras de azúcar°
y el pan° de muerto —pan en forma de huesos°.

Ciudades • México, D.F.

La Ciudad de México, fundada° en 1525, también se llama el D.F. o Distrito Federal. Muchos turistas e inmigrantes vienen a la ciudad porque es el centro cultural y económico del país. El crecimiento° de la población es de los más altos° del mundo. El D.F. tiene una población mayor que las de Nueva York, Madrid o París.

Artes • Diego Rivera y Frida Kahlo

Frida Kahlo y Diego Rivera eran° artistas mexicanos muy famosos. Se casaron° en 1929. Los dos se interesaron° en las condiciones sociales de la gente indígena de su país. Puedes ver algunas° de sus obras° en el Museo de Arte Moderno de la Ciudad de México.

Historia • Los aztecas

Los aztecas dominaron° en México del siglo° XIV al siglo XVI. Sus canales, puentes° y pirámides con templos religiosos eran muy importantes.
El fin del imperio azteca comenzó° con la llegada° de los españoles en 1519, pero la presencia azteca sigue hoy. La Ciudad de México está situada en la capital azteca de Tenochtitlán, y muchos turistas van a visitar sus ruinas.

Economía • La plata

México es el mayor productor de plata° del mundo°. Estados como Zacatecas y Durango tienen ciudades fundadas cerca de los más grandes yacimientos° de plata del país. Estas ciudades fueron° en la época colonial unas de las más ricas e importantes. Hoy en día, aún° conservan mucho de su encanto° y esplendor.

Península de Yucatán

Mérida

Cancún

olfo México

ía de peche

no de antepec

BELICE

GUATEMALA

 ¿Qué aprendiste? Responde a cada pregunta con una oración completa.

1. ¿Qué lenguas hablan los mexicanos?

2. ¿Cómo es la población del D.F. en comparación con la de otras ciudades?

3. ¿En qué se interesaron Frida Kahlo y Diego Rivera?

4. Nombra algunas de las estructuras de la arquitectura azteca.

5. ¿Dónde está situada la capital de México?

6. ¿Qué estados de México tienen los mayores yacimientos de plata?

 Conexión Internet Investiga estos temas en **vhlcentral.com**.

Practice more at **vhlcentral.com**.

1. Busca información sobre dos lugares de México. ¿Te gustaría (*Would you like*) vivir allí? ¿Por qué?

2. Busca información sobre dos artistas mexicanos. ¿Cómo se llaman sus obras más famosas?

....

fundada *founded* **crecimiento** *growth* **más altos** *highest* **eran** *were* **Se casaron** *They got married* **se interesaron** *were interested* **algunas** *some* **obras** *works* **dominaron** *dominated* **siglo** *century* **puentes** *bridges* **comenzó** *started* **llegada** *arrival* **plata** *silver* **mundo** *world* **yacimientos** *deposits* **fueron** *were* **aún** *still* **encanto** *charm*

Lección 4

Pasatiempos

andar en patineta	to skateboard
bucear	to scuba dive
escalar montañas (f., pl.)	to climb mountains
escribir una carta	to write a letter
escribir un mensaje electrónico	to write an e-mail
esquiar	to ski
ganar	to win
ir de excursión	to go on a hike
leer correo electrónico	to read e-mail
leer un periódico	to read a newspaper
leer una revista	to read a magazine
nadar	to swim
pasear	to take a walk; to stroll
pasear en bicicleta	to ride a bicycle
patinar (en línea)	to (inline) skate
practicar deportes (m., pl.)	to play sports
tomar el sol	to sunbathe
ver películas (f., pl.)	to watch movies
visitar monumentos (m., pl.)	to visit monuments
la diversión	fun activity; entertainment; recreation
el fin de semana	weekend
el pasatiempo	pastime; hobby
los ratos libres	spare (free) time
el videojuego	video game

Deportes

el baloncesto	basketball
el béisbol	baseball
el ciclismo	cycling
el equipo	team
el esquí (acuático)	(water) skiing
el fútbol	soccer
el fútbol americano	football
el golf	golf
el hockey	hockey
el/la jugador(a)	player
la natación	swimming
el partido	game; match
la pelota	ball
el tenis	tennis
el vóleibol	volleyball

Adjetivos

deportivo/a	sports-related
favorito/a	favorite

Lugares

el café	café
el centro	downtown
el cine	movie theater
el gimnasio	gymnasium
la iglesia	church
el lugar	place
el museo	museum
el parque	park
la piscina	swimming pool
la plaza	city or town square
el restaurante	restaurant

Verbos

almorzar (o:ue)	to have lunch
cerrar (e:ie)	to close
comenzar (e:ie)	to begin
conseguir (e:i)	to get; to obtain
contar (o:ue)	to count; to tell
decir (e:i)	to say; to tell
dormir (o:ue)	to sleep
empezar (e:ie)	to begin
encontrar (o:ue)	to find
entender (e:ie)	to understand
hacer	to do; to make
ir	to go
jugar (u:ue)	to play (a sport or a game)
mostrar (o:ue)	to show
oír	to hear
pedir (e:i)	to ask for; to request
pensar (e:ie)	to think
pensar (+ inf.)	to intend
pensar en	to think about
perder (e:ie)	to lose; to miss
poder (o:ue)	to be able to; can
poner	to put; to place
preferir (e:ie)	to prefer
querer (e:ie)	to want; to love
recordar (o:ue)	to remember
repetir (e:i)	to repeat
salir	to leave
seguir (e:i)	to follow; to continue
suponer	to suppose
traer	to bring
ver	to see
volver (o:ue)	to return

Decir expressions	See page 206.
Expresiones útiles	See page 191.

recursos

LM p. 244 | vhlcentral.com Lección 4

  **Audio: Vocabulary Flashcards**

contextos

1 **Los deportes** Name the sport associated with each object. Include the definite article.

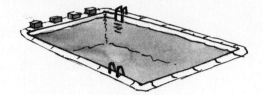

1. _____

2. _____

3. _____

4. _____

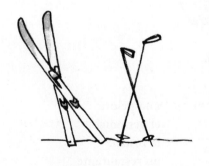

5. _____

6. _____

2 **Una es diferente** Write the word that does not belong in each group.

1. pasatiempo, diversión, ratos libres, trabajar _____

2. patinar, descansar, esquiar, nadar, bucear _____

3. baloncesto, películas, fútbol, tenis, vóleibol _____

4. museo, equipo, jugador, partido, aficionados _____

5. correo electrónico, revista, periódico, tenis _____

6. cine, deportivo, gimnasio, piscina, restaurante _____

3 **¿Qué son?** Write each of these words in the appropriate column in the chart.

andar en patineta	fútbol	montaña
baloncesto	gimnasio	natación
béisbol	jugar un videojuego	pasear
centro	leer una revista	restaurante

Deportes	Lugares	Actividades

4 **El fin de semana** Esteban is a very active young man. Complete the paragraph about his weekend with the appropriate words from the word bank.

Esteban

el cine	el monumento	una pelota
la ciudad	un museo	el periódico
deportes	la natación	la piscina
el gimnasio	el partido	un restaurante

Siempre leo (1) _____ los domingos por la mañana. Después, me gusta practicar

(2) _____. A veces, nado en (3) _____ que hay en el parque.

Cuando no nado, hago ejercicio (*exercise*) en (4) _____. Cuando hay mucho

tráfico en (5) _____, voy al gimnasio en bicicleta.

Cuando no como en casa, como en (6) _____ con mis amigos, y luego nosotros

podemos ver (7) _____ de béisbol. Algunos días, veo películas. Me gusta más ver

películas en (8) _____ que en mi casa.

estructura

4.1 Present tense of ir

1 **Vamos a la universidad** Complete the paragraph with the correct forms of **ir**.

Alina, Cristina y yo somos buenas amigas. (Nosotras) (1) _____ a la universidad a

las ocho de la mañana todos los días (*every day*). Ellas y yo (2) _____ al centro de

computación y leemos el correo electrónico. A las nueve Alina y Cristina (3) _____

a su clase de psicología y yo (4) _____ a mi clase de historia. A las diez y media

yo (5) _____ a la biblioteca a estudiar. A las doce (yo) (6) _____ a

la cafetería y como con ellas. Luego (*Afterwards*), Alina y yo (7) _____ a practicar

deportes. Yo (8) _____ a practicar fútbol y Alina (9) _____ a la

piscina. Cristina (10) _____ a trabajar en la librería. Los fines de semana Alina,

Cristina y yo (11) _____ al cine.

2 **Los planes** Mr. Díaz wants to make sure he knows about everything that is going on. Answer his questions in complete sentences using the words in parentheses.

1. ¿Adónde van Marissa y Felipe? (pasear por la ciudad)

   _____

2. ¿Cuándo van a correr los chicos? (noche)

   _____

3. ¿A qué hora van al Bosque de Chapultepec? (a las dos y media)

   _____

4. ¿Cuándo van a ir a la playa? (martes)

   _____

5. ¿Qué va a hacer Jimena en el parque? (leer un libro)

   _____

6. ¿Qué va a hacer Felipe en el parque? (jugar al fútbol)

   _____

3 **Conversación** Complete this conversation with the correct forms of **ir**.

ELENA ¡Hola, Daniel! ¿Qué tal?

DANIEL Muy bien, gracias. ¿Y tú?

ELENA Muy bien. ¿Adónde (1) _____ ahora?

DANIEL (2) _____ al cine a ver una película. ¿Quieres (3) _____ conmigo?

ELENA No, gracias. Tengo mucha prisa ahora. (4) _____ al museo de arte.

DANIEL ¿Y adónde (5) _____ hoy por la noche?

ELENA Mi compañera de cuarto y yo (6) _____ a comer en un restaurante italiano. ¿Quieres (7) _____ con nosotras?

DANIEL ¡Sí! ¿Cómo (8) _____ ustedes al restaurante?

ELENA (9) _____ en autobús. Hay un autobús que (10) _____ directamente al barrio (*neighborhood*) italiano.

DANIEL ¿A qué hora (11) _____ ustedes?

ELENA Creo que (12) _____ a llegar al restaurante a las nueve.

DANIEL ¿Desean (13) _____ a bailar luego (*afterwards*)?

ELENA ¡Sí!

DANIEL (14) _____ a invitar a nuestro amigo Pablo también. ¡Nos vemos a las nueve!

ELENA ¡Chau, Daniel!

4 **¡Vamos!** Víctor is planning a weekend out with his friends. Combine elements from each column to describe what everyone is going to do. Use the correct verb forms.

ustedes	ver películas	el domingo
nosotros	ir al estadio de fútbol	el fin de semana
Víctor	tomar el sol	al mediodía
Claudio y su primo	visitar monumentos	a las tres
tú	pasear por el parque	por la noche
yo	comer en el restaurante	por la mañana

_____

_____

_____

_____

_____

_____

_____

_____

4.2 Stem-changing verbs: e→ie, o→ue

1

¿Qué hacen? Write complete sentences using the cues provided.

1. Vicente y Francisco / jugar / al vóleibol los domingos

   _____

2. Adela y yo / empezar / a tomar clases de tenis

   _____

3. ustedes / volver / de Cancún el viernes

   _____

4. los jugadores de béisbol / recordar / el partido importante

   _____

5. la profesora / mostrar / las palabras del vocabulario

   _____

6. Adán / preferir / escalar la montaña de noche

   _____

7. (yo) / entender / el plan de estudios

   _____

8. (tú) / cerrar / los libros y te vas a dormir

   _____

2

Quiero ir Alejandro wants to go on a hike with his friends, but Gabriela says he doesn't have time. Write the correct forms of the verbs in parentheses.

ALEJANDRO ¿(1) _____ (poder) ir a la excursión con ustedes? Aunque (*Although*) tengo que volver a mi casa a las tres.

GABRIELA No, no (2) _____ (poder) venir. Nosotros (3) _____ (pensar) salir a las doce.

ALEJANDRO Yo (4) _____ (querer) ir. ¿(5) _____ (poder) ustedes volver a las dos?

GABRIELA No, tú tienes que comprender: Nosotros no (6) _____ (volver) a las dos. Nosotros (7) _____ (preferir) estar más tiempo en el pueblo.

ALEJANDRO Bueno, ¿a qué hora (8) _____ (pensar) regresar?

GABRIELA Yo no (9) _____ (pensar) volver hasta las nueve o las diez de la noche.

3   **No, no quiero**   Answer these questions negatively, using complete sentences.

> **modelo**
>
> ¿Puedes ir a la biblioteca a las once?
>
> *No, no puedo ir a la biblioteca a las once.*

1. ¿Quieren ustedes patinar en línea con nosotros?

2. ¿Recuerdan ellas los libros que necesitan?

3. ¿Prefieres jugar al fútbol a nadar en la piscina?

4. ¿Duermen tus sobrinos en casa de tu abuela?

5. ¿Juegan ustedes al baloncesto en la universidad?

6. ¿Piensas que la clase de química orgánica es difícil?

7. ¿Encuentras el programa de computadoras en la librería?

8. ¿Vuelven ustedes a casa los fines de semana?

9. ¿Puedo tomar el autobús a las once de la noche?

10. ¿Entendemos la tarea de psicología?

4   **Mensaje electrónico**   Complete this e-mail message with the correct form of the logical verb. Use each verb once.

dormir
empezar
entender
jugar
pensar
poder
preferir
querer
volver

Para Daniel Moncada	De Paco	Asunto Saludo

Hola, Daniel. Estoy con Mario en la biblioteca. Los exámenes (1) _____ mañana. Por las noches Mario y yo no (2) _____ mucho porque tenemos que estudiar. Tú (3) _____ cómo estamos, ¿no? Yo (4) _____ que los exámenes serán (*will be*) muy difíciles. Tengo muchas ganas de volver al pueblo. Cuando (5) _____ al pueblo puedo descansar. Yo (6) _____ el pueblo a la ciudad. (7) _____ volver pronto. Si (*If*) Mario y yo compramos pasajes (*tickets*) de autobús, (8) _____ pasar el fin de semana contigo. En casa (*At home*) mis hermanos y yo (9) _____ al fútbol en nuestros ratos libres.

Nos vemos,
Paco

4.3 Stem-changing verbs: e→i

1

En el cine Amalia and her brothers are going to the movies. Complete the story using the correct form of the verb provided.

1. Al entrar al cine, mis hermanos _____ (pedir) una soda.

2. Mis hermanos _____ (decir) que prefieren las películas de acción.

3. Nosotros _____ (pedir) ver la película de las seis y media.

4. Mis hermanos y yo _____ (conseguir) entradas (*tickets*) para estudiantes.

5. Yo _____ (repetir) el diálogo para mis hermanos.

6. Mis hermanos son pequeños y no _____ (seguir) bien la trama (*plot*) de la película.

2

Conversaciones Complete these conversations with the correct form of the verbs in parentheses.

(pedir)

1. —¿Qué _____ en la biblioteca, José?

2. — _____ un libro que necesito para el examen.

(conseguir)

3. —¿Dónde _____ ustedes las entradas (*tickets*) para los partidos de fútbol?

4. —Nosotros _____ las entradas en una oficina de la escuela.

(repetir)

5. —¿Quién _____ la excursión?

6. —Yo _____, me gusta mucho ese pueblo.

(seguir)

7. —¿Qué equipo _____ Manuel y Pedro?

8. —Pedro _____ a los Red Sox y Manuel _____ a los Yankees de Nueva York.

3

¿Qué haces? Imagine that you are writing in your diary. Choose at least five of these phrases and describe what you do on any given day. You should add any details you feel are necessary.

conseguir hablar español	pedir una pizza
conseguir el periódico	repetir una pregunta
pedir un libro	seguir las instrucciones

_____

_____

_____

_____

_____

4 **La película** Read the paragraph. Then answer the questions using complete sentences.

Gastón y Lucía leen el periódico y deciden ir al cine. Un crítico dice que *Una noche en el centro* es buena. Ellos siguen la recomendación. Quieren conseguir entradas (*tickets*) para estudiantes, que son más baratas. Para conseguir entradas para estudiantes, deben ir a la oficina de la escuela antes de las seis de la tarde. La oficina cierra a las seis. Ellos corren para llegar a tiempo. Cuando ellos llegan, la oficina está cerrada y la secretaria está afuera (*outside*). Ellos le piden un favor a la secretaria. Explican que no tienen mucho dinero y necesitan entradas para estudiantes. La secretaria sonríe (*smiles*) y dice: "Está bien, pero es la última vez (*last time*)".

1. ¿Qué deciden hacer Gastón y Lucía?

   _____

2. ¿Siguen la recomendación de quién?

   _____

3. ¿Por qué Gastón y Lucía quieren conseguir entradas para estudiantes?

   _____

4. ¿Cómo y cuándo pueden conseguir entradas para estudiantes?

   _____

5. ¿Qué ocurre cuando llegan a la oficina de la escuela?

   _____

   _____

6. ¿Qué le piden a la secretaria? ¿Crees que ellos consiguen las entradas?

   _____

   _____

5 **Preguntas** Answer these questions, using complete sentences.

1. ¿Cómo consigues buenas calificaciones (*grades*)?

   _____

2. ¿Dónde pides pizza?

   _____

3. ¿Sigues a algún (*any*) equipo deportivo?

   _____

4. ¿Qué dicen tus padres si no consigues buenas calificaciones?

   _____

5. ¿Qué programas repiten en la televisión?

   _____

4.4 Verbs with irregular **yo** forms

1

Hago muchas cosas Complete each sentence by choosing the best verb and writing its correct form.

1. (Yo) _____ un disco de música latina. (oír, suponer, salir)

2. (Yo) _____ la hamburguesa y la soda sobre la mesa. (poner, oír, suponer)

3. (Yo) _____ la tarea porque hay un examen mañana. (salir, hacer, suponer)

4. (Yo) _____ a mi sobrina a mi clase de baile. (traer, salir, hacer)

5. (Yo) _____ una película sobre un gran equipo de béisbol. (salir, suponer, ver)

6. (Yo) _____ a bailar los jueves por la noche. (ver, salir, traer)

7. (Yo) _____ que la película es buena, pero no estoy seguro (*sure*). (hacer, poner, suponer)

8. (Yo) _____ mi computadora portátil (*laptop*) a clase en la mochila. (traer, salir, hacer)

2

Completar Complete these sentences with the correct verb. Use each verb in the **yo** form once.

hacer	suponer
oír	traer
salir	ver

1. _____ para la clase a las dos.

2. Los fines de semana _____ mi computadora a casa.

3. _____ que me gusta trabajar los sábados por la mañana.

4. Por las mañanas, _____ música en la radio.

5. Cuando tengo hambre, _____ un sándwich.

6. Para descansar, _____ películas en la televisión.

3

Preguntas Answer these questions, using complete sentences.

1. ¿Adónde sales a bailar con tus amigos?

_____

2. ¿Ves partidos de béisbol todos los fines de semana?

_____

3. ¿Oyes música clásica?

_____

4. ¿Traes una computadora portátil (*laptop*) a clase?

_____

5. ¿Cómo supones que va a ser el examen de español?

_____

6. ¿Cuándo sales a comer?

_____

4   **La descripción**   Read this description of Marisol. Then imagine that you are Marisol, and write a description of yourself based on the information you read. The first sentence has been done for you.

Marisol es estudiante de biología en la universidad. Hace sus tareas todas (*every*) las tardes y sale por las noches a bailar o a comer en un restaurante cerca de la universidad. Los fines de semana, Marisol va a su casa a descansar, pero (*but*) trae sus libros. En los ratos libres, oye música o ve una película en el cine. Si hay un partido de fútbol, Marisol pone la televisión y ve los partidos con su papá. Hace algo (*something*) de comer y pone la mesa (*sets the table*).

Soy estudiante de biología en la universidad. _____

_____

_____

_____

_____

_____

_____

_____

Síntesis

Interview a classmate about his or her pastimes, weekend activities, and favorite sports. Use these questions as guidelines, and prepare several more before the interview. Then, write up the interview in a question-and-answer format, faithfully reporting your classmate's responses.

- ¿Cuáles son tus pasatiempos? ¿Dónde los practicas?
- ¿Cuál es tu deporte favorito? ¿Practicas ese (*that*) deporte? ¿Eres un(a) gran aficionado/a? ¿Tu equipo favorito pierde muchas veces? ¿Quién es tu jugador(a) favorito/a?
- ¿Adónde vas los fines de semana? ¿Qué piensas hacer este (*this*) viernes?
- ¿Duermes mucho los fines de semana? ¿Vuelves a casa muy tarde (*late*)?

_____

_____

_____

_____

_____

_____

_____

panorama

México _____

1 **Palabras** Use the clues to put the letters in order, spelling words in **Panorama**.

1. MGEÓINARIC _____
   resultado de la proximidad geográfica de México y los EE.UU.

2. ÍAD ED RMOTESU _____
   celebración en honor a las personas muertas

3. ALUJDAAAGRA _____
   ciudad número dos de México en población

4. ONETBI RZUEÁJ _____
   héroe nacional de México

5. CÁUNYAT _____
   península mexicana

6. ARSISTUT _____
   cl D.F. atrae a miles de ellos

7. RADIF OKLAH _____
   la esposa de Diego Rivera

8. NGADORU _____
   estado mexicano que produce mucha plata

2 **¿Cierto o falso?** Indicate if each statement is **cierto** or **falso**. Then correct the false statements.

1. El área de México es casi dos veces el área de Texas.

   _____

2. Octavio Paz era un célebre periodista y narrador mexicano.

   _____

3. La geografía de México influye en aspectos económicos y sociales.

   _____

4. No hay mucho crecimiento en la población del D.F.

   _____

5. Frida Kahlo y Diego Rivera eran escritores.

   _____

6. El fin del imperio azteca comenzó (*started*) con la llegada (*arrival*) de los españoles en 1519.

   _____

7. Los turistas van a Guadalajara a ver las ruinas de Tenochtitlán.

   _____

8. México es el mayor productor de plata en el mundo.

   _____

3 **Completar** Complete these sentences with the correct words.

1. México está localizado geográficamente al _____ de los Estados Unidos.

2. Hoy en día hay _____ de personas de ascendencia mexicana en los Estados Unidos.

3. Los idiomas que se hablan en México son el español, el _____ y _____.

4. Frida Kahlo, esposa del artista _____, es conocida por sus autorretratos (*self-portraits*).

5. El imperio _____ dominó México del siglo XIV al siglo XVI.

6. Se celebra el Día de Muertos en los _____.

4 **¿Qué hacen?** Write sentences using these cues and adding what you learned in **Panorama**.

1. la tercera (*third*) ciudad de México en población / ser

_____

2. la moneda mexicana / ser

_____

3. el Distrito Federal / atraer (*to attract*)

_____

4. muchos turistas / ir a ver las ruinas de

_____

5. el D.F. / tener una población mayor que las de

_____

6. tú / poder / ver / las obras de Diego Rivera y Frida Kahlo en

_____

5 **Preguntas** Answer these questions in complete sentences.

1. ¿Cuáles son las cinco ciudades más importantes de México?

_____

2. ¿Quiénes son seis mexicanos célebres?

_____

3. ¿Qué países hacen frontera (*border*) con México?

_____

4. ¿Cuál es un río importante de México?

_____

5. ¿Cuáles son dos sierras importantes de México?

_____

6. ¿Qué ciudad mexicana importante está en la frontera con los EE.UU.?

_____

7. ¿En qué siglo (*century*) fue (*was*) fundada la Ciudad de México?

_____

Fútbol, cenotes y mole

...

Antes de ver el video

1 **El cenote** In this episode, Miguel, Maru, Marissa, and Jimena are going to a cenote to swim. What do you think they will see? What will they talk about?

_____
_____
_____
_____
_____
_____

Mientras ves el video

2 **Verbos** These sentences are taken from **Fútbol, cenotes y mole**. As you watch this segment, fill in the blanks with the missing verbs.

1. ¿No vamos a _____? ¿Qué es un cenote?
2. Ella nada y _____ al tenis y al golf.
3. Bueno, chicos, ya es hora, ¡_____!
4. Si _____, compramos el almuerzo.

3 **¿Qué ves?** Check what you see.

____ 1. una pelota de fútbol
____ 2. un mensaje de correo electrónico
____ 3. una mochila
____ 4. un videojuego

____ 5. un periódico
____ 6. un restaurante
____ 7. una plaza
____ 8. un cine

4 **Completar** Fill in the blanks in Column A with words from Column B.

A	B
1. Miguel dice que un cenote es una _____ natural.	montañas
2. Marissa dice que donde ella vive no hay _____.	pasatiempos
3. La tía Ana María tiene muchos _____ y actividades.	almorzar
4. La tía Ana María va al cine y a los _____.	museos
5. Eduardo y Pablo dicen que hay un partido de fútbol en el _____.	nadan
6. Don Guillermo dice que hay muchos _____ buenos en Mérida.	piscina
7. Felipe desea _____ mole.	restaurantes
8. Marissa y sus amigos _____ en el cenote.	parque

Después de ver el video

5 **¿Qué hacen?** For numbers 1–11, fill in the missing letters in each word. For number 12, put the letters in the boxes in the right order.

1. Pablo dice que si no consigue más jugadores, su equipo va a ☐ __ __ d __ __.
2. Miguel dice que en México sólo hay __ __ n __ __ __ ☐ en la península de Yucatán.
3. Felipe dice que el restaurante del mole está en el __ __ __ ☐ __ o.
4. La tía Ana María sale mucho los __ __ n __ ☐ de semana.
5. Don Guillermo dice que hay un buen restaurante en la ☐ __ a __ __.
6. El mole de la tía Ana María es el __ __ v __ __ ☐ __ __ de Jimena.
7. Juan Carlos y Felipe van a __ __ __ ☐ r al fútbol con Eduardo y Pablo.
8. Eduardo juega con la p ☐ __ __ __ __ después del partido.
9. Eduardo y Pablo van a pagar lo que Felipe y Juan Carlos van a ☐ __ m __ __ __ __ __.
10. Marissa no escala ☐ __ __ t __ __ __ __.
11. Los chicos hablan con don Guillermo después de jugar al __ __ __ b ☐ __.
12. La tía Ana María tiene muchos _____.

6 **Me gusta** Fill in the chart with the activities, hobbies, or sports that you enjoy. Also say when and where you do each activity.

Mis pasatiempos favoritos	¿Cuándo?	¿Dónde?

7 **Preguntas** Answer these questions in Spanish.

1. ¿Son aficionados/as a los deportes tus amigos/as? ¿Cuáles son sus deportes favoritos?

_____

_____

_____

2. ¿Qué hacen tú y tus amigos/as cuando tienen ratos libres?

_____

_____

_____

3. ¿Qué vas a hacer esta noche? ¿Vas a estudiar? ¿Descansar? ¿Mirar televisión? ¿Ver una película? ¿Por qué? _____

_____

_____

_____

Panorama: México

Lección 4
Panorama cultural

Antes de ver el video

1 **Más vocabulario** Look over these useful words before you watch the video.

Vocabulario útil			
día *day*	estos *these*	gente *people*	sentir *to feel*
energía *energy*	fiesta *party, celebration*	para *to*	valle *valley*

2 **Describir** In this video, you will learn about the archaeological ruins of Teotihuacán where the celebration of the equinox takes place every year. Do you know what the equinox is? In English, try to write a description.

equinoccio: _____

_____

3 **Categorías** Categorize the words listed in the word bank.

arqueológicos	gente	increíble	mexicanos	Teotihuacán
capital mexicana	hacen	interesante	moderno	tienen
celebrar	hombres	jóvenes	mujeres	Valle de México
ciudad	importante	Latinoamérica	niños	van
escalar				

Lugares	Personas	Verbos	Adjetivos

Mientras ves el video

4 **Marcar** Check off the pastimes you see while watching the video.

____ 1. pasear
____ 2. nadar
____ 3. patinar
____ 4. escalar (pirámides)
____ 5. tomar el sol
____ 6. ver películas
____ 7. visitar monumentos
____ 8. bucear

Después de ver el video

5 **Completar** Fill in the blanks with the appropriate word(s).

la capital mexicana	muy interesante
la celebración del equinoccio	pasean
celebrar	sentir
comienzan	sol
manos	el Valle de México

1. Teotihuacán está a cincuenta kilómetros de _____.

2. A _____ van muchos grupos de música tradicional.

3. Todos quieren _____ la energía del sol en sus _____.

4. Ir a las pirámides de Teotihuacán es una experiencia _____.

5. Las personas _____ por las ruinas.

6 **¿Cierto o falso?** Indicate whether each statement is **cierto** or **falso**. Correct the false statements.

1. Las pirámides de Teotihuacán están lejos del Valle de México.

   _____

2. Muchas personas van a Teotihuacán todos los años para celebrar el equinoccio.

   _____

3. Turistas de muchas nacionalidades van a la celebración.

   _____

4. La gente prefiere ir a Teotihuacán los martes.

   _____

5. La celebración del equinoccio termina a las cinco de la mañana.

   _____

6. Las personas celebran la energía que reciben de Teotihuacán todos los años.

   _____

7 **Foto** Describe the video still. Write at least three sentences in Spanish.

   _____

   _____

   _____

   _____

   _____

¡Fútbol en España!

Antes de ver el video

1 **Más vocabulario** Look over these useful words before you watch the video.

Vocabulario útil		
la afición *fans*	nunca *never*	seguro/a *sure*
más allá *beyond*	se junta (con) *is intertwined (with)*	la válvula de escape *outlet*

2 **¡En español!** Look at the video still. Imagine what Mari Carmen will say about soccer in Spain, and write a two- or three-sentence introduction to this episode.

Mari Carmen Ortiz, Barcelona

¡Hola, amigos! ¡Bienvenidos a *Flash cultura*! Hoy vamos a hablar de... _____

_____

_____

_____

_____

Mientras ves el video

3 **Identificar** You might see any of these actions in a video about soccer in Spain. Check off the items you see in this episode.

___ a. celebrar un gol (*goal*)   ___ d. hablar con un jugador famoso   ___ f. pasear en bicicleta

___ b. comer churros   ___ e. jugar al fútbol   ___ g. celebrar en las calles (*streets*)

___ c. ganar un premio (*award*)   ___ h. jugar al fútbol americano

4 **Emparejar** Indicate which teams these people are affiliated with.

○ Barça
○ Real Madrid
○ no corresponde

○ Barça
○ Real Madrid
○ no corresponde

○ Barça
○ Real Madrid
○ no corresponde

Después de ver el video

5 **Completar** Complete each statement with the correct option.

| aficionados al fútbol | brasileños | guapo | feo | Red Sox |

1. En España hay muchos _____.

2. Ronaldinho y Ronaldo son dos futbolistas (*soccer players*) _____ famosos.

3. La rivalidad entre el Barça y el Real Madrid es comparable con la rivalidad entre los Yankees y los _____ en béisbol.

4. Mari Carmen piensa que David Beckham es _____.

6 **Aficionados** Who are these fans? Imagine what they would say if they introduced themselves. Write information like their name, age, origin, team affiliation, and any other details that come to mind.

> **modelo**
>
> **Aficionado:** ¡Hola! Soy José Artigas y soy de Madrid. Mi equipo favorito es el Real Madrid. Miro todos los partidos en el estadio. ¡VIVA EL REAL MADRID! ¡Nunca pierde!

_____

_____

_____

_____

_____

_____

_____

_____

7 **David Beckham** Imagine that you are Mari Carmen and you decide to interview David Beckham. Write five questions you would ask him.

> **modelo**
>
> ¿Dónde prefieres vivir: en España o en los Estados Unidos?

_____

_____

_____

_____

contextos

1 **Lugares** You will hear six people describe what they are doing. Choose the place that corresponds to the activity.

1. _____   a. el museo   e. el estadio

2. _____   b. el café   f. las montañas

3. _____   c. la piscina   g. el parque

4. _____   d. el cine   h. la biblioteca

5. _____

6. _____

2 **Describir** For each drawing, you will hear two statements. Choose the one that corresponds to the drawing.

1. a.   b.

2. a.   b.

3. a.   b.

4. a.   b.

3 **Completar** Listen to this description and write the missing words in your lab manual.

Chapultepec es un (1) _____ muy grande en el (2) _____ de

la (3) _____ de México. Los (4) _____ muchas

(5) _____ llegan a Chapultepec a pasear, descansar y practicar

(6) _____ como (*like*) el (7) _____, el fútbol, el vóleibol y

el (8) _____. Muchos turistas también (9) _____ por

Chapultepec. Visitan los (10) _____ y el (11) _____ a los

Niños Héroes.

pronunciación

Word stress and accent marks

Every Spanish syllable contains at least one vowel. When two vowels are joined in the same syllable, they form a diphthong. A monosyllable is a word formed by a single syllable.

pe - **lí** - cu - la   e - di - fi - **cio**   ver   **yo**

The syllable of a Spanish word that is pronounced most emphatically is the "stressed" syllable.

bi - blio - **te** - ca   vi - si - **tar**   **par** - que   **fút** - bol

Words that end in **n**, **s**, or a **vowel** are usually stressed on the next-to-last syllable.

pe - **lo** - ta   pis - **ci** - na   **ra** - tos   **ha** - blan

If words that end in **n**, **s**, or a **vowel** are stressed on the last syllable, they must carry an accent mark on the stressed syllable.

na - ta - **ción**   pa - **pá**   in - **glés**   Jo - **sé**

Words that do not end in **n**, **s**, or a **vowel** are usually stressed on the last syllable.

bai - **lar**   es - pa - **ñol**   u - ni - ver - si - **dad**   tra - ba - ja - **dor**

If words that do not end in **n**, **s**, or a **vowel** are stressed on the next-to-last syllable, they must carry an accent mark on the stressed syllable.

béis - bol   **lá** - piz   **ár** - bol   **Gó** - mez

1 Práctica Repeat each word after the speaker, stressing the correct syllable.

1. profesor   4. Mazatlán   7. niños   10. México
2. Puebla   5. examen   8. Guadalajara   11. están
3. ¿Cuántos?   6. ¿Cómo?   9. programador   12. geografía

2 Conversación Repeat the conversation after the speaker to practice word stress.

MARINA Hola, Carlos. ¿Qué tal?
CARLOS Bien. Oye, ¿a qué hora es el partido de fútbol?
MARINA Creo que es a las siete.
CARLOS ¿Quieres ir?
MARINA Lo siento, pero no puedo. Tengo que estudiar biología.

3 Refranes Repeat each saying after the speaker to practice word stress.

1. Quien ríe de último, ríe mejor.   2. En la unión está la fuerza.

4 Dictado You will hear six sentences. Each will be said twice. Listen carefully and write what you hear.

1. _____
2. _____
3. _____
4. _____
5. _____
6. _____

4.1 Present tense of **ir**

1 **Identificar** Listen to each sentence and mark an **X** in the column for the subject of the verb you hear.

> **modelo**
>
> *You hear:* Van a ver una película.
> *You mark:* an **X** under **ellos/ellas**.

	yo	tú	él/ella	nosotros/as	ellos/ellas
Modelo					X
1.					
2.					
3.					
4.					
5.					
6.					

2 **Cambiar** Form a new sentence using the cue you hear as the subject. Repeat the correct answer after the speaker. (*8 items*)

> **modelo**
>
> Ustedes van al Museo Frida Kahlo. (yo)
> *Yo voy al Museo Frida Kahlo.*

3 **Preguntas** Answer each question you hear using the cue in your lab manual. Repeat the correct response after the speaker.

> **modelo**
>
> *You hear:* ¿Quiénes van a la piscina?
> *You see:* Gustavo y Elisa
> *You say:* Gustavo y Elisa van a la piscina.

1. mis amigos
2. en el Café Tacuba
3. al partido de baloncesto
4. no
5. sí
6. pasear en bicicleta

4 **¡Vamos!** Listen to this conversation. Then read the statements in your lab manual and decide whether they are **cierto** or **falso**.

	Cierto	Falso
1. Claudia va a ir al gimnasio.	○	○
2. Claudia necesita comprar una mochila.	○	○
3. Sergio va a visitar a su tía.	○	○
4. Sergio va al gimnasio a las ocho de la noche.	○	○
5. Sergio va a ir al cine a las seis.	○	○
6. Claudia y Sergio van a ver una película.	○	○

4.2 Stem-changing verbs: **e→ie, o→ue**

1 **Identificar** Listen to each sentence and write the infinitive form of the verb you hear.

modelo

> *You hear:* No entiendo el problema.
> *You write:* entender

1. _____   4. _____   7. _____
2. _____   5. _____   8. _____
3. _____   6. _____

2 **Preguntas** Answer each question you hear using the cue in your lab manual. Repeat the correct response after the speaker.

modelo

> *You hear:* ¿A qué hora comienza el partido?
> *You see:* 2:15 p.m.
> *You say:* El partido comienza a las dos y cuarto de la tarde.

1. el jueves, (nosotros)   3. sí   5. leer una revista, (yo)   7. a las tres, (nosotros)
2. no, (yo)   4. sí, (ustedes)   6. mirar la televisión   8. Samuel

3 **Diversiones** Look at these listings from the entertainment section in a newspaper. Then listen to the questions and write the answers in your lab manual.

23D

MÚSICA	Pinturas de José Clemente	**Campeonato de baloncesto**
Palacio de Bellas Artes	Orozco	Los Universitarios vs. Los Toros
Ballet folclórico	De martes a domingo,	Gimnasio Municipal
Viernes 9, 8:30 p.m.	de 10:00 a.m. a 6:00 p.m.	Sábado 10, 7:30 p.m.
	Entrada libre	
Bosque de Chapultepec		**Torneo de Golf**
Concierto de música mexicana	**DEPORTES**	con Lee Treviño
Domingo, 1:00 p.m.	**Copa Internacional de Fútbol**	Club de Golf Atlas
	México vs. Guatemala	Domingo 8, 9:00 a.m.
MUSEOS	Estadio Martín	
Museo de Arte Moderno	Viernes 9, 8:30 p.m.	

1. _____
2. _____
3. _____
4. _____
5. _____

4.3 Stem-changing verbs: e→i

1 **Completar** Listen to this radio broadcast and fill in the missing words.

Este fin de semana los excursionistas (*hikers*) (1) _____ más senderos (*trails*).

Dicen que ir de (2) _____ a las montañas es una (3) _____

muy popular y (4) _____ que (5) _____ más senderos. Si lo

(6) _____, la gente va a (7) _____ muy feliz. Si no, ustedes

pueden (8) _____ la historia aquí, en Radio Montaña.

2 **Escoger** Listen to each question and choose the most logical response.

1. a. Normalmente pido tacos.   b. Voy al restaurante los lunes.
2. a. Consigo novelas en la biblioteca.   b. Consigo revistas en el centro.
3. a. Repiten la película el sábado.   b. No deseo ver la película.
4. a. Sigue un programa de baloncesto.   b. No, está buceando.
5. a. Nunca pido pizza.   b. Nunca pido perdón.
6. a. Prefiere visitar un monumento.   b. Prefiere buscar en la biblioteca.
7. a. ¿Quién fue el primer presidente?   b. A las cuatro de la tarde.
8. a. Sí, es muy interesante.   b. Sí, mi hermano juega.

3 **Conversación** Listen to the conversation and answer the questions.

1. ¿Qué quiere Paola?

   _____

2. ¿Por qué repite Paola las palabras?

   _____

3. ¿Hace Miguel el favor que pide Paola?

   _____

4. ¿Dónde puede conseguir la revista?

   _____

4.4 Verbs with irregular **yo** forms

1 **Describir** For each drawing, you will hear two statements. Choose the one that corresponds to the drawing

1. a.   b.   2. a.   b.

3. a.   b.   4. a.   b.

2 **Yo también** Listen to the following statements about Roberto and respond by saying that you do the same things. Repeat the correct answer after the speaker. (*5 items*)

> **modelo**
>
> Roberto siempre (*always*) hace ejercicio (*exercise*).
> *Yo también hago ejercicio.*

3 **Completar** Listen to this telephone conversation and complete the statements in your lab manual.

1. Cristina ve _____.

2. Manuel y Ricardo quieren ir al parque para _____.

3. Manuel y Ricardo _____ las pelotas.

4. Manuel _____ la hora porque Cristina no _____.

5. Los chicos salen para el parque _____.

vocabulario

You will now hear the vocabulary found in your textbook on the last page of this lesson. Listen and repeat each Spanish word or phrase after the speaker.

Additional Vocabulary

Additional Vocabulary

Notes

Las vacaciones

5

A PRIMERA VISTA
- ¿Están ellos en una montaña o en un museo?
- ¿Son viejos o jóvenes?
- ¿Pasean o ven una película? ¿Andan en patineta o van de excursión?
- ¿Es posible esquiar en este lugar?

Más práctica
Workbook pages 283–292
Video Manual pages 293–298
Lab Manual pages 299–304

Las vacaciones

Más vocabulario

la cama	bed
la habitación individual, doble	single, double room
el piso	floor (of a building)
la planta baja	ground floor
el campo	countryside
el paisaje	landscape
el equipaje	luggage
la estación de autobuses, del metro, de tren	bus, subway, train station
la llegada	arrival
el pasaje (de ida y vuelta)	(round-trip) ticket
la salida	departure; exit
la tabla de (wind)surf	surfboard/sailboard
acampar	to camp
estar de vacaciones	to be on vacation
hacer las maletas	to pack (one's suitcases)
hacer un viaje	to take a trip
hacer (wind)surf	to (wind)surf
ir de compras	to go shopping
ir de vacaciones	to go on vacation
ir en autobús (m.), auto(móvil) (m.), motocicleta (f.), taxi (m.)	to go by bus, car, motorcycle, taxi

Variación léxica

automóvil ⟷ coche (*Esp.*), carro (*Amér. L.*)

autobús ⟷ camión (*Méx.*), guagua (*Caribe*)

motocicleta ⟷ moto (*coloquial*)

la agente de viajes

el pasaporte

Confirma una reservación. (confirmar)

En la agencia de viajes

la habitación

el ascensor

el empleado

la llave

la huésped

el botones

el huésped

En el hotel

Saca/Toma fotos.
(sacar, tomar)

BIENVENIDOS

el avión

el viajero

la inspectora
de aduanas

En el aeropuerto

Pesca.
(pescar)

Monta a caballo.
(montar)

Va en barco.
(ir)

el mar

Juegan a las
cartas. (jugar)

la playa

En la playa

Práctica

1

Escuchar Indicate who would probably make each statement you hear. Each answer is used twice.

a. el agente de viajes   1. _____   4. _____

b. el inspector de aduanas   2. _____   5. _____

c. un empleado del hotel   3. _____   6. _____

2

¿Cierto o falso? Mario and his wife, Natalia, are planning their next vacation with a travel agent. Indicate whether each statement is **cierto** or **falso** according to what you hear in the conversation.

	Cierto	Falso
1. Mario y Natalia están en Puerto Rico.	◯	◯
2. Ellos quieren hacer un viaje a Puerto Rico.	◯	◯
3. Natalia prefiere ir a la montaña.	◯	◯
4. Mario quiere pescar en Puerto Rico.	◯	◯
5. La agente de viajes va a confirmar la reservación.	◯	◯

3

Escoger Choose the best answer for each sentence.

1. Un huésped es una persona que _____.
   a. toma fotos   b. está en un hotel   c. pesca en el mar

2. Abrimos la puerta con _____.
   a. una llave   b. un caballo   c. una llegada

3. Enrique tiene _____ porque va a viajar a otro (*another*) país.
   a. un pasaporte   b. una foto   c. una llegada

4. Antes de (*Before*) ir de vacaciones, hay que _____.
   a. pescar   b. ir en tren   c. hacer las maletas

5. Nosotros vamos en _____ al aeropuerto.
   a. autobús   b. pasaje   c. viajero

6. Me gusta mucho ir al campo. El _____ es increíble.
   a. paisaje   b. pasaje   c. equipaje

4

Analogías Complete the analogies using the words below. Two words will not be used.

auto	huésped	mar	sacar
botones	llegada	pasaporte	tren

1. acampar ⟶ campo ⊜ pescar ⟶
2. agencia de viajes ⟶ agente ⊜ hotel ⟶
3. llave ⟶ habitación ⊜ pasaje ⟶
4. estudiante ⟶ libro ⊜ turista ⟶
5. aeropuerto ⟶ viajero ⊜ hotel ⟶
6. maleta ⟶ hacer ⊜ foto ⟶

Las estaciones y los meses del año

el invierno: **diciembre, enero, febrero**

la primavera: **marzo, abril, mayo**

el verano: **junio, julio, agosto**

el otoño: **septiembre, octubre, noviembre**

—**¿Cuál es la fecha de hoy?**	*What is today's date?*
—**Es el primero de octubre.**	*It's the first of October.*
—**Es el dos de marzo.**	*It's March 2ⁿᵈ.*
—**Es el diez de noviembre.**	*It's November 10ᵗʰ.*

El tiempo

—**¿Qué tiempo hace?**	*How's the weather?*
—**Hace buen/mal tiempo.**	*The weather is good/bad.*

Hace (mucho) calor.
It's (very) hot.

Hace (mucho) frío.
It's (very) cold.

Llueve. (llover o:ue)
It's raining.

Está lloviendo.
It's raining.

Nieva. (nevar e:ie)
It's snowing.

Está nevando.
It's snowing.

Más vocabulario

Está (muy) nublado.	*It's (very) cloudy.*
Hace fresco.	*It's cool.*
Hace (mucho) sol.	*It's (very) sunny.*
Hace (mucho) viento.	*It's (very) windy.*

5 **El Hotel Regis** Label the floors of the hotel.

Números ordinales	
primer (before a masculine singular noun), **primero/a**	first
segundo/a	second
tercer (before a masculine singular noun), **tercero/a**	third
cuarto/a	fourth
quinto/a	fifth
sexto/a	sixth
séptimo/a	seventh
octavo/a	eighth
noveno/a	ninth
décimo/a	tenth

a. _____ piso
b. _____ piso
c. _____ piso
d. _____ piso
e. _____ piso
f. _____ piso
g. _____ piso
h. _____ baja

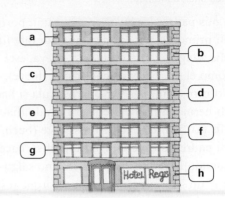

Lección 5

6 **Contestar** Look at the illustrations of the months and seasons on the previous page. In pairs, take turns asking each other these questions.

> **modelo**
>
> **Estudiante 1:** ¿Cuál es el primer mes de la primavera?
> **Estudiante 2:** marzo

1. ¿Cuál es el primer mes del invierno?
2. ¿Cuál es el segundo mes de la primavera?
3. ¿Cuál es el tercer mes del otoño?
4. ¿Cuál es el primer mes del año?
5. ¿Cuál es el quinto mes del año?
6. ¿Cuál es el octavo mes del año?
7. ¿Cuál es el décimo mes del año?
8. ¿Cuál es el segundo mes del verano?
9. ¿Cuál es el tercer mes del invierno?
10. ¿Cuál es el sexto mes del año?

7 **Las estaciones** Name the season that applies to the description.

1. Las clases terminan.
2. Vamos a la playa.
3. Acampamos.
4. Nieva mucho.
5. Las clases empiezan.
6. Hace mucho calor.
7. Llueve mucho.
8. Esquiamos.
9. el entrenamiento (*training*) de béisbol
10. el Día de Acción de Gracias (*Thanksgiving*)

8 **¿Cuál es la fecha?** Give the dates for these holidays.

> **modelo**
>
> el día de San Valentín   14 de febrero

1. el día de San Patricio
2. el día de Halloween
3. el primer día de verano
4. el Año Nuevo
5. mi cumpleaños (*birthday*)
6. mi día de fiesta favorito

9

Seleccionar Paco is talking about his family and friends. Choose the word or phrase that best completes each sentence.

1. A mis padres les gusta ir a Yucatán porque (hace sol, nieva).
2. Mi primo de Kansas dice que durante (*during*) un tornado, hace mucho (sol, viento).
3. Mis amigos van a esquiar si (nieva, está nublado).
4. Tomo el sol cuando (hace calor, llueve).
5. Nosotros vamos a ver una película si hace (buen, mal) tiempo.
6. Mi hermana prefiere correr cuando (hace mucho calor, hace fresco).
7. Mis tíos van de excursión si hace (buen, mal) tiempo.
8. Mi padre no quiere jugar al golf si (hace fresco, llueve).
9. Cuando hace mucho (sol, frío) no salgo de casa y tomo chocolate caliente (*hot*).
10. Hoy mi sobrino va al parque porque (está lloviendo, hace buen tiempo).

10

El clima With a partner, take turns asking and answering questions about the weather and temperatures in these cities. Use the model as a guide.

> **modelo**
>
> **Estudiante 1:** ¿Qué tiempo hace hoy en Nueva York?
> **Estudiante 2:** Hace frío y hace viento.
> **Estudiante 1:** ¿Cuál es la temperatura máxima?
> **Estudiante 2:** Treinta y un grados (*degrees*).
> **Estudiante 1:** ¿Y la temperatura mínima?
> **Estudiante 2:** Diez grados.

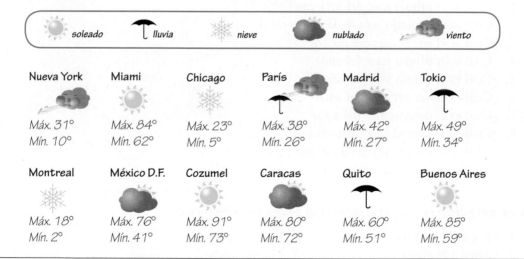

soleado   lluvia   nieve   nublado   viento

Nueva York	Miami	Chicago	París	Madrid	Tokio
Máx. 31°	Máx. 84°	Máx. 23°	Máx. 38°	Máx. 42°	Máx. 49°
Mín. 10°	Mín. 62°	Mín. 5°	Mín. 26°	Mín. 27°	Mín. 34°

Montreal	México D.F.	Cozumel	Caracas	Quito	Buenos Aires
Máx. 18°	Máx. 76°	Máx. 91°	Máx. 80°	Máx. 60°	Máx. 85°
Mín. 2°	Mín. 41°	Mín. 73°	Mín. 72°	Mín. 51°	Mín. 59°

11

Completar Complete these sentences with your own ideas.

1. Cuando hace sol, yo…
2. Cuando llueve, mis amigos y yo…
3. Cuando hace calor, mi familia…
4. Cuando hace viento, la gente…
5. Cuando hace frío, yo…
6. Cuando hace mal tiempo, mis amigos…
7. Cuando nieva, muchas personas…
8. Cuando está nublado, mis amigos y yo…
9. Cuando hace fresco, mis padres…
10. Cuando hace buen tiempo, mis amigos…

Practice more at **vhlcentral.com**.

NOTA CULTURAL

In most Spanish-speaking countries, temperatures are given in degrees Celsius. Use these formulas to convert between **grados centígrados** and **grados Fahrenheit**.

degrees C. × 9 ÷ 5 + 32 = degrees F.

degrees F. - 32 × 5 ÷ 9 = degrees C.

CONSULTA

Calor and **frío** can apply to both weather and people. Use **hacer** to describe weather conditions or climate.

(**Hace frío en Santiago.** *It's cold in Santiago.*)

Use **tener** to refer to people.

(**El viajero tiene frío.** *The traveler is cold.*)

See **Estructura 3.4**, p. 147.

Lección 5

Comunicación

12

Preguntas personales In pairs, ask each other these questions.

1. ¿Cuál es la fecha de hoy? ¿Qué estación es?
2. ¿Te gusta esta estación? ¿Por qué?
3. ¿Qué estación prefieres? ¿Por qué?
4. ¿Prefieres el mar o las montañas? ¿La playa o el campo? ¿Por qué?
5. Cuando haces un viaje, ¿qué te gusta hacer y ver?
6. ¿Piensas ir de vacaciones este verano? ¿Adónde quieres ir? ¿Por qué?
7. ¿Qué deseas ver y qué lugares quieres visitar?
8. ¿Cómo te gusta viajar? ¿En avión? ¿En motocicleta...?

13

Encuesta Your instructor will give you a worksheet. How does the weather affect what you do? Walk around the class and ask your classmates what they prefer or like to do in the weather conditions given. Note their responses on your worksheet. Make sure to personalize your survey by adding a few original questions to the list. Be prepared to report your findings to the class.

14

La reservación In pairs, imagine that one of you is a receptionist at a hotel and the other is a tourist calling to make a reservation. Read only the information that pertains to you. Then role-play the situation.

Turista

Vas a viajar a Yucatán con un amigo. Llegan a Cancún el 23 de febrero y necesitan una habitación con baño privado para cuatro noches. Ustedes quieren descansar y prefieren una habitación con vista (*view*) al mar. Averigua (*Find out*) toda la información que necesitas (el costo, cuántas camas, etc.) y decide si quieres hacer la reservación o no.

Empleado/a

Trabajas en la recepción del Hotel Oceanía en Cancún. Para el mes de febrero, sólo quedan (*remain*) dos habitaciones: una individual ($168/noche) en el primer piso y una doble ($134/noche) en el quinto piso que tiene descuento porque no hay ascensor. Todas las habitaciones tienen baño privado y vista (*view*) a la piscina.

15

Minidrama With two or three classmates, prepare a skit about people who are on vacation or are planning a vacation. The skit should take place in one of these locations.

- una agencia de viajes
- una casa
- un aeropuerto, una estación de tren/autobuses
- un hotel
- el campo o la playa

Síntesis

16

Un viaje You are planning a trip to Mexico and have many questions about your itinerary on which your partner, a travel agent, will advise you. Your instructor will give you and your partner each a sheet with different instructions for acting out the roles.

¡Vamos a la playa!

Los seis amigos hacen un viaje a la playa.

 FELIPE   JUAN CARLOS

S Video: *Fotonovela*

TÍA ANA MARÍA ¿Están listos para su viaje a la playa?

TODOS Sí.

TÍA ANA MARÍA Excelente... ¡A la estación de autobuses!

MARU ¿Dónde está Miguel?

FELIPE Yo lo traigo.

(*se escucha un grito de Miguel*)

FELIPE Ya está listo. Y tal vez enojado. Ahorita vamos.

FELIPE No está nada mal el hotel, ¿verdad? Limpio, cómodo... ¡Oye, Miguel! ¿Todavía estás enojado conmigo? (*a Juan Carlos*) Miguel está de mal humor. No me habla.

JUAN CARLOS ¿Todavía?

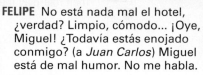

EMPLEADO Bienvenidas. ¿En qué puedo servirles?

MARU Hola. Tenemos una reservación para seis personas para esta noche.

EMPLEADO ¿A nombre de quién?

JIMENA ¿Díaz? ¿López? No estoy segura.

EMPLEADO No encuentro su nombre. Ah, no, ahora sí lo veo, aquí está. Díaz. Dos habitaciones en el primer piso para seis huéspedes.

EMPLEADO Aquí están las llaves de sus habitaciones.

MARU Gracias. Una cosa más. Mi novio y yo queremos hacer windsurf, pero no tenemos tablas.

EMPLEADO El botones las puede conseguir para ustedes.

MARISSA
 JIMENA
 MARU
 MIGUEL
 MAITE FUENTES
 ANA MARÍA
EMPLEADO

Lección 5

JUAN CARLOS ¿Qué hace este libro aquí? ¿Estás estudiando en la playa?

JIMENA Sí, es que tengo un examen la próxima semana.

JUAN CARLOS Ay, Jimena. ¡No! ¿Vamos a nadar?

JIMENA Bueno, como estudiar es tan aburrido y el tiempo está tan bonito...

MARISSA Yo estoy un poco cansada. ¿Y tú? ¿Por qué no estás nadando?

FELIPE Es por causa de Miguel.

MARISSA Hmm, estoy confundida.

FELIPE Esta mañana. ¡Sigue enojado conmigo!

MARISSA No puede seguir enojado tanto tiempo.

recursos
VM pp. 293–294
vhlcentral.com Lección 5

Expresiones útiles

Talking with hotel personnel

¿En qué puedo servirles?
How can I help you?
Tenemos una reservación.
We have a reservation.
¿A nombre de quién?
In whose name?
¿Quizás López? ¿Tal vez Díaz?
Maybe López? Maybe Díaz?
Ahora lo veo, aquí está. Díaz.
Now I see it. Here it is. Díaz.
Dos habitaciones en el primer piso para seis huéspedes.
Two rooms on the first floor for six guests.
Aquí están las llaves.
Here are the keys.

Describing a hotel

No está nada mal el hotel.
The hotel isn't bad at all.
Todo está tan limpio y cómodo.
Everything is so clean and comfortable.
Es excelente/estupendo/fabuloso/ fenomenal/increíble/magnífico/ maravilloso/perfecto.
It's excellent/stupendous/fabulous/ phenomenal/incredible/magnificent/ marvelous/perfect.

Talking about how you feel

Yo estoy un poco cansado/a.
I am a little tired.
Estoy confundido/a. *I'm confused.*
Todavía estoy/Sigo enojado/a contigo.
I'm still angry with you.

Additional vocabulary

afuera *outside*
agradable *pleasant*
el balde *bucket*
la crema de afeitar *shaving cream*
entonces *so, then*
es igual *it's the same*
el frente (frío) *(cold) front*
el grito *scream*
la temporada *period of time*

¿Qué pasó?

1 Completar Complete these sentences with the correct term from the word bank.

aburrido	botones	la llave
el aeropuerto	la estación de autobuses	montar a caballo
amable	habitaciones	reservación

1. Los amigos van a _____ para ir a la playa.
2. La _____ del hotel está a nombre de los Díaz.
3. Los amigos tienen dos _____ para seis personas.
4. El _____ puede conseguir tablas de windsurf para Maru.
5. Jimena dice que estudiar en vacaciones es muy _____ .

CONSULTA

The meaning of some adjectives, such as **aburrido**, changes depending on whether they are used with **ser** or **estar**. See **Estructura 5.3**, pp. 264–265.

2 Identificar Identify the person who would make each statement.

EMPLEADO   **MARU**   **TÍA ANA MARÍA**   **FELIPE**   **JUAN CARLOS**

1. No lo encuentro, ¿a nombre de quién está su reservación?
2. ¿Por qué estás estudiando en la playa? ¡Mejor vamos a nadar!
3. Nuestra reservación es para seis personas en dos habitaciones.
4. El hotel es limpio y cómodo, pero estoy triste porque Miguel no me habla.
5. Suban al autobús y ¡buen viaje a la playa!

3 Ordenar Place these events in the correct order.

_____ a. El empleado busca la reservación.
_____ b. Marissa dice que está confundida.
_____ c. Los amigos están listos para ir a la playa.
_____ d. El empleado da (*gives*) las llaves de las habitaciones a las chicas.
_____ e. Miguel grita (*screams*).

4 Conversar With a partner, use these cues to create a conversation between a hotel employee and a guest in Mexico.

Huésped	**Empleado/a**
Say hi to the employee and ask for your reservation.	→ Tell the guest that you can't find his/her reservation.
Tell the employee that the reservation is in your name.	→ Tell him/her that you found the reservation and that it's for a double room.
Tell the employee that the hotel is very clean and orderly.	→ Say that you agree with the guest, welcome him/her, and give him/her the keys.
Ask the employee to call the bellhop to help you with your luggage.	→ Call the bellhop to help the guest with his/her luggage.

 Practice more at **vhlcentral.com**.

Pronunciación  Audio
Spanish b and v

bueno	vóleibol	biblioteca	vivir

There is no difference in pronunciation between the Spanish letters **b** and **v**. However, each letter can be pronounced two different ways, depending on which letters appear next to them.

bonito	viajar	también	investigar

B and **v** are pronounced like the English hard *b* when they appear either as the first letter of a word, at the beginning of a phrase, or after **m** or **n**.

deber	novio	abril	cerveza

In all other positions, **b** and **v** have a softer pronunciation, which has no equivalent in English. Unlike the hard **b**, which is produced by tightly closing the lips and stopping the flow of air, the soft **b** is produced by keeping the lips slightly open.

bola	vela	Caribe	declive

In both pronunciations, there is no difference in sound between **b** and **v**. The English *v* sound, produced by friction between the upper teeth and lower lip, does not exist in Spanish. Instead, the soft **b** comes from friction between the two lips.

Verónica y su esposo cantan boleros.

When **b** or **v** begins a word, its pronunciation depends on the previous word. At the beginning of a phrase or after a word that ends in **m** or **n**, it is pronounced as a hard **b**.

Benito es de Boquerón pero vive en Victoria.

Words that begin with **b** or **v** are pronounced with a soft **b** if they appear immediately after a word that ends in a vowel or any consonant other than **m** or **n**.

Práctica Read these words aloud to practice the **b** and the **v**.

1. hablamos	4. van	7. doble	10. nublado
2. trabajar	5. contabilidad	8. novia	11. llave
3. botones	6. bien	9. béisbol	12. invierno

Oraciones Read these sentences aloud to practice the **b** and the **v**.

1. Vamos a Guaynabo en autobús.
2. Voy de vacaciones a la Isla Culebra.
3. Tengo una habitación individual en el octavo piso.
4. Víctor y Eva van en avión al Caribe.
5. La planta baja es bonita también.
6. ¿Qué vamos a ver en Bayamón?
7. Beatriz, la novia de Víctor, es de Arecibo, Puerto Rico.

Refranes Read these sayings aloud to practice the **b** and the **v**.

No hay mal que por bien no venga.¹

Hombre prevenido vale por dos.²

recursos

| LM p. 300 | vhlcentral.com Lección 5 |

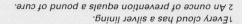

1 Every cloud has a silver lining.
2 An ounce of prevention equals a pound of cure.

Additional Reading

Las cataratas del Iguazú

Imagine the impressive and majestic Niagara Falls, the most powerful waterfall in North America. Now, if you can, imagine a waterfall four times as wide and almost twice as tall that caused Eleanor Roosevelt to exclaim "Poor Niagara!" upon seeing it for the first time. Welcome to **las cataratas del Iguazú!**

Iguazú is located in Iguazú National Park, an area of subtropical jungle where Argentina meets Brazil. Its name comes from the indigenous Guaraní word for "great water." A UNESCO World Heritage Site, **las cataratas del Iguazú** span three kilometers and comprise 275 cascades split into two main sections by San Martín Island. Most of the falls are about 82 meters (270 feet) high. The horseshoe-shaped cataract **Garganta del Diablo** (Devil's Throat) has the greatest water flow and is considered to be the most impressive; it also marks the border between Argentina and Brazil.

Each country offers different views and tourist options. Most visitors opt to use the numerous catwalks that are available on both

Garganta del Diablo

Isla San Martín

sides; however, from the Argentinean side, tourists can get very close to the falls, whereas Brazil provides more panoramic views. If you don't mind getting wet, a jet boat tour is a good choice; those looking for wildlife—such as toucans, ocelots, butterflies, and jaguars—should head for San Martín Island. Brazil boasts less conventional ways to view the falls, such as helicopter rides and rappelling, while Argentina focuses on sustainability with its **Tren Ecológico de la Selva** (*Ecological Jungle Train*), an environmentally friendly way to reach the walkways.

No matter which way you choose to enjoy the falls, you are certain to be captivated.

Más cascadas° en Latinoamérica			
Nombre	**País**	**Altura°**	**Datos**
Salto Ángel	Venezuela	979 metros	la más alta° del mundo°
Catarata del Gocta	Perú	771 metros	descubierta° en 2006
Piedra Volada	México	453 metros	la más alta de México

cascadas *waterfalls* Altura *Height* más alta *tallest* mundo *world* descubierta *discovered*

ACTIVIDADES

1 **¿Cierto o falso?** Indicate whether these statements are cierto or falso. Correct the false statements.

1. Iguazú Falls is located on the border of Argentina and Brazil.

2. Niagara Falls is four times as wide as Iguazú Falls.

3. Iguazú Falls has a few cascades, each about 82 meters.

4. Tourists visiting Iguazú can see exotic wildlife.

5. *Iguazú* is the Guaraní word for "blue water."

6. You can access the walkways by taking the **Garganta del Diablo**.

7. It is possible for tourists to visit Iguazú Falls by air.

8. **Salto Ángel** is the tallest waterfall in the world.

9. There are no waterfalls in Mexico.

10. For the best views of Iguazú Falls, tourists should visit the Brazilian side.

ASÍ SE DICE

Viajes y turismo

el asiento del medio, del pasillo, de la ventanilla	*center, aisle, window seat*
el itinerario	*itinerary*
media pensión	*breakfast and one meal included*
el ómnibus (Perú)	el autobús
pensión completa	*all meals included*
el puente	*long weekend (lit., bridge)*

EL MUNDO HISPANO

Destinos populares

- **Las playas del Parque Nacional Manuel Antonio** (Costa Rica) ofrecen° la oportunidad de nadar y luego caminar por el bosque tropical°.

- **Teotihuacán** (México) Desde antes de la época° de los aztecas, aquí se celebra el equinoccio de primavera en la Pirámide del Sol.

- **Puerto Chicama** (Perú), con sus olas° de cuatro kilómetros de largo°, es un destino para surfistas expertos.

- **Tikal** (Guatemala) Aquí puedes ver las maravillas de la selva° y ruinas de la civilización maya.

- **Las playas de Rincón** (Puerto Rico) Son ideales para descansar y observar ballenas°.

ofrecen *offer* bosque tropical *rainforest*
Desde antes de la época *Since before the time* olas *waves*
de largo *in length* selva *jungle* ballenas *whales*

PERFIL

Punta del Este

One of South America's largest and most fashionable beach resort towns is Uruguay's **Punta del Este**, a narrow strip of land containing twenty miles of pristine beaches. Its peninsular shape gives it two very different seascapes. **La Playa Mansa**, facing the bay and therefore the more protected side, has calm waters. Here, people practice water sports like swimming, water skiing, windsurfing, and diving. **La Playa Brava**, facing the east, receives the Atlantic Ocean's powerful, wave-producing winds, making it popular for surfing, body boarding, and kite surfing. Besides the beaches, posh shopping, and world-famous nightlife, **Punta** offers its 600,000 yearly visitors yacht and fishing clubs, golf courses, and excursions to observe sea lions at the **Isla de Lobos** nature reserve.

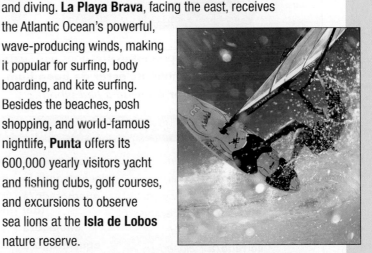

Conexión Internet

¿Cuáles son los sitios más populares para el turismo en Puerto Rico?

Go to vhlcentral.com to find more cultural information related to this Cultura section.

ACTIVIDADES

2 **Comprensión** Complete the sentences.

1. En las playas de Rincón puedes ver _____.

2. Cerca de 600.000 turistas visitan _____ cada año.

3. En el avión pides un _____ si te gusta ver el paisaje.

4. En Punta del Este, la gente prefiere nadar en la Playa _____.

5. El _____ es un medio de transporte en Perú.

3 **De vacaciones** Spring break is coming up, and you want to go on a short vacation with some friends. Working in a small group, decide which of the locations featured on these pages best suits the group's likes and interests. Come to an agreement about how you will get there, where you prefer to stay and for how long, and what each of you will do during free time. Present your trip to the class.

 Practice more at **vhlcentral.com**.

5.1 Estar with conditions and emotions

ANTE TODO As you learned in **Lecciones 1** and **2**, the verb **estar** is used to talk about how you feel and to say where people, places, and things are located. **Estar** is also used with adjectives to talk about certain emotional and physical conditions.

▶ Use **estar** with adjectives to describe the physical condition of places and things.

La habitación **está** sucia.
The room is dirty.

La puerta **está** cerrada.
The door is closed.

▶ Use **estar** with adjectives to describe how people feel, both mentally and physically.

Yo estoy cansada.

¿Están listos para su viaje?

▶ **¡Atención!** Two important expressions with **estar** that you can use to talk about conditions and emotions are **estar de buen humor** (*to be in a good mood*) and **estar de mal humor** (*to be in a bad mood*).

Adjectives that describe emotions and conditions

abierto/a	open	**contento/a**	happy; content	**listo/a**	ready
aburrido/a	bored	**desordenado/a**	disorderly	**nervioso/a**	nervous
alegre	happy; joyful	**enamorado/a (de)**	in love (with)	**ocupado/a**	busy
avergonzado/a	embarrassed			**ordenado/a**	orderly
cansado/a	tired	**enojado/a**	mad; angry	**preocupado/a (por)**	worried (about)
cerrado/a	closed	**equivocado/a**	wrong		
cómodo/a	comfortable	**feliz**	happy	**seguro/a**	sure
confundido/a	confused	**limpio/a**	clean	**sucio/a**	dirty
				triste	sad

¡INTÉNTALO! Provide the present-tense forms of **estar**, and choose which adjective best completes the sentence.

1. La biblioteca ___está___ (cerrada / nerviosa) los domingos por la noche. *cerrada*
2. Nosotros _____ muy (ocupados / equivocados) todos los lunes.
3. Ellas _____ (alegres / confundidas) porque tienen vacaciones.
4. Javier _____ (enamorado / ordenado) de Maribel.
5. Diana _____ (enojada / limpia) con su novio.
6. Yo _____ (nerviosa / abierta) por el viaje.
7. La habitación siempre _____ (ordenada / segura) cuando vienen sus padres.
8. Ustedes no comprenden; _____ (equivocados / tristes).

CONSULTA

To review the present tense of **estar**, see **Estructura 2.3**, p. 81.

• • •

To review the present tense of **ser**, see **Estructura 1.3**, p. 20.

recursos

WB
pp. 285–286

LM
p. 301

vhlcentral.com
Lección 5

Práctica y Comunicación

1

¿Cómo están? Complete Martín's statements about how he and other people are feeling. In the first blank, fill in the correct form of **estar**. In the second blank, fill in the adjective that best fits the context.

1. Yo _____ un poco _____ porque tengo un examen mañana.
2. Mi hermana Patricia _____ muy _____ porque mañana va a hacer una excursión al campo.
3. Mis hermanos Juan y José salen de la casa a las cinco de la mañana. Por la noche, siempre _____ muy _____.
4. Mi amigo Ramiro _____ _____; su novia se llama Adela.
5. Mi papá y sus colegas _____ muy _____ hoy. ¡Hay mucho trabajo!
6. Patricia y yo _____ un poco _____ por ellos porque trabajan mucho.
7. Mi amiga Mónica _____ un poco _____ porque su novio no puede salir esta noche.
8. Esta clase no es muy interesante. ¿Tú _____ _____ también?

2

Describir Describe these people and places.

1. Anabela

2. Juan y Luisa

3. la habitación de Teresa

4. la habitación de César

3

Situaciones With a partner, use **estar** to talk about how you feel in these situations.

1. Cuando hace sol…
2. Cuando tomas un examen…
3. Cuando viajas en avión…
4. Cuando estás en la clase de español…
5. Cuando ves una película con tu actor/actriz favorito/a…

4

En la tele In small groups, imagine that you are a family that stars on a reality TV show. You are vacationing together, but the trip isn't going well for everyone. Write the script of a scene from the show and then act it out. Use at least six adjectives from the previous page and be creative!

> **modelo**
>
> **Papá:** ¿Por qué estás enojada, María Rosa? El hotel es muy bonito y las habitaciones están limpias.
>
> **Mamá:** ¡Pero mira, Roberto! Las maletas de Elisa están abiertas y, como siempre, sus cosas están muy desordenadas.

 Practice more at **vhlcentral.com**.

5.2 The present progressive   (S) Tutorial

ANTE TODO   Both Spanish and English use the present progressive, which consists of the present tense of the verb *to be* and the present participle of another verb (the *-ing* form in English).

Las chicas están hablando con el empleado del hotel.

¿Estás estudiando en la playa?

▶ Form the present progressive with the present tense of **estar** and a present participle.

FORM OF **ESTAR** + PRESENT PARTICIPLE		FORM OF **ESTAR** + PRESENT PARTICIPLE	
Estoy	**pescando.**	**Estamos**	**comiendo.**
I am	*fishing.*	*We are*	*eating.*

▶ The present participle of regular **-ar**, **-er**, and **-ir** verbs is formed as follows:

INFINITIVE	STEM	ENDING	PRESENT PARTICIPLE
hablar	habl-	**-ando**	habl**ando**
comer	com-	**-iendo**	com**iendo**
escribir	escrib-	**-iendo**	escrib**iendo**

▶ **¡Atención!** When the stem of an **-er** or **-ir** verb ends in a vowel, the present participle ends in **-yendo**.

INFINITIVE	STEM	ENDING	PRESENT PARTICIPLE
leer	le-	**-yendo**	le**yendo**
oír	o-	**-yendo**	o**yendo**
traer	tra-	**-yendo**	tra**yendo**

▶ **Ir**, **poder**, and **venir** have irregular present participles (**yendo**, **pudiendo**, **viniendo**). Several other verbs have irregular present participles that you will need to learn.

▶ **-Ir** stem-changing verbs have a stem change in the present participle.

-ir stem-changing verbs

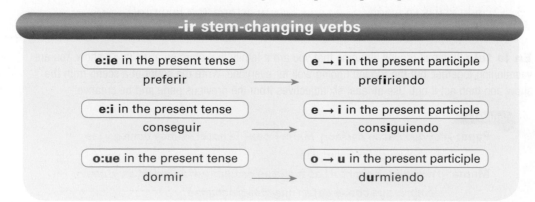

e:ie in the present tense	e → i in the present participle
preferir ⟶	prefir**i**endo
e:i in the present tense	e → i in the present participle
conseguir ⟶	consi**g**uiendo
o:ue in the present tense	o → u in the present participle
dormir ⟶	d**u**rmiendo

Lección 5

The use of the present progressive is much more restricted in Spanish than in English. In Spanish, the present progressive is mainly used to emphasize that an action is in progress at the time of speaking.

> Maru **está escuchando** música
> latina **ahora mismo**.
> *Maru is listening to Latin music*
> *right now.*

> Felipe y su amigo **todavía**
> **están jugando** al fútbol.
> *Felipe and his friend are still*
> *playing soccer.*

In English, the present progressive is often used to talk about situations and actions that occur over an extended period of time or in the future. In Spanish, the simple present tense is often used instead.

> Xavier **estudia** computación
> este semestre.
> *Xavier is studying computer*
> *science this semester.*

> Marissa **sale** mañana
> para los Estados Unidos.
> *Marissa is leaving tomorrow*
> *for the United States.*

¿Está pensando en su futuro?
Nosotros, sí.

BANCO
CONGRESO

Preparándolo para el mañana

 **¡INTÉNTALO!**   Create complete sentences by putting the verbs in the present progressive.

1. mis amigos / descansar en la playa <u>Mis amigos están descansando en la playa.</u>
2. nosotros / practicar deportes _____
3. Carmen / comer en casa _____
4. nuestro equipo / ganar el partido _____
5. yo / leer el periódico _____
6. él / pensar comprar una bicicleta _____
7. ustedes / jugar a las cartas _____
8. José y Francisco / dormir _____
9. Marisa / leer correo electrónico _____
10. yo / preparar sándwiches _____
11. Carlos / tomar fotos _____
12. ¿dormir / tú? _____

Práctica

1

Completar Alfredo's Spanish class is preparing to travel to Puerto Rico. Use the present progressive of the verb in parentheses to complete Alfredo's description of what everyone is doing.

1. Yo _____ (investigar) la situación política de la isla (*island*).
2. La esposa del profesor _____ (hacer) las maletas.
3. Marta y José Luis _____ (buscar) información sobre San Juan en Internet.
4. Enrique y yo _____ (leer) un correo electrónico de nuestro amigo puertorriqueño.
5. Javier _____ (aprender) mucho sobre la cultura puertorriqueña.
6. Y tú _____ (practicar) el español, ¿verdad?

2

¿Qué están haciendo? María and her friends are vacationing at a resort in San Juan, Puerto Rico. Complete her description of what everyone is doing right now.

CONSULTA

For more information about Puerto Rico, see **Panorama**, pp. 280–281.

1. Yo

2. Javier

3. Alejandro y Rebeca

4. Celia y yo

5. Samuel

6. Lorenzo

3

Personajes famosos Say what these celebrities are doing right now, using the cues provided.

modelo

Celine Dion
Celine Dion está cantando una canción ahora mismo.

A		B	
Stephenie Meyer	Nelly Furtado	bailar	hacer
Rachael Ray	Steve Nash	cantar	jugar
James Cameron	Las Rockettes de	correr	preparar
Venus y Serena	Nueva York	escribir	¿?
Williams	¿?	hablar	¿?
Joey Votto	¿?		

AYUDA

Stephenie Meyer: **novelas**

Rachael Ray: **televisión, negocios** (*business*)

James Cameron: **cine**

Venus y Serena Williams: **tenis**

Joey Votto: **béisbol**

Nelly Furtado: **canciones**

Steve Nash: **baloncesto**

Las Rockettes de Nueva York: **baile**

 Practice more at **vhlcentral.com**.

Comunicación

4

Preguntar With a partner, take turns asking each other what you are doing at these times.

> **modelo**
>
> 8:00 a.m.
> **Estudiante 1:** ¡Hola, Andrés! Son las *ocho de la mañana*. ¿Qué estás haciendo?
> **Estudiante 2:** Estoy desayunando.

1. 5:00 a.m.   3. 11:00 a.m.   5. 2:00 p.m.   7. 9:00 p.m.
2. 9:30 a.m.   4. 12:00 p.m.   6. 5:00 p.m.   8. 11:30 p.m.

5

Describir Work with a partner and use the present progressive to describe what is going on in this Spanish beach scene.

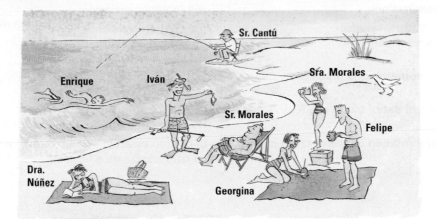

6

Conversar Imagine that you and a classmate are each babysitting a group of children. With a partner, prepare a telephone conversation using these cues. Be creative and add further comments.

Estudiante 1	**Estudiante 2**
Say hello and ask what the kids are doing.	Say hello and tell your partner that two of your kids are doing their homework. Then ask what the kids at his/her house are doing.
Tell your partner that two of your kids are running and dancing in the house.	Tell your partner that one of the kids is reading.
Tell your partner that you are tired and that two of your kids are watching TV and eating pizza.	Tell your partner that one of the kids is sleeping.
Tell your partner you have to go; the kids are playing soccer in the house.	Say goodbye and good luck (**¡Buena suerte!**).

Síntesis

7

¿Qué están haciendo? A group of classmates is traveling to San Juan, Puerto Rico, for a week-long Spanish immersion program. In order for the participants to be on time for their flight, you and your partner must locate them. Your instructor will give you each a handout to help you complete this task.

5.3   Ser and estar   Tutorial

ANTE TODO   You have already learned that **ser** and **estar** both mean *to be* but are used for different purposes. These charts summarize the key differences in usage between **ser** and **estar**.

Uses of ser

1. **Nationality and place of origin**	Juan Carlos **es** argentino. **Es** de Buenos Aires.
2. **Profession or occupation**	Adela **es** agente de viajes. Francisco **es** médico.
3. **Characteristics of people and things** . . .	José y Clara **son** simpáticos. El clima de Puerto Rico **es** agradable.
4. **Generalizations**	**¡Es** fabuloso viajar! **Es** difícil estudiar a la una de la mañana.
5. **Possession**	**Es** la pluma de Jimena. **Son** las llaves del señor Díaz.
6. **What something is made of**	La bicicleta **es** de metal. Los pasajes **son** de papel.
7. **Time and date**	Hoy **es** martes. **Son** las dos. Hoy **es** el primero de julio.
8. **Where or when an event takes place** . .	El partido **es** en el estadio Santa Fe. La conferencia **es** a las siete.

¡ATENCIÓN!

Ser de expresses not only origin (**Es de Buenos Aires.**) and possession (**Es la pluma de Maru.**), but also what material something is made of (**La bicicleta es de metal.**).

Ellos son mis amigos.

Miguel está enojado conmigo.

Uses of estar

1. **Location or spatial relationships**	El aeropuerto **está** lejos de la ciudad. Tu habitación **está** en el tercer piso.
2. **Health**	¿Cómo **estás**? **Estoy** bien, gracias.
3. **Physical states and conditions**	El profesor **está** ocupado. Las ventanas **están** abiertas.
4. **Emotional states**	Marissa **está** feliz hoy. **Estoy** muy enojado con Maru.
5. **Certain weather expressions**	**Está** lloviendo. **Está** nublado.
6. **Ongoing actions (progressive tenses)** . .	**Estamos** estudiando para un examen. Ana **está** leyendo una novela.

Lección 5

Ser and estar with adjectives

▶ With many descriptive adjectives, **ser** and **estar** can both be used, but the meaning will change.

Juan **es** delgado.	Ana **es** nerviosa.
Juan is thin.	*Ana is a nervous person.*
Juan **está** más delgado hoy.	Ana **está** nerviosa por el examen.
Juan looks thinner today.	*Ana is nervous because of the exam.*

▶ In the examples above, the statements with **ser** are general observations about the inherent qualities of Juan and Ana. The statements with **estar** describe conditions that are variable.

▶ Here are some adjectives that change in meaning when used with **ser** and **estar**.

With ser	With estar
El chico **es listo**.	El chico **está listo**.
*The boy is **smart**.*	*The boy is **ready**.*
La profesora **es mala**.	La profesora **está mala**.
*The professor is **bad**.*	*The professor is **sick**.*
Jaime **es aburrido**.	Jaime **está aburrido**.
*Jaime is **boring**.*	*Jaime is **bored**.*
Las peras **son verdes**.	Las peras **están verdes**.
*Pears are **green**.*	*The pears are **not ripe**.*
El gato **es muy vivo**.	El gato **está vivo**.
*The cat is very **lively**.*	*The cat is **alive**.*
Iván **es un hombre seguro**.	Iván no **está seguro**.
*Iván is a **confident** man.*	*Iván is **not sure**.*

¡ATENCIÓN!

When referring to objects, **ser seguro/a** means *to be safe.*
El puente es seguro.
The bridge is safe.

¡INTÉNTALO!   Form complete sentences by using the correct form of **ser** or **estar** and making any other necessary changes.

1. Alejandra / cansado
   Alejandra está cansada.

2. ellos / pelirrojo

3. Carmen / alto

4. yo / la clase de español

5. película / a las once

6. hoy / viernes

7. nosotras / enojado

8. Antonio / médico

9. Romeo y Julieta / enamorado

10. libros / de Ana

11. Marisa y Juan / estudiando

12. partido de baloncesto / gimnasio

recursos

WB
pp. 288–289

LM
p. 303

vhlcentral.com
Lección 5

Práctica

1

¿Ser o estar? Indicate whether each adjective takes **ser** or **estar**. **¡Ojo!**
Three of them can take both verbs.

	ser	estar			ser	estar
1. delgada	○	○		5. seguro	○	○
2. canadiense	○	○		6. enojada	○	○
3. enamorado	○	○		7. importante	○	○
4. lista	○	○		8. avergonzada	○	○

2

Completar Complete this conversation with the appropriate forms of **ser** and **estar**.

EDUARDO ¡Hola, Ceci! ¿Cómo (1)_____?

CECILIA Hola, Eduardo. Bien, gracias. ¡Qué guapo (2)_____ hoy!

EDUARDO Gracias. (3)_____ muy amable. Oye, ¿qué (4)_____ haciendo?
(5)¿_____ ocupada?

CECILIA No, sólo le (6)_____ escribiendo una carta a mi prima Pilar.

EDUARDO ¿De dónde (7)_____ ella?

CECILIA Pilar (8)_____ de Ecuador. Su papá (9)_____ médico en Quito. Pero
ahora Pilar y su familia (10)_____ de vacaciones en Ponce, Puerto Rico.

EDUARDO Y... ¿cómo (11)_____ Pilar?

CECILIA (12)_____ muy lista. Y también (13)_____ alta, rubia y muy bonita.

3

En el parque With a partner, take turns describing the people in the drawing. Your descriptions
should answer the questions provided.

1. ¿Quiénes son?
2. ¿Dónde están?
3. ¿Cómo son?
4. ¿Cómo están?

5. ¿Qué están haciendo?
6. ¿Qué estación es?
7. ¿Qué tiempo hace?
8. ¿Quiénes están de vacaciones?

S: Practice more at **vhlcentral.com**.

Comunicación

4

Describir With a classmate, take turns describing these people. Mention where they are from, what they are like, how they are feeling, and what they are doing right now.

> **modelo**
>
> tu compañero/a de cuarto
>
> Mi compañera de cuarto es de San Juan, Puerto Rico. Es muy inteligente. Está cansada pero está estudiando porque tiene un examen.

1. tu mejor (*best*) amigo/a
2. tu actor/actriz favorito/a
3. tu profesor(a) favorito/a
4. tu novio/a o esposo/a
5. tus abuelos
6. tus padres

5

Adivinar Get together with a partner and take turns describing a celebrity using these items as a guide. Don't mention the celebrity's name. Can your partner guess who you are describing?

- descripción física
- cómo está ahora
- origen
- dónde está ahora
- qué está haciendo ahora
- profesión u ocupación

6

En el aeropuerto In groups of three, take turns assuming the identity of a character from this drawing. Your partners will ask you questions using **ser** and **estar** until they figure out who you are.

> **modelo**
>
> **Estudiante 3:** ¿Dónde estás?
> **Estudiante 1:** Estoy cerca de la puerta.
> **Estudiante 2:** ¿Qué estás haciendo?
> **Estudiante 1:** Estoy escuchando a otra persona.
> **Estudiante 3:** ¿Eres uno de los pasajeros?
> **Estudiante 1:** No, soy empleado del aeropuerto.
> **Estudiante 2:** ¿Eres Camilo?

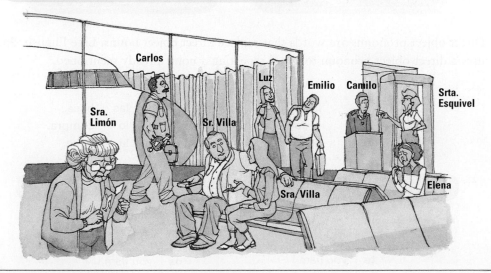

Síntesis

7

Conversación In pairs, imagine that you and your partner are two of the characters in the drawing in **Actividad 6**. After boarding, you are seated next to each other and strike up a conversation. Act out what you would say to your fellow passenger.

5.4 Direct object nouns and pronouns Tutorial

SUBJECT	VERB	DIRECT OBJECT NOUN
Juan Carlos y Jimena	están tomando	fotos.
Juan Carlos and Jimena	*are taking*	*photos.*

▶ A direct object noun receives the action of the verb directly and generally follows the verb. In the example above, the direct object noun answers the question *What are Juan Carlos and Jimena taking?*

▶ When a direct object noun in Spanish is a person or a pet, it is preceded by the word **a**. This is called the personal **a**; there is no English equivalent for this construction.

La señora Díaz visita **a** la doctora Salas.   La señora Díaz visita el café Delicias.
Mrs Díaz is visiting Dr. Salas.   *Mrs. Díaz is visiting the Delicias café.*

▶ In the first sentence above, the personal **a** is required because the direct object is a person. In the second sentence, the personal **a** is not required because the direct object is a place, not a person.

Miguel no me perdona.

No tenemos tablas de windsurf.

El botones las puede conseguir para ustedes.

▶ Direct object pronouns are words that replace direct object nouns. Like English, Spanish uses a direct object pronoun to avoid repeating a noun already mentioned.

	DIRECT OBJECT			DIRECT OBJECT PRONOUN	
Maribel hace	las maletas.		Maribel	las	hace.
Felipe compra	el sombrero.	▶	Felipe	lo	compra.
Vicky tiene	la llave.		Vicky	la	tiene.

Direct object pronouns

SINGULAR		PLURAL	
me	me	**nos**	us
te	you (fam.)	**os**	you (fam.)
lo	you (m., form.)	**los**	you (m., form.)
	him; it (m.)		them (m.)
la	you (f., form.)	**las**	you (f., form.)
	her; it (f.)		them (f.)

Lección 5

▶ In affirmative sentences, direct object pronouns generally appear before the conjugated verb. In negative sentences, the pronoun is placed between the word **no** and the verb.

Adela practica **el tenis.**	Gabriela no tiene **las llaves.**
Adela **lo** practica.	Gabriela **no las** tiene.
Carmen compra **los pasajes.**	Diego no hace **las maletas.**
Carmen **los** compra.	Diego **no las** hace.

▶ When the verb is an infinitive construction, such as **ir a** + [*infinitive*], the direct object pronoun can be placed before the conjugated form or attached to the infinitive.

Ellos van a escribir **unas postales.**
    Ellos **las** van a escribir.
    Ellos van a escribir**las.**

Lidia quiere ver **una película.**
    Lidia **la** quiere ver.
    Lidia quiere ver**la.**

▶ When the verb is in the present progressive, the direct object pronoun can be placed before the conjugated form or attached to the present participle. **¡Atención!** When a direct object pronoun is attached to the present participle, an accent mark is added to maintain the proper stress.

Gerardo está leyendo **la lección.**
    Gerardo **la** está leyendo.
    Gerardo está leyéndo**la.**

Toni está mirando **el partido.**
    Toni **lo** está mirando.
    Toni está mirándo**lo.**

CONSULTA

To learn more about accents, see **Lección 4, Pronunciación**, p. 193, **¡ADELANTE!** `DOS` **Lección 4, Ortografía**, p. 203, and **¡ADELANTE!** `DOS` **Lección 5, Ortografía**, p. 265. **¡ADELANTE!** `DOS`

¡INTÉNTALO!   Choose the correct direct object pronoun for each sentence.

1. Tienes el libro de español. *c*
   a. La tienes.   b. Los tienes.   c. Lo tienes.
2. Voy a ver el partido de baloncesto.
   a. Voy a verlo.   b. Voy a verte.   c. Voy a vernos.
3. El artista quiere dibujar a Luisa y a su mamá.
   a. Quiere dibujarme. b. Quiere dibujarla. c. Quiere dibujarlas.
4. Marcos busca la llave.
   a. Me busca.   b. La busca.   c. Las busca.
5. Rita me lleva al aeropuerto y también lleva a Tomás.
   a. Nos lleva.   b. Las lleva.   c. Te lleva.
6. Puedo oír a Gerardo y a Miguel.
   a. Puedo oírte.   b. Puedo oírlos.   c. Puedo oírlo.
7. Quieren estudiar la gramática.
   a. Quieren estudiarnos. b. Quieren estudiarlo. c. Quieren estudiarla.
8. ¿Practicas los verbos irregulares?
   a. ¿Los practicas?   b. ¿Las practicas?   c. ¿Lo practicas?
9. Ignacio ve la película.
   a. La ve.   b. Lo ve.   c. Las ve.
10. Sandra va a invitar a Mario a la excursión. También me va a invitar a mí.
    a. Los va a invitar. b. Lo va a invitar.   c. Nos va a invitar.

recursos

WB
p. 290

LM
p. 304

Ⓢ
vhlcentral.com
Lección 5

Práctica

1 Simplificar Professor Vega's class is planning a trip to Costa Rica. Describe their preparations by changing the direct object nouns into direct object pronouns.

> **modelo**
>
> La profesora Vega tiene su pasaporte.
> *La profesora Vega lo tiene.*

1. Gustavo y Héctor confirman las reservaciones.
2. Nosotros leemos los folletos (*brochures*).
3. Ana María estudia el mapa.
4. Yo aprendo los nombres de los monumentos de San José.
5. Alicia escucha a la profesora.
6. Miguel escribe las direcciones para ir al hotel.
7. Esteban busca el pasaje.
8. Nosotros planeamos una excursión.

¡LENGUA VIVA!

There are many Spanish words that correspond to *ticket*. **Billete** and **pasaje** usually refer to a ticket for travel, such as an airplane ticket. **Entrada** refers to a ticket to an event, such as a concert or a movie. **Boleto** can be used in either case.

2 Vacaciones Ramón is going to San Juan, Puerto Rico, with his friends, Javier and Marcos. Express his thoughts more succinctly using direct object pronouns.

> **modelo**
>
> Quiero hacer una excursión.
> *Quiero hacerla./La quiero hacer.*

1. Voy a hacer mi maleta.
2. Necesitamos llevar los pasaportes.
3. Marcos está pidiendo el folleto turístico.
4. Javier debe llamar a sus padres.
5. Ellos desean visitar el Viejo San Juan.
6. Puedo llamar a Javier por la mañana.
7. Prefiero llevar mi cámara.
8. No queremos perder nuestras reservaciones de hotel.

NOTA CULTURAL

Puerto Rico is a U.S. territory, so people do not need travel documents when traveling to and from Puerto Rico from the U.S. mainland. However, everyone must meet all requirements for entering the U.S. when traveling directly to Puerto Rico from abroad.

3 ¿Quién? The Garza family is preparing to go on a vacation to Puerto Rico. Based on the clues, answer the questions. Use direct object pronouns in your answers.

> **modelo**
>
> ¿Quién hace las reservaciones para el hotel? (el Sr. Garza)
> *El Sr. Garza las hace.*

1. ¿Quién compra los pasajes para el vuelo (*flight*)? (la Sra. Garza)

2. ¿Quién tiene que hacer las maletas de los niños? (María)

3. ¿Quiénes buscan los pasaportes? (Antonio y María)

4. ¿Quién va a confirmar las reservaciones de hotel? (la Sra. Garza)

5. ¿Quién busca la cámara? (María)

6. ¿Quién compra un mapa de Puerto Rico? (Antonio)

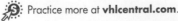
Practice more at **vhlcentral.com**.

Comunicación

4

Entrevista Take turns asking and answering these questions with a classmate. Be sure to use direct object pronouns in your responses.

1. ¿Ves mucho la televisión?
2. ¿Cuándo vas a ver tu programa favorito?
3. ¿Quién prepara la comida (*food*) en tu casa?
4. ¿Te visita mucho tu familia?
5. ¿Visitas mucho a tus abuelos?
6. ¿Nos entienden nuestros padres a nosotros?
7. ¿Cuándo ves a tus amigos/as?
8. ¿Cuándo te llaman tus amigos/as?

5

Los pasajeros Get together with a partner and take turns asking each other questions about the drawing. Use the word bank and direct object pronouns.

AYUDA

For travel-related vocabulary, see **Contextos**, pp. 246–247.

modelo

▶ **Estudiante 1:** ¿Quién está leyendo el libro?
Estudiante 2: Susana lo está leyendo./Susana está leyéndolo.

| buscar | confirmar | escribir | leer | tener | vender |
| comprar | encontrar | escuchar | llevar | traer | ¿? |

Sra. Sánchez   Orlando   Sr. López
Marta   Sr. Sánchez   Susana   Miguelito

Síntesis

6

Adivinanzas In pairs, take turns describing a person, place, or thing for your partner to guess. Each of you should give at least five descriptions.

modelo

Estudiante 1: Lo uso para (*I use it to*) escribir en mi cuaderno.
           No es muy grande y tiene borrador. ¿Qué es?
Estudiante 2: ¿Es un lápiz?
Estudiante 1: ¡Sí!

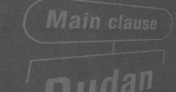

Recapitulación

 **Diagnostics**

Review the grammar concepts you have learned in this lesson by completing these activities.

1 **Completar** Complete the chart with the correct present participle of these verbs. **8 pts.**

Infinitive	Present participle	Infinitive	Present participle
hacer		estar	
acampar		ser	
tener		vivir	
venir		estudiar	

2 **Vacaciones en París** Complete this paragraph about Julia's trip to Paris with the correct form of **ser** or **estar**. **12 pts.**

Hoy (1) _____ (es/está) el 3 de julio y voy a París por tres semanas. (Yo) (2) _____ (Soy/Estoy) muy feliz porque voy a ver a mi mejor amiga. Ella (3) _____ (es/está) de Puerto Rico, pero ahora (4) _____ (es/está) viviendo en París. También (yo) (5) _____ (soy/estoy) un poco nerviosa porque (6) _____ (es/está) mi primer viaje a Francia. El vuelo (*flight*) (7) _____ (es/está) hoy por la tarde, pero ahora (8) _____ (es/está) lloviendo. Por eso (9) _____ (somos/estamos) preocupadas, porque probablemente el avión va a salir tarde. Mi equipaje ya (10) _____ (es/está) listo. (11) _____ (Es/Está) tarde y me tengo que ir. ¡Va a (12) _____ (ser/estar) un viaje fenomenal!

3 **¿Qué hacen?** Respond to these questions by indicating what people do with the items mentioned. Use direct object pronouns. **5 pts.**

> **modelo**
> ¿Qué hacen ellos con la película? (ver)
> La ven.

1. ¿Qué haces tú con el libro de viajes? (leer) _____
2. ¿Qué hacen los turistas en la ciudad? (explorar) _____
3. ¿Qué hace el botones con el equipaje? (llevar) _____
4. ¿Qué hace la agente con las reservaciones? (confirmar) _____
5. ¿Qué hacen ustedes con los pasaportes? (mostrar) _____

RESUMEN GRAMATICAL

5.1 Estar with conditions and emotions *p. 258*

▶ Yo **estoy** aburrido/a, feliz, nervioso/a.

▶ El cuarto **está** desordenado, limpio, ordenado.

▶ Estos libros **están** abiertos, cerrados, sucios.

5.2 The present progressive *pp. 260–261*

▶ The present progressive is formed with the present tense of **estar** plus the present participle.

Forming the present participle

infinitive	stem	ending	present participle
hablar	habl-	-ando	hablando
comer	com-	-iendo	comiendo
escribir	escrib-	-iendo	escribiendo

-ir stem-changing verbs

	infinitive	present participle
e:ie	preferir	prefiriendo
e:i	conseguir	consiguiendo
o:ue	dormir	durmiendo

▶ Irregular present participles: **yendo (ir), pudiendo (poder), viniendo (venir)**

5.3 Ser and estar *pp. 264–265*

▶ Uses of **ser**: nationality, origin, profession or occupation, characteristics, generalizations, possession, what something is made of, time and date, time and place of events

▶ Uses of **estar**: location, health, physical states and conditions, emotional states, weather expressions, ongoing actions

▶ Many adjectives can be used with both **ser** and **estar**, but the meaning of the adjectives will change.

Juan **es** delgado.	Juan **está** más delgado hoy.
Juan is thin.	*Juan looks thinner today.*

4 **Opuestos** Complete these sentences with the appropriate form of the verb **estar** and an antonym for the underlined adjective. **5 pts.**

> **modelo**
>
> Mis respuestas están <u>bien</u>, pero las de Susana *están mal.*

1. Las tiendas están <u>abiertas</u>, pero la agencia de viajes _____ _____.
2. No me gustan las habitaciones <u>desordenadas</u>. Incluso (*Even*) mi habitación de hotel _____ _____.
3. Nosotras estamos <u>tristes</u> cuando trabajamos. Hoy comienzan las vacaciones y _____ _____.
4. En esta ciudad los autobuses están <u>sucios</u>, pero los taxis _____ _____.
5. —El avión sale a las 5:30, ¿verdad? —No, estás <u>confundida</u>. Yo _____ _____ de que el avión sale a las 5:00.

5.4 Direct object nouns and pronouns *pp. 268–269*

Direct object pronouns

Singular		Plural	
me	lo	nos	los
te	la	os	las

In affirmative sentences:
Adela practica el tenis. → Adela **lo** practica.

In negative sentences: Adela **no lo** practica.

With an infinitive:
Adela **lo** va a practicar./Adela va a practicar**lo**.

With the present progressive:
Adela **lo** está practicando./Adela está practicándo**lo**.

Lección 5

5 **En la playa** Describe what these people are doing. Complete the sentences using the present progressive tense. **8 pts.**

1. El Sr. Camacho _____.
2. Felicia _____.
3. Leo _____.
4. Nosotros _____.

6 **Antes del viaje** Write a paragraph of at least six sentences describing the time right before you go on a trip. Say how you feel and what you are doing. You can use **Actividad 2** as a model. **12 pts.**

> **modelo**
>
> Hoy es viernes, 27 de octubre. Estoy en mi habitación...

7 **Refrán** Complete this Spanish saying by filling in the missing present participles. Refer to the translation and the drawing. **2 EXTRA points!**

¡LA CIUDAD ESTÁ MUY SUCIA!

" Se consigue más _____ que _____. "

(You can accomplish more by doing than by saying.)

Practice more at **vhlcentral.com**.

Lectura

Antes de leer

Estrategia

Scanning

Scanning involves glancing over a document in search of specific information. For example, you can scan a document to identify its format, to find cognates, to locate visual clues about the document's content, or to find specific facts. Scanning allows you to learn a great deal about a text without having to read it word for word.

Examinar el texto

Scan the reading selection for cognates and write down a few of them.

1. _____   4. _____
2. _____   5. _____
3. _____   6. _____

Based on the cognates you found, what do you think this document is about?

_____

Preguntas

Read these questions. Then scan the document again to look for answers.

1. What is the format of the reading selection?

_____

2. Which place is the document about?

_____

3. What are some of the visual cues this document provides? What do they tell you about the content of the document?

_____

4. Who produced the document, and what do you think it is for?

_____

Turismo ecológico en Puerto Rico

Hotel Vistahermosa
~ Lajas, Puerto Rico ~

- 40 habitaciones individuales
- 15 habitaciones dobles
- Teléfono/TV por cable/Internet

- Aire acondicionado
- Restaurante (Bar)
- Piscina
- Área de juegos
- Cajero automático°

El hotel está situado en Playa Grande, un pequeño pueblo de pescadores del mar Caribe. Es el lugar perfecto para el viajero que viene de vacaciones. Las playas son seguras y limpias, ideales para tomar el sol, descansar, tomar fotografías y nadar. Está abierto los 365 días del año. Hay una rebaja° especial para estudiantes universitarios.

DIRECCIÓN: Playa Grande 406, Lajas, PR 00667, cerca del Parque Nacional Foresta.

Cajero automático *ATM* rebaja *discount*

Atracciones cercanas

Playa Grande ¿Busca la playa perfecta? Playa Grande es la playa que está buscando. Usted puede pescar, sacar fotos, nadar y pasear en bicicleta. Playa Grande es un paraíso para el turista que quiere practicar deportes acuáticos. El lugar es bonito e interesante y usted va a tener muchas oportunidades para descansar y disfrutar en familia.

Valle Niebla Ir de excursión, tomar café, montar a caballo, caminar, hacer picnics. Más de cien lugares para acampar.

Bahía Fosforescente Sacar fotos, salidas de noche, excursión en barco. Una maravillosa experiencia llena de luz°.

Arrecifes de Coral Sacar fotos, bucear, explorar. Es un lugar único en el Caribe.

Playa Vieja Tomar el sol, pasear en bicicleta, jugar a las cartas, escuchar música. Ideal para la familia.

Parque Nacional Foresta Sacar fotos, visitar el Museo de Arte Nativo. Reserva Mundial de la Biosfera.

Santuario de las Aves Sacar fotos, observar aves°, seguir rutas de excursión.

llena de luz *full of light* aves *birds*

Después de leer

Listas

Which amenities of Hotel Vistahermosa would most interest these potential guests? Explain your choices.

1. dos padres con un hijo de seis años y una hija de ocho años

   _____

2. un hombre y una mujer en su luna de miel (*honeymoon*)

   _____

3. una persona en un viaje de negocios (*business trip*)

   _____

Conversaciones

With a partner, take turns asking each other these questions.

1. ¿Quieres visitar el Hotel Vistahermosa? ¿Por qué?
2. Tienes tiempo de visitar sólo tres de las atracciones turísticas que están cerca del hotel. ¿Cuáles vas a visitar? ¿Por qué?
3. ¿Qué prefieres hacer en Valle Niebla? ¿En Playa Vieja? ¿En el Parque Nacional Foresta?

Situaciones

You have just arrived at Hotel Vistahermosa. Your classmate is the concierge. Use the phrases below to express your interests and ask for suggestions about where to go.

1. montar a caballo
2. bucear
3. pasear en bicicleta
4. pescar
5. observar aves

Contestar

Answer these questions.

1. ¿Quieres visitar Puerto Rico? Explica tu respuesta.

   _____

2. ¿Adónde quieres ir de vacaciones el verano que viene? Explica tu respuesta.

   _____

Lección 5

Escritura

Estrategia

Making an outline

When we write to share information, an outline can serve to separate topics and subtopics, providing a framework for the presentation of data. Consider the following excerpt from an outline of the tourist brochure on pages 274–275.

IV. Descripción del sitio (con foto)
    A. Playa Grande
        1. Playas seguras y limpias
        2. Ideal para tomar el sol, descansar, tomar fotografías, nadar
    B. El hotel
        1. Abierto los 365 días del año
        2. Rebaja para estudiantes universitarios

Mapa de ideas

Idea maps can be used to create outlines. The major sections of an idea map correspond to the Roman numerals in an outline. The minor idea map sections correspond to the outline's capital letters, and so on. Examine the idea map that led to the outline above.

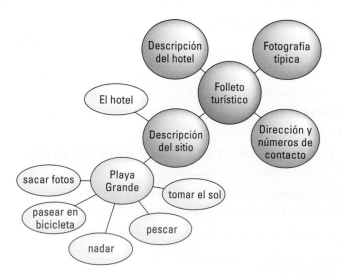

Tema

Escribir un folleto

Write a tourist brochure for a hotel or resort you have visited. If you wish, you may write about an imaginary location. You may want to include some of this information in your brochure:

▶ the name of the hotel or resort
▶ phone and fax numbers that tourists can use to make contact
▶ the hotel website that tourists can consult
▶ an e-mail address that tourists can use to request information
▶ a description of the exterior of the hotel or resort
▶ a description of the interior of the hotel or resort, including facilities and amenities
▶ a description of the surrounding area, including its climate
▶ a listing of nearby scenic natural attractions
▶ a listing of nearby cultural attractions
▶ a listing of recreational activities that tourists can pursue in the vicinity of the hotel or resort

Escuchar Audio

Estrategia

Listening for key words

By listening for key words or phrases, you can identify the subject and main ideas of what you hear, as well as some of the details.

 To practice this strategy, you will now listen to a short paragraph. As you listen, jot down the key words that help you identify the subject of the paragraph and its main ideas.

Preparación

Based on the illustration, who do you think Hernán Jiménez is, and what is he doing? What key words might you listen for to help you understand what he is saying?

Ahora escucha

Now you are going to listen to a weather report by Hernán Jiménez. Note which phrases are correct according to the key words and phrases you hear.

Santo Domingo

1. hace sol
2. va a hacer frío
3. una mañana de mal tiempo
4. va a estar nublado
5. buena tarde para tomar el sol
6. buena mañana para la playa

San Francisco de Macorís

1. hace frío
2. hace sol
3. va a nevar
4. va a llover
5. hace calor
6. mal día para excursiones

 Practice more at **vhlcentral.com**.

Comprensión

¿Cierto o falso?

Indicate whether each statement is **cierto** or **falso**, based on the weather report. Correct the false statements.

1. Según el meteorólogo, la temperatura en Santo Domingo es de 26 grados.

   _____

2. La temperatura máxima en Santo Domingo hoy va a ser de 30 grados.

   _____

3. Está lloviendo ahora en Santo Domingo.

   _____

4. En San Francisco de Macorís la temperatura mínima de hoy va a ser de 20 grados.

   _____

5. Va a llover mucho hoy en San Francisco de Macorís.

   _____

Preguntas

Answer these questions about the weather report.

1. ¿Hace viento en Santo Domingo ahora?
2. ¿Está nublado en Santo Domingo ahora?
3. ¿Está nevando ahora en San Francisco de Macorís?
4. ¿Qué tiempo hace en San Francisco de Macorís?

Lección 5

En pantalla

If you like adventure or extreme sports, Latin America might be a good destination for you. The area of Patagonia, located in Chile and Argentina, offers both breath-taking scenery and an adrenaline rush. Here, one can enjoy a variety of sports, including whitewater rafting, kayaking, trekking, and skiing. One weeklong itinerary in Argentina might include camping, hiking the granite rock of Mount Fitz Roy, and trekking across the deep blue Perito Moreno Glacier, a massive 18-mile-long sheet of ice and one of the world's few advancing glaciers.

Now, hold on to your helmets as we travel to Mexico to see what sort of adventure you can experience there.

Vocabulario útil

callejones	*alleyways, narrow streets*
calles	*streets*
carrera de bicicleta	*bicycle race*
descender (escaleras)	*to descend (stairs)*
reto, desafío	*challenge*

Preparación

Some areas attract tourists because of their unusual sports and activities. Do you know of any such destinations? Where?

Preguntas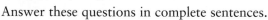

Answer these questions in complete sentences.

1. ¿Por qué viajan ciclistas (*cyclists*) a Taxco?

2. ¿Es Taxco una ciudad turística moderna o colonial?

3. ¿Hay competidores de otros (*other*) países en la carrera de bicicleta?

4. ¿Cómo está el reportero (*reporter*) después (*after*) de descender las escaleras, aburrido o cansado?

Deportes extremos

In pairs, discuss these questions: **¿Cómo son las personas que hacen deportes extremos? ¿Por qué crees que los practican? ¿Viajarías (*Would you travel*) a algún destino para practicarlos?**

menor least   *lo más alto* the highest point   *hasta* to   *diseño* design

Reportaje sobre
Down Taxco

El reto es descender en el menor° tiempo posible...

... desde lo más alto° de la ciudad hasta° la plaza central.

El principal desafío es el diseño° de la ciudad...

Video: TV Clip

Practice more at **vhlcentral.com**.

Lección 5

Between 1438 and 1533, when the vast and powerful Incan Empire was at its height, the Incas built an elaborate network of **caminos** (*trails*) that traversed the Andes Mountains and converged on the empire's capital, Cuzco. Today, hundreds of thousands of tourists come to Peru annually to walk the surviving trails and enjoy the spectacular scenery. The most popular trail, **el Camino Inca**, leads from Cuzco to **Intipunku** (*Sun Gate*), the entrance to the ancient mountain city of Machu Picchu.

Vocabulario útil

ciudadela	*citadel*
de cultivo	*farming*
el/la guía	*guide*
maravilla	*wonder*
quechua	*Quechua (indigenous Peruvian)*
sector (urbano)	*(urban) sector*

Preparación

Have you ever visited an archeological or historic site? Where? Why did you go there?

Completar

Complete these sentences. Make the necessary changes.

1. Las ruinas de Machu Picchu son una antigua _____ inca.

2. La ciudadela estaba (*was*) dividida en tres sectores: _____ , religioso y de cultivo.

3. Cada año los _____ reciben a cientos (*hundreds*) de turistas de diferentes países.

4. Hoy en día, la cultura _____ está presente en las comunidades andinas (*Andean*) de Perú.

¡Vacaciones en Perú!

Machu Picchu [...] se encuentra aislada sobre° esta montaña...

... siempre he querido° venir [...] Me encantan° las civilizaciones antiguas°.

Somos una familia francesa [...] Perú es un país muy, muy bonito de verdad.

Video: *Flash cultura*

Practice more at **vhlcentral.com**.

se encuentra aislada sobre *it is isolated on* siempre he querido *I have always wanted* Me encantan *I love* antiguas *ancient*

recursos

VM pp. 297–298   vhlcentral.com Lección 5

Puerto Rico

El país en cifras

▶ **Área:** 8.959 km² (3.459 millas²)
menor° que el área de Connecticut

▶ **Población:** 4.074.000
Puerto Rico es una de las islas más densamente pobladas° del mundo. Más de la mitad de la población vive en San Juan, la capital.

▶ **Capital:** San Juan—2.763.000

SOURCE: Population Division, UN Secretariat

▶ **Ciudades principales:** Arecibo, Bayamón, Fajardo, Mayagüez, Ponce

▶ **Moneda:** dólar estadounidense

▶ **Idiomas:** español (oficial); inglés (oficial)
Aproximadamente la cuarta parte de la población puertorriqueña habla inglés, pero en las zonas turísticas este porcentaje es mucho más alto. El uso del inglés es obligatorio para documentos federales.

Bandera
de Puerto Rico

Puertorriqueños célebres

▶ **Raúl Juliá,** actor (1940–1994)

▶ **Roberto Clemente,** beisbolista (1934–1972)

▶ **Julia de Burgos,** escritora (1914–1953)

▶ **Benicio del Toro,** actor y productor (1967–)

▶ **Rosie Pérez,** actriz y bailarina (1964–)

menor *less* pobladas *populated* río subterráneo *underground river* más largo *longest* cuevas *caves* bóveda *vault* fortaleza *fort* caber *fit*

recursos

| WB pp. 291–292 | VM pp. 295–296 | vhlcentral.com Lección 5 |

Playa en San Juan

Faro en Arecibo

Océano Atlántico

Arecibo

San Juan ★

Río Grande de Añasco

Bayamón

Mayagüez

Cordillera Central

Sierra de Cayey

Ponce

Mar Caribe

Iglesia en Ponce

Pescadores en Mayagüez

OCÉANO ATLÁNTICO

PUERTO RICO

OCÉANO PACÍFICO

¡Increíble pero cierto!

El río Camuy es el tercer río subterráneo° más largo° del mundo y tiene el sistema de cuevas° más grande del hemisferio occidental.
La Cueva de los Tres Pueblos es una gigantesca bóveda°, tan grande que toda la fortaleza° del Morro puede caber° en su interior.

Lugares • El Morro

El Morro es una fortaleza que se construyó para proteger° la bahía° de San Juan desde principios del siglo° XVI hasta principios del siglo XX. Hoy día muchos turistas visitan este lugar, convertido en un museo. Es el sitio más fotografiado de Puerto Rico. La arquitectura de la fortaleza es impresionante. Tiene misteriosos túneles, oscuras mazmorras° y vistas fabulosas de la bahía.

Artes • Salsa

La salsa, un estilo musical de origen puertorriqueño y cubano, nació° en el barrio latino de la ciudad de Nueva York. Dos de los músicos de salsa más famosos son Tito Puente y Willie Colón, los dos de Nueva York. Las estrellas° de la salsa en Puerto Rico son Felipe Rodríguez y Héctor Lavoe. Hoy en día, Puerto Rico es el centro internacional de este estilo musical. El Gran Combo de Puerto Rico es una de las orquestas de salsa más famosas del mundo°.

 • Fajardo   Isla de Culebra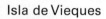

Isla de Vieques

Ciencias • El Observatorio de Arecibo

El Observatorio de Arecibo tiene uno de los radiotelescopios más grandes del mundo. Gracias a este telescopio, los científicos° pueden estudiar las propiedades de la Tierra°, la Luna° y otros cuerpos celestes. También pueden analizar fenómenos celestiales como los quasares y pulsares, y detectar emisiones de radio de otras galaxias, en busca de inteligencia extraterrestre.

Historia • Relación con los Estados Unidos

Puerto Rico pasó a ser° parte de los Estados Unidos después de° la guerra° de 1898 y se hizo° un estado libre asociado en 1952. Los puertorriqueños, ciudadanos° estadounidenses desde° 1917, tienen representación política en el Congreso, pero no votan en las elecciones presidenciales y no pagan impuestos° federales. Hay un debate entre los puertorriqueños: ¿debe la isla seguir como estado libre asociado, hacerse un estado como los otros° o volverse° independiente?

¿Qué aprendiste? Responde a las preguntas con una oración completa.

1. ¿Cuál es la moneda de Puerto Rico?
2. ¿Qué idiomas se hablan (*are spoken*) en Puerto Rico?
3. ¿Cuál es el sitio más fotografiado de Puerto Rico?
4. ¿Qué es el Gran Combo?
5. ¿Qué hacen los científicos en el Observatorio de Arecibo?

Conexión Internet Investiga estos temas en **vhlcentral.com**.

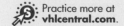 Practice more at **vhlcentral.com**.

1. Describe a dos puertorriqueños famosos. ¿Cómo son? ¿Qué hacen? ¿Dónde viven? ¿Por qué son célebres?
2. Busca información sobre lugares en los que se puede hacer ecoturismo en Puerto Rico. Luego presenta un informe a la clase.

proteger *protect* bahía *bay* siglo *century* mazmorras *dungeons* nació *was born* estrellas *stars* mundo *world* científicos *scientists* Tierra *Earth* Luna *Moon* pasó a ser *became* después de *after* guerra *war* se hizo *became* ciudadanos *citizens* desde *since* pagan impuestos *pay taxes* otros *others* volverse *to become*

Los viajes y las vacaciones

acampar	to camp
confirmar una reservación	to confirm a reservation
estar de vacaciones (f. pl.)	to be on vacation
hacer las maletas	to pack (one's suitcases)
hacer un viaje	to take a trip
hacer (wind)surf	to (wind)surf
ir de compras (f. pl.)	to go shopping
ir de vacaciones	to go on vacation
ir en autobús (m.), auto(móvil) (m.), avión (m.), barco (m.), moto(cicleta) (f.), taxi (m.)	to go by bus, car, plane, boat, motorcycle, taxi
jugar a las cartas	to play cards
montar a caballo (m.)	to ride a horse
pescar	to fish
sacar/tomar fotos (f. pl.)	to take photos
el/la agente de viajes	travel agent
el/la inspector(a) de aduanas	customs inspector
el/la viajero/a	traveler
el aeropuerto	airport
la agencia de viajes	travel agency
el campo	countryside
el equipaje	luggage
la estación de autobuses, del metro, de tren	bus, subway, train station
la llegada	arrival
el mar	sea
el paisaje	landscape
el pasaje (de ida y vuelta)	(round-trip) ticket
el pasaporte	passport
la playa	beach
la salida	departure; exit
la tabla de (wind)surf	surfboard/sailboard

El hotel

el ascensor	elevator
el/la botones	bellhop
la cama	bed
el/la empleado/a	employee
la habitación individual, doble	single, double room
el hotel	hotel
el/la huésped	guest
la llave	key
el piso	floor (of a building)
la planta baja	ground floor

Adjetivos

abierto/a	open
aburrido/a	bored; boring
alegre	happy; joyful
amable	nice; friendly
avergonzado/a	embarrassed
cansado/a	tired
cerrado/a	closed
cómodo/a	comfortable
confundido/a	confused
contento/a	happy; content
desordenado/a	disorderly
enamorado/a (de)	in love (with)
enojado/a	mad; angry
equivocado/a	wrong
feliz	happy
limpio/a	clean
listo/a	ready; smart
nervioso/a	nervous
ocupado/a	busy
ordenado/a	orderly
preocupado/a (por)	worried (about)
seguro/a	sure; safe; confident
sucio/a	dirty
triste	sad

Los números ordinales

primer, primero/a	first
segundo/a	second
tercer, tercero/a	third
cuarto/a	fourth
quinto/a	fifth
sexto/a	sixth
séptimo/a	seventh
octavo/a	eighth
noveno/a	ninth
décimo/a	tenth

Palabras adicionales

ahora mismo	right now
el año	year
¿Cuál es la fecha (de hoy)?	What is the date (today)?
de buen/mal humor	in a good/bad mood
la estación	season
el mes	month
todavía	yet; still

Seasons, months, and dates	See page 248.
Weather expressions	See page 248.
Direct object pronouns	See page 268.
Expresiones útiles	See page 253.

Audio: Vocabulary Flashcards

contextos

Lección 5

1 **Viajes** Complete these sentences with the logical words.

1. Una persona que tiene una habitación en un hotel es _____.

2. El lugar donde los pasajeros esperan el tren es _____.

3. Para viajar en avión, tienes que ir _____.

4. Antes de entrar (*enter*) en el avión, tienes que mostrar _____.

5. La persona que lleva el equipaje a la habitación del hotel es _____.

6. Para planear (*plan*) tus vacaciones, puedes ir a _____.

7. El/la agente de viajes puede confirmar _____.

8. Para subir a tu habitación, tomas _____.

9. Para abrir la puerta de la habitación, necesitas _____.

10. Cuando una persona entra a otro país, tiene que mostrar _____.

2 **De vacaciones** Complete this conversation with the logical words.

aeropuerto	equipaje	llegada	playa
agente de viajes	habitación	pasajes	sacar fotos
cama	hotel	pasaportes	salida
confirmar	llave	pasear	taxi

ANTONIO ¿Llevas todo (*everything*) lo que vamos a necesitar para el viaje, Ana?

ANA Sí. Llevo los (1) _____ de avión. También llevo

los (2) _____ para entrar (*enter*) a Costa Rica.

ANTONIO Y yo tengo el (3) _____ con todas (*all*) nuestras cosas.

ANA ¿Tienes la cámara para (4) _____?

ANTONIO Sí, está en mi mochila.

ANA ¿Vamos al (5) _____ en metro?

ANTONIO No, vamos a llamar un (6) _____. Nos lleva directamente al aeropuerto.

ANA Voy a llamar al aeropuerto para (7) _____ la reservación.

ANTONIO La (8) _____ dice que está confirmada ya (*already*).

ANA Muy bien. Tengo muchas ganas de (9) _____ por Puntarenas.

ANTONIO Yo también. Quiero ir a la (10) _____ y nadar en el mar.

ANA ¿Cuál es la hora de (11) _____ al aeropuerto de San José?

ANTONIO Llegamos a las tres de la tarde y vamos directamente al (12) _____.

3 **Los meses** Write the appropriate month next to each description or event.

1. el Día de San Valentín _____
2. el tercer mes del año _____
3. Hanukkah _____

4. el Día de las Madres _____
5. el séptimo mes del año _____
6. el Día de Año Nuevo (*New*) _____

4 **Las estaciones** Answer these questions using complete sentences.

1. ¿Qué estación sigue al invierno? _____
2. ¿En qué estación va mucha gente a la playa? _____
3. ¿En qué estación empiezan las clases? _____

5 **El tiempo** Answer these questions with complete sentences based on the weather map.

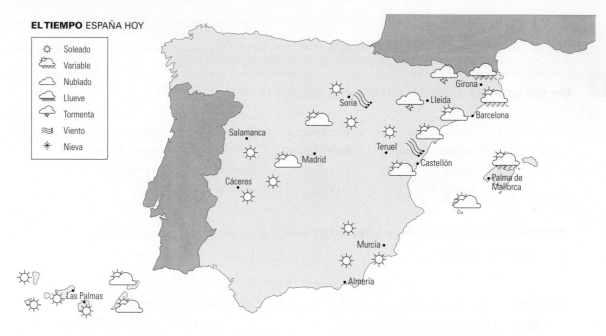

EL TIEMPO ESPAÑA HOY

☼ Soleado
⛅ Variable
☁ Nublado
🌧 Llueve
⛈ Tormenta
≋ Viento
✳ Nieva

1. ¿Hace buen tiempo en Soria? _____
2. ¿Llueve en Teruel? _____
3. ¿Hace sol en Girona? _____
4. ¿Está nublado en Murcia? _____
5. ¿Nieva en Cáceres? _____
6. ¿Qué tiempo hace en Salamanca? _____
7. ¿Hace viento cerca de Castellón? _____
8. ¿Qué tiempo hace en Almería? _____
9. ¿Está nublado en Las Palmas? _____
10. ¿Hace buen tiempo en Lleida? _____

estructura

5.1 Estar with conditions and emotions

1 **¿Por qué?** Choose the best phrase to complete each sentence.

1. José Miguel está cansado porque...
   a. trabaja mucho.
   b. su familia lo quiere.
   c. quiere ir al cine.

2. Los viajeros están preocupados porque...
   a. es la hora de comer.
   b. va a pasar un huracán (*hurricane*).
   c. estudian matemáticas.

3. Maribel y Claudia están tristes porque...
   a. nieva mucho y no pueden salir.
   b. van a salir a bailar.
   c. sus amigos son simpáticos.

4. Los estudiantes están equivocados porque...
   a. estudian mucho.
   b. pasean en bicicleta.
   c. su respuesta es incorrecta.

5. Laura está enamorada porque...
   a. tiene que ir a la biblioteca.
   b. su novio es simpático, inteligente y guapo.
   c. sus amigas ven una película.

6. Mis abuelos están felices porque...
   a. vamos a pasar el verano con ellos.
   b. mucha gente toma el sol.
   c. el autobús no llega.

2 **Completar** Complete these sentences with the correct forms of **estar** and the conditions or emotions from the list.

abierto	cerrado	desordenado	sucio
aburrido	cómodo	equivocado	triste
cansado	contento	feliz	

1. No tenemos nada que hacer; _____ muy _____.

2. Humberto _____ muy _____ en su gran cama nueva (*new*).

3. Los estudiantes de filosofía no _____ _____; ellos tienen razón.

4. Cuando Estela llega a casa a las tres de la mañana, _____ muy _____.

5. La habitación _____ _____ porque no tengo tiempo (*time*) de organizar los libros y papeles.

6. Son las once de la noche; no puedo ir a la biblioteca ahora porque _____ _____.

7. El auto de mi tío _____ muy _____ por la nieve y el lodo (*mud*) de esta semana.

8. Mi papá canta en la casa cuando _____ _____.

9. Alberto _____ _____ porque sus amigos están muy lejos.

10. Las ventanas _____ _____ porque hace calor.

3 **Marta y Juan** Complete this letter using **estar** + the correct forms of the emotions and conditions. Use each term once.

abierto	cómodo	enamorado	nervioso
aburrido	confundido	enojado	ocupado
avergonzado	contento	equivocado	seguro
cansado	desordenado	feliz	triste

Querida Marta:

¿Cómo estás? Yo (1)_____ porque mañana vuelvo a Puerto Rico y te voy a ver. Sé (I know) que tú (2)_____ porque tenemos que estar separados durante el semestre, pero (3)_____ de que (that) te van a aceptar en la universidad y que vas a venir en septiembre. La habitación en la residencia estudiantil no es grande, pero mi compañero de cuarto y yo (4)_____ aquí. Las ventanas son grandes y (5)_____ porque el tiempo es muy bueno en California. El cuarto no (6)_____ porque mi compañero de cuarto es muy ordenado. En la semana mis amigos y yo (7)_____ porque trabajamos y estudiamos muchas horas al día. Cuando llego a la residencia estudiantil por la noche, (8)_____ y me voy a dormir. Los fines de semana no (9)_____ porque hay muchas cosas que hacer en San Diego. Ahora (10)_____ porque mañana tengo que llegar al aeropuerto a las cinco de la mañana y está lejos de la universidad. Pero tengo ganas de estar contigo porque (11)_____ de ti (you) y (12)_____ porque te voy a ver mañana.

Te quiero mucho,

Juan

4 **¿Cómo están?** Read each sentence, then write a new one for each, using **estar** + an emotion or condition to tell how these people are doing or feeling.

> **modelo**
> Pepe tiene que trabajar muchas horas.
> *Pepe está ocupado.*

1. Vicente y Mónica tienen sueño. _____

2. No tenemos razón. _____

3. El pasajero tiene miedo. _____

4. Paloma se quiere casar con (*marry*) su novio. _____

5. Los abuelos de Irene van de vacaciones a Puerto Rico. _____

6. No sé (*I don't know*) si el examen va a ser fácil o difícil. _____

5.2 The present progressive

1 **Completar** Complete these sentences with the correct form of **estar** + the present participle of the verbs in parentheses.

1. Ana _____ (buscar) un apartamento en el centro de la ciudad.

2. Vamos a ver a mis primos que _____ (comer) en el café de la esquina.

3. (Yo) _____ (empezar) a entender muy bien el español.

4. Miguel y Elena _____ (vivir) en un apartamento en la playa.

5. El amigo de Antonio _____ (trabajar) en la oficina hoy.

6. (Tú) _____ (jugar) al *Monopolio* con tu sobrina y su amiga.

7. Las familias _____ (tener) muchos problemas con los hijos adolescentes.

8. El inspector de aduanas _____ (abrir) las maletas de Ramón.

9. (Nosotros) _____ (pensar) en ir de vacaciones a Costa Rica.

10. Mi compañera de cuarto _____ (estudiar) en la biblioteca esta tarde.

2 **Están haciendo muchas cosas** Look at the illustration and label what each person is doing. Use the present progressive.

1. El señor Rodríguez _____
_____ .

2. Pepe y Martita _____
_____ .

3. Paquito _____
_____ .

4. Kim _____
_____ .

5. Tus abuelos _____
_____ .

6. (Yo) _____
_____ .

7. La madre de David _____
_____ .

8. (Tú) _____
_____ .

5.3 Ser and estar

1 **Usos de *ser* y *estar*** Complete these sentences with **ser** and **estar**. Then write the letter that corresponds to the correct use of the verb in the blank at the end of each sentence.

Uses of *ser*
a. Nationality and place of origin
b. Profession or occupation
c. Characteristics of people and things
d. Generalizations
e. Possession
f. What something is made of
g. Time and date
h. Where an event takes place

Uses of *estar*
i. Location or spatial relationships
j. Health
k. Physical states or conditions
l. Emotional states
m. Certain weather expressions
n. Ongoing actions (progressive tenses)

1. El concierto de jazz _____ a las ocho de la noche. _____

2. Inés y Pancho _____ preocupados porque el examen va a ser difícil. _____

3. La playa _____ sucia porque hay muchos turistas. _____

4. No puedo salir a tomar el sol porque _____ nublado. _____

5. En el verano, Tito _____ empleado del hotel Brisas de Loíza. _____

6. Rita no puede venir al trabajo hoy porque _____ enferma. _____

7. La motocicleta nueva _____ de David. _____

8. (Yo) _____ estudiando en la biblioteca porque tengo un examen mañana. _____

9. La piscina del hotel _____ grande y bonita. _____

10. _____ importante estudiar, pero también tienes que descansar. _____

2 **¿Ser o estar?** In each of the following pairs, complete one sentence with the correct form of **ser** and the other with the correct form of **estar**.

1. Irene todavía no _____ lista para salir.
   Ricardo _____ el chico más listo de la clase.

2. Tomás no es un buen amigo porque _____ muy aburrido.
   Quiero ir al cine porque _____ muy aburrida.

3. Mi mamá está en cama porque _____ mala del estómago (*stomach*).
   El restaurante chino que está cerca del laboratorio _____ muy malo.

4. La mochila de Javier _____ verde (*green*).
   No me gustan las bananas cuando _____ verdes.

5. Elena _____ más rubia por tomar el sol.
   La hija de mi profesor _____ rubia.

6. Gabriela _____ muy delgada porque está enferma (*sick*).
   Mi hermano _____ muy delgado.

3 **En el hotel** Describe the Hotel San Juan using these cues and either **ser** or **estar** as appropriate.

1. la habitación / limpio y ordenado

_____

2. el restaurante del hotel / excelente

_____

3. la puerta del ascensor / abierta

_____

4. los otros huéspedes / franceses

_____

5. (yo) / cansada de viajar

_____

6. Paula y yo / buscando al botones

_____

7. la empleada / muy simpática

_____

8. el botones / ocupado

_____

9. ustedes / en la ciudad de San Juan

_____

10. (tú) / José Javier Fernández

_____

4 **La familia Piñero** Complete this paragraph with the correct forms of **ser** and **estar**.

Los Piñero (1) _____ de Nueva York, pero (2) _____ de vacaciones

en Puerto Rico. (3) _____ en un hotel grande en el pueblo de Dorado. Los padres

(4) _____ Elena y Manuel, y ahora (5) _____ comiendo en el

restaurante del hotel. Los hijos (6) _____ Cristina y Luis, y (7) _____

nadando en la piscina. Ahora mismo (8) _____ lloviendo, pero el sol va a salir

muy pronto (*soon*). Hoy (9) _____ lunes y la familia (10) _____

muy contenta porque puede descansar. El señor Piñero (11) _____ profesor

y la señora Piñero (12) _____ doctora. Los Piñero dicen: "¡Cuando

no (13) _____ de vacaciones, (14) _____ todo el tiempo

muy ocupados!".

5.4 Direct object nouns and pronouns

1 **Monólogo de un viajero** Complete this monologue with the correct direct object pronouns.

Hoy es lunes. El sábado voy de viaje. Tengo cinco días, ¿no? Sí, (1) _____ tengo.

Tengo que conseguir un pasaje de ida y vuelta. ¡Imprescindible! Mi hermano trabaja en una agencia

de viajes; él me (2) _____ consigue fácilmente. Tengo que buscar un buen mapa de

la ciudad. En Internet (3) _____ puedo encontrar. Y en la biblioteca puedo encontrar

libros sobre el país; libros sobre su historia, su arquitectura, su geografía, su gente...

(4) _____ voy a leer en el avión. También quiero comprar una mochila nueva.

Pero (5) _____ quiero muy grande. ¿Y dónde está mi vieja cámara de fotos?

(6) _____ tengo que buscar esta noche. Voy a tomar muchas fotos; mi familia

(7) _____ quiere ver. Y... ¿cuándo voy a hacer las maletas? (8) _____

tengo que hacer el miércoles. Y eso es todo, ¿verdad? No, no es todo. Necesito encontrar un

compañero o una compañera de viaje. Pero, hay un pequeño problema: ¿dónde

(9) _____ encuentro o (10) _____ encuentro?

Síntesis

On another sheet of paper, describe the room and the people in the illustration. Use complete
sentences. Explain what the people are doing and feeling, and why. Then choose one of the groups of
people and write a conversation that they could be having. They should discuss a vacation that they
are planning, the arrangements they are making for it, and the things that they will need to take.

panorama

Puerto Rico

1 **¿Cierto o falso?** Indicate if each statement is **cierto** or **falso**. Then correct the false statements.

1. El área de Puerto Rico es menor que (*smaller than*) la de Connecticut.

2. Todos (*All*) los puertorriqueños hablan inglés y español.

3. La fortaleza del Morro protegía (*protected*) la bahía de Mayagüez.

4. La música salsa tiene raíces españolas.

5. Los científicos detectan emisiones de radio desde (*from*) el Observatorio de Arecibo.

6. Los puertorriqueños no votan en las elecciones presidenciales de los Estados Unidos.

2 **Datos de Puerto Rico** Complete these sentences with words and expressions from **Panorama**.

1. Aproximadamente la mitad de la población de Puerto Rico vive en _____.
2. El uso del inglés es obligatorio en los documentos _____.
3. _____ fue (*was*) un beisbolista puertorriqueño famoso.
4. Hoy día _____ es el centro internacional de la salsa.
5. El Observatorio de Arecibo tiene uno de los _____ más grandes del mundo.
6. Puerto Rico se hizo parte de los EE.UU. en 1898 y se hizo un _____ en 1952.

3 **Cosas puertorriqueñas** Fill in each category with information from **Panorama**.

	Ciudades puertorriqueñas	Ríos puertorriqueños	Islas puertorriqueñas	Puertorriqueños célebres

4 **¿Lo hacen?** Answer these questions correctly using a direct object pronoun in each answer.

> **modelo**
>
> ¿Lees el artículo de Puerto Rico?
> Sí, lo leo./ No, no lo leo.

1. ¿Usan los pesos como moneda los puertorriqueños?

_____

2. ¿Habla el idioma inglés la cuarta parte de la población puertorriqueña?

_____

3. ¿Sacan fotografías del Morro muchas personas?

_____

4. ¿Tocan música salsa Felipe Rodríguez, El Gran Combo y Héctor Lavoe?

_____

5. ¿Estudian las montañas los científicos del Observatorio de Arecibo?

_____

6. ¿Pagan impuestos federales los puertorriqueños?

_____

5 **Fotos de Puerto Rico** Write the name of what is shown in each picture.

1. _____

2. _____

3. _____

4. _____

¡Vamos a la playa!

Antes de ver el video

1 **¿Qué hacen?** The six friends have just arrived at the beach. Based on the image, what do you think Maru and Jimena are doing? What do you think they will do next?

_____

_____

_____

_____

_____

_____

_____

Mientras ves el video

2 **¿Quién?** Watch the episode and write the name of the person that goes with each expression.

Expresión	Nombre
1. En Yucatán hace mucho calor.	_____
2. ¿Están listos para su viaje a la playa?	_____
3. No podemos perder el autobús.	_____
4. Bienvenidas. ¿En qué puedo servirles?	_____
5. No está nada mal el hotel, ¿verdad? Limpio, cómodo.	_____

3 **¿Qué ves?** Check what is shown.

____ 1. un inspector de aduanas ____ 5. unas maletas ____ 9. la planta baja del hotel

____ 2. el mar ____ 6. una pelota ____ 10. unas llaves

____ 3. un aeropuerto ____ 7. una agencia de viajes ____ 11. un libro

____ 4. un botones ____ 8. el campo ____ 12. personas en la playa

4 **Completar** Fill in the blanks.

1. **TÍA ANA MARÍA** Excelente, entonces... ¡A la _____ !

2. **MARU** Tenemos una _____ para seis personas para esta noche.

3. **EMPLEADO** Dos _____ en el primer piso para seis huéspedes.

4. **MIGUEL** Ellos son mis amigos. Ellos sí son _____ conmigo.

5. **MARISSA** Yo estoy un poco _____ ¿Y tú? ¿Por qué no estás nadando?

Después de ver el video

5 **¿Cierto o falso?** Say whether each statement is **cierto** or **falso**. Correct the false statements.

1. Miguel está enojado con Felipe.

_____

2. Felipe y Marissa hablan con un empleado del hotel.

_____

3. Los ascensores del hotel están a la izquierda.

_____

4. Maru y su novio quieren hacer windsurf, pero no tienen tablas.

_____

5. Felipe dice que el hotel es feo y desagradable.

_____

6. Jimena dice que estudiar en la playa es muy divertido.

_____

6 **Resumir** Write a summary of this episode in Spanish. Try not to leave out any important information.

_____

_____

_____

_____

_____

_____

_____

_____

_____

7 **Preguntas** Answer these questions in Spanish.

1. ¿Te gusta ir de vacaciones? ¿Por qué? _____

_____

_____

2. ¿Adónde te gusta ir de vacaciones? ¿Por qué? _____

_____

_____

3. ¿Con quién(es) vas de vacaciones? _____

_____

_____

Panorama: Puerto Rico

Lección 5
Panorama cultural

Antes de ver el video

1 **Más vocabulario** Look over these useful words and expressions before you watch the video.

Vocabulario útil		
angosto *narrow*	calle *street*	plaza *square*
antiguo *old*	escultura *sculpture*	promocionar *to promote*
artesanías *handicrafts*	exposición *exhibition*	sitio *site*
bahía *bay*	fuente *fountain*	vender *to sell*
barrio *neighborhood*		

2 **Preferencias** This video describes the attractions that San Juan, the capital of Puerto Rico, has to offer. In Spanish, list at least three things that you like to do when you visit a new city.

_____

_____

_____

_____

_____

_____

Mientras ves el video

3 **Cognados** Check off all the cognates you hear during the video.

_____ 1. aeropuerto

_____ 2. área

_____ 3. arte

_____ 4. artístico

_____ 5. cafés

_____ 6. calma

_____ 7. capital

_____ 8. construcciones

_____ 9. estrés

_____ 10. histórico

_____ 11. información

_____ 12. nacional

_____ 13. permanente

_____ 14. presidente

_____ 15. restaurantes

Después de ver el video

4 **Corregir** All of these statements are false. Rewrite them to correct the false information.

1. El Viejo San Juan es el barrio más moderno de la capital.

   _____

2. El Morro es el centro artístico y cultural de Puerto Rico.

   _____

3. Muchos artistas locales compran sus creaciones en las calles.

   _____

4. En diciembre se celebra la Fiesta de la Calle San Sebastián con conciertos, exposiciones especiales de arte y un carnaval.

   _____

5. En el Museo de las Américas presentan exposiciones relacionadas con la historia de Norteamérica.

   _____

6. Todos los días, más de un millón de visitantes llegan al Centro de Información de Turismo del Viejo San Juan.

   _____

5 **Completar** Complete the following sentences with words from the box.

camina	coloniales	excelente	galerías	promociona
capital	esculturas	exposición	hermoso	

1. En la bahía de la _____ de Puerto Rico está el Castillo de San Felipe del Morro.
2. Muchas de las construcciones del Viejo San Juan son _____.
3. En la mayoría de los parques hay _____ inspiradas en la historia del país.
4. El Instituto de Cultura Puertorriqueña _____ eventos culturales en la isla.
5. Hay muchas _____ de arte y museos.
6. En el Museo de San Juan hay una _____ permanente de la historia de Puerto Rico.

6 **Preferencias** Of all the places in San Juan that were described, which one did you find most interesting? In Spanish, describe this place and indicate why you found it so interesting.

_____

_____

_____

_____

_____

¡Vacaciones en Perú!

Lección 5
Flash cultura

Antes de ver el video

1 **Más vocabulario** Look over these useful words before you watch the video.

Vocabulario útil		
aislado/a *isolated*	disfrutar *to enjoy*	se salvó *was saved*
andino/a *Andean*	el esfuerzo *effort*	la selva *jungle*
ayudó *helped*	hemos contratado *we have hired*	subir *to climb, to go up*
el cultivo *farming*	la obra *work (of art)*	la vuelta al mundo *around the world*

2 **Completar** Complete these sentences. Make the necessary changes.

1. Machu Picchu es una _____ muy importante de la civilización inca. Esta (*This*) ciudad inca está rodeada (*surrounded*) de una gran _____.

2. Los incas fueron (*were*) grandes artistas y expertos en técnicas de _____ como el sistema de terrazas (*terraces*).

3. Hoy muchos turistas van a _____ de las ruinas incas y del maravilloso paisaje (*landscape*) andino.

4. Cada año miles de personas deciden _____ hasta Machu Picchu por el Camino Inca.

3 **¡En español!** Look at the video still. Imagine what Omar will say about Machu Picchu, and write a two- or three-sentence introduction to this episode.

Omar Fuentes, Perú

¡Bienvenidos a otra aventura de *Flash cultura*! Hoy estamos en…

_____

_____

_____

_____

Mientras ves el video

4 **Descripción** What does Noemí say about the lost city of Machu Picchu? Complete this quote.

"Omar, te cuento (*let me tell you*) que Machu Picchu se salvó de la invasión (1) _____

gracias a que se encuentra (*it's located*) (2) _____ sobre esta (3) _____,

como tú puedes ver. Y también la (4) _____ ayudó mucho… lo cubrió (*covered*)

rápidamente, y eso también contribuye."

5 **Emparejar** Watch the tourists describe their impressions of Machu Picchu. Match the captions to the appropriate people.

1. _____ 2. _____

3. _____ 4. _____

   a. enigma y misterio   b. magnífico y misterioso   c. algo esplendoroso, algo único…

   d. ¡Fantástico!   e. Nos encanta muchísimo.

Después de ver el video

6 **¿Cierto o falso?** Indicate whether each statement is **cierto** or **falso**.

1. Las ruinas de Machu Picchu están al lado del mar.   _____

2. Hay menos de (*less than*) cien turistas por día en el santuario (*sanctuary*) inca.   _____

3. Cuando visitas Machu Picchu, puedes contratar a un guía experto.   _____

4. Todos los turistas llegan a Machu Picchu en autobús.   _____

5. Omar pregunta a los turistas por qué visitan Machu Picchu.   _____

7 **¡La vuelta al mundo!** Imagine that you are a travel agent and that the French globetrotting family you saw in the video is planning their next destination. Write a conversation between you and the mother. Suggest an exciting destination, describe the activities the family can do together, and then work out how to get there, where to stay, and for how long.

_____

_____

_____

_____

_____

contextos

1 **Identificar** You will hear a series of words. Write the word that does not belong in each series.

1. _____
2. _____
3. _____
4. _____

5. _____
6. _____
7. _____
8. _____

2 **Describir** For each drawing, you will hear two statements. Choose the one that corresponds to the drawing.

1. a.   b.

2. a.   b.

3. a.   b.

3 **En la agencia de viajes** Listen to this conversation between Mr. Vega and a travel agent. Then read the statements in your lab manual and decide whether they are **cierto** or **falso**.

	Cierto	Falso
1. El señor Vega quiere esquiar, pescar y bucear.	○	○
2. El señor Vega va a Puerto Rico.	○	○
3. El señor Vega quiere ir de vacaciones la primera semana de mayo.	○	○
4. Una habitación en Las Tres Palmas cuesta (*costs*) $85,00.	○	○
5. El hotel tiene restaurante, piscina y *jacuzzi*.	○	○

4 **Escoger** Listen to each statement and choose the most appropriate activity for that weather condition.

1. a. Vamos a ir a la piscina.   b. Vamos a poner la televisión.
2. a. Voy a escribir una carta.   b. Voy a bucear.
3. a. Vamos al museo.   b. Vamos a tomar el sol.
4. a. Mañana voy a pasear en bicicleta.   b. Mañana voy a esquiar.
5. a. Queremos ir al cine.   b. Queremos nadar.
6. a. Voy a correr en el parque.   b. Voy a leer un libro.
7. a. Quiero escuchar música.   b. Quiero jugar al golf.

pronunciación

Spanish **b** and **v**

There is no difference in pronunciation between the Spanish letters **b** and **v**. However, each letter can be pronounced two different ways, depending on which letters appear next to them.

bueno	**v**óleibol	**b**iblioteca	**v**ivir

B and **v** are pronounced like the English hard **b** when they appear either as the first letter of a word, at the beginning of a phrase, or after **m** or **n**.

bonito	**v**iajar	tam**b**ién	investigar

In all other positions, **b** and **v** have a softer pronunciation, which has no equivalent in English. Unlike the hard **b**, which is produced by tightly closing the lips and stopping the flow of air, the soft **b** is produced by keeping the lips slightly open.

de**b**er	no**v**io	a**b**ril	cer**v**eza

In both pronunciations, there is no difference in sound between **b** and **v**. The English *v* sound, produced by friction between the upper teeth and lower lip, does not exist in Spanish. Instead, the soft **b** comes from friction between the two lips.

bola	**v**ela	Cari**b**e	decli**v**e

When **b** or **v** begins a word, its pronunciation depends on the previous word. At the beginning of a phrase or after a word that ends in **m** or **n**, it is pronounced as a hard **b**.

Verónica y su esposo cantan **b**oleros.

Words that begin with **b** or **v** are pronounced with a soft **b** if they appear immediately after a word that ends in a vowel or any consonant other than **m** or **n**.

Benito es de **B**oquerón pero **v**ive en **V**ictoria.

---

1 **Práctica** Repeat these words after the speaker to practice the **b** and the **v**.

1. hablamos	4. van	7. doble	10. nublado
2. trabajar	5. contabilidad	8. novia	11. llave
3. botones	6. bien	9. béisbol	12. invierno

---

2 **Oraciones** When you hear the number, read the corresponding sentence aloud, focusing on the **b** and **v** sounds. Then listen to the speaker and repeat the sentence.

1. Vamos a Guaynabo en autobús.
2. Voy de vacaciones a la Isla Culebra.
3. Tengo una habitación individual en el octavo piso.
4. Víctor y Eva van por avión al Caribe.
5. La planta baja es bonita también.
6. ¿Qué vamos a ver en Bayamón?
7. Beatriz, la novia de Víctor, es de Arecibo, Puerto Rico.

---

3 **Refranes** Repeat each saying after the speaker to practice the **b** and the **v**.

1. No hay mal que por bien no venga.
2. Hombre prevenido vale por dos.

---

4 **Dictado** You will hear four sentences. Each will be said twice. Listen carefully and write what you hear.

1. _____
2. _____
3. _____
4. _____

5.1 **Estar** with conditions and emotions

1 **Describir** For each drawing, you will hear two statements. Choose the one that corresponds to the drawing.

1. a.   b.

2. a.   b.

3. a.   b.

4. a.   b.

2 **Cambiar** Form a new sentence using the cue you hear as the subject. Repeat the correct answer after the speaker. (8 items)

> *modelo*
> Rubén está enojado con Patricia. (mamá)
> Mamá *está enojada con Patricia.*

3 **Preguntas** Answer each question you hear using the cues in your lab manual. Repeat the correct response after the speaker.

> *modelo*
> *You hear:* ¿Está triste Tomás?
> *You see:* no / contento/a
> *You say:* No, Tomás *está contento.*

1. no / abierto/a
2. sí, (nosotros)
3. su hermano
4. no / ordenado/a
5. no / sucio/a
6. estar de vacaciones, (yo)

4 **Situaciones** You will hear four brief conversations. Choose the statement that expresses how the people feel in each situation.

1. a. Ricardo está nervioso.   b. Ricardo está cansado.
2. a. La señora Fuentes está contenta.   b. La señora Fuentes está preocupada.
3. a. Eugenio está aburrido.   b. Eugenio está avergonzado.
4. a. Rosario y Alonso están equivocados.   b. Rosario y Alonso están enojados.

5.2 The present progressive

1 **Escoger** Listen to what these people are doing. Then read the statements in your lab manual and choose the appropriate description.

1. a. Es profesor.   b. Es estudiante.

2. a. Es botones.   b. Es inspector de aduanas.

3. a. Eres artista.   b. Eres huésped.

4. a. Son jugadoras de fútbol.   b. Son programadoras.

5. a. Es ingeniero.   b. Es botones.

6. a. Son turistas.   b. Son empleados.

2 **Transformar** Change each sentence from the present tense to the present progressive. Repeat the correct answer after the speaker. (6 *items*)

> **modelo**
>
> Adriana confirma su reservación.
> Adriana *está confirmando su reservación.*

3 **Preguntas** Answer each question you hear using the cue in your lab manual and the present progressive. Repeat the correct response after the speaker.

> **modelo**
>
> *You hear:* ¿Qué hacen ellos?
> *You see:* jugar a las cartas
> *You say:* Ellos *están jugando a las cartas.*

1. hacer las maletas   3. dormir   5. hablar con el botones

2. pescar en el mar   4. correr en el parque   6. comer en el café

4 **Describir** You will hear some questions. Look at the drawing and respond to each question. Repeat the correct answer after the speaker. (6 *items*)

5.3 Ser and estar

1 **Escoger** You will hear some questions with a beep in place of the verb. Decide which form of **ser** or **estar** should complete each question and circle it.

> **modelo**
>
> You hear: ¿Cómo (beep)?
> You circle: **estás** because the question is **¿Cómo estás?**

1. es	está	3. Es	Está	5. Es	Está
2. Son	Están	4. Es	Está	6. Es	Está

2 **¿Cómo es?** You just met Rosa Beltrán at a party. Describe her to a friend by using **ser** or **estar** with the cues you hear. Repeat the correct response after the speaker. (6 items)

> **modelo**
>
> muy amable
> Rosa es muy amable.

3 **¿Ser o estar?** You will hear the subject of a sentence. Complete the sentence using a form of **ser** or **estar** and the cue in your lab manual. Repeat the correct response after the speaker.

> **modelo**
>
> You hear: Papá
> You see: en San Juan
> You say: Papá está en San Juan.

1. inspector de aduanas
2. la estación de tren
3. a las diez
4. ocupados
5. el 14 de febrero
6. corriendo a clase

4 **¿Lógico o no?** You will hear some statements. Decide if they are **lógico** or **ilógico**.

1. Lógico   Ilógico
2. Lógico   Ilógico
3. Lógico   Ilógico
4. Lógico   Ilógico
5. Lógico   Ilógico
6. Lógico   Ilógico

5 **Ponce** Listen to Carolina's description of her vacation and answer the questions in your lab manual.

1. ¿Dónde está Ponce?

2. ¿Qué tiempo está haciendo?

3. ¿Qué es el Parque de Bombas?

4. ¿Que día es hoy?

5. ¿Por qué no va Carolina al Parque de Bombas hoy?

5.4 Direct object nouns and pronouns

1 **Escoger** Listen to each question and choose the most logical response.

1. a. Sí, voy a comprarlo.
   b. No, no voy a comprarla.
2. a. Joaquín lo tiene.
   b. Joaquín la tiene.
3. a. Sí, los puedo llevar.
   b. No, no te puedo llevar.
4. a. Irene los tiene.
   b. Irene las tiene.

5. a. Sí, te llevamos al partido.
   b. Sí, nos llevas al partido.
6. a. No, vamos a hacerlo mañana.
   b. No, vamos a hacerla mañana.
7. a. Va a conseguirlos mañana.
   b. Va a conseguirlas mañana.
8. a. Pienso visitarla el fin de semana.
   b. Pienso visitarte el fin de semana.

2 **Cambiar** Restate each sentence you hear using a direct object pronoun. Repeat the correct answer after the speaker. (6 *items*)

> **modelo**
> Isabel está mirando la televisión.
> Isabel *está mirándola.*

Isabel está mirando la televisión con Diego.

3 **No veo nada** You just broke your glasses and now you can't see anything. Respond to each statement using a direct object pronoun. Repeat the correct answer after the speaker. (6 *items*)

> **modelo**
> Allí está el Museo de Arte e Historia.
> ¿Dónde? No lo veo.

4 **Preguntas** Answer each question you hear in the negative. Repeat the correct response after the speaker. (6 *items*)

> **modelo**
> ¿Haces tu maleta?
> No, no la hago.

vocabulario

You will now hear the vocabulary found in your textbook on the last page of this lesson. Listen and repeat each Spanish word or phrase after the speaker.

Additional Vocabulary

Additional Vocabulary

Notes

Notes

¡De compras!

6

A PRIMERA VISTA
- ¿Está comprando algo la chica?
- ¿Crees que busca una maleta o una blusa?
- ¿Está contenta o enojada?
- ¿Cómo es la chica?

Más práctica
Workbook pages 341–352
Video Manual pages 353–358
Lab Manual pages 359–364

Communicative Goals
You will learn how to:
- Talk about and describe clothing
- Express preferences in a store
- Negotiate and pay for items you buy

¡De compras!

Más vocabulario

el abrigo	coat
los calcetines (el calcetín)	sock(s)
el cinturón	belt
las gafas (de sol)	(sun)glasses
los guantes	gloves
el impermeable	raincoat
la ropa	clothing; clothes
la ropa interior	underwear
las sandalias	sandals
el traje	suit
el vestido	dress
los zapatos de tenis	sneakers
el regalo	gift
el almacén	department store
el centro comercial	shopping mall
el mercado (al aire libre)	(open-air) market
el precio (fijo)	(fixed; set) price
la rebaja	sale
la tienda	shop; store
costar (o:ue)	to cost
gastar	to spend (money)
pagar	to pay
regatear	to bargain
vender	to sell
hacer juego (con)	to match (with)
llevar	to wear; to take
usar	to wear; to use

Variación léxica

calcetines	↔	medias (Amér. L.)
cinturón	↔	correa (Col., Venez.)
gafas/lentes	↔	espejuelos (Cuba, P.R.), anteojos (Arg., Chile)
zapatos de tenis	↔	zapatillas de deporte (Esp.), zapatillas (Arg., Perú)

los pantalones cortos

el traje de baño

los pantalones

la camiseta

Damas

el dependiente/el vendedor

la camisa

la clienta

el dinero en efectivo

la blusa

el suéter

la bolsa

las medias

la falda

Práctica

1

Escuchar 🎧 Listen to Juanita and Vicente talk about what they're packing for their vacations. Indicate who is packing each item. If both are packing an item, write both names. If neither is packing an item, write an **X**.

1. abrigo _____
2. zapatos de tenis _____
3. impermeable _____
4. chaqueta _____
5. sandalias _____
6. bluejeans _____

7. gafas de sol _____
8. camisetas _____
9. traje de baño _____
10. botas _____
11. pantalones cortos _____
12. suéter _____

2

¿Lógico o ilógico? 🎧 Listen to Guillermo and Ana talk about vacation destinations. Indicate whether each statement is **lógico** or **ilógico.**

1. _____
2. _____

3. _____
4. _____

3

Completar Anita is talking about going shopping. Complete each sentence with the correct word(s), adding definite or indefinite articles when necessary.

caja	medias	tarjeta de crédito
centro comercial	par	traje de baño
dependientas	ropa	vendedores

1. Hoy voy a ir de compras al _____.
2. Voy a ir a la tienda de ropa para mujeres. Siempre hay muchas rebajas y las _____ son muy simpáticas.
3. Necesito comprar _____ de zapatos.
4. Y tengo que comprar _____ porque el sábado voy a la playa con mis amigos.
5. También voy a comprar unas _____ para mi mamá.
6. Voy a pagar todo (*everything*) en _____.
7. Pero hoy no tengo dinero. Voy a tener que usar mi _____.
8. Mañana voy al mercado al aire libre. Me gusta regatear con los _____.

4

Escoger Choose the item in each group that does not belong.

1. almacén • centro comercial • mercado • sombrero
2. camisa • camiseta • blusa • botas
3. jeans • bolsa • falda • pantalones
4. abrigo • suéter • corbata • chaqueta
5. mercado • tienda • almacén • cartera
6. pagar • llevar • hacer juego (con) • usar
7. botas • sandalias • zapatos • traje
8. vender • regatear • ropa interior • gastar

el sombrero

Caballeros

un par de zapatos

los zapatos

la chaqueta

la caja

la cartera

la dependienta/la vendedora

la corbata

la tarjeta de crédito

los (blue)jeans

la bota

Los colores

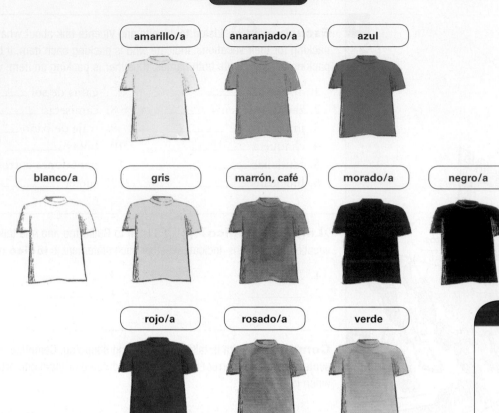

amarillo/a anaranjado/a azul

blanco/a gris marrón, café morado/a negro/a

rojo/a rosado/a verde

¡LENGUA VIVA!

The names of colors vary throughout the Spanish-speaking world. For example, in some countries, **anaranjado/a** may be referred to as **naranja**, **morado/a** as **púrpura**, and **rojo/a** as **colorado/a**.

Other terms that will prove helpful include **claro** (*light*) and **oscuro** (*dark*): **azul claro, azul oscuro**.

Adjetivos

barato/a	*cheap*
bueno/a	*good*
cada	*each*
caro/a	*expensive*
corto/a	*short (in length)*
elegante	*elegant*
hermoso/a	*beautiful*
largo/a	*long*
loco/a	*crazy*
nuevo/a	*new*
otro/a	*other; another*
pobre	*poor*
rico/a	*rich*

5

Contrastes Complete each phrase with the opposite of the underlined word.

1. una corbata <u>barata</u> • unas camisas…
2. unas vendedoras <u>malas</u> • unos dependientes…
3. un vestido <u>corto</u> • una falda…
4. un hombre muy <u>pobre</u> • una mujer muy…
5. una cartera <u>nueva</u> • un cinturón…
6. unos trajes <u>hermosos</u> • unos jeans…
7. un impermeable <u>caro</u> • unos suéteres…
8. unos calcetines <u>blancos</u> • unas medias…

CONSULTA

Like other adjectives you have seen, colors must agree in gender and number with the nouns they modify.

Ex: **las camisas verdes, el vestido amarillo.**

For a review of descriptive adjectives, see **Estructura 3.1,** pp. 134–135.

6

Preguntas Answer these questions with a classmate.

1. ¿De qué color es la rosa de Texas?
2. ¿De qué color es la bandera (*flag*) de Canadá?
3. ¿De qué color es la casa donde vive el presidente de los EE.UU.?
4. ¿De qué color es el océano Atlántico?
5. ¿De qué color es la nieve?
6. ¿De qué color es el café?
7. ¿De qué color es el dólar de los EE.UU.?
8. ¿De qué color es la cebra (*zebra*)?

 Practice more at **vhlcentral.com**.

Comunicación

7

Las maletas With a classmate, answer these questions about the drawings.

1. ¿Qué ropa hay al lado de la maleta de Carmela?

2. ¿Qué hay en la maleta?

3. ¿De qué color son las sandalias?

4. ¿Adónde va Carmela?

▶ 5. ¿Qué tiempo va a hacer?

CONSULTA

To review weather, see **Lección 5, Contextos**, p. 248.

6. ¿Qué hay al lado de la maleta de Pepe?

7. ¿Qué hay en la maleta?

8. ¿De qué color es el suéter?

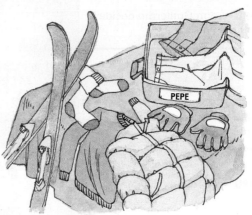

NOTA CULTURAL

Bariloche is a popular resort for skiing in South America. Located in Argentina's Patagonia region, the town is also known for its chocolate factories and its beautiful lakes, mountains, and forests.

▶ 9. ¿Qué va a hacer Pepe en Bariloche?

10. ¿Qué tiempo va a hacer?

8

El viaje Get together with two classmates and imagine that the three of you are going on vacation. Pick a destination and then draw three suitcases. Write in each one what clothing each person is taking. Present your drawings to the rest of the class, answering these questions.

- ¿Adónde van?
- ¿Qué tiempo va a hacer allí?
- ¿Qué van a hacer allí?
- ¿Qué hay en sus maletas?
- ¿De qué color es la ropa que llevan?

9

Preferencias Take turns asking and answering these questions with a classmate.

1. ¿Adónde vas a comprar ropa? ¿Por qué?
2. ¿Qué tipo de ropa prefieres? ¿Por qué?
3. ¿Cuáles son tus colores favoritos?
4. En tu opinión, ¿es importante comprar ropa nueva frecuentemente? ¿Por qué?
5. ¿Gastas mucho dinero en ropa cada mes? ¿Buscas rebajas?
6. ¿Regateas cuando compras ropa? ¿Usas tarjetas de crédito?

Lección 6

En el mercado

Los chicos van de compras al mercado. ¿Quién hizo la mejor compra?

 FELIPE

 JUAN CARLOS

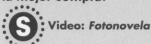

S Video: *Fotonovela*

MARISSA Oigan, vamos al mercado.

JUAN CARLOS ¡Sí! Los chicos en un equipo y las chicas en otro.

FELIPE Tenemos dos horas para ir de compras.

MARU Y don Guillermo decide quién gana.

JIMENA Esta falda azul es muy elegante.

MARISSA ¡Sí! Además, este color está de moda.

MARU Éste rojo es de algodón.

(Las chicas encuentran unas bolsas.)

VENDEDOR Ésta de rayas cuesta 190 pesos, ésta 120 pesos y ésta 220 pesos.

MARISSA ¿Me das aquella blusa rosada? Me parece que hace juego con esta falda, ¿no? ¿No tienen otras tallas?

JIMENA Sí, aquí. ¿Qué talla usas?

MARISSA Uso talla 4.

JIMENA La encontré. ¡Qué ropa más bonita!

(En otra parte del mercado)

FELIPE Juan Carlos compró una camisa de muy buena calidad.

MIGUEL *(a la vendedora)* ¿Puedo ver ésos, por favor?

VENDEDORA Sí, señor. Le doy un muy buen precio.

VENDEDOR Son 530 por las tres bolsas. Pero como ustedes son tan bonitas, son 500 pesos.

MARU Señor, no somos turistas ricas. Somos estudiantes pobres.

VENDEDOR Bueno, son 480 pesos.

MARISSA

JIMENA

MARU

MIGUEL

DON GUILLERMO

VENDEDORA

VENDEDOR

JUAN CARLOS Miren, mi nueva camisa. Elegante, ¿verdad?

FELIPE A ver, Juan Carlos... te queda bien.

MARU ¿Qué compraste?

MIGUEL Sólo esto.

MARU ¡Qué bonitos aretes! Gracias, mi amor.

JUAN CARLOS Y ustedes, ¿qué compraron?

JIMENA Bolsas.

MARU Acabamos de comprar tres bolsas por sólo 480 pesos. ¡Una ganga!

FELIPE Don Guillermo, usted tiene que decidir quién gana. ¿Los chicos o las chicas?

DON GUILLERMO El ganador es... Miguel. ¡Porque no compró nada para él, sino para su novia!

recursos

VM
pp. 353–354

vhlcentral.com
Lección 6

Expresiones útiles

Talking about clothing

¡Qué ropa más bonita!
What nice clothing!

Esta falda azul es muy elegante.
This blue skirt is very elegant.

Está de moda.
It's in style.

Éste rojo es de algodón/lana.
This red one is cotton/wool.

Ésta de rayas/lunares/cuadros es de seda.
This striped / polka-dotted / plaid one is silk.

Es de muy buena calidad.
It's very good quality.

¿Qué talla usas/llevas?
What size do you wear?

Uso/Llevo talla 4.
I wear a size 4.

¿Qué número calza?
What size shoe do you wear?

Yo calzo siete.
I wear a size seven.

Te queda bien.
That looks good on you.

Negotiating a price

¿Cuánto cuesta?
How much does it cost?

Demasiado caro/a.
Too expensive.

Es una ganga.
It's a bargain.

Saying what you bought

¿Qué compraste?/¿Qué compró usted?
What did you buy?

Sólo compré esto.
I only bought this.

¡Qué bonitos aretes!
What beautiful earrings!

Y ustedes, ¿qué compraron?
And you guys, what did you buy?

Additional vocabulary

híjole *wow*

¿Qué pasó?

1 **¿Cierto o falso?** Indicate whether each sentence is **cierto** or **falso**. Correct the false statements.

	Cierto	Falso
1. Jimena dice que la falda azul no es elegante.	○	○
2. Juan Carlos compra una camisa.	○	○
3. Marissa dice que el azul es un color que está de moda.	○	○
4. Miguel compra unas sandalias para Maru.	○	○

NOTA CULTURAL

Las guayaberas are a popular men's shirt worn in hot climates. They are usually made of cotton, linen, or silk and decorated with pleats, pockets, and sometimes embroidery. They can be worn instead of a jacket to formal occasions or as everyday clothing.

2 **Identificar** Provide the first initial of the person who would make each statement.

____ 1. ¿Te gusta cómo se me ven mis nuevos aretes?
____ 2. Juan Carlos compró una camisa de muy buena calidad.
____ 3. No podemos pagar 500, señor, eso es muy caro.
____ 4. Aquí tienen ropa de muchas tallas.
____ 5. Esta falda me gusta mucho, el color azul es muy elegante.
____ 6. Hay que darnos prisa, sólo tenemos dos horas para ir de compras.

MARU

FELIPE

JIMENA

3 **Completar** Answer the questions using the information in the **Fotonovela**.

1. ¿Qué talla es Marissa?
2. ¿Cuánto les pide el vendedor por las tres bolsas?
3. ¿Cuál es el precio que pagan las tres amigas por las bolsas?
4. ¿Qué dice Juan Carlos sobre su nueva camisa?
5. ¿Quién ganó al hacer las compras? ¿Por qué?

AYUDA

When discussing prices, it's important to keep in mind singular and plural forms of verbs.

La **camisa cuesta** diez dólares.

Las **botas cuestan** sesenta dólares.

El **precio** de las botas **es** sesenta dólares.

Los **precios** de la ropa **son** altos.

4 **Conversar** With a partner, role-play a conversation between a customer and a salesperson in an open-air market. Use these expressions and also look at **Expresiones útiles** on the previous page.

¿Qué desea?	Estoy buscando...	Prefiero el/la rojo/a.
What would you like?	*I'm looking for...*	*I prefer the red one.*

Cliente/a

Say good afternoon.

Explain that you are looking for a particular item of clothing.

Discuss colors and sizes.

Ask for the price and begin bargaining.

Settle on a price and purchase the item.

Vendedor(a)

Greet the customer and ask what he/she would like.

Show him/her some items and ask what he/she prefers.

Discuss colors and sizes.

Tell him/her a price. Negotiate a price.

Accept a price and say thank you.

 Practice more at **vhlcentral.com**.

Pronunciación

The consonants **d** and **t**

¿Dónde?   **vender**   **nadar**   **verdad**

Like **b** and **v**, the Spanish **d** can also have a hard sound or a soft sound, depending on which letters appear next to it.

Don   **dinero**   **tienda**   **falda**

At the beginning of a phrase and after **n** or **l**, the letter **d** is pronounced with a hard sound. This sound is similar to the English *d* in *dog*, but a little softer and duller. The tongue should touch the back of the upper teeth, not the roof of the mouth.

---

medias   **verde**   **vestido**   **huésped**

In all other positions, **d** has a soft sound. It is similar to the English *th* in *there*, but a little softer.

Don Diego no tiene el diccionario.

When **d** begins a word, its pronunciation depends on the previous word. At the beginning of a phrase or after a word that ends in **n** or **l**, it is pronounced as a hard **d**.

Doña Dolores es de la capital.

Words that begin with **d** are pronounced with a soft **d** if they appear immediately after a word that ends in a vowel or any consonant other than **n** or **l**.

---

traje   **pantalones**   **tarjeta**   **tienda**

When pronouncing the Spanish **t**, the tongue should touch the back of the upper teeth, not the roof of the mouth. Unlike the English *t*, no air is expelled from the mouth.

Práctica   Read these phrases aloud to practice the **d** and the **t**.

1. Hasta pronto.
2. De nada.
3. Mucho gusto.
4. Lo siento.
5. No hay de qué.
6. ¿De dónde es usted?
7. ¡Todos a bordo!
8. No puedo.
9. Es estupendo.
10. No tengo computadora.
11. ¿Cuándo vienen?
12. Son las tres y media.

Oraciones   Read these sentences aloud to practice the **d** and the **t**.

1. Don Teodoro tiene una tienda en un almacén en La Habana.
2. Don Teodoro vende muchos trajes, vestidos y zapatos todos los días.
3. Un día un turista, Federico Machado, entra en la tienda para comprar un par de botas.
4. Federico regatea con don Teodoro y compra las botas y también un par de sandalias.

Refranes   Read these sayings aloud to practice the **d** and the **t**.

En la variedad está el gusto.[1]

Aunque la mona se vista de seda, mona se queda.[2]

1 Variety is the spice of life.
2 You can't make a silk purse out of a sow's ear.

Lección 6

Additional Reading

Los mercados al aire libre

Mercados al aire libre are an integral part of commerce and culture in the Spanish-speaking world. Whether they take place daily or weekly, these markets are an important forum where tourists, locals, and vendors interact. People come to the marketplace to shop, socialize, taste local foods, and watch street performers. Wandering from one **puesto** (*stand*) to the next, one can browse for fresh fruits and vegetables, clothing, CDs and DVDs, and **artesanías** (*crafts*). Some markets offer a mix of products, while others specialize in food, fashion, or used merchandise, such as antiques and books.

When shoppers see an item they like, they can bargain with the vendor. Friendly bargaining is an expected ritual and may result in a significantly lower price. When selling food, vendors may give the customer a little extra of what they purchase; this free addition is known as **la ñapa**.

Many open-air markets are also tourist attractions. The market in Otavalo, Ecuador, is world-famous and has taken place every Saturday since pre-Incan times. This market is well-known for the colorful textiles woven by the **otavaleños**, the indigenous people of the area. One can also find leather goods and wood carvings from nearby towns. Another popular market is **El Rastro**, held every Sunday in Madrid, Spain. Sellers set up **puestos** along the streets to display their wares, which range from local artwork and antiques to inexpensive clothing and electronics.

Mercado de Otavalo

Otros mercados famosos		
Mercado	**Lugar**	**Productos**
Feria Artesanal de Recoleta	Buenos Aires, Argentina	artesanías
Mercado Central	Santiago, Chile	mariscos°, pescado°, frutas, verduras°
Tianguis Cultural del Chopo	Ciudad de México, México	ropa, música, revistas, libros, arte, artesanías
El mercado de Chichicastenango	Chichicastenango, Guatemala	frutas y verduras, flores°, cerámica, textiles

mariscos *seafood* pescado *fish* verduras *vegetables* flores *flowers*

ACTIVIDADES

1 **¿Cierto o falso?** Indicate whether these statements are **cierto** or **falso**. Correct the false statements

1. Generally, open-air markets specialize in one type of goods.

2. Bargaining is commonplace at outdoor markets.

3. Only new goods can be found at open-air markets.

4. A Spaniard in search of antiques could search at **El Rastro.**

5. If you are in Guatemala and want to buy ceramics, you can go to Chichicastenango.

6. A **ñapa** is a tax on open-air market goods.

7. The **otavaleños** weave colorful textiles to sell on Saturdays.

8. Santiago's **Mercado Central** is known for books and music.

Lección 6

La ropa

la chamarra (Méx.)	la chaqueta
de manga corta/larga	*short/long-sleeved*
los mahones (P. Rico); el pantalón de mezclilla (Méx.); los tejanos (Esp.); los vaqueros (Arg., Cuba, Esp., Uru.)	los bluejeans
la marca	*brand*
la playera (Méx.); la remera (Arg.)	la camiseta

Diseñadores de moda

- **Adolfo Domínguez** (España) Su ropa tiene un estilo minimalista y práctico. Usa telas° naturales y cómodas en sus diseños.

- **Silvia Tcherassi** (Colombia) Los colores vivos y las líneas asimétricas de sus vestidos y trajes muestran influencias tropicales.

- **Óscar de la Renta** (República Dominicana) Diseñó ropa opulenta para la mujer clásica.

- **Narciso Rodríguez** (EE.UU.) En sus diseños delicados y finos predominan los colores blanco y negro. Hizo° el vestido de boda° de Carolyn Bessette Kennedy.

telas *fabrics* Hizo *He made* de boda *wedding*

Carolina Herrera

In 1980, at the urging of some friends, **Carolina Herrera** created a fashion collection as a "test." The Venezuelan designer received such a favorable response that within one year she moved her family from Caracas to New York City and created her own label, Carolina Herrera, Ltd.

"I love elegance and intricacy, but whether it is in a piece of clothing or a fragrance, the intricacy must appear as simplicity," Herrera once stated. She quickly found that many sophisticated women agreed; from the start, her sleek and glamorous designs have been in constant demand. Over the years, Herrera has grown her brand into a veritable fashion empire that encompasses her fashion and bridal collections, cosmetics, perfume, and accessories that are sold around the globe.

 Conexión Internet

¿Qué marcas de ropa son populares en el mundo hispano?

Go to **vhlcentral.com** to find more cultural information related to this **Cultura** section.

2 **Comprensión** Complete these sentences.

1. Adolfo Domínguez usa telas _____ y _____ en su ropa.
2. Si hace fresco en el D.F., puedes llevar una _____.
3. La diseñadora _____ hace ropa, perfumes y más.
4. La ropa de _____ muestra influencias tropicales.
5. Los _____ son una ropa casual en Puerto Rico.

3 **Mi ropa favorita** Write a brief description of your favorite article of clothing. Mention what store it is from, the brand, colors, fabric, style, and any other information. Then get together with a small group, collect the descriptions, and take turns reading them aloud at random. Can the rest of the group guess whose favorite piece of clothing is being described?

 Practice more at **vhlcentral.com**.

6.1 Saber and conocer  Tutorial

ANTE TODO Spanish has two verbs that mean *to know*: **saber** and **conocer**. They cannot be used interchangeably. Note the irregular **yo** forms.

The verbs saber and conocer

		saber *(to know)*	conocer *(to know)*
SINGULAR FORMS	yo	sé	conozco
	tú	sabes	conoces
	Ud./él/ella	sabe	conoce
PLURAL FORMS	nosotros/as	sabemos	conocemos
	vosotros/as	sabéis	conocéis
	Uds./ellos/ellas	saben	conocen

▶ **Saber** means *to know a fact or piece(s) of information* or *to know how to do something.*

No **sé** tu número de teléfono.
I don't know your telephone number.

Mi hermana **sabe** hablar francés.
My sister knows how to speak French.

▶ **Conocer** means *to know* or *be familiar/acquainted* with a person, place, or thing.

¿**Conoces** la ciudad de Nueva York?
Do you know New York City?

No **conozco** a tu amigo Esteban.
I don't know your friend Esteban.

▶ When the direct object of **conocer** is a person or pet, the personal **a** is used.

¿Conoces La Habana?   *but*   ¿Conoces **a** Celia Cruz?
Do you know Havana?   *Do you know Celia Cruz?*

▶ **¡Atención! Parecer** (*to seem*) and **ofrecer** (*to offer*) are conjugated like **conocer**.

▶ **¡Atención! Conducir** (*to drive*) and **traducir** (*to translate*) also have an irregular **yo** form, but since they are **-ir** verbs, they are conjugated differently from **conocer**.

conducir	conduzco, conduces, conduce, conducimos, conducís, conducen
traducir	traduzco, traduces, traduce, traducimos, traducís, traducen

NOTA CULTURAL

Cuban singer **Celia Cruz** (1924–2003), known as the "Queen of Salsa," recorded many albums over her long career. Adored by her fans, she was famous for her colorful and lively on-stage performances.

¡INTÉNTALO! Provide the appropriate forms of these verbs.

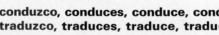

saber

1. José no __sabe__ la hora.
2. Sara y yo _____ jugar al tenis.
3. ¿Por qué no _____ tú estos verbos?
4. Mis padres _____ hablar japonés.
5. Yo _____ a qué hora es la clase.
6. Usted no _____ dónde vivo.
7. Mi hermano no _____ nadar.
8. Nosotros _____ muchas cosas.

conocer

1. Usted y yo __conocemos__ bien Miami.
2. ¿Tú _____ a mi amigo Manuel?
3. Sergio y Taydé _____ mi pueblo.
4. Emiliano _____ a mis padres.
5. Yo _____ muy bien el centro.
6. ¿Ustedes _____ la tienda Gigante?
7. Nosotras _____ una playa hermosa.
8. ¿Usted _____ a mi profesora?

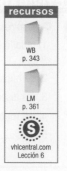

recursos

WB p. 343

LM p. 361

S

vhlcentral.com Lección 6

Práctica y Comunicación

Lección 6

1

Completar Indicate the correct verb for each sentence.

1. Mis hermanos (conocen/saben) conducir, pero yo no (sé/conozco).
2. —¿(Conocen/Saben) ustedes dónde está el estadio? —No, no lo (conocemos/sabemos).
3. —¿(Conoces/Sabes) a Lady Gaga? —Bueno, (sé/conozco) quién es, pero no la (conozco/sé).
4. Mi profesora (sabe/conoce) Cuba y también (conoce/sabe) bailar salsa.

2

Combinar Combine elements from each column to create sentences.

A	B	C
Shakira	(no) conocer	Conan O'Brien
los Yankees	(no) saber	cantar y bailar
el primer ministro		La Habana Vieja
de Canadá		muchas personas importantes
mis amigos y yo		hablar dos lenguas extranjeras
tú		jugar al béisbol

3

Preguntas In pairs, ask each other these questions. Answer with complete sentences.

1. ¿Conoces a un(a) cantante famoso/a? ¿Te gusta cómo canta?
2. En tu familia, ¿quién sabe cantar bien? ¿Tu opinión es objetiva?
3. Y tú, ¿conduces bien o mal? ¿Y tus amigos?
4. Si un(a) amigo/a no conduce muy bien, ¿le ofreces crítica constructiva?
5. ¿Cómo parece estar el/la profesor(a) hoy? ¿Y tus compañeros de clase?

4

Entrevista Jot down three things you know how to do, three people you know, and three places you are familiar with. Then, in a small group, find out what you have in common.

> **modelo**
>
> **Estudiante 1:** ¿Conocen ustedes a David Lomas?
> **Estudiante 2:** Sí, conozco a David. Vivimos en la misma residencia estudiantil.
> **Estudiante 3:** No, no lo conozco. ¿Cómo es?

5

Anuncio In groups, read the ad and answer these questions.

1. Busquen ejemplos de los verbos **saber** y **conocer**.
2. ¿Qué saben del Centro Comercial Málaga?
3. ¿Qué pueden hacer en el Centro Comercial Málaga?
4. ¿Conocen otros centros comerciales similares? ¿Cómo se llaman? ¿Dónde están?
5. ¿Conocen un centro comercial en otro país? ¿Cómo es?...

Él sabe dónde **comer** lo que más le gusta.

Él sabe cómo **jugar** cuatro horas seguidas.

Él sabe dónde está su **regalo** de cumpleaños.

Él sabe dónde **divertirse...**

... y usted sabe dónde puede encontrar un poco de todo. ¿Conoce algún otro lugar como éste?

CENTRO COMERCIAL **MÁLAGA** SABE LO QUE TE GUSTA.

 Practice more at **vhlcentral.com**.

6.2 Indirect object pronouns  Tutorial

ANTE TODO In **Lección 5**, you learned that a direct object receives the action of the verb directly. In contrast, an indirect object receives the action of the verb indirectly.

SUBJECT	I.O. PRONOUN	VERB	DIRECT OBJECT	INDIRECT OBJECT
Roberto	**le**	presta	cien pesos	**a Luisa**.
Roberto		*lends*	*100 pesos*	*to Luisa.*

An indirect object is a noun or pronoun that answers the question *to whom* or *for whom* an action is done. In the preceding example, the indirect object answers this question:
¿A quién le presta Roberto cien pesos? *To whom does Roberto lend 100 pesos?*

Indirect object pronouns

Singular forms		Plural forms	
me	(to, for) *me*	nos	(to, for) *us*
te	(to, for) *you* (fam.)	os	(to, for) *you* (fam.)
le	(to, for) *you* (form.)	les	(to, for) *you* (form.)
	(to, for) *him; her*		(to, for) *them*

▶ **¡Atención!** The forms of indirect object pronouns for the first and second persons (**me**, **te**, **nos**, **os**) are the same as the direct object pronouns. Indirect object pronouns agree in number with the corresponding nouns, but not in gender.

Bueno, le doy un descuento.

Acabo de mostrarles que sí sabemos regatear.

Using indirect object pronouns

▶ Spanish speakers commonly use both an indirect object pronoun and the noun to which it refers in the same sentence. This is done to emphasize and clarify to whom the pronoun refers.

I.O. PRONOUN	INDIRECT OBJECT	I.O. PRONOUN	INDIRECT OBJECT
Ella **le** vende la ropa **a Elena**.		**Les** prestamos el dinero **a Inés y a Álex**.	

▶ Indirect object pronouns are also used without the indirect object noun when the person for whom the action is being done is known.

Ana **le** presta la falda **a Elena**.
Ana lends her skirt to Elena.

También **le** presta unos jeans.
She also lends her a pair of jeans.

Lección 6

▶ Indirect object pronouns are usually placed before the conjugated form of the verb. In negative sentences the pronoun is placed between **no** and the conjugated verb.

Martín **me** compra un regalo.
Martín is buying me a gift.

Eva **no me** escribe cartas.
Eva doesn't write me letters.

CONSULTA

For more information on accents, see **Lección 4, Pronunciación**, p. 193, **¡ADELANTE!** DOS **Lección 4, Ortografía,** p. 203, and **¡ADELANTE!** DOS **Lección 5, Ortografía,** p. 265.

▶ When a conjugated verb is followed by an infinitive or the present progressive, the indirect object pronoun may be placed before the conjugated verb or attached to the infinitive or present participle. **¡Atención!** When an indirect object pronoun is attached to a present participle, an accent mark is added to maintain the proper stress.

Él no quiere **pagarte**./
Él no **te** quiere pagar.
He does not want to pay you.

Él está **escribiéndole** una postal a ella./
Él **le** está escribiendo una postal a ella.
He is writing a postcard to her.

▶ Because the indirect object pronouns **le** and **les** have multiple meanings, Spanish speakers often clarify to whom the pronouns refer with the preposition **a** + [*pronoun*] or **a** + [*noun*].

UNCLARIFIED STATEMENTS
Yo **le** compro un abrigo.

Ella **le** describe un libro.

CLARIFIED STATEMENTS
Yo **le** compro un abrigo **a usted/él/ella**.

Ella **le** describe un libro **a Juan**.

UNCLARIFIED STATEMENTS
Él **les** vende unos sombreros.

Ellos **les** hablan muy claro.

CLARIFIED STATEMENTS
Él **les** vende unos sombreros **a ustedes/ellos/ellas**.

Ellos **les** hablan muy claro **a los clientes**.

▶ The irregular verbs **dar** (*to give*) and **decir** (*to say; to tell*) are often used with indirect object pronouns.

The verbs dar and decir

	Singular forms				Plural forms		
		dar	decir			dar	decir
yo		doy	digo	nosotros/as		damos	decimos
tú		das	dices	vosotros/as		dais	decís
Ud./él/ella		da	dice	Uds./ellos/ellas		dan	dicen

Me dan una fiesta cada año.
They give (throw) me a party every year.

Te digo la verdad.
I'm telling you the truth.

Voy a **darle** consejos.
I'm going to give her advice.

No **les digo** mentiras a mis padres.
I don't tell lies to my parents.

recursos

WB
pp. 344–345

LM
p. 362

S
vhlcentral.com
Lección 6

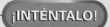

¡INTÉNTALO! Use the cues in parentheses to provide the correct indirect object pronoun for each sentence.

1. Juan ___le___ quiere dar un regalo. (*to Elena*)
2. María _____ prepara un café. (*for us*)
3. Beatriz y Felipe _____ escriben desde (*from*) Cuba. (*to me*)
4. Marta y yo _____ compramos unos guantes. (*for them*)
5. Los vendedores _____ venden ropa. (*to you, fam. sing.*)
6. La dependienta _____ muestra los guantes. (*to us*)

Práctica

1

Completar Fill in the blanks with the correct pronouns to complete Mónica's description of her family's holiday shopping.

1. Juan y yo _____ damos una blusa a nuestra hermana Gisela.
2. Mi tía _____ da a nosotros una mesa para la casa.
3. Gisela _____ da dos corbatas a su novio.
4. A mi mamá yo _____ doy un par de guantes negros.
5. A mi profesora _____ doy dos libros de José Martí.
6. Juan _____ da un regalo a mis padres.
7. Mis padres _____ dan un traje nuevo a mí.
8. Y a ti, yo _____ doy un regalo también. ¿Quieres verlo?

NOTA CULTURAL

Cuban writer and patriot **José Martí** (1853–1895) was born in **La Habana Vieja**, the old colonial center of Havana. Founded by Spanish explorers in the early 1500s, Havana, along with San Juan, Puerto Rico, served as a major stopping point for Spaniards traveling to Mexico and South America.

2

En La Habana Describe what happens on Pascual's trip to Cuba based on the cues provided.

1. ellos / cantar / canción / (mí)

2. él / comprar / libros / (sus hijos) / Plaza de Armas

3. yo / preparar el almuerzo (*lunch*) / (ti)

4. él / explicar cómo llegar / (conductor)

5. mi novia / sacar / foto / (nosotros)

6. el guía (*guide*) / mostrar / catedral de San Cristóbal / (ustedes)

NOTA CULTURAL

La Habana Vieja, Cuba, is the site of another well-known outdoor market. Located in the **Plaza de la Catedral**, it is a place where Cuban painters, artists, and sculptors sell their work, and other vendors offer handmade crafts and clothing.

3

Combinar Use an item from each column and an indirect object pronoun to create logical sentences.

> **modelo**
> Mis padres les dan regalos a mis primos.

A	B	C	D
yo	comprar	mensajes electrónicos	mí
el dependiente	dar	corbata	ustedes
el profesor Arce	decir	dinero en efectivo	clienta
la vendedora	escribir	tarea	novia
mis padres	explicar	problemas	primos
tú	pagar	regalos	ti
nosotros/as	prestar	ropa	nosotros
¿?	vender	¿?	¿?

 Practice more at **vhlcentral.com**.

Comunicación

4

Entrevista In pairs, take turns asking and answering for whom you do these activities. Use the model as a guide.

> cantar canciones de amor *(love songs)*   escribir mensajes electrónicos
> comprar ropa   mostrar fotos de un viaje
> dar una fiesta   pedir dinero
> decir mentiras   preparar comida *(food)* mexicana

> escribir mensajes electrónicos
> **Estudiante 1:** ¿A quién le escribes mensajes electrónicos?
> **Estudiante 2:** Le escribo mensajes electrónicos a mi hermano.

5

¡Somos ricos! You and your classmates chipped in on a lottery ticket and you won! Now you want to spend money on your loved ones. In groups of three, discuss what each person is buying for family and friends.

modelo

> **Estudiante 1:** Quiero comprarle un vestido de Carolina Herrera a mi madre.
> **Estudiante 2:** Y yo voy a darles un automóvil nuevo a mis padres.
> **Estudiante 3:** Voy a comprarles una casa a mis padres, pero a mis amigos no les voy a dar nada.

6

Entrevista Use these questions to interview a classmate.

1. ¿Qué tiendas, almacenes o centros comerciales prefieres?
2. ¿A quién le compras regalos cuando hay rebajas?
3. ¿A quién le prestas dinero cuando lo necesita?
4. Quiero ir de compras. ¿Cuánto dinero me puedes prestar?
5. ¿Te dan tus padres su tarjeta de crédito cuando vas de compras?

Síntesis

7

Minidrama In groups of three, take turns playing the roles of two shoppers and a clerk in a clothing store. The shoppers should talk about the articles of clothing they are looking for and for whom they are buying the clothes. The clerk should recommend several items based on the shoppers' descriptions. Use these expressions and also look at **Expresiones útiles** on page 311.

> Me queda grande/pequeño.   ¿Está en rebaja?
> *It's big/small on me.*   *Is it on sale?*
> ¿Tiene otro color?   También estoy buscando...
> *Do you have another color?*   *I'm also looking for...*

Lección 6

6.3 # Preterite tense of regular verbs  Tutorial

ANTE TODO In order to talk about events in the past, Spanish uses two simple tenses: the preterite and the imperfect. In this lesson, you will learn how to form the preterite tense, which is used to express actions or states completed in the past.

Preterite of regular -ar, -er, and -ir verbs

		-ar verbs **comprar**	-er verbs **vender**	-ir verbs **escribir**
SINGULAR FORMS	yo	compr**é** *I bought*	vend**í** *I sold*	escrib**í** *I wrote*
	tú	compr**aste**	vend**iste**	escrib**iste**
	Ud./él/ella	compr**ó**	vend**ió**	escrib**ió**
PLURAL FORMS	nosotros/as	compr**amos**	vend**imos**	escrib**imos**
	vosotros/as	compr**asteis**	vend**isteis**	escrib**isteis**
	Uds./ellos/ellas	compr**aron**	vend**ieron**	escrib**ieron**

▸ **¡Atención!** The **yo** and **Ud./él/ella** forms of all three conjugations have written accents on the last syllable to show that it is stressed.

▸ As the chart shows, the endings for regular **-er** and **-ir** verbs are identical in the preterite.

¿Qué compraste?

Compré estos aretes.

▸ Note that the **nosotros/as** forms of regular **-ar** and **-ir** verbs in the preterite are identical to the present-tense forms. Context will help you determine which tense is being used.

En invierno **compramos** ropa.
In the winter, we buy clothing.

Anoche **compramos** unos zapatos.
Last night we bought some shoes.

▸ **-Ar** and **-er** verbs that have a stem change in the present tense are regular in the preterite. They do *not* have a stem change.

	PRESENT	PRETERITE
cerrar (e:ie)	La tienda **cierra** a las seis.	La tienda **cerró** a las seis.
volver (o:ue)	Carlitos **vuelve** tarde.	Carlitos **volvió** tarde.
jugar (u:ue)	Él **juega** al fútbol.	Él **jugó** al fútbol.

▸ **¡Atención!** **-Ir** verbs that have a stem change in the present tense also have a stem change in the preterite.

CONSULTA

There are a few high-frequency irregular verbs in the preterite. You will learn more about them in *¡ADELANTE!* **DOS** Estructura 3.1, p. 152.

AYUDA

You will learn about stem-changing verbs in *¡ADELANTE!* **DOS** Estructura 2.1, p. 92.

Lección 6

▶ Verbs that end in **-car**, **-gar**, and **-zar** have a spelling change in the first person singular (**yo** form) in the preterite.

bus**car**	busc-	qu-	yo bus**qué**
lle**gar**	lleg-	gu-	yo lle**gué**
empe**zar**	empez-	c-	yo empe**cé**

▶ Except for the **yo** form, all other forms of **-car**, **-gar**, and **-zar** verbs are regular in the preterite.

▶ Three other verbs—**creer**, **leer**, and **oír**—have spelling changes in the preterite. The **i** of the verb endings of **creer**, **leer**, and **oír** carries an accent in the **yo**, **tú**, **nosotros/as**, and **vosotros/as** forms, and changes to **y** in the **Ud./él/ella** and **Uds./ellos/ellas** forms.

creer	cre-	cre**í**, cre**í**ste, cre**yó**, cre**í**mos, cre**í**steis, cre**yeron**
leer	le-	le**í**, le**í**ste, le**yó**, le**í**mos, le**í**steis, le**yeron**
oír	o-	o**í**, o**í**ste, o**yó**, o**í**mos, o**í**steis, o**yeron**

▶ **Ver** is regular in the preterite, but none of its forms has an accent.

ver ⟶ vi, viste, vio, vimos, visteis, vieron

Words commonly used with the preterite

anoche	*last night*	**pasado/a (*adj.*)**	*last; past*
anteayer	*the day before yesterday*	**el año pasado**	*last year*
		la semana pasada	*last week*
ayer	*yesterday*	**una vez**	*once; one time*
de repente	*suddenly*	**dos veces**	*twice; two times*
desde... hasta...	*from... until...*	**ya**	*already*

Ayer llegué a Santiago de Cuba.   **Anoche** oí un ruido extraño.
Yesterday I arrived in Santiago de Cuba.   *Last night I heard a strange noise.*

▶ **Acabar de** + [*infinitive*] is used to say that something has just occurred. Note that **acabar** is in the present tense in this construction.

Acabo de comprar una falda.   **Acabas de ir** de compras.
I just bought a skirt.   *You just went shopping.*

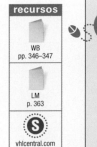

recursos

WB
pp. 346–347

LM
p. 363

vhlcentral.com
Lección 6

¡INTÉNTALO!   Provide the appropriate preterite forms of the verbs.

	comer	salir	comenzar	leer
1. ellas	comieron	salieron	comenzaron	leyeron
2. tú	_____	_____	_____	_____
3. usted	_____	_____	_____	_____
4. nosotros	_____	_____	_____	_____
5. yo	_____	_____	_____	_____

Práctica

1

Completar Andrea is talking about what happened last weekend. Complete each sentence by choosing the correct verb and putting it in the preterite.

1. El viernes a las cuatro de la tarde, la profesora Mora _____ (asistir, costar, usar) a una reunión (*meeting*) de profesores.

2. A la una, yo _____ (llegar, bucear, llevar) a la tienda con mis amigos.

3. Mis amigos y yo _____ (comprar, regatear, gastar) dos o tres cosas.

4. Yo _____ (costar, comprar, escribir) unos pantalones negros y mi amigo Mateo _____ (gastar, pasear, comprar) una camisa azul.

5. Después, nosotros _____ (llevar, vivir, comer) cerca de un mercado.

6. A las tres, Pepe _____ (hablar, pasear, nadar) con su novia por teléfono.

7. El sábado por la tarde, mi mamá _____ (escribir, beber, vivir) una carta.

8. El domingo mi tía _____ (decidir, salir, escribir) comprarme un traje.

9. A las cuatro de la tarde, mi tía _____ (beber, salir, encontrar) el traje y después nosotras _____ (acabar, ver, salir) una película.

2

Preguntas Imagine that you have a pesky friend who keeps asking you questions. Respond that you already did or have just done what he/she asks. Make sure you and your partner take turns playing the role of the pesky friend and responding to his/her questions.

> **modelo**
>
> leer la lección
> **Estudiante 1:** ¿Leíste la lección?
> **Estudiante 2:** Sí, ya la leí./Sí, acabo de leerla.

1. escribir el mensaje electrónico
2. lavar (*to wash*) la ropa
3. oír las noticias (*news*)
4. comprar pantalones cortos
5. practicar los verbos
6. pagar la cuenta (*bill*)
7. empezar la composición
8. ver la película *Diarios de motocicleta*

NOTA CULTURAL

Based on Ernesto "Che" Guevara's diaries, *Diarios de motocicleta* (2004) traces the road trip of Che (played by Gael García Bernal) with his friend Alberto Granado (played by Rodrigo de la Serna) through Argentina, Chile, Peru, Colombia, and Venezuela.

3

¿Cuándo? Use the time expressions from the word bank to talk about when you and others did the activities listed.

| anoche | anteayer | el mes pasado | una vez |
| ayer | la semana pasada | el año pasado | dos veces |

1. mi compañero/a de cuarto: llegar tarde a clase
2. mi mejor (*best*) amigo/a: salir con un(a) chico/a guapo/a
3. mis padres: ver una película
4. yo: llevar un traje/vestido
5. el presidente/primer ministro de mi país: asistir a una conferencia internacional
6. mis amigos y yo: comer en un restaurante
7. ¿?: comprar algo (*something*) bueno, bonito y barato

 Practice more at **vhlcentral.com**.

Comunicación

4

Ayer Jot down at what time you did these activities yesterday. Then get together with a classmate and find out at what time he or she did these activities. Be prepared to share your findings with the class.

1. desayunar
2. empezar la primera clase
3. almorzar
4. ver a un(a) amigo/a
5. salir de clase
6. volver a la residencia/casa

5

Las vacaciones Imagine that you took these photos on a vacation with friends. Get together with a partner and use the pictures to tell him or her about your trip.

6

El fin de semana Your instructor will give you and your partner different incomplete charts about what four employees at **Almacén Gigante** did last weekend. After you fill out the chart based on each other's information, you will fill out the final column about your partner.

Síntesis

7

Conversación Get together with a partner and have a conversation about what you did last week using verbs from the word bank. Don't forget to include school activities, shopping, and pastimes.

acampar	comer	gastar	tomar
asistir	comprar	hablar	trabajar
bailar	correr	jugar	vender
beber	escribir	leer	ver
buscar	estudiar	oír	viajar

6.4 Demonstrative adjectives and pronouns

Demonstrative adjectives  Tutorial

ANTE TODO   In Spanish, as in English, demonstrative adjectives are words that "demonstrate" or "point out" nouns. Demonstrative adjectives precede the nouns they modify and, like other Spanish adjectives you have studied, agree with them in gender and number. Observe these examples and then study the chart below.

esta camisa   **ese** vendedor   **aquellos** zapatos
this shirt   *that salesman*   *those shoes (over there)*

Demonstrative adjectives

Singular		Plural		
MASCULINE	FEMININE	MASCULINE	FEMININE	
este	**esta**	**estos**	**estas**	*this; these*
ese	**esa**	**esos**	**esas**	*that; those*
aquel	**aquella**	**aquellos**	**aquellas**	*that; those (over there)*

▶ There are three sets of demonstrative adjectives. To determine which one to use, you must establish the relationship between the speaker and the noun(s) being pointed out.

▶ The demonstrative adjectives **este**, **esta**, **estos**, and **estas** are used to point out things that are close to the speaker and the listener.

Me gustan estos zapatos.

▶ The demonstrative adjectives **ese**, **esa**, **esos**, and **esas** are used to point out things that are not close in space and time to the speaker. They may, however, be close to the listener.

Prefiero esos zapatos.

▶ The demonstrative adjectives **aquel**, **aquella**, **aquellos**, and **aquellas** are used to point out things that are far away from the speaker and the listener.

Aquel auto es de mi hermana.

Demonstrative pronouns

▶ Demonstrative pronouns are identical to their corresponding demonstrative adjectives, with the exception that they traditionally carry an accent mark on the stressed vowel. The **Real Academia** no longer requires this accent, but it is still commonly used.

Demonstrative pronouns			
Singular		**Plural**	
MASCULINE	FEMININE	MASCULINE	FEMININE
éste	**ésta**	**éstos**	**éstas**
ése	**ésa**	**ésos**	**ésas**
aquél	**aquélla**	**aquéllos**	**aquéllas**

—¿Quieres comprar **este suéter**?
Do you want to buy this sweater?

—No, no quiero **éste**. Quiero **ése**.
No, I don't want this one. I want that one.

—¿Vas a leer **estas revistas**?
Are you going to read these magazines?

—Sí, voy a leer **éstas**. También voy a leer **aquéllas**.
Yes, I'm going to read these. I'll also read those (over there).

▶ **¡Atención!** Like demonstrative adjectives, demonstrative pronouns agree in gender and number with the corresponding noun.

Este libro es de Pablito.   **Éstos** son de Juana.

▶ There are three neuter demonstrative pronouns: **esto**, **eso**, and **aquello**. These forms refer to unidentified or unspecified things, situations, ideas, and concepts. They do not change in gender or number and never carry an accent mark.

—¿Qué es **esto**?   —**Eso** es interesante.   —**Aquello** es bonito.
What's this?   *That's interesting.*   *That's pretty.*

recursos

WB
pp. 348–350

LM
p. 364

vhlcentral.com
Lección 6

¡INTÉNTALO!   Provide the correct form of the demonstrative adjective for these nouns.

1. la falda / este _____ *esta falda*
2. los estudiantes / este _____
3. los países / aquel _____
4. la ventana / ese _____

5. los periodistas / ese _____
6. el chico / aquel _____
7. las sandalias / este _____
8. las chicas / aquel _____

Lección 6

Práctica

1

Cambiar Make the singular sentences plural and the plural sentences singular.

> **modelo**
>
> Estas camisas son blancas.
> Esta camisa es blanca.

1. Aquellos sombreros son muy elegantes.
2. Ese abrigo es muy caro.
3. Estos cinturones son hermosos.
4. Esos precios son muy buenos.
5. Estas faldas son muy cortas.
6. ¿Quieres ir a aquel almacén?
7. Esas blusas son baratas.
8. Esta corbata hace juego con mi traje.

2

Completar Here are some things people might say while shopping. Complete the sentences with the correct demonstrative pronouns.

1. No me gustan esos zapatos. Voy a comprar _____. (*these*)
2. ¿Vas a comprar ese traje o _____? (*this one*)
3. Esta guayabera es bonita, pero prefiero _____. (*that one*)
4. Estas corbatas rojas son muy bonitas, pero _____ son fabulosas. (*those*)
5. Estos cinturones cuestan demasiado. Prefiero _____. (*those over there*)
6. ¿Te gustan esas botas o _____? (*these*)
7. Esa bolsa roja es bonita, pero prefiero _____. (*that one over there*)
8. No voy a comprar estas botas; voy a comprar _____. (*those over there*)
9. ¿Prefieres estos pantalones o _____? (*those*)
10. Me gusta este vestido, pero voy a comprar _____. (*that one*)
11. Me gusta ese almacén, pero _____ es mejor (*better*). (*that one over there*)
12. Esa blusa es bonita, pero cuesta demasiado. Voy a comprar _____. (*this one*)

3

Describir With your partner, look for two items in the classroom that are one of these colors: **amarillo**, **azul**, **blanco**, **marrón**, **negro**, **verde**, **rojo**. Take turns pointing them out to each other, first using demonstrative adjectives, and then demonstrative pronouns.

> **modelo**
>
> azul
> **Estudiante 1:** Esta silla es azul. Aquella mochila es azul.
> **Estudiante 2:** Ésta es azul. Aquélla es azul.

Now use demonstrative adjectives and pronouns to discuss the colors of your classmates' clothing. One of you can ask a question about an article of clothing, using the wrong color. Your partner will correct you and point out that color somewhere else in the room.

> **modelo**
>
> **Estudiante 1:** ¿Esa camisa es negra?
> **Estudiante 2:** No, ésa es azul. Aquélla es negra.

 Practice more at **vhlcentral.com**.

Comunicación

4 **Conversación** With a classmate, use demonstrative adjectives and pronouns to ask each other questions about the people around you. Use expressions from the word bank and/or your own ideas.

¿A qué hora…?	¿Cuántos años tiene(n)…?
¿Cómo es/son…?	¿De dónde es/son…?
¿Cómo se llama…?	¿De quién es/son…?
¿Cuándo…?	¿Qué clases toma(n)…?

modelo

Estudiante 1: ¿Cómo se llama esa chica?
Estudiante 2: Se llama Rebeca.
Estudiante 1: ¿A qué hora llegó aquel chico a la clase?
Estudiante 2: A las nueve.

5 **En una tienda** Imagine that you and a classmate are in Madrid shopping at Zara. Study the floor plan, then have a conversation about your surroundings. Use demonstrative adjectives and pronouns.

modelo

Estudiante 1: Me gusta este suéter azul.
Estudiante 2: Yo prefiero aquella chaqueta.

NOTA CULTURAL

Zara is an international clothing company based in Spain. Its innovative processes take a product from the design room to the manufacturing shelves in less than a month. This means that the merchandise is constantly changing to keep up with the most current trends.

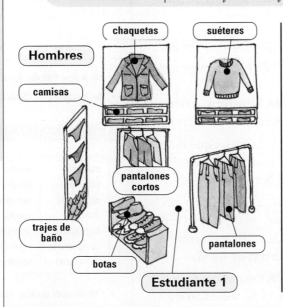

Síntesis

6 **Diferencias** Your instructor will give you and a partner each a drawing of a store. They are almost identical, but not quite. Use demonstrative adjectives and pronouns to find seven differences.

modelo

Estudiante 1: Aquellas gafas de sol son feas, ¿verdad?
Estudiante 2: No. Aquellas gafas de sol son hermosas.

Lección 6

Recapitulación

SUBJECT → Javier   CONJUGATED FORM empiezo   Main clause   Dudan

 Diagnostics

Review the grammar concepts you have learned in this lesson by completing these activities.

1 **Completar** Complete the chart with the correct preterite or infinitive form of the verbs. **15 pts.**

Infinitive	yo	ella	ellos
			tomaron
		abrió	
comprender			
	leí		
pagar			

2 **En la tienda** Look at the drawing and complete the conversation with demonstrative adjectives and pronouns. **7 pts.**

CLIENTE Buenos días, señorita. Deseo comprar (1) _____ corbata.

VENDEDORA Muy bien, señor. ¿No le interesa mirar (2) _____ trajes que están allá? Hay unos que hacen juego con la corbata.

CLIENTE (3) _____ de allá son de lana, ¿no? Prefiero ver (4) _____ traje marrón que está detrás de usted.

VENDEDORA Estupendo. Como puede ver, es de seda. Cuesta seiscientos cincuenta dólares.

CLIENTE Ah… eh… no, creo que sólo voy a comprar la corbata, gracias.

VENDEDORA Bueno… si busca algo más económico, hay rebaja en (5) _____ sombreros. Cuestan sólo treinta dólares.

CLIENTE ¡Magnífico! Me gusta (6) _____, el blanco que está hasta arriba (*at the top*). Y quiero pagar todo con (7) _____ tarjeta.

VENDEDORA Sí, señor. Ahora mismo le traigo el sombrero.

6.1 Saber and conocer *p. 316*

saber	conocer
sé	conozco
sabes	conoces
sabe	conoce
sabemos	conocemos
sabéis	conocéis
saben	conocen

▶ **saber** = to know facts/how to do something

▶ **conocer** = to know a person, place, or thing

6.2 Indirect object pronouns *pp. 318–319*

Indirect object pronouns

Singular	Plural
me	nos
te	os
le	les

▶ **dar** = doy, das, da, damos, dais, dan

▶ **decir (e:i)** = digo, dices, dice, decimos, decís, dicen

6.2 Preterite tense of regular verbs *pp. 322–323*

comprar	vender	escribir
compré	vendí	escribí
compraste	vendiste	escribiste
compró	vendió	escribió
compramos	vendimos	escribimos
comprasteis	vendisteis	escribisteis
compraron	vendieron	escribieron

Verbs with spelling changes in the preterite

▶ -car: buscar → yo busqué

▶ -gar: llegar → yo llegué

▶ -zar: empezar → yo empecé

▶ **creer:** creí, creíste, creyó, creímos, creísteis, creyeron

▶ **leer:** leí, leíste, leyó, leímos, leísteis, leyeron

▶ **oír:** oí, oíste, oyó, oímos, oísteis, oyeron

▶ **ver:** vi, viste, vio, vimos, visteis, vieron

Lección 6

3 **¿Saber o conocer?** Complete each dialogue with the correct form of **saber** or **conocer**. **10 pts.**

1. —¿Qué _____ hacer tú?
   —(Yo) _____ jugar al fútbol.
2. —¿_____ tú esta tienda de ropa?
   —No, (yo) no la _____. ¿Es buena?
3. —¿Tus padres no _____ a tu novio?
   —No, ¡ellos no _____ que tengo novio!
4. —Mi compañero de cuarto todavía no me _____ bien.
   —Y tú, ¿lo quieres _____ a él?
5. —¿_____ ustedes dónde está el mercado?
   —No, nosotros no _____ bien esta ciudad.

4 **Oraciones** Form complete sentences using the information provided. Use indirect object pronouns and the present tense of the verbs. **10 pts.**

1. Javier / prestar / el abrigo / a Maripili

2. nosotros / vender / ropa / a los clientes

3. el vendedor / traer / las camisetas / a mis amigos y a mí

4. yo / querer dar / consejos / a ti

5. ¿tú / ir a comprar / un regalo / a mí?

5 **Mi última compra** Write a short paragraph describing the last time you went shopping. Use at least four verbs in the preterite tense. **8 pts.**

> *modelo*
> El viernes pasado, busqué unos zapatos en el centro comercial...

6 **Poema** Write the missing words to complete the excerpt from the poem *Romance sonámbulo* by Federico García Lorca. **2 EXTRA points!**

> " Verde que _____ quiero verde.
> Verde viento. Verdes ramas°.
> El barco sobre la mar
> y el caballo en la montaña, [...]
> Verde que te quiero _____ (*green*). "

ramas *branches*

6.4 Demonstrative adjectives and pronouns *pp. 326–327*

Demonstrative adjectives

Singular		Plural	
Masc.	Fem.	Masc.	Fem.
este	esta	estos	estas
ese	esa	esos	esas
aquel	aquella	aquellos	aquellas

Demonstrative pronouns

Singular		Plural	
Masc.	Fem.	Masc.	Fem.
éste	ésta	éstos	éstas
ése	ésa	ésos	ésas
aquél	aquélla	aquéllos	aquéllas

Practice more at **vhlcentral.com**.

Lectura
Antes de leer

Estrategia
Skimming

Skimming involves quickly reading through a document to absorb its general meaning. This allows you to understand the main ideas without having to read word for word. When you skim a text, you might want to look at its title and subtitles. You might also want to read the first sentence of each paragraph.

Examinar el texto
Look at the format of the reading selection. How is it organized? What does the organization of the document tell you about its content?

Buscar cognados
Scan the reading selection to locate at least five cognates. Based on the cognates, what do you think the reading selection is about?

1. _____   4. _____
2. _____   5. _____
3. _____

The reading selection is about _____.

Impresiones generales
Now skim the reading selection to understand its general meaning. Jot down your impressions. What new information did you learn about the document by skimming it? Based on all the information you now have, answer these questions in Spanish.

1. Who created this document?
2. What is its purpose?
3. Who is its intended audience?

Corona

¡Corona tiene las ofertas más locas del verano!

La tienda más elegante de la ciudad con precios increíbles

Carteras
ELEGANCIA
Colores anaranjado, blanco, rosado y amarillo
Ahora: 15.000 pesos
50% de rebaja

Sandalias de playa
GINO
Números del 35 al 38
A sólo 12.000 pesos
50% de descuento

Faldas largas
ROPA BONITA
Algodón. De distintos colores
Talla mediana
Precio especial:
8.000 pesos

Blusas de seda
BAMBÚ
De cuadros y de lunares
Ahora: 21.000 pesos
40% de rebaja

Vestido de algodón
PANAMÁ
Colores blanco, azul y verde
Ahora: 18.000 pesos
30% de rebaja

Accesorios
BELLEZA
Cinturones, gafas de sol, sombreros, medias
Diversos estilos
Todos con un 40% de rebaja

Lunes a sábado de 9 a 21 horas.
Domingo de 10 a 14 horas.

¡Grandes rebajas!
Real° Liquidación°
¡La rebaja está de moda en Corona!

y con la tarjeta de crédito más conveniente del mercado.

Chaquetas
CASINO
Microfibra. Colores negro,
café y gris
Tallas: P, M, G, XG
Ahora: 22.500 pesos

Zapatos
COLOR
Italianos y franceses
Números del 40 al 45
A sólo 20.000 pesos

Pantalones
OCÉANO
Colores negro, gris y café
Ahora: 11.500 pesos
30% de rebaja

Ropa interior
ATLÁNTICO
Tallas: P, M, G
Colores blanco,
negro y gris
40% de rebaja

Traje inglés
GALES
Modelos originales
Ahora: 105.000 pesos
30% de rebaja

Accesorios
GUAPO
Gafas de sol, corbatas,
cinturones, calcetines
Diversos estilos
Todos con un 40%
de rebaja

Real *Royal* Liquidación *Clearance sale*

Por la compra de 40.000 pesos, puede llevar un regalo gratis.

- Un hermoso cinturón de señora
- Un par de calcetines
- Una corbata de seda
- Una bolsa para la playa
- Una mochila
- Unas medias

Después de leer

Completar
Complete this paragraph about the reading selection with the correct forms of the words from the word bank.

almacén	hacer juego	tarjeta de crédito
caro	increíble	tienda
dinero	pantalones	verano
falda	rebaja	zapato

En este anuncio de periódico, el _____ Corona anuncia la liquidación de _____ con grandes _____. Con muy poco _____ usted puede conseguir ropa fina y elegante. Si no tiene dinero en efectivo, puede utilizar su _____ y pagar luego. Para el caballero con gustos refinados, hay _____ importados de París y Roma. La señora elegante puede encontrar blusas de seda que _____ con todo tipo de _____ o _____. Los precios de esta liquidación son realmente _____.

¿Cierto o falso?
Indicate whether each statement is **cierto** or **falso**. Correct the false statements.

1. Hay sandalias de playa.
2. Las corbatas tienen una rebaja del 30%.
3. El almacén Corona tiene un departamento de zapatos.
4. Normalmente las sandalias cuestan 22.000 pesos.
5. Cuando gastas 30.000 pesos en la tienda, llevas un regalo gratis.
6. Tienen carteras amarillas.

Preguntas
In pairs, take turns asking and answering these questions.

1. Imagina que vas a ir a la tienda Corona. ¿Qué departamentos vas a visitar? ¿El departamento de ropa para señoras, el departamento de ropa para caballeros…?
2. ¿Qué vas a buscar en Corona?
3. ¿Hay tiendas similares a la tienda Corona en tu pueblo o ciudad? ¿Cómo se llaman? ¿Tienen muchas gangas?

Escritura

Estrategia

How to report an interview

There are several ways to prepare a written report about an interview. For example, you can transcribe the interview verbatim, you can simply summarize it, or you can summarize it but quote the speakers occasionally. In any event, the report should begin with an interesting title and a brief introduction, which may include the five Ws (*what, where, when, who, why*) and the H (*how*) of the interview. The report should end with an interesting conclusion. Note that when you transcribe dialogue in Spanish, you should pay careful attention to format and punctuation.

Writing dialogue in Spanish

- If you need to transcribe an interview verbatim, you can use speakers' names to indicate a change of speaker.

CARMELA	¿Qué compraste? ¿Encontraste muchas gangas?
ROBERTO	Sí, muchas. Compré un suéter, una camisa y dos corbatas. Y tú, ¿qué compraste?
CARMELA	Una blusa y una falda muy bonitas. ¿Cuánto costó tu camisa?
ROBERTO	Sólo diez dólares. ¿Cuánto costó tu blusa?
CARMELA	Veinte dólares.

- You can also use a dash (*raya*) to mark the beginning of each speaker's words.

  —¿Qué compraste?

  —Un suéter y una camisa muy bonitos. Y tú, ¿encontraste muchas gangas?

  —Sí... compré dos blusas, tres camisetas y un par de zapatos.

  —¡A ver!

Tema

Escribe un informe

Write a report for the school newspaper about an interview you conducted with a student about his or her shopping habits and clothing preferences. First, brainstorm a list of interview questions. Then conduct the interview using the questions below as a guide, but feel free to ask other questions as they occur to you.

Examples of questions:

- ▶ ¿Cuándo vas de compras?
- ▶ ¿Adónde vas de compras?
- ▶ ¿Con quién vas de compras?
- ▶ ¿Qué tiendas, almacenes o centros comerciales prefieres?
- ▶ ¿Compras ropa de catálogos o por Internet?
- ▶ ¿Prefieres comprar ropa cara o barata? ¿Por qué? ¿Te gusta buscar gangas?
- ▶ ¿Qué ropa llevas cuando vas a clase?
- ▶ ¿Qué ropa llevas cuando sales a bailar?
- ▶ ¿Qué ropa llevas cuando practicas un deporte?
- ▶ ¿Cuáles son tus colores favoritos? ¿Compras mucha ropa de esos colores?
- ▶ ¿Les das ropa a tu familia o a tus amigos/as?

Escuchar Audio

Marisol

Alicia

Lección 6

Estrategia

Listening for linguistic clues

You can enhance your listening comprehension by listening for specific linguistic cues. For example, if you listen for the endings of conjugated verbs, or for familiar constructions, such as **acabar de** + [*infinitive*] or **ir a** + [*infinitive*], you can find out whether an event already took place, is taking place now, or will take place in the future. Verb endings also give clues about who is participating in the action.

 To practice listening for linguistic cues, you will now listen to four sentences. As you listen, note whether each sentence refers to a past, present, or future action. Also jot down the subject of each sentence.

Preparación

Based on the photograph, what do you think Marisol has recently done? What do you think Marisol and Alicia are talking about? What else can you guess about their conversation from the visual clues in the photograph?

Ahora escucha

Now you are going to hear Marisol and Alicia's conversation. Make a list of the clothing items that each person mentions. Then put a check mark after the item if the person actually purchased it.

Marisol	Alicia
1. ___	1. ___
2. ___	2. ___
3. ___	3. ___
4. ___	4. ___

 Practice more at **vhlcentral.com**.

Comprensión

¿Cierto o falso?

Indicate whether each statement is **cierto** or **falso**. Then correct the false statements.

1. Marisol y Alicia acaban de ir de compras juntas (*together*).
2. Marisol va a comprar unos pantalones y una blusa mañana.
3. Marisol compró una blusa de cuadros.
4. Alicia compró unos zapatos nuevos hoy.
5. Alicia y Marisol van a ir al café.
6. Marisol gastó todo el dinero de la semana en ropa nueva.

Preguntas

Discuss the following questions with a classmate. Be sure to explain your answers.

1. ¿Crees que Alicia y Marisol son buenas amigas? ¿Por qué?
2. ¿Cuál de las dos estudiantes es más ahorradora (*frugal*)? ¿Por qué?
3. ¿Crees que a Alicia le gusta la ropa que Marisol compró?
4. ¿Crees que la moda es importante para Alicia? ¿Para Marisol? ¿Por qué?
5. ¿Es importante para ti estar a la moda? ¿Por qué?

En pantalla

Grocery stores in Mexico make one-stop shopping easy! Similar to the concept of a *Super-Walmart* in the U.S., most **supermercados°** in Mexico sell appliances, clothing, medicine, gardening supplies, electronics, and toys in addition to groceries. Large chains, like **Comercial Mexicana,** and smaller grocery stores alike typically sell a variety of products, allowing customers to satisfy all of their routine weekly shopping needs in one trip. Watch the **En pantalla** videoclip to see how one customer takes advantage of one-stop shopping at his local supermarket.

Vocabulario útil

con lo que ahorré	*with what I saved*
corazón	*sweetheart*
de peluche	*stuffed (toy)*
dragón	*dragon*
¿Me lo compras?	*Would you buy it for me?*

Comprensión

Indicate whether each statement is **cierto** or **falso**.

	Cierto	Falso
1. El niño quiere un elefante de peluche.	○	○
2. La señora usa un vestido rojo.	○	○
3. El niño sigue a la señora hasta la caja.	○	○
4. La señora no es la mamá del niño.	○	○

Conversar

With a partner, use these cues to create a conversation in Spanish between two friends at a clothing store.

Estudiante 1: Would you buy me a(n)...?

Estudiante 2: No, because it costs...

Estudiante 1: Please! I always (**siempre**) buy you...

Estudiante 2: OK, I will buy you this... How much does it cost?

Estudiante 1: It's on sale! It only costs....

Anuncio de Comercial Mexicana

¿Me lo compras?

No, corazón.

¿Me lo compras, me lo compras, me lo compras?

Video: TV Clip

Practice more at **vhlcentral.com**.

---

supermercados *supermarkets*

Lección 6

In the Spanish-speaking world, most city dwellers shop at large supermarkets and little stores that specialize in just one item, such as a butcher shop (**carnicería**), vegetable market (**verdulería**), perfume shop (**perfumería**), or hat shop (**sombrerería**). In small towns where supermarkets are less common, many people rely exclusively on specialty shops. This requires shopping more frequently—often every day or every other day for perishable items—but also means that the foods they consume are fresher and the goods are usually locally produced. Each neighborhood generally has its own shops, so people don't have to walk far to find fresh bread (at a **panadería**) for the midday meal.

Comprar en los mercados

Trescientos colones.

Vocabulario útil	
colones (pl.)	*currency from Costa Rica*
¿Cuánto vale?	**¿Cuánto cuesta?**
descuento	*discount*
disculpe	*excuse me*
¿Dónde queda...?	*Where is... located?*
los helados	*ice cream*
el regateo	*bargaining*

... pero me hace un buen descuento.

Preparación

Have you ever been to an open-air market? What did you buy? Have you ever negotiated a price? What did you say?

Comprensión

Select the option that best summarizes this episode.

a. Randy Cruz va al mercado al aire libre para comprar papayas. Luego va al Mercado Central. Él les pregunta a varios clientes qué compran, prueba (*tastes*) platos típicos y busca la heladería.

b. Randy Cruz va al mercado al aire libre para comprar papayas y pedir un descuento. Luego va al Mercado Central para preguntarles a los clientes qué compran en los mercados.

¿Qué compran en el Mercado Central?

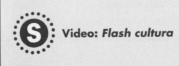
Video: *Flash cultura*

Practice more at **vhlcentral.com**.

recursos

VM
pp. 357–358

vhlcentral.com
Lección 6

Ⓢ **Video:** *Panorama cultural*
Interactive map

Cuba

El país en cifras

▶ **Área:** 110.860 km² (42.803 millas²), *aproximadamente el área de Pensilvania*
▶ **Población:** 11.213.000
▶ **Capital:** La Habana—2.100.000

La Habana Vieja fue declarada° Patrimonio° Cultural de la Humanidad por la UNESCO en 1982. Este distrito es uno de los lugares más fascinantes de Cuba. En La Plaza de Armas, se puede visitar el majestuoso Palacio de Capitanes Generales, que ahora es un museo. En la calle° Obispo, frecuentada por el autor Ernest Hemingway, hay hermosos cafés, clubes nocturnos y tiendas elegantes.

▶ **Ciudades principales:** Santiago de Cuba; Camagüey; Holguín; Guantánamo

SOURCE: Population Division, UN Secretariat

▶ **Moneda:** peso cubano
▶ **Idiomas:** español (oficial)

Bandera de Cuba

Cubanos célebres

▶ **Carlos Finlay,** doctor y científico (1833–1915)
▶ **José Martí,** político y poeta (1853–1895)
▶ **Fidel Castro,** ex primer ministro, ex comandante en jefe° de las fuerzas armadas (1926–2016)
▶ **Zoé Valdés,** escritora (1959–)
▶ **Ibrahim Ferrer,** músico (1927–2005)

fue declarada *was declared* Patrimonio *Heritage* calle *street*
comandante en jefe *commander in chief* liviano *light*
colibrí abeja *bee hummingbird* ave *bird* mundo *world*
miden *measure* pesan *weigh*

Golfo de México

ESTADOS UNIDOS

Gran Teatro de La Habana

Los coco taxis son un medio de transporte cubano muy popular.

Océano Atlántico

Plaza del Capitolio

La Habana

Cordillera de los Órganos

ESTADOS UNIDOS

CUBA

OCÉANO ATLÁNTICO

OCÉANO PACÍFICO

AMÉRICA DEL SUR

Isla de la Juventud

Mar Caribe

Camagüey

La música es parte esencial de la vida en Cuba.

recursos

WB pp. 351–352

VM pp. 355–356

Ⓢ vhlcentral.com Lección 6

¡Increíble pero cierto!

Pequeño y liviano°, el colibrí abeja° de Cuba es una de las más de 320 especies de colibrí y es también el ave° más pequeña del mundo°. Menores que muchos insectos, estas aves minúsculas miden° 5 centímetros y pesan° sólo 1,95 gramos.

Baile • Ballet Nacional de Cuba

La bailarina Alicia Alonso fundó el Ballet Nacional de Cuba en 1948, después de° convertirse en una estrella° internacional en el Ballet de Nueva York y en Broadway. El Ballet Nacional de Cuba es famoso en todo el mundo por su creatividad y perfección técnica.

Economía • La caña de azúcar y el tabaco

La caña de azúcar° es el producto agrícola° que más se cultiva en la isla y su exportación es muy importante para la economía del país. El tabaco, que se usa para fabricar los famosos puros° cubanos, es otro cultivo° de mucha importancia.

Gente • Población

La población cubana tiene raíces° muy heterogéneas. La inmigración a la isla fue determinante° desde la colonia hasta mediados° del siglo° XX. Los cubanos de hoy son descendientes de africanos, europeos, chinos y antillanos, entre otros.

Música • Buena Vista Social Club

En 1997 nace° el fenómeno musical conocido como *Buena Vista Social Club*. Este proyecto reúne° a un grupo de importantes músicos de Cuba, la mayoría ya mayores, con una larga trayectoria interpretando canciones clásicas del son° cubano. Ese mismo año ganaron un *Grammy*. Hoy en día estos músicos son conocidos en todo el mundo, y personas de todas las edades bailan al ritmo° de su música.

• Holguín

• Santiago de Cuba
   • Guantánamo

Sierra Maestra

 ¿Qué aprendiste? Responde a las preguntas con una oración completa.

1. ¿Qué autor está asociado con la Habana Vieja?
2. ¿Por qué es famoso el Ballet Nacional de Cuba?
3. ¿Cuáles son los dos cultivos más importantes para la economía cubana?
4. ¿Qué fabrican los cubanos con la planta del tabaco?
5. ¿De dónde son muchos de los inmigrantes que llegaron a Cuba?
6. ¿En qué año ganó un *Grammy* el disco *Buena Vista Social Club*?

 Conexión Internet Investiga estos temas en **vhlcentral.com**.

Practice more at **vhlcentral.com**.

1. Busca información sobre un(a) cubano/a célebre. ¿Por qué es célebre? ¿Qué hace? ¿Todavía vive en Cuba?
2. Busca información sobre una de las ciudades principales de Cuba. ¿Qué atracciones hay en esta ciudad?

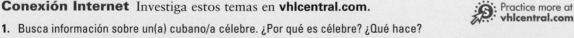

después de *after* estrella *star* caña de azúcar *sugar cane* agrícola *farming* puros *cigars* cultivo *crop* raíces *roots* determinante *deciding* mediados *halfway through* siglo *century* nace *is born* reúne *gets together* son *Cuban musical genre* ritmo *rhythm*

La ropa

el abrigo	coat
los (blue)jeans	jeans
la blusa	blouse
la bolsa	purse; bag
la bota	boot
los calcetines (el calcetín)	sock(s)
la camisa	shirt
la camiseta	t-shirt
la cartera	wallet
la chaqueta	jacket
el cinturón	belt
la corbata	tie
la falda	skirt
las gafas (de sol)	(sun)glasses
los guantes	gloves
el impermeable	raincoat
las medias	pantyhose; stockings
los pantalones	pants
los pantalones cortos	shorts
la ropa	clothing; clothes
la ropa interior	underwear
las sandalias	sandals
el sombrero	hat
el suéter	sweater
el traje	suit
el traje de baño	bathing suit
el vestido	dress
los zapatos de tenis	sneakers

Verbos

conducir	to drive
conocer	to know; to be acquainted with
ofrecer	to offer
parecer	to seem
saber	to know; to know how
traducir	to translate

Ir de compras

el almacén	department store
la caja	cash register
el centro comercial	shopping mall
el/la cliente/a	customer
el/la dependiente/a	clerk
el dinero	money
(en) efectivo	cash
el mercado (al aire libre)	(open-air) market
un par (de zapatos)	a pair (of shoes)
el precio (fijo)	(fixed; set) price
la rebaja	sale
el regalo	gift
la tarjeta de crédito	credit card
la tienda	shop; store
el/la vendedor(a)	salesperson
costar (o:ue)	to cost
gastar	to spend (money)
hacer juego (con)	to match (with)
llevar	to wear; to take
pagar	to pay
regatear	to bargain
usar	to wear; to use
vender	to sell

Adjetivos

barato/a	cheap
bueno/a	good
cada	each
caro/a	expensive
corto/a	short (in length)
elegante	elegant
hermoso/a	beautiful
largo/a	long
loco/a	crazy
nuevo/a	new
otro/a	other; another
pobre	poor
rico/a	rich

Los colores

el color	color
amarillo/a	yellow
anaranjado/a	orange
azul	blue
blanco/a	white
gris	gray
marrón, café	brown
morado/a	purple
negro/a	black
rojo/a	red
rosado/a	pink
verde	green

Palabras adicionales

acabar de (+ inf.)	to have just done something
anoche	last night
anteayer	the day before yesterday
ayer	yesterday
de repente	suddenly
desde	from
dos veces	twice; two times
hasta	until
pasado/a (adj.)	last; past
el año pasado	last year
la semana pasada	last week
prestar	to lend; to loan
una vez	once; one time
ya	already

Indirect object pronouns	See page 318.
Demonstrative adjectives and pronouns	See page 326.
Expresiones útiles	See page 311.

Audio: Vocabulary Flashcards

contextos   **Lección 6**

1 **El almacén** Look at the department store directory. Then complete the sentences with terms from the word list.

> ### Almacén Gema
>
> PRIMER PISO   Departamento de caballeros
> SEGUNDO PISO   Ropa de invierno y zapatos
> TERCER PISO   Departamento de damas y óptica
> CUARTO PISO   Ropa interior, ropa de verano y trajes de baño

abrigos	corbatas	sandalias
blusas	faldas	trajes de baño
bolsas	gafas de sol	trajes de hombre
botas	guantes	vestidos
calcetines	medias	zapatos de tenis
cinturones	pantalones de hombre	

1. En el primer piso puedes encontrar _____

_____

2. En el segundo piso puedes encontrar _____

_____

3. En el tercer piso puedes encontrar _____

_____

4. En el cuarto piso puedes encontrar _____

_____

5. Quiero unos pantalones cortos. Voy al _____ piso.

6. Buscas unos lentes. Vas al _____ piso.

7. Arturo ve una chaqueta en el _____ piso.

8. Ana ve los jeans en el _____ piso.

2 **Necesito muchas cosas** Complete these sentences with the correct terms.

1. Voy a nadar en la piscina. Necesito _____.

2. Está lloviendo mucho. Necesito _____.

3. No puedo ver bien porque hace sol. Necesito _____.

4. Voy a correr por el parque. Necesito _____.

5. Queremos entrar en muchas tiendas diferentes. Vamos al _____.

6. No tengo dinero en la cartera. Voy a pagar con la _____.

3   **Los colores** Answer these questions in complete sentences.

1. ¿De qué color es el chocolate?

   _____

2. ¿De qué color son las bananas?

   _____

3. ¿De qué color son las naranjas (*oranges*)?

   _____

4. ¿De qué colores es la bandera (*flag*) de los Estados Unidos?

   _____

5. ¿De qué color son las nubes (*clouds*) cuando está nublado?

   _____

6. ¿De qué color son los bluejeans?

   _____

7. ¿De qué color son muchos aviones?

   _____

8. ¿De qué color son las palabras de este libro?

   _____

4   **¿Qué lleva?** Look at the illustration and fill in the blanks with the names of the numbered items.

5. _____

4. _____

2. _____

10. _____

6. _____

8. _____

3. _____

1. _____

7. _____

9. _____

estructura

6.1 Saber and conocer

1 **¿Saber o conocer?** Complete the sentences, using **saber** and **conocer**.

1. (yo) No _____ a los padres de Juan Carlos.
2. Marissa _____ las ciudades de Canadá.
3. ¿(Maru, tú) _____ dónde estamos?
4. Yo _____ hablar italiano y francés.
5. La señora Díaz _____ bien la capital de México.
6. Jimena y yo no _____ a los otros turistas.

2 **¿Qué hacen?** Complete the sentences, using the verbs from the word bank. Use each verb only once.

conducir	ofrecer	saber
conocer	parecer	traducir

1. El señor Díaz _____ su automóvil todos los días.
2. Miguel _____ usar su computadora muy bien.
3. Jimena _____ ser una estudiante excelente.
4. Miguel y Maru no _____ bien al vendedor.
5. La Universidad del Mar _____ cursos muy interesantes.
6. Nosotros _____ libros a diferentes lenguas extranjeras.

3 **Oraciones completas** Create sentences, using the elements and **saber** or **conocer**.

1. Eugenia / mi amiga Frances

   _____

2. Pamela / hablar español muy bien

   _____

3. el sobrino de Rosa / leer y escribir

   _____

4. José y Laura / la ciudad de Barcelona

   _____

5. nosotros no / llegar a la residencia estudiantil

   _____

6. yo / el profesor de literatura

   _____

7. Elena y María Victoria / patinar en línea

   _____

6.2 Indirect object pronouns

1 **¿A quién?** Complete these sentences with the correct indirect object pronouns.

1. _____ pido a la profesora los libros de español.

2. Amelia _____ pregunta a nosotras adónde queremos ir.

3. El empleado _____ busca trabajo a sus primas en el almacén.

4. Julio _____ quiere dar un televisor nuevo a sus padres.

5. Los clientes _____ piden rebajas a nosotros todos los años.

6. Tu hermano no _____ presta la ropa a ti (*you*).

7. La empleada de la tienda _____ cerró la puerta a mi tía.

8. La mamá no _____ hace la tarea a sus hijos.

9. _____ deben pagar mucho dinero a ti, porque llevas ropa muy cara.

10. Las dependientas _____ traen el vestido rosado a mí.

2 **Planes** Complete this paragraph with the correct indirect object pronouns and find out Sara's plans for this summer.

Mis amigos Loles, Antonio y Karen (1)_____ preguntan a mí si quiero ir a Italia con ellos este verano. Yo (2)_____ digo: "¡Sí, sííí, síííííí!" Ellos (3)_____ quieren pedir un libro o dos a la profesora de historia del arte. Yo (4)_____ quiero dar a ellos un álbum de fotos muy interesante. El novio de mi hermana es italiano. Él tiene una colección con dos mil cuatrocientas sesenta y tres fotos de muchas ciudades y museos de su país. (5)_____ voy a preguntar a mi hermana dónde lo tiene y a mis padres (6)_____ voy a decir: "¡Mamá, papá, en agosto voy a Italia con unos amigos! La señorita Casanova (7)_____ va a prestar un par de libros y el novio de Ángeles (8)_____ va a prestar su maravilloso álbum de fotos".

Loles tiene suerte. Su tía (9)_____ va a pagar el pasaje. Antonio y Karen van a trabajar en el centro comercial los meses de junio y julio. ¿Y yo qué hago? ¿Quién (10)_____ va a pagar el pasaje a mí? ¿A quién (11)_____ pido dinero yo? ¿A papá?... Pero él (12)_____ dice: "Sarita, hija, lo siento, pero yo no (13)_____ puedo pagar tu pasaje. Tu prima (14)_____ puede dar trabajo de dependienta en su tienda de ropa". ¡¡¿Trabajo?!!

3 **Delante o detrás** Rewrite these sentences, using an alternate placement for the indirect object pronouns.

> **modelo**
>
> Me quiero comprar un coche nuevo.
> *Quiero comprarme un coche nuevo.*

1. Les vas a dar muchos regalos a tus padres.

   _____

2. Quiero comprarles unos guantes a mis sobrinos.

   _____

3. Clara va a venderle sus libros de literatura francesa a su amiga.

   _____

4. Los clientes nos pueden pagar con tarjeta de crédito.

   _____

4 **De compras** Complete the paragraph with the correct indirect object pronouns.

Isabel y yo vamos de compras al centro comercial. Yo (1)_____ tengo que comprar unas cosas a mis parientes porque voy a viajar a mi ciudad este fin de semana. A mi hermana Laura (2)_____ quiero comprar unas gafas de sol, pero ella (3)_____ tiene que comprar un traje de baño a mí. A mis dos sobrinos (4)_____ voy a comprar una pelota de béisbol. A mi padre (5)_____ llevo un libro y a mi madre (6)_____ tengo que conseguir una blusa. (7)_____ quiero llevar camisetas con el nombre de mi universidad a todos.

5 **Respuestas** Answer these questions negatively. Use indirect object pronouns in the answer.

> **modelo**
>
> ¿Le compras una camisa a tu novio?
> *No, no le compro una camisa.*

1. ¿Le escribe Rolando un mensaje electrónico a Miguel?

   _____

2. ¿Nos trae el botones las maletas a la habitación?

   _____

3. ¿Les dan gafas de sol los vendedores a los turistas?

   _____

4. ¿Te compra botas en el invierno tu mamá?

   _____

5. ¿Les muestra el traje a ustedes el dependiente?

   _____

6. ¿Me vas a buscar la revista en la librería?

   _____

6.3 Preterite tense of regular verbs

1 **El pretérito** Complete these sentences with the preterite tense of the indicated verb.

1. Marcela _____ (encontrar) las sandalias debajo de la cama.

2. Gustavo _____ (recibir) un regalo muy bonito.

3. Sara y Viviana _____ (terminar) el libro al mismo tiempo.

4. La agente de viajes _____ (preparar) un itinerario muy interesante.

5. (yo) _____ (visitar) la ciudad en invierno.

6. Los dependientes _____ (escuchar) el partido por la radio.

7. Patricia y tú _____ (viajar) a México el verano pasado.

8. (nosotras) _____ (escribir) una carta al empleado del almacén.

9. (tú) _____ (regresar) del centro comercial a las cinco de la tarde.

10. Ustedes _____ (vivir) en casa de sus padres.

2 **Ahora y en el pasado** Rewrite these sentences in the preterite tense.

1. Ramón escribe una carta al director del programa.

_____

2. Mi tía trabaja de dependienta en un gran almacén.

_____

3. Comprendo el trabajo de la clase de biología.

_____

4. La familia de Daniel vive en Argentina.

_____

5. Virginia y sus amigos comen en el café de la librería.

_____

6. Los ingenieros terminan la construcción de la tienda en junio.

_____

7. Cada día llevas ropa muy elegante.

_____

8. Los turistas caminan, compran y descansan.

_____

9. Corremos cada día en el parque.

_____

3

Confundido Your friend Mario has a terrible memory. Answer his questions negatively, indicating that what he asks already happened.

> **modelo**
>
> ¿Va a comprar ropa Silvia en el centro comercial?
> No, Silvia ya *compró ropa en el centro comercial.*

1. ¿Va a viajar a Perú tu primo Andrés?

   _____

2. ¿Vas a buscar una tienda de computadoras en el centro comercial?

   _____

3. ¿Vamos a encontrar muchas rebajas en el centro?

   _____

4. ¿Va María a pagar las sandalias en la caja?

   _____

5. ¿Van a regatear con el vendedor Mónica y Carlos?

   _____

6. ¿Va a pasear por la playa tu abuela?

   _____

4

La semana pasada Now Mario wants to know what you did last week. Write his question, then answer it affirmatively or negatively.

> **modelo**
>
> sacar fotos de los amigos
> —¿Sacaste fotos de los amigos?
> —Sí, saqué fotos de los amigos./No, no saqué fotos de los amigos.

1. pagar el abrigo con la tarjeta de crédito

   _____

   _____

2. jugar al tenis

   _____

   _____

3. buscar un libro en la biblioteca

   _____

   _____

4. llegar tarde a clase

   _____

   _____

5. empezar a escribir una carta

   _____

   _____

6.4 Demonstrative adjectives and pronouns

1 **De compras** Complete these sentences with the correct form of the adjective in parentheses.

1. Me quiero comprar _____ (*these*) zapatos porque me gustan mucho.

2. Comimos en _____ (*that*) centro comercial la semana pasada.

3. _____ (*that over there*) tienda vende las gafas de sol a un precio muy alto.

4. Las rebajas en _____ (*this*) almacén son legendarias.

5. _____ (*those*) botas hacen juego con tus pantalones negros.

6. Voy a llevar _____ (*these*) pantalones con la blusa roja.

2 **Claro que no** Your friend Mario hates shopping, and can't keep anything straight. Answer his questions negatively, using the cues in parentheses and the corresponding demonstrative adjectives.

> **modelo**
>
> ¿Compró esas medias Sonia? (cartera)
> No, *compró esa cartera.*

1. ¿Va a comprar ese suéter Gloria? (pantalones)

   _____

2. ¿Llevaste estas sandalias? (zapatos de tenis)

   _____

3. ¿Quieres ver esta ropa interior? (medias)

   _____

4. ¿Usa aquel traje David? (chaqueta negra)

   _____

5. ¿Decidió Silvia comprar esas gafas de sol? (sombrero)

   _____

6. ¿Te mostró el vestido aquella vendedora? (dependiente)

   _____

3 **Ésos no** Complete these sentences using demonstrative pronouns. Choose a pronoun for each sentence, paying attention to agreement.

1. Aquellas sandalias son muy cómodas, pero _____ son más elegantes.

2. Esos vestidos largos son muy caros; voy a comprar _____.

3. No puedo usar esta tarjeta de crédito; tengo que usar _____.

4. Esos zapatos tienen buen precio, pero _____ no.

5. Prefiero este sombrero porque _____ es muy grande.

6. Estas medias son buenas; las prefiero a _____.

4 **Éstas y aquéllas** Look at the illustration and complete this conversation with the appropriate demonstrative adjectives and pronouns.

CLAUDIA	¿Quieres comprar (1)_____ corbata, Gerardo?
GERARDO	No, no quiero comprar (2)_____. Prefiero (3)_____ del escaparate (*display case*).
CLAUDIA	(4)_____ es bonita, pero no hace juego con tu chaqueta.
GERARDO	Mira (5)_____ chaqueta. Es muy elegante y está a buen precio. Sí, puedo usar (6)_____ y darle a mi hermano ésta.
CLAUDIA	¿Y (7)_____ cinturón?
GERARDO	(8)_____ es muy elegante. ¿Es caro?
CLAUDIA	Es más barato que (9)_____ tres del escaparate.

5 **Más compras** Pilar and Marta are at the mall trying to get a new outfit for a special occasion. Write the conversation in which they talk about different clothing. Use at least six expressions from the list.

aquel vendedor	esa camisa	esos colores	esta falda
aquellas botas	ese precio	esos zapatos	este vestido

_____

_____

_____

_____

_____

_____

_____

Síntesis

Imagine that you went with your brother to an open-air market last weekend. This weekend you take a friend there. Write a conversation between you and your friend, using as many different verbs as you can from those you have learned.

- Indicate to your friend the items you saw last weekend, what you liked and didn't like, the items that you bought, how much you paid for them, and for whom you bought the items.
- Suggest items that your friend might buy and for whom he or she might buy them.

_____

_____

_____

_____

_____

_____

_____

_____

_____

_____

_____

_____

_____

_____

_____

_____

_____

_____

_____

_____

_____

_____

_____

_____

panorama

Cuba

1   **Crucigrama (*Crossword*)** Complete this crossword puzzle with the correct terms.

Horizontales

4. Nombre de la bailarina que fundó el Ballet Nacional de Cuba
5. Especie cubana de colibrí
6. Calle de la Habana Vieja frecuentada por Hemingway
9. Apellido de una escritora cubana célebre
10. Uno de los productos agrícolas más importantes en Cuba

Verticales

1. Esta organización declaró a la Habana Vieja Patrimonio Cultural de la Humanidad.
2. Apellido del ex líder del gobierno de Cuba
3. El azúcar se saca (*is extracted*) de esta planta.
7. Alicia Alonso practicaba (*practiced*) este baile.
8. Moneda cubana

2   **Preguntas de Cuba** Answer these questions about Cuba in complete sentences.

1. ¿De dónde son los antepasados de muchos cubanos de hoy en día?

2. ¿De qué colores es la bandera cubana?

3. ¿Cuál es un medio de transporte muy popular en Cuba?

4. ¿Qué es *Buena Vista Social Club*?

3 **Datos de Cuba** Complete these sentences with information from **Panorama**.

1. El _____ en la Plaza de Armas de la Habana Vieja es ahora un museo.

2. En Cuba se encuentran la Cordillera de los _____ y la Sierra _____.

3. Una isla que forma parte de Cuba es la _____.

4. Alicia Alonso fundó el _____ en 1948.

5. La _____ es un producto de exportación muy importante para Cuba.

6. El tabaco se usa para fabricar los famosos _____.

7. La inmigración fue muy importante en Cuba desde la _____ hasta mediados del siglo XX.

8. *Buena Vista Social Club* interpreta canciones clásicas del _____.

4 **Cubanos célebres** Write the name of the famous Cuban who might have said each of these quotations.

1. "Nací en 1927 y mi música es famosa."

   _____

2. "Me convertí en una estrella internacional con el Ballet de Nueva York."

   _____

3. "Soy el ex jefe de las fuerzas armadas de Cuba."

   _____

4. "Viví en el siglo (*century*) diecinueve y escribí poemas."

   _____

5. "Tengo más de cuarenta años, soy cubana y escribo libros."

   _____

6. "Curé a muchas personas enfermas y estudié las ciencias."

   _____

5 **Números cubanos** Write out the numbers in Spanish that complete these sentences about Cuba.

1. Hay _____ habitantes en la isla de Cuba.

2. Hay _____ habitantes en La Habana.

3. En el año _____ la Habana Vieja fue declarada Patrimonio Cultural de la Humanidad.

4. El área de Cuba es de _____ millas cuadradas.

5. El colibrí abeja de Cuba es una de las más de _____ especies de colibrí del mundo.

6. En el año _____ nació Fidel Castro.

En el mercado

Lección 6
Fotonovela

Antes de ver el video

1

Describir Look at the image and describe what you see, answering these questions: Where are Maru, Jimena, and Marissa? Who are they talking to? What is the purpose of their conversation?

_____
_____
_____
_____
_____
_____

Mientras ves el video

2

Ordenar Watch **En el mercado** and indicate the order in which you hear the following.

_____ a. Acabamos de comprar tres bolsas por 480 pesos.

_____ b. ¿Encontraron el restaurante?

_____ c. Esta falda azul es muy elegante.

_____ d. Le doy un muy buen precio.

_____ e. Mira, son cuatro. Roja, amarilla, blanca, azul.

_____ f. Acabo de ver una bolsa igual a ésta que cuesta 30 pesos menos.

3

Mérida Check each thing you see.

_____ 1. una tarjeta de crédito

_____ 2. una blusa

_____ 3. un mercado

_____ 4. un impermeable

_____ 5. unos aretes

_____ 6. un vendedor

4

¿Quién lo dijo? Indicate whether Marissa, Miguel, or don Guillermo said each sentence.

_____ 1. Quiero comprarle un regalo a Maru.

_____ 2. ¿Me das aquella blusa rosada? Me parece que hace juego con esta falda.

_____ 3. ¿Puedo ver ésos, por favor?

_____ 4. Hasta más tarde. Y ¡buena suerte!

_____ 5. Me contaron que los vendedores son muy simpáticos.

Después de ver el video

5 **Completar** Complete the following sentences with words from the box.

azul	hermana	novia
camisetas	mercado	regatear
en efectivo	negro	vender

1. Juan Carlos, Felipe y Miguel creen que las chicas no saben _____.

2. Los seis amigos van de compras a un _____.

3. Marissa dice que el color _____ está de moda.

4. Miguel quiere comprarle un regalo a su _____ Maru.

5. Las _____ de Juan Carlos y Felipe costaron 200 pesos.

6. Las chicas pagan 480 pesos _____ por las bolsas.

6 **Corregir** All these statements are false. Rewrite them so they are true.

1. Jimena dice que la ropa del mercado es muy fea.

_____

2. Marissa usa la talla 6.

_____

3. Maru compró una blusa.

_____

4. Miguel compró un abrigo para Maru.

_____

7 **Preguntas** Answer these questions in Spanish.

1. ¿Te gusta ir de compras? ¿Por qué? _____

_____

2. ¿Adónde vas de compras? ¿Por qué? _____

_____

3. ¿Con quién(es) vas de compras? ¿Por qué? _____

_____

4. Imagina que estás en un centro comercial y que tienes mil dólares. ¿Qué vas a comprar? ¿Por qué?

_____

_____

5. Cuando compras un auto, ¿regateas con el/la vendedor(a)?

_____

Panorama: Cuba

Lección 6
Panorama cultural

Antes de ver el video

1 **Más vocabulario** Look over these useful words before you watch the video.

Vocabulario útil	
conversar *to talk*	relacionadas *related to*
imágenes *images (in this case, of a religious nature)*	relaciones *relationships*
miembro *member*	sacerdote *priest*

2 **Responder** In this video you are going to see people visiting **santeros** to talk about their problems and their futures. In preparation for watching the video, answer the following questions about your behavior and beliefs.

1. ¿Hablas con alguien (*someone*) cuando tienes problemas? ¿Con quién?

_____

_____

_____

2. ¿Crees que hay personas que pueden "ver" el futuro?

_____

_____

_____

Mientras ves el video

3 **Marcar** Check off the activities you see while watching the video.

_____ 1. hombre escribiendo

_____ 2. hombre leyendo

_____ 3. mujer corriendo

_____ 4. mujer llorando (*crying*)

_____ 5. niño jugando

_____ 6. personas bailando

_____ 7. personas caminando

_____ 8. personas cantando

_____ 9. personas conversando

Después de ver el video

4 **Responder** Answer the questions in Spanish using complete sentences.

1. ¿Qué es la santería?

2. ¿Quiénes son los santeros?

3. ¿Qué venden en las tiendas de santería?

4. ¿Para qué visitan las personas a los santeros?

5. ¿Quiénes son los sacerdotes?

6. ¿Qué hacen los sacerdotes cuando van a las casas de las personas?

5 **¿Cierto o falso?** Indicate whether each statement is **cierto** or **falso**. Correct the false statements.

1. Cada tres horas sale un barco de La Habana con destino a Regla.

2. Regla es una ciudad donde se practica la santería.

3. La santería es una práctica religiosa muy común en algunos países latinoamericanos.

4. Los santeros no son personas importantes en su comunidad.

5. La santería es una de las tradiciones cubanas más viejas.

6 **Conversación** In this video, you see a **santero** talking with a woman. In Spanish, write a short conversation. Include what the woman would ask the **santero** and how he would respond to her problems.

Comprar en los mercados

Antes de ver el video

1 **Más vocabulario** Look over these useful words before you watch the video.

Vocabulario útil		
las artesanías *handicrafts*	la heladería *ice-cream shop*	la soda (C.R.) *food stall*
el camarón *shrimp*	el helado *ice cream*	la sopa de mondongo *tripe soup*
la carne *meat*	el pescado *fish*	suave *soft*
la flor *flower*	¡Pura vida! *Cool!, Alright!*	el/la tico/a *person from Costa Rica*
la fruta *fruit*	el regateo *haggling, bargaining*	vale *it costs*

2 **¡En español!** Look at the video still. Imagine what Randy will say about markets in Costa Rica, and write a two- or three-sentence introduction to this episode.

Randy Cruz, Costa Rica

¡Hola a todos! Hoy estamos en... _____

_____

_____

_____

_____

Mientras ves el video

3 **¿Qué compran?** Identify which item(s) these people buy at the market.

1. _____ 2. _____ 3. _____

a. frutas
d. camarones y flores

b. artesanías
e. zapatos

c. carne y pescado

4   **Completar** Watch Randy bargain, and complete this conversation.

RANDY	¿(1)_____ vale?
VENDEDOR	Trescientos (*300*) (2)_____.
RANDY	Trescientos colones el kilo. Me puede hacer un (3)_____, ¿sí?
VENDEDOR	Perfecto.
VENDEDOR	OK... (4)_____ cuatro ochenta... cuatro y medio.
RANDY	Cuatrocientos (*400*).
VENDEDOR	Cuatro (5)_____.
RANDY	Cuatrocientos cuarenta.
VENDEDOR	Sí, señor.

Después de ver el video

5   **Ordenar** Put Randy's actions in the correct order.

_____ a. Busca la heladería en el Mercado Central.

_____ b. Regatea el precio de unas papayas.

_____ c. Va al mercado al aire libre.

_____ d. Entrevista a personas en el Mercado Central.

_____ e. Toma sopa de mondongo, un plato (*dish*) típico de Costa Rica.

6   **¡Aquí no hay descuentos!** Imagine that Randy wants to buy an item of clothing that he really likes, but he doesn't have enough money to pay the full price. Write a conversation between Randy and a salesperson in which Randy negotiates the price. Be creative!

_____

_____

_____

_____

7   **Preguntas** Answer these questions.

1. ¿En qué lugares o tipos de tiendas haces las compras generalmente? ¿Pequeñas tiendas, grandes almacenes o centros comerciales? _____

2. ¿Con quién(es) sales generalmente a comprar ropa: solo/a (*alone*), con amigos o con alguien (*someone*) de tu familia? ¿Por qué? _____

3. ¿Cómo prefieres pagar tus compras: en efectivo o con tarjeta de crédito? ¿Por qué? _____

4. ¿Esperas las rebajas para comprar cosas que quieres o no te importa (*you don't mind*) pagar el precio normal? _____

contextos

Lección 6

1 **¿Lógico o ilógico?** Listen to each statement and indicate if it is **lógico** or **ilógico**.

1. Lógico   Ilógico   5. Lógico   Ilógico
2. Lógico   Ilógico   6. Lógico   Ilógico
3. Lógico   Ilógico   7. Lógico   Ilógico
4. Lógico   Ilógico   8. Lógico   Ilógico

2 **Escoger** Listen as each person talks about the clothing he or she needs to buy. Then choose the activity for which the clothing would be appropriate.

1. a. ir a la playa   b. ir al cine
2. a. jugar al golf   b. buscar trabajo (*work*)
3. a. salir a bailar   b. ir a las montañas
4. a. montar a caballo   b. jugar a las cartas
5. a. jugar al vóleibol   b. comer en un restaurante elegante
6. a. hacer un viaje   b. patinar en línea

3 **Preguntas** Respond to each question saying that the opposite is true. Repeat the correct answer after the speaker. (*6 items*)

> **modelo**
> Las sandalias cuestan mucho, ¿no?
> No, las sandalias *cuestan poco.*

4 **Describir** You will hear some questions. Look at the drawing and write the answer to each question.

Diana   Carmen

1. _____

2. _____

3. _____

4. _____

pronunciación

The consonants **d** and **t**

Like **b** and **v**, the Spanish **d** can have a hard sound or a soft sound, depending on which letters appear next to it.

¿**D**ónde?	ven**d**er	na**d**ar	ver**dad**

At the beginning of a phrase and after **n** or **l**, the letter **d** is pronounced with a hard sound. This sound is similar to the English *d* in *dog*, but a little softer and duller. The tongue should touch the back of the upper teeth, not the roof of the mouth.

Don	**d**inero	tien**d**a	fal**d**a

In all other positions, **d** has a soft sound. It is similar to the English *th* in *there*, but a little softer.

me**d**ias	ver**d**e	vesti**d**o	huéspe**d**

When **d** begins a word, its pronunciation depends on the previous word. At the beginning of a phrase or after a word that ends in **n** or **l**, it is pronounced as a hard **d**.

Don **D**iego no tiene el **d**iccionario.

Words that begin with **d** are pronounced with a soft **d** if they appear immediately after a word that ends in a vowel or any consonant other than **n** or **l**.

Doña **D**olores es **d**e la capital.

When pronouncing the Spanish **t**, the tongue should touch the back of the upper teeth, not the roof of the mouth. In contrast to the English *t*, no air is expelled from the mouth.

traje	pan**t**alones	**t**arje**t**a	**t**ienda

1 **Práctica** Repeat each phrase after the speaker to practice the **d** and the **t**.

1. Hasta pronto.
2. De nada.
3. Mucho gusto.
4. Lo siento.
5. No hay de qué.
6. ¿De dónde es usted?
7. ¡Todos a bordo!
8. No puedo.
9. Es estupendo.
10. No tengo computadora.
11. ¿Cuándo vienen?
12. Son las tres y media.

2 **Oraciones** When you hear the number, read the corresponding sentence aloud, focusing on the **d** and **t** sounds. Then listen to the speaker and repeat the sentence.

1. Don Teodoro tiene una tienda en un almacén en La Habana.
2. Don Teodoro vende muchos trajes, vestidos y zapatos todos los días.
3. Un día un turista, Federico Machado, entra en la tienda para comprar un par de botas.
4. Federico regatea con don Teodoro y compra las botas y también un par de sandalias.

3 **Refranes** Repeat each saying after the speaker to practice the **d** and the **t**.

1. En la variedad está el gusto.
2. Aunque la mona se vista de seda, mona se queda.

4 **Dictado** You will hear four sentences. Each will be said twice. Listen carefully and write what you hear.

1. _____
2. _____
3. _____
4. _____

estructura

6.1 Saber and conocer

1 **¿Saber o conocer?** You will hear some sentences with a beep in place of the verb. Decide which form of **saber** or **conocer** should complete each sentence and circle it.

> **modelo**
>
> You hear: (Beep) cantar.
> You circle: **Sé** because sentence is **Sé cantar.**

1. Sé   Conozco
2. Saben   Conocen
3. Sabemos   Conocemos
4. Sé   Conozco
5. Sabes   Conoces
6. Sabes   Conoces

2 **Cambiar** Listen to the following statements and say that you do the same activities. Repeat the correct answer after the speaker. (5 items)

> **modelo**
>
> Julia sabe nadar.
> Yo también sé nadar.

3 **Preguntas** Answer each question using the cue you hear. Repeat the correct response after the speaker. (6 items)

> **modelo**
>
> ¿Conocen tus padres Antigua? (Sí)
> Sí, mis padres conocen Antigua.

4 **Mi compañera de cuarto** Listen as Jennifer describes her roommate. Then read the statements in your lab manual and decide whether they are **cierto** or **falso**.

	Cierto	Falso
1. Jennifer conoció (met) a Laura en la escuela primaria.	○	○
2. Laura sabe hacer muchas cosas.	○	○
3. Laura sabe hablar alemán.	○	○
4. Laura sabe buscar gangas.	○	○
5. Laura sabe patinar en línea.	○	○
6. Laura conoce a algunos muchachos simpáticos.	○	○

5 **De compras** Listen to this conversation between Carmen and Rosalía. Then choose the correct answers to the questions in your lab manual.

1. ¿Cuál es el problema de Carmen cuando va de compras?
   a. Siempre encuentra gangas.   b. Nunca encuentra ofertas.
2. ¿Conoce Carmen el nuevo centro comercial?
   a. No lo conoce, pero sabe dónde está.   b. Ni lo conoce, ni sabe dónde está.
3. ¿Qué quiere comprar Rosalía en el centro comercial?
   a. Quiere comprar zapatos.   b. No quiere comprar nada.
4. ¿Cuándo van Carmen y Rosalía de compras?
   a. Mañana antes del trabajo.   b. Mañana después del trabajo.

6.2 Indirect object pronouns

1 **Escoger** Listen to each question and choose the most logical response.

1. a. Sí, le muestro el abrigo.
   b. Sí, me muestra el abrigo.
2. a. No, no le presto el suéter azul.
   b. No, no te presto el suéter azul.
3. a. Voy a comprarles ropa interior.
   b. Vamos a comprarle ropa interior.
4. a. Sí, nos dan las nuevas sandalias.
   b. Sí, me dan las nuevas sandalias.
5. a. Nos cuestan veinte dólares.
   b. Les cuestan veinte dólares.
6. a. Sí, nos trae un sombrero.
   b. Sí, te traigo un sombrero.

2 **Transformar** Cecilia is shopping. Say for whom she buys these items using indirect object pronouns. Repeat the correct answer after the speaker. (*6 items*)

> **modelo**
> Cecilia compra una bolsa para Dora.
> *Cecilia le compra una bolsa.*

3 **Preguntas** Answer each question you hear using the cue in your lab manual. Repeat the correct response after the speaker.

> **modelo**
> *You hear:* ¿Quién está esperándote?
> *You see:* Mauricio
> *You say:* Mauricio está esperándome.

1. sí
2. $50,00
3. no
4. su traje nuevo
5. Antonio
6. bluejeans

4 **En el centro comercial** Listen to this conversation and answer the questions in your lab manual.

1. ¿Quién es Gustavo?

2. ¿Qué está haciendo Gustavo?

3. ¿Qué le pregunta Gustavo a José?

4. ¿Por qué le presta dinero José?

5. ¿Cuándo va a regalarle (*to give*) la falda a Norma?

6.3 Preterite tense of regular verbs

1 **Identificar** Listen to each sentence and decide whether the verb is in the present or the preterite tense. Mark an **X** in the appropriate column.

> modelo
>
> *You hear:* Alejandro llevó un suéter marrón.
> *You mark:* an **X** under **Preterite**.

	Present	*Preterite*
Modelo		**X**
1.		
2.		
3.		
4.		
5.		
6.		
7.		
8.		

2 **Cambiar** Change each sentence from the present to the preterite. Repeat the correct answer after the speaker. (*8 items*)

> modelo
>
> Compro unas sandalias baratas.
> Compré unas sandalias baratas.

3 **Preguntas** Answer each question you hear using the cue in your lab manual. Repeat the correct response after the speaker.

> modelo
>
> *You hear:* ¿Dónde conseguiste tus botas?
> *You see:* en la tienda Lacayo
> *You say:* Conseguí mis botas en la tienda Lacayo.

1. $26,00   2. ayer   3. Marta   4. no   5. no   6. no

4 **¿Estás listo?** Listen to this conversation between Matilde and Hernán. Make a list of the tasks Hernán has already done in preparation for his trip and a list of the tasks he still needs to do.

Tareas completadas	**Tareas que necesita hacer**

6.4 Demonstrative adjectives and pronouns

1 **En el mercado** A group of tourists is shopping at an open-air market. Listen to what they say, and mark an **X** in the column for the demonstrative adjective you hear.

> *modelo*
>
> *You hear:* Me gusta mucho esa bolsa.
> *You mark:* an **X** under *that*.

	this	*that*	*these*	*those*
Modelo	_____	**X**	_____	_____
1.	_____	_____	_____	_____
2.	_____	_____	_____	_____
3.	_____	_____	_____	_____
4.	_____	_____	_____	_____

2 **Cambiar** Form a new sentence using the cue you hear. Repeat the correct answer after the speaker. (*6 items*)

> *modelo*
>
> Quiero este suéter. (chaqueta)
> *Quiero esta chaqueta.*

3 **Transformar** Form a new sentence using the cue you hear. Repeat the correct answer after the speaker. (*6 items*)

> *modelo*
>
> Aquel abrigo es muy hermoso. (corbatas)
> *Aquellas corbatas son muy hermosas.*

4 **Preguntas** Answer each question you hear in the negative using a form of the demonstrative pronoun **ése**. Repeat the correct response after the speaker. (*8 items*)

> *modelo*
>
> ¿Quieres esta blusa?
> *No, no quiero ésa.*

5 **De compras** Listen to this conversation. Then read the statements in your lab manual and decide whether they are **cierto** or **falso**.

	Cierto	Falso
1. Flor quiere ir al almacén Don Guapo.	○	○
2. Enrique trabaja en el almacén Don Guapo.	○	○
3. El centro comercial está lejos de los chicos.	○	○
4. Van al almacén que está al lado del Hotel Plaza.	○	○

vocabulario

You will now hear the vocabulary found in your textbook on the last page of this lesson. Listen and repeat each Spanish word or phrase after the speaker.

Additional Vocabulary

Additional Vocabulary

Notes

Notes

Notes

Plan de escritura

1 **Ideas y organización**

Begin by organizing your writing materials. If you prefer to write by hand, you may want to have a few spare pens and pencils on hand, as well as an eraser or correction fluid. If you prefer to use a word-processing program, make sure you know how to type Spanish accent marks, the **tilde,** and Spanish punctuation marks. Then make a list of the resources you can consult while writing. Finally, make a list of the basic ideas you want to cover. Beside each idea, jot down a few Spanish words and phrases you may want to use while writing.

2 **Primer borrador**

Write your first draft, using the resources and ideas you gathered in **Ideas y organización.**

3 **Comentario**

Exchange papers with a classmate and comment on each other's work, using these questions as a guide. Begin by mentioning what you like about your classmate's writing.

a. How can your classmate make his or her writing clearer, more logical, or more organized?

b. What suggestions do you have for making the writing more interesting or complete?

c. Do you see any spelling or grammatical errors?

4 **Redacción**

Revise your first draft, keeping in mind your classmate's comments. Also, incorporate any new information you may have. Before handing in the final version, review your work using these guidelines:

a. Make sure each verb agrees with its subject. Then check the gender and number of each article, noun, and adjective.

b. Check your spelling and punctuation.

c. Consult your **Anotaciones para mejorar la escritura** (see description below) to avoid repetition of previous errors.

5 **Evaluación y progreso**

You may want to share what you've written with a classmate, a small group, or the entire class. After your instructor has returned your paper, review the comments and corrections. On a separate sheet of paper, write the heading **Anotaciones para mejorar** (*Notes for improving*) **la escritura** and list your most common errors. Place this list and your corrected document in your writing portfolio (**Carpeta de trabajos**) and consult it from time to time to gauge your progress.

Spanish Terms for Direction Lines and Classroom Use

Below is a list of useful terms that you might hear your instructor say in class. It also includes Spanish terms that appear in the direction lines of your textbook.

En las instrucciones · *In direction lines*

Cambia/Cambien...	*Change...*
Camina/Caminen por la clase.	*Walk around the classroom.*
Ciertas o falsas	*True or false*
Cierto o falso	*True or false*
Circula/Circulen por la clase.	*Walk around the classroom.*
Completa las oraciones de una manera lógica.	*Complete the sentences logically.*
Con un(a) compañero/a...	*With a classmate...*
Contesta las preguntas.	*Answer the questions.*
Corrige las oraciones falsas.	*Correct the false statements.*
Cuenta/Cuenten...	*Tell...*
Di/Digan...	*Say...*
Discute/Discutan...	*Discuss...*
En grupos...	*In groups...*
En parejas...	*In pairs...*
Entrevista...	*Interview...*
Escúchala	*Listen to it*
Forma oraciones completas.	*Create/Make complete sentences.*
Háganse preguntas.	*Ask each other questions.*
Haz el papel de...	*Play the role of...*
Haz los cambios necesarios.	*Make the necessary changes.*
Indica/Indiquen si las oraciones...	*Indicate if the sentences...*
Intercambia/Intercambien...	*Exchange...*
Lee/Lean en voz alta.	*Read aloud.*
Pon/Pongan...	*Put...*
...que mejor completa...	*...that best completes...*
Reúnete...	*Get together...*
...se da/dan como ejemplo.	*...is/are given as a model.*
Toma nota...	*Take note...*
Tomen apuntes.	*Take notes.*
Túrnense...	*Take turns...*

Palabras útiles · *Useful words*

la adivinanza	*riddle*
el anuncio	*advertisement/ad*
los apuntes	*notes*
el borrador	*draft*
la canción	*song*
la concordancia	*agreement*
el contenido	*contents*
el cortometraje	*short film*
eficaz	*efficient*
la encuesta	*survey*
el equipo	*team*
el esquema	*outline*
el folleto	*brochure*
las frases	*phrases*
la hoja de actividades	*activity sheet/handout*
la hoja de papel	*piece of paper*
la información errónea	*incorrect information*
el/la lector(a)	*reader*
la lectura	*reading*
las oraciones	*sentences*
la ortografía	*spelling*
el papel	*role*
el párrafo	*paragraph*
el paso	*step*
la(s) persona(s) descrita(s)	*the person (people) described*
la pista	*clue*
por ejemplo	*for example*
el propósito	*purpose*
los recursos	*resources*
el reportaje	*report*
los resultados	*results*
según	*according to*
siguiente	*following*
la sugerencia	*suggestion*
el sustantivo	*noun*
el tema	*topic*
último	*last*
el último recurso	*last resort*

Verbos útiles *Useful verbs*

adivinar	*to guess*
anotar	*to jot down*
añadir	*to add*
apoyar	*to support*
averiguar	*to find out*
cambiar	*to change*
combinar	*to combine*
compartir	*to share*
comprobar (o:ue)	*to check*
corregir (e:i)	*to correct*
crear	*to create*
devolver (o:ue)	*to return*
doblar	*to fold*
dramatizar	*to act out*
elegir (e:i)	*to choose/select*
emparejar	*to match*
entrevistar	*to interview*
escoger	*to choose*
identificar	*to identify*
incluir	*to include*
informar	*to report*
intentar	*to try*
intercambiar	*to exchange*
investigar	*to research*
marcar	*to mark*
preguntar	*to ask*
recordar (o:ue)	*to remember*
responder	*to answer*
revisar	*to revise*
seguir (e:i)	*to follow*
seleccionar	*to select*
subrayar	*to underline*
traducir	*to translate*
tratar de	*to be about*

Expresiones útiles *Useful expressions*

Ahora mismo.	*Right away.*
¿Cómo no?	*But of course.*
¿Cómo se dice _____ en español?	*How do you say _____ in Spanish?*
¿Cómo se escribe _____?	*How do you spell _____?*
¿Comprende(n)?	*Do you understand?*
Con gusto.	*With pleasure.*
Con permiso.	*Excuse me.*
De acuerdo.	*Okay.*
De nada.	*You're welcome.*
¿De veras?	*Really?*
¿En qué página estamos?	*What page are we on?*
¿En serio?	*Seriously?*
Enseguida.	*Right away.*
hoy día	*nowadays*
Más despacio, por favor.	*Slower, please.*
Muchas gracias.	*Thanks a lot.*
No entiendo.	*I don't understand.*
No hay de qué.	*Don't mention it.*
No importa.	*No problem./It doesn't matter.*
¡No me digas!	*You don't say!*
No sé.	*I don't know.*
¡Ojalá!	*Hopefully!*
Perdone.	*Pardon me.*
Por favor.	*Please.*
Por supuesto.	*Of course.*
¡Qué bien!	*Great!*
¡Qué gracioso!	*How funny!*
¡Qué pena!	*What a shame/pity!*
¿Qué significa _____?	*What does _____ mean?*
Repite, por favor.	*Please repeat.*
Tengo una pregunta.	*I have a question.*
¿Tiene(n) alguna pregunta?	*Do you have any questions?*
Vaya(n) a la página dos.	*Go to page 2.*

Glossary of Grammatical Terms

ADJECTIVE A word that modifies, or describes, a noun or pronoun.

muchos libros	un hombre **rico**
many books	*a rich man*
las mujeres **altas**	
*the **tall** women*	

Demonstrative adjective An adjective that specifies which noun a speaker is referring to.

esta fiesta	**ese** chico
this party	*that boy*
aquellas flores	
those flowers	

Possessive adjective An adjective that indicates ownership or possession.

mi mejor vestido	**Éste** es **mi** hermano.
my best dress	*This is **my** brother.*

Stressed possessive adjective A possessive adjective that emphasizes the owner or possessor.

Es un libro **mío**.
*It's **my** book./It's a book **of mine**.*

Es amiga **tuya**; yo no la conozco.
*She's a friend **of yours**; I don't know her.*

ADVERB A word that modifies, or describes, a verb, adjective, or other adverb.

Pancho escribe **rápidamente**.
*Pancho writes **quickly**.*

Este cuadro es **muy** bonito.
*This picture is **very** pretty.*

ARTICLE A word that points out a noun in either a specific or a non-specific way.

Definite article An article that points out a noun in a specific way.

el libro	la maleta
the book	*the suitcase*
los diccionarios	las palabras
the dictionaries	*the words*

Indefinite article An article that points out a noun in a general, non-specific way.

un lápiz	**una** computadora
a pencil	*a computer*
unos pájaros	**unas** escuelas
some birds	*some schools*

CLAUSE A group of words that contains both a conjugated verb and a subject, either expressed or implied.

Main (or Independent) clause A clause that can stand alone as a complete sentence.

Pienso ir a cenar pronto.
I plan to go to dinner soon.

Subordinate (or Dependent) clause A clause that does not express a complete thought and therefore cannot stand alone as a sentence.

Trabajo en la cafetería **porque necesito dinero para la escuela.**
*I work in the cafeteria **because I need money for school.***

COMPARATIVE A construction used with an adjective or adverb to express a comparison between two people, places, or things.

Este programa es **más interesante que** el otro.
*This program is **more interesting** than the other one.*

Tomás no es **tan alto como** Alberto.
*Tomás is not **as tall as** Alberto.*

CONJUGATION A set of the forms of a verb for a specific tense or mood or the process by which these verb forms are presented.

Preterite conjugation of **cantar**:

cant**é**	cant**amos**
cant**aste**	cant**asteis**
cant**ó**	cant**aron**

CONJUNCTION A word used to connect words, clauses, or phrases.

Susana es de Cuba **y** Pedro es de España.
*Susana is from Cuba **and** Pedro is from Spain.*

No quiero estudiar **pero** tengo que hacerlo.
*I don't want to study, **but** I have to.*

CONTRACTION The joining of two words into one. The only contractions in Spanish are **al** and **del**.

Mi hermano fue **al** concierto ayer.
*My brother went **to the** concert yesterday.*

Saqué dinero **del** banco.
*I took money **from the** bank.*

DIRECT OBJECT A noun or pronoun that directly receives the action of the verb.

Tomás lee **el libro.**   La pagó ayer.
*Tomás reads **the book.***   *She paid **it** yesterday.*

GENDER The grammatical categorizing of certain kinds of words, such as nouns and pronouns, as masculine, feminine, or neuter.

Masculine
articles el, un
pronouns él, lo, mío, éste, ése, aquél
adjective simpático

Feminine
articles la, una
pronouns ella, la, mía, ésta, ésa, aquélla
adjective simpática

IMPERSONAL EXPRESSION A third-person expression with no expressed or specific subject.

Es muy importante.   Llueve mucho.
It's very important.   *It's raining hard.*

Aquí **se habla** español.
*Spanish **is spoken** here.*

INDIRECT OBJECT A noun or pronoun that receives the action of the verb indirectly; the object, often a living being, to or for whom an action is performed.

Eduardo **le** dio un libro a Linda.
*Eduardo gave a book **to Linda.***

La profesora **me** dio una C en el examen.
*The professor gave **me** a C on the test.*

INFINITIVE The basic form of a verb. Infinitives in Spanish end in -ar, -er, or -ir.

hablar   correr   abrir
to speak   *to run*   *to open*

INTERROGATIVE An adjective or pronoun used to ask a question.

¿**Quién** habla?   ¿**Cuántos** compraste?
Who is speaking?   *How many did you buy?*

¿**Qué** piensas hacer hoy?
What do you plan to do today?

INVERSION Changing the word order of a sentence, often to form a question.

Statement: Elena pagó la cuenta del restaurante.

Inversion: ¿Pagó Elena la cuenta del restaurante?

MOOD A grammatical distinction of verbs that indicates whether the verb is intended to make a statement or command or to express a doubt, emotion, or condition contrary to fact.

Imperative mood Verb forms used to make commands.

Di la verdad.   Caminen ustedes conmigo.
Tell the truth.   *Walk with me.*

¡Comamos ahora!
Let's eat now!

Indicative mood Verb forms used to state facts, actions, and states considered to be real.

Sé que **tienes** el dinero.
*I know that **you have** the money.*

Subjunctive mood Verb forms used principally in subordinate (dependent) clauses to express wishes, desires, emotions, doubts, and certain conditions, such as contrary-to-fact situations.

Prefieren que **hables** en español.
*They prefer that **you speak** in Spanish.*

Dudo que Luis **tenga** el dinero necesario.
*I doubt that Luis **has** the necessary money.*

NOUN A word that identifies people, animals, places, things, and ideas.

hombre   gato
man   *cat*

México   casa
Mexico   *house*

libertad   libro
freedom   *book*

NUMBER A grammatical term that refers to singular or plural. Nouns in Spanish and English have number. Other parts of a sentence, such as adjectives, articles, and verbs, can also have number.

Singular	Plural
una cosa	**unas** cosas
a thing	*some things*
el profesor	**los** profesores
the professor	*the professors*

NUMBERS Words that represent amounts.

Cardinal numbers Words that show specific amounts.

cinco minutos
five minutes

el año **dos mil veintitrés**
the year 2023

Ordinal numbers Words that indicate the order of a noun in a series.

el **cuarto** jugador   la **décima** hora
the fourth player   *the tenth hour*

PAST PARTICIPLE A past form of the verb used in compound tenses. The past participle may also be used as an adjective, but it must then agree in number and gender with the word it modifies.

Han **buscado** por todas partes.
They have searched everywhere.

Yo no había **estudiado** para el examen.
I hadn't studied for the exam.

Hay una **ventana abierta** en la sala.
There is an open window in the living room.

PERSON The form of the verb or pronoun that indicates the speaker, the one spoken to, or the one spoken about. In Spanish, as in English, there are three persons: first, second, and third.

Person	Singular		Plural	
1st	yo	*I*	nosotros/as	*we*
2nd	tú, Ud.	*you*	vosotros/as, Uds.	*you*
3rd	él, ella	*he, she*	ellos, ellas	*they*

PREPOSITION A word or words that describe(s) the relationship, most often in time or space, between two other words.

Anita es **de** California.
Anita is from California.

La chaqueta está **en** el carro.
The jacket is in the car.

Marta se peinó **antes de** salir.
Marta combed her hair before going out.

PRESENT PARTICIPLE In English, a verb form that ends in *-ing*. In Spanish, the present participle ends in **-ndo**, and is often used with **estar** to form a progressive tense.

Mi hermana está **hablando** por teléfono ahora mismo.
My sister is talking on the phone right now.

PRONOUN A word that takes the place of a noun or nouns.

Demonstrative pronoun A pronoun that takes the place of a specific noun.

Quiero **ésta**.
I want this one.

¿Vas a comprar **ése**?
Are you going to buy that one?

Juan prefirió **aquéllos**.
Juan preferred those (over there).

Object pronoun A pronoun that functions as a direct or indirect object of the verb.

Te digo la verdad.
I'm telling you the truth.

Me lo trajo Juan.
Juan brought it to me.

Reflexive pronoun A pronoun that indicates that the action of a verb is performed by the subject on itself. These pronouns are often expressed in English with *-self: myself, yourself,* etc.

Yo **me** bañé antes de salir.
I bathed (myself) before going out.

Elena **se acostó** a las once y media.
Elena went to bed at eleven-thirty.

Relative pronoun A pronoun that connects a subordinate clause to a main clause.

El chico **que** nos escribió viene de visita mañana.
*The boy **who** wrote us is coming to visit tomorrow.*

Ya sé **lo que** tenemos que hacer.
*I already know **what** we have to do.*

Subject pronoun A pronoun that replaces the name or title of a person or thing, and acts as the subject of a verb.

Tú debes estudiar más.
***You** should study more.*

Él llegó primero.
***He** arrived first.*

SUBJECT A noun or pronoun that performs the action of a verb and is often implied by the verb.

María va al supermercado.
***María** goes to the supermarket.*

(Ellos) Trabajan mucho.
***They** work hard.*

Esos **libros** son muy caros.
*Those **books** are very expensive.*

SUPERLATIVE A word or construction used with an adjective or adverb to express the highest or lowest degree of a specific quality among three or more people, places, or things.

De todas mis clases, ésta es la **más interesante**.
*Of all my classes, this is the **most interesting**.*

Raúl es el **menos simpático** de los chicos.
*Raúl is the **least pleasant** of the boys.*

TENSE A set of verb forms that indicates the time of an action or state: past, present, or future.

Compound tense A two-word tense made up of an auxiliary verb and a present or past participle. In Spanish, **estar** and **haber** are auxiliary verbs.

En este momento, **estoy estudiando**.
*At this time, **I am studying**.*

El paquete no **ha llegado** todavía.
*The package **has** not **arrived** yet.*

Simple tense A tense expressed by a single verb form.

María **estaba** enferma anoche.
*María **was** sick last night.*

Juana **hablará** con su mamá mañana.
*Juana **will speak** with her mom tomorrow.*

VERB A word that expresses actions or states of being.

Auxiliary verb A verb used with a present or past participle to form a compound tense. **Haber** is the most commonly used auxiliary verb in Spanish.

Los chicos **han** visto los elefantes.
*The children **have** seen the elephants.*

Espero que **hayas** comido.
*I hope you **have** eaten.*

Reflexive verb A verb that describes an action performed by the subject on itself and is always used with a reflexive pronoun.

Me compré un carro nuevo.
*I bought **myself** a new car.*

Pedro y Adela **se levantan** muy temprano.
*Pedro and Adela **get (themselves) up** very early.*

Spelling change verb A verb that undergoes a predictable change in spelling, in order to reflect its actual pronunciation in the various conjugations.

practicar	c→qu	practico	practiqué
dirigir	g→j	dirigí	dirijo
almorzar	z→c	almorzó	almorcé

Stem-changing verb A verb whose stem vowel undergoes one or more predictable changes in the various conjugations.

entender (e:ie)   entiendo
pedir (e:i)   piden
dormir (o:ue, u)   duermo, durmieron

Verb Conjugation Tables

The verb lists

The list of verbs below, and the model-verb tables that start on page A-11 show you how to conjugate every verb taught in **¡ADELANTE!** Each verb in the list is followed by a model verb conjugated according to the same pattern. The number in parentheses indicates where in the verb tables you can find the conjugated forms of the model verb. If you want to find out how to conjugate **divertirse**, for example, look up number 33, **sentir**, the model for verbs that follow the e:ie stem-change pattern.

How to use the verb tables

In the tables you will find the infinitive, present and past participles, and all the simple forms of each model verb. The formation of the compound tenses of any verb can be inferred from the table of compound tenses, pages A-11 and A-12, either by combining the past participle of the verb with a conjugated form of **haber** or by combining the present participle with a conjugated form of **estar**.

Verb tables

abrazar (z:c) like cruzar (37)

abrir like vivir (3) *except* past participle is **abierto**

aburrir(se) like vivir (3)

acabar de like hablar (1)

acampar like hablar (1)

acompañar like hablar (1)

aconsejar like hablar (1)

acordarse (o:ue) like contar (24)

acostarse (o:ue) like contar (24)

adelgazar (z:c) like cruzar (37)

afeitarse like hablar (1)

ahorrar like hablar (1)

alegrarse like hablar (1)

aliviar like hablar (1)

almorzar (o:ue) like contar (24) *except* (z:c)

alquilar like hablar (1)

andar like hablar (1) *except* preterite stem is **anduv-**

anunciar like hablar (1)

apagar (g:gu) like llegar (41)

aplaudir like vivir (3)

apreciar like hablar (1)

aprender like comer (2)

apurarse like hablar (1)

arrancar (c:qu) like tocar (43)

arreglar like hablar (1)

asistir like vivir (3)

aumentar like hablar (1)

ayudar(se) like hablar (1)

bailar like hablar (1)

bajar(se) like hablar (1)

bañarse like hablar (1)

barrer like comer (2)

beber like comer (2)

besar(se) like hablar (1)

borrar like hablar (1)

brindar like hablar (1)

bucear like hablar (1)

buscar (c:qu) like tocar (43)

caber (4)

caer(se) (5)

calentarse (e:ie) like pensar (30)

calzar (z:c) like cruzar (37)

cambiar like hablar (1)

caminar like hablar (1)

cantar like hablar (1)

casarse like hablar (1)

cazar (z:c) like cruzar (37)

celebrar like hablar (1)

cenar like hablar (1)

cepillarse like hablar (1)

cerrar (e:ie) like pensar (30)

cobrar like hablar (1)

cocinar like hablar (1)

comenzar (e:ie) (z:c) like empezar (26)

comer (2)

compartir like vivir (3)

comprar like hablar (1)

comprender like comer (2)

comprometerse like comer (2)

comunicarse (c:qu) like tocar (43)

confirmar like hablar (1)

conducir (c:zc) (6)

conocer (c:zc) (35)

conseguir (e:i) (g:gu) like seguir (32)

conservar like hablar (1)

consumir like vivir (3)

contaminar like hablar (1)

contar (o:ue) (24)

contestar like hablar (1)

contratar like hablar (1)

controlar like hablar (1)

conversar like hablar (1)

correr like comer (2)

costar (o:ue) like contar (24)

creer (y) (36)

cruzar (z:c) (37)

cuidar like hablar (1)

cumplir like vivir (3)

dañar like hablar (1)

dar (7)

deber like comer (2)

decidir like vivir (3)

decir (e:i) (8)

declarar like hablar (1)

dejar like hablar (1)

depositar like hablar (1)

desarrollar like hablar (1)

desayunar like hablar (1)

descansar like hablar (1)

descargar like llegar (41)

describir like vivir (3) *except* past participle is **descrito**

descubrir like vivir (3) *except* past participle is **descubierto**

desear like hablar (1)

despedirse (e:i) like pedir (29)

despertarse (e:ie) like pensar (30)

destruir (y) (38)

dibujar like hablar (1)

dirigir (g:j) like vivir (3) *except* (g:j)

disfrutar like hablar (1)

divertirse (e:ie) like sentir (33)

divorciarse like hablar (1)

doblar like hablar (1)

doler (o:ue) like volver (34) *except* past participle is regular

dormir(se) (o:ue, u) (25)

ducharse like hablar (1)

dudar like hablar (1)

durar like hablar (1)

echar like hablar (1)

elegir (e:i) like pedir (29) *except* (g:j)

emitir like vivir (3)

empezar (e:ie) (z:c) (26)

enamorarse like hablar (1)

encantar like hablar (1)
encontrar(se) (o:ue) like contar (24)
enfermarse like hablar (1)
engordar like hablar (1)
enojarse like hablar (1)
enseñar like hablar (1)
ensuciar like hablar (1)
entender (e:ie) (27)
entrenarse like hablar (1)
entrevistar like hablar (1)
enviar (envío) (39)
escalar like hablar (1)
escanear like hablar (1)
escoger (g:j) like proteger (42)
escribir like vivir (3) *except* past participle is escrito
escuchar like hablar (1)
esculpir like vivir (3)
esperar like hablar (1)
esquiar (esquío) like enviar (39)
establecer (c:zc) like conocer (35)
estacionar like hablar (1)
estar (9)
estornudar like hablar (1)
estudiar like hablar (1)
evitar like hablar (1)
explicar (c:qu) like tocar (43)
faltar like hablar (1)
fascinar like hablar (1)
firmar like hablar (1)
fumar like hablar (1)
funcionar like hablar (1)
ganar like hablar (1)
gastar like hablar (1)
grabar like hablar (1)
graduarse (gradúo) (40)
guardar like hablar (1)
gustar like hablar (1)
haber (hay) (10)
hablar (1)
hacer (11)
importar like hablar (1)
imprimir like vivir (3)
indicar (c:qu) like tocar (43)
informar like hablar (1)
insistir like vivir (3)
interesar like hablar (1)
invertir (e:ie) like sentir (33)

invitar like hablar (1)
ir(se) (12)
jubilarse like hablar (1)
jugar (u:ue) (g:gu) (28)
lastimarse like hablar (1)
lavar(se) like hablar (1)
leer (y) like creer (36)
levantar(se) like hablar (1)
limpiar like hablar (1)
llamar(se) like hablar (1)
llegar (g:gu) (41)
llenar like hablar (1)
llevar(se) like hablar (1)
llover (o:ue) like volver (34) *except* past participle is regular
luchar like hablar (1)
mandar like hablar (1)
manejar like hablar (1)
mantener(se) (e:ie) like tener (20)
maquillarse like hablar (1)
mejorar like hablar (1)
merendar (e:ie) like pensar (30)
mirar like hablar (1)
molestar like hablar (1)
montar like hablar (1)
morir (o:ue, u) like dormir (25) *except* past participle is muerto
mostrar (o:ue) like contar (24)
mudarse like hablar (1)
nacer (c:zc) like conocer (35)
nadar like hablar (1)
navegar (g:gu) like llegar (41)
necesitar like hablar (1)
negar (e:ie) like pensar (30) *except* (g:gu)
nevar (e:ie) like pensar (30)
obedecer (c:zc) like conocer (35)
obtener (e:ie) like tener (20)
ocurrir like vivir (3)
odiar like hablar (1)
ofrecer (c:zc) like conocer (35)
oír (13)
olvidar like hablar (1)
pagar (g:gu) like llegar (41)
parar like hablar (1)
parecer (c:zc) like conocer (35)

pasar like hablar (1)
pasear like hablar (1)
patinar like hablar (1)
pedir (e:i) (29)
peinarse like hablar (1)
pensar (e:ie) (30)
perder (e:ie) like entender (27)
pescar (c:qu) like tocar (43)
pintar like hablar (1)
planchar like hablar (1)
poder (o:ue) (14)
poner(se) (15)
practicar (c:qu) like tocar (43)
preferir (e:ie) like sentir (33)
preguntar like hablar (1)
prender like comer (2)
preocuparse like hablar (1)
preparar like hablar (1)
presentar like hablar (1)
prestar like hablar (1)
probar(se) (o:ue) like contar (24)
prohibir (prohíbo) like vivir (3)
proteger (g:j) (42)
publicar (c:qu) like tocar (43)
quedar(se) like hablar (1)
querer (e:ie) (16)
quitar(se) like hablar (1)
recetar like hablar (1)
recibir like vivir (3)
reciclar like hablar (1)
recoger (g:j) like proteger (42)
recomendar (e:ie) like pensar (30)
recordar (o:ue) like contar (24)
reducir (c:zc) like conducir (6)
regalar like hablar (1)
regatear like hablar (1)
regresar like hablar (1)
reír(se) (e:i) (31)
relajarse like hablar (1)
renunciar like hablar (1)
repetir (e:i) like pedir (29)
resolver (o:ue) like volver (34)
respirar like hablar (1)
revisar like hablar (1)

rogar (o:ue) like contar (24) *except* (g:gu)
romper(se) like comer (2) *except* past participle is roto
saber (17)
sacar (c:qu) like tocar (43)
sacudir like vivir (3)
salir (18)
saludar(se) like hablar (1)
secar(se) (c:qu) like tocar (43)
seguir (e:i) (32)
sentarse (e:ie) like pensar (30)
sentir(se) (e:ie) (33)
separarse like hablar (1)
ser (19)
servir (e:i) like pedir (29)
solicitar like hablar (1)
sonar (o:ue) like contar (24)
sonreír (e:i) like reír(se) (31)
sorprender like comer (2)
subir like vivir (3)
sudar like hablar (1)
sufrir like vivir (3)
sugerir (e:ie) like sentir (33)
suponer like poner (15)
temer like comer (2)
tener (e:ie) (20)
terminar like hablar (1)
tocar (c:qu) (43)
tomar like hablar (1)
torcerse (o:ue) like volver (34) *except* (c:z) and past participle is regular; e.g., yo tuerzo
toser like comer (2)
trabajar like hablar (1)
traducir (c:zc) like conducir (6)
traer (21)
transmitir like vivir (3)
tratar like hablar (1)
usar like hablar (1)
vender like comer (2)
venir (e:ie) (22)
ver (23)
vestirse (e:i) like pedir (29)
viajar like hablar (1)
visitar like hablar (1)
vivir (3)
volver (o:ue) (34)
votar like hablar (1)

Regular verbs: simple tenses

	INDICATIVE						SUBJUNCTIVE		IMPERATIVE
Infinitive	**Present**	**Imperfect**	**Preterite**	**Future**	**Conditional**		**Present**	**Past**	
1 hablar	hablo	hablaba	hablé	hablaré	hablaría		hable	hablara	
	hablas	hablabas	hablaste	hablarás	hablarías		hables	hablaras	habla tú (no hables)
	habla	hablaba	habló	hablará	hablaría		hable	hablara	hable Ud.
Participles:	hablamos	hablábamos	hablamos	hablaremos	hablaríamos		hablemos	habláramos	hablemos
hablando	habláis	hablabais	hablasteis	hablaréis	hablaríais		habléis	hablarais	hablad (no habléis)
hablado	hablan	hablaban	hablaron	hablarán	hablarían		hablen	hablaran	hablen Uds.
2 comer	como	comía	comí	comeré	comería		coma	comiera	
	comes	comías	comiste	comerás	comerías		comas	comieras	come tú (no comas)
	come	comía	comió	comerá	comería		coma	comiera	coma Ud.
Participles:	comemos	comíamos	comimos	comeremos	comeríamos		comamos	comiéramos	comamos
comiendo	coméis	comíais	comisteis	comeréis	comeríais		comáis	comierais	comed (no comáis)
comido	comen	comían	comieron	comerán	comerían		coman	comieran	coman Uds.
3 vivir	vivo	vivía	viví	viviré	viviría		viva	viviera	
	vives	vivías	viviste	vivirás	vivirías		vivas	vivieras	vive tú (no vivas)
	vive	vivía	vivió	vivirá	viviría		viva	viviera	viva Ud.
Participles:	vivimos	vivíamos	vivimos	viviremos	viviríamos		vivamos	viviéramos	vivamos
viviendo	vivís	vivíais	vivisteis	viviréis	viviríais		viváis	vivierais	vivid (no viváis)
vivido	viven	vivían	vivieron	vivirán	vivirían		vivan	vivieran	vivan Uds.

All verbs: compound tenses

PERFECT TENSES

INDICATIVE

Present Perfect		Past Perfect		Future Perfect		Conditional Perfect	
he	hablado	había	hablado	habré	hablado	habría	hablado
has	comido	habías	comido	habrás	comido	habrías	comido
ha	vivido	había	vivido	habrá	vivido	habría	vivido
hemos		habíamos		habremos		habríamos	
habéis		habíais		habréis		habríais	
han		habían		habrán		habrían	

SUBJUNCTIVE

Present Perfect		Past Perfect	
haya	hablado	hubiera	hablado
hayas	comido	hubieras	comido
haya	vivido	hubiera	vivido
hayamos		hubiéramos	
hayáis		hubierais	
hayan		hubieran	

PROGRESSIVE TENSES

	INDICATIVE				SUBJUNCTIVE	
	Present Progressive	Past Progressive	Future Progressive	Conditional Progressive	Present Progressive	Past Progressive
	estoy	estaba	estaré	estaría	esté	estuviera
	estás	estabas	estarás	estarías	estés	estuvieras
	está hablando	estaba hablando	estará hablando	estaría hablando	esté hablando	estuviera hablando
	estamos comiendo	estábamos comiendo	estaremos comiendo	estaríamos comiendo	estemos comiendo	estuviéramos comiendo
	estáis viviendo	estabais viviendo	estaréis viviendo	estaríais viviendo	estéis viviendo	estuvierais viviendo
	están	estaban	estarán	estarían	estén	estuvieran

Irregular verbs

Infinitive	INDICATIVE					SUBJUNCTIVE		IMPERATIVE
	Present	Imperfect	Preterite	Future	Conditional	Present	Past	
caber	**quepo**	cabía	**cupe**	**cabré**	**cabría**	**quepa**	**cupiera**	
	cabes	cabías	**cupiste**	**cabrás**	**cabrías**	**quepas**	**cupieras**	cabe tú (no **quepas**)
Participles:	cabe	cabía	**cupo**	**cabrá**	**cabría**	**quepa**	**cupiera**	**quepa** Ud.
cabiendo	cabemos	cabíamos	**cupimos**	**cabremos**	**cabríamos**	**quepamos**	**cupiéramos**	**quepamos**
cabido	cabéis	cabíais	**cupisteis**	**cabréis**	**cabríais**	**quepáis**	**cupierais**	cabed (no **quepáis**)
	caben	cabían	**cupieron**	**cabrán**	**cabrían**	**quepan**	**cupieran**	**quepan** Uds.
caer(se)	**caigo**	caía	caí	caeré	caería	**caiga**	**cayera**	
	caes	caías	**caíste**	caerás	caerías	**caigas**	**cayeras**	cae tú (no **caigas**)
Participles:	cae	caía	**cayó**	caerá	caería	**caiga**	**cayera**	**caiga** Ud.
cayendo	caemos	caíamos	**caímos**	caeremos	caeríamos	**caigamos**	**cayéramos**	**caigamos**
caído	caéis	caíais	**caísteis**	caeréis	caeríais	**caigáis**	**cayerais**	caed (no **caigáis**)
	caen	caían	**cayeron**	caerán	caerían	**caigan**	**cayeran**	**caigan** Uds.
conducir	**conduzco**	conducía	**conduje**	conduciré	conduciría	**conduzca**	**condujera**	
(c:zc)	conduces	conducías	**condujiste**	conducirás	conducirías	**conduzcas**	**condujeras**	conduce tú (no **conduzcas**)
	conduce	conducía	**condujo**	conducirá	conduciría	**conduzca**	**condujera**	**conduzca** Ud.
Participles:	conducimos	conducíamos	**condujimos**	conduciremos	conduciríamos	**conduzcamos**	**condujéramos**	**conduzcamos**
conduciendo	conducís	conducíais	**condujisteis**	conduciréis	conduciríais	**conduzcáis**	**condujerais**	conducid (no **conduzcáis**)
conducido	conducen	conducían	**condujeron**	conducirán	conducirían	**conduzcan**	**condujeran**	**conduzcan** Uds.

4

5

6

Verb tables

7. dar
Participles: dando, dado

	INDICATIVE					SUBJUNCTIVE		IMPERATIVE
	Present	Imperfect	Preterite	Future	Conditional	Present	Past	
	doy	daba	di	daré	daría	dé	diera	
	das	dabas	diste	darás	darías	des	dieras	da tú (no des)
	da	daba	dio	dará	daría	dé	diera	dé Ud.
	damos	dábamos	dimos	daremos	daríamos	demos	diéramos	demos
	dais	dabais	disteis	daréis	daríais	deis	dierais	dad (no deis)
	dan	daban	dieron	darán	darían	den	dieran	den Uds.

8. decir (e:i)
Participles: diciendo, dicho

	INDICATIVE					SUBJUNCTIVE		IMPERATIVE
	Present	Imperfect	Preterite	Future	Conditional	Present	Past	
	digo	decía	dije	diré	diría	diga	dijera	
	dices	decías	dijiste	dirás	dirías	digas	dijeras	di tú (no digas)
	dice	decía	dijo	dirá	diría	diga	dijera	diga Ud.
	decimos	decíamos	dijimos	diremos	diríamos	digamos	dijéramos	digamos
	decís	decíais	dijisteis	diréis	diríais	digáis	dijerais	decid (no digáis)
	dicen	decían	dijeron	dirán	dirían	digan	dijeran	digan Uds.

9. estar
Participles: estando, estado

	INDICATIVE					SUBJUNCTIVE		IMPERATIVE
	Present	Imperfect	Preterite	Future	Conditional	Present	Past	
	estoy	estaba	estuve	estaré	estaría	esté	estuviera	
	estás	estabas	estuviste	estarás	estarías	estés	estuvieras	está tú (no estés)
	está	estaba	estuvo	estará	estaría	esté	estuviera	esté Ud.
	estamos	estábamos	estuvimos	estaremos	estaríamos	estemos	estuviéramos	estemos
	estáis	estabais	estuvisteis	estaréis	estaríais	estéis	estuvierais	estad (no estéis)
	están	estaban	estuvieron	estarán	estarían	estén	estuvieran	estén Uds.

10. haber
Participles: habiendo, habido

	INDICATIVE					SUBJUNCTIVE		IMPERATIVE
	Present	Imperfect	Preterite	Future	Conditional	Present	Past	
	he	había	hube	habré	habría	haya	hubiera	
	has	habías	hubiste	habrás	habrías	hayas	hubieras	
	ha	había	hubo	habrá	habría	haya	hubiera	
	hemos	habíamos	hubimos	habremos	habríamos	hayamos	hubiéramos	
	habéis	habíais	hubisteis	habréis	habríais	hayáis	hubierais	
	han	habían	hubieron	habrán	habrían	hayan	hubieran	

11. hacer
Participles: haciendo, hecho

	INDICATIVE					SUBJUNCTIVE		IMPERATIVE
	Present	Imperfect	Preterite	Future	Conditional	Present	Past	
	hago	hacía	hice	haré	haría	haga	hiciera	
	haces	hacías	hiciste	harás	harías	hagas	hicieras	haz tú (no hagas)
	hace	hacía	hizo	hará	haría	haga	hiciera	haga Ud.
	hacemos	hacíamos	hicimos	haremos	haríamos	hagamos	hiciéramos	hagamos
	hacéis	hacíais	hicisteis	haréis	haríais	hagáis	hicierais	haced (no hagáis)
	hacen	hacían	hicieron	harán	harían	hagan	hicieran	hagan Uds.

12. ir
Participles: yendo, ido

	INDICATIVE					SUBJUNCTIVE		IMPERATIVE
	Present	Imperfect	Preterite	Future	Conditional	Present	Past	
	voy	iba	fui	iré	iría	vaya	fuera	
	vas	ibas	fuiste	irás	irías	vayas	fueras	ve tú (no vayas)
	va	iba	fue	irá	iría	vaya	fuera	vaya Ud.
	vamos	íbamos	fuimos	iremos	iríamos	vayamos	fuéramos	vamos
	vais	ibais	fuisteis	iréis	iríais	vayáis	fuerais	id (no vayáis)
	van	iban	fueron	irán	irían	vayan	fueran	vayan Uds.

13. oír (y)
Participles: oyendo, oído

	INDICATIVE					SUBJUNCTIVE		IMPERATIVE
	Present	Imperfect	Preterite	Future	Conditional	Present	Past	
	oigo	oía	oí	oiré	oiría	oiga	oyera	
	oyes	oías	oíste	oirás	oirías	oigas	oyeras	oye tú (no oigas)
	oye	oía	oyó	oirá	oiría	oiga	oyera	oiga Ud.
	oímos	oíamos	oímos	oiremos	oiríamos	oigamos	oyéramos	oigamos
	oís	oíais	oísteis	oiréis	oiríais	oigáis	oyerais	oíd (no oigáis)
	oyen	oían	oyeron	oirán	oirían	oigan	oyeran	oigan Uds.

14 poder (o:ue) — Participles: **pudiendo**, podido

	INDICATIVE					SUBJUNCTIVE		IMPERATIVE
	Present	Imperfect	Preterite	Future	Conditional	Present	Past	
	puedo	podía	**pude**	**podré**	**podría**	**pueda**	**pudiera**	
	puedes	podías	**pudiste**	**podrás**	**podrías**	**puedas**	**pudieras**	**puede** tú (no **puedas**)
	puede	podía	**pudo**	**podrá**	**podría**	**pueda**	**pudiera**	**pueda** Ud.
	podemos	podíamos	**pudimos**	**podremos**	**podríamos**	podamos	**pudiéramos**	podamos
	podéis	podíais	**pudisteis**	**podréis**	**podríais**	podáis	**pudierais**	poded (no podáis)
	pueden	podían	**pudieron**	**podrán**	**podrían**	**puedan**	**pudieran**	**puedan** Uds.

15 poner — Participles: poniendo, **puesto**

	INDICATIVE					SUBJUNCTIVE		IMPERATIVE
	Present	Imperfect	Preterite	Future	Conditional	Present	Past	
	pongo	ponía	**puse**	**pondré**	**pondría**	**ponga**	**pusiera**	
	pones	ponías	**pusiste**	**pondrás**	**pondrías**	**pongas**	**pusieras**	**pon** tú (no **pongas**)
	pone	ponía	**puso**	**pondrá**	**pondría**	**ponga**	**pusiera**	**ponga** Ud.
	ponemos	poníamos	**pusimos**	**pondremos**	**pondríamos**	**pongamos**	**pusiéramos**	**pongamos**
	ponéis	poníais	**pusisteis**	**pondréis**	**pondríais**	**pongáis**	**pusierais**	poned (no **pongáis**)
	ponen	ponían	**pusieron**	**pondrán**	**pondrían**	**pongan**	**pusieran**	**pongan** Uds.

16 querer (e:ie) — Participles: queriendo, querido

	INDICATIVE					SUBJUNCTIVE		IMPERATIVE
	Present	Imperfect	Preterite	Future	Conditional	Present	Past	
	quiero	quería	**quise**	**querré**	**querría**	**quiera**	**quisiera**	
	quieres	querías	**quisiste**	**querrás**	**querrías**	**quieras**	**quisieras**	**quiere** tú (no **quieras**)
	quiere	quería	**quiso**	**querrá**	**querría**	**quiera**	**quisiera**	**quiera** Ud.
	queremos	queríamos	**quisimos**	**querremos**	**querríamos**	queramos	**quisiéramos**	**queramos**
	queréis	queríais	**quisisteis**	**querréis**	**querríais**	queráis	**quisierais**	quered (no queráis)
	quieren	querían	**quisieron**	**querrán**	**querrían**	**quieran**	**quisieran**	**quieran** Uds.

17 saber — Participles: sabiendo, sabido

	INDICATIVE					SUBJUNCTIVE		IMPERATIVE
	Present	Imperfect	Preterite	Future	Conditional	Present	Past	
	sé	sabía	**supe**	**sabré**	**sabría**	**sepa**	**supiera**	
	sabes	sabías	**supiste**	**sabrás**	**sabrías**	**sepas**	**supieras**	sabe tú (no **sepas**)
	sabe	sabía	**supo**	**sabrá**	**sabría**	**sepa**	**supiera**	**sepa** Ud.
	sabemos	sabíamos	**supimos**	**sabremos**	**sabríamos**	**sepamos**	**supiéramos**	**sepamos**
	sabéis	sabíais	**supisteis**	**sabréis**	**sabríais**	**sepáis**	**supierais**	sabed (no **sepáis**)
	saben	sabían	**supieron**	**sabrán**	**sabrían**	**sepan**	**supieran**	**sepan** Uds.

18 salir — Participles: saliendo, salido

	INDICATIVE					SUBJUNCTIVE		IMPERATIVE
	Present	Imperfect	Preterite	Future	Conditional	Present	Past	
	salgo	salía	salí	**saldré**	**saldría**	**salga**	saliera	
	sales	salías	saliste	**saldrás**	**saldrías**	**salgas**	salieras	**sal** tú (no **salgas**)
	sale	salía	salió	**saldrá**	**saldría**	**salga**	saliera	**salga** Ud.
	salimos	salíamos	salimos	**saldremos**	**saldríamos**	**salgamos**	saliéramos	**salgamos**
	salís	salíais	salisteis	**saldréis**	**saldríais**	**salgáis**	salierais	salid (no **salgáis**)
	salen	salían	salieron	**saldrán**	**saldrían**	**salgan**	salieran	**salgan** Uds.

19 ser — Participles: siendo, sido

	INDICATIVE					SUBJUNCTIVE		IMPERATIVE
	Present	Imperfect	Preterite	Future	Conditional	Present	Past	
	soy	**era**	**fui**	seré	sería	**sea**	**fuera**	
	eres	**eras**	**fuiste**	serás	serías	**seas**	**fueras**	**sé** tú (no **seas**)
	es	**era**	**fue**	será	sería	**sea**	**fuera**	**sea** Ud.
	somos	**éramos**	**fuimos**	seremos	seríamos	**seamos**	**fuéramos**	**seamos**
	sois	**erais**	**fuisteis**	seréis	seríais	**seáis**	**fuerais**	sed (no **seáis**)
	son	**eran**	**fueron**	serán	serían	**sean**	**fueran**	**sean** Uds.

20 tener (e:ie) — Participles: teniendo, tenido

	INDICATIVE					SUBJUNCTIVE		IMPERATIVE
	Present	Imperfect	Preterite	Future	Conditional	Present	Past	
	tengo	tenía	**tuve**	**tendré**	**tendría**	**tenga**	**tuviera**	
	tienes	tenías	**tuviste**	**tendrás**	**tendrías**	**tengas**	**tuvieras**	**ten** tú (no **tengas**)
	tiene	tenía	**tuvo**	**tendrá**	**tendría**	**tenga**	**tuviera**	**tenga** Ud.
	tenemos	teníamos	**tuvimos**	**tendremos**	**tendríamos**	**tengamos**	**tuviéramos**	**tengamos**
	tenéis	teníais	**tuvisteis**	**tendréis**	**tendríais**	**tengáis**	**tuvierais**	tened (no **tengáis**)
	tienen	tenían	**tuvieron**	**tendrán**	**tendrían**	**tengan**	**tuvieran**	**tengan** Uds.

21 — traer

Participles: **trayendo**, **traído**

	INDICATIVE					SUBJUNCTIVE		IMPERATIVE
	Present	Imperfect	Preterite	Future	Conditional	Present	Past	
	traigo	traía	**traje**	traeré	traería	**traiga**	**trajera**	
	traes	traías	**trajiste**	traerás	traerías	**traigas**	**trajeras**	trae tú (no **traigas**)
	trae	traía	**trajo**	traerá	traería	**traiga**	**trajera**	**traiga** Ud.
	traemos	traíamos	**trajimos**	traeremos	traeríamos	**traigamos**	**trajéramos**	**traigamos**
	traéis	traíais	**trajisteis**	traeréis	traeríais	**traigáis**	**trajerais**	traed (no **traigáis**)
	traen	traían	**trajeron**	traerán	traerían	**traigan**	**trajeran**	**traigan** Uds.

22 — venir (e:ie)

Participles: **viniendo**, venido

	INDICATIVE					SUBJUNCTIVE		IMPERATIVE
	Present	Imperfect	Preterite	Future	Conditional	Present	Past	
	vengo	venía	**vine**	**vendré**	**vendría**	**venga**	**viniera**	
	vienes	venías	**viniste**	**vendrás**	**vendrías**	**vengas**	**vinieras**	**ven** tú (no **vengas**)
	viene	venía	**vino**	**vendrá**	**vendría**	**venga**	**viniera**	**venga** Ud.
	venimos	veníamos	**vinimos**	**vendremos**	**vendríamos**	**vengamos**	**viniéramos**	**vengamos**
	venís	veníais	**vinisteis**	**vendréis**	**vendríais**	**vengáis**	**vinierais**	venid (no **vengáis**)
	vienen	venían	**vinieron**	**vendrán**	**vendrían**	**vengan**	**vinieran**	**vengan** Uds.

23 — ver

Participles: **viendo**, **visto**

	INDICATIVE					SUBJUNCTIVE		IMPERATIVE
	Present	Imperfect	Preterite	Future	Conditional	Present	Past	
	veo	**veía**	**vi**	veré	vería	**vea**	**viera**	
	ves	**veías**	**viste**	verás	verías	**veas**	**vieras**	**ve** tú (no **veas**)
	ve	**veía**	**vio**	verá	vería	**vea**	**viera**	**vea** Ud.
	vemos	**veíamos**	**vimos**	veremos	veríamos	**veamos**	**viéramos**	**veamos**
	veis	**veíais**	**visteis**	veréis	veríais	**veáis**	**vierais**	ved (no **veáis**)
	ven	**veían**	**vieron**	verán	verían	**vean**	**vieran**	**vean** Uds.

Stem-changing verbs

24 — contar (o:ue)

Participles: contando, contado

	INDICATIVE					SUBJUNCTIVE		IMPERATIVE
	Present	Imperfect	Preterite	Future	Conditional	Present	Past	
	cuento	contaba	conté	contaré	contaría	**cuente**	cortara	
	cuentas	contabas	contaste	contarás	contarías	**cuentes**	contaras	**cuenta** tú (no **cuentes**)
	cuenta	contaba	contó	contará	contaría	**cuente**	contara	**cuente** Ud.
	contamos	contábamos	contamos	contaremos	contaríamos	contemos	contáramos	contemos
	contáis	contabais	contasteis	contaréis	contaríais	contéis	contarais	contad (no contéis)
	cuentan	contaban	contaron	contarán	contarían	**cuenten**	contaran	**cuenten** Uds.

25 — dormir (o:ue)

Participles: **durmiendo**, dormido

	INDICATIVE					SUBJUNCTIVE		IMPERATIVE
	Present	Imperfect	Preterite	Future	Conditional	Present	Past	
	duermo	dormía	dormí	dormiré	dormiría	**duerma**	**durmiera**	
	duermes	dormías	dormiste	dormirás	dormirías	**duermas**	**durmieras**	**duerme** tú (no **duermas**)
	duerme	dormía	**durmió**	dormirá	dormiría	**duerma**	**durmiera**	**duerma** Ud.
	dormimos	dormíamos	dormimos	dormiremos	dormiríamos	**durmamos**	**durmiéramos**	**durmamos**
	dormís	dormíais	dormisteis	dormiréis	dormiríais	**durmáis**	**durmierais**	dormid (no **durmáis**)
	duermen	dormían	**durmieron**	dormirán	dormirían	**duerman**	**durmieran**	**duerman** Uds.

26 — empezar (e:ie) (z:c)

Participles: empezando, empezado

	INDICATIVE					SUBJUNCTIVE		IMPERATIVE
	Present	Imperfect	Preterite	Future	Conditional	Present	Past	
	empiezo	empezaba	**empecé**	empezaré	empezaría	**empiece**	empezara	
	empiezas	empezabas	empezaste	empezarás	empezarías	**empieces**	empezaras	**empieza** tú (no **empieces**)
	empieza	empezaba	empezó	empezará	empezaría	**empiece**	empezara	**empiece** Ud.
	empezamos	empezábamos	empezamos	empezaremos	empezaríamos	**empecemos**	empezáramos	**empecemos**
	empezáis	empezabais	empezasteis	empezaréis	empezaríais	**empecéis**	empezarais	empezad (no **empecéis**)
	empiezan	empezaban	empezaron	empezarán	empezarían	**empiecen**	empezaran	**empiecen** Uds.

Verb tables

27. entender (e:ie) — Participles: entendiendo, entendido

	INDICATIVE					SUBJUNCTIVE		IMPERATIVE
	Present	Imperfect	Preterite	Future	Conditional	Present	Past	
	entiendo	entendía	entendí	entenderé	entendería	entienda	entendiera	
	entiendes	entendías	entendiste	entenderás	entenderías	entiendas	entendieras	entiende tú (no entiendas)
	entiende	entendía	entendió	entenderá	entendería	entienda	entendiera	entienda Ud.
	entendemos	entendíamos	entendimos	entenderemos	entenderíamos	entendamos	entendiéramos	entendamos
	entendéis	entendíais	entendisteis	entenderéis	entenderíais	entendáis	entendierais	entended (no entendáis)
	entienden	entendían	entendieron	entenderán	entenderían	entiendan	entendieran	entiendan Uds.

28. jugar (u:ue) (g:gu) — Participles: jugando, jugado

	INDICATIVE					SUBJUNCTIVE		IMPERATIVE
	Present	Imperfect	Preterite	Future	Conditional	Present	Past	
	juego	jugaba	jugué	jugaré	jugaría	juegue	jugara	
	juegas	jugabas	jugaste	jugarás	jugarías	juegues	jugaras	juega tú (no juegues)
	juega	jugaba	jugó	jugará	jugaría	juegue	jugara	juegue Ud.
	jugamos	jugábamos	jugamos	jugaremos	jugaríamos	juguemos	jugáramos	juguemos
	jugáis	jugabais	jugasteis	jugaréis	jugaríais	juguéis	jugarais	jugad (no juguéis)
	juegan	jugaban	jugaron	jugarán	jugarían	jueguen	jugaran	jueguen Uds.

29. pedir (e:i) — Participles: pidiendo, pedido

	INDICATIVE					SUBJUNCTIVE		IMPERATIVE
	Present	Imperfect	Preterite	Future	Conditional	Present	Past	
	pido	pedía	pedí	pediré	pediría	pida	pidiera	
	pides	pedías	pediste	pedirás	pedirías	pidas	pidieras	pide tú (no pidas)
	pide	pedía	pidió	pedirá	pediría	pida	pidiera	pida Ud.
	pedimos	pedíamos	pedimos	pediremos	pediríamos	pidamos	pidiéramos	pidamos
	pedís	pedíais	pedisteis	pediréis	pediríais	pidáis	pidierais	pedid (no pidáis)
	piden	pedían	pidieron	pedirán	pedirían	pidan	pidieran	pidan Uds.

30. pensar (e:ie) — Participles: pensando, pensado

	INDICATIVE					SUBJUNCTIVE		IMPERATIVE
	Present	Imperfect	Preterite	Future	Conditional	Present	Past	
	pienso	pensaba	pensé	pensaré	pensaría	piense	pensara	
	piensas	pensabas	pensaste	pensarás	pensarías	pienses	pensaras	piensa tú (no pienses)
	piensa	pensaba	pensó	pensará	pensaría	piense	pensara	piense Ud.
	pensamos	pensábamos	pensamos	pensaremos	pensaríamos	pensemos	pensáramos	pensemos
	pensáis	pensabais	pensasteis	pensaréis	pensaríais	penséis	pensarais	pensad (no penséis)
	piensan	pensaban	pensaron	pensarán	pensarían	piensen	pensaran	piensen Uds.

31. reír(se) (e:i) — Participles: riendo, reído

	INDICATIVE					SUBJUNCTIVE		IMPERATIVE
	Present	Imperfect	Preterite	Future	Conditional	Present	Past	
	río	reía	reí	reiré	reiría	ría	riera	
	ríes	reías	reíste	reirás	reirías	rías	rieras	ríe tú (no rías)
	ríe	reía	rió	reirá	reiría	ría	riera	ría Ud.
	reímos	reíamos	reímos	reiremos	reiríamos	riamos	riéramos	riamos
	reís	reíais	reísteis	reiréis	reiríais	riáis	rierais	reíd (no riáis)
	ríen	reían	rieron	reirán	reirían	rían	rieran	rían Uds.

32. seguir (e:i) (gu:g) — Participles: siguiendo, seguido

	INDICATIVE					SUBJUNCTIVE		IMPERATIVE
	Present	Imperfect	Preterite	Future	Conditional	Present	Past	
	sigo	seguía	seguí	seguiré	seguiría	siga	siguiera	
	sigues	seguías	seguiste	seguirás	seguirías	sigas	siguieras	sigue tú (no sigas)
	sigue	seguía	siguió	seguirá	seguiría	siga	siguiera	siga Ud.
	seguimos	seguíamos	seguimos	seguiremos	seguiríamos	sigamos	siguiéramos	sigamos
	seguís	seguíais	seguisteis	seguiréis	seguiríais	sigáis	siguierais	seguid (no sigáis)
	siguen	seguían	siguieron	seguirán	seguirían	sigan	siguieran	sigan Uds.

33. sentir (e:ie) — Participles: sintiendo, sentido

	INDICATIVE					SUBJUNCTIVE		IMPERATIVE
	Present	Imperfect	Preterite	Future	Conditional	Present	Past	
	siento	sentía	sentí	sentiré	sentiría	sienta	sintiera	
	sientes	sentías	sentiste	sentirás	sentirías	sientas	sintieras	siente tú (no sientas)
	siente	sentía	sintió	sentirá	sentiría	sienta	sintiera	sienta Ud.
	sentimos	sentíamos	sentimos	sentiremos	sentiríamos	sintamos	sintiéramos	sintamos
	sentís	sentíais	sentisteis	sentiréis	sentiríais	sintáis	sintierais	sentid (no sintáis)
	sienten	sentían	sintieron	sentirán	sentirían	sientan	sintieran	sientan Uds.

34 — volver (o:ue)

Participles: volviendo, **vuelto**

	INDICATIVE Present	Imperfect	Preterite	Future	Conditional	SUBJUNCTIVE Present	Past	IMPERATIVE
	vuelvo	volvía	volví	volveré	volvería	**vuelva**	volviera	
	vuelves	volvías	volviste	volverás	volverías	**vuelvas**	volvieras	**vuelve** tú (no **vuelvas**)
	vuelve	volvía	volvió	volverá	volvería	**vuelva**	volviera	**vuelva** Ud.
	volvemos	volvíamos	volvimos	volveremos	volveríamos	volvamos	volviéramos	volvamos
	volvéis	volvíais	volvisteis	volveréis	volveríais	volváis	volvierais	volved (no volváis)
	vuelven	volvían	volvieron	volverán	volverían	**vuelvan**	volvieran	**vuelvan** Uds.

Verbs with spelling changes only

35 — conocer (c:zc)

Participles: conociendo, conocido

	INDICATIVE Present	Imperfect	Preterite	Future	Conditional	SUBJUNCTIVE Present	Past	IMPERATIVE
	conozco	conocía	conocí	conoceré	conocería	**conozca**	conociera	
	conoces	conocías	conociste	conocerás	conocerías	**conozcas**	conocieras	conoce tú (no **conozcas**)
	conoce	conocía	conoció	conocerá	conocería	**conozca**	conociera	**conozca** Ud.
	conocemos	conocíamos	conocimos	conoceremos	conoceríamos	**conozcamos**	conociéramos	**conozcamos**
	conocéis	conocíais	conocisteis	conoceréis	conoceríais	**conozcáis**	conocierais	conoced (no **conozcáis**)
	conocen	conocían	conocieron	conocerán	conocerían	**conozcan**	conocieran	**conozcan** Uds.

36 — creer (y)

Participles: **creyendo**, **creído**

	INDICATIVE Present	Imperfect	Preterite	Future	Conditional	SUBJUNCTIVE Present	Past	IMPERATIVE
	creo	creía	**creí**	creeré	creería	crea	**creyera**	
	crees	creías	**creíste**	creerás	creerías	creas	**creyeras**	cree tú (no creas)
	cree	creía	**creyó**	creerá	creería	crea	**creyera**	crea Ud.
	creemos	creíamos	**creímos**	creeremos	creeríamos	creamos	**creyéramos**	creamos
	creéis	creíais	**creísteis**	creeréis	creeríais	creáis	**creyerais**	creed (no creáis)
	creen	creían	**creyeron**	creerán	creerían	crean	**creyeran**	crean Uds.

37 — cruzar (z:c)

Participles: cruzando, cruzado

	INDICATIVE Present	Imperfect	Preterite	Future	Conditional	SUBJUNCTIVE Present	Past	IMPERATIVE
	cruzo	cruzaba	**crucé**	cruzaré	cruzaría	**cruce**	cruzara	
	cruzas	cruzabas	cruzaste	cruzarás	cruzarías	**cruces**	cruzaras	cruza tú (no **cruces**)
	cruza	cruzaba	cruzó	cruzará	cruzaría	**cruce**	cruzara	**cruce** Ud.
	cruzamos	cruzábamos	cruzamos	cruzaremos	cruzaríamos	**crucemos**	cruzáramos	**crucemos**
	cruzáis	cruzabais	cruzasteis	cruzaréis	cruzaríais	**crucéis**	cruzarais	cruzad (no **crucéis**)
	cruzan	cruzaban	cruzaron	cruzarán	cruzarían	**crucen**	cruzaran	**crucen** Uds.

38 — destruir (y)

Participles: **destruyendo**, destruido

	INDICATIVE Present	Imperfect	Preterite	Future	Conditional	SUBJUNCTIVE Present	Past	IMPERATIVE
	destruyo	destruía	destruí	destruiré	destruiría	**destruya**	**destruyera**	
	destruyes	destruías	destruiste	destruirás	destruirías	**destruyas**	**destruyeras**	**destruye** tú (no **destruyas**)
	destruye	destruía	**destruyó**	destruirá	destruiría	**destruya**	**destruyera**	**destruya** Ud.
	destruimos	destruíamos	destruimos	destruiremos	destruiríamos	**destruyamos**	**destruyéramos**	**destruyamos**
	destruís	destruíais	destruisteis	destruiréis	destruiríais	**destruyáis**	**destruyerais**	destruid (no **destruyáis**)
	destruyen	destruían	**destruyeron**	destruirán	destruirían	**destruyan**	**destruyeran**	**destruyan** Uds.

39 — enviar (envío)

Participles: enviando, enviado

	INDICATIVE Present	Imperfect	Preterite	Future	Conditional	SUBJUNCTIVE Present	Past	IMPERATIVE
	envío	enviaba	envié	enviaré	enviaría	**envíe**	enviara	
	envías	enviabas	enviaste	enviarás	enviarías	**envíes**	enviaras	**envía** tú (no **envíes**)
	envía	enviaba	envió	enviará	enviaría	**envíe**	enviara	**envíe** Ud.
	enviamos	enviábamos	enviamos	enviaremos	enviaríamos	**enviemos**	enviáramos	enviemos
	enviáis	enviabais	enviasteis	enviaréis	enviaríais	**enviéis**	enviarais	enviad (no **enviéis**)
	envían	enviaban	enviaron	enviarán	enviarían	**envíen**	enviaran	**envíen** Uds.

Verb tables

40. graduarse (gradúo)
Participles: graduando, graduado

	INDICATIVE					SUBJUNCTIVE		IMPERATIVE
	Present	Imperfect	Preterite	Future	Conditional	Present	Past	
	gradúo	graduaba	gradué	graduaré	graduaría	gradúe	graduara	
	gradúas	graduabas	graduaste	graduarás	graduarías	gradúes	graduaras	gradúa tú (no gradúes)
	gradúa	graduaba	graduó	graduará	graduaría	gradúe	graduara	gradúe Ud.
	graduamos	graduábamos	graduamos	graduaremos	graduaríamos	graduemos	graduáramos	graduemos
	graduáis	graduabais	graduasteis	graduaréis	graduaríais	graduéis	graduarais	graduad (no graduéis)
	gradúan	graduaban	graduaron	graduarán	graduarían	gradúen	graduaran	gradúen Uds.

41. llegar (g:gu)
Participles: llegando, llegado

	INDICATIVE					SUBJUNCTIVE		IMPERATIVE
	Present	Imperfect	Preterite	Future	Conditional	Present	Past	
	llego	llegaba	llegué	llegaré	llegaría	llegue	llegara	
	llegas	llegabas	llegaste	llegarás	llegarías	llegues	llegaras	llega tú (no llegues)
	llega	llegaba	llegó	llegará	llegaría	llegue	llegara	llegue Ud.
	llegamos	llegábamos	llegamos	llegaremos	llegaríamos	lleguemos	llegáramos	lleguemos
	llegáis	llegabais	llegasteis	llegaréis	llegaríais	lleguéis	llegarais	llegad (no lleguéis)
	llegan	llegaban	llegaron	llegarán	llegarían	lleguen	llegaran	lleguen Uds.

42. proteger (g:j)
Participles: protegiendo, protegido

	INDICATIVE					SUBJUNCTIVE		IMPERATIVE
	Present	Imperfect	Preterite	Future	Conditional	Present	Past	
	protejo	protegía	protegí	protegeré	protegería	proteja	protegiera	
	proteges	protegías	protegiste	protegerás	protegerías	protejas	protegieras	protege tú (no protejas)
	protege	protegía	protegió	protegerá	protegería	proteja	protegiera	proteja Ud.
	protegemos	protegíamos	protegimos	protegeremos	protegeríamos	protejamos	protegiéramos	protejamos
	protegéis	protegíais	protegisteis	protegeréis	protegeríais	protejáis	protegierais	proteged (no protejáis)
	protegen	protegían	protegieron	protegerán	protegerían	protejan	protegieran	protejan Uds.

43. tocar (c:qu)
Participles: tocando, tocado

	INDICATIVE					SUBJUNCTIVE		IMPERATIVE
	Present	Imperfect	Preterite	Future	Conditional	Present	Past	
	toco	tocaba	toqué	tocaré	tocaría	toque	tocara	
	tocas	tocabas	tocaste	tocarás	tocarías	toques	tocaras	toca tú (no toques)
	toca	tocaba	tocó	tocará	tocaría	toque	tocara	toque Ud.
	tocamos	tocábamos	tocamos	tocaremos	tocaríamos	toquemos	tocáramos	toquemos
	tocáis	tocabais	tocasteis	tocaréis	tocaríais	toquéis	tocarais	tocad (no toquéis)
	tocan	tocaban	tocaron	tocarán	tocarían	toquen	tocaran	toquen Uds.

Guide to Vocabulary

All active vocabulary in **¡ADELANTE!** is presented in this glossary. The first number after an entry refers to the volume of **¡ADELANTE!** where the word is activated; the second refers to the lesson number.

aceite 2.2 (Activated in **¡ADELANTE! DOS**, Lección 2)

posible 3.1 (Activated in **¡ADELANTE! TRES**, Lección 1)

Note on alphabetization

For purposes of alphabetization, **ch** and **ll** are not treated as separate letters, but **ñ** follows **n**. Therefore, in this glossary you will find that **año**, for example, appears after **anuncio**.

Abbreviations used in this glossary

adj.	adjective	*form.*	formal	*pl.*	plural
adv.	adverb	*indef.*	indefinite	*poss.*	possessive
art.	article	*interj.*	interjection	*prep.*	preposition
conj.	conjunction	*i.o.*	indirect object	*pron.*	pronoun
def.	definite	*m.*	masculine	*ref.*	reflexive
d.o.	direct object	*n.*	noun	*sing.*	singular
f.	feminine	*obj.*	object	*sub.*	subject
fam.	familiar	*p.p.*	past participle	*v.*	verb

Spanish-English

A

a *prep.* at; to 1.1
  ¿A qué hora...? At what time...? 1.1
  a dieta on a diet 3.3
  a la derecha to the right 1.2
  a la izquierda to the left 1.2
  a la plancha grilled 2.2
  a la(s) + *time* at + *time* 1.1
  a menos que unless 3.1
  a menudo *adv.* often 2.4
  a nombre de in the name of 1.5
  a plazos in installments 3.4
  A sus órdenes. At your service.
  a tiempo *adv.* on time 2.4
  a veces *adv.* sometimes 2.4
  a ver let's see 1.2
¡Abajo! *adv.* Down! 3.3
abeja *f.* bee
abierto/a *adj.* open 1.5, 3.2
abogado/a *m., f.* lawyer 3.4
abrazar(se) *v.* to hug; to embrace (each other) 2.5
abrazo *m.* hug
abrigo *m.* coat 1.6
abril *m.* April 1.5
abrir *v.* to open 1.3
abuelo/a *m., f.* grandfather; grandmother 1.3
abuelos *pl.* grandparents 1.3
aburrido/a *adj.* bored; boring 1.5

aburrir *v.* to bore 2.1
aburrirse *v.* to get bored 3.5
acabar de (+ *inf.*) *v.* to have just done something 1.6
acampar *v.* to camp 1.5
accidente *m.* accident 2.4
acción *f.* action 3.5
  de acción action (genre) 3.5
aceite *m.* oil 2.2
aceptar: ¡Acepto casarme contigo! I'll marry you! 3.5
ácido/a *adj.* acid 3.1
acompañar *v.* to accompany 3.2
aconsejar *v.* to advise 2.6
acontecimiento *m.* event 3.6
acordarse (de) (o:ue) *v.* to remember 2.1
acostarse (o:ue) *v.* to go to bed 2.1
activo/a *adj.* active 3.3
actor *m.* actor 3.4
actriz *f.* actor 3.4
actualidades *f., pl.* news; current events 3.6
acuático/a *adj.* aquatic 1.4
adelgazar *v.* to lose weight; to slim down 3.3
además (de) *adv.* furthermore; besides 2.4
adicional *adj.* additional
adiós *m.* good-bye 1.1
adjetivo *m.* adjective
administración de empresas *f.* business administration 1.2
adolescencia *f.* adolescence 2.3
¿adónde? *adv.* where (to)? (destination) 1.2
aduana *f.* customs 1.5

aeróbico/a *adj.* aerobic 3.3
aeropuerto *m.* airport 1.5
afectado/a *adj.* affected 3.1
afeitarse *v.* to shave 2.1
aficionado/a *adj.* fan 1.4
afirmativo/a *adj.* affirmative
afuera *adv.* outside 1.5
afueras *f., pl.* suburbs; outskirts 2.6
agencia de viajes *f.* travel agency 1.5
agente de viajes *m., f.* travel agent 1.5
agosto *m.* August 1.5
agradable *adj.* pleasant 1.5
agua *f.* water 2.2
  agua mineral mineral water 2.2
aguantar *v.* to endure, to hold up 3.2
ahora *adv.* now 1.2
  ahora mismo right now 1.5
ahorrar *v.* to save (money) 3.2
ahorros *m.* savings 3.2
aire *m.* air 1.5
ajo *m.* garlic 2.2
al (*contraction of* **a** + **el**) 1.2
  al aire libre open-air 1.6
  al contado in cash 3.2
  (al) este (to the) east 3.2
  al fondo (de) at the end (of) 2.6
  al lado de beside 1.2
  (al) norte (to the) north 3.2
  (al) oeste (to the) west 3.2
  (al) sur (to the) south 3.2
alcoba *f.* bedroom 2.6
alcohol *m.* alcohol 3.3
alcohólico/a *adj.* alcoholic 3.3

alegrarse (de) *v.* to be happy 3.1
alegre *adj.* happy; joyful 1.5
alegría *f.* happiness 2.3
alemán, alemana *adj.* German 1.3
alérgico/a *adj.* allergic 2.4
alfombra *f.* carpet; rug 2.6
algo *pron.* something; anything 2.1
algodón *m.* cotton 1.6
alguien *pron.* someone; somebody; anyone 2.1
algún, alguno/a(s) *adj.* any; some 2.1
alimento *m.* food
   alimentación *f.* diet
aliviar *v.* to reduce 3.3
   aliviar el estrés/la tensión to reduce stress/tension 3.3
allá *adv.* over there 1.2
allí *adv.* there 1.2
   allí mismo right there 3.2
alma *f.* soul 2.3
almacén *m.* department store 1.6
almohada *f.* pillow 2.6
almorzar (o:ue) *v.* to have lunch 1.4
almuerzo *m.* lunch 2.2
aló *interj.* hello (*on the telephone*) 2.5
alquilar *v.* to rent 2.6
alquiler *m.* rent (payment) 2.6
altar *m.* altar 2.3
altillo *m.* attic 2.6
alto/a *adj.* tall 1.3
aluminio *m.* aluminum 3.1
ama de casa *m., f.* housekeeper; caretaker 2.6
amable *adj.* nice; friendly
amarillo/a *adj.* yellow 1.6
amigo/a *m., f.* friend 1.3
amistad *f.* friendship 2.3
amor *m.* love 2.3
   amor a primera vista love at first sight 2.3
anaranjado/a *adj.* orange 1.6
ándale *interj.* come on 3.2
andar *v.* **en patineta** to skateboard 1.4
ángel *m.* angel 2.3
anillo *m.* ring 3.5
animal *m.* animal 3.1
aniversario (de bodas) *m.* (wedding) anniversary 2.3
anoche *adv.* last night 1.6
anteayer *adv.* the day before yesterday 1.6
antes *adv.* before 2.1
   antes (de) que *conj.* before 3.1
   antes de *prep.* before 2.1
antibiótico *m.* antibiotic 2.4
antipático/a *adj.* unpleasant 1.3
anunciar *v.* to announce; to advertise 3.6
anuncio *m.* advertisement 3.4
año *m.* year 1.5
   año pasado last year 1.6
apagar *v.* to turn off 2.5

aparato *m.* appliance
apartamento *m.* apartment 2.6
apellido *m.* last name 1.3
apenas *adv.* hardly; scarcely 2.4
aplaudir *v.* to applaud 3.5
apreciar *v.* to appreciate 3.5
aprender (a + *inf.*) *v.* to learn 1.3
apurarse *v.* to hurry; to rush 3.3
aquel, aquella *adj.* that (over there) 1.6
aquél, aquélla *pron.* that (over there) 1.6
aquello *neuter, pron.* that; that thing; that fact 1.6
aquellos/as *pl. adj.* those (over there) 1.6
aquéllos/as *pl. pron.* those (ones) (over there) 1.6
aquí *adv.* here 1.1
   Aquí está(n)... Here is/ are... 1.5
árbol *m.* tree 3.1
archivo *m.* file 2.5
arete *m.* earring 1.6
Argentina *f.* Argentina 1.1
argentino/a *adj.* Argentine 1.3
armario *m.* closet 2.6
arqueología *f.* archaeology 1.2
arqueólogo/a *m., f.* archaeologist 3.4
arquitecto/a *m., f.* architect 3.4
arrancar *v.* to start (*a car*) 2.5
arreglar *v.* to fix; to arrange 2.5; to neaten; to straighten up 2.6
arreglarse v. to get ready 2.1; to fix oneself (*clothes, hair, etc., to go out*) 2.1
arriba: hasta arriba to the top 3.3
arroba *f.* @ symbol 2.5
arroz *m.* rice 2.2
arte *m.* art 1.2
artes *f., pl.* arts 3.5
artesanía *f.* craftsmanship; crafts 3.5
artículo *m.* article 3.6
artista *m., f.* artist 1.3
artístico/a *adj.* artistic 3.5
arveja *f.* pea 2.2
asado/a *adj.* roast 2.2
ascenso *m.* promotion 3.4
ascensor *m.* elevator 1.5
así *adv.* like this; so (*in such a way*) 2.4
asistir (a) *v.* to attend 1.3
aspiradora *f.* vacuum cleaner 2.6
aspirante *m., f.* candidate; applicant 3.4
aspirina *f.* aspirin 2.4
atún *m.* tuna 2.2
aumentar *v.* to grow; to get bigger 3.1
aumentar *v.* **de peso** to gain weight 3.3
aumento *m.* increase 3.4
   aumento de sueldo pay raise 3.4

aunque although
autobús *m.* bus 1.1
automático/a *adj.* automatic
auto(móvil) *m.* auto(mobile) 1.5
autopista *f.* highway 2.5
ave *f.* bird 3.1
avenida *f.* avenue
aventura *f.* adventure 3.5
   de aventura adventure (genre) 3.5
avergonzado/a *adj.* embarrassed 1.5
avión *m.* airplane 1.5
¡Ay! *interj.* Oh!
   ¡Ay, qué dolor! Oh, what pain!
ayer *adv.* yesterday 1.6
ayudar(se) *v.* to help (each other) 2.5, 2.6
azúcar *m.* sugar 2.2
azul *adj. m., f.* blue 1.6

B

bailar *v.* to dance 1.2
bailarín/bailarina *m., f.* dancer 3.5
baile *m.* dance 3.5
bajar(se) de *v.* to get off of/out of (a vehicle) 2.5
bajo/a *adj.* short (*in height*) 1.3
bajo control under control 2.1
balcón *m.* balcony 2.6
balde *m.* bucket 1.5
ballena *f.* whale 3.1
baloncesto *m.* basketball 1.4
banana *f.* banana 2.2
banco *m.* bank 3.2
banda *f.* band 3.5
bandera *f.* flag
bañarse *v.* to bathe; to take a bath 2.1
baño *m.* bathroom 2.1
barato/a *adj.* cheap 1.6
barco *m.* boat 1.5
barrer *v.* to sweep 2.6
   barrer el suelo to sweep the floor 2.6
barrio *m.* neighborhood 2.6
bastante *adv.* enough; rather 2.4
basura *f.* trash 2.6
baúl *m.* trunk 2.5
beber *v.* to drink 1.3
bebida *f.* drink 2.2
   bebida alcohólica *f.* alcoholic beverage 3.3
béisbol *m.* baseball 1.4
bellas artes *f., pl.* fine arts 3.5
belleza *f.* beauty 3.2
beneficio *m.* benefit 3.4
besar(se) *v.* to kiss (each other) 2.5
beso *m.* kiss 2.3
biblioteca *f.* library 1.2
bicicleta *f.* bicycle 1.4
bien *adj.* well 1.1
bienestar *m.* well-being 3.3
bienvenido(s)/a(s) *adj.* welcome 1.1

billete *m.* paper money; ticket
billón *m.* trillion
biología *f.* biology 1.2
bisabuelo/a *m.*, *f.* great-grand-father/great-grandmother 1.3
bistec *m.* steak 2.2
bizcocho *m.* biscuit
blanco/a *adj.* white 1.6
blog *m.* blog 2.5
(blue)jeans *m.*, *pl.* jeans 1.6
blusa *f.* blouse 1.6
boca *f.* mouth 2.4
boda *f.* wedding 2.3
boleto *m.* ticket 1.2, 3.5
bolsa *f.* purse, bag 1.6
bombero/a *m.*, *f.* firefighter 3.4
bonito/a *adj.* pretty 1.3
borrador *m.* eraser 1.2
borrar *v.* to erase 2.5
bosque *m.* forest 3.1
　bosque tropical tropical forest; rain forest 3.1
bota *f.* boot 1.6
botella *f.* bottle 2.3
　botella de vino bottle of wine 2.3
botones *m.*, *f. sing.* bellhop 1.5
brazo *m.* arm 2.4
brindar *v.* to toast (*drink*) 2.3
bucear *v.* to scuba dive 1.4
bueno *adv.* well
buen, bueno/a *adj.* good 1.3, 1.6
　buena forma good shape (*physical*) 3.3
　Buenas noches. Good evening; Good night. 1.1
　Buenas tardes. Good afternoon. 1.1
　buenísimo/a extremely good
　Bueno. Hello. (on telephone) 2.5
　Buenos días. Good morning. 1.1
bulevar *m.* boulevard
buscar *v.* to look for 1.2
buzón *m.* mailbox 3.2

C

caballero *m.* gentleman, sir 2.2
caballo *m.* horse 1.5
cabe: no cabe duda de there's no doubt 3.1
cabeza *f.* head 2.4
cada *adj. m.*, *f.* each 1.6
caerse *v.* to fall (down) 2.4
café *m.* café 1.4; *adj. m.*, *f.* brown 1.6; *m.* coffee 2.2
cafeína *f.* caffeine 3.2
cafetera *f.* coffee maker 2.6
cafetería *f.* cafeteria 1.2
caído/a *p.p.* fallen 3.2
caja *f.* cash register 1.6
cajero/a *m.*, *f.* cashier 3.2
　cajero automático *m.* ATM 3.2
calavera de azúcar *f.* skull made out of sugar 2.3

calcetín (calcetines) *m.* sock(s) 1.6
calculadora *f.* calculator 1.2
calentamiento global *m.* global warming 3.1
calentarse (e:ie) *v.* to warm up 3.3
calidad *f.* quality 1.6
calle *f.* street 2.5
caloría *f.* calorie 3.3
calzar *v.* to take size... shoes 1.6
cama *f.* bed 1.5
cámara digital *f.* digital camera 2.5
cámara de video *f.* video camera 2.5
camarero/a *m.*, *f.* waiter/waitress 2.2
camarón *m.* shrimp 2.2
cambiar (de) *v.* to change 2.3
cambio: de cambio in change 2.3
cambio *m.* **climático** climate change 3.1
cambio *m.* **de moneda** currency exchange
caminar *v.* to walk 1.2
camino *m.* road
camión *m.* truck; bus
camisa *f.* shirt 1.6
camiseta *f.* t-shirt 1.6
campo *m.* countryside 1.5
canadiense *adj.* Canadian 1.3
canal *m.* (TV) channel 2.5, 3.5
canción *f.* song 3.5
candidato/a *m.*, *f.* candidate 3.6
canela *f.* cinnamon 2.4
cansado/a *adj.* tired 1.5
cantante *m.*, *f.* singer 3.5
cantar *v.* to sing 1.2
capital *f.* capital city 1.1
capó *m.* hood 2.5
cara *f.* face 2.1
caramelo *m.* caramel 2.3
carne *f.* meat 2.2
　carne de res *f.* beef 2.2
carnicería *f.* butcher shop 3.2
caro/a *adj.* expensive 1.6
carpintero/a *m.*, *f.* carpenter 3.4
carrera *f.* career 3.4
carretera *f.* highway 2.5
carro *m.* car; automobile 2.5
carta *f.* letter 1.4; (playing) card 1.5
cartel *m.* poster 2.6
cartera *f.* wallet 1.4, 1.6
cartero *m.* mail carrier 3.2
casa *f.* house; home 1.2
casado/a *adj.* married 2.3
casarse (con) *v.* to get married (to) 2.3
casi *adv.* almost 2.4
catorce fourteen 1.1
cazar *v.* to hunt 3.1
cebolla *f.* onion 2.2
cederrón *m.* CD-ROM 2.5
celebrar *v.* to celebrate 2.3
cementerio *m.* cemetery 2.3
cena *f.* dinner 2.2
cenar *v.* to have dinner 1.2

centro *m.* downtown 1.4
　centro comercial shopping mall 1.6
cepillarse los dientes/el pelo *v.* to brush one's teeth/one's hair 2.1
cerámica *f.* pottery 3.5
cerca de *prep.* near 1.2
cerdo *m.* pork 2.2
cereales *m.*, *pl.* cereal; grains 2.2
cero *m.* zero 1.1
cerrado/a *adj.* closed 1.5, 3.2
cerrar (e:ie) *v.* to close 1.4
cerveza *f.* beer 2.2
césped *m.* grass
ceviche *m.* marinated fish dish 2.2
　ceviche de camarón *m.* lemon-marinated shrimp 2.2
chaleco *m.* vest
champán *m.* champagne 2.3
champiñón *m.* mushroom 2.2
champú *m.* shampoo 2.1
chaqueta *f.* jacket 1.6
chau *fam. interj.* bye 1.1
cheque *m.* (bank) check 3.2
　cheque (de viajero) *m.* (traveler's) check 3.2
chévere *adj.*, *fam.* terrific
chico/a *m.*, *f.* boy/girl 1.1
chino/a *adj.* Chinese 1.3
chocar (con) *v.* to run into
chocolate *m.* chocolate 2.3
choque *m.* collision 3.6
chuleta *f.* chop (*food*) 2.2
　chuleta de cerdo *f.* pork chop 2.2
cibercafé *m.* cybercafé
ciclismo *m.* cycling 1.4
cielo *m.* sky 3.1
cien(to) one hundred 1.2
ciencia *f.* science 1.2
　ciencias ambientales environmental sciences 1.2
　de ciencia ficción *f.* science fiction (genre) 3.5
científico/a *m.*, *f.* scientist 3.4
cierto/a *adj.* certain 3.1
　es cierto it's certain 3.1
　no es cierto it's not certain 3.1
cima *f.* top, peak 3.3
cinco five 1.1
cincuenta fifty 1.2
cine *m.* movie theater 1.4
cinta *f.* (audio)tape
cinta caminadora *f.* treadmill 3.3
cinturón *m.* belt 1.6
circulación *f.* traffic 2.5
cita *f.* date; appointment 2.3
ciudad *f.* city 1.4
ciudadano/a *m.*, *f.* citizen 3.6
Claro (que sí). *fam.* Of course.
clase *f.* class 1.2
　clase de ejercicios aeróbicos *f.* aerobics class 3.3
clásico/a *adj.* classical 3.5
cliente/a *m.*, *f.* customer 1.6
clínica *f.* clinic 2.4

cobrar *v.* to cash (a check) 3.2
coche *m.* car; automobile 2.5
cocina *f.* kitchen; stove 2.3, 2.6
cocinar *v.* to cook 2.6
cocinero/a *m., f.* cook, chef 3.4
cofre *m.* hood 3.2
cola *f.* line 3.2
colesterol *m.* cholesterol 3.3
color *m.* color 1.6
comedia *f.* comedy; play 3.5
comedor *m.* dining room 2.6
comenzar (e:ie) *v.* to begin 1.4
comer *v.* to eat 1.3
comercial *adj.* commercial;
   business-related 3.4
comida *f.* food; meal 1.4, 2.2
como like; as 2.2
¿cómo? what?; how? 1.1
   ¿Cómo es...? What's... like? 1.3
   ¿Cómo está usted? *form.*
      How are you? 1.1
   ¿Cómo estás? *fam.* How are
      you? 1.1
   ¿Cómo les fue...? *pl.* How
      did... go for you? 3.3
   ¿Cómo se llama usted?
      (form.) What's your name? 1.1
   ¿Cómo te llamas? *(fam.)*
      What's your name? 1.1
cómoda *f.* chest of drawers 2.6
cómodo/a *adj.* comfortable 1.5
compañero/a de clase *m., f.*
   classmate 1.2
compañero/a de cuarto *m., f.*
   roommate 1.2
compañía *f.* company; firm 3.4
compartir *v.* to share 1.3
completamente *adv.* completely
   1.5, 3.4
compositor(a) *m., f.* composer 3.5
comprar *v.* to buy 1.2
compras *f., pl.* purchases 1.5
   ir de compras to go shopping 1.5
comprender *v.* to understand 1.3
comprobar *v.* to check
comprometerse (con) *v.* to get
   engaged (to) 2.3
computación *f.* computer
   science 1.2
computadora *f.* computer 1.1
computadora portátil *f.* portable
   computer; laptop 2.5
comunicación *f.* communication 3.6
comunicarse (con) *v.* to
   communicate (with) 3.6
comunidad *f.* community 1.1
con *prep.* with 1.2
   Con él/ella habla. Speaking.
      (on phone) 2.5
   con frecuencia *adv.*
      frequently 2.4
   Con permiso. Pardon me;
      Excuse me. 1.1
   con tal (de) que provided
      (that) 3.1
concierto *m.* concert 3.5
concordar *v.* to agree

concurso *m.* game show;
   contest 3.5
conducir *v.* to drive 1.6, 2.5
conductor(a) *m., f.* driver 1.1
conexión *f.* **inalámbrica** wireless
   (connection) 2.5
confirmar *v.* to confirm 1.5
confirmar *v.* **una reservación** *f.*
   to confirm a reservation 1.5
confundido/a *adj.* confused 1.5
congelador *m.* freezer 2.6
congestionado/a *adj.* congested;
   stuffed-up 2.4
conmigo *pron.* with me 1.4, 2.3
conocer *v.* to know; to be
   acquainted with 1.6
conocido *adj.; p.p.* known
conseguir (e:i) *v.* to get; to
   obtain 1.4
consejero/a *m., f.* counselor;
   advisor 3.4
consejo *m.* advice
conservación *f.* conservation 3.1
conservar *v.* to conserve 3.1
construir *v.* to build
consultorio *m.* doctor's office 2.4
consumir *v.* to consume 3.3
contabilidad *f.* accounting 1.2
contador(a) *m., f.* accountant 3.4
contaminación *f.* pollution 3.1
   contaminación del aire/del
      agua air/water pollution 3.1
contaminado/a *adj.* polluted 3.1
contaminar *v.* to pollute 3.1
contar (o:ue) *v.* to count; to tell 1.4
contento/a *adj.* happy; content 1.5
contestar *v.* to answer 1.2
contigo *fam. pron.* with
   you 1.5, 2.3
contratar *v.* to hire 3.4
control *m.* control 2.1
   control remoto remote
      control 2.5
controlar *v.* to control 3.1
conversación *f.* conversation 1.1
conversar *v.* to converse, to chat 1.2
copa *f.* wineglass; goblet 2.6
corazón *m.* heart 2.4
corbata *f.* tie 1.6
corredor(a) *m., f.* **de bolsa**
   stockbroker 3.4
correo *m.* mail; post office 3.2
   correo de voz *m.*
      voice mail 2.5
   correo electrónico *m.*
      e-mail 1.4
correr *v.* to run 1.3
cortesía *f.* courtesy
cortinas *f., pl.* curtains 2.6
corto/a *adj.* short *(in length)* 1.6
cosa *f.* thing 1.1
Costa Rica *f.* Costa Rica 1.1
costar (o:ue) *v.* to cost 1.6
costarricense *adj.* Costa
   Rican 1.3
cráter *m.* crater 3.1

creer *v.* to believe 3.1
   creer (en) *v.* to believe (in) 1.3
   no creer (en) *v.* not to
      believe (in) 3.1
creído/a *adj., p.p.* believed 3.2
crema de afeitar *f.* shaving
   cream 1.5, 2.1
crimen *m.* crime; murder 3.6
cruzar *v.* to cross 3.2
cuaderno *m.* notebook 1.1
cuadra *f.* (city) block 3.2
¿cuál(es)? which?; which
   one(s)? 1.2
   ¿Cuál es la fecha de hoy?
      What is today's date? 1.5
cuadro *m.* picture 2.6
cuadros *m., pl.* plaid 1.6
cuando when 2.1; 3.1
¿cuándo? when? 1.2
¿cuánto(s)/a(s)? how much/how
   many? 1.1
   ¿Cuánto cuesta...? How
      much does... cost? 1.6
   ¿Cuántos años tienes? How
      old are you? 1.3
cuarenta forty 1.2
cuarto de baño *m.* bathroom 2.1
cuarto *m.* room 1.2, 2.1
cuarto/a *adj.* fourth 1.5
   menos cuarto quarter to
      (time) 1.1
   y cuarto quarter after (time) 1.1
cuatro four 1.1
cuatrocientos/as four
   hundred 1.2
Cuba *f.* Cuba 1.1
cubano/a *adj.* Cuban 1.3
cubiertos *m., pl.* silverware
cubierto/a *p.p.* covered
cubrir *v.* to cover
cuchara *f.* (table or large) spoon 2.6
cuchillo *m.* knife 2.6
cuello *m.* neck 2.4
cuenta *f.* bill 2.3; account 3.2
   cuenta corriente *f.* checking
      account 3.2
   cuenta de ahorros *f.* savings
      account 3.2
cuento *m.* short story 3.5
cuerpo *m.* body 2.4
cuidar *v.* to take care of 3.1
cultura *f.* culture 1.2, 3.5
cumpleaños *m., ing.*
   birthday 2.3
cumplir años *v.* to have a
   birthday 2.3
cuñado/a *m., f.* brother-in-law;
   sister-in-law 1.3
currículum *m.* résumé 3.4
curso *m.* course 1.2

D

danza *f.* dance 3.5
dañar *v.* to damage; to break
   down 2.4

dar *v.* to give 1.6, 2.3
  dar un consejo *v.* to give advice 1.6
  darse con *v.* to bump into; to run into (something) 2.4
  darse prisa *v.* to hurry; to rush 3.3
de *prep.* of; from 1.1
  ¿De dónde eres? *fam.* Where are you from? 1.1
  ¿De dónde es usted? *form.* Where are you from? 1.1
  ¿De parte de quién? Who is speaking/calling? (*on phone*) 2.5
  ¿de quién...? whose...? (*sing.*) 1.1
  ¿de quiénes...? whose...? (*pl.*) 1.1
  de algodón (made) of cotton 1.6
  de aluminio (made) of aluminum 3.1
  de buen humor in a good mood 1.5
  de compras shopping 1.5
  de cuadros plaid 1.6
  de excursión hiking 1.4
  de hecho in fact
  de ida y vuelta roundtrip 1.5
  de la mañana in the morning; A.M. 1.1
  de la noche in the evening; at night; P.M. 1.1
  de la tarde in the afternoon; in the early evening; P.M. 1.1
  de lana (made) of wool 1.6
  de lunares polka-dotted 1.6
  de mal humor in a bad mood 1.5
  de mi vida of my life 3.3
  de moda in fashion 1.6
  De nada. You're welcome. 1.1
  de niño/a as a child 2.4
  de parte de on behalf of 2.5
  de plástico (made) of plastic 3.1
  de rayas striped 1.6
  de repente suddenly 1.6
  de seda (made) of silk 1.6
  de vaqueros western (genre) 3.5
  de vez en cuando from time to time 2.4
  de vidrio (made) of glass 3.1
debajo de *prep.* below; under 1.2
deber (+ *inf.*) *v.* should; must; ought to 1.3
  Debe ser... It must be... 1.6
deber *m.* responsibility; obligation 3.6
debido a due to (the fact that)
débil *adj.* weak 3.3
decidido/a *adj.* decided 3.2
decidir (+ *inf.*) *v.* to decide 1.3
décimo/a *adj.* tenth 1.5

decir (e:i) *v.* (**que**) to say (that); to tell (that) 1.4, 2.3
  decir la respuesta to say the answer 1.4
  decir la verdad to tell the truth 1.4
  decir mentiras to tell lies 1.4
declarar *v.* to declare; to say 3.6
dedo *m.* finger 2.4
dedo del pie *m.* toe 2.4
deforestación *f.* deforestation 3.1
dejar *v.* to let 2.6; to quit; to leave behind 3.4
  dejar de (+ *inf.*) *v.* to stop (*doing something*) 3.1
  dejar una propina *v.* to leave a tip 2.3
del (*contraction of* **de + el**) of the; from the
delante de *prep.* in front of 1.2
delgado/a *adj.* thin; slender 1.3
delicioso/a *adj.* delicious 2.2
demás *adj.* the rest
demasiado *adj., adv.* too much 1.6
dentista *m., f.* dentist 2.4
dentro de (diez años) within (ten years) 3.4; inside
dependiente/a *m., f.* clerk 1.6
deporte *m.* sport 1.4
deportista *m.* sports person
deportivo/a *adj.* sports-related 1.4
depositar *v.* to deposit 3.2
derecha *f.* right 1.2
  a la derecha de to the right of 1.2
derecho *adv.* straight (ahead) 3.2
derechos *m., pl.* rights 3.6
desarrollar *v.* to develop 3.1
desastre (natural) *m.* (natural) disaster 3.6
desayunar *v.* to have breakfast 1.2
desayuno *m.* breakfast 2.2
descafeinado/a *adj.* decaffeinated 3.3
descansar *v.* to rest 1.2
descargar *v.* to download 2.5
descompuesto/a *adj.* not working; out of order 2.5
describir *v.* to describe 1.3
descrito/a *p.p.* described 3.2
descubierto/a *p.p.* discovered 3.2
descubrir *v.* to discover 3.1
desde *prep.* from 1.6
desear *v.* to wish; to desire 1.2
desempleo *m.* unemployment 3.6
desierto *m.* desert 3.1
desigualdad *f.* inequality 3.6
desordenado/a *adj.* disorderly 1.5
despacio *adv.* slowly 2.4
despedida *f.* farewell; good-bye
despedir (e:i) *v.* to fire 3.4
despedirse (de) (e:i) *v.* to say good-bye (to) 2.1
despejado/a *adj.* clear (*weather*)
despertador *m.* alarm clock 2.1
despertarse (e:ie) *v.* to wake up 2.1

después *adv.* afterwards; then 2.1
  después de after 2.1
  después de que *conj.* after 3.1
destruir *v.* to destroy 3.1
detrás de *prep.* behind 1.2
día *m.* day 1.1
  día de fiesta holiday 2.3
diario *m.* diary 1.1; newspaper 3.6
diario/a *adj.* daily 2.1
dibujar *v.* to draw 1.2
dibujo *m.* drawing 3.5
  dibujos animados *m., pl.* cartoons 3.5
diccionario *m.* dictionary 1.1
dicho/a *p.p.* said 3.2
diciembre *m.* December 1.5
dictadura *f.* dictatorship 3.6
diecinueve nineteen 1.1
dieciocho eighteen 1.1
dieciséis sixteen 1.1
diecisiete seventeen 1.1
diente *m.* tooth 2.1
dieta *f.* diet 3.3
  comer una dieta equilibrada to eat a balanced diet 3.3
diez ten 1.1
difícil *adj.* difficult; hard 1.3
Diga. Hello. (*on phone*) 2.5
diligencia *f.* errand 3.2
dinero *m.* money 1.6
dirección *f.* address 3.2
  dirección electrónica *f.* e-mail address 2.5
director(a) *m., f.* director; (*musical*) conductor 3.5
dirigir *v.* to direct 3.5
disco compacto compact disc (CD) 2.5
discriminación *f.* discrimination 3.6
discurso *m.* speech 3.6
diseñador(a) *m., f.* designer 3.4
diseño *m.* design
disfraz *m.* costume
disfrutar (de) *v.* to enjoy; to reap the benefits (of) 3.3
disminuir *v.* to reduce 3.6
diversión *f.* fun activity; entertainment; recreation 1.4
divertido/a *adj.* fun 2.1
divertirse (e:ie) *v.* to have fun 2.3
divorciado/a *adj.* divorced 2.3
divorciarse (de) *v.* to get divorced (from) 2.3
divorcio *m.* divorce 2.3
doblar *v.* to turn 3.2
doble *adj.* double
doce twelve 1.1
doctor(a) *m., f.* doctor 1.3, 2.4
documental *m.* documentary 3.5
documentos de viaje *m., pl.* travel documents
doler (o:ue) *v.* to hurt 2.4
dolor *m.* ache; pain 2.4
  dolor de cabeza *m.* headache 2.4
doméstico/a *adj.* domestic 2.6

domingo *m.* Sunday 1.2
don *m.* Mr.; sir 1.1
doña *f.* Mrs.; ma'am 1.1
donde *adv.* where
   ¿Dónde está...? *Where is...?* 1.2
   ¿dónde? where? 1.1
dormir (o:ue) *v.* to sleep 1.4
dormirse (o:ue) *v.* to go to sleep;
   to fall asleep 2.1
dormitorio *m.* bedroom 2.6
dos two 1.1
   dos veces *f.* twice; two times 1.6
doscientos/as two hundred 1.2
drama *m.* drama; play 3.5
dramático/a *adj.* dramatic 3.5
dramaturgo/a *m., f.* playwright 3.5
droga *f.* drug 3.3
drogadicto/a *adj.* drug addict 3.3
ducha *f.* shower 2.1
ducharse *v.* to shower; to take a
   shower 2.1
duda *f.* doubt 3.1
dudar *v.* to doubt 3.1
   no dudar *v.* not to doubt 3.1
dueño/a *m., f.* owner; landlord 2.2
dulces *m., pl.* sweets; candy 2.3
durante *prep.* during 2.1
durar *v.* to last 3.6

E

e *conj. (used instead of y before
   words beginning with i and hi)*
   and 1.4
echar *v.* to throw
   echar (una carta) al buzón *v.*
     to put (a letter) in the
     mailbox; to mail 3.2
ecología *f.* ecology 3.1
ecológico/a *adj.* ecological 3.1
ecologista *m., f.* ecologist 3.1
economía *f.* economics 1.2
ecoturismo *m.* ecotourism 3.1
Ecuador *m.* Ecuador 1.1
ecuatoriano/a *adj.* Ecuadorian 1.3
edad *f.* age 2.3
edificio *m.* building 2.6
   edificio de apartamentos
     apartment building 2.6
(en) efectivo *m.* cash 1.6
ejercer *v.* to practice/exercise (a
   degree/profession) 3.4
ejercicio *m.* exercise 3.3
   ejercicios aeróbicos
     aerobic exercises 3.3
   ejercicios de estiramiento
     stretching exercises 3.3
ejército *m.* army 3.6
el *m., sing., def. art.* the 1.1
él *sub. pron.* he 1.1;
   obj. pron. him
elecciones *f., pl.* election 3.6
electricista *m., f.* electrician 3.4
electrodoméstico *m.* electric
   appliance 2.6
elegante *adj. m., f.* elegant 1.6

elegir (e:i) *v.* to elect 3.6
ella *sub. pron.* she 1.1; *obj. pron.* her
ellos/as *sub. pron.* they 1.1; them
embarazada *adj.* pregnant 2.4
emergencia *f.* emergency 2.4
emitir *v.* to broadcast 3.6
emocionante *adj. m., f.* exciting
empezar (e:ie) *v.* to begin 1.4
empleado/a *m., f.* employee 1.5
empleo *m.* job; employment 3.4
empresa *f.* company; firm 3.4
en *prep.* in; on; at 1.2
   en casa at home 2.1
   en caso (de) que in case
     (that) 3.1
   en cuanto as soon as 3.1
   en efectivo in cash 3.2
   en exceso in excess; too
     much 3.3
   en línea in-line 1.4
   en mi nombre in my name
   en punto on the dot; exactly;
     sharp *(time)* 1.1
   en qué in what; how 1.2
   ¿En qué puedo servirles?
     How can I help you? 1.5
   en vivo live 2.1
enamorado/a (de) *adj.* in
   love (with) 1.5
enamorarse (de) *v.* to fall in love
   (with) 2.3
encantado/a *adj.* delighted;
   pleased to meet you 1.1
encantar *v.* to like very much;
   to love *(inanimate objects)* 2.1
   ¡Me encantó! *I* loved it! 3.3
encima de *prep.* on top of 1.2
encontrar (o:ue) *v.* to find 1.4
encontrar(se) (o:ue) *v.* to meet
   (each other); to run into (each
   other) 2.5
   encontrarse con to meet up
     with 2.1
encuesta *f.* poll; survey 3.6
energía *f.* energy 3.1
   energía nuclear nuclear
     energy 3.1
   energía solar solar energy 3.1
enero *m.* January 1.5
enfermarse *v.* to get sick 2.4
enfermedad *f.* illness 2.4
enfermero/a *m., f.* nurse 2.4
enfermo/a *adj.* sick 2.4
enfrente de *adv.* opposite; facing 3.2
engordar *v.* to gain weight 3.3
enojado/a *adj.* mad; angry 1.5
enojarse (con) *v.* to get angry
   (with) 2.1
ensalada *f.* salad 2.2
ensayo *m.* essay 1.3
enseguida *adv.* right away
enseñar *v.* to teach 1.2
ensuciar *v.* to get (something)
   dirty 2.6
entender (e:ie) *v.* to understand 1.4
enterarse *v.* to find out 3.4
entonces *adv.* so, then 1.5, 2.1

entrada *f.* entrance 2.6; ticket 3.5
entre *prep.* between; among 1.2
entregar *v.* to hand in 2.5
entremeses *m., pl.* hors
   d'oeuvres; appetizers 2.2
entrenador(a) *m., f.* trainer 3.3
entrenarse *v.* to practice; to
   train 3.3
entrevista *f.* interview 3.4
entrevistador(a) *m., f.*
   interviewer 3.4
entrevistar *v.* to interview 3.4
envase *m.* container 3.1
enviar *v.* to send; to mail 3.2
equilibrado/a *adj.* balanced 3.3
equipado/a *adj.* equipped 3.3
equipaje *m.* luggage 1.5
equipo *m.* team 1.4
equivocado/a *adj.* wrong 1.5
eres *fam.* you are 1.1
es he/she/it is 1.1
   Es bueno que... It's good
     that... 2.6
   Es de... He/She is from... 1.1
   es extraño it's strange 3.1
   es igual it's the same 1.5
   Es importante que... It's
     important that... 2.6
   es imposible it's impossible 3.1
   es improbable it's
     improbable 3.1
   Es malo que... It's bad
     that... 2.6
   Es mejor que... It's better
     that... 2.6
   Es necesario que... It's
     necessary that... 2.6
   es obvio it's obvious 3.1
   es ridículo it's ridiculous 3.1
   es seguro it's sure 3.1
   es terrible it's terrible 3.1
   es triste it's sad 3.1
   Es urgente que... It's urgent
     that... 2.6
   Es la una. It's one o'clock. 1.1
   es una lástima it's a shame 3.1
   es verdad it's true 3.1
esa(s) *f., adj.* that; those 1.6
ésa(s) *f., pron.* that (one);
   those (ones) 1.6
escalar *v.* to climb 1.4
   escalar montañas *v.* to climb
     mountains 1.4
escalera *f.* stairs; stairway 2.6
escalón *m.* step 3.3
escanear *v.* to scan 2.5
escoger *v.* to choose 2.2
escribir *v.* to write 1.3
   escribir un mensaje
     electrónico to write an
     e-mail message 1.4
   escribir una postal
     to write a postcard 1.4
   escribir una carta to write a
     letter 1.4
escrito/a *p.p.* written 3.2
escritor(a) *m., f.* writer 3.5

escritorio *m.* desk 1.2
escuchar *v.* to listen to 1.2
  escuchar la radio to listen (to) the radio 1.2
  escuchar música to listen (to) music 1.2
escuela *f.* school 1.1
esculpir *v.* to sculpt 3.5
escultor(a) *m., f.* sculptor 3.5
escultura *f.* sculpture 3.5
ese *m., sing., adj.* that 1.6
ése *m., sing., pron.* that one 1.6
eso *neuter, pron.* that; that thing 1.6
esos *m., pl., adj.* those 1.6
ésos *m., pl., pron.* those (ones) 1.6
España *f.* Spain 1.1
español *m.* Spanish (language) 1.2
español(a) *adj. m., f.* Spanish 1.3
espárragos *m., pl.* asparagus 2.2
especialidad: las especialidades del día today's specials 1.2
especialización *f.* major 1.2
espectacular *adj.* spectacular 3.3
espectáculo *m.* show 3.5
espejo *m.* mirror 2.1
esperar *v.* to hope; to wish 3.1
  esperar (+ *inf.*) *v.* to wait (for); to hope 1.2
esposo/a *m., f.* husband/wife; spouse 1.3
esquí (acuático) *m.* (water) skiing 1.4
esquiar *v.* to ski 1.4
esquina *m.* corner 3.2
está he/she/it is, you are
  Está (muy) despejado. It's (very) clear. (*weather*)
  Está lloviendo. It's raining. 1.5
  Está nevando. It's snowing. 1.5
  Está (muy) nublado. It's (very) cloudy. (*weather*) 1.5
  Está bien. That's fine. 2.5
esta(s) *f., adj.* this; these 1.6
  esta noche tonight 1.4
ésta(s) *f., pron.* this (one); these (ones) 1.6
  Ésta es... *f.* This is... (*introducing someone*) 1.1
establecer *v.* to establish 3.4
estación *f.* station; season 1.5
  estación de autobuses bus station 1.5
  estación del metro subway station 1.5
  estación de tren train station 1.5
estacionamiento *m.* parking lot 3.2
estacionar *v.* to park 2.5
estadio *m.* stadium 1.2
estado civil *m.* marital status 2.3
Estados Unidos *m., pl.* (EE.UU.; E.U.) United States 1.1
estadounidense *adj. m., f.* from the United States 1.3

estampado/a *adj.* print
estampilla *f.* stamp 3.2
estante *m.* bookcase; bookshelves 2.6
estar *v.* to be 1.2
  estar a dieta to be on a diet 3.3
  estar aburrido/a to be bored 1.5
  estar afectado/a (por) to be affected (by) 3.1
  estar bajo control to be under control 2.1
  estar cansado/a to be tired 1.5
  estar contaminado/a to be polluted 3.1
  estar de acuerdo to agree 3.4
  Estoy de acuerdo. I agree. 3.4
  No estoy de acuerdo. I don't agree. 3.4
  estar de moda to be in fashion 1.6
  estar de vacaciones *f., pl.* to be on vacation 1.5
  estar en buena forma to be in good shape 3.3
  estar enfermo/a to be sick 2.4
  estar harto/a de... to be sick of 3.6
  estar listo/a to be ready 3.3
  estar perdido/a to be lost 3.2
  estar roto/a to be broken 2.4
  estar seguro/a to be sure 1.5
  estar torcido/a to be twisted; to be sprained 2.4
  No está nada mal. It's not bad at all. 1.5
estatua *f.* statue 3.5
este *m.* east 3.2
este *m., sing., adj.* this 1.6
éste *m., sing., pron.* this (one) 1.6
  Éste es... *m.* This is... (*introducing someone*) 1.1
estéreo *m.* stereo 2.5
estilo *m.* style
estiramiento *m.* stretching 3.3
esto *neuter pron.* this; this thing 1.6
estómago *m.* stomach 2.4
estornudar *v.* to sneeze 2.4
estos *m., pl., adj.* these 1.6
éstos *m., pl., pron.* these (ones) 1.6
estrella *f.* star 3.1
  estrella de cine *m., f.* movie star 3.5
estrés *m.* stress 3.3
estudiante *m., f.* student 1.1, 1.2
estudiantil *adj. m., f.* student 1.2
estudiar *v.* to study 1.2
estufa *f.* stove 2.6
estupendo/a *adj.* stupendous 1.5
etapa *f.* stage 2.3
evitar *v.* to avoid 3.1
examen *m.* test; exam 1.2
  examen médico physical exam 2.4
excelente *adj. m., f.* excellent 1.5

exceso *m.* excess; too much 3.3
excursión *f.* hike; tour; excursion 1.4
excursionista *m., f.* hiker
experiencia *f.* experience 3.6
explicar *v.* to explain 1.2
explorar *v.* to explore
expresión *f.* expression
extinción *f.* extinction 3.1
extranjero/a *adj.* foreign 3.5
extrañar *v.* to miss 3.4
extraño/a *adj.* strange 3.1

F

fábrica *f.* factory 3.1
fabuloso/a *adj.* fabulous 1.5
fácil *adj.* easy 1.3
falda *f.* skirt 1.6
faltar *v.* to lack; to need 2.1
familia *f.* family 1.3
famoso/a *adj.* famous 3.4
farmacia *f.* pharmacy 2.4
fascinar *v.* to fascinate 2.1
favorito/a *adj.* favorite 1.4
fax *m.* fax (machine) 2.5
febrero *m.* February 1.5
fecha *f.* date 1.5
¡Felicidades! Congratulations! 2.3
¡Felicitaciones! Congratulations! 2.3
feliz *adj.* happy 1.5
  ¡Feliz cumpleaños! Happy birthday! 2.3
fenomenal *adj.* great, phenomenal 1.5
feo/a *adj.* ugly 1.3
festival *m.* festival 3.5
fiebre *f.* fever 2.4
fiesta *f.* party 2.3
fijo/a *adj.* fixed, set 1.6
fin *m.* end 1.4
  fin de semana weekend 1.4
finalmente *adv.* finally 3.3
firmar *v.* to sign (*a document*) 3.2
física *f.* physics 1.2
flan (de caramelo) *m.* baked (caramel) custard 2.3
flexible *adj.* flexible 3.3
flor *f.* flower 3.1
folclórico/a *adj.* folk; folkloric 3.5
folleto *m.* brochure
fondo *m.* end 2.6
forma *f.* shape 3.3
formulario *m.* form 3.2
foto(grafía) *f.* photograph 1.1
francés, francesa *adj. m., f.* French 1.3
frecuentemente *adv.* frequently 2.4
frenos *m., pl.* brakes
frente (frío) *m.* (cold) front 1.5
fresco/a *adj.* cool 1.5
frijoles *m., pl.* beans 2.2
frío/a *adj.* cold 1.5
frito/a *adj.* fried 2.2

fruta *f.* fruit 2.2
frutería *f.* fruit store 3.2
fuera *adv.* outside
fuerte *adj. m., f.* strong 3.3
fumar *v.* to smoke 3.3
  (no) fumar *v.* (not) to smoke 3.3
funcionar *v.* to work 2.5; to function
fútbol *m.* soccer 1.4
fútbol americano *m.* football 1.4
futuro/a *adj.* future 3.4
  en el futuro in the future 3.4

G

gafas (de sol) *f., pl.* (sun) glasses 1.6
gafas (oscuras) *f., pl.* (sun)glasses
galleta *f.* cookie 2.3
ganar *v.* to win 1.4; to earn (money) 3.4
ganga *f.* bargain 1.6
garaje *m.* garage; (mechanic's) repair shop 2.5; garage (*in a house*) 2.6
garganta *f.* throat 2.4
gasolina *f.* gasoline 2.5
gasolinera *f.* gas station 2.5
gastar *v.* to spend (*money*) 1.6
gato *m.* cat 3.1
gemelo/a *m., f.* twin 1.3
genial *adj.* great 3.4
gente *f.* people 1.3
geografía *f.* geography 1.2
gerente *m., f.* manager 2.2, 3.4
gimnasio *m.* gymnasium 1.4
gobierno *m.* government 3.1
golf *m.* golf 1.4
gordo/a *adj.* fat 1.3
grabar *v.* to record 2.5
gracias *f., pl.* thank you; thanks 1.1
  Gracias por invitarme. Thanks for inviting me. 2.3
graduarse (de/en) *v.* to graduate (from/in) 2.3
gran, grande *adj.* big; large 1.3
grasa *f.* fat 3.3
gratis *adj. m., f.* free of charge 3.2
grave *adj.* grave; serious 2.4
grillo *m.* cricket
gripe *f.* flu 2.4
gris *adj. m., f.* gray 1.6
gritar *v.* to scream, to shout 2.1
grito *m.* scream 1.5
guantes *m., pl.* gloves 1.6
guapo/a *adj.* handsome; good-looking 1.3
guardar *v.* to save (on a computer) 2.5
guerra *f.* war 3.6
guía *m., f.* guide
gustar *v.* to be pleasing to; to like 1.2
  Me gustaría... I would like...

gusto *m.* pleasure 1.1
  El gusto es mío. The pleasure is mine. 1.1
  Mucho gusto. Pleased to meet you. 1.1
  ¡Qué gusto verlo/la! *(form.)* How nice to see you! 3.6
  ¡Qué gusto verte! *(fam.)* How nice to see you! 3.6

H

haber *(auxiliar)* *v.* to have (done something) 3.3
habitación *f.* room 1.5
  habitación doble double room 1.5
  habitación individual single room 1.5
hablar *v.* to talk; to speak 1.2
hacer *v.* to do; to make 1.4
  Hace buen tiempo. The weather is good. 1.5
  Hace (mucho) calor. It's (very) hot. (*weather*) 1.5
  Hace fresco. It's cool. (*weather*) 1.5
  Hace (mucho) frío. It's (very) cold. (*weather*) 1.5
  Hace mal tiempo. The weather is bad. 1.5
  Hace (mucho) sol. It's (very) sunny. (*weather*) 1.5
  Hace (mucho) viento. It's (very) windy. (*weather*) 1.5
  hacer cola to stand in line 3.2
  hacer diligencias to run errands 3.2
  hacer ejercicio to exercise 3.3
  hacer ejercicios aeróbicos to do aerobics 3.3
  hacer ejercicios de estiramiento to do stretching exercises 3.3
  hacer el papel (de) to play the role (of) 3.5
  hacer gimnasia to work out 3.3
  hacer juego (con) to match (with) 1.6
  hacer la cama to make the bed 2.6
  hacer las maletas to pack (one's) suitcases 1.5
  hacer quehaceres domésticos to do household chores 2.6
  hacer (wind)surf to (wind)surf 1.5
  hacer turismo to go sightseeing
  hacer un viaje to take a trip 1.5
  ¿Me harías el honor de casarte conmigo? Would you do me the honor of marrying me? 3.5

hacia *prep.* toward 3.2
hamburguesa *f.* hamburger 2.2
hasta *prep.* until 1.6; toward
  Hasta la vista. See you later. 1.1
  Hasta luego. See you later. 1.1
  Hasta mañana. See you tomorrow. 1.1
  Hasta pronto. See you soon. 1.1
  hasta que until 3.1
hay there is; there are 1.1
  Hay (mucha) contaminación. It's (very) smoggy.
  Hay (mucha) niebla. It's (very) foggy.
  Hay que It is necessary that 3.2
  No hay de qué. You're welcome. 1.1
  No hay duda de There's no doubt 3.1
hecho/a *p.p.* done 3.2
heladería *f.* ice cream shop 3.2
helado/a *adj.* iced 2.2
helado *m.* ice cream 2.3
hermanastro/a *m., f.* stepbrother/stepsister 1.3
hermano/a *m., f.* brother/sister 1.3
hermano/a mayor/menor *m., f.* older/younger brother/sister 1.3
hermanos *m., pl.* siblings (brothers and sisters) 1.3
hermoso/a *adj.* beautiful 1.6
hierba *f.* grass 3.1
hijastro/a *m., f.* stepson/stepdaughter 1.3
hijo/a *m., f.* son/daughter 1.3
  hijo/a único/a *m., f.* only child 1.3
  hijos *m., pl.* children 1.3
híjole *interj.* wow 1.6
historia *f.* history 1.2; story 3.5
hockey *m.* hockey 1.4
hola *interj.* hello; hi 1.1
hombre *m.* man 1.1
  hombre de negocios *m.* businessman 3.4
hora *f.* hour 1.1; the time
horario *m.* schedule 1.2
horno *m.* oven 2.6
  horno de microondas *m.* microwave oven 2.6
horror *m.* horror 3.5
  de horror horror (genre) 3.5
hospital *m.* hospital 2.4
hotel *m.* hotel 1.5
hoy *adv.* today 1.2
  hoy día *adv.* nowadays
  Hoy es... Today is... 1.2
hueco *m.* hole 1.4
huelga *f.* strike (*labor*) 3.6
hueso *m.* bone 2.4
huésped *m., f.* guest 1.5
huevo *m.* egg 2.2
humanidades *f., pl.* humanities 1.2
huracán *m.* hurricane 3.6

I

ida *f.* one way (*travel*)
idea *f.* idea 1.4
iglesia *f.* church 1.4
igualdad *f.* equality 3.6
igualmente *adv.* likewise 1.1
impermeable *m.* raincoat 1.6
importante *adj. m., f.* important 1.3
importar *v.* to be important to; to matter 2.1
imposible *adj. m., f.* impossible 3.1
impresora *f.* printer 2.5
imprimir *v.* to print 2.5
improbable *adj. m., f.* improbable 3.1
impuesto *m.* tax 3.6
incendio *m.* fire 3.6
increíble *adj. m., f.* incredible 1.5
indicar cómo llegar *v.* to give directions 3.2
individual *adj.* private (*room*) 1.5
infección *f.* infection 2.4
informar *v.* to inform 3.6
informe *m.* report; paper (*written work*) 3.6
ingeniero/a *m., f.* engineer 1.3
inglés *m.* English (*language*) 1.2
inglés, inglesa *adj.* English 1.3
inodoro *m.* toilet 2.1
insistir (en) *v.* to insist (on) 2.6
inspector(a) de aduanas *m., f.* customs inspector 1.5
inteligente *adj. m., f.* intelligent 1.3
intento *m.* intent 2.5
intercambiar *v.* to exchange
interesante *adj. m., f.* interesting 1.3
interesar *v.* to be interesting to; to interest 2.1
internacional *adj. m., f.* international 3.6
Internet Internet 2.5
inundación *f.* flood 3.6
invertir (e:ie) *v.* to invest 3.4
invierno *m.* winter 1.5
invitado/a *m., f.* guest 2.3
invitar *v.* to invite 2.3
inyección *f.* injection 2.4
ir *v.* to go 1.4
  ir a (+ inf.) to be going to do something 1.4
  ir de compras to go shopping 1.5
  ir de excursión (a las montañas) to go for a hike (in the mountains) 1.4
  ir de pesca to go fishing
  ir de vacaciones to go on vacation 1.5
  ir en autobús to go by bus 1.5
  ir en auto(móvil) to go by auto(mobile); to go by car 1.5
  ir en avión to go by plane 1.5
  ir en barco to go by boat 1.5

  ir en metro to go by subway
  ir en motocicleta to go by motorcycle 1.5
  ir en taxi to go by taxi 1.5
  ir en tren to go by train
irse *v.* to go away; to leave 2.1
italiano/a *adj.* Italian 1.3
izquierda *f.* left 1.2
  a la izquierda de to the left of 1.2

J

jabón *m.* soap 2.1
jamás *adv.* never; not ever 2.1
jamón *m.* ham 2.2
japonés, japonesa *adj.* Japanese 1.3
jardín *m.* garden; yard 2.6
jefe, jefa *m., f.* boss 3.4
jengibre *m.* ginger 2.4
joven *adj. m., f., sing.* (**jóvenes** *pl.*) young 1.3
  joven *m., f., sing.* (**jóvenes** *pl.*) youth; young person 1.1
joyería *f.* jewelry store 3.2
jubilarse *v.* to retire (from work) 2.3
juego *m.* game
jueves *m., sing.* Thursday 1.2
jugador(a) *m., f.* player 1.4
jugar (u:ue) *v.* to play 1.4
  jugar a las cartas *f., pl.* to play cards 1.5
jugo *m.* juice 2.2
  jugo de fruta *m.* fruit juice 2.2
julio *m.* July 1.5
jungla *f.* jungle 3.1
junio *m.* June 1.5
juntos/as *adj.* together 2.3
juventud *f.* youth 2.3

K

kilómetro *m.* kilometer 1.1

L

la *f., sing., def. art.* the 1.1
la *f., sing., d.o. pron.* her, it, *form.* you 1.5
laboratorio *m.* laboratory 1.2
lago *m.* lake 3.1
lámpara *f.* lamp 2.6
lana *f.* wool 1.6
langosta *f.* lobster 2.2
lápiz *m.* pencil 1.1
largo/a *adj.* long 1.6
las *f., pl., def. art.* the 1.1
las *f., pl., d.o. pron.* them; form. you 1.5
lástima *f.* shame 3.1
lastimarse *v.* to injure oneself 2.4
  lastimarse el pie to injure one's foot 2.4

lata *f.* (*tin*) can 3.1
lavabo *m.* sink 2.1
lavadora *f.* washing machine 2.6
lavandería *f.* laundromat 3.2
lavaplatos *m., sing.* dishwasher 2.6
lavar *v.* to wash 2.6
  lavar (el suelo, los platos) to wash (the floor, the dishes) 2.6
lavarse *v.* to wash oneself 2.1
  lavarse la cara to wash one's face 2.1
  lavarse las manos to wash one's hands 2.1
le *sing., i.o. pron.* to/for him, her, *form.* you 1.6
  Le presento a... *form.* I would like to introduce you to (name). 1.1
lección *f.* lesson 1.1
leche *f.* milk 2.2
lechuga *f.* lettuce 2.2
leer *v.* to read 1.3
  leer correo electrónico to read e-mail 1.4
  leer un periódico to read a newspaper 1.4
  leer una revista to read a magazine 1.4
leído/a *p.p.* read 3.2
lejos de *prep.* far from 1.2
lengua *f.* language 1.2
  lenguas extranjeras *f., pl.* foreign languages 1.2
lentes de contacto *m., pl.* contact lenses
  lentes (de sol) (sun)glasses
lento/a *adj.* slow 2.5
les *pl., i.o. pron.* to/for them, *form.* you 1.6
letrero *m.* sign 3.2
levantar *v.* to lift 3.3
  levantar pesas to lift weights 3.3
levantarse *v.* to get up 2.1
ley *f.* law 3.1
libertad *f.* liberty; freedom 3.6
libre *adj. m., f.* free 1.4
librería *f.* bookstore 1.2
libro *m.* book 1.2
licencia de conducir *f.* driver's license 2.5
limón *m.* lemon 2.2
limpiar *v.* to clean 2.6
  limpiar la casa *v.* to clean the house 2.6
limpio/a *adj.* clean 1.5
línea *f.* line 1.4
listo/a *adj.* ready; smart 1.5
literatura *f.* literature 1.2
llamar *v.* to call 2.5
  llamar por teléfono to call on the phone
llamarse *v.* to be called; to be named 2.1
llanta *f.* tire 2.5
llave *f.* key 1.5; wrench 2.5
llegada *f.* arrival 1.5

llegar *v.* to arrive 1.2
llenar *v.* to fill 2.5, 3.2
  llenar el tanque to fill the
    tank 2.5
  llenar (un formulario) to fill
    out (a form) 3.2
lleno/a *adj.* full 2.5
llevar *v.* to carry 1.2; to wear;
  to take 1.6
  llevar una vida sana to lead
    a healthy lifestyle 3.3
  llevarse bien/mal (con) to
    get along well/badly (with) 2.3
llorar *v.* to cry 3.3
llover (o:ue) *v.* to rain 1.5
  Llueve. It's raining. 1.5
lluvia *f.* rain
lo *m., sing. d.o. pron.* him, it, *form.*
  you 1.5
  ¡Lo he pasado de película!
    I've had a fantastic time! 3.6
  lo que that which; what 2.6
  Lo siento. I'm sorry. 1.1
loco/a *adj.* crazy 1.6
locutor(a) *m., f.* (TV or radio)
  announcer 3.6
lodo *m.* mud
los *m., pl., def. art.* the 1.1
los *m. pl., d.o. pron.* them, *form.*
  you 1.5
luchar (contra/por) *v.* to fight;
  to struggle (against/for) 3.6
luego *adv.* later 1.1; then 2.1
lugar *m.* place 1.2, 1.4
luna *f.* moon 3.1
lunares *m.* polka dots 1.6
lunes *m., sing.* Monday 1.2
luz *f.* light; electricity 2.6

M

madrastra *f.* stepmother 1.3
madre *f.* mother 1.3
madurez *f.* maturity; middle age 2.3
maestro/a *m., f.* teacher 3.4
magnífico/a *adj.* magnificent 1.5
maíz *m.* corn 2.2
mal, malo/a *adj.* bad 1.3
maleta *f.* suitcase 1.1
mamá *f.* mom 1.3
mandar *v.* to order 2.6; to send;
  to mail 3.2
manejar *v.* to drive 2.5
manera *f.* way 3.4
mano *f.* hand 1.1
manta *f.* blanket 2.6
mantener *v.* to maintain 3.3
  mantenerse en forma to stay
    in shape 3.3
mantequilla *f.* butter 2.2
manzana *f.* apple 2.2
mañana *f.* morning, a.m. 1.1;
  tomorrow 1.1
mapa *m.* map 1.2
maquillaje *m.* makeup 2.1
maquillarse *v.* to put on
  makeup 2.1

mar *m.* sea 1.5
maravilloso/a *adj.* marvelous 1.5
mareado/a *adj.* dizzy; nauseated 2.4
margarina *f.* margarine 2.2
mariscos *m., pl.* shellfish 2.2
marrón *adj. m., f.* brown 1.6
martes *m., sing.* Tuesday 1.2
marzo *m.* March 1.5
más *pron.* more 1.2
  más de (+ *number*) more
    than 2.2
  más tarde later (on) 2.1
  más... que more... than 2.2
masaje *m.* massage 3.3
matemáticas *f., pl.* mathematics 1.2
materia *f.* course 1.2
matrimonio *m.* marriage 2.3
máximo/a *adj.* maximum 2.5
mayo *m.* May 1.5
mayonesa *f.* mayonnaise 2.2
mayor *adj.* older 1.3
  el/la mayor *adj.* eldest 2.2;
    oldest
me *sing., d.o. pron.* me 1.5;
  sing. i.o. pron. to/for me 1.6
  Me duele mucho. It hurts me
    a lot. 2.4
  Me gusta... I like... 1.2
  No me gustan nada. I don't
    like them at all. 1.2
  Me gustaría(n)... I would
    like... 3.5
  Me llamo... My name is... 1.1
  Me muero por... I'm dying to
    (for)...
mecánico/a *m., f.* mechanic 2.5
mediano/a *adj.* medium
medianoche *f.* midnight 1.1
medias *f., pl.* pantyhose,
  stockings 1.6
medicamento *m.* medication 2.4
medicina *f.* medicine 2.4
médico/a *m., f.* doctor 1.3;
  adj. medical 2.4
medio/a *adj.* half 1.3
  medio ambiente *m.*
    environment 3.1
  medio/a hermano/a *m., f.*
    half-brother/half-sister 1.3
  mediodía *m.* noon 1.1
  medios de comunicación *m.,*
    pl. means of communication;
    media 3.6
  y media thirty minutes past the
    hour (time) 1.1
mejor *adj.* better 2.2
  el/la mejor *m., f.* the best 2.2
mejorar *v.* to improve 3.1
melocotón *m.* peach 2.2
menor *adj.* younger 1.3
  el/la menor *m., f.* youngest 2.2
menos *adv.* less 2.4
  menos cuarto..., menos
    quince... *quarter* to... (time) 1.1
  menos de (+ *number*) fewer
    than 2.2
  menos... que less... than 2.2

mensaje *m.* **de texto** text
  message 2.5
mensaje electrónico *m.* e-mail
  message 1.4
mentira *f.* lie 1.4
menú *m.* menu 2.2
mercado *m.* market 1.6
  mercado al aire libre open-air
    market 1.6
merendar (e:ie) *v.* to snack 2.2;
  to have an afternoon snack
merienda *f.* afternoon snack 3.3
mes *m.* month 1.5
mesa *f.* table 1.2
mesita *f.* end table 2.6
  mesita de noche night
    stand 2.6
meterse en problemas *v.* to get
  into trouble 3.1
metro *m.* subway 1.5
mexicano/a *adj.* Mexican 1.3
México *m.* Mexico 1.1
mí *pron., obj. of prep.* me 2.2
mi(s) *poss. adj.* my 1.3
microonda *f.* microwave 2.6
  horno de microondas *m.*
    microwave oven 2.6
miel *f.* honey 2.4
mientras *conj.* while 2.4
miércoles *m., sing.*
  Wednesday 1.2
mil *m.* one thousand 1.2
  mil millones billion
milla *f.* mile 2.5
millón *m.* million 1.2
millones (de) *m.* millions (of)
mineral *m.* mineral 3.3
minuto *m.* minute 1.1
mío(s)/a(s) *poss.* my; (of)
  mine 2.5
mirar *v.* to look (at); to watch 1.2
  mirar (la) televisión to watch
    television 1.2
mismo/a *adj.* same 1.3
mochila *f.* backpack 1.2
moda *f.* fashion 1.6
módem *m.* modem
moderno/a *adj.* modern 3.5
molestar *v.* to bother; to annoy 2.1
monitor *m.* (computer) monitor 2.5
  monitor(a) *m., f.* trainer
mono *m.* monkey 3.1
montaña *f.* mountain 1.4
montar v. a caballo to ride a
  horse 1.5
montón: un montón de a lot
  of 1.4
monumento *m.* monument 1.4
morado/a *adj.* purple 1.6
moreno/a *adj.* brunet(te) 1.3
morir (o:ue) *v.* to die 2.2
mostrar (o:ue) *v.* to show 1.4
motocicleta *f.* motorcycle 1.5
motor *m.* motor
muchacho/a *m., f.* boy; girl 1.3
mucho/a *adj., adv.* a lot of;
  much 1.2; many 1.3

(Muchas) gracias. Thank you (very much); Thanks (a lot). **1.1**

muchas veces *adv.* a lot; many times **2.4**

Mucho gusto. Pleased to meet you. **1.1**

muchísimo very much **1.2**

mudarse *v.* to move (from one house to another) **2.6**

muebles *m., pl.* furniture **2.6**

muela *f.* tooth

muerte *f.* death **2.3**

muerto/a *p.p.* died **3.2**

mujer *f.* woman **1.1**

mujer de negocios *f.* business woman **3.4**

mujer policía *f.* female police officer

multa *f.* fine

mundial *adj. m., f.* worldwide

mundo *m.* world **2.1, 3.1**

muro *m.* wall **3.3**

músculo *m.* muscle **3.3**

museo *m.* museum **1.4**

música *f.* music **1.2, 3.5**

musical *adj. m., f.* musical **3.5**

músico/a *m., f.* musician **3.5**

muy adv. very **1.1**

(Muy) bien, gracias. (Very) well, thanks. **1.1**

N

nacer *v.* to be born **2.3**

nacimiento *m.* birth **2.3**

nacional *adj. m., f.* national **3.6**

nacionalidad *f.* nationality **1.1**

nada nothing **1.1**; not anything **2.1**

nada mal not bad at all **1.5**

nadar *v.* to swim **1.4**

nadie *pron.* no one, nobody, not anyone **2.1**

naranja *f.* orange **2.2**

nariz *f.* nose **2.4**

natación *f.* swimming **1.4**

natural *adj. m., f.* natural **3.1**

naturaleza *f.* nature **3.1**

navegador *m.* **GPS** GPS **2.5**

navegar (en Internet) *v.* to surf (the Internet) **2.5**

Navidad *f.* Christmas **2.3**

necesario/a *adj.* necessary **2.6**

necesitar (+ inf.) *v.* to need **1.2**

negar (e:ie) *v.* to deny **3.1**

no negar (e:ie) *v.* not to deny **3.1**

negocios *m., pl.* business; commerce **3.4**

negro/a *adj.* black **1.6**

nervioso/a *adj.* nervous **1.5**

nevar (e:ie) *v.* to snow **1.5**

Nieva. It's snowing. **1.5**

ni... ni neither... nor **2.1**

niebla *f.* fog

nieto/a *m., f.* grandson/ granddaughter **1.3**

nieve *f.* snow

ningún, ninguno/a(s) *adj.* no; none; not any **2.1**

niñez *f.* childhood **2.3**

niño/a *m., f.* child **1.3**

no no; not **1.1**

¿no? right? **1.1**

No cabe duda de... There is no doubt... **3.1**

no es seguro it's not sure **3.1**

no es verdad it's not true **3.1**

No está nada mal. It's not bad at all. **1.5**

no estar de acuerdo to disagree

No estoy seguro. I'm not sure.

no hay there is not; there are not **1.1**

No hay de qué. You're welcome. **1.1**

No hay duda de... There is no doubt... **3.1**

¡No me diga(s)! You don't say!

No me gustan nada. I don't like them at all. **1.2**

no muy bien not very well **1.1**

No quiero. I don't want to. **1.4**

No sé. I don't know.

No se preocupe. (*form.*) Don't worry. **2.1**

No te preocupes. (*fam.*) Don't worry. **2.1**

no tener razón to be wrong **1.3**

noche *f.* night **1.1**

nombre *m.* name **1.1**

norte *m.* north **3.2**

norteamericano/a *adj.* (North) American **1.3**

nos *pl., d.o. pron.* us **1.5**; *pl., i.o. pron.* to/for us **1.6**

Nos vemos. See you. **1.1**

nosotros/as *sub. pron.* we **1.1**; *obj. pron.* us

noticia *f.* news **2.5**

noticias *f., pl.* news **3.6**

noticiero *m.* newscast **3.6**

novecientos/as nine hundred **1.2**

noveno/a *adj.* ninth **1.5**

noventa ninety **1.2**

noviembre *m.* November **1.5**

novio/a *m., f.* boyfriend/ girlfriend **1.3**

nube *f.* cloud **3.1**

nublado/a *adj.* cloudy **1.5**

Está (muy) nublado. It's very cloudy. **1.5**

nuclear *adj. m., f.* nuclear **3.1**

nuera *f.* daughter-in-law **1.3**

nuestro(s)/a(s) *poss. adj.* our **1.3**; (of ours) **2.5**

nueve nine **1.1**

nuevo/a *adj.* new **1.6**

número *m.* number **1.1**; (shoe) size **1.6**

nunca *adv.* never; not ever **2.1**

nutrición *f.* nutrition **3.3**

nutricionista *m., f.* nutritionist **3.3**

O

o or **2.1**

o... o either... or **2.1**

obedecer *v.* to obey **3.6**

obra *f.* work (*of art, literature, music, etc.*) **3.5**

obra maestra *f.* masterpiece **3.5**

obtener *v.* to obtain; to get **3.4**

obvio/a *adj.* obvious **3.1**

océano *m.* ocean

ochenta eighty **1.2**

ocho eight **1.1**

ochocientos/as eight hundred **1.2**

octavo/a *adj.* eighth **1.5**

octubre *m.* October **1.5**

ocupación *f.* occupation **3.4**

ocupado/a *adj.* busy **1.5**

ocurrir *v.* to occur; to happen **3.6**

odiar *v.* to hate **2.3**

oeste *m.* west **3.2**

oferta *f.* offer

oficina *f.* office **2.6**

oficio *m.* trade **3.4**

ofrecer *v.* to offer **1.6**

oído *m.* (sense of) hearing; inner ear **2.4**

oído/a *p.p.* heard **3.2**

oír *v.* to hear **1.4**

Oiga/Oigan. *form., sing./pl.* Listen. (*in conversation*) **1.1**

Oye. *fam., sing.* Listen. (*in conversation*) **1.1**

ojalá (que) *interj.* I hope (that); I wish (that) **3.1**

ojo *m.* eye **2.4**

olvidar *v.* to forget **2.4**

once eleven **1.1**

ópera *f.* opera **3.5**

operación *f.* operation **2.4**

ordenado/a *adj.* orderly **1.5**

ordinal *adj.* ordinal (*number*)

oreja *f.* (outer) ear **2.4**

organizarse *v.* to organize oneself **2.6**

orquesta *f.* orchestra **3.5**

ortografía *f.* spelling

ortográfico/a *adj.* spelling

os *fam., pl. d.o. pron.* you **1.5**; *fam., pl. i.o. pron.* to/for you **1.6**

otoño *m.* autumn **1.5**

otro/a *adj.* other; another **1.6**

otra vez again

P

paciente *m., f.* patient **2.4**

padrastro *m.* stepfather **1.3**

padre *m.* father **1.3**

padres *m., pl.* parents **1.3**

pagar *v.* to pay **1.6, 2.3**

pagar a plazos to pay in installments **3.2**

pagar al contado to pay in cash **3.2**

pagar en efectivo to pay in cash 3.2

pagar la cuenta to pay the bill 2.3

página *f.* page 2.5

página principal *f.* home page 2.5

país *m.* country 1.1

paisaje *m.* landscape 1.5

pájaro *m.* bird 3.1

palabra *f.* word 1.1

paleta helada *f.* popsicle 1.4

pálido/a *adj.* pale 3.2

pan *m.* bread 2.2

pan tostado *m.* toasted bread 2.2

panadería *f.* bakery 3.2

pantalla *f.* screen 2.5

pantalla táctil *f.* touch screen 2.5

pantalones *m., pl.* pants 1.6

pantalones cortos *m., pl.* shorts 1.6

pantuflas *f.* slippers 2.1

papa *f.* potato 2.2

papas fritas *f., pl.* fried potatoes; French fries 2.2

papá *m.* dad 1.3

papás *m., pl.* parents 1.3

papel *m.* paper 1.2; role 3.5

papelera *f.* wastebasket 1.2

paquete *m.* package 3.2

par *m.* pair 1.6

par de zapatos pair of shoes 1.6

para *prep.* for; in order to; by; used for; considering 2.5

para que so that 3.1

parabrisas *m., sing.* windshield 2.5

parar *v.* to stop 2.5

parecer *v.* to seem 1.6

pared *f.* wall 2.6

pareja *f.* (married) couple; partner 2.3

parientes *m., pl.* relatives 1.3

parque *m.* park 1.4

párrafo *m.* paragraph

parte: de parte de on behalf of 2.5

partido *m.* game; match (*sports*) 1.4

pasado/a *adj.* last; past 1.6

pasado *p.p.* passed

pasaje *m.* ticket 1.5

pasaje de ida y vuelta *m.* roundtrip ticket 1.5

pasajero/a *m., f.* passenger 1.1

pasaporte *m.* passport 1.5

pasar *v.* to go through 1.5

pasar la aspiradora to vacuum 2.6

pasar por el banco to go by the bank 3.2

pasar por la aduana to go through customs

pasar tiempo to spend time

pasarlo bien/mal to have a good/bad time 2.3

pasatiempo *m.* pastime; hobby 1.4

pasear *v.* to take a walk; to stroll 1.4

pasear en bicicleta to ride a bicycle 1.4

pasear por to walk around 1.4

pasillo *m.* hallway 2.6

pasta *f.* **de dientes** toothpaste 2.1

pastel *m.* cake; pie 2.3

pastel de chocolate *m.* chocolate cake 2.3

pastel de cumpleaños *m.* birthday cake

pastelería *f.* pastry shop 3.2

pastilla *f.* pill; tablet 2.4

patata *f.* potato 2.2

patatas fritas *f., pl.* fried potatoes; French fries 2.2

patinar (en línea) *v.* to (in-line) skate 1.4

patineta *f.* skateboard 1.4

patio *m.* patio; yard 2.6

pavo *m.* turkey 2.2

paz *f.* peace 3.6

pedir (e:i) *v.* to ask for; to request 1.4; to order (*food*) 2.2

pedir prestado *v.* to borrow 3.2

pedir un préstamo *v.* to apply for a loan 3.2

Todos me dijeron que te pidiera disculpas de su parte. They all told me to ask you to excuse them/ forgive them. 3.6

peinarse *v.* to comb one's hair 2.1

película *f.* movie 1.4

peligro *m.* danger 3.1

peligroso/a *adj.* dangerous 3.6

pelirrojo/a *adj.* red-haired 1.3

pelo *m.* hair 2.1

pelota *f.* ball 1.4

peluquería *f.* beauty salon 3.2

peluquero/a *m., f.* hairdresser 3.4

pensar (e:ie) *v.* to think 1.4

pensar (+ inf.) *v.* to intend to; to plan to (*do something*) 1.4

pensar en *v.* to think about 1.4

pensión *f.* boardinghouse

peor *adj.* worse 2.2

el/la peor *adj.* the worst 2.2

pequeño/a *adj.* small 1.3

pera *f.* pear 2.2

perder (e:ie) *v.* to lose; to miss 1.4

perdido/a *adj.* lost 3.1, 3.2

Perdón Pardon me.; Excuse me. 1.1

perezoso/a *adj.* lazy

perfecto/a *adj.* perfect 1.5

periódico *m.* newspaper 1.4

periodismo *m.* journalism 1.2

periodista *m., f.* journalist 1.3

permiso *m.* permission

pero *conj.* but 1.2

perro *m.* dog 3.1

persona *f.* person 1.3

personaje *m.* character 3.5

personaje principal *m.* main character 3.5

pesas *f. pl.* weights 3.3

pesca *f.* fishing

pescadería *f.* fish market 3.2

pescado *m.* fish (*cooked*) 2.2

pescar *v.* to fish 1.5

peso *m.* weight 3.3

pez *m., sing.* (**peces** *pl.*) fish (*live*) 3.1

pie *m.* foot 2.4

piedra *f.* stone 3.1

pierna *f.* leg 2.4

pimienta *f.* black pepper 2.2

pintar *v.* to paint 3.5

pintor(a) *m., f.* painter 3.4

pintura *f.* painting; picture 2.6, 3.5

piña *f.* pineapple

piscina *f.* swimming pool 1.4

piso *m.* floor (*of a building*) 1.5

pizarra *f.* blackboard 1.2

planchar la ropa *v.* to iron the clothes 2.6

planes *m., pl.* plans 1.4

planta *f.* plant 3.1

planta baja *f.* ground floor 1.5

plástico *m.* plastic 3.1

plato *m.* dish (*in a meal*) 2.2; *m.* plate 2.6

plato principal *m.* main dish 2.2

playa *f.* beach 1.5

plaza *f.* city or town square 1.4

plazos *m., pl.* periods; time 3.2

pluma *f.* pen 1.2

plumero *m.* duster 2.6

población *f.* population 3.1

pobre *adj. m., f.* poor 1.6

pobrecito/a *adj.* poor thing 1.3

pobreza *f.* poverty

poco/a *adj.* little; few 1.5; 2.4

poder (o:ue) *v.* to be able to; can 1.4

¿Podría pedirte algo? Could I ask you something? 3.5

¿Puedo dejar un recado? May I leave a message? 2.5

poema *m.* poem 3.5

poesía *f.* poetry 3.5

poeta *m., f.* poet 3.5

policía *f.* police (force) 2.5

política *f.* politics 3.6

político/a *m., f.* politician 3.4; *adj.* political 3.6

pollo *m.* chicken 2.2

pollo asado *m.* roast chicken 2.2

ponchar *v.* to go flat

poner *v.* to put; to place 1.4; to turn on (*electrical appliances*) 2.5

poner la mesa to set the table 2.6

poner una inyección to give an injection 2.4

ponerle el nombre to name someone/something 2.3

ponerse (+ *adj.*) *v.* to become (+ *adj.*) 2.1; to put on 2.1
por *prep.* in exchange for; for; by; in; through; around; along; during; because of; on account of; on behalf of; in search of; by way of; by means of 2.5
por aquí around here 2.5
por ejemplo for example 2.5
por eso that's why; therefore 2.5
por favor please 1.1
por fin finally 2.5
por la mañana in the morning 2.1
por la noche at night 2.1
por la tarde in the afternoon 2.1
por lo menos *adv.* at least 2.4
¿por qué? why? 1.2
Por supuesto. Of course.
por teléfono by phone; on the phone
por último finally 2.1
porque *conj.* because 1.2
portátil *adj. m., f.* portable 2.5
portero/a *m., f.* doorman/doorwoman 1.1
porvenir *m.* future 3.4
por el porvenir for/to the future 3.4
posesivo/a *adj.* possessive 1.3
posible *adj.* possible 3.1
es posible it's possible 3.1
no es posible it's not possible 3.1
postal *f.* postcard
postre *m.* dessert 2.3
practicar *v.* to practice 1.2
practicar deportes *m., pl.* to play sports 1.4
precio (fijo) *m.* (fixed; set) price 1.6
preferir (e:ie) *v.* to prefer 1.4
pregunta *f.* question
preguntar *v.* to ask (*a question*) 1.2
premio *m.* prize; award 3.5
prender *v.* to turn on 2.5
prensa *f.* press 3.6
preocupado/a (por) *adj.* worried (about) 1.5
preocuparse (por) *v.* to worry (about) 2.1
preparar *v.* to prepare 1.2
preposición *f.* preposition
presentación *f.* introduction
presentar *v.* to introduce; to present 3.5; to put on (*a performance*) 3.5
Le presento a... I would like to introduce you to (name). (*form.*) 1.1
Te presento a... I would like to introduce you to (name). (*fam.*) 1.1
presiones *f., pl.* pressures 3.3
prestado/a *adj.* borrowed

préstamo *m.* loan 3.2
prestar *v.* to lend; to loan 1.6
primavera *f.* spring 1.5
primer, primero/a *adj.* first 1.2, 1.5
primo/a *m., f.* cousin 1.3
principal *adj. m., f.* main 2.2
prisa *f.* haste
darse prisa *v.* to hurry; to rush 3.3
probable *adj. m., f.* probable 3.1
es probable it's probable 3.1
no es probable it's not probable 3.1
probar (o:ue) *v.* to taste; to try 2.2
probarse (o:ue) *v.* to try on 2.1
problema *m.* problem 1.1
profesión *f.* profession 1.3, 3.4
profesor(a) *m., f.* teacher 1.1, 1.2
programa *m.* 1.1
programa de computación *m.* software 2.5
programa de entrevistas *m.* talk show 3.5
programa de realidad *m.* reality show 3.5
programador(a) *m., f.* computer programmer 1.3
prohibir *v.* to prohibit 2.4; to forbid
pronombre *m.* pronoun
pronto *adv.* soon 2.4
propina *f.* tip 2.3
propio/a *adj.* own 3.4
proteger *v.* to protect 3.1
proteína *f.* protein 3.3
próximo/a *adj.* next 1.3, 3.4
proyecto *m.* project 2.5
prueba *f.* test; quiz 1.2
psicología *f.* psychology 1.2
psicólogo/a *m., f.* psychologist 3.4
publicar *v.* to publish 3.5
público *m.* audience 3.5
pueblo *m.* town 1.4
puerta *f.* door 1.2
Puerto Rico *m.* Puerto Rico 1.1
puertorriqueño/a *adj.* Puerto Rican 1.3
pues *conj.* well
puesto *m.* position; job 3.4
puesto/a *p.p.* put 3.2
puro/a *adj.* pure 3.1

Q

que *pron.* that; which; who 2.6
¿En qué...? In which...? 1.2
¡Qué...! How...!
¡Qué dolor! What pain!
¡Qué ropa más bonita! What pretty clothes! 1.6
¡Qué sorpresa! What a surprise!
¿qué? what? 1.1
¿Qué día es hoy? What day is it? 1.2

¿Qué hay de nuevo? What's new? 1.1
¿Qué hora es? What time is it? 1.1
¿Qué les parece? What do you (*pl.*) think?
¿Qué onda? What's up? 3.2
¿Qué pasa? What's happening? What's going on? 1.1
¿Qué pasó? What happened? 2.5
¿Qué precio tiene? What is the price?
¿Qué tal...? How are you?; How is it going? 1.1
¿Qué talla lleva/usa? What size do you wear? 1.6
¿Qué tiempo hace? How's the weather? 1.5
quedar *v.* to be left over; to fit (*clothing*) 2.1; to be left behind; to be located 3.2
quedarse *v.* to stay; to remain 2.1
quehaceres domésticos *m., pl.* household chores 2.6
quemar (un CD/DVD) *v.* to burn (a CD/DVD)
querer (e:ie) *v.* to want; to love 1.4
queso *m.* cheese 2.2
quien(es) *pron.* who; whom; that 2.6
¿quién(es)? who?; whom? 1.1
¿Quién es...? Who is...? 1.1
¿Quién habla? Who is speaking/calling? (*phone*) 2.5
química *f.* chemistry 1.2
quince fifteen 1.1
menos quince quarter to (time) 1.1
y quince quarter after (time) 1.1
quinceañera *f.* young woman celebrating her fifteenth birthday 2.3
quinientos/as *adj.* five hundred 1.2
quinto/a *adj.* fifth 1.5
quisiera *v.* I would like 3.5
quitar el polvo *v.* to dust 2.6
quitar la mesa *v.* to clear the table 2.6
quitarse *v.* to take off 2.1
quizás *adv.* maybe 1.5

R

racismo *m.* racism 3.6
radio *f.* radio (*medium*) 1.2; *m.* radio (set) 1.2
radiografía *f.* X-ray 2.4
rápido *adv.* quickly 2.4
ratón *m.* mouse 2.5
ratos libres *m., pl.* spare (free) time 1.4
raya *f.* stripe 1.6
razón *f.* reason
rebaja *f.* sale 1.6
receta *f.* prescription 2.4
recetar *v.* to prescribe 2.4

recibir *v.* to receive 1.3
reciclaje *m.* recycling 3.1
reciclar *v.* to recycle 3.1
recién casado/a *m.,*
    f. newlywed 2.3
recoger *v.* to pick up 3.1
recomendar (e:ie) *v.* to
    recommend 2.2, 2.6
recordar (o:ue) *v.* to remember 1.4
recorrer *v.* to tour an area
recuperar *v.* to recover 2.5
recurso *m.* resource 3.1
    recurso natural *m.* natural
      resource 3.1
red *f.* network; Web 2.5
reducir *v.* to reduce 3.1
refresco *m.* soft drink 2.2
refrigerador *m.* refrigerator 2.6
regalar *v.* to give (a gift) 2.3
regalo *m.* gift 1.6
regatear *v.* to bargain 1.6
región *f.* region; area 3.1
regresar *v.* to return 1.2
regular *adv.* so-so; OK 1.1
reído *p.p.* laughed 3.2
reírse (e:i) *v.* to laugh 2.3
relaciones *f., pl.* relationships
relajarse *v.* to relax 2.3
reloj *m.* clock; watch 1.2
renovable *adj.* renewable 3.1
renunciar (a) *v.* to resign
    (from) 3.4
repetir (e:i) *v.* to repeat 1.4
reportaje *m.* report 3.6
reportero/a *m., f.* reporter;
    journalist 3.4
representante *m., f.*
    representative 3.6
reproductor de CD *m.* CD
    player 2.5
reproductor de DVD *m.* DVD
    player 2.5
reproductor de MP3 *m.* MP3
    player 2.5
resfriado *m.* cold (*illness*) 2.4
residencia estudiantil *f.*
    dormitory 1.2
resolver (o:ue) *v.* to resolve;
    to solve 3.1
respirar *v.* to breathe 3.1
responsable *adj.* responsible 2.2
respuesta *f.* answer
restaurante *m.* restaurant 1.4
resuelto/a *p.p.* resolved 3.2
reunión *f.* meeting 3.4
revisar *v.* to check 2.5
    revisar el aceite *v.* to check
      the oil 2.5
revista *f.* magazine 1.4
rico/a *adj.* rich 1.6; *adj.* tasty;
    delicious 2.2
ridículo/a *adj.* ridiculous 3.1
río *m.* river 3.1
rodilla *f.* knee 2.4
rogar (o:ue) *v.* to beg; to
    plead 2.6
rojo/a *adj.* red 1.6

romántico/a *adj.* romantic 3.5
romper *v.* to break 2.4
    romperse la pierna *v.* to break
      one's leg 2.4
romper (con) *v.* to break up
    (with) 2.3
ropa *f.* clothing; clothes 1.6
    ropa interior *f.* underwear 1.6
rosado/a *adj.* pink 1.6
roto/a *adj.* broken 2.4, 3.2
rubio/a *adj.* blond(e) 1.3
ruso/a *adj.* Russian 1.3
rutina *f.* routine 2.1
    rutina diaria *f.* daily routine 2.1

S

sábado *m.* Saturday 1.2
saber *v.* to know; to know how 1.6;
    to taste 2.2
    saber a to taste like 2.2
sabrosísimo/a *adj.* extremely
    delicious 2.2
sabroso/a *adj.* tasty; delicious 2.2
sacar *v.* to take out
    sacar buena notas to get
      good grades 1.2
    sacar fotos to take photos 1.5
    sacar la basura to take out
      the trash 2.6
    sacar(se) un diente to have a
      tooth removed 2.4
sacudir *v.* to dust 2.6
    sacudir los muebles to dust
      the furniture 2.6
sal *f.* salt 2.2
sala *f.* living room 2.6; room
    sala de emergencia(s)
      emergency room 2.4
salario *m.* salary 3.4
salchicha *f.* sausage 2.2
salida *f.* departure; exit 1.5
salir *v.* to leave 1.4; to go out
    salir (con) to go out (with);
      to date 2.3
    salir de to leave from
    salir para to leave for (*a place*)
salmón *m.* salmon 2.2
salón de belleza *m.* beauty
    salon 3.2
salud *f.* health 2.4
saludable *adj.* healthy 2.4
saludar(se) *v.* to greet (each
    other) 2.5
saludo *m.* greeting 1.1
    saludos a... greetings to... 1.1
sandalia *f.* sandal 1.6
sandía *f.* watermelon
sándwich *m.* sandwich 2.2
sano/a *adj.* healthy 2.4
se *ref. pron.* himself, herself,
    itself, *form.* yourself,
    themselves, yourselves 2.1
se *impersonal* one 2.4
    Se hizo... He/she/it became...
secadora *f.* clothes dryer 2.6

secarse *v.* to dry oneself 2.1
sección de (no) fumar *f.* (non)
    smoking section 2.2
secretario/a *m., f.* secretary 3.4
secuencia *f.* sequence
seda *f.* silk 1.6
sedentario/a *adj.* sedentary;
    related to sitting 3.3
seguir (e:i) *v.* to follow; to
    continue 1.4
según according to
segundo/a *adj.* second 1.5
seguro/a *adj.* sure; safe 1.5
seis six 1.1
seiscientos/as six hundred 1.2
sello *m.* stamp 3.2
selva *f.* jungle 3.1
semáforo *m.* traffic light 3.2
semana *f.* week 1.2
    fin *m.* **de semana** weekend 1.4
    semana f. pasada last week 1.6
semestre *m.* semester 1.2
sendero *m.* trail; trailhead 3.1
sentarse (e:ie) *v.* to sit down 2.1
sentir(se) (e:ie) *v.* to feel 2.1;
    to be sorry; to regret 3.1
señor (Sr.); don *m.* Mr.; sir 1.1
señora (Sra.); doña *f.* Mrs.;
    ma'am 1.1
señorita (Srta.) *f.* Miss 1.1
separado/a *adj.* separated 2.3
separarse (de) *v.* to separate
    (from) 2.3
septiembre *m.* September 1.5
séptimo/a *adj.* seventh 1.5
ser *v.* to be 1.1
    ser aficionado/a (a) to be a
      fan (of) 1.4
    ser alérgico/a (a) to be allergic
      (to) 2.4
    ser gratis to be free of
      charge 3.2
serio/a *adj.* serious
servicio *m.* service 3.3
servilleta *f.* napkin 2.6
servir (e:i) *v.* to help 1.5; to
    serve 2.2
sesenta sixty 1.2
setecientos/as seven hundred 1.2
setenta seventy 1.2
sexismo *m.* sexism 3.6
sexto/a *adj.* sixth 1.5
sí *adv.* yes 1.1
si *conj.* if 1.4
SIDA *m.* AIDS 3.6
sido *p.p.* been 3.3
siempre *adv.* always 2.1
siete seven 1.1
silla *f.* seat 1.2
sillón *m.* armchair 2.6
similar *adj. m., f.* similar
simpático/a *adj.* nice; likeable 1.3
sin *prep.* without 1.2, 3.1
    sin duda without a doubt
    sin embargo however
    sin que *conj.* without 3.1
sino but (rather)

síntoma *m.* symptom 2.4
sitio *m.* place 1.3
sitio *m.* **web** website 2.5
situado/a *p.p.* located
sobre *m.* envelope 3.2; *prep.* on; over 1.2
   sobre todo above all 3.1
(sobre)población *f.* (over)population 3.1
sobrino/a *m., f.* nephew; niece 1.3
sociología *f.* sociology 1.2
sofá *m.* couch; sofa 2.6
sol *m.* sun 1.4; 1.5; 3.1
solar *adj. m., f.* solar 3.1
soldado *m., f.* soldier 3.6
soleado/a *adj.* sunny
solicitar *v.* to apply (*for a job*) 3.4
solicitud (de trabajo) *f.* (job) application 3.4
sólo *adv.* only 1.3
solo/a *adj.* alone
soltero/a *adj.* single 2.3
solución *f.* solution 3.1
sombrero *m.* hat 1.6
Son las dos. It's two o'clock. 1.1
sonar (o:ue) *v.* to ring 2.5
sonreído *p.p.* smiled 3.2
sonreír (e:i) *v.* to smile 2.3
sopa *f.* soup 2.2
sorprender *v.* to surprise 2.3
sorpresa *f.* surprise 2.3
sótano *m.* basement; cellar 2.6
soy I am 1.1
   Soy de... I'm from... 1.1
su(s) *poss. adj.* his; her; its; *form.* your; their 1.3
subir(se) a *v.* to get on/into (*a vehicle*) 2.5
sucio/a *adj.* dirty 1.5
sudar *v.* to sweat 3.3
suegro/a *m., f.* father-in-law; mother-in-law 1.3
sueldo *m.* salary 3.4
suelo *m.* floor 2.6
suéter *m.* sweater 1.6
sufrir *v.* to suffer 2.4
   sufrir muchas presiones to be under a lot of pressure 3.3
   sufrir una enfermedad to suffer an illness 2.4
sugerir (e:ie) *v.* to suggest 2.6
supermercado *m.* supermarket 3.2
suponer *v.* to suppose 1.4
sur *m.* south 3.2
sustantivo *m.* noun
suyo(s)/a(s) *poss.* (of) his/her; (of) hers; (of) its; (of) *form.* your, (of) yours, (of) their 2.5

T

tabla de (wind)surf *f.* sufboard/sailboard 1.3
tal vez *adv.* maybe 1.5
talentoso/a *adj.* talented 3.5
talla *f.* size 1.6
   talla grande *f.* large

taller *m.* **mecánico** garage; mechanic's repairshop 2.5
también *adv.* also; too 1.2; 2.1
tampoco *adv.* neither; not either 2.1
tan *adv.* so 1.5
   tan... como as... as 2.2
   tan pronto como *conj.* as soon as 3.1
tanque *m.* tank 2.5
tanto *adv.* so much
   tanto... como as much... as 2.2
tantos/as como as many... as 2.2
tarde *f.* afternoon; evening; P.M. 1.1; *adv.* late 2.1
tarea *f.* homework 1.2
tarjeta *f.* (post) card
tarjeta de crédito *f.* credit card 1.6
tarjeta postal *f.* postcard
taxi *m.* taxi 1.5
taza *f.* cup 2.6
te *sing., fam., d.o. pron.* you 1.5; *sing., fam., i.o. pron.* to/for you 1.6
   Te presento a... *fam.* I would like to introduce you to (name). 1.1
   ¿Te gustaría? Would you like to? 3.5
   ¿Te gusta(n)... ? Do you like... ? 1.2
té *m.* tea 2.2
   té helado *m.* iced tea 2.2
teatro *m.* theater 3.5
teclado *m.* keyboard 2.5
técnico/a *m., f.* technician 3.4
tejido *m.* weaving 3.5
teleadicto/a *m., f.* couch potato 3.3
teléfono (celular) *m.* (cell) phone 2.5
telenovela *f.* soap opera 3.5
teletrabajo *m.* telecommuting 3.4
televisión *f.* television 1.2; 2.5
televisión por cable *f.* cable television 2.5
televisor *m.* television set 2.5
temer *v.* to fear 3.1
temperatura *f.* temperature 2.4
temporada *f.* period of time 1.5
temprano *adv.* early 2.1
tenedor *m.* fork 2.6
tener *v.* to have 1.3
   tener... años to be... years old 1.3
   Tengo... años. I'm... years old. 1.3
   tener (mucho) calor to be (very) hot 1.3
   tener (mucho) cuidado to be (very) careful 1.3
   tener dolor to have pain 2.4
   tener éxito to be successful 3.4
   tener fiebre to have a fever 2.4
   tener (mucho) frío to be (very) cold 1.3

tener ganas de (+ *inf.*) to feel like (*doing something*) 1.3
tener (mucha) hambre *f.* to be (very) hungry 1.3
tener (mucho) miedo (de) to be (very) afraid (of); to be (very) scared (of) 1.3
tener miedo (de) que to be afraid that
tener planes *m., pl.* to have plans 1.4
tener (mucha) prisa to be in a (big) hurry 1.3
tener que (+ *inf.*) *v.* to have to (*do something*) 1.3
tener razón *f.* to be right 1.3
tener (mucha) sed *f.* to be (very) thirsty 1.3
tener (mucho) sueño to be (very) sleepy 1.3
tener (mucha) suerte to be (very) lucky 1.3
tener tiempo to have time 1.4
tener una cita to have a date; to have an appointment 2.3
tenis *m.* tennis 1.4
tensión *f.* tension 3.3
tercer, tercero/a *adj.* third 1.5
terco/a *adj.* stubborn 2.4
terminar *v.* to end; to finish 1.2
   terminar de (+ *inf.*) *v.* to finish (*doing something*) 1.4
terremoto *m.* earthquake 3.6
terrible *adj. m., f.* terrible 3.1
ti *obj. of prep., fam.* you
tiempo *m.* time 1.4; weather 1.5
   tiempo libre free time
tienda *f.* shop; store 1.6
tierra *f.* land; soil 3.1
tinto/a *adj.* red (wine) 2.2
tío/a *m., f.* uncle; aunt 1.3
tíos *m., pl.* aunts and uncles 1.3
título *m.* title 3.4
tiza *f.* chalk 1.2
toalla *f.* towel 2.1
tobillo *m.* ankle 2.4
tocar *v.* to play (*a musical instrument*) 3.5; to touch
todavía *adv.* yet; still 1.3, 1.5
todo *m.* everything 1.5
   Todo está bajo control. Everything is under control. 2.1
todo(s)/a(s) *adj.* all 1.4; whole
todos *m., pl.* all of us; *m., pl.* everybody; everyone
todos los días *adv.* every day 2.4
tomar *v.* to take; drink 1.2
   tomar clases *f., pl.* to take classes 1.2
   tomar el sol to sunbathe 1.4
   tomar en cuenta to take into account
   tomar fotos *f., pl.* to take photos 1.5
   tomar la temperatura to take someone's temperature 2.4

tomar una decisión to make a decision 3.3
tomate *m.* tomato 2.2
tonto/a *adj.* silly; foolish 1.3
torcerse (o:ue) (el tobillo) *v.* to sprain (one's ankle) 2.4
torcido/a *adj.* twisted; sprained 2.4
tormenta *f.* storm 3.6
tornado *m.* tornado 3.6
tortuga (marina) *f.* (sea) turtle 3.1
tos *f., sing.* cough 2.4
toser *v.* to cough 2.4
tostado/a *adj.* toasted 2.2
tostadora *f.* toaster 2.6
trabajador(a) *adj.* hard-working 1.3
trabajar *v.* to work 1.2
trabajo *m.* job; work 3.4
traducir *v.* to translate 1.6
traer *v.* to bring 1.4
tráfico *m.* traffic 2.5
tragedia *f.* tragedy 3.5
traído/a *p.p.* brought 3.2
traje *m.* suit 1.6
  traje (de baño) *m.* (bathing) suit 1.6
trajinera *f.* type of barge 1.3
tranquilo/a *adj.* calm; quiet 3.3
  Tranquilo. Don't worry.; Be cool. 2.1
  Tranquilo, cariño. Relax, sweetie. 2.5
transmitir *v.* to broadcast 3.6
tratar de (+ inf.) *v.* to try (*to do something*) 3.3
trece thirteen 1.1
treinta thirty 1.1, 1.2
  y treinta thirty minutes past the hour (time) 1.1
tren *m.* train 1.5
tres three 1.1
trescientos/as three hundred 1.2
trimestre *m.* trimester; quarter 1.2
triste *adj.* sad 1.5
tú *fam. sub. pron.* you 1.1
  Tú eres... You are... 1.1
tu(s) *fam. poss. adj.* your 1.3
turismo *m.* tourism 1.5
turista *m., f.* tourist 1.1
turístico/a *adj.* touristic
tuyo(s)/a(s) *fam. poss. pron.* your; (of) yours 2.5

Ud. *form. sing.* you 1.1
Uds. *form., pl.* you 1.1
último/a *adj.* last 2.1
  la última vez the last time 2.1
un, uno/a *indef. art.* a; one 1.1
  uno/a *m., f., sing. pron.* one 1.1
  a la una at one o'clock 1.1
  una vez once; one time 1.6
  una vez más one more time 2.3

único/a *adj.* only 1.3; unique 2.3
universidad *f.* university; college 1.2
unos/as *m., f., pl. indef. art.* some 1.1
  los unos a los otros each other 2.5
  unos/as *pron.* some 1.1
urgente *adj.* urgent 2.6
usar *v.* to wear; to use 1.6
usted (Ud.) *form. sing.* you 1.1
  ustedes (Uds.) *form., pl.* you 1.1
útil *adj.* useful
uva *f.* grape 2.2

V

vaca *f.* cow 3.1
vacaciones *f. pl.* vacation 1.5
valle *m.* valley 3.1
vamos *let's go* 1.4
vaquero *m.* cowboy 3.5
  de vaqueros *m., pl.* western (genre) 3.5
varios/as *adj. m. f., pl.* various; several 2.2
vaso *m.* glass 2.6
veces *f., pl.* times 1.6
vecino/a *m., f.* neighbor 2.6
veinte twenty 1.1
veinticinco twenty-five 1.1
veinticuatro twenty-four 1.1
veintidós twenty-two 1.1
veintinueve twenty-nine 1.1
veintiocho twenty-eight 1.1
veintiséis twenty-six 1.1
veintisiete twenty-seven 1.1
veintitrés twenty-three 1.1
veintiún, veintiuno/a twenty-one 1.1
vejez *f.* old age 2.3
velocidad *f.* speed 2.5
  velocidad máxima *f.* speed limit 2.5
vencer *v.* to expire 2.2
vendedor(a) *m., f.* salesperson 1.6
vender *v.* to sell 1.6
venir *v.* to come 1.3
ventana *f.* window 1.2
ver *v.* to see 1.4
  a ver *v.* let's see 1.2
  ver películas *f., pl.* to see movies 1.4
verano *m.* summer 1.5
verbo *m.* verb
verdad *f.* truth
  ¿verdad? right? 1.1
verde *adj., m. f.* green 1.6
verduras *pl., f.* vegetables 2.2
vestido *m.* dress 1.6
vestirse (e:i) *v.* to get dressed 2.1
vez *f.* time 1.6
viajar *v.* to travel 1.2
viaje *m.* trip 1.5
viajero/a *m., f.* traveler 1.5
vida *f.* life 2.3

video *m.* video 1.1, 2.5
videoconferencia *f.* videoconference 3.4
videojuego *m.* video game 1.4
vidrio *m.* glass 3.1
viejo/a *adj.* old 1.3
viento *m.* wind 1.5
viernes *m., sing.* Friday 1.2
vinagre *m.* vinegar 2.2
vino *m.* wine 2.2
  vino blanco *m.* white wine 2.2
  vino tinto *m.* red wine 2.2
violencia *f.* violence 3.6
visitar *v.* to visit 1.4
  visitar monumentos *m., pl.* to visit monuments 1.4
visto/a *p.p.* seen 3.2
vitamina *f.* vitamin 3.3
viudo/a *adj.* widower/widow 2.3
vivienda *f.* housing 2.6
vivir *v.* to live 1.3
vivo/a *adj.* bright; lively; living
volante *m.* steering wheel 2.5
volcán *m.* volcano 3.1
vóleibol *m.* volleyball 1.4
volver (o:ue) *v.* to return 1.4
volver a ver(te, lo, la) *v.* to see (you, him, her) again 3.6
vos *pron.* you
vosotros/as *fam., pl.* you 1.1
votar *v.* to vote 3.6
vuelta *f.* return trip
vuelto/a *p.p.* returned 3.2
vuestro(s)/a(s) *poss. adj.* your 1.3; (of) yours *fam.* 2.5

W

walkman *m.* walkman

Y

y *conj.* and 1.1
  y cuarto quarter after (time) 1.1
  y media half-past (time) 1.1
  y quince quarter after (time) 1.1
  y treinta thirty (minutes past the hour) 1.1
  ¿Y tú? *fam.* And you? 1.1
  ¿Y usted? *form.* And you? 1.1
ya *adv.* already 1.6
yerno *m.* son-in-law 1.3
yo *sub. pron.* I 1.1
  Yo soy... I'm... 1.1
yogur *m.* yogurt 2.2

Z

zanahoria *f.* carrot 2.2
zapatería *f.* shoe store 3.2
zapatos de tenis *m., pl.* tennis shoes, sneakers 1.6

English-Spanish

A

a **un/a** *m., f., sing.; indef. art.* 1.1
@ (*symbol*) **arroba** *f.* 2.5
A.M. **mañana** *f.* 1.1
able: be able to **poder (o:ue)** *v.* 1.4
above all **sobre todo** 3.1
accident **accidente** *m.* 2.4
accompany **acompañar** *v.* 3.2
account **cuenta** *f.* 3.2
  on account of **por** *prep.* 2.5
accountant **contador(a)** *m., f.* 3.4
accounting **contabilidad** *f.* 1.2
ache **dolor** *m.* 2.4
acquainted: be acquainted
  with **conocer** *v.* 1.6
action (genre) **de acción** *f.* 3.5
active **activo/a** *adj.* 3.3
actor **actor** *m.*, **actriz** *f.* 3.4
addict (*drug*) **drogadicto/a** *adj.* 3.3
additional **adicional** *adj.*
address **dirección** *f.* 3.2
adjective **adjetivo** *m.*
adolescence **adolescencia** *f.* 2.3
adventure (genre) **de aventura** *f.* 3.5
advertise **anunciar** *v.* 3.6
advertisement **anuncio** *m.* 3.4
advice **consejo** *m.* 1.6
  give advice **dar consejos** 1.6
advise **aconsejar** *v.* 2.6
advisor **consejero/a** *m., f.* 3.4
aerobic **aeróbico/a** *adj.* 3.3
  aerobics class **clase de
    ejercicios aeróbicos** 3.3
  to do aerobics **hacer ejercicios
    aeróbicos** 3.3
affected **afectado/a** *adj.* 3.1
  be affected (by) **estar** *v.*
    afectado/a (por) 3.1
affirmative **afirmativo/a** *adj.*
afraid: be (very) afraid (of) **tener
  (mucho) miedo (de)** 1.3
  be afraid that **tener miedo
    (de) que**
after **después de** *prep.* 2.1;
  después de que *conj.* 3.1
afternoon **tarde** *f.* 1.1
afterward **después** *adv.* 2.1
again **otra vez**
age **edad** *f.* 2.3
agree **concordar** *v.*
agree **estar** *v.* **de acuerdo** 3.4
  I agree. **Estoy de acuerdo.** 3.4
  I don't agree. **No estoy de
    acuerdo.** 3.4
agreement **acuerdo** *m.* 3.4
AIDS **SIDA** *m.* 3.6
air **aire** *m.* 3.1
  air pollution **contaminación
    del aire** 3.1
airplane **avión** *m.* 1.5
airport **aeropuerto** *m.* 1.5
alarm clock **despertador** *m.* 2.1
alcohol **alcohol** *m.* 3.3

to consume alcohol **consumir
  alcohol** 3.3
alcoholic **alcohólico/a** *adj.* 3.3
all **todo(s)/a(s)** *adj.* 1.4
  all of us **todos** 1.1
  all over the world **en todo el
    mundo**
allergic **alérgico/a** *adj.* 2.4
  be allergic (to) **ser alérgico/a
    (a)** 2.4
alleviate **aliviar** *v.*
almost **casi** *adv.* 2.4
alone **solo/a** *adj.*
along **por** *prep.* 2.5
already **ya** *adv.* 1.6
also **también** *adv.* 1.2; 2.1
altar **altar** *m.* 2.3
aluminum **aluminio** *m.* 3.1
  (made) of aluminum **de
    aluminio** 3.1
always **siempre** *adv.* 2.1
American (*North*)
  norteamericano/a *adj.* 1.3
among **entre** *prep.* 1.2
amusement **diversión** *f.*
and **y** 1.1, **e** (*before words
  beginning with* **i** *or* **hi**) 1.4
  And you? **¿Y tú?** *fam.* 1.1;
    ¿Y usted? *form.* 1.1
angel **ángel** *m.* 2.3
angry **enojado/a** *adj.* 1.5
  get angry (with) **enojarse** *v.*
    (con) 2.1
animal **animal** *m.* 3.1
ankle **tobillo** *m.* 2.4
anniversary **aniversario** *m.* 2.3
  (wedding) anniversary
    aniversario *m.*
    (de bodas) 2.3
announce **anunciar** *v.* 3.6
announcer (*TV/radio*) **locutor(a)**
  m., f. 3.6
annoy **molestar** *v.* 2.1
another **otro/a** *adj.* 1.6
answer **contestar** *v.* 1.2;
  respuesta *f.*
antibiotic **antibiótico** *m.* 2.4
any **algún, alguno/a(s)** *adj.* 2.1
anyone **alguien** *pron.* 2.1
anything **algo** *pron.* 2.1
apartment **apartamento** *m.* 2.6
apartment building **edificio de
  apartamentos** 2.6
appear **parecer** *v.*
appetizers **entremeses** *m., pl.* 2.2
applaud **aplaudir** *v.* 3.5
apple **manzana** *f.* 2.2
appliance (electric)
  electrodoméstico *m.* 2.6
applicant **aspirante** *m., f.* 3.4
application **solicitud** *f.* 3.4
  job application **solicitud de
    trabajo** 3.4
apply (*for a job*) **solicitar** *v.* 3.4
  apply for a loan **pedir (e:i)** *v.*
    un préstamo 3.2
appointment **cita** *f.* 2.3

have an appointment **tener** *v.*
  una cita 2.3
appreciate **apreciar** *v.* 3.5
April **abril** *m.* 1.5
aquatic **acuático/a** *adj.*
archaeologist **arqueólogo/a**
  m., f. 3.4
archaeology **arqueología** *f.* 1.2
architect **arquitecto/a** *m., f.* 3.4
area **región** *f.* 3.1
Argentina **Argentina** *f.* 1.1
Argentine **argentino/a** *adj.* 1.3
arm **brazo** *m.* 2.4
armchair **sillón** *m.* 2.6
army **ejército** *m.* 3.6
around **por** *prep.* 2.5
  around here **por aquí** 2.5
arrange **arreglar** *v.* 2.5
arrival **llegada** *f.* 1.5
arrive **llegar** *v.* 1.2
art **arte** *m.* 1.2
  (fine) arts **bellas artes** *f., pl.* 3.5
article **artículo** *m.* 3.6
artist **artista** *m., f.* 1.3
artistic **artístico/a** *adj.* 3.5
arts **artes** *f., pl.* 3.5
as **como** 2.2
  as a child **de niño/a** 2.4
  as... as **tan... como** 2.2
  as many... as **tantos/as...
    como** 2.2
  as much... as **tanto...
    como** 2.2
  as soon as **en cuanto** *conj.* 3.1;
    tan pronto como *conj.* 3.1
ask (*a question*) **preguntar** *v.* 1.2
  ask for **pedir (e:i)** *v.* 1.4
asparagus **espárragos** *m., pl.* 2.2
aspirin **aspirina** *f.* 2.4
at **a** *prep.* 1.1; **en** *prep.* 1.2
  at + *time* **a la(s)** + *time* 1.1
  at home **en casa** 2.1
  at least **por lo menos** 2.4
  at night **por la noche** 2.1
  at the end (of) **al fondo (de)** 2.6
  At what time...? **¿A qué
    hora...?** 1.1
  At your service. **A sus
    órdenes.**
ATM **cajero automático** *m.* 3.2
attempt **intento** *m.* 2.5
attend **asistir (a)** *v.* 1.3
attic **altillo** *m.* 2.6
attract **atraer** *v.* 1.4
audience **público** *m.* 3.5
August **agosto** *m.* 1.5
aunt **tía** *f.* 1.3
  aunts and uncles **tíos** *m., pl.* 1.3
automobile **automóvil** *m.* 1.5;
  carro *m.*; **coche** *m.* 2.5
autumn **otoño** *m.* 1.5
avenue **avenida** *f.*
avoid **evitar** *v.* 3.1
award **premio** *m.* 3.5

B

backpack **mochila** *f.* 1.2
bad **mal, malo/a** *adj.* 1.3
　It's bad that… **Es malo
　　que…** 2.6
　It's not at all bad. **No está
　　nada mal.** 1.5
bag **bolsa** *f.* 1.6
bakery **panadería** *f.* 3.2
balanced **equilibrado/a** *adj.* 3.3
　to eat a balanced diet **comer
　　una dieta equilibrada** 3.3
balcony **balcón** *m.* 2.6
ball **pelota** *f.* 1.4
banana **banana** *f.* 2.2
band **banda** *f.* 3.5
bank **banco** *m.* 3.2
bargain **ganga** *f.* 1.6;
　regatear *v.* 1.6
baseball (*game*) **béisbol** *m.* 1.4
basement **sótano** *m.* 2.6
basketball (*game*) **baloncesto**
　m. 1.4
bathe **bañarse** *v.* 2.1
bathing suit **traje** *m.* **de baño** 1.6
bathroom **baño** *m.* 2.1;
　cuarto de baño *m.* 2.1
be **ser** *v.* 1.1; **estar** *v.* 1.2
　be… years old **tener… años** 1.3
　be sick of… **estar harto/a
　　de…** 3.6
beach **playa** *f.* 1.5
beans **frijoles** *m., pl.* 2.2
beautiful **hermoso/a** *adj.* 1.6
beauty **belleza** *f.* 3.2
　beauty salon **peluquería** *f.* 3.2;
　　salón *m.* **de belleza** 3.2
because **porque** *conj.* 1.2
　because of **por** *prep.* 2.5
become (+ *adj.*) **ponerse**
　(+ *adj.*) 2.1; **convertirse** *v.*
bed **cama** *f.* 1.5
　go to bed **acostarse (o:ue)** *v.* 2.1
bedroom **alcoba** *f.*; **dormitorio** *m.*
　2.6; **recámara** *f.*
beef **carne de res** *f.* 2.2
been **sido** *p.p.* 3.3
beer **cerveza** *f.* 2.2
before **antes** *adv.* 2.1; **antes de**
　prep. 2.1; **antes (de) que**
　conj. 3.1
beg **rogar (o:ue)** *v.* 2.6
begin **comenzar (e:ie)** *v.* 1.4;
　empezar (e:ie) *v.* 1.4
behalf: on behalf of **de parte de** 2.5
behind **detrás de** *prep.* 1.2
believe (in) **creer** *v.* **(en)** 1.3;
　creer *v.* 3.1
　not to believe **no creer** 3.1
believed **creído/a** *p.p.* 3.2
bellhop **botones** *m., f. sing.* 1.5
below **debajo de** *prep.* 1.2
belt **cinturón** *m.* 1.6
benefit **beneficio** *m.* 3.4
beside **al lado de** *prep.* 1.2
besides **además (de)** *adv.* 2.4

best **mejor** *adj.*
　the best **el/la mejor** *m., f.* 2.2;
better **mejor** *adj.* 2.2
　It's better that… **Es mejor
　　que…** 2.6
between **entre** *prep.* 1.2
beverage **bebida** *f.*
　alcoholic beverage **bebida
　　alcohólica** *f.* 3.3
bicycle **bicicleta** *f.* 1.4
big **gran, grande** *adj.* 1.3
bill **cuenta** *f.* 2.3
billion **mil millones**
biology **biología** *f.* 1.2
bird **ave** *f.* 3.1; **pájaro** *m.* 3.1
birth **nacimiento** *m.* 2.3
birthday **cumpleaños** *m., sing.* 2.3
　have a birthday **cumplir** *v.*
　　años 2.3
black **negro/a** *adj.* 1.6
blackboard **pizarra** *f.* 1.2
blanket **manta** *f.* 2.6
block (city) **cuadra** *f.* 3.2
blog **blog** *m.* 2.5
blond(e) **rubio/a** *adj.* 1.3
blouse **blusa** *f.* 1.6
blue **azul** *adj. m., f.* 1.6
boarding house **pensión** *f.*
boat **barco** *m.* 1.5
body **cuerpo** *m.* 2.4
bone **hueso** *m.* 2.4
book **libro** *m.* 1.2
bookcase **estante** *m.* 2.6
bookshelves **estante** *m.* 2.6
bookstore **librería** *f.* 1.2
boot **bota** *f.* 1.6
bore **aburrir** *v.* 2.1
bored **aburrido/a** *adj.* 1.5
　be bored **estar** *v.* **aburrido/a** 1.5
　get bored **aburrirse** *v.* 3.5
boring **aburrido/a** *adj.* 1.5
born: be born **nacer** *v.* 2.3
borrow **pedir (e:i)** *v.*
　prestado 3.2
borrowed **prestado/a** *adj.*
boss **jefe** *m.*, **jefa** *f.* 3.4
bother **molestar** *v.* 2.1
bottle **botella** *f.* 2.3
　bottle of wine **botella de
　　vino** 2.3
bottom **fondo** *m.*
boulevard **bulevar** *m.*
boy **chico** *m.* 1.1;
　muchacho *m.* 1.3
boyfriend **novio** *m.* 1.3
brakes **frenos** *m., pl.*
bread **pan** *m.* 2.2
break **romper** *v.* 2.4
　break (one's leg) **romperse
　　(la pierna)** 2.4
　break down **dañar** *v.* 2.4
　break up (with) **romper** *v.*
　　(con) 2.3
breakfast **desayuno** *m.* 1.2, 2.2
　have breakfast **desayunar** *v.* 1.2
breathe **respirar** *v.* 3.1
bring **traer** *v.* 1.4

broadcast **transmitir** *v.* 3.6;
　emitir *v.* 3.6
brochure **folleto** *m.*
broken **roto/a** *adj.* 2.4, 3.2
　be broken **estar roto/a** 2.4
brother **hermano** *m.* 1.3
　brother-in-law **cuñado** *m., f.* 1.3
　brothers and sisters **hermanos**
　　m., pl. 1.3
brought **traído/a** *p.p.* 3.2
brown **café** *adj.* 1.6;
　marrón *adj.* 1.6
brunet(te) **moreno/a** *adj.* 1.3
brush **cepillar** *v.* 2.1
　brush one's hair **cepillarse el
　　pelo** 2.1
　brush one's teeth **cepillarse los
　　dientes** 2.1
bucket **balde** *m.* 1.5
build **construir** *v.* 1.4
building **edificio** *m.* 2.6
bump into (*something
　accidentally*) **darse con** 2.4;
　(*someone*) **encontrarse** *v.* 2.5
burn (a CD/DVD) **quemar** *v.*
　(un CD/DVD)
bus **autobús** *m.* 1.1
　bus station **estación** *f.* **de
　　autobuses** 1.5
business **negocios** *m. pl.* 3.4
　business administration
　　administración *f.* **de
　　empresas** 1.2
　business-related **comercial**
　　adj. 3.4
businessperson **hombre** *m.* **/
　mujer** *f.* **de negocios** 3.4
busy **ocupado/a** *adj.* 1.5
but **pero** *conj.* 1.2; (*rather*) **sino**
　conj. (*in negative sentences*)
butcher shop **carnicería** *f.* 3.2
butter **mantequilla** *f.* 2.2
buy **comprar** *v.* 1.2
by **por** *prep.* 2.5; **para** *prep.* 2.5
　by means of **por** *prep.* 2.5
　by phone **por teléfono** 2.5
　by way of **por** *prep.* 2.5
bye **chau** *interj. fam.* 1.1

C

cable television **televisión** *f.*
　por cable *m.* 2.5
café **café** *m.* 1.4
cafeteria **cafetería** *f.* 1.2
caffeine **cafeína** *f.* 3.3
cake **pastel** *m.* 2.3
　chocolate cake **pastel de
　　chocolate** *m.* 2.3
calculator **calculadora** *f.* 1.2
call **llamar** *v.* 2.5
　be called **llamarse** *v.* 2.1
　call on the phone **llamar
　　por teléfono**
calm **tranquilo/a** *adj.* 3.3
calorie **caloría** *f.* 3.3

camera **cámara** *f.* 2.5
camp **acampar** *v.* 1.5
can (*tin*) **lata** *f.* 3.1
can **poder (o:ue)** *v.* 1.4
  Could I ask you something?
    ¿Podría pedirte algo? 3.5
Canadian **canadiense** *adj.* 1.3
candidate **aspirante** *m., f.* 3.4;
  candidato/a *m., f.* 3.6
candy **dulces** *m., pl.* 2.3
capital city **capital** *f.* 1.1
car **coche** *m.* 2.5; **carro** *m.* 2.5;
  auto(móvil) *m.* 1.5
caramel **caramelo** *m.* 2.3
card **tarjeta** *f.;* (*playing*)
  carta *f.* 1.5
care: take care of **cuidar** *v.* 3.2
career **carrera** *f.* 3.4
careful: be (very) careful **tener** *v.*
  (mucho) cuidado 1.3
caretaker **ama** *m., f.* **de casa** 2.6
carpenter **carpintero/a** *m., f.* 3.4
carpet **alfombra** *f.* 2.6
carrot **zanahoria** *f.* 2.2
carry **llevar** *v.* 1.2
cartoons **dibujos** *m, pl.*
  animados 3.5
case: in case (that) **en caso (de)**
  que 3.1
cash (a check) **cobrar** *v.* 3.2;
  cash **(en) efectivo** 1.6
  cash register **caja** *f.* 1.6
  pay in cash **pagar** *v.* **al contado**
    3.2; **pagar en efectivo** 3.2
cashier **cajero/a** *m., f.*
cat **gato** *m.* 3.1
CD **disco compacto** *m.* 2.5
CD player **reproductor de**
  CD *m.* 2.5
CD-ROM **cederrón** *m.* 2.5
celebrate **celebrar** *v.* 2.3
celebration **celebración** *f.*
cellar **sótano** *m.* 2.6
(cell) phone **(teléfono)**
  celular *m.* 2.5
cemetery **cementerio** *m.* 2.3
cereal **cereales** *m., pl.* 2.2
certain **cierto/a** *adj.;*
  seguro/a *adj.* 3.1
  it's (not) certain **(no) es**
    cierto/seguro 3.1
chalk **tiza** *f.* 1.2
champagne **champán** *m.* 2.3
change **cambiar** *v.* **(de)** 2.3
change: in change **de cambio** 1.2
channel (*TV*) **canal** *m.* 2.5; 3.5
character (*fictional*) **personaje**
  m. 2.5, 3.5
  (main) character **personaje**
    (principal) *m.* 3.5
chat **conversar** *v.* 1.2
cheap **barato/a** *adj.* 1.6
check **comprobar (o:ue)** *v.;*
  revisar *v.* 2.5; (*bank*) **cheque**
  m. 3.2
  check the oil **revisar el**
    aceite 2.5

checking account **cuenta** *f.*
  corriente 3.2
cheese **queso** *m.* 2.2
chef **cocinero/a** *m., f.* 3.4
chemistry **química** *f.* 1.2
chest of drawers **cómoda** *f.* 2.6
chicken **pollo** *m.* 2.2
child **niño/a** *m., f.* 1.3
childhood **niñez** *f.* 2.3
children **hijos** *m., pl.* 1.3
Chinese **chino/a** *adj.* 1.3
chocolate **chocolate** *m.* 2.3
  chocolate cake **pastel** *m.* **de**
    chocolate 2.3
cholesterol **colesterol** *m.* 3.3
choose **escoger** *v.* 2.2
chop (*food*) **chuleta** *f.* 2.2
Christmas **Navidad** *f.* 2.3
church **iglesia** *f.* 1.4
cinnamon **canela** *f.* 2.4
citizen **ciudadano/a** *m., f.* 3.6
city **ciudad** *f.* 1.4
class **clase** *f.* 1.2
  take classes **tomar clases** 1.2
classical **clásico/a** *adj.* 3.5
classmate **compañero/a** *m., f.* **de**
  clase 1.2
clean **limpio/a** *adj.* 1.5;
  limpiar *v.* 2.6
  clean the house *v.* **limpiar la**
    casa 2.6
clear (*weather*) **despejado/a** *adj.*
  clear the table **quitar la**
    mesa 2.6
  It's (very) clear. (*weather*)
    Está (muy) despejado.
clerk **dependiente/a** *m., f.* 1.6
climate change **cambio**
  climático *m.* 3.1
climb **escalar** *v.* 1.4
  climb mountains **escalar**
    montañas 1.4
clinic **clínica** *f.* 2.4
clock **reloj** *m.* 1.2
close **cerrar (e:ie)** *v.* 1.4
closed **cerrado/a** *adj.* 1.5
closet **armario** *m.* 2.6
clothes **ropa** *f.* 1.6
  clothes dryer **secadora** *f.* 2.6
clothing **ropa** *f.* 1.6
cloud **nube** *f.* 3.1
cloudy **nublado/a** *adj.* 1.5
  It's (very) cloudy. **Está (muy)**
    nublado. 1.5
coat **abrigo** *m.* 1.6
coffee **café** *m.* 2.2
  coffee maker **cafetera** *f.* 2.6
cold **frío** *m.* 1.5;
  (*illness*) **resfriado** *m.* 2.4
  be (*feel*) (very) cold **tener**
    (mucho) frío 1.3
  It's (very) cold. (*weather*) **Hace**
    (mucho) frío. 1.5
college **universidad** *f.* 1.2
collision **choque** *m.* 3.6
color **color** *m.* 1.6
comb one's hair **peinarse** *v.* 2.1

come **venir** *v.* 1.3
come on **ándale** *interj.* 3.2
comedy **comedia** *f.* 3.5
comfortable **cómodo/a** *adj.* 1.5
commerce **negocios** *m., pl.* 3.4
commercial **comercial** *adj.* 3.4
communicate (with) **comunicarse**
  v. **(con)** 3.6
communication **comunicación**
  f. 3.6
  means of communication
    medios *m. pl.* **de**
    comunicación 3.6
community **comunidad** *f.* 1.1
company **compañía** *f.* 3.4;
  empresa *f.* 3.4
comparison **comparación** *f.*
completely **completamente**
  adv. 3.4
composer **compositor(a)** *m., f.* 3.5
computer **computadora** *f.* 1.1
  computer monitor **monitor**
    m. 2.5
  computer programmer
    programador(a) *m., f.* 1.3
  computer science **computación**
    f. 1.2
concert **concierto** *m.* 3.5
conductor (*musical*) **director(a)**
  m., f. 3.5
confirm **confirmar** *v.* 1.5
  confirm a reservation **confirmar**
    una reservación 1.5
confused **confundido/a** *adj.* 1.5
congested **congestionado/a**
  adj. 2.4
Congratulations! **¡Felicidades!;**
  ¡Felicitaciones! *f. pl.* 2.3
conservation **conservación** *f.* 3.1
conserve **conservar** *v.* 3.1
considering **para** *prep.* 2.3
consume **consumir** *v.* 3.3
container **envase** *m.* 3.1
contamination **contaminación** *f.*
content **contento/a** *adj.* 1.5
contest **concurso** *m.* 3.5
continue **seguir (e:i)** *v.* 1.4
control **control** *m.;* **controlar** *v.* 3.1
  be under control **estar bajo**
    control 2.1
conversation **conversación** *f.* 1.1
converse **conversar** *v.* 1.2
cook **cocinar** *v.* 2.6;
  cocinero/a *m., f.* 3.4
cookie **galleta** *f.* 2.3
cool **fresco/a** *adj.* 1.5
  Be cool. **Tranquilo.** 2.1
  It's cool. (weather) **Hace**
    fresco. 1.5
corn **maíz** *m.* 2.2
corner **esquina** *f.* 3.2
cost **costar (o:ue)** *v.* 1.6
Costa Rica **Costa Rica** *f.* 1.1
Costa Rican **costarricense** *adj.* 1.3
costume **disfraz** *m.*
cotton **algodón** *f.* 1.6
  (made of) cotton **de algodón** 1.6

couch **sofá** *m.* 2.6
couch potato **teleadicto/a**
   m., f. 3.3
cough **tos** *f.* 2.4; **toser** *v.* 2.4
counselor **consejero/a** *m., f.* 3.4
count **contar (o:ue)** *v.* 1.4
country (*nation*) **país** *m.* 1.1
countryside **campo** *m.* 1.5
(married) couple **pareja** *f.* 2.3
course **curso** *m.* 1.2; **materia** *f.* 1.2
courtesy **cortesía** *f.*
cousin **primo/a** *m., f.* 1.3
cover **cubrir** *v.*
covered **cubierto/a** *p.p.*
cow **vaca** *f.* 3.1
crafts **artesanía** *f.* 3.5
craftsmanship **artesanía** *f.* 3.5
crater **cráter** *m.* 3.1
crazy **loco/a** *adj.* 1.6
create **crear** *v.*
credit **crédito** *m.* 1.6
   credit card **tarjeta** *f.* **de**
      crédito 1.6
crime **crimen** *m.* 3.6
cross **cruzar** *v.* 3.2
cry **llorar** *v.* 3.3
Cuba **Cuba** *f.* 1.1
Cuban **cubano/a** *adj.* 1.3
culture **cultura** *f.* 1.2, 3.5
cup **taza** *f.* 2.6
currency exchange **cambio** *m.*
   de moneda
current events **actualidades** *f.,*
   pl. 3.6
curtains **cortinas** *f., pl.* 2.6
custard (*baked*) **flan** *m.* 2.3
custom **costumbre** *f.* 1.1
customer **cliente/a** *m., f.* 1.6
customs **aduana** *f.* 1.5
   customs inspector **inspector(a)**
      m., f. **de aduanas** 1.5
cybercafé **cibercafé** *m.*
cycling **ciclismo** *m.* 1.4

D

dad **papá** *m.* 1.3
daily **diario/a** *adj.* 2.1
   daily routine **rutina** *f.* **diaria** 2.1
damage **dañar** *v.* 2.4
dance **bailar** *v.* 1.2; **danza** *f.* 3.5;
   baile *m.* 3.5
dancer **bailarín/bailarina** *m.,*
   f. 3.5
danger **peligro** *m.* 3.1
dangerous **peligroso/a** *adj.* 3.6
date (*appointment*) **cita** *f.* 2.3;
   (*calendar*) **fecha** *f.* 1.5;
   (*someone*) **salir** *v.* **con**
   (alguien) 2.3
   have a date **tener una cita** 2.3
daughter **hija** *f.* 1.3
daughter-in-law **nuera** *f.* 1.3
day **día** *m.* 1.1
   day before yesterday
      anteayer *adv.* 1.6

deal: It's not a big deal.
   No es para tanto. 2.6
death **muerte** *f.* 2.3
decaffeinated **descafeinado/a**
   adj. 3.3
December **diciembre** *m.* 1.5
decide **decidir** *v.* (+ *inf.*) 1.3
decided **decidido/a** *adj. p.p.* 3.2
declare **declarar** *v.* 3.6
deforestation **deforestación** *f.* 3.1
delicious **delicioso/a** *adj.* 2.2;
   rico/a *adj.* 2.2; **sabroso/a**
   adj. 2.2
delighted **encantado/a** *adj.* 1.1
dentist **dentista** *m., f.* 2.4
deny **negar (e:ie)** *v.* 3.1
   not to deny **no dudar** 3.1
department store **almacén** *m.* 1.6
departure **salida** *f.* 1.5
deposit **depositar** *v.* 3.2
describe **describir** *v.* 1.3
described **descrito/a** *p.p.* 3.2
desert **desierto** *m.* 3.1
design **diseño** *m.*
designer **diseñador(a)** *m., f.* 3.4
desire **desear** *v.* 1.2
desk **escritorio** *m.* 1.2
dessert **postre** *m.* 2.3
destroy **destruir** *v.* 3.1
develop **desarrollar** *v.* 3.1
diary **diario** *m.* 1.1
dictatorship **dictadura** *f.* 3.6
dictionary **diccionario** *m.* 1.1
die **morir (o:ue)** *v.* 2.2
died **muerto/a** *p.p.* 3.2
diet **dieta** *f.* 3.3; **alimentación**
   balanced diet **dieta**
      equilibrada 3.3
   be on a diet **estar a dieta** 3.3
difficult **difícil** *adj. m., f.* 1.3
digital camera **cámara** *f.*
   digital 2.5
dining room **comedor** *m.* 2.6
dinner **cena** *f.* 1.2, 2.2
   have dinner **cenar** *v.* 1.2
direct **dirigir** *v.* 3.5
director **director(a)** *m., f.* 3.5
dirty **ensuciar** *v.*; **sucio/a** *adj.* 1.5
   get (something) dirty **ensuciar**
      v. 2.6
disagree **no estar de acuerdo**
disaster **desastre** *m.* 3.6
discover **descubrir** *v.* 3.1
discovered **descubierto/a** *p.p.* 3.2
discrimination **discriminación**
   f. 3.6
dish **plato** *m.* 2.2, 2.6
   main dish **plato principal** *m.* 2.2
dishwasher **lavaplatos** *m.,*
   sing. 2.6
disorderly **desordenado/a** *adj.* 1.5
dive **bucear** *v.* 1.4
divorce **divorcio** *m.* 2.3
divorced **divorciado/a** *adj.* 2.3
   get divorced (from) **divorciarse**
      v. **(de)** 2.3
dizzy **mareado/a** *adj.* 2.4

do **hacer** *v.* 1.4
   do aerobics **hacer ejercicios**
      aeróbicos 3.3
   do household chores **hacer**
      quehaceres domésticos 2.6
   do stretching exercises **hacer**
      ejercicios de estiramiento 3.3
   (I) don't want to. **No quiero.** 1.4
doctor **doctor(a)** *m., f.* 1.3; 2.4;
   médico/a *m., f.* 1.3
documentary (*film*) **documental**
   m. 3.5
dog **perro** *m.* 3.1
domestic **doméstico/a** *adj.*
   domestic appliance
      electrodoméstico *m.*
done **hecho/a** *p.p.* 3.2
door **puerta** *f.* 1.2
doorman/doorwoman
   portero/a *m., f.* 1.1
dormitory **residencia** *f.*
   estudiantil 1.2
double **doble** *adj.* 1.5
   double room **habitación** *f.*
      doble 1.5
doubt **duda** *f.* 3.1; **dudar** *v.* 3.1
   not to doubt **no dudar** 3.1
   There is no doubt that...
      No cabe duda de 3.1;
      No hay duda de 3.1
Down with... ! **¡Abajo el/la...!**
download **descargar** *v.* 2.5
downtown **centro** *m.* 1.4
drama **drama** *m.* 3.5
dramatic **dramático/a** *adj.* 3.5
draw **dibujar** *v.* 1.2
drawing **dibujo** *m.* 3.5
dress **vestido** *m.* 1.6
   get dressed **vestirse (e:i)** *v.* 2.1
drink **beber** *v.* 1.3; **bebida**
   f. 2.2; **tomar** *v.* 1.2
drive **conducir** *v.* 1.6; **manejar**
   v. 2.5
driver **conductor(a)** *m., f.* 1.1
drug **droga** *f.* 3.3
   drug addict **drogadicto/a**
      adj. 3.3
dry oneself **secarse** *v.* 2.1
during **durante** *prep.* 2.1; **por**
   prep. 2.5
dust **sacudir** *v.* 2.6;
   quitar *v.* **el polvo** 2.6
   dust the furniture **sacudir los**
      muebles 2.6
duster **plumero** *m.* 2.6
DVD player **reproductor** *m.* **de**
   DVD 2.5

E

each **cada** *adj.* 1.6
each other **los unos a los**
   otros 2.5
eagle **águila** *f.*
ear (*outer*) **oreja** *f.* 2.4
early **temprano** *adv.* 2.1

earn **ganar** v. 3.4
earring **arete** m. 1.6
earthquake **terremoto** m. 3.6
ease **aliviar** v.
east **este** m. 3.2
  to the east **al este** 3.2
easy **fácil** adj. m., f. 1.3
eat **comer** v. 1.3
ecological **ecológico/a** adj. 3.1
ecologist **ecologista** m., f. 3.1
ecology **ecología** f. 3.1
economics **economía** f. 1.2
ecotourism **ecoturismo** m. 3.1
Ecuador **Ecuador** m. 1.1
Ecuadorian **ecuatoriano/a** adj. 1.3
effective **eficaz** adj. m., f.
egg **huevo** m. 2.2
eight **ocho** 1.1
eight hundred **ochocientos/as** 1.2
eighteen **dieciocho** 1.1
eighth **octavo/a** 1.5
eighty **ochenta** 1.2
either… or **o… o** conj. 2.1
eldest **el/la mayor** 2.2
elect **elegir** v. 3.6
election **elecciones** f. pl. 3.6
electric appliance
  electrodoméstico m. 2.6
electrician **electricista** m., f. 3.4
electricity **luz** f. 2.6
elegant **elegante** adj. m., f. 1.6
elevator **ascensor** m. 1.5
eleven **once** 1.1
e-mail **correo** m. **electrónico** 1.4
  e-mail message **mensaje** m.
    electrónico 1.4
  read e-mail **leer** v. **el correo**
    electrónico 1.4
e-mail address **dirrección** f.
  electrónica 2.5
embarrassed **avergonzado/a**
  adj. 1.5
embrace (each other) **abrazar(se)**
  v. 2.5
emergency **emergencia** f. 2.4
  emergency room **sala** f. **de**
    emergencia 2.4
employee **empleado/a** m., f. 1.5
employment **empleo** m. 3.4
end **fin** m. 1.4; **terminar** v. 1.2
  end table **mesita** f. 2.6
endure **aguantar** v. 3.2
energy **energía** f. 3.1
engaged: get engaged (to)
  comprometerse v. **(con)** 2.3
engineer **ingeniero/a** m., f. 1.3
English (language) **inglés** m. 1.2;
  inglés, inglesa adj. 1.3
enjoy **disfrutar** v. **(de)** 3.3
enough **bastante** adv. 2.4
entertainment **diversión** f. 1.4
entrance **entrada** f. 2.6
envelope **sobre** m. 3.2
environment **medio ambiente**
  m. 3.1
environmental sciences **ciencias**
  ambientales 1.2

equality **igualdad** f. 3.6
equipped **equipado/a** adj. 3.3
erase **borrar** v. 2.5
eraser **borrador** m. 1.2
errand **diligencia** f. 3.2
essay **ensayo** m. 1.3
evening **tarde** f. 1.1
event **acontecimiento** m. 3.6
every day **todos los días** 2.4
everything **todo** m. 1.5
  Everything is under control.
    Todo está bajo control. 2.1
exactly **en punto** 1.1
exam **examen** m. 1.2
excellent **excelente** adj. 1.5
excess **exceso** m. 3.3
  in excess **en exceso** 3.3
exchange **intercambiar** v.
  in exchange for **por** 2.5
exciting **emocionante** adj. m., f.
excursion **excursión** f.
excuse **disculpar** v.
Excuse me. (May I?) **Con**
  permiso. 1.1; (I beg your
  pardon.) **Perdón.** 1.1
exercise **ejercicio** m. 3.3;
  hacer v. **ejercicio** 3.3; (a
  degree/profession) **ejercer** v. 3.4
exit **salida** f. 1.5
expensive **caro/a** adj. 1.6
experience **experiencia** f. 3.6
expire **vencer** v. 3.2
explain **explicar** v. 1.2
explore **explorar** v.
expression **expresión** f.
extinction **extinción** f. 3.1
eye **ojo** m. 2.4

F

fabulous **fabuloso/a** adj. 1.5
face **cara** f. 2.1
facing **enfrente de** prep. 3.2
fact: in fact **de hecho**
factory **fábrica** f. 3.1
fall (down) **caerse** v. 2.4
  fall asleep **dormirse (o:ue)**
    v. 2.1
  fall in love (with) **enamorarse**
    v. **(de)** 2.3
fall (season) **otoño** m. 1.5
fallen **caído/a** p.p. 3.2
family **familia** f. 1.3
famous **famoso/a** adj. 3.4
fan **aficionado/a** adj. 1.4
  be a fan (of) **ser aficionado/a**
    (a) 1.4
far from **lejos de** prep. 1.2
farewell **despedida** f.
fascinate **fascinar** v. 2.1
fashion **moda** f. 1.6
  be in fashion **estar de moda** 1.6
fast **rápido/a** adj.
fat **gordo/a** adj. 1.3; **grasa** f. 3.3
father **padre** m. 1.3
father-in-law **suegro** m. 1.3

favorite **favorito/a** adj. 1.4
fax (machine) **fax** m. 2.5
fear **temer** v. 3.1
February **febrero** m. 1.5
feel **sentir(se) (e:ie)** v. 2.1
  feel like (doing something) **tener**
    ganas de (+ inf.) 1.3
festival **festival** m. 3.5
fever **fiebre** f. 2.4
  have a fever **tener** v. **fiebre** 2.4
few **pocos/as** adj. pl.
  fewer than **menos de**
    (+ number) 2.2
field: major field of study
  especialización f.
fifteen **quince** 1.1
  fifteen-year-old girl celebrating her
    birthday **quinceañera** f. 2.3
fifth **quinto/a** 1.5
fifty **cincuenta** 1.2
fight (for/against) **luchar** v. **(por/**
  contra) 3.6
figure (number) **cifra** f.
file **archivo** m. 2.5
fill **llenar** v. 2.5
  fill out (a form) **llenar (un**
    formulario) 3.2
  fill the tank **llenar el tanque** 2.5
finally **finalmente** adv. 3.3; **por**
  último 2.1; **por fin** 2.5
find **encontrar (o:ue)** v. 1.4
  find (each other) **encontrar(se)**
  find out **enterarse** v. 3.4
fine **multa** f.
  (fine) arts **bellas artes** f., pl. 3.5
finger **dedo** m. 2.4
finish **terminar** v. 1.2
  finish (doing something)
    terminar v. **de (+ inf.)** 1.4
fire **incendio** m. 3.6; **despedir**
  (e:i) v. 3.4
firefighter **bombero/a** m., f. 3.4
firm **compañía** f. 3.4; **empresa**
  f. 3.4
first **primer, primero/a** 1.2, 1.5
fish (food) **pescado** m. 2.2;
  pescar v. 1.5; (live) **pez** m.,
  sing. **(peces** pl.**)** 3.1
  fish market **pescadería** f. 3.2
fishing **pesca** f.
fit (clothing) **quedar** v. 2.1
five **cinco** 1.1
five hundred **quinientos/as** 1.2
fix (put in working order) **arreglar**
  v. 2.5; (clothes, hair, etc. to go
  out) **arreglarse** v. 2.1
fixed **fijo/a** adj. 1.6
flag **bandera** f.
flexible **flexible** adj. 3.3
flood **inundación** f. 3.6
floor (of a building) **piso** m. 1.5;
  suelo m. 2.6
  ground floor **planta baja** f. 1.5
  top floor **planta** f. **alta**
flower **flor** f. 3.1
flu **gripe** f. 2.4
fog **niebla** f.

folk **folclórico/a** *adj.* 3.5
follow **seguir (e:i)** *v.* 1.4
food **comida** *f.* 1.4, 2.2
foolish **tonto/a** *adj.* 1.3
foot **pie** *m.* 2.4
football **fútbol** *m.* **americano** 1.4
for **para** *prep.* 2.5; **por** *prep.* 2.5
  for example **por ejemplo** 2.5
  for me **para mí** 2.2
forbid **prohibir** *v.*
foreign **extranjero/a** *adj.* 3.5
  foreign languages **lenguas**
    f., pl. **extranjeras** 1.2
forest **bosque** *m.* 3.1
forget **olvidar** *v.* 2.4
fork **tenedor** *m.* 2.6
form **formulario** *m.* 3.2
forty **cuarenta** *m.* 1.2
four **cuatro** 1.1
four hundred **cuatrocientos/**
  as 1.2
fourteen **catorce** 1.1
fourth **cuarto/a** *m., f.* 1.5
free **libre** *adj. m., f.* 1.4
  be free (of charge) **ser**
    gratis 3.2
  free time **tiempo libre;** spare
    (free) time **ratos libres** 1.4
freedom **libertad** *f.* 3.6
freezer **congelador** *m.* 2.6
French **francés, francesa** *adj.* 1.3
  French fries **papas** *f., pl.*
    fritas 2.2; **patatas** *f., pl.*
    fritas 2.2
frequently **frecuentemente**
  adv. 2.4; **con frecuencia**
  adv. 2.4
Friday **viernes** *m., sing.* 1.2
fried **frito/a** *adj.* 2.2
  fried potatoes **papas** *f., pl.*
    fritas 2.2; **patatas** *f., pl.*
    fritas 2.2
friend **amigo/a** *m., f.* 1.3
friendly **amable** *adj. m., f.*
friendship **amistad** *f.* 2.3
from **de** *prep.* 1.1; **desde** *prep.* 1.6
  from the United States
    estadounidense *m., f.*
    adj. 1.3
  from time to time **de vez en**
    cuando 2.4
  He/She/It is from... **Es de...;**
    I'm from... **Soy de...** 1.1
front: (cold) front **frente**
  (frío) *m.* 1.5
fruit **fruta** *f.* 2.2
  fruit juice **jugo** *m.* **de fruta** 2.2
  fruit store **frutería** *f.* 3.2
full **lleno/a** *adj.* 2.5
fun **divertido/a** *adj.* 2.1
  fun activity **diversión** *f.* 1.4
  have fun **divertirse (e:ie)** *v.* 2.3
function **funcionar** *v.*
furniture **muebles** *m., pl.* 2.6
furthermore **además (de)** *adv.* 2.4
future **futuro** *adj.* 3.4; **porvenir**
  m. 3.4

for/to the future **por el**
  porvenir 3.4
in the future **en el futuro** 3.4

G

gain weight **aumentar** *v.* **de**
  peso 3.3; **engordar** *v.* 3.3
game **juego** *m.;* *(match)*
  partido *m.* 1.4
  game show **concurso** *m.* 3.5
garage *(in a house)* **garaje** *m.* 2.6;
  garaje *m.* 2.5; **taller**
  (mecánico) 2.5
garden **jardín** *m.* 2.6
garlic **ajo** *m.* 2.2
gas station **gasolinera** *f.* 2.5
gasoline **gasolina** *f.* 2.5
gentleman **caballero** *m.* 2.2
geography **geografía** *f.* 1.2
German **alemán, alemana** *adj.* 1.3
get **conseguir (e:i)** *v.* 1.4;
  obtener *v.* 3.4
  get along well/badly (with)
    llevarse bien/mal (con) 2.3
  get bigger **aumentar** *v.* 3.1
  get bored **aburrirse** *v.* 3.5
  get good grades **sacar buenas**
    notas 1.2
  get into trouble **meterse en**
    problemas 3.1
  get off of (a vehicle) **bajar(se)** *v.*
    de 2.5
  get on/into (a vehicle) **subir(se)**
    v. **a** 2.5
  get out of (a vehicle) **bajar(se)**
    v. **de** 2.5
  get ready **arreglarse** *v.* 2.1
  get up **levantarse** *v.* 2.1
gift **regalo** *m.* 1.6
ginger **jengibre** *m.* 2.4
girl **chica** *f.* 1.1; **muchacha** *f.* 1.3
girlfriend **novia** *f.* 1.3
give **dar** *v.* 1.6, 2.3;
  (as a gift) **regalar** 2.3
  give directions **indicar cómo**
    llegar 3.2
glass *(drinking)* **vaso** *m.* 2.6;
  vidrio *m.* 3.1
  (made) of glass **de vidrio** 3.1
glasses **gafas** *f., pl.* 1.6
  sunglasses **gafas** *f., pl.* **de sol** 1.6
global warming **calentamiento**
  global *m.* 3.1
gloves **guantes** *m., pl.* 1.6
go **ir** *v.* 1.4
  go away **irse** 2.1
  go by boat **ir en barco** 1.5
  go by bus **ir en autobús** 1.5
  go by car **ir en auto(móvil)** 1.5
  go by motorcycle **ir en**
    motocicleta 1.5
  go by plane **ir en avión** 1.5
  go by taxi **ir en taxi** 1.5
  go by the bank **pasar por el**
    banco 3.2

go down; **bajar(se)** *v.*
go on a hike (in the mountains)
  ir de excursión (a las
  montañas) 1.4
go out **salir** *v.* 2.3
go out (with) **salir** *v.* **(con)** 2.3
go up **subir** *v.*
Let's go. **Vamos.** 1.4
goblet **copa** *f.* 2.6
going to: be going to *(do something)*
  ir a (+ *inf.*) 1.4
golf **golf** *m.* 1.4
good **buen, bueno/a** *adj.* 1.3, 1.6
  Good afternoon. **Buenas**
    tardes. 1.1
  Good evening. **Buenas**
    noches. 1.1
  Good morning. **Buenos días.** 1.1
  Good night. **Buenas noches.** 1.1
  It's good that... **Es bueno**
    que... 2.6
goodbye **adiós** *m.* 1.1
  say goodbye (to) **despedirse** *v.*
    (de) (e:i) 2.1
good-looking **guapo/a** *adj.* 1.3
government **gobierno** *m.* 3.1
GPS **navegador GPS** *m.* 2.5
graduate (from/in) **graduarse** *v.*
  (de/en) 2.3
grains **cereales** *m., pl.* 2.2
granddaughter **nieta** *f.* 1.3
grandfather **abuelo** *m.* 1.3
grandmother **abuela** *f.* 1.3
grandparents **abuelos** *m., pl.* 1.3
grandson **nieto** *m.* 1.3
grape **uva** *f.* 2.2
grass **hierba** *f.* 3.1
grave **grave** *adj.* 2.4
gray **gris** *adj. m., f.* 1.6
great **fenomenal** *adj. m., f.* 1.5;
  genial *adj.* 3.4
great-grandfather **bisabuelo** *m.* 1.3
great-grandmother **bisabuela** *f.* 1.3
green **verde** *adj. m., f.* 1.6
greet (each other) **saludar(se)** *v.* 2.5
greeting **saludo** *m.* 1.1
  Greetings to... **Saludos a...** 1.1
grilled **a la plancha** 2.2
ground floor **planta baja** *f.* 1.5
grow **aumentar** *v.* 3.1
guest *(at a house/hotel)* **huésped**
  m., f. 1.5; *(invited to a function)*
  invitado/a *m., f.* 2.3
guide **guía** *m., f.* 3.1
gymnasium **gimnasio** *m.* 1.4

H

hair **pelo** *m.* 2.1
hairdresser **peluquero/a** *m., f.* 3.4
half **medio/a** *adj.* 1.3
  half-brother **medio**
    hermano 1.3
  half-sister **media hermana** 1.3
  half-past... *(time)* **...y media** 1.1
hallway **pasillo** *m.* 2.6

ham **jamón** *m.* 2.2
hamburger **hamburguesa** *f.* 2.2
hand **mano** *f.* 1.1
hand in **entregar** *v.* 2.5
handsome **guapo/a** *adj.* 1.3
happen **ocurrir** *v.* 3.6
happiness **alegría** *v.* 2.3
Happy birthday! **¡Feliz
   cumpleaños!** 2.3
happy **alegre** *adj.* 1.5; **contento/a**
   adj. 1.5; **feliz** *adj. m., f.* 1.5
   be happy **alegrarse** *v.* **(de)** 3.1
hard **difícil** *adj. m., f.* 1.3
hard-working **trabajador(a)**
   adj. 1.3
hardly **apenas** *adv.* 2.4
hat **sombrero** *m.* 1.6
hate **odiar** *v.* 2.3
have **tener** *v.* 1.3
   have time **tener tiempo** 1.4
   have to (*do something*) **tener que
      (+ *inf.*)** 1.3; **deber (+ *inf.*)**
   have a tooth removed **sacar(se)
      un diente** 2.4
he **él** 1.1
head **cabeza** *f.* 2.4
headache **dolor** *m.* **de cabeza** 2.4
health **salud** *f.* 2.4
healthy **saludable** *adj. m., f.* 2.4;
   sano/a *adj.* 2.4
   lead a healthy lifestyle **llevar** *v.*
      una vida sana 3.3
hear **oír** *v.* 1.4
heard **oído/a** *p.p.* 3.2
hearing: sense of hearing **oído** *m.* 2.4
heart **corazón** *m.* 2.4
Hello. **Hola.** 1.1; (*on the
   telephone*) **Aló.** 2.5;
   Bueno. 2.5; **Diga.** 2.5
help **ayudar** *v.* 2.6; **servir
   (e:i)** *v.* 1.5
   help each other **ayudarse** *v.* 2.5
her **su(s)** *poss. adj.* 1.3; (of) hers
   suyo(s)/a(s) *poss.* 2.5
   her **la** *f., sing., d.o. pron.* 1.5
   to/for her **le** *f., sing., i.o. pron.* 1.6
here **aquí** *adv.* 1.1
   Here is/are... **Aquí está(n)...** 1.5
Hi. **Hola.** 1.1
highway **autopista** *f.* 2.5;
   carretera *f.* 2.5
hike **excursión** *f.* 1.4
   go on a hike **hacer una excursión**
      1.5; **ir de excursión** 1.4
hiker **excursionista** *m., f.*
hiking **de excursión** 1.4
him: to/for him **le** *m., sing., i.o.
   pron.* 1.6
hire **contratar** *v.* 3.4
his **su(s)** *poss. adj.* 1.3; (of) his
   suyo(s)/a(s) *poss. pron.* 2.5
   his **lo** *m., sing., d.o. pron.* 1.5
history **historia** *f.* 1.2; 3.5
hobby **pasatiempo** *m.* 1.4
hockey **hockey** *m.* 1.4
hold up **aguantar** *v.* 3.2
hole **hueco** *m.* 1.4

holiday **día** *m.* **de fiesta** 2.3
home **casa** *f.* 1.2
   home page **página** *f.*
      principal 2.5
homework **tarea** *f.* 1.2
honey **miel** *f.* 2.4
hood **capó** *m.* 2.5; **cofre** *m.* 2.5
hope **esperar** *v.* **(+ *inf.*)** 1.2;
   esperar *v.* 3.1
   I hope (that) **ojalá (que)** 3.1
horror (genre) **de horror** *m.* 3.5
hors d'oeuvres **entremeses** *m.,
   pl.* 2.2
horse **caballo** *m.* 1.5
hospital **hospital** *m.* 2.4
hot: be (*feel*) (very) hot **tener
   (mucho) calor** 1.3
   It's (very) hot. **Hace (mucho)
      calor.** 1.5
hotel **hotel** *m.* 1.5
hour **hora** *f.* 1.1
house **casa** *f.* 1.2
household chores **quehaceres** *m.
   pl.* **domésticos** 2.6
housekeeper **ama** *m., f.* **de casa** 2.6
housing **vivienda** *f.* 2.6
How... ! **¡Qué...!**
   how **¿cómo?** *adv.* 1.1
   How are you? **¿Qué tal?** 1.1
   How are you? **¿Cómo estás?**
      fam. 1.1
   How are you? **¿Cómo está
      usted?** *form.* 1.1
   How can I help you? **¿En qué
      puedo servirles?** 1.5
   How did it go for you...?
      ¿Cómo le/les fue...? 3.3
   How is it going? **¿Qué tal?** 1.1
   How is the weather? **¿Qué
      tiempo hace?** 3.3
   How much/many?
      ¿Cuánto(s)/a(s)? 1.1
   How much does... cost?
      ¿Cuánto cuesta...? 1.6
   How old are you? **¿Cuántos
      años tienes?** *fam.* 1.3
however **sin embargo**
hug (each other) **abrazar(se)** *v.* 2.5
humanities **humanidades** *f., pl.* 1.2
hundred **cien, ciento** 1.2
hungry: be (very) hungry **tener** *v.*
   (mucha) hambre 1.3
hunt **cazar** *v.* 3.1
hurricane **huracán** *m.* 3.6
hurry **apurarse** *v.* 3.3; **darse
   prisa** *v.* 3.3
   be in a (big) hurry **tener** *v.*
      (mucha) prisa 1.3
hurt **doler (o:ue)** *v.* 2.4
   It hurts me a lot... **Me duele
      mucho...** 2.4
husband **esposo** *m.* 1.3

I

I **yo** 1.1

I am... **Yo soy...** 1.1
I hope (that) **Ojalá (que)**
   interj. 3.1
I wish (that) **Ojalá (que)**
   interj. 3.1
ice cream **helado** *m.* 2.3
   ice cream shop **heladería** *f.* 3.2
iced **helado/a** *adj.* 2.2
   iced tea **té** *m.* **helado** 2.2
idea **idea** *f.* 1.4
if **si** *conj.* 1.4
illness **enfermedad** *f.* 2.4
important **importante** *adj.* 1.3
   be important to **importar** *v.* 2.1
   It's important that... **Es
      importante que...** 2.6
impossible **imposible** *adj.* 3.1
   it's impossible **es imposible** 3.1
improbable **improbable** *adj.* 3.1
   it's improbable **es
      improbable** 3.1
improve **mejorar** *v.* 3.1
in **en** *prep.* 1.2; **por** *prep.* 2.5
   in the afternoon **de la tarde** 1.1;
      por la tarde 2.1
   in a bad mood **de mal
      humor** 1.5
   in the direction of **para** *prep.* 1.1
   in the early evening **de la
      tarde** 1.1
   in the evening **de la noche** 1.1;
      por la tarde 2.1
   in a good mood **de buen
      humor** 1.5
   in the morning **de la
      mañana** 1.1; **por la
      mañana** 2.1
   in love (with)
      enamorado/a (de) 1.5
   in search of **por** *prep.* 2.5
in front of **delante de** *prep.* 1.2
increase **aumento** *m.* 3.4
incredible **increíble** *adj.* 1.5
inequality **desigualdad** *f.* 3.6
infection **infección** *f.* 2.4
inform **informar** *v.* 3.6
injection **inyección** *f.* 2.4
   give an injection **poner una
      inyección** *v.* 2.4
injure (oneself) **lastimarse** 2.4
   injure (one's foot) **lastimarse** *v.*
      (el pie) 2.4
inner ear **oído** *m.* 2.4
inside **dentro** *adv.*
insist (on) **insistir** *v.* **(en)** 2.6
installments: pay in installments
   pagar *v.* **a plazos** 3.2
intelligent **inteligente** *adj.* 1.3
intend to **pensar** *v.* **(+ *inf.*)** 1.4
interest **interesar** *v.* 2.1
interesting **interesante** *adj.* 1.3
   be interesting to **interesar** *v.* 2.1
international **internacional**
   adj. m., f. 3.6
Internet **Internet** 2.5
interview **entrevista** *f.* 3.4;
   interview **entrevistar** *v.* 3.4

interviewer **entrevistador(a)** *m.,*
  f. 3.4
introduction **presentación** *f.*
  I would like to introduce you to
  (name)... **Le presento a...**
  form. 1.1; **Te presento a...**
  fam. 1.1
invest **invertir (e:ie)** *v.* 3.4
invite **invitar** *v.* 2.3
iron (clothes) **planchar** *v.* **la**
  ropa 2.6
it **lo/la** *sing., d.o., pron.* 1.5
Italian **italiano/a** *adj.* 1.3
its **su(s)** *poss. adj.* 1.3,
  suyo(s)/a(s) *poss. pron.* 2.5
it's the same **es igual** 1.5

J

jacket **chaqueta** *f.* 1.6
January **enero** *m.* 1.5
Japanese **japonés, japonesa**
  adj. 1.3
jeans **(blue)jeans** *m., pl.* 1.6
jewelry store **joyería** *f.* 3.2
job **empleo** *m.* 3.4; **puesto**
  m. 3.4; **trabajo** *m.* 3.4
  job application **solicitud** *f.* **de**
    trabajo 3.4
jog **correr** *v.*
journalism **periodismo** *m.* 1.2
journalist **periodista** *m., f.* 1.3;
  reportero/a *m., f.* 3.4
joy **alegría** *f.* 2.3
  give joy **dar** *v.* **alegría** 2.3
joyful **alegre** *adj.* 1.5
juice **jugo** *m.* 2.2
July **julio** *m.* 1.5
June **junio** *m.* 1.5
jungle **selva, jungla** *f.* 3.1
just **apenas** *adv.*
  have just done something
    acabar de (+ inf.) 1.6

K

key **llave** *f.* 1.5
keyboard **teclado** *m.* 2.5
kilometer **kilómetro** *m.* 2.5
kiss **beso** *m.* 2.3
  kiss each other **besarse** *v.* 2.5
kitchen **cocina** *f.* 2.3, 2.6
knee **rodilla** *f.* 2.4
knife **cuchillo** *m.* 2.6
know **saber** *v.* 1.6; **conocer** *v.* 1.6
know how **saber** *v.* 1.6

L

laboratory **laboratorio** *m.* 1.2
lack **faltar** *v.* 2.1
lake **lago** *m.* 3.1
lamp **lámpara** *f.* 2.6
land **tierra** *f.* 3.1
landlord **dueño/a** *m., f.* 2.2

landscape **paisaje** *m.* 1.5
language **lengua** *f.* 1.2
laptop (computer) **computadora**
  f. **portátil** 2.5
large **grande** *adj.* 1.3
large (*clothing size*) **talla**
  grande
last **durar** *v.* 3.6; **pasado/a**
  adj. 1.6; **último/a** *adj.* 2.1
  last name **apellido** *m.* 1.3
  last night **anoche** *adv.* 1.6
  last week **semana** *f.* **pasada** 1.6
  last year **año** *m.* **pasado** 1.6
  the last time **la última vez** 2.1
late **tarde** *adv.* 2.1
later (on) **más tarde** 2.1
  See you later. **Hasta la vista.** 1.1;
    Hasta luego. 1.1
laugh **reírse (e:i)** *v.* 2.3
laughed **reído** *p.p.* 3.2
laundromat **lavandería** *f.* 3.2
law **ley** *f.* 3.1
lawyer **abogado/a** *m., f.* 3.4
lazy **perezoso/a** *adj.*
learn **aprender** *v.* **(a + inf.)** 1.3
least, at **por lo menos** *adv.* 2.4
leave **salir** *v.* 1.4; **irse** *v.* 2.1
  leave a tip **dejar una**
    propina 2.3
  leave behind **dejar** *v.* 3.4
  leave for (*a place*) **salir para**
  leave from **salir de**
left **izquierda** *f.* 1.2
  be left over **quedar** *v.* 2.1
  to the left of **a la izquierda**
    de 1.2
leg **pierna** *f.* 2.4
lemon **limón** *m.* 2.2
lend **prestar** *v.* 1.6
less **menos** *adv.* 2.4
  less... than **menos... que** 2.2
  less than **menos de (+ *number*)**
lesson **lección** *f.* 1.1
let **dejar** *v.* 2.6
let's see **a ver**
letter **carta** *f.* 1.4, 3.2
lettuce **lechuga** *f.* 2.2
liberty **libertad** *f.* 3.6
library **biblioteca** *f.* 1.2
license (*driver's*) **licencia** *f.* **de**
  conducir 2.5
lie **mentira** *f.* 1.4
life **vida** *f.* 2.3
  of my life **de mi vida** 3.3
lifestyle: lead a healthy lifestyle
  llevar una vida sana 3.3
lift **levantar** *v.* 3.3
  lift weights **levantar pesas** 3.3
light **luz** *f.* 2.6
like **gustar** *v.* 1.2; **como**
  prep. 2.2
  I don't like them at all. **No me**
    gustan nada. 1.2
  I like... **Me gusta(n)...** 1.2
  like this **así** *adv.* 2.4
  like very much **encantar** *v.;*
    fascinar *v.* 2.1

Do you like...? **¿Te**
  gusta(n)...? 1.2
likeable **simpático/a** *adj.* 1.3
likewise **igualmente** *adv.* 1.1
line **línea** *f.* 1.4; **cola** (*queue*) *f.* 3.2
listen (to) **escuchar** *v.* 1.2
  Listen! (*command*) **¡Oye!** *fam.,*
    sing. 1.1; **¡Oiga/Oigan!**
    form., sing./pl. 1.1
  listen to music **escuchar**
    música 1.2
  listen (to) the radio **escuchar la**
    radio 1.2
literature **literatura** *f.* 1.2
little (*quantity*) **poco/a** *adj.* 1.5;
  poco *adv.* 2.4
live **vivir** *v.* 1.3; **en vivo** *adj.* 2.1
living room **sala** *f.* 2.6
loan **préstamo** *m.* 3.2; **prestar**
  v. 1.6, 3.2
lobster **langosta** *f.* 2.2
located **situado/a** *adj.*
  be located **quedar** *v.* 3.2
long **largo/a** *adj.* 1.6
look (at) **mirar** *v.* 1.2
look for **buscar** *v.* 1.2
lose **perder (e:ie)** *v.* 1.4
  lose weight **adelgazar** *v.* 3.3
lost **perdido/a** *adj.* 3.1, 3.2
  be lost **estar perdido/a** 3.2
lot, a **muchas veces** *adv.* 2.4
lot of, a **mucho/a** *adj.* 1.2, 1.3;
  un montón de 1.4
love (*another person*) **querer**
  (e:ie) *v.* 1.4; (*inanimate objects*)
  encantar *v.* 2.1; **amor** *m.* 2.3
  in love **enamorado/a** *adj.* 1.5
  I loved it! **¡Me encantó!** 3.3
  love at first sight **amor a**
    primera vista 2.3
lucky: be (very) lucky **tener**
  (mucha) suerte 1.3
luggage **equipaje** *m.* 1.5
lunch **almuerzo** *m.* 1.4, 2.2
  have lunch **almorzar (o:ue)**
    v. 1.4

M

ma'am **señora (Sra.); doña** *f.* 1.1
mad **enojado/a** *adj.* 1.5
magazine **revista** *f.* 1.4
magnificent **magnífico/a** *adj.* 1.5
mail **correo** *m.* 3.2; **enviar** *v.,*
  mandar *v.* 3.2; **echar**
  (una carta) al buzón 3.2
  mail carrier **cartero** *m.* 3.2
mailbox **buzón** *m.* 3.2
main **principal** *adj. m., f.* 2.2
maintain **mantener** *v.* 3.3
major **especialización** *f.* 1.2
make **hacer** *v.* 1.4
  make a decision **tomar una**
    decisión 3.3
  make the bed **hacer la**
    cama 2.6

makeup **maquillaje** *m.* 2.1
  put on makeup **maquillarse** *v.* 2.1
man **hombre** *m.* 1.1
manager **gerente** *m., f.* 2.2, 3.4
many **mucho/a** *adj.* 1.3
  many times **muchas veces** 2.4
map **mapa** *m.* 1.2
March **marzo** *m.* 1.5
margarine **margarina** *f.* 2.2
marinated fish **ceviche** *m.* 2.2
  lemon-marinated shrimp **ceviche** *m.* **de camarón** 2.2
marital status **estado** *m.* **civil** 2.3
market **mercado** *m.* 1.6
  open-air market **mercado al aire libre** 1.6
marriage **matrimonio** *m.* 2.3
married **casado/a** *adj.* 2.3
  get married (to) **casarse** *v.* **(con)** 2.3
  I'll marry you! **¡Acepto casarme contigo!** 3.5
marvelous **maravilloso/a** *adj.* 1.5
massage **masaje** *m.* 3.3
masterpiece **obra maestra** *f.* 3.5
match (*sports*) **partido** *m.* 1.4
match (with) **hacer** *v.* **juego (con)** 1.6
mathematics **matemáticas** *f., pl.* 1.2
matter **importar** *v.* 2.1
maturity **madurez** *f.* 2.3
maximum **máximo/a** *adj.* 2.5
May **mayo** *m.* 1.5
May I leave a message? **¿Puedo dejar un recado?** 2.5
maybe **tal vez** 1.5; **quizás** 1.5
mayonnaise **mayonesa** *f.* 2.2
me **me** *sing., d.o. pron.* 1.5
  to/for me **me** *sing., i.o. pron.* 1.6
meal **comida** *f.* 1.4, 2.2
means of communication **medios** *m., pl.* **de comunicación** 3.6
meat **carne** *f.* 2.2
mechanic **mecánico/a** *m., f.* 2.5
  mechanic's repair shop **taller mecánico** 2.5
media **medios** *m., pl.* **de comunicación** 3.6
medical **médico/a** *adj.* 2.4
medication **medicamento** *m.* 2.4
medicine **medicina** *f.* 2.4
medium **mediano/a** *adj.*
meet (each other) **encontrar(se)** *v.* 2.5; **conocer(se)** *v.* 2.2
  meet up with **encontrarse con** 2.1
meeting **reunión** *f.* 3.4
menu **menú** *m.* 2.2
message **mensaje** *m.*
Mexican **mexicano/a** *adj.* 1.3
Mexico **México** *m.* 1.1
microwave **microonda** *f.* 2.6
  microwave oven **horno** *m.* **de microondas** 2.6
middle age **madurez** *f.* 2.3

midnight **medianoche** *f.* 1.1
mile **milla** *f.* 2.5
milk **leche** *f.* 2.2
million **millón** *m.* 1.2
  million of **millón de** 1.2
mine **mío(s)/a(s)** *poss.* 2.5
mineral **mineral** *m.* 3.3
  mineral water **agua** *f.* **mineral** 2.2
minute **minuto** *m.* 1.1
mirror **espejo** *m.* 2.1
Miss **señorita (Srta.)** *f.* 1.1
miss **perder (e:ie)** *v.* 1.4; **extrañar** *v.* 3.4
mistaken **equivocado/a** *adj.*
modern **moderno/a** *adj.* 3.5
mom **mamá** *f.* 1.3
Monday **lunes** *m., sing.* 1.2
money **dinero** *m.* 1.6
monitor **monitor** *m.* 2.5
monkey **mono** *m.* 3.1
month **mes** *m.* 1.5
monument **monumento** *m.* 1.4
moon **luna** *f.* 3.1
more **más** 1.2
  more… than **más… que** 2.2
  more than **más de (+ *number*)** 2.2
morning **mañana** *f.* 1.1
mother **madre** *f.* 1.3
mother-in-law **suegra** *f.* 1.3
motor **motor** *m.*
motorcycle **motocicleta** *f.* 1.5
mountain **montaña** *f.* 1.4
mouse **ratón** *m.* 2.5
mouth **boca** *f.* 2.4
move (*from one house to another*) **mudarse** *v.* 2.6
movie **película** *f.* 1.4
  movie star **estrella** *f.* **de cine** 3.5
  movie theater **cine** *m.* 1.4
MP3 player **reproductor** *m.* **de MP3** 2.5
Mr. **señor (Sr.); don** *m.* 1.1
Mrs. **señora (Sra.); doña** *f.* 1.1
much **mucho/a** *adj.* 1.2, 1.3
  very much **muchísimo/a** *adj.* 1.2
mud **lodo** *m.*
murder **crimen** *m.* 3.6
muscle **músculo** *m.* 3.3
museum **museo** *m.* 1.4
mushroom **champiñón** *m.* 2.2
music **música** *f.* 1.2, 3.5
musical **musical** *adj., m., f.* 3.5
musician **músico/a** *m., f.* 3.5
must **deber** *v.* **(+ *inf.*)** 3
  It must be… **Debe ser…** 1.6
my **mi(s)** *poss. adj.* 1.3; **mío(s)/a(s)** *poss. pron.* 2.5

name **nombre** *m.* 1.1
  be named **llamarse** *v.* 2.1
  in the name of **a nombre de** 1.5

last name **apellido** *m.* 1.3
My name is… **Me llamo…** 1.1
name someone/ something **ponerle el nombre** 2.3
napkin **servilleta** *f.* 2.6
national **nacional** *adj. m., f.* 3.6
nationality **nacionalidad** *f.* 1.1
natural **natural** *adj. m., f.* 3.1
  natural disaster **desastre** *m.* **natural** 3.6
  natural resource **recurso** *m.* **natural** 3.1
nature **naturaleza** *f.* 3.1
nauseated **mareado/a** *adj.* 2.4
near **cerca de** *prep.* 1.2
neaten **arreglar** *v.* 2.6
necessary **necesario/a** *adj.* 2.6
  It is necessary that… **Hay que…** 2.6, 3.2
neck **cuello** *m.* 2.4
need **faltar** *v.* 2.1; **necesitar** *v.* **(+ *inf.*)** 1.2
neighbor **vecino/a** *m., f.* 2.6
neighborhood **barrio** *m.* 2.6
neither **tampoco** *adv.* 2.1
neither… nor **ni… ni** *conj.* 2.1
nephew **sobrino** *m.* 1.3
nervous **nervioso/a** *adj.* 1.5
network **red** *f.* 2.5
never **nunca** *adj.* 2.1; **jamás** 2.1
new **nuevo/a** *adj.* 1.6
newlywed **recién casado/a** *m., f.* 2.3
news **noticias** *f., pl.* 3.6; **actualidades** *f., pl.* 3.6; **noticia** *f.* 2.5
newscast **noticiero** *m.* 3.6
newspaper **periódico** 1.4; **diario** *m.* 3.6
next **próximo/a** *adj.* 1.3, 3.4
  next to **al lado de** *prep.* 1.2
nice **simpático/a** *adj.* 1.3; **amable** *adj. m., f.*
niece **sobrina** *f.* 1.3
night **noche** *f.* 1.1
  night stand **mesita** *f.* **de noche** 2.6
nine **nueve** 1.1
nine hundred **novecientos/as** 1.2
nineteen **diecinueve** 1.1
ninety **noventa** 1.2
ninth **noveno/a** 1.5
no **no** 1.1; **ningún, ninguno/a(s)** *adj.* 1
  no one **nadie** *pron.* 2.1
nobody **nadie** 2.1
none **ningún, ninguno/a(s)** *adj.* 2.1
noon **mediodía** *m.* 1.1
nor **ni** *conj.* 2.1
north **norte** *m.* 3.2
  to the north **al norte** 3.2
nose **nariz** *f.* 2.4
not **no** 1.1
  not any **ningún, ninguno/a(s)** *adj.* 2.1

not anyone **nadie** *pron.* 2.1
not anything **nada** *pron.* 2.1
not bad at all **nada mal** 1.5
not either **tampoco** *adv.* 2.1
not ever **nunca** *adv.* 2.1;
　jamás *adv.* 2.1
not very well **no muy bien** 1.1
not working **descompuesto/a**
　adj. 2.5
notebook **cuaderno** *m.* 1.1
nothing **nada** 1.1; 2.1
noun **sustantivo** *m.*
November **noviembre** *m.* 1.5
now **ahora** *adv.* 1.2
nowadays **hoy día** *adv.*
nuclear **nuclear** *adj. m., f.* 3.1
　nuclear energy **energía**
　　nuclear 3.1
number **número** *m.* 1.1
nurse **enfermero/a** *m., f.* 2.4
nutrition **nutrición** *f.* 3.3
nutritionist **nutricionista**
　m., f. 3.3

O

o'clock: It's... o'clock **Son**
　las... 1.1
　It's one o'clock. **Es la una.** 1.1
obey **obedecer** *v.* 3.6
obligation **deber** *m.* 3.6
obtain **conseguir (e:i)** *v.* 1.4;
　obtener *v.* 3.4
obvious **obvio/a** *adj.* 3.1
　it's obvious **es obvio** 3.1
occupation **ocupación** *f.* 3.4
occur **ocurrir** *v.* 3.6
October **octubre** *m.* 1.5
of **de** *prep.* 1.1
　Of course. **Claro que sí.;**
　　Por supuesto.
offer **oferta** *f.*; **ofrecer**
　(c:zc) *v.* 1.6
office **oficina** *f.* 2.6
　doctor's office **consultorio** *m.* 2.4
often **a menudo** *adv.* 2.4
Oh! **¡Ay!**
oil **aceite** *m.* 2.2
OK **regular** *adj.* 1.1
　It's okay. **Está bien.**
old **viejo/a** *adj.* 1.3
old age **vejez** *f.* 2.3
older **mayor** *adj. m., f.* 1.3
　older brother, sister **hermano/a**
　　mayor *m., f.* 1.3
oldest **el/la mayor** 2.2
on **en** *prep.* 1.2; **sobre** *prep.* 1.2
　on behalf of **por** *prep.* 2.5
　on the dot **en punto** 1.1
　on time **a tiempo** 2.4
　on top of **encima de** 1.2
once **una vez** 1.6
one **un, uno/a** *m., f., sing. pron.* 1.1
　one hundred **cien(to)** 1.2
　one million **un millón** *m.* 1.2
　one more time **una vez más** 2.3

one thousand **mil** 1.2
one time **una vez** 1.6
onion **cebolla** *f.* 2.2
only **sólo** *adv.* 1.3; **único/a**
　adj. 1.3
　only child **hijo/a único/a**
　　m., f. 1.3
open **abierto/a** *adj.* 1.5, 3.2;
　abrir *v.* 1.3
open-air **al aire libre** 1.6
opera **ópera** *f.* 3.5
operation **operación** *f.* 2.4
opposite **enfrente de** *prep.* 3.2
or **o** *conj.* 2.1
orange **anaranjado/a** *adj.* 1.6;
　naranja *f.* 2.2
orchestra **orquesta** *f.* 3.5
order **mandar** 2.6; *(food)* **pedir**
　(e:i) *v.* 2.2
　in order to **para** *prep.* 2.5
orderly **ordenado/a** *adj.* 1.5
ordinal *(numbers)* **ordinal** *adj.*
organize oneself
　organizarse *v.* 2.6
other **otro/a** *adj.* 1.6
ought to **deber** *v.* **(+ *inf.*)** *adj.* 1.3
our **nuestro(s)/a(s)** *poss.*
　adj. 1.3; *poss. pron.* 2.5
out of order **descompuesto/a**
　adj. 2.5
outside **afuera** *adv.* 1.5
outskirts **afueras** *f., pl.* 2.6
oven **horno** *m.* 2.6
over **sobre** *prep.* 1.2
(over)population **(sobre)**
　población *f.* 3.1
over there **allá** *adv.* 1.2
own **propio/a** *adj.* 3.4
owner **dueño/a** *m., f.* 2.2

P

p.m. **tarde** *f.* 1.1
pack (one's suitcases) **hacer** *v.* **las**
　maletas 1.5
package **paquete** *m.* 3.2
page **página** *f.* 2.5
pain **dolor** *m.* 2.4
　have pain **tener** *v.* **dolor** 2.4
paint **pintar** *v.* 3.5
painter **pintor(a)** *m., f.* 3.4
painting **pintura** *f.* 2.6, 3.5
pair **par** *m.* 1.6
　pair of shoes **par** *m.* **de**
　　zapatos 1.6
pale **pálido/a** *adj.* 3.2
pants **pantalones** *m., pl.* 1.6
pantyhose **medias** *f., pl.* 1.6
paper **papel** *m.* 1.2; *(report)*
　informe *m.* 3.6
Pardon me. *(May I?)* **Con**
　permiso. 1.1; *(Excuse me.)*
　Pardon me. **Perdón.** 1.1
parents **padres** *m., pl.* 1.3;
　papás *m., pl.* 1.3

park **estacionar** *v.* 2.5; **parque**
　m. 1.4
parking lot **estacionamiento**
　m. 3.2
partner *(one of a married couple)*
　pareja *f.* 2.3
party **fiesta** *f.* 2.3
passed **pasado/a** *p.p.*
passenger **pasajero/a** *m., f.* 1.1
passport **pasaporte** *m.* 1.5
past **pasado/a** *adj.* 1.6
pastime **pasatiempo** *m.* 1.4
pastry shop **pastelería** *f.* 3.2
patient **paciente** *m., f.* 2.4
patio **patio** *m.* 2.6
pay **pagar** *v.* 1.6
　pay in cash **pagar** *v.* **al**
　　contado; pagar en
　　efectivo 3.2
　pay in installments **pagar** *v.* **a**
　　plazos 3.2
　pay the bill **pagar la**
　　cuenta 2.3
pea **arveja** *m.* 2.2
peace **paz** *f.* 3.6
peach **melocotón** *m.* 2.2
peak **cima** *f.* 3.3
pear **pera** *f.* 2.2
pen **pluma** *f.* 1.2
pencil **lápiz** *m.* 1.1
people **gente** *f.* 1.3
pepper *(black)* **pimienta** *f.* 2.2
per **por** *prep.* 2.5
perfect **perfecto/a** *adj.* 1.5
period of time **temporada** *f.* 1.5
person **persona** *f.* 1.3
pharmacy **farmacia** *f.* 2.4
phenomenal **fenomenal** *adj.* 1.5
photograph **foto(grafía)** *f.* 1.1
physical *(exam)* **examen** *m.*
　médico 2.4
physician **doctor(a), médico/a**
　m., f. 1.3
physics **física** *f. sing.* 1.2
pick up **recoger** *v.* 3.1
picture **cuadro** *m.* 2.6;
　pintura *f.* 2.6
pie **pastel** *m.* 2.3
pill (tablet) **pastilla** *f.* 2.4
pillow **almohada** *f.* 2.6
pineapple **piña** *f.*
pink **rosado/a** *adj.* 1.6
place **lugar** *m.* 1.2, 1.4; **sitio** *m.*
　1.3; **poner** *v.* 1.4
plaid **de cuadros** 1.6
plans **planes** *m., pl.* 1.4
　have plans **tener planes** 1.4
plant **planta** *f.* 3.1
plastic **plástico** *m.* 3.1
　(made) of plastic **de**
　　plástico 3.1
plate **plato** *m.* 2.6
play **drama** *m.* 3.5; **comedia**
　f. 3.5; **jugar (u:ue)** *v.* 1.4; *(a*
　musical instrument) **tocar** *v.*
　3.5; *(a role)* **hacer el papel**
　de 3.5; *(cards)* **jugar a (las**

cartas) 1.5; (*sports*)
practicar deportes 1.4
player **jugador(a)** *m., f.* 1.4
playwright **dramaturgo/a**
m., f. 3.5
plead **rogar (o:ue)** *v.* 2.6
pleasant **agradable** *adj.* 1.5
please **por favor** 1.1
Pleased to meet you. **Mucho
gusto.** 1.1; **Encantado/a.**
adj. 1.1
pleasing: be pleasing to **gustar** *v.* 2.1
pleasure **gusto** *m.* 1.1
The pleasure is mine. **El gusto
es mío.** 1.1
poem **poema** *m.* 3.5
poet **poeta** *m., f.* 3.5
poetry **poesía** *f.* 3.5
police (force) **policía** *f.* 2.5
political **político/a** *adj.* 3.6
politician **político/a** *m., f.* 3.4
politics **política** *f.* 3.6
polka-dotted **de lunares** 1.6
poll **encuesta** *f.* 3.6
pollute **contaminar** *v.* 3.1
polluted **contaminado/a** *m., f.* 3.1
be polluted **estar
contaminado/a** 3.1
pollution **contaminación** *f.* 3.1
pool **piscina** *f.* 1.4
poor **pobre** *adj., m., f.* 1.6
poor thing **pobrecito/a** *adj.* 1.3
popsicle **paleta helada** *f.* 1.4
population **población** *f.* 3.1
pork **cerdo** *m.* 2.2
pork chop **chuleta** *f.* **de
cerdo** 2.2
portable **portátil** *adj.* 2.5
portable computer
computadora *f.*
portátil 2.5
position **puesto** *m.* 3.4
possessive **posesivo/a** *adj.* 1.3
possible **posible** *adj.* 3.1
it's (not) possible **(no) es
posible** 3.1
post office **correo** *m.* 3.2
postcard **postal** *f.*
poster **cartel** *m.* 2.6
potato **papa** *f.* 2.2; **patata** *f.* 2.2
pottery **cerámica** *f.* 3.5
practice **entrenarse** *v.* 3.3;
practicar *v.* 1.2; (a degree/
profession) **ejercer** *v.* 3.4
prefer **preferir (e:ie)** *v.* 1.4
pregnant **embarazada** *adj. f.* 2.4
prepare **preparar** *v.* 1.2
preposition **preposición** *f.*
prescribe (medicine) **recetar**
v. 2.4
prescription **receta** *f.* 2.4
present **regalo** *m.* 1.6;
presentar *v.* 3.5
press **prensa** *f.* 3.6
pressure **presión** *f.*
be under a lot of pressure **sufrir
muchas presiones** 3.3

pretty **bonito/a** *adj.* 1.3
price **precio** *m.* 1.6
(fixed, set) price **precio** *m.*
fijo 1.6
print **estampado/a** *adj.;*
imprimir *v.* 2.5
printer **impresora** *f.* 2.5
private (*room*) **individual** *adj.*
prize **premio** *m.* 3.5
probable **probable** *adj.* 3.1
it's (not) probable **(no) es
probable** 3.1
problem **problema** *m.* 1.1
profession **profesión** *f.* 1.3; 3.4
professor **profesor(a)** *m., f.*
program **programa** *m.* 1.1
programmer **programador(a)**
m., f. 1.3
prohibit **prohibir** *v.* 2.4
project **proyecto** *m.* 2.5
promotion (*career*)
ascenso *m.* 3.4
pronoun **pronombre** *m.*
protect **proteger** *v.* 3.1
protein **proteína** *f.* 3.3
provided (that) **con tal (de)
que** *conj.* 3.1
psychologist **psicólogo/a**
m., f. 3.4
psychology **psicología** *f.* 1.2
publish **publicar** *v.* 3.5
Puerto Rican **puertorriqueño/a**
adj. 1.3
Puerto Rico **Puerto Rico** *m.* 1.1
pull a tooth **sacar una muela**
purchases **compras** *f., pl.* 1.5
pure **puro/a** *adj.* 3.1
purple **morado/a** *adj.* 1.6
purse **bolsa** *f.* 1.6
put **poner** *v.* 1.4; **puesto/a**
p.p. 3.2
put (a letter) in the mailbox
**echar (una carta) al
buzón** 3.2
put on (*a performance*)
presentar *v.* 3.5
put on (*clothing*) **ponerse**
v. 2.1
put on makeup **maquillarse**
v. 2.1

quality **calidad** *f.* 1.6
quarter (academic) **trimestre**
m. 1.2
quarter after (*time*) **y cuarto** 1.1;
y quince 1.1
quarter to (*time*) **menos
cuarto** 1.1; **menos
quince** 1.1
question **pregunta** *f.* 1.2
quickly **rápido** *adv.* 2.4
quiet **tranquilo/a** *adj.* 3.3
quit **dejar** *v.* 3.4
quiz **prueba** *f.* 1.2

racism **racismo** *m.* 3.6
radio (*medium*) **radio** *f.* 1.2
radio (set) **radio** *m.* 2.5
rain **llover (o:ue)** *v.* 1.5;
lluvia *f.*
It's raining. **Llueve.** 1.5; **Está
lloviendo.** 1.5
raincoat **impermeable** *m.* 1.6
rain forest **bosque** *m.* **tropical** 3.1
raise (*salary*) **aumento de
sueldo** 3.4
rather **bastante** *adv.* 2.4
read **leer** *v.* 1.3; **leído/a** *p.p.* 3.2
read e-mail **leer correo
electrónico** 1.4
read a magazine **leer una
revista** 1.4
read a newspaper **leer un
periódico** 1.4
ready **listo/a** *adj.* 1.5
(Are you) ready? **¿(Están)
listos?** 3.3
reality show **progama de
realidad** *m.* 3.5
reap the benefits (of) **disfrutar** *v.*
(de) 3.3
receive **recibir** *v.* 1.3
recommend **recomendar (e:ie)**
v. 2.2; 2.6
record **grabar** *v.* 2.5
recover **recuperar** *v.* 2.5
recreation **diversión** *f.* 1.4
recycle **reciclar** *v.* 3.1
recycling **reciclaje** *m.* 3.1
red **rojo/a** *adj.* 1.6
red-haired **pelirrojo/a** *adj.* 1.3
reduce **reducir** *v.* 3.1; disminuir *v.* 3.4
reduce stress/tension **aliviar el
estrés/la tensión** 3.3
refrigerator **refrigerador** *m.* 2.6
region **región** *f.* 3.1
regret **sentir (e:ie)** *v.* 3.1
related to sitting **sedentario/a**
adj. 3.3
relatives **parientes** *m., pl.* 1.3
relax **relajarse** *v.* 2.3
Relax, sweetie. **Tranquilo/a,
cariño.** 2.5
remain **quedarse** *v.* 2.1
remember **recordar (o:ue)** *v.* 1.4;
acordarse (o:ue) *v.* **(de)** 2.1
remote control **control remoto**
m. 2.5
renewable **renovable** *adj.* 3.1
rent **alquilar** *v.* 2.6; (payment)
alquiler *m.* 2.6
repeat **repetir (e:i)** *v.* 1.4
report **informe** *m.* 3.6; **reportaje**
m. 3.6
reporter **reportero/a** *m., f.* 3.4
representative **representante**
m., f. 3.6
request **pedir (e:i)** *v.* 1.4
reservation **reservación** *f.* 1.5
resign (from) **renunciar (a)** *v.* 3.4

resolve **resolver (o:ue)** v. 3.1
resolved **resuelto/a** p.p. 3.2
resource **recurso** m. 3.1
responsibility **deber** m. 3.6;
   responsabilidad f.
responsible **responsable** adj. 2.2
rest **descansar** v. 1.2
restaurant **restaurante** m. 1.4
résumé **currículum** m. 3.4
retire (from work) **jubilarse** v. 2.3
return **regresar** v. 1.2; **volver**
   (o:ue) v. 1.4
returned **vuelto/a** p.p. 3.2
rice **arroz** m. 2.2
rich **rico/a** adj. 1.6
ride a bicycle **pasear** v. **en**
   bicicleta 1.4
ride a horse **montar** v. **a**
   caballo 1.5
ridiculous **ridículo/a** adj. 3.1
   it's ridiculous **es ridículo** 3.1
right **derecha** f. 1.2
   be right **tener razón** 1.3
   right? (question tag) **¿no?** 1.1;
      ¿verdad? 1.1
   right away **enseguida** adv.
   right now **ahora mismo** 1.5
   right there **allí mismo** 3.2
   to the right of **a la**
      derecha de 1.2
rights **derechos** m. 3.6
ring **anillo** m. 3.5
ring (a doorbell) **sonar (o:ue)** v. 2.5
river **río** m. 3.1
road **camino** m.
roast **asado/a** adj. 2.2
roast chicken **pollo** m. **asado** 2.2
rollerblade **patinar en línea** v.
romantic **romántico/a** adj. 3.5
room **habitación** f. 1.5; **cuarto**
   m. 1.2; 2.1
   living room **sala** f. 2.6
roommate **compañero/a**
   m., f. **de cuarto** 1.2
roundtrip **de ida y vuelta** 1.5
   roundtrip ticket **pasaje** m. **de**
      ida y vuelta 1.5
routine **rutina** f. 2.1
rug **alfombra** f. 2.6
run **correr** v. 1.3
   run errands **hacer**
      diligencias 3.2
   run into (have an accident)
      chocar (con) v.; (meet
      accidentally) **encontrar(se)**
      (o:ue) v. 2.5; (run into
      something) **darse (con)** 2.4
   run into (each other)
      encontrar(se) (o:ue) v. 2.5
rush **apurarse, darse prisa** v. 3.3
Russian **ruso/a** adj. 1.3

S

sad **triste** adj. 1.5; 3.1
   it's sad **es triste** 3.1

safe **seguro/a** adj. 1.5
said **dicho/a** p.p. 3.2
sailboard **tabla de**
   windsurf f. 1.5
salad **ensalada** f. 2.2
salary **salario** m. 3.4; **sueldo**
   m. 3.4
sale **rebaja** f. 1.6
salesperson **vendedor(a)** m., f. 1.6
salmon **salmón** m. 2.2
salt **sal** f. 2.2
same **mismo/a** adj. 1.3
sandal **sandalia** f. 1.6
sandwich **sándwich** m. 2.2
Saturday **sábado** m. 1.2
sausage **salchicha** f. 2.2
save (on a computer) **guardar**
   v. 2.5; save (money) **ahorrar**
   v. 3.2
savings **ahorros** m. 3.2
   savings account **cuenta** f. **de**
      ahorros 3.2
say **decir** v. 1.4; **declarar** v. 3.6
say (that) **decir (que)** v. 1.4, 2.3
   say the answer **decir la**
      respuesta 1.4
scan **escanear** v. 2.5
scarcely **apenas** adv. 2.4
scared: be (very) scared (of) **tener**
   (mucho) miedo (de) 1.3
schedule **horario** m. 1.2
school **escuela** f. 1.1
science **ciencia** f. 1.2
   science fiction **ciencia ficción**
      f. 3.5
scientist **científico/a** m., f. 3.4
scream **grito** m. 1.5; **gritar**
   v. 2.1
screen **pantalla** f. 2.5
scuba dive **bucear** v. 1.4
sculpt **esculpir** v. 3.5
sculptor **escultor(a)** m., f. 3.5
sculpture **escultura** f. 3.5
sea **mar** m. 1.5
   (sea) turtle **tortuga**
      (marina) f. 3.1
season **estación** f. 1.5
seat **silla** f. 1.2
second **segundo/a** 1.5
secretary **secretario/a** m., f. 3.4
sedentary **sedentario/a** adj. 3.3
see **ver** v. 1.4
   see (you, him, her) again **volver**
      a ver(te, lo, la) 3.6
   see movies **ver películas** 1.4
   See you. **Nos vemos.** 1.1
   See you later. **Hasta la vista.** 1.1;
      Hasta luego. 1.1
   See you soon. **Hasta**
      pronto. 1.1
   See you tomorrow. **Hasta**
      mañana. 1.1
seem **parecer** v. 1.6
seen **visto/a** p.p. 3.2
sell **vender** v. 1.6
semester **semestre** m. 1.2
send **enviar; mandar** v. 3.2

separate (from) **separarse** v.
   (de) 2.3
separated **separado/a** adj. 2.3
September **septiembre** m. 1.5
sequence **secuencia** f.
serious **grave** adj. 2.4
serve **servir (e:i)** v. 2.2
service **servicio** m. 3.3
set (fixed) **fijo/a** adj. 1.6
   set the table **poner la mesa** 2.6
seven **siete** 1.1
seven hundred **setecientos/as** 1.2
seventeen **diecisiete** 1.1
seventh **séptimo/a** 1.5
seventy **setenta** 1.2
several **varios/as** adj. pl. 2.2
sexism **sexismo** m. 3.6
shame **lástima** f. 3.1
   it's a shame **es una lástima** 3.1
shampoo **champú** m. 2.1
shape **forma** f. 3.3
   be in good shape **estar en**
      buena forma 3.3
   stay in shape **mantenerse en**
      forma 3.3
share **compartir** v. 1.3
sharp (time) **en punto** 1.1
shave **afeitarse** v. 2.1
shaving cream **crema** f. **de**
   afeitar 1.5, 2.1
she **ella** 1.1
shellfish **mariscos** m., pl. 2.2
ship **barco** m.
shirt **camisa** f. 1.6
shoe **zapato** m. 1.6
   shoe size **número** m. 1.6
   shoe store **zapatería** f. 3.2
   tennis shoes **zapatos** m., pl. **de**
      tenis 1.6
shop **tienda** f. 1.6
shopping, to go **ir de**
   compras 1.5
   shopping mall **centro**
      comercial m. 1.6
short (in height) **bajo/a** adj. 1.3;
   (in length) **corto/a** adj. 1.6
short story **cuento** m. 3.5
shorts **pantalones cortos**
   m., pl. 1.6
should (do something) **deber** v.
   (+ inf.) 1.3
shout **gritar** v. 2.1
show **espectáculo** m. 3.5;
   mostrar (o:ue) v. 1.4
   game show **concurso** m. 3.5
shower **ducha** f. 2.1; **ducharse**
   v. 2.1
shrimp **camarón** m. 2.2
siblings **hermanos/as** pl. 1.3
sick **enfermo/a** adj. 2.4
   be sick **estar enfermo/a** 2.4
   get sick **enfermarse** v. 2.4
sign **firmar** v. 3.2; **letrero** m. 3.2
silk **seda** f. 1.6
   (made of) silk **de seda** 1.6
silly **tonto/a** adj. 1.3
since **desde** prep.

sing **cantar** *v.* 1.2
singer **cantante** *m., f.* 3.5
single **soltero/a** *adj.* 2.3
   single room **habitación** *f.*
     individual 1.5
sink **lavabo** *m.* 2.1
sir **señor (Sr.), don** m. 1.1;
   caballero *m.* **2.2**
sister **hermana** *f.* 1.3
sister-in-law **cuñada** *f.* 1.3
sit down **sentarse (e:ie)** *v.* 2.1
six **seis** 1.1
six hundred **seiscientos/as** 1.2
sixteen **dieciséis** 1.1
sixth **sexto/a** 1.5
sixty **sesenta** 1.2
size **talla** *f.* 1.6
   shoe size **número** *m.* 1.6
(in-line) skate **patinar (en línea)** 1.4
skateboard **andar en patineta**
   v. 1.4
ski **esquiar** *v.* 1.4
skiing **esquí** *m.* 1.4
   water-skiing **esquí** *m.*
     acuático 1.4
skirt **falda** *f.* 1.6
skull made out of sugar **calavera**
   de azúcar *f.* 2.3
sky **cielo** *m.* 3.1
sleep **dormir (o:ue)** *v.* 1.4
   go to sleep **dormirse**
     (o:ue) *v.* 2.1
sleepy: be (very) sleepy **tener**
   (mucho) sueño 1.3
slender **delgado/a** *adj.* 1.3
slim down **adelgazar** *v.* 3.3
slippers **pantuflas** *f.* 2.1
slow **lento/a** *adj.* 2.5
slowly **despacio** *adv.* 2.4
small **pequeño/a** *adj.* 1.3
smart **listo/a** *adj.* 1.5
smile **sonreír (e:i)** *v.* 2.3
smiled **sonreído** *p.p.* 3.2
smoggy: It's (very) smoggy. **Hay**
   (mucha) contaminación.
smoke **fumar** *v.* 2.2; 3.3
   (not) to smoke **(no) fumar** 3.3
smoking section **sección** *f.* **de**
   fumar 2.2
   (non) smoking section **sección**
     de (no) fumar *f.* 2.2
snack **merendar** *v.* 2.2; 3.3;
   afternoon snack **merienda** *f.* 3.3
   have a snack **merendar** *v.*
sneakers **los zapatos de tenis** 1.6
sneeze **estornudar** *v.* 2.4
snow **nevar (e:ie)** *v.* 1.5; **nieve** *f.*
snowing: It's snowing. **Nieva.** 1.5;
   Está nevando. 1.5
so (*in such a way*) **así** *adv.* 2.4;
   tan *adv.* 1.5
   so much **tanto** *adv.*
   so-so **regular** 1.1
   so that **para que** *conj.* 3.1
soap **jabón** *m.* 2.1
soap opera **telenovela** *f.* 3.5
soccer **fútbol** *m.* 1.4

sociology **sociología** *f.* 1.2
sock(s) **calcetín (calcetines)**
   m. 1.6
sofa **sofá** *m.* 2.6
soft drink **refresco** *m.* 2.2
software **programa** *m.* **de**
   computación 2.5
soil **tierra** *f.* 3.1
solar **solar** *adj., m., f.* 3.1
   solar energy **energía solar** 3.1
soldier **soldado** *m., f.* 3.6
solution **solución** *f.* 3.1
solve **resolver (o:ue)** *v.* 3.1
some **algún, alguno/a(s)** *adj.*
   2.1; **unos/as** *pron./ m., f., pl;*
   indef., art. 1.1
somebody **alguien** *pron.* 2.1
someone **alguien** *pron.* 2.1
something **algo** *pron.* 2.1
sometimes **a veces** *adv.* 2.4
son **hijo** *m.* 1.3
song **canción** *f.* 3.5
son-in-law **yerno** *m.* 1.3
soon **pronto** *adv.* 2.4
   See you soon. **Hasta pronto.** 1.1
sorry: be sorry **sentir (e:ie)** *v.* 3.1
   I'm sorry. **Lo siento.** 1.1
soul **alma** *f.* 2.3
soup **sopa** *f.* 2.2
south **sur** *m.* 3.2
   to the south **al sur** 3.2
Spain **España** *f.* 1.1
Spanish (*language*) **español**
   m. 1.2; **español(a)** *adj.* 1.3
spare (free) time **ratos libres** 1.4
speak **hablar** *v.* 1.2
   Speaking. (*on the phone*) **Con**
     él/ella habla. 2.5
special: today's specials **las**
   especialidades del día 2.2
spectacular **espectacular** *adj. m.,*
   f. 3.3
speech **discurso** *m.* 3.6
speed **velocidad** *f.* 2.5
   speed limit **velocidad** *f.*
     máxima 2.5
spelling **ortografía** *f.,*
   ortográfico/a *adj.*
spend (*money*) **gastar** *v.* 1.6
spoon (*table or large*) **cuchara**
   f. 2.6
sport **deporte** *m.* 1.4
   sports-related **deportivo/a**
     adj. 1.4
spouse **esposo/a** *m., f.* 1.3
sprain (one's ankle) **torcerse**
   (o:ue) *v.* **(el tobillo)** 2.4
sprained **torcido/a** *adj.* 2.4
   be sprained **estar torcido/a** 2.4
spring **primavera** *f.* 1.5
(city or town) square **plaza** *f.* 1.4
stadium **estadio** *m.* 1.2
stage **etapa** *f.* 2.3
stairs **escalera** *f.* 2.6
stairway **escalera** *f.* 2.6
stamp **estampilla** *f.* 3.2; **sello**
   m. 3.2

stand in line **hacer** *v.* **cola** 3.2
star **estrella** *f.* 3.1
start (*a vehicle*) **arrancar** *v.* 2.5
station **estación** *f.* 1.5
statue **estatua** *f.* 3.5
status: marital status **estado** *m.*
   civil 2.3
stay **quedarse** *v.* 2.1
   stay in shape **mantenerse en**
     forma 3.3
steak **bistec** *m.* 2.2
steering wheel **volante** *m.* 2.5
step **escalón** *m.* 3.3
stepbrother **hermanastro** *m.* 1.3
stepdaughter **hijastra** *f.* 1.3
stepfather **padrastro** *m.* 1.3
stepmother **madrastra** *f.* 1.3
stepsister **hermanastra** *f.* 1.3
stepson **hijastro** *m.* 1.3
stereo **estéreo** *m.* 2.5
still **todavía** *adv.* 1.5
stockbroker **corredor(a)** *m., f.* **de**
   bolsa 3.4
stockings **medias** *f., pl.* 1.6
stomach **estómago** *m.* 2.4
stone **piedra** *f.* 3.1
stop **parar** *v.* 2.5
   stop (*doing something*) **dejar de**
     (+ inf.) 3.1
store **tienda** *f.* 1.6
storm **tormenta** *f.* 3.6
story **cuento** *m.* 3.5; **historia**
   f. 3.5
stove **cocina, estufa** *f.* 2.6
straight **derecho** *adv.* 3.2
   straight (ahead) **derecho** 3.2
straighten up **arreglar** *v.* 2.6
strange **extraño/a** *adj.* 3.1
   it's strange **es extraño** 3.1
street **calle** *f.* 2.5
stress **estrés** *m.* 3.3
stretching **estiramiento** *m.* 3.3
   do stretching exercises **hacer**
     ejercicios *m. pl.* **de**
     estiramiento 3.3
strike (*labor*) **huelga** *f.* 3.6
stripe **raya** *f.* 1.6
   striped **de rayas** 1.6
stroll **pasear** *v.* 1.4
strong **fuerte** *adj. m., f.* 3.3
struggle (for/against) **luchar** *v.*
   (por/contra) 3.6
student **estudiante** *m., f.* 1.1; 1.2;
   estudiantil *adj.* 1.2
study **estudiar** *v.* 1.2
stuffed-up (*sinuses*)
   congestionado/a *adj.* 2.4
stupendous **estupendo/a** *adj.* 1.5
style **estilo** *m.*
suburbs **afueras** *f., pl.* 2.6
subway **metro** *m.* 1.5
   subway station **estación** *f.*
     del metro 1.5
successful: be successful **tener**
   éxito 3.4
such as **tales como**
suddenly **de repente** *adv.* 1.6

suffer **sufrir** *v.* 2.4
   suffer an illness **sufrir una enfermedad** 2.4
sugar **azúcar** *m.* 2.2
suggest **sugerir (e:ie)** *v.* 2.6
suit **traje** *m.* 1.6
suitcase **maleta** *f.* 1.1
summer **verano** *m.* 1.5
sun **sol** *m.* 1.5; 3.1
sunbathe **tomar** *v.* **el sol** 1.4
Sunday **domingo** *m.* 1.2
(sun)glasses **gafas** *f., pl.* **(de sol)** 1.6
sunny: It's (very) sunny. **Hace (mucho) sol.** 1.5
supermarket **supermercado** *m.* 3.2
suppose **suponer** *v.* 1.4
sure **seguro/a** *adj.* 1.5
   be sure **estar seguro/a** 1.5
surf (*the Internet*) **navegar** *v.* **(en Internet)** 2.5
surfboard **tabla de surf** *f.* 1.5
surprise **sorprender** *v.* 2.3; **sorpresa** *f.* 2.3
survey **encuesta** *f.* 3.6
sweat **sudar** *v.* 3.3
sweater **suéter** *m.* 1.6
sweep the floor **barrer el suelo** 2.6
sweets **dulces** *m., pl.* 2.3
swim **nadar** *v.* 1.4
swimming **natación** *f.* 1.4
   swimming pool **piscina** *f.* 1.4
symptom **síntoma** *m.* 2.4

T

table **mesa** *f.* 1.2
tablespoon **cuchara** *f.* 2.6
tablet (*pill*) **pastilla** *f.* 2.4
take **tomar** *v.* 1.2; **llevar** *v.* 1.6
   take care of **cuidar** *v.* 3.1
   take someone's temperature **tomar** *v.* **la temperatura** 2.4
   take (wear) a shoe size **calzar** *v.* 1.6
   take a bath **bañarse** *v.* 2.1
   take a shower **ducharse** *v.* 2.1
   take off **quitarse** *v.* 2.1
   take out the trash **sacar la basura** *v.* 2.6
   take photos **tomar** *v.* **fotos** 1.5; **sacar** *v.* **fotos** 1.5
talented **talentoso/a** *adj.* 3.5
talk **hablar** *v.* 1.2
   talk show **programa** *m.* **de entrevistas** 3.5
tall **alto/a** *adj.* 1.3
tank **tanque** *m.* 2.5
taste **probar (o:ue)** *v.* 2.2; **saber** *v.* 2.2
   taste like **saber a** 2.2
tasty **rico/a** *adj.* 2.2; **sabroso/a** *adj.* 2.2
tax **impuesto** *m.* 3.6
taxi **taxi** *m.* 1.5
tea **té** *m.* 2.2

teach **enseñar** *v.* 1.2
teacher **profesor(a)** *m., f.* 1.1, 1.2; **maestro/a** *m., f.* 3.4
team **equipo** *m.* 1.4
technician **técnico/a** *m., f.* 3.4
telecommuting **teletrabajo** *m.* 3.4
telephone **teléfono** 2.5
television **televisión** *f.* 1.2; 2.5
   television set **televisor** *m.* 2.5
tell **contar** *v.* 1.4; **decir** *v.* 1.4
tell (that) **decir** *v.* **(que)** 1.4, 2.3
   tell lies **decir mentiras** 1.4
   tell the truth **decir la verdad** 1.4
temperature **temperatura** *f.* 2.4
ten **diez** 1.1
tennis **tenis** *m.* 1.4
   tennis shoes **zapatos** *m., pl.* **de tenis** 1.6
tension **tensión** *f.* 3.3
tenth **décimo/a** 1.5
terrible **terrible** *adj. m., f.* 3.1
   it's terrible **es terrible** 3.1
terrific **chévere** *adj.*
test **prueba** *f.* 1.2; **examen** *m.* 1.2
text message **mensaje** *m.* **de texto** 2.5
Thank you. **Gracias.** *f., pl.* 1.1
   Thank you (very much). **(Muchas) gracias.** 1.1
   Thanks (a lot). **(Muchas) gracias.** 1.1
   Thanks for inviting me. **Gracias por invitarme.** 2.3
that **que, quien(es), lo que** *pron.* 2.6
   that (one) **ése, ésa, eso** *pron.* 1.6; **ese, esa,** *adj.* 1.6
   that (*over there*) **aquél, aquélla, aquello** *pron.* 1.6; **aquel, aquella** *adj.* 1.6
   that which **lo que** *conj.* 2.6
   that's why **por eso** 2.5
the **el** *m.*, **la** *f. sing.*, **los** *m.*, **las** *f., pl.* 1.1
theater **teatro** *m.* 3.5
their **su(s)** *poss. adj.* 1.3; **suyo(s)/a(s)** *poss. pron.* 2.5
them **los/las** *pl., d.o. pron.* 1.5
   to/for them **les** *pl., i.o. pron.* 1.6
then (*afterward*) **después** *adv.* 2.1; (*as a result*) **entonces** *adv.* 1.5, 2.1; (*next*) **luego** *adv.* 2.1; **pues** *adv.* 3.3
there **allí** *adv.* 1.2
   There is/are… **Hay…** 1.1
   There is/are not… **No hay…** 1.1
therefore **por eso** 2.5
these **éstos, éstas** *pron.* 1.6; **estos, estas** *adj.* 1.6
they **ellos** *m.*, **ellas** *f. pron.*
   They all told me to ask you to excuse them/forgive them. **Todos me dijeron que te pidiera disculpas de su parte.** 3.6
thin **delgado/a** *adj.* 1.3
thing **cosa** *f.* 1.1

think **pensar (e:ie)** *v.* 1.4; (believe) **creer** *v.*
   think about **pensar en** *v.* 1.4
third **tercero/a** 1.5
thirsty: be (very) thirsty **tener (mucha) sed** 1.3
thirteen **trece** 1.1
thirty **treinta** 1.1; 1.2; thirty (*minutes past the hour*) **y treinta; y media** 1.1
this **este, esta** *adj.*; **éste, ésta, esto** *pron.* 1.6
   This is… (*introduction*) **Éste/a es…** 1.1
those **ésos, ésas** *pron.* 1.6; **esos, esas** *adj.* 1.6
those (over there) **aquéllos, aquéllas** *pron.* 1.6; **aquellos, aquellas** *adj.* 1.6
thousand **mil** *m.* 1.6
three **tres** 1.1
three hundred **trescientos/as** 1.2
throat **garganta** *f.* 2.4
through **por** *prep.* 2.5
Thursday **jueves** *m., sing.* 1.2
thus (*in such a way*) **así** *adv.*
ticket **boleto** *m.* 1.2, 3.5; **pasaje** *m.* 1.5
tie **corbata** *f.* 1.6
time **tiempo** *m.* 1.4; **vez** *f.* 1.6
   have a good/bad time **pasarlo bien/mal** 2.3
   I've had a fantastic time. **Lo he pasado de película.** 3.6
   What time is it? **¿Qué hora es?** 1.1
   (At) What time…? **¿A qué hora…?** 1.1
times **veces** *f., pl.* 1.6
   many times **muchas veces** 2.4
   two times **dos veces** 1.6
tip **propina** *f.* 2.3
tire **llanta** *f.* 2.5
tired **cansado/a** *adj.* 1.5
   be tired **estar cansado/a** 1.5
to **a** *prep.* 1.1
toast (*drink*) **brindar** *v.* 2.3
   toast **pan** *m.* **tostado**
toasted **tostado/a** *adj.* 2.2
   toasted bread **pan tostado** *m.* 2.2
toaster **tostadora** *f.* 2.6
today **hoy** *adv.* 1.2
   Today is… **Hoy es…** 1.2
toe **dedo** *m.* **del pie** 2.4
together **juntos/as** *adj.* 2.3
toilet **inodoro** *m.* 2.1
tomato **tomate** *m.* 2.2
tomorrow **mañana** *f.* 1.1
   See you tomorrow. **Hasta mañana.** 1.1
tonight **esta noche** *adv.* 1.4
too **también** *adv.* 1.2; 2.1
   too much **demasiado** *adv.* 1.6; **en exceso** 3.3
tooth **diente** *m.* 2.1
toothpaste **pasta** *f.* **de dientes** 2.1

top **cima** *f.* 3.3
   to the top **hasta arriba** *f.* 3.3
tornado **tornado** *m.* 3.6
touch **tocar** *v.* 3.5
touch screen **pantalla táctil** *f.* 2.5
tour **excursión** *f.* 1.4;
   recorrido *m.* 3.1
tour an area **recorrer** *v.*
tourism **turismo** *m.* 1.5
tourist **turista** *m., f.* 1.1;
   turístico/a *adj.*
toward **hacia** *prep.* 3.2;
   para *prep.* 2.5
towel **toalla** *f.* 2.1
town **pueblo** *m.* 1.4
trade **oficio** *m.* 3.4
traffic **circulación** *f.* 2.5;
   tráfico *m.* 2.5
   traffic light **semáforo** *m.* 3.2
tragedy **tragedia** *f.* 3.5
trail **sendero** *m.* 3.1
   trailhead **sendero** *m.* 3.1
train **entrenarse** *v.* 3.3;
   tren *m.* 1.5
   train station **estación** *f.* **de**
   tren *m.* 1.5
trainer **entrenador(a)** *m., f.* 3.3
translate **traducir** *v.* 1.6
trash **basura** *f.* 2.6
travel **viajar** *v.* 1.2
   travel agent **agente** *m., f.*
   de viajes 1.5
traveler **viajero/a** *m., f.* 1.5
   (traveler's) check **cheque (de**
   viajero) 3.2
treadmill **cinta caminadora** *f.* 3.3
tree **árbol** *m.* 3.1
trillion **billón** *m.*
trimester **trimestre** *m.* 1.2
trip **viaje** *m.* 1.5
   take a trip **hacer un viaje** 1.5
tropical forest **bosque** *m.*
   tropical 3.1
true: it's (not)
   true **(no) es verdad** 3.1
trunk **baúl** *m.* 2.5
truth **verdad** *f.*
try **intentar v.; probar**
   (o:ue) *v.* 2.2
   try (*to do something*) **tratar de**
   (+ inf.) 3.3
   try on **probarse (o:ue)** *v.* 2.1
t-shirt **camiseta** *f.* 1.6
Tuesday **martes** *m., sing.* 1.2
tuna **atún** *m.* 2.2
turkey **pavo** *m.* 2.2
turn **doblar** *v.* 3.2
   turn off (*electricity/appliance*)
   apagar *v.* 2.5
   turn on (*electricity/appliance*)
   poner *v.* 2.5; **prender** *v.* 2.5
twelve **doce** 1.1
twenty **veinte** 1.1
twenty-eight **veintiocho** 1.1
twenty-five **veinticinco** 1.1
twenty-four **veinticuatro** 1.1
twenty-nine **veintinueve** 1.1

twenty-one **veintiún,**
   veintiuno/a 1.1
twenty-seven **veintisiete** 1.1
twenty-six **veintiséis** 1.1
twenty-three **veintitrés** 1.1
twenty-two **veintidós** 1.1
twice **dos veces** 1.6
twin **gemelo/a** *m., f.* 1.3
twisted **torcido/a** *adj.* 2.4
   be twisted **estar torcido/a** 2.4
two **dos** 1.1
   two hundred **doscientos/as** 1.2
   two times **dos veces** 1.6

U

ugly **feo/a** *adj.* 1.3
uncle **tío** *m.* 1.3
under **bajo** *adv.* 2.1;
   debajo de *prep.* 1.2
understand **comprender** *v.* 1.3;
   entender (e:ie) *v.* 1.4
underwear **ropa interior** 1.6
unemployment **desempleo** *m.* 3.6
unique **único/a** *adj.* 2.3
United States **Estados Unidos**
   (EE.UU.) *m. pl.* 1.1
university **universidad** *f.* 1.2
unless **a menos que** *conj.* 3.1
unpleasant **antipático/a** *adj.* 1.3
until **hasta** *prep.* 1.6; **hasta que**
   conj. 3.1
up **arriba** *adv.* 3.3
urgent **urgente** *adj.* 2.6
   It's urgent that... **Es urgente**
   que... 3.6
us **nos** *pl., d.o. pron.* 1.5
   to/for us **nos** *pl., i.o. pron.* 1.6
use **usar** *v.* 1.6
used for **para** *prep.* 2.5
useful **útil** *adj. m., f.*

V

vacation **vacaciones** *f., pl.* 1.5
   be on vacation **estar de**
   vacaciones 1.5
   go on vacation **ir de**
   vacaciones 1.5
vacuum **pasar** *v.* **la aspiradora** 2.6
   vacuum cleaner **aspiradora** *f.* 2.6
valley **valle** *m.* 3.1
various **varios/as** *adj. m., f. pl.* 2.2
vegetables **verduras** *pl., f.* 2.2
verb **verbo** *m.*
very **muy** *adv.* 1.1
   very much **muchísimo** *adv.* 1.2
   (Very) well, thank you. **(Muy)**
   bien, gracias. 1.1
video **video** *m.* 1.1
   video camera **cámara** *f.* **de**
   video 2.5
videoconference
   videoconferencia *f.* 3.4
video game **videojuego** *m.* 1.4
vinegar **vinagre** *m.* 2.2

violence **violencia** *f.* 3.6
visit **visitar** *v.* 1.4
   visit monuments **visitar**
   monumentos 1.4
vitamin **vitamina** *f.* 3.3
voice mail **correo de voz** *m.* 2.5
volcano **volcán** *m.* 3.1
volleyball **vóleibol** *m.* 1.4
vote **votar** *v.* 3.6

W

wait (for) **esperar** *v.* **(+ inf.)** 1.2
waiter/waitress **camarero/a**
   m., f. 2.2
wake up **despertarse (e:ie)**
   v. 2.1
walk **caminar** *v.* 1.2
   take a walk **pasear** *v.* 1.4
   walk around **pasear por** 1.4
walkman **walkman** *m.*
wall **pared** *f.* 2.6; **muro** *m.* 3.3
wallet **cartera** *f.* 1.4, 1.6
want **querer (e:ie)** *v.* 1.4
war **guerra** *f.* 3.6
warm (oneself) up **calentarse**
   (e:ie) *v.* 3.3
wash **lavar** *v.* 2.6
   wash one's face/hands **lavarse**
   la cara/las manos 2.1
   wash (the floor, the dishes)
   lavar (el suelo, los
   platos) 2.6
   wash oneself **lavarse** *v.* 2.1
washing machine **lavadora** *f.* 2.6
wastebasket **papelera** *f.* 1.2
watch **mirar** *v.* 1.2; **reloj** *m.* 1.2
   watch television **mirar (la)**
   televisión 1.2
water **agua** *f.* 2.2
   water pollution **contaminación**
   del agua 3.1
   water-skiing **esquí** *m.*
   acuático 1.4
way **manera** *f.* 3.4
we **nosotros(as)** *m., f.* 1.1
weak **débil** *adj. m., f.* 3.3
wear **llevar** *v.* 1.6; **usar** *v.* 1.6
weather **tiempo** *m.*
   The weather is bad. **Hace mal**
   tiempo. 1.5
   The weather is good. **Hace**
   buen tiempo. 1.5
weaving **tejido** *m.* 3.5
Web **red** *f.* 2.5
website **sitio** *m.* **web** 2.5
wedding **boda** *f.* 2.3
Wednesday **miércoles** *m.,*
   sing. 1.2
week **semana** *f.* 1.2
weekend **fin** *m.* **de semana** 1.4
weight **peso** *m.* 3.3
   lift weights **levantar** *v.* **pesas**
   f., pl. 3.3
welcome **bienvenido(s)/a(s)**
   adj. 1.1

well: (Very) well, thanks. **(Muy) bien, gracias.** 1.1
well-being **bienestar** *m.* 3.3
well organized **ordenado/a** *adj.*
west **oeste** *m.* 3.2
   to the west **al oeste** 3.2
western (*genre*) **de vaqueros** 3.5
whale **ballena** *f.* 3.1
what **lo que** *pron.* 2.6
what? **¿qué?** 1.1
   At what time...? **¿A qué hora...?** 1.1
   What a pleasure to... ! **¡Qué gusto (+ inf.)...** 3.6
   What day is it? **¿Qué día es hoy?** 1.2
   What do you guys think? **¿Qué les parece?** 2.3
   What happened? **¿Qué pasó?** 2.5
   What is today's date? **¿Cuál es la fecha de hoy?** 1.5
   What nice clothes! **¡Qué ropa más bonita!** 1.6
   What size do you wear? **¿Qué talla lleva (usa)?** 1.6
   What time is it? **¿Qué hora es?** 1.1
   What's going on? **¿Qué pasa?** 1.1
   What's happening? **¿Qué pasa?** 1.1
   What's... like? **¿Cómo es...?** 1.3
   What's new? **¿Qué hay de nuevo?** 1.1
   What's the weather like? **¿Qué tiempo hace?** 1.5
   What's up? **¿Qué onda?** 3.2
   What's wrong? **¿Qué pasó?** 2.5
   What's your name? **¿Cómo se llama usted?** *form.* 1.1; **¿Cómo te llamas (tú)?** *fam.* 1.1
when **cuando** *conj.* 2.1; 3.1
When? **¿Cuándo?** 1.2
where **donde**
where (to)? (*destination*) **¿adónde?** 1.2; (*location*) **¿dónde?** 1.1
   Where are you from? **¿De dónde eres (tú)?** (*fam.*) 1.1; **¿De dónde es (usted)?** (*form.*) 1.1
   Where is...? **¿Dónde está...?** 1.2
   (to) where? **¿adónde?** 1.2
which **que** *pron.*, **lo que** *pron.* 2.6
which? **¿cuál?** 1.2; **¿qué?** 1.2
   In which...? **¿En qué...?** 1.2
   which one(s)? **¿cuál(es)?** 1.2
while **mientras** *conj.* 2.4
white **blanco/a** *adj.* 1.6
   white wine **vino blanco** 2.2
who **que** *pron.* 2.6; **quien(es)** *pron.* 2.6

who? **¿quién(es)?** 1.1
Who is...? **¿Quién es...?** 1.1
   Who is calling/speaking? (*on phone*) **¿De parte de quién?** 2.5
   Who is speaking? (*on phone*) **¿Quién habla?** 2.5
whole **todo/a** *adj.*
whom **quien(es)** *pron.* 2.6
whose? **¿de quién(es)?** 1.1
why? **¿por qué?** 1.2
widower/widow **viudo/a** *adj.* 2.3
wife **esposa** *f.* 1.3
win **ganar** *v.* 1.4
wind **viento** *m.* 1.5
window **ventana** *f.* 1.2
windshield **parabrisas** *m.*, *sing.* 2.5
windy: It's (very) windy. **Hace (mucho) viento.** 1.5
wine **vino** *m.* 2.2
   red wine **vino tinto** 2.2
   white wine **vino blanco** 2.2
wineglass **copa** *f.* 2.6
winter **invierno** *m.* 1.5
wireless (connection) **conexión inalámbrica** *f.* 2.5
wish **desear** *v.* 1.2; **esperar** *v.* 3.1
   I wish (that) **ojalá (que)** 3.1
with **con** *prep.* 1.2
   with me **conmigo** 1.4; 2.3
   with you **contigo** *fam.* 1.5, 2.3
within (ten years) **dentro de (diez años)** *prep.* 3.4
without **sin** *prep.* 1.2; 3.1; 3.3; **sin que** *conj.* 3.1
woman **mujer** *f.* 1.1
wool **lana** *f.* 1.6
   (made of) wool **de lana** 1.6
word **palabra** *f.* 1.1
work **trabajar** *v.* 1.2; **funcionar** *v.* 2.5; **trabajo** *m.* 3.4
   work (*of art, literature, music, etc.*) **obra** *f.* 3.5
   work out **hacer gimnasia** 3.3
world **mundo** *m.* 2.2, 3.1
worldwide **mundial** *adj. m., f.*
worried (about) **preocupado/a (por)** *adj.* 1.5
worry (about) **preocuparse** *v.* **(por)** 2.1
   Don't worry. **No se preocupe.** *form.* 2.1; **Tranquilo.; No te preocupes.**; *fam.* 2.1
worse **peor** *adj. m., f.* 2.2
worst **el/la peor** 2.2
Would you like to...? **¿Te gustaría...?** *fam.* 1.4
Would you do me the honor of marrying me? **¿Me harías el honor de casarte conmigo?** 3.5
wow **híjole** *interj.* 1.6
wrench **llave** *f.* 2.5
write **escribir** *v.* 1.3
   write a letter/post card/e-mail

message **escribir una carta/postal/mensaje electrónico** 1.4
writer **escritor(a)** *m., f* 3.5
written **escrito/a** *p.p.* 3.2
wrong **equivocado/a** *adj.* 1.5
   be wrong **no tener razón** 1.3

X

X-ray **radiografía** *f.* 2.4

Y

yard **jardín** *m.* 2.6; **patio** *m.* 2.6
year **año** *m.* 1.5
   be... years old **tener... años** 1.3
yellow **amarillo/a** *adj.* 1.6
yes **sí** *interj.* 1.1
yesterday **ayer** *adv.* 1.6
yet **todavía** *adv.* 1.5
yogurt **yogur** *m.* 2.2
you **tú** *fam.* **usted (Ud.)** *form. sing.* **vosotros/as** *m., f. fam.* **ustedes (Uds.)** *form.* 1.1; (to, for) you *fam. sing.* **te** *pl.* **os** 1.6; *form. sing.* **le** *pl.* **les** 1.6
   you **te** *fam., sing.,* **lo/la** *form., sing.,* **os** *fam., pl.,* **los/las** *form., pl, d.o. pron.* 1.5
You don't say! **¡No me digas!** *fam.;* **¡No me diga!** *form.* 2.5
You are... **Tú eres...** 1.1
You're welcome. **De nada.** 1.1; **No hay de qué.** 1.1
young **joven** *adj. sing.* (**jóvenes** pl.) 1.3
   young person **joven** *m., f. sing.* (**jóvenes** pl.) 1.1
   young woman **señorita (Srta.)** *f.*
younger **menor** *adj. m., f.* 1.3
younger: younger brother, sister **hermano/a menor** *m., f.* 1.3
youngest **el/la menor** *m., f.* 2.2
your **su(s)** *poss. adj. form.* 1.3
   your **tu(s)** *poss. adj. fam. sing.* 1.3
   your **vuestro/a(s)** *poss. adj. form. pl.* 1.3
   your(s) *form.* **suyo(s)/a(s)** *poss. pron. form.* 2.5
   your(s) **tuyo(s)/a(s)** *poss. fam. sing.* 2.5
   your(s) **vuestro(s)/a(s)** *poss. fam.* 2.5
youth *f.* **juventud** 2.3

Z

zero **cero** *m.* 1.1

As in the glossary, the level and lesson of ¡**ADELANTE**! where each item is found is indicated by the two numbers separated by a decimal:

- 1.6 = ¡*ADELANTE!* **UNO** , Lección 6
- 3.4 = ¡*ADELANTE!* **TRES** , Lección 4

Índice

Comic Credits

31 "Ovejitas" ©©Joaquín Salvador Lavado (QUINO) *Toda Mafalda* – Ediciones de La Flor, 1993.

Film Credits

156 "Tears & Tortillas" By permission of Xochitl Dorsey.

Television Credits

34 "Mastercard-Perrito" By permission of Edgardo Tettamanti.
94 "Jumbo Mountainbike" By permission of Cencosud.
216 "Totofútbol" By permission of Diego Reves.
278 "Down Taxco" By permission of Univision.com.
336 "¿Me lo compras?" © Comercial Mexicana.

Photography and Art Credits

All images © Vista Higher Learning unless otherwise noted. Fotonovela photos provided by Carolina Zapata.

Cover: (full pg) José Blanco.

Front Matter (IAE): IAE-36 (t) Amy Baron; (b) Martín Bernetti; **IAE-37 (t)** Janet Dracksdorf; (m) Carolina Zapata; (b) Martín Bernetti.

Lesson One: 1 (full pg) Paula Díez; **2** © John Henley/Corbis; **3** Martín Bernetti; **4** Martín Bernetti; **10** (l) Rachel Distler; (r) Ali Burafi; **11** (t) © Hans Georg Roth/Corbis; (bl) © Mark Mainz/Getty Images; (br) Paola Ríos-Schaaf; **12** (l) Janet Dracksdorf; (r) © Tom Grill/Corbis; **16** (l) © José Girarte/iStockphoto; (r) © Blend Images/Alamy; **19** (m) Anne Loubet; (r) © Digital Vision/Getty Images; **28** (tl, tr, bl) Martín Bernetti; **31** (tl) Ana Cabezas Martín; (tml) Martín Bernetti; (tmr) © Serban Enache/Dreamstime.com; (tr) Vanessa Bertozzi; (bl) © Corey Hochachka/Design Pics/Corbis; (br) Ramiro Isaza © Fotocolombia.com; **32** Carolina Zapata; **33** Paula Díez; **36** (t) © Robert Holmes/Corbis; (m) © Jon Arnold Images Ltd./Alamy; (b) © Andresr/Shutterstock.com; **37** (tl) © PhotoLink/Getty Images; (tr) © Tony Arruza/Corbis; (bl) © Shaul Schwarz/Sygma/Corbis; (br) Marta Mesa.

Lesson Two: 61 (full pg) Paula Díez; **64** Martín Bernetti; **70** (l) Mauricio Arango; (r) © Pablo Corral V/Corbis; **71** (t) © Murle/Dreamstime.com; (b) © Paul Almasy/Corbis; **79** © Stephen Coburn/Shutterstock.com; **81** (l) Paola Rios-Schaaf; (r) © Image Source/Corbis; **89** (l) © Rick Gomez/Corbis; (r) © Hola Images/Workbook.com; **90** José Blanco; **91** (l) Pascal Pernix; (r) Mauricio Osorio; **92** (t, b) Martín Bernetti; **93** Nora y Susana © Fotocolombia.com; **96** (tl, tr) José Blanco; (m) © Elke Stolzenberg/Corbis; (b) © Reuters/Corbis; **97** (t) Photo courtesy of Charles Ommanney; (ml, mr) José Blanco; (bl) © Iconotec/Fotosearch; (br) © Owen Franken/Corbis; **110** (l) © Owen Franken/Corbis; (m) © Elke Stolzenberg/Corbis; (r) José Blanco.

Lesson Three: 123 (full pg) © Ronnie Kaufman/Corbis; **125** Martín Bernetti; **126** (tl) Anne Loubet; (tr) © Blend Images/Alamy; (mtl) Ana Cabezas Martín; (mtr) Ventus Pictures; (mbl, mbr, bl, br) Martín Bernetti; **132** (tl) © David Cantor/AP Wide World Photos; (tr) © Rafael Perez/Reuters/Corbis; (b) © Martial Trezzini/epa/Corbis; **133** (t) © Dani Cardona/Reuters/Corbis; (b) © Ballesteros/epa/Corbis; **136** (l) Martín Bernetti; (r) José Blanco; **138** © Andres Rodriguez/Alamy; **143** (l) © Tyler Olson/Fotolia.com; (r) Martín Bernetti; **144** Martín Bernetti; **152** (all) Martín Bernetti; **153** (t) Nora y Susana © Fotocolombia.com; (m) © Chuck Savage/Corbis; (b) Martín Bernetti; **154** © Tom & Dee Ann McCarthy/Corbis; **155** Martín Bernetti; **158** (t, ml, b) Martín Bernetti; (mm) Iván Mejía; (mr) Lauren Krolick; **159** (tl, ml, b) Martín Bernetti; (tr) Oswaldo Guayasamín. *Madre y niño en azul.* 1986. Cortesía Fundación Guayasamín. Quito, Ecuador.; (br) © Gerardo Mora; **172** (tl) Lauren Krolick; (bl) Martín Bernetti; (r) Iván Mejía; **181** Martín Bernetti.

About the Author

José A. Blanco founded Vista Higher Learning in 1998. A native of Barranquilla, Colombia, Mr. Blanco holds degrees in Literature and Hispanic Studies from Brown University and the University of California, Santa Cruz. He has worked as a writer, editor, and translator for Houghton Mifflin and D.C. Heath and Company and has taught Spanish at the secondary and university levels. Mr. Blanco is also the co-author of several other Vista Higher Learning programs: **Panorama, Aventuras,** and **¡Viva!** at the introductory level, **Ventanas, Facetas, Enfoques, Imagina,** and **Sueña** at the intermediate level, and **Revista** at the advanced conversation level.

About the Illustrators

Yayo, an internationally acclaimed illustrator, was born in Colombia. He has illustrated children's books, newspapers, and magazines, and has been exhibited around the world. He currently lives in Montreal, Canada.

Pere Virgili lives and works in Barcelona, Spain. His illustrations have appeared in textbooks, newspapers, and magazines throughout Spain and Europe.

Born in Caracas, Venezuela, **Hermann Mejía** studied illustration at the *Instituto de Diseño de Caracas*. Hermann currently lives and works in the United States.